Throwing the Dice of History with Marx

Historical Materialism Book Series

The Historical Materialism Book Series is a major publishing initiative of the radical left. The capitalist crisis of the twenty-first century has been met by a resurgence of interest in critical Marxist theory. At the same time, the publishing institutions committed to Marxism have contracted markedly since the high point of the 1970s. The Historical Materialism Book Series is dedicated to addressing this situation by making available important works of Marxist theory. The aim of the series is to publish important theoretical contributions as the basis for vigorous intellectual debate and exchange on the left.

The peer-reviewed series publishes original monographs, translated texts, and reprints of classics across the bounds of academic disciplinary agendas and across the divisions of the left. The series is particularly concerned to encourage the internationalization of Marxist debate and aims to translate significant studies from beyond the English-speaking world.

For a full list of titles in the Historical Materialism Book Series available in paperback from Haymarket Books, visit: www.haymarketbooks.org/series_collections/1-historical-materialism.

Throwing the Dice of History with Marx

The Plurality of Historical Worlds from Epicurus to Modern Science

Marcus Bajema

Haymarket Books
Chicago, IL

First published in 2023 by Brill Academic Publishers, The Netherlands
© 2023 Koninklijke Brill NV, Leiden, The Netherlands

Published in paperback in 2024 by
Haymarket Books
P.O. Box 180165
Chicago, IL 60618
773-583-7884
www.haymarketbooks.org

ISBN: 979-8-88890-207-3

Distributed to the trade in the US through Consortium Book Sales and
Distribution (www.cbsd.com) and internationally through Ingram
Publisher Services International (www.ingramcontent.com).

This book was published with the generous support of Lannan
Foundation, Wallace Action Fund, and the Marguerite Casey Foundation.

Special discounts are available for bulk purchases by organizations and
institutions. Please call 773-583-7884 or email info@haymarketbooks.org
for more information.

Cover art and design by David Mabb. Cover art is a detail from *Painting
6, Long Live the New! Morris & Co. Hand Printed Wallpapers and Kazimir
Malevich's Suprematism*. Acrylic on wallpaper mounted on canvas (2016).

Library of Congress Cataloging-in-Publication data is available.

I was especially inclined to laugh at the people who quarrelled about boundary-lines, and at those who plumed themselves on working the plain of Sicyon or possessing the district of Oenoe in Marathon or owning a thousand acres in Acharnae. As a matter of fact, since the whole of Greece as it looked to me then from on high was no bigger than four fingers, on that scale surely Attica was infinitesimal. I thought, therefore, how little there was for our friends the rich to be proud of; for it seemed to me that the widest-acred of them all had but a single Epicurean atom under cultivation.

LUCIAN, Icaromenippus (Harmon 1915, p. 299)

∴

Contents

Introduction

Of the spectres haunting Marxism, stadialism may be one of the most pernicious. The notion that through a sequence of historical stages there will be an inevitable transition to communism has been discredited in most quarters. It has been replaced by a reverse thesis, holding that the idea of a transition to a communist form of social life is inevitably doomed to fail. This thesis further seems to suggest that any attempt to achieve communism denies historical reality, or alternatively, that such attempts are based on the faulty application of grand narratives that cannot be accepted in the discourse of postmodern capitalism. The main thrust of this book is to provide philosophical ideas and scientific evidence that allow us to think history in a way that departs from stadialism, with the aim of conceiving alternatives to both the communist past and the capitalist present. It seeks to be part of a broader movement to break the 'bonds of fate' of notions of historical inevitability to which Marxism has been shackled, to its own misfortune.

Intellectually, it draws upon the recognition of the aleatory current in philosophy that grew out of the work of the *Lire Capital* group of Althusser, Balibar, Macherey and others, and since has been taken up by succeeding generations. The aleatory here refers to the role of chance and unpredictability in history, which demolish the notion of an inevitable sequence of stages of social development. It opens up a perspective that recognises a plurality of past, present, and future historical trajectories. Of particular importance in this perspective is the thesis of plural temporality, which recognises the interweaving of different elements and temporalities. As such, this thesis renders the notion of discrete historical stages obsolete and presents a more nuanced, richer view of historical causality that can incorporate the aleatory. This book argues the case for a complementary thesis to that of plural temporality, that of the plurality of worlds. In a basic sense, this thesis adds a spatial dimension to the temporal one, in this way recognising distinct spatio-temporal forms.

In more concrete terms such forms constitute the major word-historical regions, such as China, Mesoamerica, the Mediterranean, and so on. Recognising these forms enables comparative studies of their characteristics and trajectories of development. From the perspective of the thesis of the plurality of worlds, it is precisely 'worlds' that form the lifeblood of history, while abstract notions such as the mode of production are used to facilitate comparative analysis. In this way it closely relates to the distinction between teleological and aleatory conceptions of the mode of production recognised in the aleatory current of philosophy. It will be argued here that the thesis of the plurality of worlds derives from ancient Epicurean ideas on the relation of humankind and nature, as well as its early history. This adds a new body of work so far absent in the debates on the aleatory current, which has focused on the ontology of atoms and void in Epicurus and Lucretius, and on tracing the reception and reworking of these ideas in later European philosophers.

This absence is unfortunate for its neglect of a rich source of inspiration for modern ideas about history, namely the fifth book of Lucretius' *De rerum natura*.[1] In Lucretius it is possible to recognise the basic principles of an aleatory conception of history from early humans to contemporary civilisation, using basic principles that can also be found in the more limited surviving writings of Epicurus. For the ancient atomists, humankind in its interaction with its physical and cultural environments has the ability to adapt not just to those conditions but to change them as well, something captured in the Greek term *phusiopoiei*.[2] Accidental encounters with natural phenomena form the basis for specific technical inventions, just as those between people generated new social arrangements. As can best be seen in Lucretius, together this series of encounters forms the tapestry that is the history of humankind. Furthermore, this history in turn depends on the preceding encounters that led to the emergence of the *kosmos* and of life in general and humans specifically.

The thesis of the plurality of worlds is specifically based on the parallel established by Epicurus between the variation between the different *kosmoi* in the universe on the one hand, and different trajectories of distinct regions. This perspective became more pronounced and explicit in receptions of Epicurean ideas in Renaissance Europe, where the thesis became intertwined with the newly discovered American continent and its cultures. In the hands of Montaigne, it became a means to understand the indigenous American civilisations in their own terms, distinct both from the western Europe of his own time and from Greco-Roman antiquity. However, Eurocentric and colonialist perspectives sought to diminish these civilisations, placing them rather on the lower rungs of an ascending series of stages. This stadialist perspective was powerfully captured in John Locke's notion that the indigenous cultures of the Americas presented the beginnings of human development everywhere, a perspective that found a powerful echo in Adam Smith.

It is also precisely this notion that makes it possible to delineate different strands within Marxism, as they relate to both the aleatory current in general and the thesis of the plurality of worlds in particular. Use will be made in this

---

1   Hereafter abbreviated as DRN.
2   As used by Democritus, see Taylor 1999, p. 15.

regard especially of the work of Lewis Henry Morgan, as his *Ancient society* has occupied pride of place in Marxist understandings of early history. Morgan was in fact greatly influenced by Lucretius' account of the history of humankind, as can be inferred not only from references in the book itself but especially from an unpublished chapter. Furthermore, other published and unpublished texts of Morgan also shine an important light on Morgan's relation to Epicurean ideas about the history of humankind. Yet at the same time he put forward a strongly unilinear and stadialist account of development. It will be argued that his work in this sense is of a somewhat contradictory and conflicted character, showing the influence of more progressive and aleatory views while at the same time denying civilisational status to indigenous American civilisations and placing them in the lower phases of a stadialist straitjacket.

Morgan's work is especially useful not only because it draws out these contradictions, but also because of how these played out in different reception contexts within Marxism. Clearly, the adaptation of his ideas occupy pride of place in this reception, and have to be understood as part of the later work of Engels such as the *Anti-Dühring* and *Dialectics of Nature*. These works were quite distinct from any kind of Epicurean heritage, and indeed, as recent work on the aleatory current has demonstrated, were part of a teleological, or more precisely teleonomic, perspective. In that sense, it is important to consider the reception of Morgan by Marx himself, as evidenced in his notebooks on *Ancient Society* and related works. By 'annotating' these notes with reference to Marx's positions in other late works, greater insights can be gained; and these in turn can be related to the volumes of *Capital* and its preparatory studies such as the *Grundrisse*. In this way, both the contrasts and similarities can be discerned. It is also important to trace Marx's own engagement with Epicureanism, as well as other thinkers who are part of the aleatory current. This engagement provides further insights into his conception of dialectics, as well as its differences with dialectical materialism.

It will be argued that in Marx a version of the thesis of the plurality of worlds can be discerned that contrasts with the stadialism of Morgan and Engels. Furthermore, his dialectics included not only the realist and historical aspects that can also be found in Engels, but also a critical perspective that is sharply different from any teleological or teleonomic notions. In order to demonstrate more powerfully the differences between Engelsian stadialism and Marx's version of plurality, the results of twentieth century and contemporary archaeological science will be used. Particular attention in this regard will be given to Soviet archaeology, which took the ideas of Morgan and Engels further than anyone else in its version of stadialism. The combination of new scientific evidence and theoretical critiques eventually demonstrated the inability of this scheme to understand the world, let alone to be able to change it. To show this in precise terms is important, for it supplies one clue for understanding the failure of the Soviet Union's developmental path.

By contrast, the elements of the thesis of the plurality of worlds as they can be recognised in Marx hold up rather well in the light of recent scientific work. In particular, we can think here of the metabolism of humans and nature, as well as the emergence of commodity exchange in Eurasia. Furthermore, Marx's insights into different developmental pathways in the pre-Columbian Americas are now increasingly being recognised by archaeologists as well. In fact, these go even further, in a sense, by outlining the persistence of more equal forms of social life in the face of further growth in the scale of both settlements and states. All of this goes to show that there is a viable alternative to stadialism in Marxism, and that both Marxist historical studies and political praxis can draw upon this alternative to move in new directions. It is argued in this book that this alternative can potentially seek to develop Walter Benjamin's call for an alternative to the universal history of the victors, that of a history of the oppressed that functions as a means for their liberation.

The argument of the book is spread out across six chapters, occupied with four main themes. Chapter 1 is the most eclectic, locating the aleatory current loosely within the context of the demise of Marxism as a dominant political force during the so-called Short Twentieth Century of 1917–91. The aim here is not to provide an overview of the different currents in Marxist thought in this era, but rather to relate the aleatory perspective to the age within which it emerged, as well as to highlight potential (abortive) alternatives. The second main theme concerns ideas about the early history of humankind in Epicureanism and the reception thereof in Renaissance and later European philosophy, which are respectively treated in Chapters 2 and 3. Particular attention is paid in Chapter 3 to the question of Epicurean ideas about early forms of social life and civilisation in relation to the newly discovered Americas. It will be shown that the thesis of the plurality of worlds came into its own in this encounter, especially in the *Essais* of Montaigne, and that this question is one that deserves to be considered as part of the debates on the aleatory current in philosophy.

Chapters 4 and 5 deal with the third theme of the book, that of the reception of the Epicurean ideas on early humankind in the Marxist tradition. The work of Morgan played a crucial role in this, and distinctions in the responses of Engels and Marx to his work *Ancient society* serve to delineate broader differences between the two men. The Engelsian notion of *Wechselwirkung* does not recur in Marx, whose work instead seems to conform more easily to the theses of plural temporality and the plurality of worlds. It will be argued that Marx's own early engagement with Epicureanism had something to do with this appreciation of pluralism and the consequent differences with Engels. The final argument will be laid out in Chapter 6. In effect it takes the different approaches of Marx and Engels laid out in the two previous chapters and subjects them to the test of modern science, in the form of archaeological evidence for early humankind and the development of class systems. As noted earlier, this evidence demonstrates the existence of pluralism and exposes the narrowness and consequent revolutionary unsuitability of a stadialist approach like the Soviet *pyatichlenka*.

Finally, it is important to emphasise that this book is written from a very specific perspective that largely leaves out topics considered central to the Marxist tradition. First of all, it leaves out the thorny question of the relation of Marx to Hegel and German idealism at large, a perilous but at the same time necessary omission. The peril in this is to abstract Marx from his immediate intellectual context, which of course cannot be ignored in his development as a thinker and revolutionary. At the same time, it is necessary to do so here in order to grasp Marx from a perspective more removed from his origins, namely that of the aleatory current in philosophy. The aim in this is not to create a hypostasis of Marx, underwriting an ideal form of materialism, but rather to draw out aspects of his thought that have never been considered in this light. In that sense, this work is complementary to other works in showing neglected features of Marxism, and should not be taken to represent a new orthodoxy to replace previous ones. Rather it has to be grasped within the plurality of approaches that characterises historical materialism today, and makes it all the better for it.

The Aleatory Current in Philosophy and the Present Conjuncture

This chapter will introduce the aleatory current in philosophy and show its relevance for the present conjuncture. It starts with an interpretation of the courses of the great socialist revolutions of the twentieth century, arguing that their conceptual frameworks were structured in large part by a stadialist perspective on history. Stadialism in this sense leads to a sense of the inevitability of communism, or conversely of its equally inevitable demise. In effect this can be seen as a *cul de sac* of socialist historiography, one that prevents the recognition of the inherent pluralism of history and the political consequences that result from it. Critiques along these lines in western European Marxism were first formulated by Benjamin and Bloch, but became more systematically grounded in the engagement of various Marxist thinkers with Spinoza. This engagement brought with it new complexities, as Macherey's critique of Althusser's notion of structure shows.

This critique, however, pointed the way to new insights with regard to significant convergences, though certainly not identities, between Spinoza's ideas and those of ancient Epicureanism. Especially in relation to the former's notion of singular things, these convergences allowed for the preliminary recognition of an aleatory current in philosophy in the later work of Althusser. Formulated in a rather fragmentary manner, these ideas have since been developed much further and in a more systematic way. Particular use in this regard is made of the work of Morfino, who has extended and deepened specific philosophical theses which may serve as comparative concepts to understand the various thinkers associated with it. In order to understand this better, as well as to grasp the distinctions with other versions of Marxism, these theses are connected to specific aspects of the Marxist view of history. This allows us not just to understand the distinctiveness of the aleatory perspective generally, but also relates it to the *cul de sac* of stadialism and its 'thesis of inevitability'.

1   Stadialism and the 'Thesis of Inevitability'

Before turning to the aleatory current in philosophy and its relation to Marxism, it is important to outline in some detail the ideas in opposition to which it was first formulated. The ideas in question are those of the dialectical and historical materialism that formed the philosophical mainstay of the communist movement in the Short Twentieth Century.[1] Although Stalin's 1938 text on the matter should not be seen as a blanket covering this movement, it nevertheless acted as a focal point for imitation, emulation, and opposition.[2] Written at the time of the Purges, a period aptly termed 'the midnight of the century',[3] Stalin's words merit philosophical attention for their practical efficacy. These ideas were powerful not in the sense of being in the hands of the masses, as Marx envisaged, but rather as props in the claws of a repressive state bureaucracy.[4] As such, they were shaped by the Soviet notion of *partiinost*, party-mindedness, the Party itself being a subject of the state.

The basic position adopted by Stalin concerned the primacy of the material over the ideational, adding to this the dialectical view of nature as a whole in a continuous state of flux, developing through the struggle of opposites and dialectical leaps.[5] These elements of dialectical materialism were directly applied to social life, through the science of historical materialism. This can be seen in Stalin's insistence that the primacy of matter over ideas translates into a determining role for the productive forces, with the instruments of production being the decisive force within these.[6] These instruments he supposed to be in a continuous state of development, giving a short summary of the history of tools to illustrate his arguments. The forces of production have corresponding relations of production (and beyond them social institutions

----

1 Marked at the beginning by the breakdown of the European imperialist order with the advent of the First World War in 1914, and at the end by the collapse of the USSR in 1991. This century was further subdivided by Hobsbawm into an Age of Catastrophe (1914 – late 1940s), a Golden Age (1950s – late 1970s), and an Age of Crisis (from the late 1970s onwards), Hobsbawm 1994, pp. 5–11.

2 As noted by the editors of a recent critical edition of the book, over forty million copies in a dozen languages were in circulation, serving as a 'master narrative' for not just the USSR itself but for the communist parties aligned with it as well, Brandenberger and Zelenov 2019, pp. 1–2.

3 The term comes from Victor Serge's novel on the purging of Left Oppositionists, Serge 2014.

4 The subversion of the Party by the state bureaucracy is traced in Lewin 2005, see especially chapters twelve and thirteen for what may be termed 'mature Stalinism', and its ideological accompaniment of Zhdanovism. Despite the attempt at comprehensive de-Stalinisation, the bureaucratic forces that had 'taken hold' in this period never really relinquished their grip on power, something recognised by Andropov in the 1980s, Lewin 2005, pp. 264–67.

5 Stalin 1939, pp. 106–9. Also important in this regard is a later text on economics, where Stalin clarifies his conception of laws in natural science and political economy alike, see Stalin 1952, pp. 5–13.

6 Stalin 1939, pp. 111–14, 119–21.

in the broadest sense), which unlike the former develop not gradually but rather through qualitative leaps.

Such leaps demarcate different modes of production, of which Stalin recognises five in successive order, the *pyatichlenka* (set of five) of the 'primitive' communal mode, the first states based on slave-holding and feudal modes, capitalism, and finally socialism.[7] The result is a vision of history that has been described as 'productive forces determinism', which entails that the underlying process of historical development (based in the instruments of production) is continuous and linear.[8] Such a perspective cannot incorporate plural temporalities, something that becomes clear when Stalin denounces geographical determinism. The only role of the environment is to delay or speed up the continuous development of the productive forces, as the longer timescale of geological processes rules out a determining impact on social life:

> In the space of three thousand years three different social systems have been successively superseded in Europe: the primitive communal system, the slave system and the feudal system. In the eastern part of Europe, in the U.S.S.R., even four social systems have been superseded. Yet during this period geographical conditions have either not changed at all, or have changed so slightly that geography takes no note of them. And that is quite natural. Changes in geographical environment of any importance require millions of years, whereas a few hundred or a couple of thousand years are enough for even very important changes in the system of human society.[9]

While geographical determinism is hardly defensible, neither is Stalin's improbable critique of it based on the different timescales of geological and social changes.[10] More subtle approaches existed in Soviet science, taking into

---

7   Stalin 1939, pp. 123–7. The reasons for the absence of Marx's Asiatic mode of production in this scheme, despite its explicit inclusion among Marx's outline of the distinct modes of production, will be discussed in the epilogue.

8   Lekas 1988, pp. 42–50.

9   Stalin 1939, p. 118. In partial contradistinction to the influential view of Plekhanov on the influence of geographical factors, notably in his review of Mechnikov's work on the 'great historical rivers', Plekhanov 1981. See for the work of Plekhanov in relation to both Stalin and the post-Stalin era chapter three of Sawer 1977.

10   In the later *Economic problems of socialism in the USSR*, Stalin expands on the difference between the natural world and human history with reference to natural laws. Both are reflections of objective processes independent of human will, allowing only understanding and limited action, yet the laws of nature are permanent while those of political

account geographical differences and the interplay of temporalities, as in the work of Nikolai Vavilov, murdered by Stalin's apparatus and then intellectually reassessed in the 1960s.[11] By contrast, for Stalin the environment was either delaying or speeding up the continuous process of the growth of the productive forces, in effect flattening historical time to this single dimension. These views were justified using a limited and highly partial set of quotations from Marx, Engels, and Lenin, and as such cannot be conflated with Marxism as such. Yet they can serve as a grotesque example of what the aleatory perspective outlined in this book argues against, namely the linear and stadialist view of inevitable historical development. Concomitant with this is the critique of violence as a means to bring such development about, a chilling example of which can be found in Stalin's quote of Marx on force being a midwife in the transition of one society to the next.[12]

It would be wrong to equate Stalinism and the broader communist and socialist movements even in the era of his rule, given that clear alternatives existed. Most notable among them was Trotsky's outline of history as structured by combined and uneven development, which was conducive to an internationalist perspective rather than the nationalism of 'socialism in one country' in Stalin's stadialism.[13] Yet whereas his crimes were condemned by the Party, and his version of its history repudiated, the stadial framework retained its hold over historiography and, most importantly, over policy as well. This can be seen in Khrushchev's report to the twenty second congress of the CPSU in 1961. In this report, he outlined a vision in which the Soviet Union would develop the main features of communism by 1980.[14] The confidence with which this aim was proclaimed was based on two things. First of all, the planning mechanism that had sustained high levels of growth during the previous decades, which had given credence to the idea of extrapolating these figures into the future.[15]

---

economy are historical, in the sense that their validity holds only for a specific period, Stalin 1952, p. 8.

11   Vavilov was a botanist and geneticist, whose work included a pioneering study of the origins of agriculture on the different continents, in part based on his own fieldwork there, Vavilov 1996. See for a later application of his ideas on domestication and early agriculture, Andrianov 2016, especially fig. 12, pp. 266–7.

12   Stalin 1939, p. 130. See in this regard also the analysis of violence in chapter five of Morfino 2014b.

13   See in this regard also the pertinent description of Bukharin and Stalin as 'the organisers of defeats' with regard to the failed Chinese revolution of 1927, Trotsky 1969, p. 241.

14   Khrushchev 1961, p. 128.

15   See the figures in Khrushchev 1961, p. 14. That high growth occurred in the USSR until the early 1970s is clear, see Allen 2003 for an insightful analysis. Spufford 2010 provides an imaginative reconstruction of the era.

This can be seen as a practical demonstration of the primacy of the productive forces.

Secondly, the stadialist model retained its overall popularity, as Stalin's *pyatichlenka* was never repudiated and remained a strong presence in textbooks and scholarly discourse.[16] However, more debates can be noted on the specific questions, some of which will be discussed in the epilogue of this book. The stadialist perspective and the economic successes bolstered Khrushchev in his prediction, which only seems like folly today because we know what actually transpired in the 1980s. Income levels in the Soviet Union by this time had stabilised around 60 to 65% relative to those of Western Europe.[17] Although this was not bad in itself, it was certainly insufficient for the 'catch up and overtake' slogan applied to the even higher levels of the USA. As such the era of Brezhnev and his immediate successors came to be seen as one of stagnation. Yet it was so in relation to its competitors, while in terms of consumer prosperity it was sometimes described in Golden Age terms (though also relative to the other eras of Soviet and Russian history).[18]

Officially the period was described as 'developed socialism', posited as a stage of development in its own right.[19] The real problem with 'developed socialism', however, lay not merely with the stagnation of income levels relative to Western Europe and the USA, nor with the well-known problems facing the Soviet Union in the 1970s and 1980s.[20] Rather, there were important structural elements in the Soviet system that prevented a transition to communism, and arguably were one of the main reasons behind the return to capitalism. In Marx's conception of the first phase of communism in the *Critique of the Gotha programme*, renumeration was still based on the input of labour, if it was no longer based on wage-labour.[21] In the USSR, wages remained the means to remunerate labour, precisely for the same reason that Marx sought to distinguish between labour inputs: the need to increase productivity through spe-

---

16   Gellner 1988, pp. 39–41; Markwick 2001, pp. 45–6.

17   Piketty 2020, fig. 12.3, p. 586. Note here the early peak in the later Stalin era, declining thereafter on account of the Western European recovery and welfare state policies.

18   Cockburn 1991, p. 167.

19   See Evans 1986 for the vicissitudes of this concept. See also Zweynert 2014 on how its economic content continued to shape Soviet economic ideas in the perestroika era.

20   Among others the impact of the arms race and the war in Afghanistan on the Soviet economy, which would be further hit by declining oil prices in the 1980s, as well as demographic imbalances, the nationality question, as well as the problems in Poland and other Eastern European satellite countries.

21   Marx 1989, pp. 85–7. See Chapter 5 for a more extensive analysis of Marx's conception of communism.

cialist labour.[22] Yet as wage-labour and the value-form persisted in the Soviet system, contrary to what Marx had envisaged, so did the accumulation of property remain a potential risk.

The effects of this came to be increasingly visible as the era of 'developed socialism' progressed, and strongly clashed with the notion of social justice as based upon the principle of remuneration according to work.[23] Instead, a host of forms of accumulation of 'unearned incomes' emerged separate from the planned economy, or, more seriously, parasitical on it, including through corruption and crime.[24] New social attitudes of 'knowing how to live' brought individualist notions that clashed with collectivist norms, thereby seriously undermining the latter.[25] Furthermore, the problem was exacerbated by an absence of both progressive taxation and an inheritance tax.[26] All of this was not just bad in the sense that it increased inequality, but also in that it undermined economic development based on the rewarding of productive labour, that is labour towards fulfilling the goals of the planned economy.[27] In the mature Brezhnev years such inequalities seem to have become entrenched and social mobility accordingly decreased.[28]

---

22   In the discussions on political economy in preparation for the first Soviet handbook on the topic, Stalin emphasised this point, specifically arguing for differential wages as a way to engage the interests of workers, acting as powerful levers through which 'there will be no limit to growth in production', cited in Pollock 2001, p. 24. See also his *Economic problems of socialism in the USSR* on the persistence of the law of value, Stalin 1952, pp. 23–6.

23   According to the principle that 'money breeds money', based on social advantages, Naumova and Rogovin 1989, p. 160. These social advantages, until 1991, would have been primarily located within the bureaucracy. The corrosive effects of this can be seen in different letters cited in Rogovin 1989, pp. 149–50. See also Filtzer 2014 for an overview of the different forms of inequality in the Soviet Union.

24   As the evidence assembled in Rogovin 1989 shows. Notably, 'official' income inequality declined during the 1980s, but as the authors of that study note, the growth of the 'shadow economy' is, in lieu of reliable evidence, not factored in here and would demand an upward adjustment of the figures, Alexeev and Gabby 1993, pp. 32–3.

25   Naumova and Rogovin 1989, collect many examples of such attitudes. In effect, however, the phrase was more a reference to 'knowing how to cheat and steal', Rogovin 1989, p. 150.

26   Rogovin 1989, p. 152.

27   Lewin clearly points out the dilemma, namely that the state from the 1960s onwards was in a constant search for scarce labour reserves, while at the same time labour productivity stubbornly remained low, or even declined, which exacerbated existing demographic imbalances: see the discussion in chapter twenty-four of Lewin 2005.

28   The 'performance principle' by now had become effectively an ideological and mystifying concept, in the sense that it did not lead to the limitless expansion of productivity that Stalin had expected it would; while increased wealth, as there might be from the fossil fuel reserves of the USSR, would merely reinforce and exacerbate the existing inequalities, as pointed out in Sawer 1980, p. 61.

Intertwined with this development of inequality was the paramount role of the bureaucracy, which was unaccountable not only to the people but even in some measure to the Party itself. The system's inability to run the planned economy effectively resulted in imbalances in the planning process and a colossal waste of resources, which were recognised but not addressed.[29] As a result, new mechanisms of a 'shadow economy' started to emerge, which were not separate but intertwined with the planned economy, forming the basis for the proliferation of 'unearned incomes'.[30] In this sense, the failure of bureaucracy, the shadow economy, and new forms of inequality were closely connected with each other. Given the continued presence if limited scope of the law of value in the Soviet system, there was always the potential for it to reassert itself as the basic principle, that is, as part of a capitalist mode of production. Arguably, this is in fact what happened, as the bureaucracy had made itself independent from the Party and the people:

> This allowed the latter [top state officials] to take a further step in their 'emancipation': although formally subject to all sorts of rules, they now existed as an uncontrollable bureaucracy, free of all curbs. They began to attack the sacrosanct principle of state ownership of the economy. The spontaneous processes at work emptied a series of ideological and political principles of any content. The most important of them – state ownership of assets and the means of production – was slowly eroded, initially issuing in the formation of veritable fiefdoms inside ministries, and then in the de facto privatization of enterprises by their managers. This process must be called by its real name: the crystallization of a proto-capitalism within the state-owned economy.[31]

Of course, with Gorbachev's 'new thinking', the policies of *perestroika* and *glasnost*, the course taken was not to remedy inequality but rather to return to market mechanisms. This in turn led to the familiar story of the unravelling of the planning mechanism, along with the strange form of capitalism that

---

29   Lewin 2005, pp. 329–33.
30   This shadow economy had been present in limited size earlier, but from the 1970s onwards, and especially from the early 1980s, greatly increased in size, and with a great role for personal gain, Lewin 2005, pp. 363–5. Notably, profits gained in this way could rarely be reinvested into the development of the productive forces, despite the fact that the shadow economy was entirely parasitical relative to the social and educational services provided by the official economy.
31   Lewin 2005, p. 369.

emerged from this.[32] The role played by the bureaucracy here can be seen as the second divergence from Marx's ideas, for in his writings on the Paris commune the need to make the state subservient to the people had always been paramount.[33] Certainly, 'developed socialism' did not conform much to Marx's writings, and this was not a question, as Stalin would have it, of the 'need to work with your own heads and not string together quotations'.[34] For in retaining the value-form, in setting up a bureaucracy impermeable to account-ability, with a planning mechanism consequently burdened with these, the Soviet system was different from Marx's ideas not just in details but in spirit. Indeed, even the capitalism that emerged from its collapse was quite unlike the 'original version' of Western Europe, which could at least be appreciated for its reinvestment of surplus-value in the development of the productive forces.[35]

An important side-effect of capitalist restoration was the demise of Soviet stadialism, unsurprisingly given the utter failure of 'developed socialism' and what now seemed the utopianism of genuine communism. This development had ramifications beyond the now defunct Soviet bloc, in that the notion of a universal historical trajectory culminating in the attainment of a world-historical stage of communism was thoroughly discredited.[36] Furthermore, it can be argued that it was precisely the stadialist mould that encouraged the shift to capitalism, with 'reformers' positing a market society rather than social-ism as the universal stage of historical development.[37] In effect the 'set of five'

---

32   Ironically, the soothing comments made by Gorbachev in a 1990 'pep talk' to the CPSU plenum about unfounded fears of the shift of the market leading to a situation where 'property will end up in the hands of wheeler-dealers in the shadow economy and of nouveaux riches' (*Current Digest of the Soviet Press*, vol. 41, no. 31, p. 3), turned out to be an actual prediction of the coming state of affairs. Something on the order of a year's worth of GNP, at the very least, has been 'moved' to tax havens, Piketty 2020, pp. 599–601.

33   In his writings on the Commune, Marx had described the bourgeois state as a parasitical, pointing instead to the great changes of the 'people's state' brought about in the Com-mune, Marx 1986, pp. 484, 488–90. Compare this to the perks of those in the Soviet state apparatus, Lewin 2005, pp. 230–32, the impact of which on labour productivity is doubt-ful.

34   Cited in Pollock 2001, p. 23.

35   See Kolganov 2016 for a Marxist analysis of late Soviet patterns representing a new form of capitalism, one that does little either for labour productivity or for the reproduction of the labour force itself.

36   See the articles in Blackburn 1991 for a selection of contemporary views.

37   See Gorbachev in his speech to the Twenty-eight CPSU congress, where he argued that 'The ideology of socialism will be shaped in the country's inclusion in the overall progress

became the 'set of four', a sequence that now ended in the capitalist mode of production rather than in the socialist one. The failure to develop an alternative to the orthodoxy of the *pyatichlenka* thus had significant repercussions when this scheme, and the broader perspective from which it derived, became untenable as state support vanished during *perestroika*.

For as one observer of Soviet historical debates in the post-Stalin period observed, the lack of a new critical perspective and discourse on history merely led to one kind of orthodoxy being replaced by another. In this way the faulty logic of the past is applied in a modified form to the future, without taking into account the specific historical situation of Russia at the time:

> The politicians and intellektualy who unleashed the perestroika process, their convictions sapped by the careerist cynicism of the 'period of stagnation', were a pale reflection of the new intelligenty of the 1960s. Now in the successor states to the Soviet Union the flight from Marxism and 'totalitarianism' has been accompanied by a search for the elusive path that will take them to capitalism and democracy, whatever the social costs. In this sense, the quest for a theory of history and society that opens up alternative paths and perspectives of development possesses as much aktual'nost' for the Soviet successor states in the new millennium as it did for the Soviet Union in the 1960s.[38]

The surviving countries ruled by communist parties are too small and marginal to be able to formulate ambitious plans for building communism, with the exception of China. The current chairman of the CPC, Xi Jinping, has outlined a vision of a 'Chinese dream' similar in scope to that of Khrushchev, announcing that China will attain the status of a moderately prosperous society by 2021 (the centenary of the CPC) and that of a modern socialist country by 2049 (the centenary of the Chinese revolution).[39] These goals are not mere political slogans, but reflect a sustained, decades-long adaptation of Marxist principles to suit the specific situation China finds itself in ('socialism with Chinese characteristics').[40] The main features of this reinterpretation is that China has only attained what is called the 'primary stage of socialism', in which pre-socialist elements

---

of civilization' (*Current Digest of the Soviet Press*, vol. 41, no. 34, p. 18). Earlier in the same speech that overall progress had been identified with market forces, the role of socialism being limited to regulation of markets and securing social safeguards.

38   Markwick 2001, p. 247.

39   Xi 2014, p. 47.

40   See Sun 1995 for this rethinking effort, including a comparison with the Soviet case.

such as market forces still have important roles to play in development.[41] In this stage the emphasis lies on developing the productive forces, doubling GDP every decade and thus attaining the status of a 'middle level developed country' by the middle of the twenty-first century.[42]

Stadialist thinking has clearly influenced such plans, and indeed official histories of China show the influence of the Soviet scheme of five stages, starting with the matriarchal communes and moving to the slave owning and feudal modes.[43] There is a twist here, however, in that the intrusion of European colonial powers on Chinese development takes centre stage. During the late Ming and early Qing dynasties the growth of the productive forces was argued to have generated some early forms of capitalism, but these were stunted by the resistance of feudal forces.[44] With the invasions and exploitation of the Europeans, a new situation developed that has been called 'semi colonial and semi feudal society'.[45] In this era, Chinese development was stunted by these two exploitative forces from without and within, which held back but did not destroy a newly emergent form of capitalism in the nineteenth century.[46] As such there emerged not just opposing forces from the peasantry and the nascent bourgeoisie, but at the same time a new proletariat of urban workers was emerging as well.

The 1911 revolution stimulated the development of industrial capitalism in China, but was unable to make a clear break from the fetters of feudalism and colonialism.[47] It was only with the coming to power of the CPC in 1949 that

---

41   The so-called 'primary stage of socialism' was adopted by the CPC at its 13th congress in 1987. Xi also accepts this stage, noting that China will be in it for a long time, see Xi 2014, p. 44.

42   Sun 1995, pp. 201–2.

43   Bai 2002, note again the absence of the Asiatic mode of production in this outline. A more recent collective edited work follows the same plot but without the references to modes of production, see Hui 2012, pp. 139–44 on the shift from kin to class relations. Note that in the discussion of transition between historical eras, the productive forces are emphasised as playing the determining role, as in the transition from slave-holding to feudal mode of production, Bai 2002, pp. 92–8. However, it would be wrong to see this as a dogmatic application, given that this study recognises the persistence of slavery in some industries, and elsewhere emphasises the huge scales of peasant uprisings, for example those at the end of the Ming dynasty, Bai 2002, pp. 329–32.

44   Bai 2002, pp. 365–77.

45   The 'semi colonial and semi feudal' formulation derived from the Comintern in the 1920s and was used in Maoism to think through the specific circumstances of China within its revolutionary conjuncture, being intrinsically connected to revolutionary practice and strategy: see Barlow 2019.

46   Bai 2002, pp. 411–13.

47   Bai 2002, pp. 581–89.

a decisive break with the past could be made, with the newly created 'state-owned economy' forming both spearhead and mainstay of China's development.[48] Arguments could be supplied, in a somewhat Trotskyist vein, for seeing China as especially suited for catching up with the capitalist powers, but this does not seem to be the CPC position. In fact, the specificity of the country's trajectory and its focus on 'Chinese characteristics' has led some to decry the lack of universalism in its chosen path of development, unlike what the Marxism-Leninist *pyatichlenka* pretended to offer.[49] Yet it should be recognised that it is precisely China's history of resistance toward colonialism and imperialism and the desire for a national rejuvenation that is fundamental to the CPC's policies and legitimacy.[50]

The Chinese focus on the growth of productive forces in the self-defined stage of primary socialism points to the postponement of any transformation of the relations of production into proper socialist ones, and the acceptance of high levels of inequality.[51] The focus on 'Chinese characteristics' has led to an emphasis on the distinguishing features of Chinese civilisation, with historians tracing out a long-term trajectory spanning five millennia.[52] In that sense it is intrinsically different from the Soviet focus on presenting its version of socialism as a universal historical pathway, and later re-joining a purported universal Western path. Thus, while its future fate is likely to be radically different from that of the October revolution, the Chinese revolution has been caught in a similar *cul de sac*. In both countries the stadialist perspective and planning mechanism produced the conception of intermediate inter-stages, neither of which can actually conceive even in theory a transition to social-

---

48   Bai 2002, pp. 719–21.

49   In the sense that in the notion of uneven and combined development there is the potential capacity for skipping stages of development. Especially relevant here is the notion described as the 'privilege of backwardness', which gives a country an advantage relative to more advanced ones, Van der Linden 2007, pp. 148–9.

50   Xi announced his 'Chinese dream' precisely in this context, as part of an exhibition on 'the road to rejuvenation' of the Chinese nation, and the responsibilities of CPC members in this, Xi 2014, pp. 37–9. The anti-imperialist aspect and the desire for China's independence played an important role in the 1980s debates, Sun 1995, pp. 226–7.

51   The concomitant decrease of the state sector and the rise of income inequality to unprecedented levels, second only to the USA, is clear, Piketty 2020, figs. 12.6–7, pp. 607–8, fig. 12.8, p. 618. Also notable is the case of Hong Kong, where the inheritance tax was scrapped on its return to China, consequently becoming 'the sole case of a capitalist country that became more inegalitarian by joining a Communist regime', Piketty 2020, p. 622.

52   See the outline of civilisation or *wenming* of China, both for its history and main characteristics, in the introduction of a four-volume history of China originally published in Beijing, Xingpei and Knechtges 2012.

ism. Other socialist countries and parties are either facing the same problem,[53] or turning to a left populism that cannot think any radical break with capitalist hegemony.[54]

In this way, the spectre of the inevitability of communism has given way to its ideological reverse, namely that of its inevitable demise or compromise. Fukuyama's 'end of history' thesis captures this 'reverse inevitability' well. Using the interpretation of Hegel by Kojève that emphasises a struggle for recognition as the origin and driving force of political life, he combines it in a rather crude way with empirical evidence to argue for the victory of liberal democracy.[55] In a way, Fukuyama repeats the worst aspect of economic determinism by positing the primacy of the development of technology,[56] as well as the worst aspect of humanism by positing a strongly determining role for the dialectic of masters and slaves.[57] The result is a strongly unitary perspective on history, which, if a bit ambivalently, posits liberal democracy and capitalism as the end-point of history and, concomitantly, the demise of the Marxist-Leninist states as inevitable.[58] Even though such arguments are hardly satisfactory on an intellectual level, the post-Soviet conjuncture provides sufficient ideological struts to prevent challenges to this 'reverse inevitability' thesis.[59]

Yet, like Marx's old mole, alternatives to what may be termed the two theses of inevitability have been burrowing their way under the surface of intellectual life. They constitute a set of Marxist perspectives on history that incorporate contingency not as an extraneous factor but rather as fundamentally intrinsic to the historical process. Thus they mark a decisive break with stadialism not

---

53 This is not to discount those efforts in countries like Cuba to move forward to alternatives, some examples of which are described in Fuentes-Ramirez 2017.

54 Or even serve the people effectively, see the sorry response of Syriza to the *Oxi* (No) referendum mandate given to them by the Greek people, Varoufakis 2017, chapter seventeen. In this regard the comments by Kouvelakis on the nihilism inherent in such politics bear repeating: 'like the former Comecon *nomenklaturists*, who led the most ferocious neoliberal reforms: when your inner world collapses, you become a bearer of nihilism – you will do anything in order to stay in power', Kouvelakis 2016, p. 68.

55 Going even further in a later book by stating that the Hegelian desire for recognition can be directly traced to specific biological factors, or as he notes 'when a monkey or a human being succeeds in achieving high status, levels of serotine, a critical neurotransmitter, are elevated', Fukuyama 2011, p. 41.

56 Fukuyama 1992, pp. 71–81.

57 Fukuyama 1992, pp. 192–8.

58 In effect this approach can aptly be described as a version of the Marxist interpretation of history that leads to a non-Marxist outcome, Fukuyama 1992, p. 131.

59 See Barker 2017 for a take on the 'bleak left' emerging after 1992.

just in recognising a plurality of historical pathways rather than a singular one, but in demolishing the conceptual foundations on which it is based. As noted by Michael Löwy, an initial formulation of such a perspective can be found in Walter Benjamin's theses on the philosophy of history, written in 1940 when Stalin's *Short Course* ruled the communist world. For him, they constitute a 'Marxism of unpredictability' that rejects the concept of progress and notions of inevitability, and instead opens up a rich set of opportunities and possible strategies.[60]

This 'Marxism of unpredictability' seeks to provide an alternative to a historical materialism that is wedded to progressive change as an automatic movement through empty and homogeneous space, a notion that Benjamin critiqued in one of his earliest texts.[61] In theses XI and XIII, he specifically targets the social-democrats for adhering to the notion of inevitable and boundless progress through work and industry, in which the natural world is only factored in externally as something to be exploited.[62] Such a view has proved itself conducive to the organisation of political defeats of the working class, both in a lack of adaptability to revolutionary situations and in denying the enduring potential of extreme reactionary forces such as fascism.[63] Although Marx is not his target in these critiques, Benjamin points out that it may be useful to replace his image of revolutions as the chief locomotives of world history with that of humankind 'reaching for the emergency break'.[64]

This emergency break for Benjamin is conceived within a different kind of temporality, one that would blow up the continuum of history and replace it with *Jetztzeit* (now-time).[65] Using the temporal realm of this *Jetztzeit*, he articulated a very different conception of history. In substance, it consists of the history of oppressed humanity since the advent of class society, which, as in the view of Engels, is taken to be coeval with written history. This history is shot through with a messianic aspect, also traceable to Benjamin's earliest writings, that conceived of the post-revolutionary situation according to Judaic *tikkun* or

---

60   Löwy 2005, p. 109. The reference to Epicurean terms such as the *clinamen* by Löwy here doesn't reflect usage in the work of Benjamin, but can be said to be congruent with his statement that: 'to grasp the eternity of historical events is really to appreciate the eternity of their transience', Benjamin 2006a, p. 407.

61   Löwy 2005, pp. 6–7.

62   Benjamin 2006b, pp. 393–95.

63   Löwy 2005, pp. 57–60.

64   Benjamin 2006a, p. 402.

65   See thesis XIV, where the example used is that of the French revolution in relation to ancient Rome, Benjamin 2006b, p. 395, an example also known from Marx's *Eighteenth Brumaire*, Marx 1989, pp. 103–5.

Christian *apokatastasis*: the redemption of oppressed humankind.[66] The historical materialist can grasp this process through the dialectical image, which can be seen as a monad that concentrates historical totality, a constellation that for a revolutionary conjuncture provides a specific connection between past and present.[67]

For example, in the German Spartacist uprising of 1919, there are the events themselves, but also the conjuncture started in 1917, which itself has to be grasped as part of a revolutionary tradition that stretches back not just centuries but across the millennia to Spartacus and the pre-capitalist slave uprisings. But this presents itself not as a narrative of oppression through homogeneous time, as a kind of counter-progress, but rather as a very specific connection between past and present that is captured in a fleeting image. In fact, Benjamin in his *Arcades* book suggested the use of montage to show such connections, and the influence of his ideas can be seen in Bertolt Brecht's work on Julius Caesar.[68] As such, the dialectical image provides a counterpoint to universal history as the narrative written by the victors, that is the enemies of oppressed humankind, as well as the forms of high culture that they have sustained on the basis of the barbarous exploitation of fellow humans.[69]

Historical materialism conceived in this way can be used to blast a hole in the continuum of empty and homogeneous historical time, forming the theoretical counterpart of the physical assault on the clock towers during the July Days of 1830.[70] As such, the kind of historical materialism that can be gleaned from Benjamin's writings is admirable in that it restores to it the primacy of the abolition of class society and the redemption of oppressed humankind, through the relentless and necessary critique of the concept of progress. However, it should be noted that the materialistic aspect is rather ill-defined, although nature, following Fourier, is held not to be external to human history.[71] Thesis XVIII gives a general overview of the relation between history and nature:

---

66   The meaning of this redemption here is not just a restoration of an original state, but rather its adaptation to a future, utopian one, inspired in part by Leskov's use of *apokatastasis*, Löwy 2005, pp. 35–6.

67   Benjamin 2006b, pp. 390–91.

68   Benjamin 1999, p. 460, see also his references to the notion of 'primal history' and Ur-phenomena on pp. 461–3, the connection with Brecht's work on Caesar is discussed in Phelan 2013.

69   Benjamin 2006b, p. 392.

70   Benjamin 206b, p. 395.

71   Löwy 2005, pp. 71–7.

'In relation to the history of all organic life on earth', writes a modern biologist, 'the paltry fifty-millennia history of homo sapiens equates to something like two seconds at the close of a twenty-four-hour day. On this scale, the history of civilized mankind would take up one-fifth of the last second of the last hour'. Now-time, which, as a model of messianic time, comprises the entire history of mankind in a tremendous abbreviation, coincides exactly with the figure which the history of mankind describes in the universe.[72]

Powerful as this image is, it is by itself hardly sufficient for clarifying the interconnections between natural and human history. Writing slightly later, Ernst Bloch addressed the same relation more directly, arguing contrary to Stalin that the slower pace of geological change doesn't mean it had no impact on social change.[73] Even with regard to the Marxist notion of the humanisation of nature, Bloch argues that it entails an interweaving of past and future, not a superseding of natural history. Although clear differences can be noted between Benjamin and Bloch, the latter shared the former's critique of progress as occurring in empty, homogeneous time, as a fetish and automaton of social democracy.[74] Unlike Benjamin, Bloch also addressed another important question: the place of the non-Western world in relation to the Eurocentric focus of stadialism. As noted by him, the concept of progress creates a 'lack of historical space' that shuts out the world-historical importance of the specific trajectories of the Indian and Chinese civilisations.[75] Hence the need to look at the 'interweaving of epochs' in larger geographical spaces.

Despite their differences, both Benjamin and Bloch made incisive and comprehensive criticisms of the stadialist Marxism of their day. Overall, three key aspects can be recognised in their critiques:

1. Emphasised by both is the critique of progress as occurring in empty and homogeneous time, as well as the autonomy of human history from natural history.
2. Benjamin's foregrounding of the oppressed and the intellectual dynamiting of the universal history that kept them in their subordinate position, at the same time unshackling them from the narrow role assigned to them as agents of transition in the stadialist perspective.

---

72   Benjamin 2006b, p. 396.
73   Bloch 1970, pp. 133–8.
74   Bloch 1970, pp. 112–15. See for the differences between Benjamin and Bloch, Farnesi Camellone 2018, p. 151.
75   Bloch 1970, pp. 120–4.

3.   In Bloch the obfuscation of the non-Western world in Eurocentric accounts of progress is highlighted, and the need for an alternative accounts
that includes them is recognised. The importance of this question for the
transition to socialism is also stressed.

All three points have subsequently been proven to resonate powerfully, both
intellectually and politically. We can think here of the postmodern denial of
grand narratives of progress, the question of global warming and the concept
of the Anthropocene, the notion of the multitude as a political force, and the
debates on post-colonial theory. What is significant in both thinkers, however,
is that these questions are combined comprehensively, in a way less commonly seen in today's debates. This combination can be traced back to their
engagement with Marx's work, bypassing Stalinist dogma. In his text, Bloch
used the 1857 introduction to the *Grundrisse* to argue for disparities in the co-
development of base and superstructure.[76] In a section of his *Arcades* book,
Benjamin addresses precisely the same text, through the work of Karl Korsch.[77]
Yet while both authors certainly engaged with Marx's work, there was no sustained, critical analysis of its philosophical premises. Such a philosophical analysis is, however, necessary, to provide not just fragments but rather a comprehensive alternative Marxist theory of history to that of the Stalinist distortion.

2   From Dialectics to the Encounter

Commenting on the relevance of Benjamin's theses on history for today, Löwy
had connected the critique of homogeneous historical time with what was
described in the previous section as a 'Marxism of unpredictably'. Reflecting
further on this unpredictability, he adds the following:

> What is the meaning today, at the dawn of the twenty-first century, sixty
> years after Benjamin's death, of this opening-up of history? First, on the
> cognitive level, it throws light on a new horizon for thought: the search for
> a dialectical rationality, which, shattering the smooth mirror of uniform
> temporality, rejects the pitfalls of 'scientific prediction' of the positivist
> type and brings within its purview the **clinamen** rich in possibilities, the
> kairos pregnant with strategic opportunities.[78]

---

76   Bloch 1970, pp. 115–18.
77   Benjamin 1999, p. 484.
78   Löwy 2005, p. 109, emphasis added.

The reference to the *clinamen* immediately brings to mind Lucretius, a thinker not unknown to Benjamin but at the same time hardly figuring in his writings.[79] It is hardly surprising that Lucretius, and ancient atomism in general, were greatly valued by Marxists as materialist philosophers and precursors to dialectical materialism. Lenin, for example, recognised in the work of Epicurus a perspective both materialist and with dialectical potential.[80] He also posited the existence of two (and two only) philosophical parties, based either on the primacy of ideas over matter (idealism) or the reverse (materialism).[81] In effect this became the 'basic philosophical question' when Lenin's views were taken up by the partisans of Marxism-Leninism.[82] For Lenin, idealism and materialism faced each other as opposite camps in a subtle dialectical process.[83] Hence, the development of philosophical ideas has to be grasped historically, as the unfolding struggle between the two camps, as part of the overall development of social formations.

According to the Leninist perspective, this process can be seen as a series of circles of thought in particular eras, such as between Democritus, Plato, and Heraclitus in ancient Greece, or between Descartes and Gassendi (and possibly Spinoza as well) in the Renaissance. These circles are shaped not so much by the idiosyncrasies of these men, but rather by the struggle of the opposites of materialism and idealism.[84] In terms of the overall process of the development of knowledge it moves, in Lenin's view, not through a straight line but instead through a series of these circles, which together form a spiralling movement. Later Soviet scholars would develop this perspective with much greater historiographical detail, arguing for a close connection with broader history:

> Study of the comparative role of materialism and idealism in the history of humanity thus suggests an organic inclusion of these main philosophical trends in a real socio-economic context. The philosophical ideology

79   In a letter to a friend, Benjamin describes reading Lucretius on Ibiza, in a faraway spot in the forest, affording him 'some of the most pleasant hours of reading I have been granted since my boyhood', Benjamin 1994, p. 464.
80   See his comments on Hegel's section of Epicurus in the *History of philosophy*, Lenin 1981, pp. 289–95.
81   Lenin 1977, p. 165.
82   Oizerman 1988 provides a good example of how this 'basic question', as well as the opposition of the idealist and materialist camps were grasped both in philosophical and historical terms.
83   As they derived from the distinction of the primacy of matter over ideas and vice versa, Lenin 1977, pp. 335–46.
84   Lenin 1981, pp. 245, 260–1.

of the bourgeoisie who were storming feudalism was revolutionary even when it bore an idealist or even religious character. The materialist philosophy of the bourgeoisie who came to power, on the contrary, was conservative; such, for example, was vulgar materialism in Germany in the nineteenth century. In other, less developed capitalist countries, incidentally, this form of materialism played a progressive role.[85]

Hence the development of philosophy, for all its dialectical complexities, follows the development of socio-economic life. In other words it is tied up with the *pyatichlenka* and originates in the slave-holding mode, in the social formations of ancient Greece. In the Soviet perspective, then, we have a stadialist view that cannot, despite its dialectical subtleties, address the question of disjointed temporality. It cannot explain from these premises the contemporaneous worth of Greek art and philosophy, a question that, as we shall see in Chapter 5, influenced Marx's view of historical temporality. Within Marxism-Leninism, however, the tendency is for thinkers to become signposts on the progressive path to socialism and communism. Thus while Lucretius was celebrated in both the Soviet Union,[86] as well as by the Communist Parties in its orbit,[87] his Epicurean philosophical perspective was more like an ancient ornament than something of contemporary critical relevance. The same can be seen to some degree for Spinoza, though this story is more complex.[88]

This is because Spinoza had been the subject of critical debates in the early USSR with regard to his legacy for Marxism, a response inspired by the work of Plekhanov and the newly published *Dialectics of Nature* of Engels.[89] The arguments used in these debates are of considerable importance for understanding the development of dialectical materialism, and especially its distinctions from a Marxism that values pluralism and unpredictability. The main thing that attracted Engels, Plekhanov, and the participants in the Soviet debates to Spinoza was his perception of a universe in which the constant flux of singular things is grasped as part of an interconnected, infinite, and eternal whole, one that is self-caused (*causa sui*).[90] Yet the interpretations of this general world-

---

85   Oizerman 1988, pp. 218–19.

86   Vavilov 1948.

87   See the selection of passages from Lucretius and the commentary in Cogniot 1954.

88   See the collection of articles in Kline 1952, as well as the work by Ilyenkov and others, Maidansky 2003.

89   The publication of this work in 1925 formed something of a watershed. The contents of this work of Engels will be discussed more fully in Chapter 4, in relation to his ideas on the development of humans and of history.

90   Kline 1952, pp. 33–4, 46.

view would be harshly disputed by what in the main can be recognised as two tendencies, or even 'parties'.[91] On the one hand there were the 'mechanists', a more eclectic group that tended more to the natural sciences and was associated with Nikolai Bukharin, but in fact was shared more broadly.[92] On the other hand Abram Deborin and his followers tended more to philosophy, including Hegelianism.

The term 'mechanists' derived from an initial dispute between Ivan Skvortsov-Stepanov and Yan Sten on the meaning of mechanism in contemporary science.[93] The former saw mechanism in terms of the modern scientific understanding of the absorption of energy by plant life through chemical and physical processes. By contrast, Sten decried this as a return to the mechanical philosophies of the seventeenth and eighteenth centuries, which had been harshly criticised by Engels in the *Dialectics of Nature* and was seen as having been superseded by dialectical materialism. In Sten's view, mechanism held a view in which the whole was nothing but the sum of its parts, whereas in Engels each particular form of motion should be understood in its own terms. Hence for biology, it was biological processes that were primary, while chemical and physical ones were secondary.[94] Based on the dialectical law of the transition of quantity into quality, it made no sense to consider primary processes in terms of the secondary ones.[95]

What the 'mechanists' rather proposed was to think the specificity of the whole through its parts, starting from mechanisms such as metabolism. This involves a rather different conception of dialectics, one that starts not from general dialectical laws but infers the dialectical connections between parts based on the investigation of nature.[96] As such, it involves a chain of reasoning that starts with the more simple mechanisms, then considering how they combine together in a complex whole that has a distinct form within nature:

---

91   Initially these were not partisan in a *partiinost* sense, but this would change at the turn of the 1930s; see chapter four of Yakhot 2012 for the trajectory of these debates from relative freedom to strong ideological circumscription.

92   Most notably, what little material there is from Trotsky on these more theoretical issues, peripheral to his political focus, also shows him to be in the 'mechanist' camp, Joravsky 1961, pp. 97–9.

93   Yakhot 2012, pp. 21–7.

94   Yakhot 2012, pp. 24, 111.

95   These conceptions could still be seen in the mature, post-Stalin conception of dialectical materialism, which retained this aspect, as well as the focus on internal factors of development, Graham 1971, pp. 63–4.

96   The reading of dialectical principles into nature was compared by one of the 'mechanists' with the use of Aristotle's philosophical ideas in medieval scholasticism, Yakhot 2012, p. 106.

While studying the cell on a molecular level, scientists get to know the organism as a whole. Only when they had managed to study nucleic acids (chemistry) could they decipher the genetic code (biology). Hence there is no 'reduction' of biology to chemistry, of the higher to the lower, of the complex to the simple, of the whole to its parts. And as true scientists, the mechanists understood the genetic reducibility of life to physical and chemical processes not as an isolated part of cognition, but as a path to discovering the specificity of life, its qualitative distinctness.[97]

As such, there is little reason to conflate this perspective with that of the mechanical philosophy of the seventeenth and eighteenth centuries, and the charges by Deborin and his followers against the 'mechanists' on this score do not hold true. The latter also turned the tables on the former, charging them with Hegelian idealism, in the sense that they used ready-made dialectical formulae to pass judgments on scientific reasoning. Even so, this did not matter in the end, as Deborin's party used administrative measures to ensure the victory of their position.[98] Such charges and methods would become much more serious later on, when Mark Mitin and others introduced intense ideological struggles in philosophy, as well as a host of scientific fields. The results of this for Soviet science are well known, as the case of Lysenkoism and the fate of genetics under Stalin show.[99] This result was hardly an inevitable outcome, however, and it can still be instructive to trace the early debates for their intrinsic value and relevance to a 'Marxism of unpredictability'.

A good way to grasp the differences between the 'mechanists' and Deborin and his followers is through their different understandings of Spinoza's ontology, and by extension also the question of his status as a materialist thinker. The 'mechanists' are harder to pin down as a group, but in general terms they emphasised 'lawfulness' as the central concept in Spinozism. This perspective can be seen very well in the work of Lyubov Akselrod, a former member of 1917 Menshevik central committee and a disciple of Plekhanov.[100] In her major article on Spinoza, she developed Plekhanov's qualifications of Spinoza's system

---

97   Yakhot 2012, p. 110.
98   Yakhot 2012, pp. 36–7, see also Joravsky 1961, pp. 205–14.
99   Highly significant in this regard is also that after repudiating his ideas, Lysenko remained a member of the scientific elite. Furthermore, the theoretical consequences of the former embracing of his ideas were not thought through in a self-critical way, see Lecourt 1977, pp. 129–34; Yakhot 2012, pp. 219–26. Or as Althusser put it: 'The history of Lysenko is finished. The history of the causes of Lysenko continues', introduction to Lecourt 1977, p. 16.
100   Yakhot 2012, p. 243.

as retaining some of the trappings of theology despite its wholesale deconstruction of conventional theology. Placing Spinoza as a man relative to the Jewish community at the time, she argued that he remained at heart a believer, relentlessly pursuing a struggle against anthropomorphic views of God and teleological conceptions of nature. Intrinsic to this struggle is his geometrical method, which is used to show that every finite thing conforms to a strict determinism and causality.[101]

This understanding of causality is completely distinct from any teleology, being placed in a series of causal events that extend into infinity. No part of this can thus lead to a conception of the whole, but inferring from it interests and desires that emphasise human perspectives can create such illusions. As such teleology has (causal) efficacy in social context, but Spinoza's philosophy shows its limits:

> Yet on a closer, objectively scientific inspection all ends, whatever their nature or content, are seen to be invoked and conditioned in the most rigorous manner according to the law of mechanical causality; hence if follows that *teleology itself is only a variety of mechanical causality.* Thus it is evident that the law of absolute necessity, that is, the rigorous conformity to law which characterizes all events, is in Spinoza's system the supreme sovereign law which governs the entire universe. *And this absolute, sovereign law is Spinoza's substance, or what amounts to the same thing, Spinoza's God.*[102]

However, Akselrod does not treat the relation between substance and its modes beyond the general notions of causality and lawfulness, focusing instead on the attributes of extension (understood by her as matter) and thought. She notes that the theological trappings present in Spinoza's work result in a static view of these parallel attributes, even if they come together in the union of body and mind in human beings.[103] Pointing to the primacy of the body and the formation of ideas in the interaction of the senses and the world, she argues that therein lies Spinoza's materialism. No connection is made here between the perspective of lawfulness in substance as such and the modal existence of human beings. More insights in this regard can be found in the work of V.K. Brushlinsky. From his article of 1927 it is clear that he shares Akselrod's view of the role of lawfulness in Spinoza, arguing that the dominant notion

---

101   Akselrod 1952, pp. 70–1.
102   Akselrod 1952, p. 71.
103   Akselrod 1952, pp. 75–7.

in his work was 'strict determinism and strict conformity to law'.[104] His main concern is to grasp the relation between substance as such and its modes.

Brushlinsky notes the various oppositions between the two, substance being infinite, timeless, and conceived through itself, while modal existence is finite, has duration, and is conceived not only by itself but also through other things.[105] He rejects the notion that the latter has emerged from the former, even if substance is by nature prior to its modifications, positing that instead of a process of dialectical unfolding there exists a dialectical correlation between the substance and modes.[106] The main example given here is of the scholium of proposition fifteen of part I of the *Ethics*, with its distinction between water as substance, hence indivisible and impermeable to change, and as water itself, and divisible and ephemeral.[107] It is clear here that there is no sense of transformation, of a cosmogony of modes from some primeval substance, or as Brushlinsky phrases it: 'the causal chain of finite things has neither beginning nor end, and at no point can it come to rest in the finite things from which, according to Spinoza, these things must flow'.[108]

Rather the dialectics Brushlinsky recognises in Spinoza is one of correlation between substance and its modes, based on the lawfulness inherent in considering modes not in isolation but as part of the order of nature, that is: according to substance. At the same time, he points to proposition sixteen of part I of the *Ethics* to show that while substance exists in itself, it is only manifested in its modes. Hence just as the parts cannot be understood without reference to the whole, that is with regard to their causal interconnections, so the whole cannot be understood unless through its parts. Even more so, Brushlinsky points to part I of the *Ethics* again to argue that if the modes were of a different nature, then substance would be different too.[109] This point emphasises the immanence of substance, as he concludes of its dialectical character, it: 'necessarily presupposes within itself an infinite series of finite modes, and in a certain sense is entirely exhausted by this series'.[110]

Brushlinsky in this way nuances Akselrod's view of Spinoza's conception of substance and its attributes as static, showing rather its immanence in the infinite plurality of modal existences. Lawfulness in this sense is nothing else

104   Brushlinski 1952, p. 122.
105   Brushlinski 1952, pp. 120–2.
106   Brushlinski 1952, p. 129.
107   Spinoza 1985, p. 424.
108   Brushlinski 1952, p. 129.
109   Brushlinski 1952, p. 123.
110   Brushlinski 1952, p. 130.

than the causal interplay between finite things, grasped from the infinite series of them that constitutes substance. In this sense extension and thought are not to be seen as if they were elementary particles, so to speak, of an ontology that unfolds from simple to complex. Rather they potentially but not necessarily occur together in modal existences, as in the case where the interactions of human bodies and other extended things exists parallel with human knowledge of those extended things. In this regard, the 'mechanists' were radically different from Deborin and his followers. The latter focused not so much on lawfulness and causality in Spinoza, but rather on the 'central problem' in philosophy of the relation of matter and thought as it follows from the parallel attributes of extension and thought.[111]

Deborin argued that to identify Spinoza's extension with matter is misguided; rather substance itself should be seen as matter, and by virtue of its attribute of thought 'matter itself is capable of thinking'.[112] Needless to say the notion of identifying substance with matter was a major point of contention with the 'mechanists'.[113] One problem that Deborin's position brings up is that it brings up the question of panpsychism and even hylozoism, an issue that appears rather unresolved not just in Deborin himself, but also in Engels, Lenin, and Plekhanov.[114] Given the analysis presented above, this issue is not present in the 'mechanists', as substance was not identified with matter in Akselrod and Brushlinsky. The difference is accentuated when we consider that in their work the dialectical correspondence between substance and its modes was grasped in theoretical terms of lawfulness, whereas in Deborin it becomes a historical relation. That is, the more advanced forms of thought in human beings must have unfolded dialectically from simple matter, and to support this claim Deborin cites from the then recently published *Dialectics of Nature* of Engels:

> The point is, however, that mechanism (and also the materialism of the eighteenth century) does not get away from abstract necessity, and hence not from chance either. That matter evolves out of itself the thinking human brain is for him a pure accident, although necessarily determined, step by step, where it happens. But the truth is that it is the nature of matter to advance to the evolution of thinking beings, hence, too, this

---

111   Already present in Plekhanov, Kline 1952, pp. 15, 26.

112   Deborin 1952, p. 112.

113   Yakhot 2012, p. 182.

114   Some qualifications have to be made, as Soviet authors saw Plekhanov as conceiving of sensation as inherent in matter, but only potentially so in Engels and Lenin, Kline 1952, pp. 27–8.

always necessarily occurs whenever the conditions for it (not necessarily identical at all places and times) are present.[115]

As will be discussed in Chapter 4, this understanding of Spinoza in Engels is closely connected to his use of Hegel, creating something of a philosophical triad, one recognised by Deborin in outlining his differences with the 'mechanists'. For when faced with the opposition between finite modes and infinite substance in Spinoza's thought, Deborin ducks the issue, and argues instead that the dialectic between them was developed further by Hegel in his *Logic*.[116] In this way a Hegelian take on Spinozist concepts can be applied retrospectively. This can be seen especially well for the notion of *Omnis determinatio est negatio*, which is understood by Deborin to apply to the dialectic between substance and modal existences.[117] His argument is twofold. On the one hand there is the inherent potential of negation in finite, ephemeral things (modal existences). On the other hand, from the perspective of nature as a whole (as substance) negation is impossible, and only positive, absolute affirmations can be recognised.

In this way each negation of a finite thing turns, dialectically, into an affirmation in nature as a whole, given that no finite thing exists in isolation and is connected to other finite things through 'reciprocal action'.[118] The Hegelian concept of 'reciprocal action' or *Wechselwirkung* in German is especially notable, given its centrality in Engels and dialectical materialism, in contradistinction to the aleatory current in philosophy (discussed in the final section of this chapter). In Deborin's argument it serves to duck another argument, that of the question of change given the timelessness of substance, referring to reciprocal action in the transformation of finite things and different forms of motion in Engels.[119] These forms of motion include organic life, emerging from other forms of motion such as that of chemistry. Here we see again the different conception of biological processes as primary relative to the secondary chemical and physical ones, as discussed above for the general differences between Deborin and his followers and the 'mechanists'.

The overall contrast between the two camps has important implications for their understanding of the role of contingency. In the Hegelian and Engelsian view of dialectics, chance is objective, but pertains only to phenomena that do

---

115   Cited in Deborin 1952, p. 114.
116   Deborin 1952, p. 108.
117   Deborin 1952, pp. 109–11.
118   Deborin 1952, p. 111.
119   Engels 1987b, p. 511, these ideas of Engels are discussed in more detail in chapter four.

not pertain to the 'innate essence' of a process.[120] Hence the focus lies on the unfolding process according to its internal logic, as in the inherent development of thinking minds from simple matter. The retrospective application of this dialectics to Spinoza shows the differences with the 'mechanists' in this regard very clearly. For in their focus on lawfulness in Spinoza, they argued that contingency was subjective rather than objective, in the sense that chance only stems from an ignorance of causes that are strictly determinist.[121] This position can hardly be seen as an endorsement of unpredictability, but in his commentary on this debate, Yehoshua Yakhot nuances the opposition of subjective contingency and objective causal necessity:

> There is, however, another form of chance. If hail destroys the harvest in a given field, then even knowledge of the causes leading to this result does not eliminate the accidental character of this process: *for the field in question*, the destruction of the harvest always remains something external, accidental, and unrelated to its intrinsic nature. Chance here functions as something relative, but not subjective.

> Let us turn our attention to one more aspect of the problem. Contingencies are characterized by the following traits: first, by the transient and temporary nature of the relations; second, by the fact that it is not obligatory that they occur; third, that the form in which they occur is a matter of indifference, i.e., they could arise in one or another form; and fourth, they arise in space and time in a completely *unpredictable* way.[122]

This perspective does not negate strict causality and lawfulness, but it certainly does negate the perspective of Deborin and his followers, where processes unfold according to dialectical laws and chance only plays a secondary role. Yakhot's conception of chance and unpredictability may not have been formulated by the 'mechanists' themselves, but it certainly is not incompatible with the conception of the relation between substance and its modes in Brushlinsky. For if, as we saw in his work, the former is nothing but an infinite series

---

120	Yakhot 2012, p. 115.
121	The reference is to Bukharin, who as part of a broader argument against teleology opposed contingency to necessity, citing from Spinoza's *Ethics* to argue that the accidental is merely the result of an ignorance of causes, Bukharin 1965, p. 44. This is qualified, however, in the sense that 'accidents' understood as secondary to processes themselves are also causes, and that social determinism should not be understood in a fatalistic way, Bukharin 1965, pp. 45–6, 51.
122	Yakhot 2012, p. 116, emphasis in the original.

of finite things, then there is no inherent tendency in this series, no process of unfolding from simple matter to complex consciousness. Rather, life and mind are grasped in the specificity of the relations between their constituent parts, existing in a metabolic interaction with external things. We are close here to the perspective of the aleatory current in philosophy, not in terms of a worked out set of philosophical theses, but rather in the provisional working out of an alternative to the emerging dialectical materialism.

The major obstacle to this alternative in its Soviet context was that its conception of materialism sat uneasily with conventional interpretations, the Leninist division of philosophy into the camps of idealism and materialism. For it emphasised the critique of teleology and emphasised mechanical causality, rather than taking matter in itself as its alpha and omega. Also important in Akselrod's account was the primacy of the body relative to thought, an aspect that she relates historically to the later influence of Spinozist ideas on Holbach and La Mettrie.[123] According to her they applied Spinoza's principles in a more thoroughly materialist way, including most notably in the relation between this conception of nature and the human collective endeavour for freedom and happiness.[124] Akselrod also noted the famous passage from the letter to Boxel in which Spinoza distanced himself from Aristotle and Plato and aligned himself with the 'founders of materialism', namely the ancient atomists Democritus, Epicurus, and Lucretius.[125]

All of this points to the recognition of a materialist philosophy that is not easily captured through the criterion of the relation between matter and thought, on the basis of which thinkers would be assigned either to the idealist or materialist camps.[126] At the end of this chapter, these early Soviet debates will be related to the later critiques of Soviet 'diamat', which led to the recognition of an aleatory current in philosophy. Here we shall see that it was precisely the concepts retrospectively added by Deborin and his followers to Spinoza, Hegel's dialectics and the reworking thereof by Engels, that were targeted in the later critiques. Later treatments of Spinoza by Soviet philosophers are important, notably the work of Evald Ilyenkov, but dealt with other questions than those that animated the debates between the 'mechanists' and Deborin and his followers. Indeed, in Ilyenkov the same passage of Engels, that it is in the

---

123   Akselrod 1952, pp. 78–82.
124   On the one hand the 'Stoic', fatalist philosophical attitude of Spinoza was emphasised, whole on the other hand the active, political striving for a commonwealth than increases the wellbeing of its subjects, Akselrod 1952, pp. 82–4, 86–7.
125   Akselrod 1952, p. 88.
126   Yakhot 2012, pp. 188–9.

nature of matter to evolve into thinking beings given the right conditions, is prominently present as well.[127] Hence, even if Ilyenkov's work is valuable in many ways, it does not qualify as a 'Marxism of unpredictability'.[128]

Ilyenkov's engagement with Spinoza was paralleled by more or less contemporary work by Marxist thinkers in Western Europe, who unlike him sought to break more radically with Hegelianism.[129] Furthermore, the most significant works produced by these thinkers looked beyond the triad of Marx, Hegel, and Spinoza to reconsider the history of philosophy. In this way they were able to move beyond the 'basic question' of philosophy, transcending the dialectic of an unfolding battle of materialism and idealism. The difficulty of doing so should be clear, however, as can be demonstrated when we look at the case of Antonio Negri. As a professor of political philosophy, Negri was a key figure in the Italian movement of *Operaismo* or 'workerism', emphasising direct class struggle in the factories rather than the parliamentary road of the PCI. As such, it is hardly surprising that Negri sought to develop a Marxist perspective more attuned to the changes that occurred after the events of 1968.[130] It was this quest that lay behind the famous writings on the fragment on machines in the *Grundrisse*, even if later analyses have questioned the kinds of interpretations and uses of this fragment for revisioning Marxist value theory.[131]

As noted by Cooper, it was precisely Negri's engagement with the *Grundrisse* and his rethinking of value theory that led him to reconsider materialism in his *Alma Venus* of 2000.[132] The result was a new conception of temporality, one that counterposed the *clinamen* of Lucretius to an Aristotelian-Hegelian philosophy of time.[133] Some caution needs to be expressed here with regard to the primacy of Lucretius, for Negri sees the *clinamen* as a 'hesitant' notion, expressed more coherently and strongly in Spinoza's philosophy of desire and *conatus*.[134] Indeed, Negri's reflections on materialism can scarcely be separated

---

127   See chapter two on Spinoza in his book Dialectical logic, Ilyenkov 1977. The passage from
        Engels is also present in his remarkable account of cosmology, Ilyenkov 2017, p. 165.
128   The most significant aspect of his work may be his thorough analysis of the notion of the
        'ideal', in relation to the Spinozist parallelism of extension and thought, Ilyenkov 2012, see
        also the interpretation of his work in Bakhurst 1991.
129   Maidansky 2017 traces the differences between Ilyenkov and Althusser and other Euro-
        pean Marxists.
130   See the introduction by Mandari to his *Alma Venus*, Negri 2003, for his intellectual-
        political trajectory.
131   Heinrich 2013; Tomba and Bellofiore 2014.
132   Cooper 2003, pp. 130–7.
133   Cooper 2003, p. 141.
134   Negri 2003, p. 173.

from his analysis of the 'savage Spinoza', in particular with regard to the relation between *conatus* and multitude.[135] Morfino has argued convincingly that in Negri's concept of the multitude, there exists a disarticulation between ontology and history, or more precisely that ontology grounds history.[136] Hence a notion like Spinoza's democracy is seen not as a historical form but rather as ontological, whereas such forms have to be grasped in an intrinsically historical way, as will be argued below instead as a Lucretian intertwining of temporalities.

This argument applies to the engagement with materialism in *Alma Venus* as well. Here, instead of a plurality of times, Negri recognises eternity and what he calls *kairòs*. According to him, *kairòs* is the instant, a rupture and opening of temporality, creative in the sense 'that it is being (*einai*) in the form of generation (*gignetai*)'.[137] Each instant of *kairòs* is invested in the eternal, which is not simply the accumulated past but in terms of generation is 'the power of accumulated life'.[138] In this way Negri arrives at a philosophy of praxis based on a view of temporality as the ontological matter of materialism.[139] This fabric is defined by the curious meeting of the temporal extremes of *kairòs* and eternity. The result is a remarkable vision of human history, the persuasive power of which can be readily grasped from the following passage:

> 'From the destiny of the 'centaur' (Man merged with nature), Man arrives at the destiny of 'man-man' (Man constructed through *praxis*), through to the emergence of the destiny of 'machine-man' (Man transfigured in production, developing his being artificially): second, third, nth natures ... In each of these epochs the common progressively assumes different forms. Different but not metaphysical, nor axiological, nor historicist, nor eschatological. 'Being-centaur', 'being-man-man' and 'being-man-machine' is as progressive as the progress in time from life to death'.[140]

Though stated in an extremely succinct form, Negri's outline is certainly not lacking in analytical clarity and incisiveness, as his take on slavery in the ancient world shows.[141] Yet as a perspective based on the recognition of a plur-

135 Negri 1990, pp. 134–5.
136 Morfino 2014a, see also Morfino 2014b, pp. 7–9.
137 Negri 2003, p. 144.
138 Negri 2003, p. 155.
139 Negri 2003, pp. 158–69.
140 Negri 2003, p. 173.
141 See especially the remarks on the conceptual exclusion of the slaves from the human

ality of temporalities would demonstrate, antiquity was not just defined by the relation of humans and nature. For, as Marx recognised, commercial relations were certainly present at its margins.[142] Furthermore, at least conceptually the notion of machines had been explored as well.[143] All of which goes to show that, while there certainly is a lot of elegance and explanatory power to Negri's provisional outline of history, it ultimately is insufficient owing to its emphasis on ontological unity over pluralism. However much Negri may emphasise the intervening power of *kairòs*, his eternity as a sequence of distinct phases carries with it significant aspects of stadialism. Something like this can be seen in his view of 1968 as the transition to the era of postmodernity, which for him marks a radical break, as the two following passages show:

> That is precisely what is happening: since 1968 the history of humanity has taken this course; the materialist teleology of the common is engaged in this task. And it is precisely at the moment when Power celebrated its most propagandized success – that is, postmodern globalization – that the genealogy of the common transformed itself into a technology of love and began to emerge.[144]

> The epochal break between modernity and postmodernity is 1968. For in 1968 mass intellectuality presented itself for the first time in hegemonic form, that is, as a hegemonic constellation in and of the multitude.[145]

It is not hard to understand the seductive pull of Negri's elaborate outline of the current era, as can be seen in the success of Negri's collaborative work with Michael Hardt as well.[146] However, as a 'Marxism of unpredictability' Negri's ideas hardly fit the bill, given his insistence on a stadialist-like conception of eras. One suspects that his analysis represents merely another *cul de sac*, much like the orthodox Marxism of the Eastern Bloc discussed above. For let us not forget that Marxism-Leninism was quite powerful in its day as well. Both, however, failed to take into account that the intrinsic plurality of history prevents the demarcation of clear-cut stages, and that policies based on

---

species itself, as it is defined by social categories rooted in kinship relations, Negri 2003, pp. 183–4.
142   See chapter five for an analysis of Marx's take on this.
143   Mayor 2018.
144   Negri 2003, p. 208.
145   Negri 2003, p. 215.
146   Hardt and Negri 2000.

such an understanding of history fail to foresee the surprises that come their way. The need to accommodate the shifting sands of time is evident in the latest rethinking by Negri and Hardt, in the face of movements that move away from globalisation and the need to reaffirm the primacy of their conception of the postmodern stage of history.[147] As a Marxism that can address the unpredictable and layered, plural character of history, Negri's is hardly a satisfactory approach.

It will be argued here that it was through the work of Althusser and those closely associated with him, especially Balibar and Macherey, that a truly satisfactorily aleatory approach to philosophy was eventually developed.[148] This perspective hardly sprung fully armed from the head of Zeus, like in the myth of Athena, but rather was wrung out in a sustained, collaborative philosophical effort that lasted decades.[149] As in Marxism-Leninism, this group viewed philosophy as a struggle of idealism and materialism, but like Negri they conceptualised materialism in a very different way. This philosophical perspective dates from the late 1960s, and is developed especially in writings from the 1970s and in the texts on aleatory materialism.[150] It is necessary, however, to consider the relation of these texts to Althusser's early analyses of Marxist philosophy, something that can be seen especially well in the collaborative work on Marx's *Capital* of the early to middle 1960s. Of course, the mainstay of the work of this period is the collaborative volume *Lire Capital* from 1965.

An important aspect of Althusser's contribution to this book is his critique of Origins, that is of the idea that the present is connected to a fixed point in the past, being tethered to it by a shared essence. We can give an example from *Lire Capital*, where the Marxist critique of (classical) political economy is ultimately located in the exposition of its silent, underlying anthropology: its conception of humankind as the 'subject of needs'.[151] Furthermore, this per-

---

147 Hardt and Negri 2019.

148 Which has since been much elaborated by many thinkers, constituting a collaborative effort of sorts. Hence it would be unfair to frame this approach to philosophy in terms of Althusser's own tragic life, as some are wont to do, for example Israel 2019, pp. 921–2.

149 An overview and critical analysis of all the different facets of Althusser's thought can be found in Sotiris 2020, a work that arrived too late to be considered here in the depth it merits.

150 An important early text from 1968 discusses the 'camps' of materialism and idealism in a discussion on Lenin and his view of philosophy, Althusser 1990, pp. 191–6, a position elaborated in Althusser 2017a and 2017b. In a letter to Fernanda Navarro from 1984, Althusser discusses the work of his student Pierre Raymond on the complex interplay between materialism and idealism, thus qualifying the Leninist notion of 'camps', Althusser 2006, pp. 222–5.

151 Althusser 2015b, pp. 314–17.

spective on human origins and nature is more flexible in ideological terms, as a variety of moral, religious, and technocratic notions can be incorporated into it.[152] Despite these variations, the core import of the 'subject of needs' is that it forms the fundament for the theoretical framework of political economy. In a metaphysical sense the subject exists in the space between Origin and End, which can be said here to be represented as their respective sides by the state of nature and the perfected form of commercial society. In effect, we are dealing here with what can be seen as a trans-historical, ideal category that can be applied to all of history:

> And if this anthropology seems **absent** from the immediate reality of the phenomena themselves, it is in the interval between origins and ends, and also by virtue of its universality which is merely repetition. As all the subjects are equally subjects of needs, their effects can be dealt with by bracketing out the ensemble of these subjects: their universality is then reflected in the universality of the laws of the effects of their needs – which naturally leads Political Economy towards its pretensions to deal with economic phenomena in the absolute, in all forms of society, past, present and future.[153]

Althusser continues by noting that this 'false eternity' of political economy derives not primarily from contemporary political reasons, but rather from a theoretical cause, one that actually had preceded bourgeois philosophy. It is here that we can acquire a first inkling of what later becomes the great argument on idealism and various forms of materialism. In *Lire Capital*, however, the main focus still lies on political economy. In a positive sense, this critique of classical political economy allowed for the development of a new historical perspective. Althusser had earlier, in the essay on contradiction and overdetermination in *For Marx*, targeted the Hegelian notion of totality, where each part expresses the essence of the whole (as a *pars totalis*).[154] Instead from a Marxist perspective the mutual determination between different levels has to be seen as contradictory, in which the economic determines only in the last instance.[155] As a consequence a different view of totality as a 'structure of structures' is formulated, which is developed further in *Lire Capital*.

---

152   See Montag 2012a for Adam Smith's ethical concerns.
153   Althusser 2015, p. 316, emphasis in the original.
154   Althusser 1977, pp. 102–4.
155   Althusser 1977, pp. 111–16.

In that book he addressed the lack of explicit expositions of philosophy in Marx's work by teasing out the implicit positions through a procedure of 'symptomatic reading', following here Marx's own critique of classical political economy.[156] From this vantage point it was possible for him to show both the negative and positive movements of Marx's critique. Negatively, Marx was able to point out the conceptual inadequacies and absences of the political economists. Examples are the absence of a general notion of surplus value, rather than just a list of its specific forms,[157] as well as the 'hidden anthropology' of the subject discussed above. In a positive sense, the critique of classical political economy allowed for the development of a new perspective. For according to Althusser, it was the critique of the temporality of political economy, and of the Hegelian concept of historical time, that allowed for a break with the *pars totalis* argument, grasped as an 'essential section'.[158]

This critique allowed Marx to formulate a comprehensive theory of history. According to Althusser, this theory signalled the shift from an ideological to a scientific take on history, an 'immense theoretical revolution' that can be likened to the discovery of a new continent of knowledge.[159] This discovery is in fact coeval with a change in Marx's way of reading, as interpreted by Althusser, for both needed each other in order to break with the Hegelian notion of essence. So whereas in the 1844 manuscripts, human essence is read straightforwardly 'at sight', the mature Marx exposes such essentialism as illusory, a fetishism, and instead history needs to be read according to Althusser's alternative conception of structures:

> It was essential to turn to history to track down this myth of reading to its lair, for it was from the history in which they offered it the cult of their religions and philosophies that men had projected it onto nature, so as not to perish in the daring project of knowing it. Only from history as thought, the theory of history, was it possible to account for the historical religion of reading: by discovering that the history of men, which survives in Books, is however not a text written on the pages of a Book, discovering that the truth of history cannot be read in its manifest discourse, because the text of history is not a text in which a voice (the Logos) speaks, but **the inaudible and illegible notation of the effects of a structure of structures.**[160]

---

156 Althusser 2015b, pp. 16–26.
157 Althusser 2015b, pp. 20–2.
158 Althusser 2015c, pp. 240–3.
159 Analogous to the discoveries of the continents of mathematics by the Greeks, that of physics by Galileo, that of the unconscious by Freud, Althusser 2017a, p. 24.
160 Althusser 2015b, p. 15, emphasis added.

We can more easily grasp what this means if we turn to the thinker to whom Althusser attributes this different way of reading, this conception of the relation between 'reading' and 'structure': Spinoza. In chapter seven of his *Tractatus Theologico-Politicus*, Spinoza outlines his strategy of reading Scripture on its own terms, in line with his desire to avoid adding to it superfluous philosophical ideas such as those of Plato and Aristotle.[161] Exactly as in the study of nature, the interpretation of Scripture should be guided by the natural light, putting together its history, and definitions should be inferred from that history: *ex ipsius historia*.[162] A number of hermeneutic procedures have to be followed to achieve this, starting with the Hebrew language of the text and its ambiguities. Then, an index of subjects has to be created, and the authorship, transmission, and reception of the different books determined. In sum: the critical work of interpretation that renders the text of Scripture legible.

Yet that is not the end of it, as Spinoza's hermeneutics is not merely a circular relation between interpreter and text. For, as he notes, to grasp Scripture it is also necessary to grasp the nation and era for which its teachings were intended, to separate those aspects still relevant today and those aspects which are limited to their original context.[163] Here it is important to realise that Spinoza's emphasis, that interpretation is to be guided by the same natural light as the study of nature, is not merely methodological, but ontological in the sense that humankind does not constitute a separate domain within nature.[164] We should therefore turn to the causal chains connecting Scripture with the rest of nature, starting with the nation and period from which it emerged: the first Hebrew commonwealth. Our concern here is less with the characteristics or historicity of this particular state than with the question of what a commonwealth is for Spinoza. The answer, to speak with Althusser, is that it constitutes a 'singular thing'.[165]

The best account of singular things in Spinoza can be found in part II of his *Ethics*. In definition seven of part II, they are explained to be things that are finite and determined, that is: as resulting from a combination of internal and external causes.[166] Furthermore, if a multiplicity of singular things together cause a single effect, then they can be considered a singular thing as well. More

161   Spinoza 2016, p. 172.
162   Spinoza 2016, pp. 71–3.
163   Spinoza 2016, p. 175.
164   Spinoza, preface to part III of the *Ethics*, Spinoza 1985, p. 491. As emphasised in the *Tractatus Theologico-Politicus*, the same methods apply to the interpretation of Scripture as for the study of nature, Spinoza 2016, p. 171.
165   Althusser 2006, p. 179.
166   Spinoza 1985, p. 447.

details can be found in proposition thirteen of part II, an exposition of sorts of Spinoza's 'physics', starting with the motion of simple bodies to an infinite series of ever larger composite, yet singular things.[167] One of these composites is the human body (and mind), which itself consists of many different kinds of individuals (again, which are themselves composite), and which is constantly affected by external bodies as well.[168] Like any singular thing, humans strive to preserve themselves, in accordance with their power, and this forms the basis for their natural right.[169] Yet, for security and prosperity, the human singular thing is better off in a civil than in a natural state.

This civil state, as it combines multiple causes into a single effect, is also a singular individual, as embodied in the covenant of the *Tractatus Theologico-Politicus*, and later the multitude in the *Tractatus Politicus*.[170] The connection between the collectivity and its members can be understood better from a passage on the supposed election of the Hebrew nation by God.[171] Spinoza here notes how God's guidance (that is, the order of nature) is both internal, in human nature and its powers, and external, in advantages from outside causes (fortune). As such, any social order derives from the interplay of both, and the less it is subject to the whims of external fortune, the more durable it will prove to be. The favour of God bestowed upon the Hebrews, then, can be seen in the success and longevity of their commonwealth. As a singular thing, this commonwealth shares with other states human nature and its powers, but is distinguished from them in the particular order that results from its combination with external causes.[172]

Hence there is no ideal template or form of the state, and variations are not marginal to it but rather constitute the essence of a particular state as a singular thing, just as, contrary to Plato and Aristotle, human beings cannot be brought under a single rubric.[173] There are certain invariants that make the Hebrew

---

167   Spinoza 1985, pp. 457–62.

168   Spinoza 1985, p. 462.

169   Spinoza 2016, pp. 282–5.

170   As emphasised by Curley in his editorial introduction to the *Tractatus Politicus*, there is no social contract theory in the strong, theoretical sense of the word even in the *Tractatus Theologico-Politicus*, even if words that are superficially suggestive of such a concept appear with greater frequency in the earlier work, Spinoza 2016, pp. 493–4.

171   Spinoza 2016, pp. 112–15.

172   See in this regard also the distinction between the state of nature and the state of religion, as embodied in the covenant of the first Hebrew commonwealth, in the *Tractatus Theologico-Politicus*, Spinoza 2016, pp. 292–4.

173   See the remarks in the *Ethics* on the concept of 'Man' as a universal, referring to Plato's term 'featherless biped' and Aristotle's 'rational animal', Spinoza 2016, p. 477.

commonwealth comparable with others, and provide valuable lessons for the Dutch Republic in which Spinoza lived,[174] but to know it properly demands that we take into account its specific history and characteristics. We can now grasp the quotation given earlier from Althusser on the relation between reading and structure better. Reading Scripture *ex ipsius historia* means not just to consider it from a philological perspective, but also through the singular thing of the Hebrew commonwealth and its constituent singular individuals. This represents a fundamentally different way of reading than the Hegelian one attacked by Althusser, where reading on the basis of the *pars totalis* argument can infer the whole from any of its parts.

As shown by Goshgarian and Sotiris, Spinoza's singular thing was of crucial importance in Althusser's evolving theory of the encounter, the problematic of which goes back to a 1959 work on Montesquieu.[175] As he himself explained in the 1970s, it was Spinoza that allowed him to think the Marxist topography of base and superstructures away from the Hegelianism of the essential section discussed above.[176] Instead of each element reflecting the whole, they represent real and distinct forces within a larger causal structure. Singular things come to the fore not just in the unpublished material analysed by Goshgarian, but also in several key texts by Althusser – even if Spinoza goes unnamed here.[177] However, in a 1966 article on the anthropologist Levi-Strauss, he mentions Spinoza's 'singular essences' that allow for thinking singularity, the hallmark of modern science.[178] The main point of this article is to criticise the notion of an original 'primitive' society, as the foundation for an anthropological ideological conception of the essence of humankind.

Instead of through the pairing of Origin and End and the 'hidden anthropology' of classical political economy, following Marx, the earliest modes of production of humankind have to be thought in their singularity. That is, instead of being subjected to a single template, it is necessary to formulate the specific laws and concepts that are appropriate to their particular characteristics:

> When we observe them, we discover that while, in principle, things function in accordance with the same laws of necessity in primitive social formations, they take different forms. We discover, for instance, that the

---

174   Spinoza 2016, pp. 322–31.
175   Goshgarian 2013, pp. 91–4; Sotiris 2014 provides a broader overview of Althusser's trajectory.
176   Althusser 1976, pp. 138–41.
177   Goshgarian 2013, pp. 100–3.
178   Althusser 2003, p. 30.

function of the relations of production is not accomplished by the same 'elements' in primitive societies as in ours; that the political, the ideological and, in general, the instances do not take the same form or, consequently, occupy exactly the same fields as they do in our societies, but, rather, include other elements, relations, and forms. These differences. however, are intelligible only on the basis of Marx's fundamental theoretical concepts (social formation, mode of production, etc.), the appropriate differential forms of which have to be produced if the mechanisms of primitive social formations are to be rendered intelligible.[179]

Hence there are invariants for the mode of production as a general theoretical concept, but for singular cases specific concepts have to be formulated. In that sense we can say that it is already possible to see in the Althusser of the mid-1960s a close connection being made between Marx and Spinoza, in the sense of shared key philosophical points. Exchanges with Macherey during this period would lead to a broadening of this connection into a 'current' of philosophy.[180] Macherey's point was that Althusser's view of Marxist topography retained the notion of the whole, with connotations of organicism and hidden essences possibly creeping in through the back door. In order to break more comprehensively with any latent notion of the whole, Macherey brought up not just Spinoza but also an article on Lucretius by Deleuze. Indeed, the interpretation of Lucretius offered by Deleuze implicitly points to many similarities with Spinoza, who in a later iteration of the article actually appears in the text.[181] The exchange with Macherey had a considerable influence on Althusser, leading to changes in his chapters of *Lire Capital*, as well as the first brief formulation in notes from 1966 on Epicureanism and the theory of the encounter and conjuncture.[182]

3   Convergences of Spinozism and Epicureanism

Before turning to Althusser's later theory of the encounter, however, it is necessary to make a detour by looking at the Spinoza-Epicureanism connection, taking Deleuze's article as a starting point but also incorporating more recent

---

179   Althusser 2003, pp. 28–9.
180   See for an account of the interaction between Althusser and Macherey on this question Montag 2013, pp. 73–100.
181   Deleuze 1990, p. 273.
182   See below in the section on the aleatory current in philosophy.

work on the same topic.[183] The basic thrust of Deleuze is that the Lucretian swerve or *clinamen* reflects not the contingency of an oblique movement, but rather determination within a causal series characterised by an irreducible plurality.[184] That is, there exist laws for particular things, but not a single law that governs all things as a whole.[185] Other aspects treated by Deleuze that are common to the Epicureans and Spinoza are the role of myth in the history of humankind and the critique of finalism. Here the discussion will be limited to the common rejection of the whole and the expounding of an infinite causal series of singular things. This convergence in an ontological sense may surprise readers, given Spinoza's explicit rejection of indivisible bodies and vacuum, the two basic foundations of ancient atomism.[186]

Yet the main critique of this very same argument is levelled against those who think corporeal and extended substance to be finite rather than infinite, as it is for Spinoza.[187] In the philosophical struggle this can be seen as a strong move against a key idealist position. But what of potential affinities with atomism, given Spinoza's apparent rejection of their ontology of atoms and void? Here Deleuze's interpretation of the atom as the minimum of thought, on analogy with the minimal sensible object for perception, is of importance.[188] As a reconstruction of Epicurean physics this is not detailed enough, for the atomic parts identified by Epicurus would necessitate important qualifications.[189] Yet Deleuze's thesis reveals, in a sense, much about the difference between the ancient atomists and Spinoza with regard to minimal particles. For unlike them, Spinoza makes a distinction between *natura naturans* and *natura nat-*

---

183   The connection is only hinted at briefly in the work of Althusser, Deleuze, and Macherey, and until recently existed more on the margins of scholarship on Spinozism, e.g. Klever 2005, pp. 65–77, Moreau 2006, pp. 15–26, as well as on the reception of Epicureanism, Wilson 2008. More recent studies by Montag, Morfino, and Vardoulakis are cited below. The shifting perspectives on the connection between Spinoza and Epicureanism can be readily noted in the series of books on the radical Enlightenment. In the first book Epicurus and Lucretius are hardly mentioned at all, only in a few passing references, Israel 2001. This changes in the latest instalment, where the role of Epicureanism in what is called a radical Renaissance is highlighted, and compared with the radical Enlightenment dominated by Spinoza, including a comparison of their doctrines, Israel 2019, pp. 75–96.

184   Deleuze 1990, pp. 269–70.

185   Deleuze 1990, p. 267.

186   However, Spinoza's conception of a vacuum seems to have been akin to 'extended nothingness', Bennett 1980, and as such is different from the Epicurean understanding of it as the negation of the occupation of space by atoms.

187   Spinoza 1985, pp. 420–4.

188   Deleuze 1990, p. 268.

189   See for this the *Letter to Herodotus* (57–9), Inwood and Gerson 1994, pp. 11–12.

urata.[190] The former is defined by substance and its attributes (such as thought and extension), which is infinite, unique and indivisible, and the latter denotes the mass of singular things, which are finite, divisible, and composed of parts.

This division is fundamentally different than the ideas on this of the ancient atomists, who distinguished between indivisible atoms and divisible compound bodies, both of which belong in Spinoza to the attribute of extension. Hence we can see in Spinoza a different ontological grid. This grid, however, also shares important features with Epicureanism.[191] An important proof of this was provided by Macherey, with his interpretation of Spinoza's so-called 'infinite modes'.[192] These modes form a set of intermediate steps between substance and singular things, without connotations of a hierarchical whole as in Plato's *Timaeus*.[193] These steps start with the attributes of thought and extension, moving on to movement and rest for the latter, and further to the *facies totius universis* (the entire universe). All these steps are still within infinity, in *natura naturans*. The boundary between this domain and that of *natura naturata* is the series from simple bodies to the entire collection of singular things in the *facies totius universis*. As noted by Macherey, the universe considered from the perspective infinity is a series without beginning or end.[194]

Yet from a finite perspective, like that of humankind, abstract limits are set both in a minimal sense (for simple bodies) and maximally in the universe. Here the resemblances with Epicureanism begin. Citing Deleuze, Macherey argues that the *facies totius universis* viewed (abstractly) as a single individual, resembles the atomistic universe of the Epicurean 'sum of things', or *to pan* in Greek.[195] Both are unchanging and eternal, their constituent bodies varying in infinite ways and unable to be combined into a single combination. Hence their view of the universe as the sum of singular things and their inherent plurality is similar. Even so, it should not be forgotten that for Spinoza this is an abstraction that should not be conflated with a really existing singular thing. In Epicureanism, it is represented in more physical terms, in the infinite num-

---

190   Spinoza 1985, pp. 433–5.
191   Montag 2016, p. 171.
192   Macherey 2011, pp. 146–9.
193   As designed and directed by the *demiurge*, Campbell 2006, pp. 12–14, notes that Plato uses similar notions as his atomist adversary Democritus and other materialists, but for diametrically opposite purposes.
194   Macherey 2011, pp. 154–7. Note here the resemblance to the interpretation of the relation between Spinoza's modes and substance by Brushlinsky discussed in the previous section.
195   Macherey 2011, pp. 158–9, see for the Epicurean sources the *Letter to Herodotus* (39–45) of Epicurus, Inwood and Gerson 1994, pp. 6–8, and DRN I.540–627, Smith 1992, pp. 44–53.

ber of finite worlds, as well as the interstices between them where the Gods dwell.[196] Hence seen from the outside, as physical representations or cosmograms, the Spinozist and Epicurean universes seem quite dissimilar.

The similarities lie rather in the generic features of their conceptions of 'totality', and in this regard another convergence can be found in the temporality of the 'sum of things'. In both philosophical perspectives, duration is not in the 'sum of things', since it is eternal, but rather is an effect of the plurality of either singular things or atoms and compounds. Time in both 'schools' is not intrinsic to things, as Epicurus puts it in his *Letter to Herodotus* (72–3), but rather is a qualification given by humans to things based on their experience of natural phenomena such as day and night.[197] It is significant that this statement of Epicurus occurred just before his discussion of the plurality of worlds. These worlds come into being from 'the unlimited' and are structured in similar and different ways, just as with the diversity of historical trajectories of distinct peoples. For this underscores the connection between the plurality of things and their distinct durations, nothing being reducible to a single, homogeneous time valid for all things.

The same can also be seen in Lucretius. In a passage of book I of the DRN, time is held to be an accident of things, and seen as the human sense of the durability of things.[198] This includes historical events, which are seen as accidents of previous sequences of events, a Lucretian view that will be further explored in Chapter 2. The notion that time only pertains to the durability of specific things implies that its main use is comparative, in using the duration of one singular thing to measure that of another. Time as comparison can also be found in Spinoza, as the following passage from an early work makes clear:

> But to determine this duration, we compare it with the duration of other things which have a certain and determinate motion. **This comparison** is called **time**. Time, therefore, is not an affection of things, but only a mere mode of thinking, **or**, as we have already said, a being of reason. For it is a mode of thinking that serves to explain duration. We should also note here – since it will be of use later, when we speak of eternity – that duration is conceived of as being greater or lesser, and as composed of parts, and finally, that it is only an attribute of existence, and not of essence.[199]

---

196   DRN V.146–155, Smith 1992, pp. 388–91.
197   Inwood and Gerson 1994, p. 15.
198   DRN I.449–482, Smith 1992, pp. 39–41.
199   Spinoza 1985, p. 310, emphasis in the original.

Furthermore, in the *Ethics* duration is held to be the indefinite perseverance of a (singular) thing, its end, or rather transformation, being determined by external causes.[200] As Morfino has shown, the sum of these different durations can be understood as a *connexio*, an interweaving of things and their temporal rhythms, based on the infinite series of encounters between them.[201] He locates this view of plural temporality within a broader philosophical current that includes not just the Epicureans but also Machiavelli and Marx, as it is precisely what underlies the critique of Hegelian time discussed in the previous section.[202] From the perspective of the Epicureans and Spinoza alike, as well as the broader current, time cannot be seen as continuous and homogeneous, except in the imagination as we shall see below. Instead the plurality of things also implies a plurality of durations, with time being the comparison between those durations as they are interwoven with each other in the infinite series of cause and effect.

The plot of the Spinoza-Epicureanism connection thickens when we consider Spinoza's simple bodies. These, as Macherey notes, are not indivisible but rather used as mental abstractions.[203] That is, they act as universals that allow for the understanding of nature. When we consider the various discussions of such simple bodies in Spinoza, something Macherey did not explore further, more resemblances to atomism come to the fore. The best place to start for this is Spinoza's exposition of the philosophy of Descartes, as laid down in his *Principles of philosophy*. This work is important for understanding the influence of Descartes on Spinoza, who certainly took from him the denial of indivisible particles and the void, if not the outright rejection of Democritean atomism.[204] Despite this explicit opposition, also seen in the polemics with Gassendi, and his idealist separation of mind and body, hints remain of Descartes as a kind of 'double agent' in the civil war of philosophy.[205]

For in part III of his *Principles*, he put forward a 'fictitious' account of the development of the heavenly bodies, plants, and humans from 'seeds', as well as his vortex theory of the formation of worlds.[206] Both are treated in Spinoza's

---

200   Spinoza 1985, pp. 447 (II D5), 499 (III P8).
201   Morfino 2014b, p. 149.
202   Morfino 2014b, pp. 143–8, 156–64.
203   Macherey 2011, p. 157, see Spinoza's *Treatise on the emendation of the intellect*, Spinoza 1985, p. 41.
204   Descartes 1985, pp. 287–8.
205   See Wilson 2008, pp. 23–4, for contemporary doubts about the susceptibility of Descartes to atomism.
206   Descartes 1985, pp. 256–58.

exposition, but the first is most pertinent for our purposes. The basic impetus is that to know something, it is necessary to grasp its causes, which can be achieved through a historical understanding of those causes:

> Next, since the best way to understand the nature of Plants and of Man is to consider how they gradually come to be and are generated from seeds, we shall have to devise such principles as are very simple and very easy to know, from which we may demonstrate how the stars, earth and finally all those things that we find in this visible world, could have arisen, as if from certain seeds – even though we may know very well that they never did arise this way. For by doing this we shall exhibit their nature far better than if we only described what they now are.

> I say that we seek principles that are simple and easy to know; for if they are not, we shall not need them. We only ascribe seeds to things fictitiously, in order to get to know their nature more easily, and in the matter of the Mathematicians, to ascend from the clearest things to the more obscure, and from the simplest to the more composite.[207]

The description of these seeds as fictitious should not be seen as a ruse to defuse potential charges of atomism, for like the *facies totius universis* they are beings of reason, not real things. At the same time, their use as such made it possible for Spinoza to think the generation of singular things in terms that are strikingly like those of Epicureanism. Letter 4 from Spinoza to Oldenburg shows this, as here he argues that humans are not created but rather generated, their bodies deriving from things that existed before in different forms.[208] Significantly, he adds to this that even if one part of matter were to be destroyed (as matter), then extension itself would disappear. A close parallel can be seen here with Lucretius and his argument that nothing can be reduced to nothing, which follows from a preceding argument that nothing can come from nothing.[209] Both arguments are demonstrated by the generation of different things from other things as they can be observed in nature, the same context that Spinoza uses in his reply to Oldenburg, consistent with other passages in his work.[210]

---

207   Spinoza 1985, p. 295.

208   Spinoza 1985, p. 172. The connection with Epicureanism here was also noted in Klever 2005, n. 20, p. 69.

209   DRN I.146–264, Smith 1992, pp. 14–23.

210   Also relevant are passages from the early work *Appendix on metaphysical thoughts*, Spinoza 1985, p. 334, and from the *Tractatus Theologico-Politicus*, Spinoza 2016, p. 105.

The similarity in fact strengthens the convergence discussed earlier between the Epicurean *to pan* and Spinoza's *facies totius universis*. For that nothing can come from nothing, nor disappear into nothing, is a logical consequence of the eternal and unchanging 'sum of things'.[211] It demonstrates that this convergence was not just incidental, but that the similarities in ontology are consistent and run deep into the respective philosophical frameworks. A further demonstration of this can be found in the motion of simple and complex bodies, especially as it is constitutive of the inherent plurality of the series of causal determinations. Once again, Deleuze points the way:

> The **clinamen** or swerve has nothing to do with an oblique movement which would come accidentally to modify a vertical fall. It has always been present: it is not a secondary movement, nor a secondary determination of the movement, which would be produced at any time, at any place. The **clinamen** is the original determination of the direction of the movement of the atom. It is a kind of **conatus** – a differential of matter and, by the same token, a differential of thought, based on the method of exhaustion.[212]

Deleuze here cites a specific passage from Lucretius that bolsters his case that the *clinamen* was not an accidental diversion from an existing motion, but rather was intrinsic to the first-beginnings of things.[213] In that sense his interpretation is in line with the text and with an important revisionist line of interpretation of the *clinamen*, away from the distortions that philosophical adversaries loaded onto it.[214] As we saw earlier, Deleuze's interpretation of the atom as thought minimum is less secure, but this hardly undermines his other points here. With regard to the connection between the *conatus* and *clinamen*, it is important in this regard to explore in more detail how Lucretius relates the latter concept to human action. From the observation that humans and living beings in general go where pleasure takes them, not just from the impact of external forces but from their own will, Lucretius infers the *clinamen*.[215] For nothing can come from nothing, and hence if the swerve had not been part of the first-beginnings of things, then it would never have been possible

---

211   See the letter (10) to Simon de Vries, Spinoza 1985, p. 196.
212   Deleuze 1990, p. 269, emphasis in the original.
213   Deleuze cites DRN II. 243–50, the connection of the *clinamen* with first-beginnings follows immediately after in lines 251–262, Smith 1992, p. 115.
214   As recognised by Marx in his doctoral dissertation, Marx 1975, pp. 46–8.
215   DRN II.251–291, Smith 1992, pp. 115–19.

to break the 'bonds of fate'. Consequently, humans would have been completely determined by external forces.

How humans actually exert their will is described elsewhere in another part of the poem.[216] First an image of an action impacts our mind, followed by the conception in the mind of a desire, which sets in motion a further chain of action that lead to the body to spring to action. It is important to stress here that there is not some incorporeal entity that can direct the body, but rather that all elements like mind, soul, and body, form part of a larger chain of intersecting powers in which human agency is located.[217] In that sense, Deleuze's use of the term *conatus* doesn't seem wholly inappropriate, for the *clinamen* is what makes it possible for living creatures to exert power and to persevere in their existence. Naturally, what is especially interesting is the implicit connection with Spinoza, even if Deleuze doesn't make this explicit in this part of his overall argument.

Here it is necessary to recall how for Spinoza simple bodies are 'beings of reason', not existing in reality, but nevertheless useful for explaining phenomena such as the generation of human beings from different kinds of bodies. Given that these particles are notional, and that Spinoza rejects the ontology of indivisible atoms and void, it is not surprising that no formulation of a *clinamen* are to be found in his work. Yet nevertheless his conception of *conatus* in animate and inanimate bodies can be said to be compatible with it. Montag has noted the connection between the discussion of bodies in part II of the *Ethics* and that of *conatus* in part III.[218] The *conatus* has to be seen as a verb, with both animate and inanimate things persisting according to their power, and this constitutes their essence, that is, what distinguishes them from other singular things. The result is a theory of encounter without atoms and void, with encounters (and non-encounters) between singular things based on the intersection of their powers. As Montag argues, this can be seen as a translation of the language of atoms of Lucretius to a different ontological grid of singular things in Spinoza.[219]

Even more fascinatingly, one phrase of Lucretius is not in fact translated but retained as it was in the original, even if Spinoza may well have taken it from

---

216   DRN IV.877–897, Smith 1992, pp. 345–7.

217   In this regard the fragments from book XXV of *On nature* by Epicurus are of relevance too, Inwood and Gerson 1994, pp. 76–7. While the interpretation of this fragment is complex, it is clear that it addresses the interaction between different factors that shape human actions, some of which are within and others outside human powers.

218   Montag 2016, p. 170.

219   Montag 2016, p. 171.

Descartes. The phrase in question is '*quantum in se est*', which is used four times in the context of the exposition of the motion of atoms in Lucretius, and is usually translated '*as far as in them lies*'.[220] In all four occasions, this phrase refers to the tendency of atoms to move downward through the void, when not affected by other bodies. Most notable is line 247 of book II, where *quantum in se est* is used to disprove the possibility of oblique movement in atoms, as they cannot go against their natural tendency, except for the tiniest, minimal swerve. In his commentary on the *clinamen* argument of Lucretius, Fowler also points in passing to a relation of the phrase to the occurrence of *quantum* in line 302 of book II.[221] The context of this passage is the relation of the permanence of matter and motion. Based on that, the conditions for compounds to form remain eternally the same, each of them having power 'as much as' granted by the *foederae naturae*, the 'laws' governing specific compounds.[222]

Hence the motion of atoms is inherent, modified only by external factors, whereas the motion of compounds is based on the 'laws' deriving from the specific configuration of atoms that constitute them. In terms of later reception of this Epicurean notion, an argument has been made that the phrase *quantum in se est* was of considerable influence on the formulation of what became to be known as the principle of inertia, as can be seen in its occurrence in the work of Descartes and Newton.[223] It was through the former that Spinoza also encountered it, for the phrase first occurs in the exposition of his *Principles of Philosophy*, paraphrasing the 'first law of nature' of Descartes that simple and undivided bodies continue 'in so far as they can'.[224] The only modification to a body can come from external bodies, and as Spinoza states in a later proposition, a body suffering variation from such external forces will strive for the least possible modifications to itself.[225]

That Spinoza is not just following Descartes here can be seen in the recurrence of *quantum in se est* in proposition six of the third part of the *Ethics*, where it is used to describe the power of each singular thing to persevere in its being: that is, *conatus*.[226] A still more interesting occurrence of *quantum in se*

---

220 DRN II.190, 201, 205, and 247, Smith 1992, pp. 108–9, 110–11, 114–15.

221 Fowler 2002, p. 278.

222 DRN II. 294–307, Smith 1992, pp. 118–19. See Fowler 2002, pp. 377–81, for further discussion of this term, which seems closely bound up with duration.

223 As argued in Cohen 1964, see also Hine 1995.

224 Descartes 1985, pp. 240–41; Spinoza 1985, p. 277.

225 Spinoza 1985, p. 283.

226 Spinoza 1985, pp. 498–9. The phrase 'as far as it can' also occurs later in the same part of the *Ethics*, describing human striving in relation to the passions, as in proposition thirty-three, Spinoza 1985, p. 513.

est can be found in the *Tractatus Theologico-Politicus*, in the context of the discussion of natural right. After observing that the power of the whole of nature is nothing more than the sum of the power of all singular things together, Spinoza continues the argument by stating:

> Now the supreme law of nature is that each thing strives to persevere in its state, **as far as it can** by its own power, and does this, not account of anything else, but only of itself. From this it follows that each individual has the supreme right to do this, i.e. (as I have said), to exist and have effects as it is naturally determined to do.

> Nor do we recognize here any difference between men and other individuals in nature, nor between men endowed with reason and those others who are ignorant of true reason, nor between fools and madmen, and those who are sensible and sane. For whatever each thing does according to the laws of its nature, it does with supreme right, because it acts as it has been determined to do according to nature, and cannot do otherwise.[227]

With this we return to the discussion of the civil state as a singular thing earlier in this chapter. This state, as a multiplicity of singular things with a common effect, depended on the combination of human nature and its powers and the fortune of external things. We can now see that this internal power of human beings, their essence, is like any other thing in nature, the ability to persist 'as far as it can' (*quantum in se est*). This ability, this power, derives from nature's laws. It is possible to see the same distinction between internal power and external circumstances in Lucretius, where the power of compound beings to act derived from the *clinamen* that broke the 'bonds of fate'.[228] Hence, even considering that Spinoza posited no atoms and void, but solely singular things, the interplay of things follows similar principles. In both philosophies, the internal power of bodies sets up the possibility of encountering external bodies, yet prevents subsumption into a concurrent whole.

In other words, both philosophies privilege the encounter over the form, the encounter in both embodied in intrinsically transient combinations. The Epicurean and Spinozist wholes can instead be found in the 'sum of things', the infinite causal series of a plurality of combinations, each with distinct durations that cannot be reduced to a single, abstract time. This series is under-

---

227   Spinoza 2016, pp. 282–3, emphasis added.
228   This is captured in the ability to act *sponte sua*, without external constraint, see the next chapter and especially the section on anthropogony for the significance of this phrase.

pinned by the eternal truth that nothing can come from nothing, or pass into nothing. Instead, something is always generated from some other thing, whether it concerns worlds, human beings, or commonwealths. The critique of finalism, of origin and end, derives from the generic characteristics of their respective ontologies, and the hence the noted affinity of Lucretius and Spinoza on this score reinforces the argument on the convergence, if not identity, of their ideas.

As noted by Macherey and Morfino, there is a close resemblance between the critique of finalism in the appendix of part I of Spinoza's *Ethics* and the anti-teleological perspective that suffuses Lucretius.[229] Here it is important to trace the connection noted by Morfino between the rejection of finalism and the understanding of causality it entails. In his critique, Lucretius argues that to suppose the parts of the body to have been made for an end reverses cause and effect, for unlike artefacts they were not intentionally made for specific purposes.[230] In the preface to part IV of the *Ethics*, Spinoza notes that the human tendency to form universal ideas leads them to confuse the ends and perfection of artificial things to apply also to natural things.[231] In this passage he refers the reader back to the appendix of part I, where the argument that nature does nothing on account of an end led to the conclusion that any inference of an end implies a reversal of cause and effect.

Therefore, we can see in Spinoza and Lucretius alike the argument that finalism entails a faulty understanding of cause and effect. Furthermore, this error derives at least in part from imputing to nature the same kind of design and uses that exist for the artefacts created by human hands, or more broadly from the human body. Another famous passage from letter 32 to Oldenburg is significant in this regard as well, since it cogently sketches the finalist position:

> Let us feign now, if you please, that there is a little worm living in the blood which is capable of distinguishing by sight the particles of the blood, of lymph, [A: of chyle], etc., and capable of observing by reason how each particle, when it encounters another, either bounces back, or communicates a part of its motion, etc. Indeed, it would live in this blood as we do in this part of the universe, and would consider each part of the blood as

229 Morfino 2014b, pp. 75–6, see also Macherey commentary on Spinoza's *Ethics*, Macherey 1998, p. 238.
230 DRN IV.823–857, Smith 1992, pp. 340–3.
231 Spinoza 1985, p. 544.

a whole, not as a part. It could not know how all the parts of the blood are regulated by the universal nature of the blood, and compelled to adapt themselves to one another, as the universal nature of the blood requires, so that they agree with one another in a definite way.[232]

This finite perspective can be transcended by the philosophical perspective that sees the infinity of nature, rather than the limited perspective provided by human affections.[233] At the same time, there is another philosophical perspective that, Spinoza argues, actually proceeds from finalism, hence moves in the wrong order. In one early work, he noted how the notion of confusion of nature follows from the application of universal ideas to judge particular things.[234] Perfection and imperfection are ascribed to particular things based on these universals, even if these are for Spinoza as non-existent in nature as centaurs.[235] Specific examples of this way of reasoning noted by him are the philosophies of Plato and Aristotle, both of whom ascribed universal ideas to God. The connection here with the 'worm in the blood' argument quoted above should be clear. Plato and Aristotle wrongly infer a whole from the small part on which 'universals' are based, and then reverse gears to provide a finalist perspective on the small part.

Another early work of Spinoza supplies a small clue as to his view the historical development of such philosophical views, even if no specific philosophers are named here.[236] Here the ordinary use of words precedes philosophy, with true and false acquiring their meaning in narratives of human action. This meaning was then falsely applied to mute nature, to denote the relation between ideas and objects, resulting in notions of 'true' and 'false' for materials like gold that do not apply to it. Historically, then, finalist philosophies seem to derive from the common prejudices. Proceeding in the wrong order philosophically can also be seen in the *Ethics*, most notably in the appendix to part I.[237] Here Spinoza gives an example of a man killed by a stone falling from a roof.

---

232   Spinoza 2016, p. 19.
233   See the passage of DRN I.72–75, Smith 1992, pp. 8–9, where Epicurus is described as going beyond the 'flaming walls of the world' to traverse the infinite universe with his mind and imagination.
234   Spinoza 1985, pp. 86–7.
235   See the comments on centaurs in a letter (54) to Boxel, Spinoza 2016, p. 415, and earlier in the work *Appendix on metaphysical thoughts*, Spinoza 1985, p. 307.
236   Spinoza 1985, p. 312.
237   Spinoza 1985, p. 443, the notion of proceeding in the 'wrong order' in philosophy by proceeding from fictions toward God, recurs in the scholium of P10 of part II of the *Ethics*, Spinoza 1985, p. 455.

From the finalist perspective, such an event cannot happen but on account of an end, for otherwise an infinite regression of causes stops only at God's feet.

Morfino has linked this passage to Aristotle's *Physics*, where he addressed the notion that the world originated by chance, as exemplified by the cosmogony of the vortex theory of Democritus.[238] Here we can see Aristotle ascribing chance as caused by the occasional encounter of causal processes, whether purely accidental (*automaton*) or involving intention (*tuche*).[239] Furthermore, he entertains the notion that things might actually come about through the intersection of causal processes, which results both in successful species and in the perishing 'man-faced ox-progeny' of Empedocles. Yet, in the end form takes precedence over matter, in other words final causes rule over the secondary, accidental ones produced by the encounters of distinct causal chains. By contrast, as stressed by Morfino, in Spinoza it is precisely these encounters that constitute the plural and infinite series of a diversity of singular things.[240] The similarity with Epicureanism here has already been discussed.

In this sense, it is hardly surprising that in rejecting the finalist account of ghosts by Boxel, Spinoza in letter 56 praises Democritus, Epicurus, and Lucretius, while belittling Plato, Aristotle, and Socrates.[241] His perception of the adversity between these different schools is brought to the fore by highlighting Plato's desire to burn the works of Democritus. Quite notable, too, is that in the same passage Spinoza also discusses the atomists as defending the existence of invisible rather than indivisible particles, thus avoiding distancing himself from them on account of his own argument in the *Ethics* and elsewhere against indivisibility.[242] There is no reason to question here the observation that Spinoza's ontology was not one of atoms and void, nor by extension was his cosmology an atomist one. Yet, an unquestionable similarity for the critique of finalism runs as a red thread through his work and that of Epicurus and Lucretius alike, and as discussed here these derive from shared basic philosophical positions. These positions, furthermore, set both philosophical streams apart from the systems of Plato, Aristotle, and their epigones.

---

238 Morfino 2014b, p. 102.

239 See the section on the 'two rains' in the next chapter for a full discussion of precisely these passages of Aristotle.

240 Morfino 2014b, pp. 86–7.

241 Spinoza 2016, p. 423.

242 Spinoza's phrasing literally refers to 'Epicurus, Democritus, Lucretius, or any of the Atomists, or defenders of invisible particles', Spinoza 2016, p. 423.

Finally, new work by Vardoulakis has emphasised that the similarities be-tween the conception of the whole and critique of teleology in both schools can be connected to their ethical concerns, in particular the calculation of util-ity.[243] A number of strands can be recognised in his work:

1. The Epicurean notion of *phronesis*, as instrumental knowledge required for action, is central to its philosophical outlook,[244] This includes Epicur-ean ethics with its focus on utility and in that it is similar to Spinoza's ethics, for which important similarities can be discerned.[245] Indeed, the close connection between virtue and utility can be observed for the con-ception of law in both schools as well.[246]

2. *Phronesis* as the starting-point of philosophy is intrinsically connected to the rejection of creation *ex nihilo* and the conception of the totality (*to pan*), and in this way is also closely comparable to the Spinozist con-ception of the whole.[247] Following from this and common to both is the critique of teleology.[248]

3. Yet *phronesis* is not a straightforward matter, as it can be distorted both from the internal factor of overwhelming passions, and the external one of power relations.[249] A historical aspect can be noted in this, notably in the account of Lucretius of the beginning and further development of social life.[250] Here the role of religious fear in bolstering the authority (the Spinozist *potestas*) of a kings like Agamemnon is significant, for the con-trast between this kind of power and the unconstrained use of *phronesis* is present in Spinoza too.[251]

---

243   Unfortunately, his book on the topic arrived too late to consider here.

244   Vardoulakis 2019a, pp. 1015–16.

245   Vardoulakis points in particular to the scholium of proposition twenty of part IV of the *Ethics*, where *conatus* is connected to utility, Spinoza 1985, p. 557. He points out that this is close to the historical use of *phronesis* in the account of early human history in book V of the DRN of Lucretius, in the sense that it revolves around a similar kind of dialectic of between authority and utility, Vardoulakis 2020, p. 47.

246   Vardoulakis 2019b.

247   Vardoulakis 2020, p. 1015.

248   In this regard he also points to the historical character of *phronesis* in Lucretius and the denial of divine creation, also evident, if implicitly and generically, in the appendix to part I of Spinoza's *Ethics*, Vardoulakis 2019a, p. 44.

249   Vardoulakis 2020, pp. 1016–17.

250   In particular in his emphasis on the delicate balance between progress and retrogression in the sequence of forms of socio-political life, as grasped through *phronesis*, Vardoulakis 2019a, p. 46.

251   Vardoulakis 2019a, pp. 42–4.

4. The conception of philosophy, then, is one of the active powers (Spinoza's *potentia*), which is free and to be contrasted to the oppression of *potestas*, especially in the kind that is based on the use of (religious) fear for political ends.[252]

From these observed similarities in the connection between *phronesis*, the conceptions of ontology, and the historical forms of human life defined by states and religions, follows another question: that of the political import of philosophy. So far any similarities between Spinozism and Epicureanism with regard to this aspect seem not to have been investigated. No doubt such an investigation is made enormously complex by the fact that, as with ontology, the political grids of the social forms in which Epicurus, Lucretius, and Spinoza lived were radically different.[253] Perhaps it is more prudent to say that it is possible to recognise the role of Epicurean ideas in early modern ideas on the social contract in Western Europe. Certainly, their influence on Hobbes has been noted, and was reckoned among the aleatory current in philosophy by Althusser.[254] It might well be that similarities in ethics between Epicureanism and Spinoza led to a view of political life and the state that was as different from the latter as their respective conceptions of the universe. Yet they would share certain views on justice and law, and the role of religion in public life, that are striking and should be noted.

4 The Aleatory Current in Philosophy

Having made this rather lengthy detour we can now return to our point of departure, namely the impact of Deleuze's article on Lucretius and Macherey, and through him on Althusser. Having here outlined the many convergences between Epicureanism and Spinoza, especially on the latter's notion of singular things so important to Althusser, this impact can now be appreciated more comprehensively. The immediate impact on Althusser can be seen in brief notes of his from 1966 on Macherey's book *A Theory of Literary Production* (published the same year), as reproduced by Goshgarian:

> Theory of the encounter or **conjunction** (= genesis ...) (cf. Epicurus, clinamen, Cournot) (theory of the deviation cf. **Epicurus**) ... 2. Theory of the conjuncture (= structure) .... Philosophy as general theory of the **conjuncture**

---

252 Vardoulakis 2019a, p. 44.
253 See for the 'political grid' of Spinoza, Balibar 1998.
254 Althusser 2006, pp. 179–83.

And, surrounded by curly brackets and underlined four times:

Theory of the clinamen[.] First theory of the encounter![255]

References to Epicureanism thereafter can be found with increasing frequency in Althusser's work. Examples can be found in the contexts of the critique of finalism in biology,[256] and the beginnings of states.[257] The connection between Marx and Epicurus is also described as having important repercussions for the understanding of the former in a 1972 letter to Francine Markovits.[258] In the same year Althusser gave a course on Rousseau's *Second Discourse*, bringing out the aleatory aspects of that work in a way that powerfully foreshadows the later work.[259] In this text, Lucretius is mentioned only once, in the context of negating the fear of death that so troubles human beings.[260] Of great importance, too, is the role of Epicureanism in a number of texts on Marxism and philosophy, developing a topic prominent in *Lire Capital*. For example, in one text from 1976, Althusser briefly notes that the materialism of Epicurus and Machiavelli can help to find a way to understand the philosophical silence of Marx in *Capital*.[261] Most notably, in a text from the previous year he had used both Spinoza and Epicurus to grasp the connection between Marx and Hegel:

> Marx was close to Hegel in his critique of the legal subject and of the social contract, in his critique of the moral subject, in short of every philosophical ideology of the Subject, which whatever the variation involved gave classical bourgeois philosophy the means of guaranteeing its ideas, practices and goals by not simply reproducing but philosophically elaborating the notions of the dominant legal ideology. And if you consider the

---

255   Goshgarian 2013, p. 107, emphasis in the original.
256   Althusser 1990, p. 154.
257   Althusser 1999, p. 36.
258   Althusser 2017a, note 7, p. 150. Goshgarian also points to an intensive study by Althusser of the ancient atomists around the same time, most likely in 1973, noting that this led to them being promoted to the rank of Marx's 'most important', albeit indirect, 'ancestors', see Goshgarian's introduction to Althusser 2006, p. xvii.
259   Vargas traces the changes in Althusser's conception of Rousseau in the various courses he gave on him from 1956 onwards, also pointing to the differences between the 1972 lectures and the section on Rousseau in the 1982 text on aleatory materialism, noting the absence of the notion of the circle in the latter text, Vargas in Althusser 2019, pp. 21–8.
260   Althusser 2019, p. 112, see also Althusser 2017b, p. 35 on the Epicurean conception of death.
261   Althusser 1990, pp. 260–1.

grouping of these critical themes, you have to admit that Marx was close to Hegel just in respect to those features which Hegel had openly borrowed from Spinoza, because all this can be found in the *Ethics* and the *Tractatus Theologico-Politicus*. These deep-rooted affinities are normally passed over in pious silence; they nevertheless constitute, from Epicurus to Spinoza and Hegel, the premises of Marx's materialism.[262]

In a work from the same period, Althusser highlights the Epicurean conception of the plurality of worlds and atomic movement as the basis for a theory of the encounter of simple and composite bodies.[263] In the sense that this theory reverberated in the later thinkers of the aleatory current, the ancient atomists are our contemporaries; in effect they are fellow fighters in the Great War of materialism and idealism.[264] Another text, written in 1978, outlines the importance of Epicureanism in the struggle of idealism and materialism. Against the idealist notion of a world-order with an absolute point of Origin out of nothing, *creatio ex nihilo*, Epicurean atomism located the beginning of plural things in encounters between atoms.[265] Furthermore, even if philosophy starts with Plato's appropriation of mathematics, the lost writings of Democritus on this topic may in fact have been the actual starting point.[266] What we can see in these writings of Althusser from the 1970s is that Epicurus and other atomists were closely related to the theory of the encounter.

This theory aligns Epicurus, Lucretius, and also Democritus with a varying set of other thinkers, especially Machiavelli, Spinoza, Rousseau, and Marx. Hence it is indeed hard to see the famous 1982 text on 'aleatory materialism' as marking a radical break in Althusser's thought.[267] All the same, we are not dealing with a restatement of past work. Rather, Althusser seems in this text to have thought through in a more comprehensive way aspects earlier expressed separately.[268] In addition to this, the relation of atomism to Marxist philosophy

---

262 Althusser 1990, p. 216. He goes on to outline how the rejection of Origin in these thinkers goes hand in hand with their use of dialectics to posit alternative philosophical categories, noting that this philosophical strategy strongly connects 'the materialism to be found in Epicurus, Spinoza and Hegel', Althusser 1990, p. 217.

263 Althusser 2017a, pp. 100–1.

264 Althusser 2017a, p. 37.

265 Althusser 2017b, pp. 28–30.

266 Althusser 2017b, pp, 170–1.

267 Goshgarian 2013, 2019.

268 Here we can think not just of the brief references to Epicureanism in earlier writings, but also the treatment of figures like Machiavelli, Spinoza, and Rousseau, now abbreviated and put into a new framework.

now comes to the fore, in that there is not one materialism opposed to idealism, but rather two different kinds of materialisms:

> That is the first point which – revealing my main thesis from the start – I would like to bring out: the existence of an almost completely unknown materialist tradition in the history of philosophy: the 'materialism' (we shall have to have some word to distinguish it as a tendency) of the rain, the swerve, the encounter, the take [prise]. I shall develop all these concepts. To simplify matters, let us say, for now, a materialism of the encounter, and therefore of the aleatory and of contingency. This materialism is opposed, as a wholly different mode of thought, to the various materialisms on record, including that widely ascribed to Marx, Engels and Lenin, which, like every other materialism in the rationalist tradition, is a materialism of necessity and teleology, that is to say, a transformed, disguised form of idealism.[269]

Foundational to this tradition are the Epicurean rain of atoms and their potential for deviation in the *clinamen*, which forms the basis for a plurality of worlds, species, and social forms. The atomists as 'friends of the Earth' break here with the logocentrism of the 'friends of the Forms', as well as with the inverted materialism associated with the latter.[270] That is, in Epicureanism there is no question of following what Heidegger termed the 'principle of reason', which would imply a *logos* anterior to the plurality of things. Althusser's main concern, however, is not with ancient thought, but rather with tracing the presence of a 'materialism of the encounter' in thinkers as diverse as Machiavelli, Hobbes, Spinoza, Rousseau, and Marx.[271] For each of them an aspect of their thought is related to this aleatory current, which, despite the brief and sometimes cursory treatment of individual thinkers, shows an overall consistency in their intellectual affinity. What these thinkers share is not a common system, but rather shared similar theses, in the sense of occupying similar positions in the struggle between idealism and materialism in philosophy.[272]

Here it is useful to recall how earlier in this chapter we saw how in the Soviet historiography the 'basic problem of philosophy', of the primacy of matter over ideas or vice versa, was the basis for the definition of the two camps. Furthermore, it was shown how the 'mechanists' and their views on Spinoza could

---

269   Althusser 2006, pp. 167–8.
270   Althusser 2006, pp. 271–2.
271   Also Deleuze, Derrida, Heidegger, Wittgenstein, see Althusser 2006, pp. 168–9, 189–90.
272   Althusser 2006, pp. 222–4, 267.

not fit in this framework, given their emphasis on causality and the critique of teleology. In contrast to this, Deborin and his followers, as well as the heavily *partiinost* philosophy of 'diamat' that followed, accepted Spinozist substance as matter, and hence as primary relative to thought (and to extension). Their philosophy is in fact close to what Althusser describes as one of teleology, a masked idealism, in the quotation given above. The 'mechanists' in this sense provide an earlier example of the same central feature of the aleatory current, the comprehensive critique of any kind of teleology. However, it was noted as well that their view of chance in purely subjective terms, following from strictly determinist causality, obscured the objective character of chance.

Yet the recognition in Brushlinsky of Spinozist substance as an infinite series of finite modes, exhausted by this series, was compatible with Yakhot's observation on an objective side to chance in terms of relation. This observation, and the example of rain falling on a field, brings him in fact very close to the aleatory current.[273] It was precisely the emphasis on the aleatory that was developed into a new direction, one that was not possible in the Soviet Union after the establishment of dialectical materialism. The clearest example of this is in the discussion of the capitalist mode of production in Althusser's 1982 text. Incidentally, many of these ideas in this fragment can already be seen in writings from the second half of the 1970s, most notably in *Philosophy for Non-Philosophers* and the *Book on Imperialism*.[274] The first aspect of capitalism discussed in the 1982 text is that it is the result of an encounter, in England, between the 'owners of money' and a proletariat devoid of all economic means but their labour-power.[275]

The most significant fact about this encounter, however, is that it may well have never taken place, or when it did take place at other times and places it failed to endure, for example in the late medieval city-states of the Po valley.[276] As such, a number of elements are involved in the encounter that results in capitalism, each with a specific history that cannot be reduced to an overarching teleological process: in a sense they can be said to be 'floating' prior to their combination in a mode of production. In this way, the theory of encounter as formulated in the text on aleatory materialism also refigures Althusser's notion

---

273 The same passage is emphasised in Morfino 2014b, pp. 101–4.

274 The former book makes more or less the same argument as the 1982 text, see Althusser 2017b.

275 Althusser 2006, p. 197.

276 Althusser 2006, p. 198, emphasis in the original. See also the *Book on Imperialism*, where Althusser notes how the political form of city-states was not appropriate and that instead a nation-state was required, Althusser 2020, p. 130.

of structure, as expounded earlier in *Lire Capital* and elsewhere. For the initial encounter is not, as we might say, superseded by 'taking hold' in a new configuration, as the aleatory is present in the very core of capitalism:

> It would, moreover, be a mistake to think that this process of the aleatory encounter was confined to the English fourteenth century. It has always gone on, and *is going on even today* – not only in the countries of the Third World, which provide the most striking example of it, but also in France, by way of the dispossession of agricultural producers and their transformation into semi-skilled workers (consider Sandouville: Bretons running machines) – as a permanent process that puts the aleatory at the heart of the survival of the capitalist 'mode of production', and also, let us add, at the heart of the so-called socialist 'mode of production' itself.[277]

As such, the encounter that brought about a mode of production like capitalism, results in a situation where its emergence is embodied in so-called 'tendential laws'. Yet at the same time these 'laws' still carry within them the possibility for radical change. Tendential laws, understood in this sense, can change on the spur of a moment or at the drop of a hat.[278] This view is diametrically opposed to a teleological conception of the mode of production, resulting from the materialism such as 'diamat' that is in effect a disguised idealism. From such a perspective the bourgeoisie and the proletariat were produced by, respectively, feudalism and capitalism, acting as inexorable forces in the dissolution of these modes of production.[279] The reference to the socialist mode of production is significant in this regard as well, for this concept had come in for harsh criticism in the fragments from the *Book on Imperialism* from the 1970s. There Althusser argued against a transitory mode of production between capitalism and communism, taking aim at views in the PCF of the 1970s that the crisis of monopoly capitalism in the West would act as an 'antechamber' to socialism.[280]

Instead of being conceived as a mode of production in its own right and as a discrete stage in a sequence of modes of production, for Althusser social-

---

277 Althusser 2006, p. 199, emphasis in the original.
278 Althusser 2006, pp. 194–6.
279 Althusser 2006, pp. 201–2. The question of the bourgeoisie was treated earlier by Althusser in his work on Montesquieu from the late 1950s, see the introduction of Goshgarian in Althusser 2006, pp. xxx–xxxiii.
280 Althusser 2020, pp. 120–1.

ism can be better understood as a social formation.[281] A social formation can be seen as the conditions of existence for a mode of production, which in the case of socialism involved a co-existence of elements of both the capitalist and communist modes. Crucially, the wage relation persisted, as did commodity exchange, as the communist elements are located primarily at the political plane: state ownership of the means of production and working-class power. Thus, rather than marking a decisive break with the past, in socialism everything is still 'up in the air', that is, it contains certain (political) conditions that might result in a transition to a communist mode of production. Given that socialism is not a form, but rather the conditions for the existence (or non-existence) of a new form, that of the communist mode of production, the actuality of the latter is far from pre-determined.[282]

Even from this brief discussion, the revolutionary impact of these ideas on Marxism should be clear. For if the 'mechanists' had posited an alternative for a dialectical materialism based on an unfolding of stages according to a teleological logic, they had not thought through the role of the aleatory in objective terms. Instead, the perspective sketched above can think through causation and historical law in a way that is radically distinct from dialectics conceived as a system of laws, as a science with a subject: matter in an ontological sense, as the *logos* of the dialectics of nature and society.[283] Instead of providing such a system of dialectical laws, Althusser formulated theses (positions). In his text three main aleatory theses are given, supplemented by three derivative, supporting ones.[284] These six theses can be summed up in the following order, starting with the three main ones:

1. The world is everything that is; it is outside historical development itself but in it take place the encounters that form the mainstay of historical change.

2. Encounters result in combinations of atoms, which have 'taken hold' based on affinity.

3. From the encounter, atoms derive being, as there is no 'first philosophy' of materialism.

4. Any being of any kind depends on an encounter having taken place.

---

281   Althusser 2020, pp. 62–3. The fallacy of seeing 'developed socialism' as a mode of production was recognised in Soviet scholarship, but imposed as orthodoxy by Sergey Trapeznikov, Markwick 2001, p. 239.

282   Althusser 2020, p. 99.

283   Althusser 2017b, pp. 188–92.

284   Althusser 2006, pp. 190–4.

5.   Encounters take place between a series of beings, which are in turn, from theses 3 and 4, themselves the result of a series of further encounters.
6.   Each encounter is aleatory not merely in its beginnings but also in its effects (in tendential laws). That is, what results from it is in no way prefigured by the elements taking part in it. As a corollary of this any reconstruction of the structural features of an encounter necessitates working backward from the result to the series of encounters that generated it.

With the outline of these theses we come to the limits of Althusser's 1982 text. There are two aspects to this. The first, likely owing to its fragmentary and heavily edited character, is that the text is rather cluttered with all kinds of asides on the various thinkers that are argued to be part of this aleatory current. Not all of these can be related to the theses listed above, and some of them appear rather unconvincing.[285] The second point is that the Althusserian theses are limited, reflecting some of the elements of the convergences between Epicureanism and Spinoza discussed in the previous section, without an added critical perspective and rather leaving out much that is of relevance.[286] It is important therefore, to use his writings as a point of departure, and recognise how from the first instance it has always been part of a collective effort, from the seminar that produced *Lire Capital* to the later work on the aleatory current. Althusser is notable for his recognition of the aleatory current in philosophy, but more systematic analyses can be found in the work of other scholars, most notably Macherey and Morfino.

Macherey, as we saw in the previous section, had noted affinities with regard to the conception of totality between Epicureanism and Spinoza. In this study, however, his main argument concerned the misreading of Spinoza by Hegel, which set up the potential for a critical revaluation of Hegel and his influence

---

285   As in the part on Spinoza, where the 'rain of atoms' is used to grasp the 'parallelism without encounter' of matter and mind in the body, except that in another sense it is held to be an encounter, Althusser 2006, p. 177.

286   Most notably the account of the history of humankind in Lucretius. Althusser came close to the conception of the relation of humans and nature in Greco-Roman atomism as shaped through accidental encounters, pointing out with regard to prehistoric inventions that 'they can only have emerged from elements already present, from an encounter between various earlier techniques and, doubtless, a "chance event" (an event or element that might not have been present) which precipitated a discovery in an unforeseen encounter of completely disparate elements', Althusser 2017b, p. 61. Althusser makes no reference here, however, to ancient atomism, which, as we shall see in the next chapter, had a more comprehensive conception of the human-nature relationship that is only tentatively intimated by in this passage.

in the Marxist tradition. In particular, Macherey demonstrated in sophisticated detail the teleological properties of the Hegelian dialectic, and through Spinoza pointed to the potential of a materialist dialectic free from this influence.[287] Morfino's work is also of great interest given his sustained engagement with the thinkers of the aleatory current and the interconnections between them, notably Lucretius, Machiavelli, Spinoza, and Marx.[288] Like Macherey, he has pointed out the distinctions between Spinoza and Hegel, thus distancing the latter from the aleatory current.[289] Most importantly, as we saw in the previous section, Morfino has grasped and thought through the convergences between Epicureanism and Spinozism.

Based on his studies of these thinkers, Morfino formulated three more generic theses, which are arguably more critical and comprehensive, and lend themselves better to the comparative analysis of different philosophical thinkers. Furthermore, in order to address the specifics of each thinker, more detailed theses can be formulated, as we shall see for the discussion of Machiavelli in Chapter 3. Apart from the intrinsic worth of the theses themselves, Morfino also showed that they have to be grasped as mutually depending on each other. Accordingly their content and relations can be summarised in the following way:

1. The thesis of trans-individuality, that is the primacy of the relation over the elements, which is constituted by a complex interlocking of elements rather than any kind of essential being. These elements are structured by the specific relation, but retain a degree of autonomy. In concrete terms, this denies essentialist conceptions of concepts such as Marx's 'species being' and the Marxist use of multitude, which rather have to be grasped intrinsically as relational to other elements that are interwoven in complex ways.[290]

2. The thesis of trans-individuality necessarily follows from the thesis of the primacy of the encounter over form (what Morfino here calls the thesis of the aleatory). Relations are the result of a series of encounters, which are aleatory both in the encounter itself and its effects. That is, no relation is prefigured in the elements it structures, nor can it be taken as a form that precedes the aleatory sequence of encounters. Here the contrast is with teleological views of form, notably using Darwin as a contrary example

287 Macherey 2011, pp. 202–13.
288 See especially the article on Marx and Lucretius, Morfino 2012a.
289 Morfino 2012b.
290 Morfino 2014b, pp. 9–11.

of how seemingly stable forms have in reality resulted from an aleatory sequence of encounters.[291] This thesis effectively captures the six theses of Althusser discussed above.

3.   Both preceding theses in turn depend on a third thesis: that of plural temporality. Given that relations and encounters both take place in a complex series that cannot be reduced to a single dimension, but has to be seen as an interweaving of temporalities. Here Spinoza's notion of eternity is used specifically as the weave of infinite modes, here also referring to the Lucretian weave of temporalities to conceive of the multitude.[292]

The theses as outlined here will orient our comparison of the various thinkers discussed in the coming chapters. As noted in the introduction, a special focus will be placed here on the ideas on early humankind and the trajectories of social development in ancient Epicureanism. Their conceptions will be related to the theses of the aleatory current. In so doing, a supplementary thesis to the thesis of plural temporality will be proposed, emphasising the consequences of the Epicurean conception of the plurality of worlds for their view of historical development. Furthermore, this thesis of the plurality of worlds also played an important role in the later encounter of Epicurean ideas with Renaissance thought, in particular in relation to the implications of the European discovery of the Americas. Both this genealogy of ideas on history and the development of humankind and the theses of the aleatory current will then be used to grasp the distinctions between Morgan, Engels, and Marx on these topics. Particular attention in this regard will be given to Morfino's analyses of the role of *Wechselwirkung* and the role of force in Engels.

---

291   Morfino 2014b, pp. 11–12.
292   Morfino 2014b, pp. 12–17.

The Ancient Atomists on Nature, Humankind and History

In the previous chapter the main characteristics of what was described as an aleatory current in philosophy were outlined. One major lacuna in their work was a lack of engagement with the ideas of the ancient atomists on humankind and its history, as part of their broader philosophy of nature. This was not for a lack of engagement with history as such, as shown by the notion of the beginning of capitalism as based on the taking hold of the encounter between the owners of money and the owners of labour. Furthermore, this historical perspective was understood as part of the unending, plural sequence of encounters that constitutes the universe. What this chapter will add is the account of the history of humankind by the ancient atomists themselves, as reconstructed by modern philology. While the analysis will draw upon a plethora of mostly fragmentary sources, the most important one will be the mostly complete *De rerum natura* (DRN) by Lucretius.

The analysis presented in this chapter will focus on outlining those aspects of ancient Epicureanism that are 'philological' in character. That is, we will focus on outlining the different invariants of the historical ideas of the ancient atomists, which form the basis for the 'constants' in later contexts of reception. As such, the analysis follows the theses of the aleatory current as outlined at the end of the previous chapter. At the same time, there are clear limits to the analysis here in that the context of ancient Epicureanism itself is largely ignored. Following the ideas of Althusser discussed in the previous chapter, it is possible to argue that a degree of autonomy for philosophical discourse allows one to adopt such an approach. Yet, as noted in Chapter 1, philosophy is closely tied to class society and the ideologies underpinning it. As will become clear below, the existence of two main philosophical parties with distinct ideas about humankind and its history has clear political implications.

Using an 'archaeological' approach, these ideas could be tied closely to their original conjunctures, as summarised in table 2.1 below. Here we can see how the different thinkers discussed below have to be placed not just temporally, but also as part of distinctive political conjunctures of the ancient world. As outlined by Althusser, important connections can be made between these conjunctures and the philosophical ideas formulated within them,[1] based on the

---

1 Althusser 2014, pp. 14–17.

TABLE 2.1   Main periods of the aleatory current in antiquity

Period	Political conjuncture	Philosophers aleatory current
Classical period Greece (500–323 BC)	Apogee of the Athenian *polis* and naval league, Peloponnesian war	Democritus, Leucippus
Hellenistic period Greece (323–146 BC)	Transition from world of the *polis* to the larger Hellenistic empires.	Epicurus, Hermarchus, Metrodorus
Late Roman republic (146–27 BC)	Roman republic facing civil wars and slave revolts.	Lucretius, Philodemus, Vitruvius
Mature Roman empire (27 BC–AD 395)	*Pax Romana*	Diogenes of Oenoanda, Lucian of Samosata[a]

a   Lucian is not strictly speaking a philosopher nor an undisputed Epicurean, yet Epicurean and generally aleatory ideas are present in his work, notably in *Zeus rants, Icaromennipus, Alexander the false prophet*, and *The double indictment*.

underlying premise discussed in the previous chapter of the intimate relation between philosophy and class struggle. Looking at ancient atomism in its varied contexts would warrant another book-length treatment. This would necessitate looking not just at textual traces but also at the material remains of the places in which they were found, and the broader political conjunctures in which they existed. In essence this is like an 'archaeological' reconstruction, in which disparate elements have to be connected coherently.

The 'philological' approach is sufficient, however, to grasp the reception of ideas in later periods in general and for the Marxist tradition in specific. Lucretius is here used as the main guide. For it is in the DRN that a complete account of humankind from the first generation of human bodies from the earth to contemporary philosophical discourse can be found. The chapter starts by placing this account in the broader context of Greco-Roman ideas on this topic, noting in this and succeeding sections the distinguishing features of Epicureanism. After noting how plural temporality characterises the chronological framework of Lucretius, a number of sections follow on specific topics. These topics include anthropogony and the early life of humans, moving on to the first form of social life, the emergence of language and technology, as well as of states and property. Qualifications on viewing this sequence as a progressive one followed from Epicurean considerations of nature and ethics, which informed notions of using philosophical therapy as a practical means to remedy social ills.

1   Two Rains, Two Histories

Unfortunately, the vagaries of textual survival over the centuries have resulted in a situation where the text of Lucretius is one of the very few surviving examples from a diverse set of (often highly fragmentary) Greco-Roman discussions of the history of humankind.[2] The account by Lucretius is unique for its length and its detailed descriptions, finding only a partial match in book three of Plato's *Laws*. It is important first of all to consider, if only briefly, the DRN in the overall context of the emergence and historical trajectory of philosophy as it developed in the Mediterranean in the first millennium BC. Ultimately, all of the texts concerned with the history, including the DRN, can be seen as outgrowths of the *historia peri phuseos* (history of nature) accounts that were first developed by pre-Socratic Ionian philosophers such as Anaximander in the Sixth century BC.[3]

Greek *phuseos*, usually translated into the modern term nature, derives from the Indo-European root **bhŭ*.[4] This root signifies growth and development, especially in the context of vegetation, something that can also be seen for the Latin term *natura*. Based on the occurrence of *phuseos* in Homer and the later philosophical sources, Naddaf suggests that the *peri phuseos* of the philosophers signifies an insight into the nature of a thing by reference to a triad of origin (*arche*), a process of growth, and, lastly, ordered, mature existence (*kosmos*).[5] The accounts of the Ionian philosophers stretched from the emergence of the world (cosmogony) to the origin of animals (zoogony) and humankind (anthropogony). These early Ionian philosophers are thought to have included a discussion on the origins of social life as well, although the first unambiguous evidence for such accounts can only be recognised for the fifth-century BC.[6]

---

2 Most of these fragments are known from doxographic reports of the positions of philosophers by others, which were selected with specific philosophical or other concerns in mind, see Mansfeld 2016. Hence by no means should these reports be taken as unambiguously representative of the views of the philosopher in question.

3 Naddaf 2005 provides an overview of the different accounts of pre-Socratic philosophers in these terms, including among them the doctrines of Democritus.

4 Naddaf 2005, p. 12.

5 Naddaf 2005, p. 20.

6 Naddaf 2005, pp. 92–106 makes an argument for Anaximander. A fragment of Xenophanes has also been connected to cultural development, see O'Brien 1985, but this is controversial for Lesher 1991. See Guthrie 1969, pp. 79–84 for a variety of sources on the beginnings of social life from the fifth century. A more extensive overview covering the entire Greco-Roman trajectory can be found in Lovejoy and Boas 1935.

The development of atomistic philosophy by Leucippus and Democritus in the fifth-century BC can be seen as the outgrowth of the *historia peri phuseos* accounts of the Ionian philosophers.[7] The key doctrine of the atomists is that all derives from atoms and void,[8] the interaction of these atoms resulting in composite bodies. It is important to remember that the term *kosmos* can denote phenomena of many kinds, including in a fragment of Democritus where it refers to Homer's ordering of verses.[9] Different *kosmoi* are notable in other fragments of Democritus, from the world at large to the *mikros kosmos* of the human body in fragment DK 68 B34,[10] to the societal order (*en panti kosmoi*) of fragments DK 68 B258 and B259.[11] The principles of atomistic philosophy are behind all these phenomena.[12] An infinite sum of atoms constantly forms *kosmoi* that inevitably dissolve again, which consequently are innumerable as well, a process which is devoid of any teleological principles of design. The atoms form the fundamental constituents of *kosmoi*, and therefore they are conceptualised both as material particles and as basic principles, which are the *archai* for Epicurus and the *principia* for Lucretius.[13]

The use of atomistic terms and the broader set of metaphors associated with them also shows a clear connection to vegetative metaphoric templates in the formation and dissolution of *kosmoi*, in line with the meanings of Greek *phuseos* and its Indo-European root **bhŭ*. This is true both for Democritus and for the Epicureans.[14] It is especially pronounced in Lucretius, and in his poem is extended to life-cycles in general, as with the young, fertile earth giving way to the later barren version that humans now inhabit.[15] Through the metaphoric

---

7   Naddaf 2005, pp. 152–61.

8   Taylor 1999, p. 9.

9   The term *kosmos* in Greek refers primarily to an ordering, whether in nature or among human beings, Liddell and Scott 1940. It can be found in settings as diverse as decoration and a state official in Crete. Its use in a philosophical context goes back to the pre-Socratic thinkers. In this chapter *kosmos* is used, unless stated otherwise, to denote the bounded space that encompasses both the earth and the heavens, which acted as a basic template of Greco-Roman cosmology, see Furley 1989, pp. 229–33.

10   Taylor 1999, p. 149.

11   Taylor 1999, p. 41.

12   A consequence is that instead of dividing the fragments of Democritus into modern categories such as physics, mathematics and ethics, as in Taylor 1999, a sequence can instead move from different kinds of *kosmoi*. All of these are structured by atomistic principles, see Morel 2007, pp. 120–2.

13   Morel 2009, p. 65.

14   Taylor 1999, p. 197; Taub 2009, pp. 117–18. Indeed, the lack of a clear divide between animate and inanimate matter is a key factor distinguishing the ancient atomists from modern mechanical physics, Furley 1989, pp. 228–33.

15   Campbell 2003, pp. 60–1. The metaphor is used skilfully by Lucretius to demonstrate key

extension of the underlying principles of atoms and void to a broad variety of phenomena, a *historia peri phuseos* can be provided from the processes of cosmogony to the latest historical era. Such all-encompassing accounts were given in Epicurus' *On Nature*, and likely also in either one or multiple works of Democritus, which are known only through fragments and testimonia.[16] Only in book five of Lucretius' DRN is it possible to see a full *historia peri phuseos* based on atomist philosophical principles, although this account is thought to have based closely on Epicurus' *On nature*.[17]

Important differences exist between the Democritean and Epicurean strands of ancient atomism, based on the precise conceptions of atoms and their movements. These differences concern the precise details of the way atoms are conceived by Democritus and Epicurus, which were influenced by broader debates on physics in Greek philosophy.[18] Not all of these differences are significant for the conception of the history of humankind, but two main distinctions between the philosophers should be noted. The first of these is the well-known distinction between the role of necessity and chance in Democritus and Epicurus, the latter placing a greater emphasis on the role of contingent events.[19] Lucretius' use of the *clinamen* or swerve of atoms, to account for the creation of composite bodies, best captures this.[20] By contrast, for Democritus composite bodies result from necessity, and for him the *kosmos* originated from a vortex or swirl of atoms.[21]

Another key difference between Democritean and Epicurean philosophy concerns the way they conceived of composite bodies. For Democritus every-

---

points, but it is also made clear by him at crucial points that such analogies should not be overextended to support strongly anthropomorphic accounts of the earth, Schrijvers 2007, pp. 267–70.

16 See for an outline of Epicurus' *On nature* chapter four of Sedley 1998, the contents of the books of Democritus that pertain to this topic are discussed in Leszl 2007, pp. 29–30, 43–44.

17 Sedley 1998, pp. 152–4.

18 Aristotle provides the main counterpoint to Democritean atomism, and as such has often been assumed to have partly influenced the Epicurean reworking of atomist ideas, i.e. Morel 2009, pp. 73–5. It is hard to trace the precise influences, however, and other philosophers of Aristotle's school (the Peripatetics) such as Theophrastus may also have had an impact on Epicurus, see Sedley 1998, pp. 182–5.

19 Of course this difference was the main point of Marx's dissertation, Marx 1975, the main thrust of which was later accepted by influential Classical scholars of Epicureanism, see Bailey 1928.

20 See Fowler 2002 for a commentary on this crucial passage of book two of Lucretius' DRN.

21 Taylor 1999, p. 58. The notion of an initial 'whirlpool' of atoms creates problems for the interpretation of motion in Democritus, which some still argue to be downward, Furley 1989, chapters seven and eight.

thing but atoms and void is conventional (DK 68 B9).[22] This perspective implies a more sceptical approach to sense-experience, as perceptible phenomena such as colour, taste, and temperature are opposed to the fundamental truth of atoms and void. By contrast, Epicurus did recognise intrinsic properties for composite bodies, privileging the evidence of the senses.[23] Not only are secondary properties real, the relation between atoms and composites is different as well.[24] The atoms are not merely constitutive parts of larger wholes, but are a generative, active force in a process of spontaneous selection that generates composite bodies.[25] These composite bodies in turn possess characteristics that cannot be reduced to the sum of the atoms constituting them. As humans are one particular kind of composite body, the differences in the atomistic physics of Democritus and Epicurus had ramifications for their ideas about psychology, as will be discussed in the section on anthropogony below.

Despite these important differences, as elucidated by Marx in his doctoral dissertation, the Democritean and Epicurean strands of ancient atomism shared the most important basic principles. These similarities include an ontology based on atoms and void, an infinite number of atoms forming and dissolving an infinite number of *kosmoi*, and the absence of any teleological design. In this they were opposed to the philosophical schools of Plato and Aristotle, echoed in the Marxist view of two philosophical camps of idealism and materialism discussed in Chapter 1.[26] In a letter to Fernanda Navarro, Althusser cited Plato's distinction in his *Sophist* between the friends (or party) of the Forms and those of the Earth, who are likened respectively to the warring Olympian gods and the giants.[27] Althusser saw this opposition as a key for understanding the history of Western philosophy.[28] In this passage from the *Sophist*, Plato

---

22   Taylor 1999, p. 9.
23   For Epicurus to contradict the evidence of the senses leads one down a slippery slope, see his *Principal Doctrines* XXIII–XXIV, Inwood and Gerson 1994, p. 34.
24   Morel 2009, pp. 78–83.
25   As for the *kosmos*, see DRN V. 416–508, Smith 1992, pp. 410–17.
26   Furley 1989, pp. 225. He notes that despite differences in doctrine, as well as a clear political difference of the early Stoics, there is not enough to distinguish the Stoics from Plato and Aristotle to warrant giving them a separate third position, see Furley 1989, pp. 204–5. The contrast between Epicurean and Stoic doctrines is explored by Cicero in his *De natura deorum*, Rackham 1951, and Lucian in his *Zeus rants*, Harmon 1915.
27   See Plato *Sophist* (245e–247e), Fowler 1921, pp. 370–9. The battle between the giants and the Olympians (the Gigantomachy), also recurs in Lucretius, see for example DRN V. 110–25. Here Lucretius accepts the charge of Plato, which has consequences also on the perspective on the ordering of social life, as we shall see below.
28   Althusser 2006, p. 216.

TABLE 2.2   Outline of the two cosmological perspectives, adapted from Furley 1989, p. 225.

Atomist philosophers	Aristotle and teleological philosophers
Primacy accident	Primacy of design, order
Explanation through matter-in-motion	Explanation based on ends (teleological)
Universe is infinite	Universe is finite
Transience *kosmos*	*Kosmos* eternal or cyclical
Plurality of *kosmoi*	*Kosmos* is unique
Ontology of atoms and void	Denial of void within the *kosmos*
Atomic matter	Continuous matter
Dynamics are linear	Dynamics are centrifocal
Earth is flat	Earth is spherical
Soul is material	Soul is immaterial (not for Stoics)
Evolution	Eternity or creation

reacted not only against the Ionian philosophers but also against Democritus, whose work he apparently wished to burn completely.[29]

Here, then, we have the main opposition within ancient philosophy. This is not to say that there did not exist important differences within the two 'parties', as we saw for the differences between Epicurus and Democritus, but which can also be noted for Plato's dialectics and Aristotelian logic. Instead, what is shared within each party is a more basic outlook, one that led to a consistent set of similar theses. Furley has recognised one such division specifically for cosmological ideas, showing a consistent difference as outlined in table 2.2. Given that the concern here is to provide an outline of Epicurean ideas on the history of humankind, no such complete comparison between the two parties on this topic will be attempted here. It is necessary, however, to show the basic opposition between them on this question, too, for certain emphases in the work of Lucretius would be incomprehensible without it. To that end, the contrast set up by Morfino between the 'two rains' of Aristotle and Epicurus will be developed further here with regard to the former's conception of humankind, both in its relation to nature and in historical development.[30]

The Epicurean rain, as we have amply discussed in this chapter and the previous one, is a rain of atoms that swerve from their downward trajectory and

29   Taylor 1999, pp. 56–7.
30   Morfino 2014b, pp. 100–4.

thereby encounter each other to form the composite bodies of the *kosmos*. It is this rain that encapsulates the atomist doctrine as expounded by Epicurus and his followers, and which constitutes the foundation of the *historia peri phuseos* account of book five of Lucretius' DRN. The seemingly immutable and immovable structures of the world are in reality based on contingent encounters, and are therefore susceptible to dissolution, even of the entire *kosmos*, as we shall see below. Yet there is another kind of rain, that of Aristotle as he expressed it in book II of his *Physics*. Arguing from the perspective of his opponents, he asks why rain could not fall from necessity alone, rather than for an end, having both beneficial and negative results. And he extends this to ask why living forms should not derive from necessity, too:

> Why not say, it is asked, that nature acts as Zeus drops the rain, not to make the corn grow, but of necessity (for the rising vapour must needs be condensed into water by the cold, and must then descend and incidentally, when this happens, the corn grows), just as, when a man loses his corn on the threshing-floor, it did not rain on purpose to destroy the crop, but the result was merely incidental to the raining? So why should it not be the same with natural organs like the teeth? Why should it not be a coincidence that the front teeth come up with an edge, suited to dividing the food, and the back ones flat and good for grinding it, without there being any design in the matter? And so with all the other bodies that seem to embody a purpose. In cases where a coincidence brought about such a combination as might have been arranged on purpose, the creatures, it is urged, having been suitably formed by the operation of chance, survived; otherwise they perished, and still perish, as Empedocles says of his 'man-faced oxen'.[31]

Aristotle was positing this notion precisely in order to forestall his adversaries in the battlefield of philosophy. For just before introducing this rain, Aristotle had discussed the ideas of Democritus and Empedocles, who, according to himself, attributed the origin of an infinite number of worlds to chance.[32] Yet for Aristotle chance was secondary and does not inhere to the essence of things.[33] This follows from another distinction he drew between his own position and that of Democritus and Empedocles, namely that they only considered mat-

---

31   Wicksteed and Cornford 1957, p. 171.
32   Wicksteed and Cornford 1957, pp. 142–5.
33   Wicksteed and Cornford 1957, pp. 146–55.

ter and not form.[34] His own outline of physics involved not just these two, but a set of four increasingly important kinds of causation: material, formal, efficient, and final (for an end).[35] According to this perspective, the earlier steps in a process of development happen for a predetermined end. In this regard it is highly significant that Aristotle brings up the theories of zoogony and anthropogony of Empedocles in the context of his broader argument on chance being secondary and inessential.

The account of zoogony and anthropogony by Empedocles, even if known only through fragments and testimonia like that of Aristotle, is certainly a topic in its own right. Aristotle merely focuses on one particular aspect of it, the notion that separate body parts were combined to form bodies, which could lead to monstrosities such as man-faced oxen. He argues cogently against this idea, basing his critique on his view of physics as being ultimately determined by final causes, form being primary over matter, on analogy with human artifice:

> Thus, if in art there are cases in which the correct procedure serves a purpose, and attempts that fail are aimed at a purpose but miss it, we must take it to be the same in Nature, and monstrosities will be like failures of purpose in Nature. So if, in the primordial combinations, such 'ox-creatures' as could not reach an equilibrium and goal, should appear, it would be by the miscarriage of some principle, as monstrous births are actually produced now by abortive developments of sperm. Besides, the sperm must precede the formation of the animal, and Empedocles' 'primal all-generative' is no other than such sperm.[36]

Aristotle's perspective is an entirely different take on the development of living species in general, and of humans in particular, compared to the Epicurean view of chance combinations resulting from a sequence of encounters. It is not true that Lucretius accepts the viability of man-faced oxen, but rather that the process that has led to the emergence of humankind was not pre-determined by any final causes.[37] This difference extends not just to the formation of humankind, but also especially to its relation to nature. As will be discussed below in the section on anthropogony, the atomist view of the human rela-

34   Wicksteed and Cornford 1957, pp. 114–23.
35   Wicksteed and Cornford 1957, pp. 128–31.
36   Wicksteed and Cornford 1957, p. 177.
37   See for the complex interplay between Empedocles and Lucretius, as well as in other authors like Ovid, Garani 2013.

tion to nature lies in a process of adapting natural features in technology and art, brought about by accidental encounters. By contrast, Aristotle views the human faculties through a finalist lens. An example of this comes from what may be seen as an adaptation of the argument of Anaxagoras on the import-ance of the hand for humankind in *On the Parts of Animals* (4.10 687a7):

> Anaxagoras says that man is the most intelligent of animals because he has hands; but it would be better to say he has hands because he is the most intelligent. For the hands are a tool, and nature always distributes each tool to the animal that is able to use it, just as an intelligent man would.[38]

In the *Physics*, Aristotle argues furthermore that the arts either imitate nature or improve upon it, and that both follow a process of development in which the initial phases are the precursors of a given end.[39] Similar views on the hand and human development can be seen in philosophers of the same ilk, notably in Cicero.[40] Another characteristic that for Aristotle distinguishes humans from animals is speech, which, unlike the cries of animals, allows for moral discourse and hence marks off humanity as a political animal (*zoon politikon*).[41] In the *Politics*, he furthermore explores the development of the socio-political organ-isation of this animal. Again, the procedure is one of reasoning from an end, in this case from the realisation of the good life in the *polis*. This perspective entails two interrelated aspects. Firstly, the whole (the *polis*) is said to be prior to its parts, the parts in this case being the households and individuals that constitute its citizen body.[42] Secondly, and building on the first, the relation between the earliest phases of history and its end result also follows the same template of the whole being prior to its constituent parts.

Hence the household, being the main foundational part of the polis, while it was chronologically prior to the state, nevertheless existed to serve as a means to achieve political life. Hence its earlier development has to be understood

---

38   Cited in Curd 2007, p. 122.
39   Wicksteed and Cornford 1957, pp. 172–7.
40   Of particular interest here is the argument attributed to the Stoic philosopher Balbus in book II of Cicero's *De natura deorum*. There the superiority of humans over animals is demonstrated using the example of the unique dexterity of the human hand, the result of divine design, which affords humans a unique place in nature, for 'by means of our hands we essay to create as it were a second world in the world of nature', Rackham 1951, p. 271.
41   Rackham 1944, pp. 10–11.
42   Rackham 1944, pp. 9–13. Later in the same book, a similar teleological argument is used to argue that animals have the natural purpose to serve humankind, Rackham 1944, pp. 36–7.

with that end in mind. The household itself was based on two things, namely the natural sexual union of men and women, together with the natural sub-jection of the weaker (slaves) to the stronger.[43] These factors were the basis for the origin of the household, which then saw the aggregation of households into villages, later merging into the city-state.[44] This process of development unfolded for a teleological end: the life of the *zoon politikon* in the city-state. The notion of a life outside this state, or even its precursors, negates this end and is described in highly negative terms, as being worse than the life of wild beasts.[45] The process of development sketched here is rather generic, even if Aristotle in the same book of the *Politics* also points to the impact of distinct subsistence regimes upon forms of socio-political organisation.[46] Among these regimes, farming has the highest status, owing to its role in sustaining the pop-ulation of the *polis*.

More insights can be gained from a fragment of Aristotle's *On Philosophy*, as preserved in the work of the Sixth century AD philosopher and theologian Philoponus. The fragment outlines the trajectory of human development after a cataclysmic event had reduced it to a very basic level of existence, much as in book III of Plato's *Laws*.[47] What is notable in the text of Aristotle, however, is that the account of historical change is structured by the development of *sophia* (wisdom). In the initial, post-apocalyptic era, *sophia* was ascribed to the development of things to satisfy basic needs:

> These survivors, then, not having the means of sustenance, were forced by necessity to think of useful devices – the grinding of corn, sowing, and the like – and they gave the name of wisdom to such thought, thought which discovered what was useful with a view to the necessities of life, and the name of wise to anyone who had such thoughts. Again they devised arts, as the poet says, 'at the prompting of Athene' – arts not limited to the necessities of life, but going on to the production of beauty and elegance; and this again men have called wisdom, and its discoverer wise, as in the phrase 'A wise craftsman framed it', 'knowing well by Athene's prompting of wisdom'. For, because of the excellence of the discoveries, they ascribed the thought of these things to God.[48]

43   Rackham 1944, pp. 4–9.
44   Rackham 1944, pp. 8–9.
45   Rackham 1944, pp. 8–13.
46   Rackham 1944, pp. 34–7.
47   Bury 1926, pp. 174–79.
48   *On Philosophy* fragment 8, Ross 1952, p. 81.

The invention of technologies in Aristotle's view came about by necessity, as in the materialist accounts of the fifth-century BC. However, there is also a clear connection between degrees of *sophia* and the sophistication of the arts, as they move from necessities to the more beautiful and elegant forms of production. The increase in levels of wisdom can be even more clearly seen in the succeeding phases of development, where the ultimate end of this development is brought out:

> Again, they turned their attention to politics, and invented laws, and all the things that hold a state together; and such thought they called wisdom; for such were the Seven Wise Men – men who attained political virtues. Then they went farther and proceeded to bodies themselves and the nature that fashions them, and this they called by the special name of natural science, and its possessors we describe as wise in the affairs of nature. Fifthly, men applied the name in connexion with things divine, supramundane, and completely unchangeable, and called the knowledge of these things the highest wisdom.[49]

Hence for Aristotle history is a teleological process that leads to increasingly sophisticated versions of wisdom, much as in the development of the *polis* out of pre-existing social groupings existing separately. The role of the hand in this is to play its designated part at the first, lower levels of the historical sequence, as befits its teleological function. By contrast, in the aleatory materialist perspective on the history of humankind outlined in the sections below, the hand, together with other human features, builds civilisation through a series of accidental encounters without following a plan set in advance. These encounters stretch from the formation of the *kosmos* to the emergence of life and humankind, and further to the first forms of social life and the subsequent development of civilisation. This series has no *telos*, no unfolding according to a predetermined end, but rather occurs according to the Lucretian term *sponte sua*, that is, without external determination.[50] In this way, Lucretius argues, the

---

49   *On Philosophy* fragment 8, Ross 1952, pp. 81–2.

50   The term *sponte sua* occurs widely in Lucretius, including in human history as we shall see below, and in its basic meaning refers to changes or actions occurring without external constraint, Johnson 2013, pp. 105–6; Fowler 2002, pp. 280–1. Perhaps most important is the passage where nature is held to be able to change without the help of the gods, see DRN II.1090–1092, Smith 1992, pp. 178–81, something also prominent in Galen's critique of Epicurus on account of his notion that 'everything happens without design', cited in Berryman 2009, p. 209.

kosmos, the earth, and living beings come about without intention or design, due to the chance encounters of atoms.[51]

2 The Weave of Historical Temporalities

Stadialism has long been used as a way to grasp the ancient atomist perspective on humankind and its history, starting with Democritus. Although the available fragments of Democritus that can shed light on developmental stages are small in number, textual comparisons have been used to connect them to a detailed outline of inventions and social changes.[52] Although this outline is too elaborate in comparison to the sparse evidence, the basic contentions that aetiological reasoning is used to explain the past by means of the present, and that development was cumulative, are accepted.[53] The use of such aetiologies can be seen in Democritus, for example in his connection between the contemporary killing of those who are harmful and the killing of wild animals and enemies by ancestral law.[54] Furthermore, it is plausible that Democritus followed a general template of technological and social change that can be recognised for different Greek authors of fifth-century BC,[55] and which can be outlined according to the following tripartite scheme:

1. An initial phase of anthropogony and a struggle for survival against natural elements, based on necessity for survival, a criterion for usefulness to meet basic needs, and a focus on practical intelligence in technological development. Although no account of anthropogony is present in the surviving fragments of Democritus, his account of human nature as the basis for cultural development (discussed in the section on anthropogony) logically presupposes an initial phase of development.

2. The second stage is that of the establishment of a social compact, enabling the founding of cities. A contrast has been proposed between an early perspective emphasising mutuality in this phase, giving way to a later view that emphasised the victory of the weak over the strong.[56]

---

51 DRN II.1058–1063, Smith 1992, pp. 176–7.
52 Cole 1990, table 1, p. 26. A longer section on technological and social development in book I.8 of Diodorus Siculus' *Library of History*, Oldfather 1933, pp. 28–31, has also been connected to Democritus, but the connection is controversial and the text is not included in Taylor 1999.
53 Cole 1990, pp. 58–9.
54 Taylor 1999, p. 41.
55 Rose 1976, pp. 51–6.
56 Rose 1976, p. 53.

Democritus seems to belong in the former group, and note has be taken in this regard also of his views of early regions and the notion of ancestral law.

3. The third stage is that of contemporary society, with a strong fifth-century association between democracy and ideas about the history of human-kind, as well as a stress on Pan-Hellenic unity. The fragments seem to point to a Democritean connection between past and present in his account of contemporary social life, which has been argued to reflect the perspective of a 'moderate democrat'.[57]

Epicurus and his followers developed their ideas based on these fifth-century templates, though certainly modified in important ways.[58] Like Democritus, Lucretius made ample use of aetiologies connecting present and past. Examples of this are his connection of the growth of feathers and bristles on animals and the emergence of grasses on the young earth,[59] and also in likening the roaming movements of the first humans to that of wild beasts.[60] Analogies like these existed alongside other devices, such as the negation of aspects of contemporary social life in that of early humans.[61] Yet these aetiologies are not mere abstractions, but rather are based on the traces or *vestigia* that were briefly referred to at the end of the previous chapter. To understand this better, it is necessary to look in more detail to Lucretius 'traces' of early times. From considering the broader context of the passage, it is clear that these traces stem from the period before the advent of civilisation, and especially of writing:

> Now they lived their lives fenced in by strong fortifications, and the earth had been parcelled out and divided up, and brought under cultivation; the sea was already blooming with wind-swept sails ... and they had made treaties and formed pacts and alliances, when the poets began to hand down stories of exploits in song; for writing had been invented not long

---

57   Taylor 1999, p. 231. Luria's commentary on Democritus' fragments in relation to democracy is among the most perceptive and comprehensive on this question, see Luria 2016, pp. 685–722.

58   Especially relevant for the human capacity for adapting to nature and also to develop in new ways unknown to it, see for further details the section on anthropogony below.

59   DRN V.788–789, Smith 1992, pp. 440–1.

60   DRN V.931–932, Smith 1992, pp. 450–1.

61   Campbell 2003, pp. 189–90; Gale 1994, p. 161. Description by negation can also work the other way around in evolutionary terms, to show human childhood distinguishes human-kind from animals, see Holmes 2013.

before. That is why our age cannot look back to what happened earlier, unless reason somehow shows us traces.[62]

It is significant that the emergence of poetry is discussed immediately prior to these traces, for most of the history of humankind in Lucretius is based on poetry and mythology, or more precisely on the rational analysis of their contents. Hence it should be clear that Lucretius therefore cannot transcend the rich poetry and mythology of the Greco-Roman world, for these constitute the traces to reconstruct the earliest times. Indeed, he himself highlights the use of poetry in sweetening the cup of wisdom.[63] In that sense it is clearly different from modern science and its procedures of verification and experimentation. Yet, as we shall see in succeeding chapters, the outline of long-term history in the DRN formed an influential template in the formative stages of the science of archaeology. Furthermore, in Chapter 5 the relevance of *vestigia* for understanding Marx's historical approach will become clear as well.

When it comes to the general outline of the history of humankind in book five of DRN, different ways have been proposed to understand its perspective on history. The most common one is that of a diachronic sequence of different phases of development, starting from the earliest humans and moving through a series of intermediate steps to contemporary civilisation. Various versions of stadialism have been proposed to make sense of the Lucretian material. These range from a basic opposition between civilisation and the *vita prior*,[64] to outlines of as much as five stages that distinguish between different forms of social life.[65] A common pattern between these stages is that they are defined by social forms, that is in each of them human beings live together (or are separated from each other) according to distinct kinds of social relations. These stadialist interpretations of Lucretius capture an important part of his account, but problems also arise.

For example, it has been observed that not only is the chronology kept vague, but also the moral evaluation of the different stages varies, making it

---

62   DRN V.1440–1447, Smith 1992, pp. 490–1.

63   DRN I.935–950, Smith 1992, pp. 78–9. The question whether Epicurus approved of the use of poetry for didactic purposes, and possible differences between Epicurus and Lucretius on this point, are much debated.

64   Farrington 1953.

65   Fowler 1989, pp. 142–3; Schiesaro 2007a, pp. 43–5. These stages are: 1) pre-social life of early humans, 2) the first form of social life based on family and friendship, 3) the first kingdoms, 4) the introduction of convention-based property and the resulting destruction of the first kingdoms, and 5) republics bound by law.

impossible to ascertain an unambiguous directional trend of progress.[66] Furthermore, a number of elements such as metallurgy, warfare, religion, music,
astronomy, and poetry are discussed separately from the outline of stages of
social forms and cannot be clearly fitted into that framework.[67] Indeed, some
of these have phases of development of their own, as can be seen for religion.[68]
These observations have led to the formulation of different ideas, such as a synchronic perspective to accompany the diachronic one. Farrell has noted that
there is a structural opposition between 'softness' and 'hardness' that recurs at
different parts of the Lucretian history of humankind.[69] For him this opposition explains why Lucretius is ambivalent about whether history can be seen
as progressive, because each phase merely reorders elements already present
at the beginning.

The synchronic perspective on history, then, provides an overview of the
general human condition as actualised in different ways in specific historical
settings. Yet it cannot provide a satisfactory explanation for the vagueness
of the chronology of the stages of historical development, and the aspects
that cannot easily be placed within the stadialist framework. Instead of the
focus on diachronic or synchronic, it may be more useful to consider the
theses of aleatory materialism to grasp Lucretian and Epicurean accounts of
(early) human history. Doing this effectively retraces the analysis of Althusser,
Morfino, and others, which were based on ancient atomism in the first place,
back to antiquity itself. The theses of aleatory materialism that are of the
greatest importance here, are the thesis of the primacy of the encounter over
the form and the thesis of plural temporality.[70]

There are several reasons why this would capture the diversity seen in the
historical account of Lucretius better. The first is that it allows each element to
be evaluated on its own terms, with its own temporality.[71] Different elements
combine in a new framework after an encounter, which imposes structural features on their relations but does not negate their own, independent existence.
As noted by Morfino, the best way to understand the relations between these
elements is through the metaphor of a weave,[72] which in fact is one that occurs
widely throughout Lucretius' DRN.[73] The weave is used not just to describe the

66   Farrell 1994.
67   Gale 2009, p. 196.
68   See the section on religion and social change below.
69   Farrell 1994, p. 95.
70   See the discussion in chapter one for the details on these theses.
71   Morfino 2014b, pp. 143–5.
72   Morfino 2014b, p. 163.
73   Snyder 1983.

relations between atoms in a compound, but also the connections between compound elements in the first-beginnings (*exordia*) of phenomena such as the earth, the sea, the sky, and living creatures.[74] Needless to say, these first-beginnings derive from an encounter, and the weave that follows it constitutes the combination of the different elements.

Of course, as noted in Chapter 1, this weave and its 'tendential laws' can change at the spur of a moment.[75] Warning his patron Memmius, Lucretius points out that the *foedus natura* ruling our world can dissolve in an instance:

> For the rest – not to put you off with promises any longer – first look at the seas, lands and sky: their three-fold substance, these three bodies, Memmius, these three elements so dissimilar in appearance, these three great fabrics, a single day will bring to destruction, and the massive machinery of the world, maintained for so many years, will fall in ruin. Nor does it escape my attention how novel and astonishing an idea the future destruction of heaven and earth appears to the mind, and how difficult it is for me to win you over to it with my words; as happens when one reports an idea unheard of previously, something that cannot be subjected to the gaze of the eyes nor touched with the hands – the means by which the high road of belief leads most directly into the human heart and the precincts of the mind.[76]

Lucretius does not explicitly refer to his historical account as a weave, but in the short syllabus at the start of book five of DRN he does seamlessly integrate the history of humankind within the first-beginnings of the *kosmos* and of life.[77] Therefore, it's not implausible to extend the weaving metaphor to human history as well, in order to be able to understand the relations between distinct elements within the process as a whole. In fact, it is important to consider cosmogony and zoogony, or specifically anthropogony, as part of the account of history as well. For in Lucretius history is at multiple occasions situated in the

---

74   DRN V. 430–1, Smith 1992, pp. 412–13, see also lines 94, 331, 430, 471 and 677 of the same book for other examples. The term *exordia* is the plural of *exordium*, the start of laying a warp, see Snyder 1983, pp. 39–40.

75   Perhaps one of the reasons why mechanical analogies were treated wearily by the Epicureans, most notably in the critique of mechanical models of the *kosmos* by Epicurus, Berryman 2009, pp. 148–50.

76   DRN V.91–103, Smith 1992, pp. 384–7. The notion of the 'machinery of the world', *machina mundi*, should not be interpreted as implying mechanical ideas, but rather more generically as organisation, Berryman 2009, pp. 38–9.

77   DRN V.65–81, Smith 1992, pp. 384–5.

context of the *kosmos*,[78] which in any case is the prerequisite for humankind to exist at all. Further support can be found in the combination of cosmogony and history in a reconstruction of book twelve of the lost work *On Nature* by Epicurus, which has been argued to have acted as a template for book five of DRN.[79]

Hence the analysis of the history of humankind in Lucretius cannot be seen as separate from the broader processes deriving from the first-beginnings of the *kosmos*, since it is interwoven with it in many ways. Further support for this can be found in the Epicurean notion of an infinite number of worlds, which derives from Democritus and other fifth-century BC materialist philosophers.[80] One notable passage on this can be found in Lucretius, in lines 1023–1089 of book II of the DRN, following the exposition of the *clinamen* and the generation of compound forms from encounters. He starts by pointing to the wondrous spectacle of the new, imagining the heavens to be revealed to subterranean dwellers out of the blue, implicitly counterposing his argument to the connection made between such wonder and attributions of the cosmic divine in Aristotle.[81]

He uses this example to argue not for a an immutable *kosmos* with fixed movements, as Aristotle does, but rather to exhort the reader not to be terrified of the universe that lies beyond the 'walls of the world' (that is, the *kosmos* in which humans dwell). We break out of our mundane vantage point and suddenly behold the infinite number of *kosmoi* in the whole (the sum of things). The universe is not only immeasurable, but as noted immediately after the passage on the plurality of worlds, it is also not made or controlled by the gods.[82] The plurality of worlds derives from the endless sequence of the emergence and dissolution of compounds, based on the chance encounters of atoms, without intention or design, yet generating worlds and life.[83] Given the abundance of matter and the recurrence of the right circumstances for such encounters to take place, it cannot be that the earth and humankind are unique. The principle of plenitude argues against this, for while the number of worlds are said to be infinite, the variation between worlds is also bound by limits.[84]

---

78   DRN V.330–334, Smith 1992, pp. 404–5.

79   Sedley 1998, p. 122.

80   See for Democritus the testimonia gathered in Taylor 1999, pp. 94–7.

81   As in fragment 18 of *On Philosophy*, Ross 1952, pp. 88–9.

82   DRN II.1090–1104, Smith 1992, pp. 178–81 That for Lucretius nature was without direction can also be seen in DRN V.1204–1217, Smith 1992, pp. 472–3.

83   DRN II.991–1022, Smith 1992, pp. 172–5.

84   See on this the analogy made between letters and atoms located just before the discussion of the plurality of worlds, arguing that the letters are the same, but they are placed

The cosmological thesis on the plurality of worlds was closely connected with human history, as the following quotation from Epicurus, from the *Letter to Herodotus* (74–5), demonstrates:

> Again, one must not believe that the cosmoi necessarily have one kind of shape ... For no one could demonstrate that a cosmos of one sort would not have included the sort of seeds from which animals, plants, and the rest of the observable things are formed as compounds, or that a [cosmos of a] different sort *could* not have [included the same things].

> Further, one must suppose that [human] nature was taught a large number of different lessons just by the facts themselves, and compelled [by them]; and that reasoning later made more precise what was handed over to it [by nature] and made additional discoveries – more quickly among some peoples, and more slowly among others and in some periods of time ⟨making greater advances⟩ and in others smaller ones.[85]

This passage follows immediately upon the discussion of the relative character of time as being not a reflection of things, but rather as constituted by the interplay of the relative durations of things and the human perception thereof.[86] In this sense, the theses of the plurality of temporality and of the plurality of worlds are complementary, forming two sides of the same coin. For the sequence of encounters that constitutes the emergence and dissolutions of worlds, within the infinity of the sum of things, is inherently plural in its accidental properties, which includes the duration of those properties. The difference with the teleological conception of the *kosmos* and human history, as discussed in the previous section, should be clear from the Aristotelian outline of development. The importance of regular cycles is evident from other sources as well,[87] most notably for political life in the outline of a sequence of political

---

in different positions, resulting in different words or compound bodies, DRN II.1015–1022, Smith 1992, pp. 174–5. In DRN I.823–829 uses this analogy to demonstrate that 'the elements that are the beginnings of things can bring with them more kinds of variety', Smith 1992, pp. 68–9. As these 'first-beginnings' have a limited number of shapes, DRN II.478–499, Smith 1992, pp. 132–35, conform the doctrine of Epicurus, see the *Letter to Herodotus* (42), Inwood and Gerson 1994, p. 7, variation of compound bodies is limited, as reflected also in the argument against Centaurs and Chimaeras, DRN II.700–17, Smith 1992, pp. 150–1.

85   Inwood and Gerson 1994, p. 16, emphasis in the original.
86   See the *Letter to Herodotus* (72–3), Inwood and Gerson 1994, p. 15.
87   For example in Cicero, in his *De natura deorum*, Rackham 1951, pp. 172–5, 234–7, specific-

regimes by Polybius. Here a cycle of political forms of monarchy, aristocracy, democracy and their negatives is traced to natural laws.[88]

In the next chapter, we will see the impact of Polybius on Machiavelli, and his differences with this teleological conception of history. Here it is important to emphasise that the difference between aleatory and teleological conceptions can be understood in the spatio-temporal sense as a plurality of worlds and temporalities opposing a unitary and cyclical *kosmos*. Hence the aetiologies discussed at the beginning of this section can never more than reflect the specific conditions resulting from encounters, with specific durations, rather than immutable and eternal natural laws. For cosmology, this is reflected in the Epicurean predilection for multiple explanations, which are rarely present in the discussion of human history.[89] However, the earlier noted reliance on traces, or *vestigia*, for grasping prehistory has the same effect of limiting knowledge to the properties of the phenomena and the human perception thereof, rather than seeking solace in the idealism of eternal forms. The case of the formation of humankind itself, of anthropogony, is the first example thereof.

3   Anthropogony and the Human Capacity for Cultural Development

The first age, that of zoogony and anthropogony, is characterised by a lack of social relations, being a largely pre-social stage. The Lucretian account zoogony will not be discussed in great depth here, except to note two major points. The first of these concerns once again the metaphoric relation between the *makros kosmos* of the earth and the *mikros kosmos* of a generic animate body. In his account of zoogony in lines 783–924 of book five of DRN, Lucretius not only presents the earth as a body, but also very specifically as the body of a mother that has brought forth a variety of life forms.[90] These forms also include human beings, who initially grew inside wombs in the earth and after emerging from

---

ally arguing against the Epicurean notion of the world order deriving from the chance collisions of atoms in an extensive section at pp. 202–15. The cosmic cycle is also present in the famous dream of Scipio in his *Republic*, Keyes 1928, pp. 260–83.

88   Paton 2010, pp. 298–301, 314–15.

89   The only exception being the discussion of the disastrous impact of the use of wild animals in battle, an event so bizarre and horrific that it leads Lucretius to wonder if it happened in some other world, structured around different principles, somewhere else in the universe at large, DRN V.1341–1349, Smith 1992, pp. 482–3.

90   Specifically through a combination of heat and moisture, a template stretching back to the pre-Socratic Ionians, with water as life-giving and small particles of heat as a generative force, Campbell 2003, pp. 61–5.

these wombs were nourished by a milk-like sap pouring out from the earth's veins.[91] However, as with an animal mother, there is a limit in time of the child-bearing phase.

A shift can therefore be noted from the earth as generating species to a new phase of the sexual reproduction of the existing species that derive from the 'motherhood' of the earth. This brings us to the second major point of Lucretian zoogony to be discussed here, that of the survival of the most suitable species of living beings. While the earth has brought forth a great variety of organisms, based on the non-teleological views of the Epicureans these are not all well-suited to survive because they are unable to reproduce themselves sexually. It is important to emphasise here that new species only emerge by being generated by the earth, afterwards remaining completely fixed. In the account of Lucretius no mutation of the characteristics of species, nor the branching off of new ones, occurs through sexual selection, a notion that is of course fundamental to modern evolutionary biology.[92] As noted by Lucretius, contemporary animals have succeeded in reproducing themselves through their fixed qualities, such as strength, speed, or cleverness.[93]

Moving forward to the account of anthropogony, the specific characteristics of humans as an animal species become clear. As with the account of zoogony, the detailed reconstruction of the process of anthropogony is based on analogies between past and present, especially between the wild animals of today and the earliest human beings.[94] The first human beings were held by Lucretius to have been bigger and more robust than the bodies of humans in subsequent ages. His account of anthropogony in lines 925–1025 of book five of DRN outlines a number of other features. First of all the earliest humans wandered around the earth in the manner of wild beasts, being without the *technê* of agriculture and having to depend upon what the earth gives naturally such as acorns and berries.[95] Yet a limited amount of craft can be observed for the dwellings in groves, caves, and woods, with beds made of foliage and leaves. Also, Lucretius notes the use of rocks and clubs to pursue wild beasts.[96] This use can be seen as another example of the adaptation of the natural fruits of the earth by humankind.

---

91   DRN V.808–820, Smith 1992, pp. 440–3.

92   Campbell 2003, pp. 108–9.

93   DRN V.855–59, Smith 1992, pp. 444–5.

94   Gale 2009, p. 177.

95   Acorns are extremely common in Greco-Roman accounts of the earliest humans, see Campbell 2003, p. 343.

96   DRN V.966–72, Smith 1992, pp. 452–5.

In fact, the basis of technology for the ancient atomists lay in the adaptation of natural features. This notion derives from the Greek philosophers of the sixth and fifth centuries BC discussed earlier, but a new twist was added by Democritus based on his conception of the human body as a conglomeration of atoms. The basis for perception for Democritus can be found in thin layers of atoms called *eidola* that constantly flake off the surfaces of macroscopic bodies.[97] These *eidola* are perceived by the mind-atoms, which were conceived of by Democritus as spherical and hot, which are distributed throughout the human body.[98] The key distinction of mind-atoms from other atoms is their animating power to induce motion, as due to their spherical form they can penetrate through other atoms. Mind-atoms were present in animals and plants as well, perhaps even in stones as indicated by a fragment describing an Democritean account of the generation of a stone.[99]

Soul and mind were held to be identical (captured in the overarching term *psyche*) by Democritus, even if the role of thought is less clear in his surviving work.[100] Although no detailed account of anthropogony and early humans of Democritus has survived, there is enough material to connect this atomic view of psychology to the human qualities that make a process of cultural development possible. A crucial fragment to consider in this regard is DK 68 B33:

> Nature and teaching are similar. For teaching reshapes the man, and in reshaping makes his nature.[101]

The role of the notion of *phusiopoiei* in fragment DK 68 B33 is of crucial importance in grasping the position of humans in nature in the thought of Democritus.[102] It relates the soul-atoms, which are present in other forms of life as well, to human action and the process of teaching. A number of fragments

---

97   Taylor 1999, p. 119.
98   The *eidola* do not directly impact the mind, for there is a mixture of them in the air (which then impresses the body). Even the perception of phenomena in sleep (including deceased persons) can be grasped as sense impressions. Hence there is a distinction between the sense perception of *eidola* and the true nature of things, as atoms cannot be readily perceived. This follows from the argument of Democritus that everything but atoms and void is conventional, as discussed in the previous section on atoms and *kosmoi*.
99   Taylor 1999, p. 135.
100   Taylor 1999, pp. 200–6.
101   Taylor 1999, p. 15. The fragment aligns Democritus with Protagoras and this view was criticised by Aristotle, as noted by Luria 2016, p. 710. This statement of Democritus has a good parallel in Lucretius, see DRN III.294–322, which will be discussed in Chapter 3.
102   Morel 2007, pp. 117–19. It is also the only fragment from Democritus for which Taylor 1999, pp. 232–33, does accept a strong reading for the connection between atoms and ethics.

suggest that for Democritus nature was the proper teacher of humankind. One example of this is DK 68 A151–5, which relates humans discovering mule-breeding by watching the violation of a mare by an ass.[103] Democritus argues in DK 68 B154 that humans should not ridicule animals, having learned these techniques from them.[104] Other fragments of Democritus also point to the specific characteristics of human beings. For example, DK 68 B198 states that things grasp their need but humans do not,[105] and DK 68 B278 that animals care for their offspring naturally but that humans expect a return from child-rearing.[106] While god has given humans good things, Democritus argues in DK 68 B175, humans have run into bad things from failing to apply their minds, and therefore teaching is required for overturning bad things.[107]

Humans learning from nature through imitation and adaptation by way of accidental encounters can also be found in the Epicurean version of ancient atomism. The clearest and most expansive example can be seen in the Lucretian account of the early development of metallurgy at a later phase in history.[108] However, an important difference between the Epicureans and Democritus needs to be taken into account here, which derives from their distinct ideas about perception. In Democritus the mind-atoms were distributed throughout the body in a unity of mind and soul in *pysche*, which would be reordered through the process of *phusiopoiei*. Yet in Epicureanism there exists a clear distinction if not a dualism between the feeling body and the mind or rational part located in the chest.[109] The former cannot perceive without the latter, while the latter cannot survive without the former.[110] Furthermore, there

---

103   Taylor 1999, p. 131. See also the commentary of Luria 2016, pp. 632–38 on this and other fragments on nature as the teacher of humankind.

104   Taylor 1999, p. 147.

105   Taylor 1999, p. 27.

106   Taylor 1999, p. 47.

107   Taylor 1999, p. 19. As can also be seen in fragment DK 68 B172, Taylor 1999, p. 19, In that fragment it is stated that things can bring both evil and advantage, as in the example of the human encounter with deep waters and the resulting danger of drowning. The result of this encounter is of nature teaching human beings to swim, thereby bringing about the possibility of gaining advantage.

108   DRN V.1243–1268, Smith 1992, pp. 474–77. See also fragment 12 of Diogenes of Oenoanda, Smith 1993, p. 373.

109   Democritus and Epicurus shared the notion that perception works through the impression of *eidola* on the mind. The basic template for understanding this in Epicurean texts is through visualisation, with some minor role for hearing, see Long and Sedley 1987, p. 76. A strong correlation exists for the relation between external objects and their impression upon the senses, for this is a physical process.

110   The notion that the soul and mind are substances in the vessel of the body recurs throughout the DRN, Gale 2009, p. 122, including in book five in a passage where it is used

exists an important role is for the notion of *prolepseis* in the process of adapting natural features for human use.

Best understood as 'anticipation' or 'preconception', *prolepsis* refers to the idea of Epicurus that sense-perception is structured by the perceiver based on a sequence of previous sense-impressions.[111] It is clear, therefore, that the Epicurean account of psychology places a stronger emphasis on naturalism, as in the idea that justice is based on (natural) *prolepseis* rather than on false opinions or the imperfect conventions of *logismos*.[112] Hence in Epicureanism *phusiopoiei* is constrained to a much greater degree by natural factors, which place logical constraints on the kinds of development that can occur.[113] As can be seen in Epicurus' *Letter to Herodotus* (75), a result is that new developments are first compelled by nature but later inventions can emerge by convention (that is, from human thought).[114] This is true as much for technologies as for the development of language, as will be further discussed in the section on the first form of social life below.

Epicurus is ambiguous about convention, holding that sense-perception cannot be false, and that errors derive from what is added to sense-perception by opinion.[115] For example, the main danger in the limited existence of the first

---

as an analogy to demonstrate that the *kosmos* and its parts are not alive in any way. The soul and mind can only function within the human body, which acts as their vessel, not as distributed throughout all kinds of things, as is evident from DRN v.138–145, Smith 1992, pp. 388–9:

> But since in our bodies too there is a settled disposition, and it seems to be fixed and determined where the soul and the mind can each exist and grow, we must deny a fortiori that they can endure right outside the body and animal form, in crumbling clods of earth or in the sun's fire or in water or the lofty realms of aether. So these things are not endowed with divine sensation, since indeed they cannot be alive and animate.

111   Morel 2008, p. 47, stressed that the *prolepsis* is not just a mental image or movement of thought, but both at the same time. He outlines fives major roles of the 'proleptic method' in Epicurean philosophy: 1) 'natural use' of the recollection of past image-impressions, 2) 'conventional use' of linguistic self-evidence between things and preconceptions, 3) use as an 'indemonstrable principle', a beginning that avoids an infinite regress, 4) regulatory use for the variation sense-experience, and 5) use as means of confirmation and criterion for opinions on sensory-experience.

112   Cole 1990, pp. 75–9.

113   The changed Epicurean conception has been connected to a broader shift in the Hellenistic period, away from notions of utility and calculation towards different conceptions of friendship and common humanity, see Cole 1990, pp. 131–47. For Cole this is a negative development, which results in the Epicurean Garden being an essentially closed and conservative entity compared to the democratic political perspective of Democritean atomism.

114   Inwood and Gerson 1994, p. 16.

115   In the *Letter to Herodotus* (49), Inwood and Gerson 1994, p. 9.

humans was from attacks of wild beasts, who often became the 'living tombs' of early humans.[116] Yet Lucretius and the Epicureans are not deploring the original state of humankind, nor were they lauding it as a primitivist would.[117] Lucretius notes that in this first age natural needs are met by what the earth naturally supplies, without harmful luxuries.[118] Furthermore, he also argues that, while with the development of civilisation the danger of wild beasts has been mitigated, at the same time war and navigation of the sea have emerged as new mortal dangers.[119] Civilisation, then, is a double-edged sword that mitigates the imperfections of the past but also creates new dangers to human well-being.

Most *prolepseis* will be discussed as part of the development of language and justice in the first form of social life in the next chapter, but there is one set that can plausibly be situated in the first phase of humankind just after anthropogony. This concerns the *prolepseis* of the gods, which modern scholars of Epicureanism have seen as either physical beings existing remote from the *kosmos* or as projections of the human mind.[120] From the perspective of the history of humankind, it is the position of the gods as material entities that fits the available texts best. Firstly there is the Lucretian account of the emergence of religion, which begins with the perception of the *eidola* of imperishable, perfect beings by humans both when awake and asleep in dreams.[121] The era in which this takes place is unclear, but there is a clear opposition between the physical perception of the *eidola* of the gods and the attribution of false, conventional attributes to them.[122]

Much the same pattern can be seen in the extant fragments of *On piety* by Philodemus. In that book the idea of the imperishable nature of the gods is attributed to what are termed 'the first people',[123] again in opposition to later elaborations of false religious beliefs and customs.[124] It is important to note here that the lack of a precise temporal location for the gods underscores the need to see Epicurean history as a weave of different developments, rather than according to a strict stadialist scheme. There may well have been an overlap in

116   DRN V.990–993, Smith 1992, pp. 454–5.
117   Campbell 2006, p. 57.
118   DRN V.937–944, Smith 1992, pp. 450–53.
119   DRN V.999–1010, Smith 1992, pp. 456–57.
120   See for opposing accounts Konstan 2011 and Sedley 2011, with references.
121   DRN V.1169–1182, Smith 1992, pp. 468–71.
122   Furley 1989, pp. 216–19.
123   Obbink 1996, p. 310.
124   Konstan 2008, n. 11, pp. 87–8.

the perception of the gods during the period just after anthropogony and the period of the development of the first form of social life. Partly this may be because the first era of humankind was ill-defined in terms of its duration.[125] Perhaps the most interesting part of the account by Lucretius of the earliest humans is that they are solitary in their wanderings around the earth, having no conception of the common good and relying solely on their own instincts for survival.[126] The only exception to this solitary, beast-like wandering is the occasional union of the sexes when they encounter each other:

> They could not look to the common good, they did not know how to govern their intercourse by custom and law. Whatever price fortune gave to each, that he carried off, every man taught to live and be strong for himself at his own will.

> And Venus joined lovers' bodies in the woods: for each woman was won over either by mutual desire, or by the man's violent strength and urgent lust, or by a fee of acorns, arbutus-berries and choice pears.[127]

Two aspects are especially significant in this quotation. The first is how each individual was self-taught according to their own volition. The precise Latin term here is *sponte sua*, corresponding to Greek *automaton*, which refers to spontaneous action without external determination.[128] It is used in many parts of the poem of Lucretius, as well as in other Greco-Roman authors, most notably with regard to zoogony. In the passage on the earliest humans just cited, it clearly shows how they act according to their own will. Most notably, *sponte sua* also occurs in line 1147 of book five.[129] Here it is part of the passage where Lucretius describes how, after the violence caused by the overthrowing of the first kings, people spontaneously submitted to laws to ensure peace. In broad terms, the Lucretian argument is comparable to that of the humans in the pure state of nature in the forest in Rousseau's *Second discourse*. Both describe a condition that completely negates social life, yet at the same time also highlight

---

125   Gale 2009, p. 178.

126   Hence there is no original communism in Lucretius as the earliest humans are unable to establish the social bonds necessary for sharing, yet clearly it is a phase without property as well, Campbell 2003, pp. 221–2.

127   DRN V.958–65, Smith 1992, pp. 452–3.

128   Johnson 2013 gives an overview of the different occurrences of the term *sponte sua* in the DRN, as well as in other Latin sources and for *automaton* in Greek ones.

129   Smith 1992, pp. 468–9.

capabilities (or rather potentialities) that will later be crucial in bringing about a more durable form of society in the face of a state of violence.[130]

The second aspect in this passage to consider is the relation between sexuality and sociality as such. The imagery of Venus bringing about the union of the sexes in procreation recalls many other Lucretian examples of this particular goddess aiding humankind. Numerous passages in the DRN describe Venus in the role of a creative force.[131] As such, there seems to be a general focus on generation, which carries over from zoogony and anthropogony to the emergence of social life. For the sexual union of male and female is the only feature of the earliest humans that has an aspect of social interaction. In fact, there is not only a direct interaction based on desire but also the slightly more subtle exchange of a gift of food. In that sense, a degree of sociality can be noted even here, together with the first examples of the use and adaptation of nature, as well as the first *prolepseis* of the gods. These three features will be elaborated in the development of social life and civilisation, to which we will now turn.

4 The First Form of Social Life

Turning now to the development of the first forms of social life, in this regard it can be seen that the earliest form of sociality in sexual unions occupies a central place in the shift to a new phase. Right at the beginning of the account of the emergence of society and the further development of social instincts in book five of DRN, Lucretius discusses the cohabitation of men and women and the consequent recognition of their children as their own.[132] Together with the bodily comforts provided by huts, skins, and fire, the love for spouse and children softens humans from their originally larger and sturdier constitution. As noted by Gale, this pleasure in being with others leads to a natural response to want to care for others as an end in itself.[133] This response also forms the basis

---

130 See the discussion of Rousseau in Chapter 3; the notion of humans acting *sponte sua*, spontaneous, that is, of their own accord, can be related to the Althusserian notion of a potentiality turning into an actuality through an encounter, see Goshgarian 2019. For human beings can *sponte sua* teach themselves, or they can join together in a state of law. This implies that the potentiality for the latter is already present among the earliest humans, in some form or another, even if it is not actualised. The wide application of *sponte sua* to various natural phenomena confirms that it should not be seen as intentional, in a kind of anthropomorphic conception of nature, Johnson 2013, pp. 110–14.
131 Campbell 2003, pp. 224–6.
132 DRN V.1012–1013, Smith 1992, pp. 456–7.
133 Gale 2009, 185–6.

for Epicurean ideas of natural friendship, and is distinct from the Democritean emphasis on social actions as based on calculations of self-interest.[134]

As we shall see below, the notion of calculation was later superimposed over natural instincts. The natural response to care for others in the first form of social life extends to neighbours as well, based not on love but rather on the feeling that pity should be taken for the weaker and in recognition of the mutual benefits of non-violence. Lucretius outlines how this social principle was initially established by communicating through stammering sounds and making gestures.[135] From the very survival of the human race it is clear that taking pity on the weak was for the most part followed, bringing about the *prolepsis* of the common good that forms the basis for justice. In that sense the *foedus amicitiae* (pact of friendship) supplements the biological pact deriving from sexual unions, and thereby forms the basis for any form of social life in which membership extends beyond the narrow boundaries of blood ties.[136]

Closely related to the emergence of communal social life is the development of language. As noted in the section on anthropogony, for Epicurus new developments were first compelled by nature and then could be added to through convention. As such it is no surprise that both naturalist and conventionalist elements can be noted in the Epicurean conception of language, with the latter being superimposed upon the former in a three-stage account that can be found in Diogenes of Oenoanda, Epicurus, Lucretius, as well as other sources.[137] For Lucretius language derives naturally from the connection between vocalisations and emotions that follow the encounter with a phenomenon.[138] He

---

134   Cole 1990, pp. 77–8. Roskam takes hedonistic calculation to be one of the key axioms for Epicureanism, see Roskam 2007, pp. 35–6. His argument, however, does not take the historical dimension sufficiently into account, and as a result ignores the historical priority of natural *prolepseis* over convention-based calculation. See in this regard also the remarks on *phronesis* in the previous chapter in the section on the convergences between Spinoza and Epicureanism.

135   DRN V.1019–1027, Smith 1992, pp. 456–9.

136   The account of Lucretius does not discuss kin relations beyond what seems to resemble a nuclear family, certainly nothing like a 'community of wives'. In a fragment of Hermarchus in Porphyry's *On abstinence*, there is a relation between community and kinship, see Clark 2000, p. 34. Kinship did play a role in the analysis of early Greek history, as can be seen in a fragment of Dicaearchus' *Life of Greece*, see Fortenbaugh and Schutrumpf 2001, p. 73. Interestingly, the aims of Dicaearchus and others may have been, at least partially, polemical, but were treated as more factual by Morgan and others in the nineteenth century, see further the discussion of Morgan in Chapter 4.

137   See Long and Sedley 1987, pp. 97–100, for the relevant sources.

138   DRN V.1056–1090, Smith 1992, pp. 460–3.

uses the analogy of animals uttering different sounds for different emotions, and therefore it should not be surprising that humans naturally came to use specific sounds for particular things.[139]

The account of the origins of language in book five of *DRN* is located just after the establishment of social life, with nature compelling the names of things through utility.[140] The physical aspect of the origin of names is emphasised by Epicurus in his *Letter to Herodotus* (75), where the specific local conditions of a tribe cause its members to expel air in specific ways.[141] The initial vocalisations (or 'first thought-objects') are sustained as a pattern based on the repetition of sensory and emotional experiences, which are plausibly connected to the notion of *prolepsis* discussed in the previous chapter in the section on anthropogony. Hence the local conditions noted by Epicurus in the *Letter to Herodotus* refer not just to feelings, but also to durable patterns of preconceptions (*prolepseis*).

Such are the basic psychological conditions for the development of language, which is then supplemented by a second stage in which convention refines the meaning of words within a community of language users, a feature expounded by Diogenes of Oenoanda, Epicurus, and Lucretius alike.[142] 'The third and final stage is that of historical society, where people are able to manipulate words with greater ease, something brought on by the introduction of metaphor and the consequent ability for analogy'.[143] Grasped within the context of history, language is a factor that accompanies the development of sociality, being stimulated by it and enabling in turn the further development of communities. An emphasis on nature as the original stimulating force can also be noted for the adaptation of fire for human use and for the development of cooking in Lucretius.[144]

Together with the effects of social life, these inventions result in the softening of human bodies and temperaments. Just as with language, technology stimulates the further development of social life. In that sense a nexus of the

---

139   DRN V.1087–1090, Smith 1992, pp. 462–3.

140   DRN V.1028–1029, Smith 1992, pp. 458–9.

141   Inwood and Gerson 1994, p. 16.

142   Gera 2003, pp. 170–9.

143   This can be seen especially well in a fragment from *On poems* (5) by Philodemus, Mackey 2015. This third phase signals both the precondition for distortion through 'empty words', that is without real referents, and its solution in the application of (Epicurean) reason to reveal the actual connection between words and referents.

144   DRN V.1091–1104, Smith 1992, pp. 462–5. Cooking also plays an important role in the account of early humans in *On Ancient Medicine* (3–7), Schiefsky 2005, pp. 76–83.

elements of social life, language, and technology can said to define the first form of social life. A rather similar account can be found in *De architectura* by Vitruvius, where the same elements of fire, language and social life are discussed, in the context of the emergence of the first human dwellings.[145] The relation between Vitruvius and the atomists is enhanced by his insistence in this passage on humans adapting their earliest technology from natural examples,[146] as well as his referencing of atomic principles in a following passage.[147] As we shall see in the next chapter, Vitruvius was also one of the main conduits through which the Epicurean or atomist perspective on the earliest phases of human history was transmitted to Renaissance Europe. However, he captured just a fragment of the history of humankind, not including the emergence of states, property, and metallurgy, specifically to illustrate the development of early architecture.

The key question then is how this generic picture of the initial development of social life can be situated historically. Only little on this can be found in Lucretius and other Epicurean authors, who offer rather generic accounts of historical development that are hard to connect to any specific region.[148] Nor are the internal dynamics and later demise of this first form of social life elaborated in his work. Some insights can be gained, however, when we recall the thesis on the plurality of worlds from the section on the weave of temporalities above. There differential development was attributed both to natural and conventional distinctions between regions.[149] An important application of this thesis can be seen in the Epicurean account of the historical variations of justice, which as we shall see below offers important clues on the dissolution of the first form of social life. With the addition of new discoveries based on reason, there is more leeway for historical development to occur in distinct

---

145   Rowland 1999, pp. 34–5.
146   If not deriving his ideas from Lucretius, Vitruvius may have drawn them from another materialist thinker, who Cole argued may have been Democritus himself, see Cole 1990, table 1, p. 26, based on the close similarities that may have sprung from a common source dated to the fifth-century BC.
147   Rowland 1999, pp. 35. As has been noted, however, the references to atomism exist side by side with notions that the *kosmos* was the result of divine craftmanship, Di Pasquale 2016. Indeed the post-Renaissance connection between mechanics and atomism is not present in the Greco-Roman sources, Berryman 2009, pp. 9–20.
148   Campbell 2003, pp. 12–15.
149   Some very limited application of this thesis for regional differences may be noted in Epicurean authors. In DRN V.14–17, Smith 1992, pp. 378–81, Lucretius notes the existence of tribes who do not cultivate grains and the vine, which were key hallmarks of Greco-Roman civilisation.

ways. As Epicurus argues in his *Principal Doctrines*, notions of justice are adaptable to changes in the objective circumstances within which they have to be applied,[150] hence in doctrine XXXVI an emphasis on regional plurality can be noted as well:

> In general outline justice is the same for everyone; for it was something useful in mutual associations. But with respect to the peculiarities of a region or of other [relevant] causes, it does not follow that the same thing is just for everyone.[151]

Expanding upon this, it was noted earlier in the section on anthropogony that with new discoveries through reason, there was the drawback of the potential introduction of falsehoods. This is because convention works through assumptions, or *hupolepseis*, that can either be false or correct, unlike the *prolepseis*, which are based on sense-perception and are therefore always true. Words are especially susceptible to the introduction of misleading opinions, for they are material entities in themselves in the sense that they act as *eidola* on listeners.[152] Hence the physicality of words is the way through which the symbols of convention can (literally) impact persons. This makes the word a double-edged sword, one with the potential to create an artificial world that obscures the natural relations between words and things captured in the *prolepseis* that derive from natural sources.[153] Because of this, language can be seen as one of the main culprits in the dissolution of the first form of social life, even if it is never explicitly assigned this role by Lucretius.[154]

The same is true of religion, in that psychological motivations such as fear lead people to attribute things to the gods that are not true, such as the divinity of the heavenly bodies and the control of the gods over their movements.[155] One idea about the dissolution of the first form of social life is that it was undone by a nexus of 'empty words' (that is, words inducing the belief in falsehoods), religious error, and injustice.[156] It is not possible to recognise the nexus of misleading words, wayward religious beliefs, and injustice directly in the surviving texts on this historical phase, however, even if it is consist-

---

150   See doctrines XXXVI–XXXVIII, Inwood and Gerson 1994, pp. 35–6.
151   Inwood and Gerson 1994, p. 35.
152   DRN IV.524–7, Smith 1992, pp. 316–17.
153   Holmes 2005, pp. 564–6.
154   Holmes 2005, pp. 534–8.
155   See below the section on religion and social change.
156   Konstan 2008, p. 107.

ent with Epicurean ideas. For justice it is possible to gain some direct insights through a fragment from Hermarchus, which seems to discuss the dissolution of the first form of social life. It starts from the instinctive realisation that peace is beneficial not just directly for individual safeguarding, but also because of the mutual advantage of being in a numerous community.[157] Yet this advantage at some point in time became obscured, leading to important changes:

> Separating themselves out, and doing nothing to injure those who had gathered in the same place, was useful not just for excluding animals of other kinds, but also for dealing with human beings who came to do harm. For a time, then, they held back from their kinsman inasmuch he was entering the same community for providing necessities and was making some contributions to both the purposes mentioned. But as time went on and reproduction greatly increased, other kinds of animals (and their dragging away of victims) had been driven out, some people acquired a rational analysis of what was advantageous in their sustenance of each other, not just a non-rational memory. So they tried to achieve more secure restraints on those who readily destroyed each other and who weakened mutual assistance because they forgot the past.[158]

Hermarchus goes on to describe how these select individuals set up legislation to regulate the killing of animals and human beings. What is notable in this are two aspects. First of all, it is clear that there occurs a shift from the natural *prolepsis* of justice (the 'non-rational memory'), which is said to have been weakened and partly forgotten, to a conception of justice based on rational thought. Here convention supplants nature in providing justice, in the concrete form of the first laws.[159] The second notable aspect is the intervention of certain persons in this process, who take up leadership roles in the community, moving beyond earlier interventions with regard to the introduction of fire. It is precisely these initial law-givers that provide the connection with the next phase in the development of humanity, that of the emergence of the first kingdoms and civilisation.

---

157 Konstan 2008, pp. 94–6.

158 The account of Hermarchus is given in Porphyry's *On abstinence*, Clarke 2000, pp. 34–5.

159 Here again the difference with Democritus can be noted, for Democritus, in keeping with his view that everything but atoms and void is conventional, stresses the conventional character of early law, see Luria 2016, p. 645.

5   From the First Kingdoms to Law-Bound Republics

As in the fragment of Hermarchus on the dissolution of the first form of social life, the account of the first kingdoms in Lucretius starts by noting the role of specific individuals distinguished by their intelligence and quickness from the others.[160] Whereas earlier they had a limited role in teaching their fellows the use of fire in a communal setting, they now acquired leadership roles that can be described as kingly.[161] It is not made clear precisely how these kings emerged in the Lucretian account, in particular whether they were chosen or established themselves by force.[162] More emphasis is rather placed on what they did once they were established. The first kings founded cities and established citadels above them (*akropoleis*) for their own security, dividing the land and livestock among their followers according to the intrinsic qualities of these people such as their beauty, strength, and intelligence.[163] It is possible that an account later in the poem on the relation between metallurgy and warfare can also be related to this period, given the coeval emergence of bronze tools for war and for tilling the soil, but this connection is not made explicit in Lucretius.[164]

Hence this new age of social life sees a coeval development of three completely new elements: civilisation (life in cities), politics (kingship), and property. For the last element of property a shift can also be discerned in the internal development of the era, which involves a shift in the way property is distributed from intrinsic personal qualities to monetary wealth. As the following quotation from Lucretius makes clear, he did not view the development of property based on monetary wealth as a particularly positive development:

---

160 DRN V.1105–1107, Smith 1992, pp. 464–5.
161 The role of such figures in Lucretius is argued to have been relatively minor, with the emphasis laying on forces and collective achievements, Gale 2009, p. 192. This view can be contrasted to that of Plato and Aristotle, where kingship is foreshadowed in the authority of patriarchal figures, see Fowler 1989, p. 143.
162 Gale 2009, pp. 192–3.
163 It should be emphasised that Greco-Roman conceptions of kingship are distinct in many ways from the feudal and absolutist models of medieval and post-medieval Europe, see for an elaboration of this point the discussion on Greek kingship in Morgan, Engels, and Marx in Chapters 4 and 5.
164 DRN V.1289–1292, Smith 1992, pp. 478–9, see Chapter 6 for the broader significance of this passage for the development of archaeology and for the early modern conception of the Americas.

Afterwards, wealth was invented and gold discovered, which easily deprived both the strong and the beautiful of honour; for people for the most part follow the party of the wealthy, however strong they may be, and however beautiful their bodies. But if one were to steer the course of his life according to true reasoning, it is great wealth for a person to live a simple life with tranquil mind; for there is never any shortage of a little. But people want to be famous and powerful, so that their fortune would stand firm on a strong foundation and so that they could live a peaceful life in affluence – in vain, since, as they struggled to reach the highest rank, they made their pathway perilous, and sometimes envy struck them nonetheless, like a bolt of lightning, and hurled them down contemptuously from the heights into vile Tartarus; for envy, like lightning, usually scorches the highest peaks and whatever is elevated above other things; so that peaceful subjection is much better than the desire to hold sway over nations and rule kingdoms.[165]

This passage is highly significant for a number of reasons. First of all it shows that two different property regimes followed each other, which were based on distinct ways of allocating land and livestock. The first one was based on the natural qualities of people, while the second one was based on the convention of wealth based on gold. Secondly, and even more importantly, is the negative valuation of seeking wealth beyond what is needed to live a simple, fulfilling life.[166] This second aspect can be connected with the distinction of desires by Epicurus in his *Principal doctrines* (XXIX).[167] Here he distinguished firstly between natural and necessary desires, secondly natural but unnecessary desires, and thirdly unnatural and unnecessary desires that follow from unfounded opinions. The notion of 'natural wealth' in Epicurean philosophy follows from this distinction between these kinds of desires, and provides the basis for a rejection of seeking wealth for its own sake as being inimical to natural needs.[168]

---

165   DRN V.1113–1130, Smith 1992, pp. 464–7.
166   This point strongly resonates with Democritus' ideas on unnecessary desires being brought about by bad states of mind, in fragments DK B219, B223 and B224, Taylor 1999, p. 31. See on this also Lucian, both in the qualification of the benefits of riches in his *Saturnalia*, Kilburn 1959, pp. 124–7, as well as his pronunciation of the victory of the Epicurean ethics of pleasure over their Stoic counterpart in the *Double indictment*, Harmon 1921, pp. 124–31.
167   Inwood and Gerson 1994, p. 34.
168   Even so, Epicurus rejected the idea of his disciples pooling their property within the set-

For the process of cultural development, a significant aspect is that the unnatural and unnecessary desires follow from opinion.[169] As noted earlier, the initial phase of development was spurred by nature and later supplanted by rational inventions based on convention. Unfounded opinion can be seen as a conventionalist aspect that is superimposed over the *prolepsis* of natural wealth based on natural and necessary desires. From the account given by Lucretius quoted above, the seeking of wealth to satisfy the unnatural and unnecessary desires, as stimulated by conventional constructions or 'empty words', results in an unstable and risky life path. Furthermore, seeking unnatural wealth presents dangers to the community as it creates envy and factionalism.[170] Such factionalism is seen by both the Epicureans and Democritus as one of the main problems facing humankind.[171]

One reading of the surviving texts has suggested that the striving for wealth and power stems from insecurity, and ultimately from the fear of death.[172] Indeed, the fear of death is an important psychological problem that Epicureanism seeks to address through its teachings, especially captured in the second part of the four-fold cure or *tetrapharmakos*.[173] The historical outline of Lucretius shows that fears can be connected to specific developments such as the emergence of the state and property. Again the role of 'empty words' comes to the fore, for as noted in the previous section, they are the means through which convention-based ideas impact individuals through sense-impressions. Yet it is not the words themselves that have a negative role, but rather the proliferation of hearsay that results from the striving for wealth and the envy this brings with it.[174] Here the connection of 'empty words' and injustice tentatively noted in the previous section appears much stronger, and arguably presents one of the first accounts of alienation in Western philosophy.[175]

---

ting of his Garden, Dawson 1992, note 3, p. 44. Nor, as noted earlier, was there an original communism of goods and wives in Epicureanism.

169 The crucial Epicurean of 'natural wealth' specifically opposes it to wealth as defined by conventionalist opinion, as can be inferred from Epicurus' *Principal doctrines* (xv), Inwood and Gerson 1994, p. 33: 'Natural wealth is both limited and easy to acquire. But wealth [as defined by] groundless opinions extend without limit'.

170 The term *secta* used in DRN V.1115 literally means 'path' or 'course of action', but is most plausibly rendered here as the party or faction of the wealthy, see Gale 2009, p. 193.

171 See for an overview of statements McConnell 2012.

172 Farrington 1955, pp. 7–9. See also the diagram in Fowler 1989, p. 137.

173 As found in his *Principal doctrines* (III), Inwood and Gerson 1994, p. 32.

174 Holmes 2005, p. 570.

175 Specifically, the Latin term for alienation (though clearly not as in the modern philosophical concept) is used by Lucretius in the context of one's thoughts coming from the lips

The first kingdoms, then, were founded on the unstable foundations of unnatural wealth and power, with the former creating envy and factionalism and thereby eroding the latter. Hence it is perhaps not surprising that the kings of the third age came to grief in Lucretius' account, despite the sense of foreboding they demonstrated by constructing defensive citadels. Lucretius describes how the kings were murdered, with a mob trampling on their bloodied corpses.[176] This mob not only killed the kings, but they also overthrew the notion of monarchy itself by breaking their sceptres and thrones.[177] This violent episode therefore ends the era of the first kingdoms, and is followed by a situation in which complete disorder rules and everyone fends for themselves without thinking of the common good.[178] As noted in the section on anthropogony, the development of civilisation can lead to conditions even more dangerous than the wild animals attacking the earliest humans.

What follows the overthrowing of the monarchy is a situation of complete disorder in which violence rules, but the people eventually tire from this and follow (as we saw: *sponte sua*) those who argue for a system of law and order with elected magistrates.[179] It is important to emphasise that unlike wealth, the republican rule of law and magistrates is a conventional construction that works well, even if it is not ideal.[180] Ultimately based upon the natural *prolepsis* of justice of the first form of social life, convention-based law succeeds through inducing fear of punishment: even in those who think they have evaded responsibility for crimes carried out in the past.[181] As will be discussed in the next section, there is a connection here with religion with regards to the inducement of fears. Thus the age of the law-bound republics demonstrates what was observed earlier in the previous section, namely that justice is derived from a natural *prolepsis*, but proves itself to be adaptable to new circumstances by deploying the possibilities of convention-based language.

---

of another person in DRN V.1133: 'quandoquidem sapiunt alieno ex ore petuntque', Smith 1992, p. 466.

176   DRN V.1136–1140, Smith 1992, pp. 466–7.

177   Here there are indications that these events might be suggestive, if in a more generic sense, with the first kings of Rome and Etruscan kingship, see Gale 2009, p. 195 and Fowler 1989, p. 144.

178   DRN V.1141–1142, Smith 1992, pp. 466–7.

179   DRN V.1145–1150, Smith 1992, pp. 466–9.

180   See the last section of this chapter for one Epicurean view of a future state better than the present one.

181   DRN V.1156–1160, Smith 1992, pp. 468–9.

6   Religion and Social Change

The discussion of the history of humankind in book five of DRN does not cease with the coming of republican law. Instead it continues the account further by discussing the origins and further development of phenomena such as religion, metallurgy and its applications, clothing, advanced agricultural technologies, music, astronomy, and finally poetry and writing. As discussed earlier, these different elements have to be understood as part of a broader weave, one that grants each elements its own particular temporality. Therefore, these phenomena need to be discussed in their own right, separately but at the same time connected to the chronological sequence that stretched from anthropogony to republics bound by law codes.[182] Yet although they are treated as elements in their own right, their intersections with other elements are treated as well. This can be seen very well for the element of religion, which in its later history is closely connected with the question of justice.

For the ancient atomists, the interaction between humans and gods was one of the former perceiving the latter as material phenomena. As with Democritus, the gods in Epicurean accounts are not bodies of atoms but rather *eidola* that float around. Unlike the gods Democritus, however, the Epicurean gods do not possess active powers that allow them to exert agency within the *kosmos* inhabited by humankind.[183] As noted earlier, the gods in the Lucretian account do not control the movements of the heavenly bodies nor are these bodies divine in themselves. Instead the gods dwell in *intermundia* between worlds, and they are not concerned with the fate of the *kosmos* in general nor with that of humankind in particular. The only connection of humans to the gods is the perception of them through the very fine *eidola* that reach us from the *intermundia*.

As discussed in the section on anthropogony, the earliest human beings perceived these *eidola* and this resulted in them forming a *prolepsis* of the gods as imperishable, perfectly blessed beings. As time went on, however, Lucretius notes that different things were attributed to the gods, in particular control over the regular movement of the heavenly bodies and the seasons.[184] Lacking knowledge of the true causes of astronomical and seasonal cycles, the ruler-

---

182   Gale 2009, p. 196.
183   Like the gods of Epicurus, the gods of Democritus are *eidola*, yet they are able to influence events within the *kosmos* in which humankind lives, Taylor 1999, pp. 211–16.
184   DRN V.1183–1193, Smith 1992, pp. 470–1. In fragment 12a of *On Philosophy*, Aristotle likewise attributes the emergence of humankind's ideas about the gods both to psychological factors and to observations of the movement of the heavenly bodies, Ross 1952, p. 84.

ship over them attributed to the gods emerges as one of the main reasons for the anxiety of humans.[185] Lucretius points out that such fears are not surprising, as human beings are often at the mercy of violent natural forces, such as earthquakes destroying entire cities.[186] Yet it is a self-induced fear, and seeking out of fear to address such calamities by appealing to the gods does not resolve anything: for the magnificent stone temples set up for worship will themselves be subjected to withering decay.[187]

From all this, and from the Epicurean exhortation that the study of nature holds the key to a good life,[188] it is not surprising that the Lucretian account of the origin of religion has been viewed in atheist terms. There is no controversy in the fact that many early modern and later atheists have used his account to bolster their arguments,[189] but from the perspective of wanting to understand Epicurean thought in its own terms the claim falls flat. The main problem with the view that Epicureanism was an atheist doctrine is the understanding of the gods as material beings. As one of the key axioms of Epicurus is that nothing comes from nothing, the *eidola* of the gods have to be accounted for. One of the key debates on Epicureanism is precisely on the materiality of the gods, which as noted earlier focuses on two alternatives. Briefly, one holds that the Epicurean position of the gods as physical entities dwelling in the *intermundia* can be accepted as a valid part of their philosophy,[190] the other outlines a position in which the gods are projections of the human mind,[191] and, furthermore, that the statements on the gods as *eidola* are a ruse to avoid charges of atheism.[192]

---

185   DRN V.1204–1217, Smith 1992, pp. 472–3.
186   DRN V.1236–1240, Smith 1992, pp. 474–5. Here we can also consider the impact of the 1755 Lisbon earthquake and its impact on the thought of the era, for example in the exchange between Rousseau and Voltaire. Closely following the arguments of the Epicureans, Rousseau rejected teleology comprehensively, see Gourevitch 2000, pp. 603–5.
187   DRN V.306–10, Smith 1992, pp. 402–3. Here is noted that the shrines to the gods cannot rebel against the *foedera naturae*, and hence are as susceptible to decay and dissolution as any other composite structure in the *kosmos*.
188   See Epicurus *Principal doctrines* X–XII, Inwood and Gerson 1994, p. 33.
189   Greenblatt 2011; Stewart 2014.
190   Konstan 2011, with references, see also the discussion of Philodemus' *On the gods* (III) in Essler 2011, which greatly bolsters the realist position.
191   Sedley 2011.
192   Interesting in this regard is the argument that Epicurean ideas on religion were so successful in deflecting charges of atheism, that some of his followers actually sincerely believed in them and erected their own defences of Epicurean theology, Long and Sedley 1987, pp. 147–9. Indeed, this supposed 'ruse' was apparently so effective that there are records of Epicureans acting as priests in various polytheistic religions, see Smith 1996.

Considering the question from the perspective of the history of humankind, the idealist position of the gods as existing solely in the mind's eye seems highly questionable. The basic problem for the idealists is that the initial *prolepseis* of the gods are formed at the earliest phases of history, when according to Epicurus human perception was compelled solely by nature. It is only during later phases, with the impact of conventional words and signs, that humans can develop ideas of their own, in the sense that they are not necessarily derivative from what nature supplies. The result is that the Epicurean critique of religion can be understood in a very different sense from a concealed version of atheism. Instead, it can be argued that Epicureanism questions not the existence of the gods in themselves, but rather criticise the historical development of human ideas on the gods and the way they are worshipped.[193] Such a view is not incompatible with the DRN, but it receives even more support from the extant fragments of Philodemus's *On Piety*.

In his work Philodemus offers a more refined historical account of the development of religion than that of Lucretius, and also connects it to the questions of atheism and justice. First of all it is possible to recognise four distinct phases in the development of religion in *On Piety* (lines 225–318),[194] which can be summarised as follows:

1. As with Lucretius, the earliest humans perceive the gods as external and imperishable.[195]

2. The same disturbances impacting all living beings are attributed to the gods. Interestingly, the use of analogy, which as noted in the section on sources was an important method, is seen as inappropriate.[196]

3. Through attending processions and sacrifices, the fear of death is connected with the gods. Prayers are now addressed to the gods to seek favour, but this is unworthy as the gods are blessed and imperishable, and furthermore do not intervene in human affairs.

4. Certain persons introduce myths telling of the sufferings of the gods, based on a supposed similarity with the sufferings of human beings. Their actions are in contrast and opposition to the beliefs of 'the many', who retain the original *prolepseis* of the gods.

---

193   Konstan 2008, pp. 115–16.

194   Obbink 1996, pp. 120–7.

195   In his commentary, Obbink stresses the lack of disputes by early humans over the gods, see Obbink 1996, p. 310.

196   Obbink 1996, p. 311. However, not all analogies between humans and the gods are faulty, as they do have a human form. Rather, the false analogy consists of attributing human weaknesses to them.

Two things are notable in this sequence. The first is that the psychological factors behind changes in religious belief are made clearer, especially with regard to the inappropriate use of analogy between the human condition and that of the gods. Secondly, there are individuals who introduce myths that extend such analogies, in a way that opposes the customs of 'the many'.[197] A recurring theme in On piety is to attack those who introduce new myths on the gods, especially in the passage citing book twelve of On nature where Epicurus attacks Prodicus, Diagoras, and Critias for their atheism.[198] The basic criticism is of etymological explanations given by such men of the gods, which remove them from 'the sum of things' and enable them to be seen as convention-based constructions.[199] There is also a more sinister charge of trickery, which seems to be in line with the account of religion in the Sisyphus fragment that has been attributed to Critias.[200]

In the Sisyphus fragment, Critias (or another author) posits a lawless state of the earliest humans, until justice was established when a man frightened the multitude with false tales of the gods.[201] These invented gods are all-seeing and punish the wicked, controlling the heavens and the forces of nature such as thunderstorms. All of these ideas are in clear opposition to the Epicurean doctrines on the gods as perfect and non-intervening beings. In lines 1189–1217 of On Piety, Philodemus succinctly describes the ideas of his opponents, drawing out their political implications:

> And preparing an immense deception against the rest, they subsequently rush into terrible, hidden injustices, since they no longer feared anyone believed to be all-knowing. Therefore it was safer to keep silent. Consequently that was what those of the theologians who were just did. For the truth did not escape them, but since they observed that evil deeds were held in check by the tales because foreboding hung over the more

---

197 Such exceptional figures are also discussed by Democritus in fragment DK B18, though in more neutral terms, as the first people who pointed to the sky and named Zeus as the king of all things, Taylor 1999, p. 9.

198 In lines 520–32 of On Piety, Obbink 1996, p. 143. A similar attack on the same grounds is made by Diogenes of Oenoanda, as can be seen in fragment 16 of his inscription, Smith 1993, p. 375.

199 Obbink 1996, p. 349.

200 This is the first mention of Critias as an atheist, here specifically in the role of deceiver by changing the letters of the names of the gods, Obbink 1996, pp. 353–55. The language here recalls the Sisyphus fragment, which is connected to Critias here, though modern scholars also emphasise the possible authorship of Euripides.

201 See the translation given in Kahn 1997, pp. 247–8.

foolish of mankind, in order that we might not render life as a whole a beastly form of existence ...[202]

The notion of a beast-like existence directly recalls the *Sisyphus* fragment, where the life of early humans was ruled by force.[203] This conception of the life of early humans stands in clear contrast to the Epicurean idea of the natural basis for the *prolepseis* of the gods and of justice. Philodemus does not dispute that the introduction of false myths about the gods occurred, locating it historically with the need for security of their inventors from the multitude and to keep the peace among them.[204] Although given the inexactness of the chronology it is impossible to be sure, it is plausible that this political adaptation of religion can be associated with the first kingdoms. Note, however, that the development of religion follows its own trajectory. There is no indication at all in the surviving Epicurean texts that the false analogies of the gods, as well as addressing the gods through prayer, derive from political rather than from psychological reasons.

It is rather through the encounter of the political and religious elements that deceptive myths about the gods are deployed for political reasons. While acknowledging this encounter as a historical factor, the Epicureans reject it as beneficial to contemporary social life.[205] Instead, following the path set out by Epicurus, the original *prolepseis* of the gods as imperishable, blessed and not concerned with human affairs, can be recovered from the false myths added later of the gods as tyrants. The result of this would be that people would imitate the blessedness of the gods, thereby refrain from doing harm to others.[206] In this sense piety and justice are practically the same thing, but in a way that completely reverses the logic of the *Sisyphus* fragment. Instead of endorsing the view that the few impose lies on the many to escape a beastly existence, the original conceptions of the gods of the many are reaffirmed as the basis for a just and blessed life.

A practical demonstration of these Epicurean doctrines can be found in Lucian's *Alexander the False Prophet*, a book that describes the trickery of Alex-

---

202   Obbink 1996, pp. 188–9.
203   Cited in Kahn 1997, p. 247.
204   See the account in lines 2142–2182 of *On piety*, Obbink 1996, pp. 252–5.
205   The rejection of the role of false myths as beneficial to political life may well be one of the reasons why the Epicureans were charged with atheism by their philosophical opponents, Obbink 1996, p. 491.
206   As can also be discerned in a papyrus fragment from the Egyptian town of Oxyrhynchus, see Obbink 1984.

ander of Abonoteichus in setting up a cult of his own to swindle people. It was dedicated to his Epicurean friend Celsus. Lucian describes the cunning devices that were used by Alexander to set up the temple and its rites, noting how they called for a Democritus, Epicurus, or Metrodorus to expose them as fraudulent.[207] Aware of the danger they posed, Alexander incited his followers against both the Epicureans and the Christians,[208] going so far as to organise book burnings of works of Epicurus. Here we see in very practical terms the way in which religious deceit led humans from their freedom to a condition of superstition and servitude to people like Alexander, or a Critias for that matter. The writings of Epicurus that were burned, especially the summary of his doctrines, were, however, extolled by Lucian:

> But the scoundrel had no idea what blessings that book creates for its readers and what peace, tranquillity, and freedom it engenders in them, liberating them as it does from terrors and apparitions and portents, from vain hopes and extravagant cravings, developing in them intelligence and truth, and truly purifying their understanding, not with torches and squills and that sort of foolery, but with straight thinking, truthfulness and frankness.[209]

7 From Metallurgy to the Arts

There are still other aspects of cultural development to be discussed, most notably the emergence of metallurgy and a number of other crafts and arts. The teaching role of nature features prominently these passages, not least in the extended account of the development of metallurgy in lines 1241–1349 of book five of DRN. Here nature teaches humans that metals can be melted by fire and be moulded into certain shapes through chance observations of molten metal being shaped into certain forms. Yet the Lucretian account also gives a twist to these accidental circumstances that lead to such teaching events. For the great forest fires that cause the metal ores to melt and be shaped into new forms are not just the result of natural phenomena such as lightning, but also of the human use of fire in warfare and hunting. The further development of metal-

---

207   Harmon 1925, pp. 198–201, yet the followers of Chrysippus, Plato, and Pythagoras are described as friends of Alexander, Harmon 1925, pp. 208–9, reflecting the division of schools along theological lines.
208   Harmon 1925, pp. 224–5.
209   Harmon 1925, p. 235.

lurgy develops through a series of phases, which may be seen as a rationalisation of the more mythologically-inspired ages defined by metals of Hesiod's *Work and Days*.[210]

The Lucretian phases were not just distinguished between the metals being worked, moving from bronze to iron, but metals are also held in esteem in different rankings in the different phases, which suggests that apart from natural qualities, values based on convention play an important part too.[211] In terms of uses, a parallel track can be noted between the applications of metals in agriculture and in war, or between their respective patron deities Ceres and Mars. Unlike in most Greco-Roman accounts of cultural development, in Lucretius weapons and war exist before metallurgy is introduced. Yet after it is introduced, war brings one invention after the other. Here the Lucretian account moves from metallurgy proper to the follies of war, which includes at one point in time the use of untamed animals like wild bulls, boars, and lions in battles. Unable to be contained and directed, these animals inflict casualties on both friend and foe. This episode brings out the self-destructive character of warfare at its sharpest, leading Lucretius to reflect:

> But I can scarcely bring myself to believe that they could not anticipate and see in their mind's eye what would happen, before ghastly disaster struck all alike; and you could more easily assert that this happened somewhere in the universe, in all the different worlds made in different ways, than on any one particular planet. But they wanted to do it – those who

---

210   Cf. Gale 2009, p. 203.

211   As noted by Gale 2009, p. 203, the changes between ranking the esteem of different materials in different phases has a close semantic parallel in lines 830–3 earlier in book five. That passage followed the explanation as to why the earth has exhausted her potential for bearing new species, going into the general aspect of time changing the nature of things. The implication is that time has the same impact upon human civilisation and the trajectory of metal use, which after the teachings of nature gained by accident led to the first metal tools, is further expanded upon by Lucretius in DRN V.1269–1280, Smith 1992, p. 477:

> At first they made to do these things no less with silver and gold than with the violent force of strong bronze – in vain, since their resistance was overcome and gave way, nor were they equally able to endure hard use. For bronze was more highly valued and gold lay neglected because of the uselessness of a dull and blunted point. Now bronze has been brought low, and gold has come up into the highest esteem. Thus the whirligig of time alters the status of things. What was once valued comes at last to be held in no esteem; but another thing comes up in its place and emerges from obscurity, and is more sought after day by day; when found, it is highly praised and amazingly esteemed amongst the human race.

had no confidence in numbers and lacked weaponry – not so much in the hope of winning, as to give the enemy cause to mourn before they themselves perished.[212]

Next in the Lucretian account of cultural development are the developments of clothing and agriculture, which are traced in their respective sequences. For agriculture in particular, the notion of nature as a teacher of humankind in its technological development is once again clearly present.[213] The same is true for the longer treatment of the origin of music and dancing by Lucretius.[214] According to him, humans start to make music by imitating the sounds of birds with their lips, and also blow in hollow stalks of hemlock to mimic the sound of wind blowing through hollow reeds. The notion of humans imitating bird song can also be seen in Democritus and may have been borrowed from his account.[215] Lucretius emphasises the pastoral settings of the initial development of music, placing great stress on the sweetness of rustic pleasures and the satisfaction of basic bodily needs, although this depends to a degree on a fairer climate.

The rustic scenes also include the development of dancing in settings which, as pointed out by Gale, act as reminders of the development of friendship and social life discussed earlier in the section on the first form of social life.[216] The simple joys of the pastoral life are not improved upon by later developments in music. Here Lucretius points to the phenomenon that new discoveries tend to produce a scorn for earlier ones, such as acorns and berries, beds of leaves and grass and so on. Yet improvements in techniques for him do not automatically lead to a greater satisfaction of needs, but can in fact result in consequences contrary to natural needs:

> So too clothing of animal skins fell into scorn, though I imagine that, when it was first discovered, it aroused such envy that the person who first wore it met his death by treachery, and yet even so it was destroyed, torn apart between them with much bloodshed, and could not be turned to use. So at that time it was animal skins, now it is gold and purple that rack human

---

212   DRN V.1342–1349, Smith 1992, pp. 482–3.
213   In that sense, humans observed and then imitated the planting of seeds, gradually leading to the disappearance of the forest in the face of expanding fields, DRN I.1361–1378, Smith 1992, pp. 484–5. The metaphor of the shrinking of the woods in the face of the advent of civilisation became a later commonplace, as we shall see in succeeding chapters.
214   DRN V.1379–1435, Smith 1992, pp. 486–9.
215   Gale 2009, p. 210.
216   Gale 2009, p. 212.

life with anxiety and wear us out with war; so that, in my view, the greater fault lies with us. For without skins, the earthborn people in their nakedness were tortured by cold; but the lack of a purple robe, decorated with huge emblems worked in gold, does us no harm, so long as we have a common garment to protect us. Thus the human race toils ever in vain and for nothing and wears out its life with empty anxieties, because, to be sure, they do not know what limit there is to ownership and in general how far true pleasure can be increased. This, then, gradually launched life further into the deep sea and stirred up a great swell of war from the depths.[217]

Based on this, Lucretius and Epicureans in general might be considered to have been primitivists, extolling the initial conditions of humankind over later phases of development. It is clear that there are aspects of primitivism in Lucretius, but as noted earlier the labels of primitivism and progressivism are not really suitable. Instead, for the Epicureans the contribution of a specific development toward enabling *ataraxia* is what is important, as other moral features are for other Greco-Roman philosophical schools.[218] Certainly, many of the *prolepseis* that constitute the criteria for *ataraxia* have developed in the second phase of cultural development, and are, if not hard-wired biologically, certainly instinctual. The convention-based phases of development that follow can go against the fulfilment of *ataraxia*, as seen dramatically in the use of wild animals in war. Yet, in the end the process of cultural development results in the gradual mastering of the useful and luxurious arts. In the last lines of DRN book five, Lucretius emphasises the progressive characteristics of his account, the process bringing out things into the open, into the light of reason. The same reason allows us to reconstruct the phases of cultural development through the traces present in the writings of the first poets, providing a link between the poet's own craft and the past.[219]

8   Social Reform and the Good Life

From the outline of the Epicurean perspective of the history of humankind given above, it is clear that the perennial philosophical question of how to live was intrinsic to this account. The emergence of states, property, and conven-

---

217   DRN V.1418–1435, Smith 1992, p. 489.
218   Long and Sedley 1987, pp. 121–5.
219   See for the conception of Lucretius of philosopher-poets in his own time Hardie 1986, pp. 17–22.

tion-based religion led humans astray, but at the same time the fears and dangers of the earliest humans were noted too. Perhaps the first form of social life is the era that finds the most favour in the Epicurean perspective. Yet this should not be taken to imply a desire to return to that era, as some have implied,[220] for as we saw the Epicurean view of development is neither one of primitivism nor a celebration of progress. Further clarity can be gained through understanding the role of Epicurus himself in the historical process and the role of philosophical therapy, especially as contrasted to the doctrines of Plato, Aristotle, and the Stoics.

One hint from the historical position ascribed by Lucretius to Epicurus comes from his discussion of cosmogony, where the youthfulness of the earth is argued for based upon the recentness of many developments, including the ideas of Epicurus.[221] The connection between Epicurus and history is even clearer at the beginning of book six of DRN, where Athens is cited for two great contributions to humankind: agriculture and law.[222] However, despite these advances the lives of humans were still plagued by anxiety, and it was Epicurus who acted as the Athenian remedy to this, teaching his philosophy for the benefit of humankind:

> Therefore with words of truth he purged people's minds by laying down limits to desire and fear; he explained the nature of the supreme good that is our ultimate goal, and indicated the way, the short and straight path, by which we might reach it; he pointed out what evil there is in human affairs, and how the various forms of it arise and fly about from natural causes – either from chance or from necessity, according as nature has ordained; he showed from what gates one should sally out to encounter each of these ills; and he proved that human beings have no reason for the most part to arouse within their breasts the rolling billows of bitter care ... The terrifying darkness that enshrouds the mind must be dispelled not by the sun's rays and the dazzling darts of day, but by study of the superficial aspect and underlying principle of nature.[223]

The praise of Epicurus as a culture-hero akin to the traditional, mythological ones that brought humankind technologies and other beneficial things, has

---

220   Farrington 1953, pp. 61–2.
221   DRN V.330–337, Smith 1992, pp. 404–5.
222   DRN VI.1–6, Smith 1992, pp. 492–93.
223   DRN VI.24–41, Smith 1992, pp. 494–5.

wide parallels beyond Lucretius. Examples are Lucian's *Alexander the False Prophet*, where Epicurus is described as a saviour,[224] as well as the inscription commissioned by Diogenes of Oenoanda that holds Epicurean philosophy to be the benefactor of humankind.[225] Also, in the Garden of Epicurus after his death there was the cult that honoured Epicurus and Metrodorus on the twentieth of each month, a monthly cycle usually reserved for gods.[226] In this sense, the notion of Epicurus as hero, saviour, and benefactor is closely related to the conception of him as a god, which was also highlighted by Lucretius at the start of book five of DRN.[227] At this juncture, it is important to recall the distinction between the atomists and Plato and Aristotle, as similar to that between the Giants and the Olympian gods in the Gigantomachy. It is precisely this distinction that makes clear the divinity ascribed to Epicurus, and the 'political' implications that follow from it.

Sometimes confused in antiquity with the Titanomachy (which came first in mythological history), the Gigantomachy was the epic battle between the Olympian gods and the Giants, who were the offspring of *Ge* (Earth).[228] The basic template of this struggle is that between disorder and order, but this generic perspective does not adequately capture the mythological layers expressed in a rich variety of literary works and visual art. This is not the place to expand on such events as the killing of the Giant named Polybotes, which involved such notable events as Poseidon breaking off and throwing a piece of the island of Kos at him.[229] One thing to be further explored here, however, concerns the location of the Gigantomachy. One of the earliest sources, Pindar, locates the battle at the plain of Phlegra, which is situated in the Chalkidiki peninsula in northern Greece.[230] The name Phlegra refers to 'burning fields' and has been

---

224   Addressing himself to his friend Celsus, a follower of Epicurus, he extolls the philosopher, describing Epicurus not just as a 'liberator' who refuted falsehoods and established right and truthful doctrines, but also more powerfully as 'a man truly saintly and divine in his nature', Harmon 1925, p. 253.

225   Erler 2009, pp. 52–9.

226   Clay 2009, pp. 22–6.

227   DRN V.6–12, Smith 1992, pp. 378–9. All of these roles can also be seen in the surviving statues of Epicurus, as an extensive iconological analysis has shown, see Frischer 1982, pp. 201–61.

228   Hanfmann 1998, p. 304. Hence Althusser makes the distinction between the friends of the Earth (the Giants and the atomists) and the friends of the Forms (the Olympian gods and Platonists and Peripatetics), see Althusser 2006, p. 224.

229   As from Apollodorus' narrative of the Gigantomachy in his *Library* book I vi.2, Frazer 1921, pp. 46–7.

230   In his *Nemean odes* I.65–70, Sandys 1937, pp. 322–5.

associated with different locations in the ancient Mediterranean, some of these areas also yielding large fossil bones.[231]

Of particular note are the Phlegraean fields west of Naples, which are the result of a collapsed caldera and witness much geological activity, including the eruption of gases. This area is often highlighted by later Classical authors as one of the places in which the Gigantomachy occurred, as can be seen in Diodorus Siculus and Strabo.[232] Now, as a place of earthly disorder, the mythological associations of the Phlegraean fields are exemplary for the Epicurean notion of false religion inducing unnecessary fears. In fact, Lucretius specifically addresses this location. Within the larger area there was a lake in a volcanic crater called Avernus, which was feared by the ancient Italians as the entrance to Hades.[233] One of the reasons for this belief was that birds flying over this lake would drop from the sky, and it is this aspect of a 'birdless place' that drew in Lucretius.[234] For him, the effect of the lake resulting in birds falling to their deaths can be explained by natural causes, also seen at other locations, as part of a broader aetiology of certain diseases that stemmed from substances emanating from under the earth's surface.[235]

These aetiologies of disease culminate in Lucretius' haunting account of the Athenian plague of 430 BC in book six of DRN, which he saw as much as the result of despair as of physical causes.[236] It provides a stunning counterpoint to the opening of the book, where he extolled the contributions of Athens to human well-being in the forms of agriculture, law, and the philosophy of Epicurus. The central point of the sixth and last book of DRN, however, is that fear of the unknown can be replaced by understanding. By considering the 'sum of things' (the all, *to pan*), disease is explained through the language of atoms and cosmology.[237] The implication is, therefore, that despair can be avoided through knowledge, and that this enables humankind to overcome the obstacles to the good life it has imposed on itself. Locations where the Gigan-

---

231   Mayor 2000, p. 197.
232   See Strabo *Geography* book V iv.6, Jones 1923, pp. 446–7, where he describes the hot water and sulphuric gases as emanating from the wounds of the fallen Giants. Diodorus Siculus tells of multiple wars against the Giants, including in Crete, Phrygia, Phlegra, and the Phlegraean fields, see his Library of history book V 71, Oldfather 1939, pp. 288–91.
233   As in Virgil's *Aeneid* book VI.121–141, Fairclough 1935, pp. 514–17.
234   DRN VI.740–748, Smith 1992, pp. 548–9.
235   DRN VI.769–780, Smith 1992, pp. 550–1.
236   DRN VI.1138–1286, Smith 1992, pp. 578–91. Also notable in this passage is the connection between the plague and the breakdown of social concord as in civil strife, Schiesaro 2007a, pp. 55–7.
237   DRN VI.647–79, Smith 1992, pp. 540–3.

tomachy was supposed to have taken place, such as the Phlegraean fields, are thereby stripped of the fears ascribed to them by false religion.

In this way the Giants may be said to have the last laugh, as the victory of the Olympian gods has been voided by Epicurean philosophy. Lucretius certainly does not keep this victory a quiet affair, for at the start of DRN he announces the feats of Epicurus in boisterous terms:

> When man's life lay for all to see foully grovelling upon the ground, crushed beneath the weight of Superstition, which displayed her head from the regions of heaven, lowering over mortals with horrible aspect, a man of Greece was the first that dared to uplift mortal eyes against her, the first to make stand against her; for neither fables of the gods could quell him, nor thunderbolts, nor heaven with menacing roar, but all the more they goaded the eager courage of his soul, so that he should desire, first of all men, to shatter the confining bars of nature's gates. Therefore the lively power of his mind prevailed, and forth he marched far beyond the flaming walls of the world, as he traversed the immeasurable universe in thought and imagination; whence victorious he returns bearing his prize, the knowledge what can come into being, what can not in a word, how each thing has its powers limited and its deep-set boundary mark.[238]

As a result, the superstition induced by false religion was brought to heel, but Lucretius hastens to add that this should not be seen as being blasphemous. It is rather a false kind of religion that induces human beings to morally despicable acts, as exemplified by the sacrificial murder of Agamemnon's daughter Iphigenia. All of this underlines the point from the earlier discussion in the section on religion and social change, namely that what Epicurus challenged were convention-based deviations from the natural conceptions of the gods, including those connected to the emergence of states. In this sense, the attainment of *ataraxia* through the understanding of nature inevitably entails the study of human social development, for it was during the course of history that the impediments preventing the good life emerged. It is therefore important to recall here the sequence of the supplementation of naturally-imposed words by convention-based words and signs.

---

238   DRN I.62–77, Smith 1992, pp. 6–9. The thunderbolt in line 68 of course stands for Zeus (Roman Jupiter), who used it to kill various Giants in the Gigantomachy, see Apollodorus *Library* book I vi.2, Frazer 1921, pp. 44–7.

There it was noted that the shift to conventionalism led to the emergence of 'empty words', which obscured or distorted the *prolepseis* that captured the natural connection between words and things. One result of this, apart from religion, was the weakening of the natural *prolepsis* of justice, thus undermining the natural pacts of friendship of the first form of social life. Leadership figures now assumed a regulatory role, including by instituting a first form of property, with allocation based on natural characteristics. When the allocative form shifted from nature to convention in the form of wealth as gold, however, Pandora's box was thrown wide open, leading to the limitless proliferation of unnatural and unnecessary desires. The drive to satisfy such desires, enmeshed with powerful psychological factors such as the fear of death, led to envy, factionalism, and civil strife, which the law could only contain through the threat of punishment.

Through the philosophical understanding of the historical emergence of these social ills, as part of the broader account of the nature and emergence of things, Epicurus was able to formulate concrete solutions. Fundamental in this regard is the notion of philosophical therapy, as captured for a broad audience in the form of the 'four-fold cure' or *tetrapharmakos*.[239] Therapeutic solutions such as this were not meant to be a solitary undertaking, but rather as part of the life of a community of friends, most notably in the Garden established by Epicurus in Athens.[240] This community was noteworthy for including women among its members, who wrote philosophical treatises alongside their male friends,[241] something for which Epicureanism was greatly abused by its philosophical adversaries.[242] Furthermore, Epicurus also let his slaves participate in the study of philosophy, in particular one slave named Mys (mouse).[243] What this shows is that the Epicureans recognised the capability of women and slaves for philosophy, and consequently also the ability to live wisely.

One caveat should be made, however, as one fragment from Clement of Alexandria has been used to argue that Epicurus thought that only Greeks are

---

239   As expressed in the doctrines I through IV of the *Principal doctrines*, Inwood and Gerson 1994, p. 32.

240   See Clay 2009 for an account of the early Garden in Athens.

241   Works that have been completely eradicated from the surviving textual record, except in the survival of a vitriolic hostility towards both femininity and materialist philosophy, see Gordon 2012, pp. 72–108.

242   Resulting in abuse from enemies of Epicureanism, to the effect that the conversions to Epicurean philosophy is likened to becoming an eunuch, Gordon 2012, pp. 160–1.

243   Gordon 2012, p. 99. See also DRN I.455–8, Smith 1992, pp. 38–9, where Lucretius describes slavery as an accidental state of being, in contrast to the essential properties.

capable of practising philosophy.[244] However, the plurality of the Hellenistic and especially the Roman world rendered this idea untenable. In the quotation of Lucretius at the beginning of this section, Epicurus and Athens are hailed as the benefactors of humankind, with philosophy having made the leap from Greek to Latin. In the later inscription of Diogenes of Oenoanda, one fragment signals a clear cosmopolitanism by espousing the notion that people from different places of origin are not really foreigners to each other, for the earth is the true country of all humans.[245] Even more importantly, we can see in this Diogenes a vision as to what kind of society could potentially be brought about if philosophical therapy were to be applied comprehensively, for in fragment fifty-six he states that:

> [So we shall not achieve wisdom universally], since not all are capable of it. But if we assume it to be possible, then truly the life of the gods will pass to men. For everything will be full of justice and mutual love, and there will be no need of fortifications or laws and all the things which we contrive on account of one another. As for the necessaries derived from agriculture, since we shall have no [slaves at that time] (for indeed [we ourselves shall plough] and dig and tend [the plants] and [divert] rivers and watch over [the crops), we shall] ... such things as ... not ... time ..., and such activities, [in accordance with what is] needful, will interrupt the continuity of the [shared] study of philosophy; for [the] farming operations [will provide what our] nature wants.[246]

Hence we can see here not a return to primitive conditions, in that agriculture is practised and nature is changed by the diversion of rivers. Even if such a description of a future state cannot be found in other Epicurean sources, its main features are hardly incompatible with its philosophical tenets. Especially notable is the notion of Diogenes that in such a state, humans will enjoy the same kind of life as that of the gods. This statement allows for a reconsideration of the notion of Epicurus himself as a god (or Giant), as discussed at the beginning of this section. This idea should be understood not as a new mytho-

---

244 Smith 1993b, pp. 140–1. The same notion might be recognised in a report of Diogenes Laërtius (X.117) that ethnic origin or bodily condition could prevent people from becoming wise, Inwood and Gerson 1994, pp. 42–3.

245 Smith 1993, p. 381.

246 Smith 1993, p. 395. The first line of not all humans being able to grasp wisdom was added by the translator, and not everyone is convinced of this and other additions to the text, Gordon 1996, n. 83, p. 126.

logy, as the introduction of a new religion or cult, but rather in the sense that through his philosophy Epicurus was able to share the *ataraxy* that marks the life of the gods. The ability to live like gods can also be recognised in the Lucretian account of human psychology. After discussing the materialist basis for the characteristics of different animal species and the psychological make-up of individual humans,[247] he argues that the problems that remain for human nature are so slight that there is little to prevent us from living as gods.[248]

These problems were addressed through the *tetrapharmakos*. It was precisely with regards to this use of philosophical therapy that, again, the Epicureans were distinguished from the philosophies of Aristotle, Plato, and the Stoics, none of whom were much concerned with philosophical therapy nor with the inclusion of women and slaves in their philosophical schools.[249] They were rather seeking to reform the state, and Plutarch specifically upbraided the Epicureans for their seeming avoidance of public affairs, praising instead Plato and the Academy for their political designs.[250] Such designs, it should be added, naturally flow from the teleological conception of the development of humankind outlined in the section on the two rains and the two histories above. There we saw that the unfolding of a series of forms, from household to *polis*, is assumed to happen for an end, namely the good life in the city and philosophy. The final form, the whole, preceded its constituent parts.

Hence it is hardly surprising that there should exist an ideal form of the *polis*, one that exists not as a result of a historical process, but, by defining its goal, precedes it. Various examples can be found in Aristotle, the Stoics, and most famously in Plato's *Republic*, where the Althusserian emphasis on logocentrism in idealist philosophy, as discussed in the previous chapter, is brought out well:

---

247   See for this also the fragments of book xxv of Epicurus' *On Nature*, Inwood and Gerson 1994, pp. 76–7. These fragments have given rise to different theories about freedom of Epicurus, see for an overview O'Keefe 2005 table 1,1, p. 18. From the historical perspective, the notion of 'developments' within individual personalities should be viewed in the broader context of the interaction between humans, as well as between humans and nature, in different eras. The fragments certainly do argue against an essentialist conception of human nature.

248   DRN III.319–322, Smith 1993a, pp. 212–13.

249   The only outlier in this was Plato's *Republic*, but it is unclear to what extent the communism of property and sexual relations is valid for the citizen body as a whole, rather than just an elite guardian class that needs to stay incorruptible, and at any rate slavery remains current in this city-state, see Dawson 1990, pp. 77–91 for an in-depth discussion. It should be noted, in any case, that Plato never held the multitude to be able to attain the capacity for philosophical refection, as can be seen in book VI of the Republic, Shorey 1937, pp. 42–7, 66–77.

250   In two tracts against the Epicurean school, Einarson and De Lacy 1967, pp. 303–15, 331.

'I understand', he said; 'you mean the city whose establishment we have described, the city whose home is in the **ideal**; for I think it can be found nowhere on earth'. 'Well', said I, 'perhaps there is a pattern of it laid up in heaven for him who wishes to contemplate it and so beholding to constitute himself its citizen. But it makes no difference whether it exists now or ever will come into being'.[251]

Here, then, we see how the two parties in philosophy meet the political, or rather two distinct views of the relation between philosophy and politics. One view seeking to use philosophy to determine a plan for the ideal life. A perspective that intersects with class interests as in Aristotle's notion of natural slavery,[252] or in Cicero's invective against agrarian laws and the cancellation of debts, as well as his praise for the assassinations of the Gracchi brothers.[253] Yet contrary to this are the seemingly more egalitarian positions of Stoics such as Zeno,[254] and in some readings Plato himself as well.[255] By contrast, Epicureanism seeks to circumvent politics through therapeutic means, in philosophical communities separate from the state. The future state posited by Diogenes of Oenoanda negates the ill effects brought about by convention-based wealth, civil strife, and religious fear. No plan of government is specified, however, for it is rather the praxis of the shared study of philosophy, along with the tilling the soil and diversion of rivers, that defines this state.

Much more can be said about the connection between Epicureanism and actual politics, and this holds for the materialist theories of Democritus and others in the fifth-century BC as well. As noted at the beginning of this chapter, this would require a book-length 'archaeological' study rather than a 'philological' approach. The scope of the investigation should be clear when we consider the various studies on Democritus and fifth-century democratic politics, the relation of Epicurus and the first generation of his school to the Hellenistic kings, Lucretius as providing an incisive critique of Roman civilisation, the more reformist position of Philodemus, the Epicureanism of Cassius and other participants in the fierce political struggles at the end of the Roman republic.

---

251   Shorey 1935, pp. 414–17, emphasis added. The word here translated as ideal is the Greek *logos*.

252   The theory of 'natural slavery' as expounded by Aristotle and others rather saw slaves as being servile by nature, Ste. Croix 1981, pp. 416–18. See book I of Aristotle's *Politics* for the classic argument, Rackham 1944, pp. 14–31.

253   In his *On Duties*, Miller 1913, pp. 213, 247–65.

254   Dawson 1992, pp. 177–8, see pp. 195–206 for the shift between the early and later Stoics on this score, the latter moving away from an egalitarian focus due to Roman influences.

255   Note the attraction of Plato to someone like Badiou today, see Badiou 2012.

Apart from these political aspects, there is also the religious one, as in the battle of Epicureans and Christians with the fraudulent oracle-monger Alexander of Abonoteichus, prompting wider reflections on the relation of atomist philosophy and Christianity. Finally a technological aspect should be noted as well, especially in relation to Vitruvius, as well as Epicurean valuations of labour.

All of these aspects await future (Marxist) scholarship on the history of philosophy and its connections to the social formations and mode of production of the ancient world. Hopefully, an aleatory perspective can show these interconnections in a radically new light. For present purposes, the 'philological' approach used in this chapter has yielded an outline of Epicurean ideas on the emergence of humankind within the broader series of encounters that constitutes nature, as well as the further development of humankind in various social forms. How, then, does this outline relate to the three theses outlined in the previous chapter, that of trans-individuality, of the primacy of the encounter over form, and of plural temporality? All three resonate powerfully in Lucretius and the other sources, and, furthermore, the interdependence between them can be observed quite well in the Lucretian outline of history.

Starting with the thesis on trans-individuality, humankind was the result of a series of encounters that started with the formation of the *kosmos*, of the earth, and zoogony. As a particular variant of zoogony, human beings emerged and adapted natural features in order to survive, thereby altering their own atomic constitution (captured in the Democritean term *phusiopoiei*). Examples are the development of speech and the softening of the body following the initial development of technology and social life. In a later phase these natural modifications were supplemented by the addition of convention-based symbols, acting as a kind of 'second nature' that was not always beneficial to humanity. Most importantly, this process of learning was *sponte sua*, without external direction or the teleological unfolding according to a pre-determined end, resulting instead from accidental encounters with natural phenomena and people.

Here we are already concerned with the thesis of the primacy of the encounter over the form, as the pre-existing elements of the encounter do not determine its outcome but rather are captured by it. A good example is the Lucretian outline of the sequence of distinct modes of social life, from the first form of social life to kingdoms and law-bound republics. Unlike in the Aristotelian conception, where the end-result of the *polis* precedes the simpler antecedent forms, in Lucretius the emergence of new modes creates unforeseen problems that potentially can lead to their dissolution. Even the law-bound republics that resulted from the violent breakdown of the first kingdoms, due to property-induced factionalism, are inherently unstable, as the troubles of the Roman republic demonstrate. Notably, as with the process of learning from nature, this submission to the law also occurred *sponte sua*, reflecting the ability of people to adapt to new conditions.

Another aspect of the thesis of the primacy of the encounter over the form is that distinct kinds of encounters can be recognised from the earliest period of humankind onwards, as in the adaptation of nature, in the modes of sociality, and, finally, in conceptions of the gods. These different kinds of encounters cannot be reduced to each other, even if they clearly intersect, as in an interwoven tapestry. Here the thesis of plural temporality comes into play. For there is no reduction of all phenomena to a singular time, whether linear or cyclical. Instead, following the Epicurean conception of time, the relative autonomy of things is reflected in their distinct durations. Indeed, Epicurus himself had emphasised that the very tempo of historical change varied between different eras, just as it varied between different regions. These regional differences in development derived from both natural and conventional distinctions.

Such historical and regional variety can be understood as part of another thesis, that of the plurality of worlds, whether they concern different parts of the earth or the infinite number of *kosmoi* in the universe at large. In the Epicurean accounts of history this thesis was developed only in a more rudimentary sense, as they tended to more generic outlines rather than the detailed descriptions of different regional histories one can find in Herodotus or Strabo. In a sense it follows from the thesis of plural temporality, in that both theses on plurality reflect that in Epicureanism compound bodies are always contingent phenomena resulting from encounters within the infinite 'sum of things'. As discussed in the next chapter, the thesis of the plurality of worlds came to the fore in the European encounter with the Americas, helping to shape a powerful aleatory perspective alongside the dominant stadialist and colonialist one. A perspective that, incidentally, is of crucial importance for realising the revitalisation of Marxist historiography.

Encounters with Ancient and New Worlds

Turning now from Epicureanism as a strand of Greco-Roman philosophy to its later reception in different cultural contexts, the question of Eurocentrism inevitably rears its head. Just as with any kind of history, the history of ideas can fall foul of stadialist logic. Given that the 'West' sees itself as the successor to the ancient Mediterranean civilisations, this immediately entails Eurocentrism as well. This chapter addresses that question in a twofold manner. First of all, the reception of Greco-Roman ideas in Renaissance and post-Renaissance Europe should be seen as an encounter, existing in a plurality of reception contexts. That the reception of Epicurean ideas 'took hold' in Europe in the way that it did was far from a foregone conclusion. Alternative receptive cultural locations existed in Byzantium and Islam, with closer ties especially to ancient Greek thought. This is not to mention the existence of fully-fledged alternative streams of philosophy, for example in China.

The second question relating to Eurocentrism concerns the universal validity of the trajectory of human development outlined by Lucretius. In this sense the European encounter with the Americas is of crucial importance, since Epicurean ideas about the first form of social life were of great influence in the first philosophical accounts of American indigenous cultures by European thinkers. Here we need to recall the materialist philosopher who jumps on a passing train without knowing its destination, as related at the end of Chapter 1. In this case the invariant constants of the generic Epicurean history of humankind were brought into contact with the singular case of the Americas. Writers such as Montaigne appreciated the plurality of historical pathways demonstrated by the Americas, being irreducible to a single template yet understandable through comparison. Yet his perspective failed to take hold, with different versions of stadialism providing the dominant paradigm. As we shall see in the succeeding chapters, this had important consequences for the development of Marxism.

1   Transcending Eurocentrism

As we saw in Chapter 1, from a Marxist perspective the history of philosophy can easily be conceived of as a dialectical unfolding. The contradictions between materialism and idealism would lead to new systems of thought, in an overall progressive movement that culminated in dialectical materialism. As for history in general, this view can be seen as an inversion of Hegel's conception of history,[1] applied here specifically to philosophy. In Hegel's hands the history of philosophy was shaped into a strongly Eurocentric mould, not from an ignorance of alternatives but from the need to conform to his general ideas on the dialectical unfolding of Spirit.[2] Writing his doctoral dissertation on ancient Greek atomism in the shadow of Hegel's towering influence, Karl Marx struck a dissident note on its reception. Rather than the unfolding of consciousness in Hegel, from its beginning in the East to German philosophy, Marx sought to question a priori models of historical change, positing instead a close kinship between past and present:

> To be sure, it is a commonplace that birth, flowering and decline constitute the iron circle in which everything human is enclosed, through which it must pass. Thus it would not have been surprising if Greek philosophy, after having reached its zenith in Aristotle, should then have withered. But the death of the hero resembles the setting of the sun, not the bursting of an inflated frog.

> And then: birth, flowering and decline are very general, very vague notions under which, to be sure, everything can be arranged, but through which nothing can be understood. Decay itself is prefigured in the living; its shape should therefore be just as much grasped in its specific characteristics as the shape of life.

> Finally, when we glance at history, are Epicureanism, Stoicism and Scepticism particular phenomena? Are they not the prototypes of the Roman mind, the shape in which Greece wandered to Rome? Is not their essence so full of character, so intense and eternal that the modern world has to admit them to full spiritual citizenship?[3]

Neither is this perspective limited to the young Marx, for it recurs in the passage on Greek art in the *Grundrisse*, where a contradiction is noted between a stadialist view of the Greeks as belonging to the childhood of humankind and the great aesthetic appeal that their art holds for us today.[4] This contradiction was

---

1   Morfino 2014b, pp. 39–45.
2   Hegel 1955, pp. 53–5.
3   Marx 1975, p. 35.
4   Marx 1986, pp. 46–8.

never resolved by Marx, owing to his inability to find sufficient time to write his books on Greek philosophy and on art.[5] The question is of great significance for thinking the history of philosophy in aleatory terms, to grasp it from its potentialities, including the non-encounters and the encounters that failed to take hold. Such a historical perspective should move beyond the confines of European philosophical history, to consider its parallels on a global scale. There existed a number of clear alternatives and parallels to the reformulation of atomism in the Renaissance. In different circumstances the social formations in which these were formulated would have eclipsed Europe, and as a result their philosophies would have gained a hegemonic roles.

Given that this did not occur, however, the relevant sources are often underused and not integrated in global histories of philosophy. Starting with independent parallels, here the picture is highly variable and subject to a great deal of new and insightful research. For civilisations like those of the pre-Columbian Americas, only now is evidence becoming available that allows for the recognition of their systems of thought.[6] Althusser's contention that a different name should be found for these systems in order to distinguish them from philosophy proper, owing to their lack of mathematical abstraction, is in fact highly doubtful.[7] Pioneering work has shown the high sophistication of philosophical and scientific work in ancient civilisations, and comparative work is now bringing these insights into contrast with Europe, resulting in overviews of their similarities and differences.[8]

Needless to say, this includes philosophically-inspired accounts of the history of humankind, a topic that comes to the fore especially in Chinese thought. During the Warring States period (c. 475–221 BC), a period of political fragmentation wedged in between the Zhou and Qin dynasties, a great variety of philosophical schools developed in China. Each of these also had their own perspective on history. For example, Legalist scholars such as Han Feizi and Shan Yang provided accounts of a shift from kin-ordered society to social strat-

---

5 Rose 1984 provides a good overview of Marx's ambitions in this regard, including the influence of ideas drawn from his study of aesthetics on the 1844 manuscripts, Rose 1984, p. 72.

6 For example, we may note the remarkable conception of cosmology and the sequence of ages in Aztec thought, placing great emphasis on weaving metaphors, see Maffie 2013, chapter eight.

7 Althusser 2014, p. 17. The remarkable series *Science and civilisation in ancient China*, established by the British Marxist scholar Joseph Needham, put this idea to rest for 'Western' audiences. See volume 3 for mathematics and his general reflections in part 2 of volume 7, Needham 1959, 2004.

8 Especially fruitful in this regard are comparisons between Greece and China, Lloyd and Zhao 2018, Tanner 2009.

ification and the state, with the former emphasising demographic and technological factors.[9] Such theories presented a change from a Confucian focus on preserving the wisdom of the past, instead positing a dynamic process of change. The same can be seen in the Taoist masterwork *Chuang Tzu*, where the notoriously cruel Robber Chih describes the first form of social life to Confucius, who had come to enlist him to work in the state's interest:

> What is more, I have heard that in the past the birds and animals were many and the people few. As a result, the people lived in nests to escape the animals. During daylight they gathered acorns and chestnuts and during darkness they hid in their tree nests. This is why they were known as the Nest-Building People. In the ancient past the people didn't know how to make clothes. During the summer they gathered firewood and in the winter they kept warm by burning it. This is why they were called the People who Know how to Keep Alive. In the time of Shen Nung the people lay down in peace and contentment and rose in serene security. The people knew their mothers but not their fathers, and they lived side by side with the elks and deer. They ploughed and ate, they wove and made clothes, never dreaming of harming others, for this was the era of the perfect Virtue.[10]

It was the sages that overturned this harmonious state of equality of humankind within the 'myriad of things', introducing false hierarchies that alienated humans from each other and from nature.[11] Hence even the most cruel robber can provide a rebuttal to Confucius, that paragon of courtly power. Underlying the difference between the two schools is the Taoist insistence on the primacy of naturalism over human conventionality, which carries with it an anti-teleological perspective as well. This perspective can be discerned from a quotation from another Taoist work called Lieh Tzu:

> My lord is wrong! All life is born in the same way that we are and we are all of the same kind. One species is not nobler than another; it is simply that the strongest and cleverest rule over the weaker and more stupid. Things eat each other and are eaten, but they were not bred for this. To be sure, we take the things which we can eat and consume them, but you cannot

---

9   Pines and Shelach 2005, pp. 134–40.
10   Palmer 1996, p. 264.
11   Pines and Shelach 2005, pp. 140–2.

claim that Heaven made them in the first place just for us to eat. After all, mosquitoes and gnats bite our skin, tigers and wolves eat our flesh. Does this mean Heaven originally created us for the sake of the mosquitoes, gnats, tigers and wolves?[12]

In contrast to these Taoist views, the Confucian thinker Xunzi elaborated a perspective that emphasised a sharp contrast between humans and animals, with the former distinguished by their social organisation and the inevitable social stratification this entails.[13] Given that this Confucianist perspective, in a simplified form, became a standard one in the new dynastical eras, it is tempting to see the parallels here of Taoism an 'underground current' in Chinese philosophy. In this sense analogues, if rather loose ones, can be noted between Taoism and the Epicurean critiques of teleology and their qualifications of the benefits of civilisation and the state. Even so, these general similarities do not extend to the specifics of each case, with regard to the atomist doctrines and so on, which was based on an more general Greek ontological framework quite distinct from that of China.[14] Furthermore, despite the similarities between Chinese and European philosophically-inspired views of the history of humankind, their differences should not be neglected either.[15]

Moving from the parallels to alternative reception contexts of ancient atomism, enough can be said to sketch at least their existence. For example, atomism was present in the medieval Byzantine and Islamic civilisations. Here seemingly isolated fragments present the surface features of what must have been more extensive underground currents. The Islamic case is especially notable as the Greek influence in philosophy, captured under the term *Falsafa*, was counterposed to the *Kalam* stream of Muslim theology.[16] Yet it was the latter that was 'atomistic', if not in an Epicurean sense. In that sense, Greco-Roman atomism is only present at the margins in Islamic philosophy, as through the work

---

12   Cited in Palmer 1996, pp. xxiv–xxv.
13   Pines and Shelach 2005, pp. 142–6.
14   Lloyd 2012, pp. 87–9.
15   See for a comparative analysis Pines and Shelach 2005, pp. 158–61. Notably distinct in Chinese thought are ideas on the emphasis of the primacy of the collective over the individual, the absence of warfare as forcing social change, and the key role that sages play in cultural development.
16   Shlomo Pines was highly influential in tracing the particular Islamic traditions in atomist ideas, see Pines 1997, and also McGinnis 2019 for more recent work along the same lines. It is clear that *Kalam* theology cannot be identified with or be closely related to Greco-Roman atomism.

of Galen.[17] The great Islamic account of the development of life and human civilisation was written by Ibn Khaldun, who was rather influenced by Aristotle and the *Falsafa* stream of Muslim philosophy. Of great worth in itself, Khaldun's *Muqaddimah* doesn't constitute a chapter in the reception of ancient atomist ideas on the history of humankind.[18]

As such, the Islamic case straddles between parallelism and alternative, while the Byzantine Greek case more clearly constitutes an alternative reception context. The term 'alternative' is something of a misnomer here, however, as the Byzantine state was the direct successor not just of the Roman and Greek states, but also of the thought and culture of its people. The fact that this was a Christian rather than a polytheistic, pagan culture, should not lead to a presumption that atomist philosophy was not present here. During the period of the transition from paganism to Christianity in the Roman empire, many notable encounters of Christian thinkers with Epicureanism can be seen, not all of them complete rejections, with some marginal gnostic groups even adopting core doctrines.[19] This included the early history of humankind, as with the fourth-century poet Prudentius, who engaged with the 'hard' Lucretian view of prehistory.[20] In later Byzantine times, the twelfth-century poet and grammarian Tzetzes, in his commentary on Hesiod, shows great familiarity with Greco-Roman ideas on the early phases of humankind, and great skill in their philological interpretation.[21]

A direct reference to Epicureanism can be seen in in the ninth-century epigram of the influential Leo the Mathematician, who wished himself a life according to Epicurean prescriptions.[22] A more detailed picture emerges from the twelfth-century writer Theodore Prodromos, who in his witty dialogue *Amarantos* presents a dialogue set in ancient Athens between two Democritean philosophers and a follower of Epicurus. Two important points emerge from this dialogue. The first concerns the distinction between a mechanical

---

17   Langermann 2009. One thinker evidencing Epicurean influences more directly was al-Razi, see Goodman 2015.

18   See for the intellectual parallels and relations between Ibn Khaldun's historical perspective and that of ancient Greece and later European thought, Dale 2006.

19   See Erler 2009, pp. 60–4, for mainstream Christian engagement with Epicureanism, characterised by ambivalence, while the materials related to the Gnostics are collected in Luria 2016, pp. 676–84.

20   Goodrum 2002, pp. 75–6.

21   Such that it provides an important source for understanding Greco-Roman sources, see for the role of Tzetzes in a comparative analysis of accounts on early humankind, Cole 1990, pp. 25–46.

22   Kaldellis 2012, p. 135.

materialism and divine providence, something seen in pointed rejections of works such as Lucian's *Zeus rants*.[23] This theme remained present in post-Renaissance European philosophy for a long time and powerfully impacted ideas on history as well. The other theme rather shows the convergence of Christians and Epicureans with regard to wealth and poverty. When the Epicurean character in the dialogue comments on the fate of a young girl married off to an old man for the sake of money, it is notable how the Epicurean view of unnatural wealth is presented, as alienating humans from the natural and the good:

> By Hercules, Amarantos, what misery! All things are slaves under wealth, everything dominated by gold. Even beauty, free by nature, is sold. For my part, at least, my laughter is turned into tears when I think about how this woman will endure those trembling embraces, suffer his unpleasant kisses, and wretchedly wipe the drool from her bridegroom's face. It would certainly have been better for her to work with her father in his garden; to live in poverty with the hyacinths and go hungry amongst the myrtle berries; to sing along with the nightingales, sleep by the streams and myrtle branches, or eat by the golden manure and recline at the table of silvery dirt.[24]

The dialogue is significant for two reasons. First of all it shows that aspects of Epicureanism were still in play in the most powerful successor to Greco-Roman antiquity, and that they were to some extent congenial to what was now a thoroughly Christian culture. This is precisely the template according to which the early Renaissance reception of Epicureanism occurred, through the focus on ethics of property and wealth, as we shall see for Erasmus and More below. It shows the potentiality of a more comprehensive reengagement with ancient atomism. The second reason of its significance follows from the first, namely as that potentiality, encompassing the broader sphere of Byzantine philosophy, denies the notion of a dialectical unfolding from East to West, from Oriental despotism to Western freedom.[25] Where the Chinese case showed a parallel track, the Islamic one with both parallels and receptions, the Byzantine case

---

23 Cullhed 2017, pp. 154–5, see also the Epicurean connection in the critique of mechanical philosophy by Gregory of Nyssa, one of the Church Fathers, Berryman 2009, pp. 213–15.

24 Cited in Cullhed 2017, p. 160.

25 Hegel is far from atypical among Western Europeans in describing the Byzantine empire as 'a disgusting picture of imbecility', Hegel 2001, p. 538.

shows that, given the right conditions, its potentiality could have developed earlier, perhaps better given its sophisticated philological traditions.[26]

What is meant with 'the right conditions' is of course those circumstances that allow an encounter to occur and 'take hold'. In order to truly transcend Eurocentrism, however, it is necessary to move beyond history as purely conceived in terms of temporality. For to be able to consider parallels and alternatives in different civilisational contexts and make a decisive break with Eurocentric historiography, it is necessary also to bring up geography. The theoretical means for doing so are provided by the revitalisation of Trotsky's notions of 'uneven and combined development'. As outlined in his historical account of the Russian revolution, this model captures both the unevenness between the development of different social formations and the combination of archaic and advanced elements in so-called peripheral regions like Russia.[27] As a result of this combination Russia could develop advanced industrial elements, being able, by the 'privilege of backwardness', to skip over the stages of development that had originally generated these elements.[28]

Although obscured by the ideological impact of Stalinism and its version of stadialism, Trotsky's theory has recently re-emerged as a potent model for making sense of capitalism in general and its international dimension in particular.[29] The advantage of models based on uneven and combined development is that they can address the weak points of other strands of interpretation of the origin of capitalism, such as world-systems theory and political Marxism.[30] By being able to tackle both 'internal' and 'external' factors not just together but in a way that shows their interrelationships, this approach can make a break with Eurocentrism in a way that is also sensitive to post-colonial critiques.[31] From a methodological perspective, notably, uneven and combined development is not to be seen so much as a theory, but rather has to be seen as a method that is generative of particular theories tailored to specific historical conjunctures:

---

26   The articles in Kaldellis and Siniossoglou 2017 for a broad overview of Byzantine intellectual traditions, including their connection to later Greek thought. In that sense the Greek Enlightenment should not be seen as only the radical break with the past, though that was there too, see for the complexities Kitromilides 2013.

27   Trotsky 1974, pp. 1–15.

28   Trotsky 1969, pp. 239–43.

29   See Van der Linden 2007 for a critical evaluation of the intellectual trajectory of the notion of 'uneven and combined development' after Trotsky, and Davidson 2018 for contemporary debates.

30   Anievas and Nisancioglu 2015, pp. 14–32.

31   Anievas and Nisancioglu 2015, pp. 36–9.

As our exposition demonstrates, the **ontology** of uneven and combined development postulates that historical processes are always the outcome of a **multiplicity of spatially diverse nonlinear causal chains** that combine in any given conjuncture. What this compels historians and sociologists to do methodologically is to analyse history from a multiplicity of different spatiotemporal vantage points – or overlapping spatiotemporal 'vectors' of uneven and combined development – in order to uncover these causal chains. In this schema, an emphasis on the origins of capitalism in Europe, or the English countryside à la Brenner, would constitute one of many spatiotemporal vectors of uneven and combined development – one that must be complemented and combined with other determinations analysed from alternative vantage points. It would be one that is, in turn, related to a number of extra-European determinations bound up in the histories of colonialism, slavery and the Asian merchant trades.[32]

The resulting framework is not at all incompatible with Althusser's aleatory conception of the mode of production, or with the emphasis on plural temporality emphasised by Morfino.[33] The notion of combined and uneven development shares with their work an anti-teleological emphasis on the chance interplay of elements in specific conjunctures, which resulted in the series of historical encounters that generated capitalism. The notion of communism emerging in the interstices of the capitalist world also suggest a convergence on this level. Combined and uneven development adds to aleatory materialism a spatial perspective, one that allows for embedding questions such as the history of philosophy or of modes of production in their specific context. Most importantly, it is also a way in which the Epicurean thesis of the plurality of worlds and its historical implications can be brought more explicitly to the fore. As we shall see in the sections below, it was precisely the geographical encounter with new lands, less pronounced in Greco-Roman antiquity, that gave the historical aspect of Epicureanism its distinctly western European flavour.

For example, from the perspective of uneven and combined development it has been pointed out that the Mongolian hegemony over much of Eurasia during the Long Thirteenth Century (AD 1210–1350), greatly impacted the sub-

---

32   Anievas and Nisancioglu 2015, p. 61, emphasis in the original.

33   As will be argued in the conclusion of Chapter 6, the thesis of the plurality of worlds is a potential bridge between combined and uneven development, and plural temporality and the aleatory conception of the mode of production.

sequent trajectory of Europe.[34] Not only did Mongolian rule enable an increase in trade and the transfer of key technologies from China to Europe, it also greatly facilitated the travels of the Black Death. The demographic impact of that disease in Europe had major ramifications for feudal relations of production, furthering its crisis and opening up spaces for new developments. The resulting historical perspective is quite different from that of stadialism, showing how Europe's advantage was in effect the result of a chance interaction of elements, and far from inevitable.[35] Precisely in the same way, it may be observed that the potentiality of the Byzantine empire was crushed by its enemies from both Europe and the Middle East, leading to the capture of Constantinople by the Ottoman Turks in 1453. The resulting partial transfer of its sophisticated philological tradition to Italy was in fact one of the main stimuli for the flourishing of Classical scholarship in Italy at that time, later broadening to the rest of Europe.[36]

2   The Renaissance Encounter with Lucretius

Within these broader developments, there emerged in fifteenth-century Europe a strand of philosophy that we defined in Chapter 1 as an 'aleatory current'. It should be emphasised, however, that this emergence was not so much an encounter in 1417 between a man (Poggio Bracciolini) and a book (DRN), as one recent best-selling account has suggested.[37] For the DRN was never really lost or completely forgotten in the Catholic part of Europe. Much as in the Byzantine and Islamic worlds it is possible to see occasional sparks of engagement with Epicureanism here too, as can be seen for the Carolingian age.[38] Furthermore, important passages from the DRN were known from more widely circulating ancient works, such as the *Saturnalia* of Macrobius.[39] What set the Renaissance encounter with atomism apart from these medieval episodes is something that

---

34   Anievas and Nisancioglu 2015, pp. 71–7.
35   See Robinson 2002 for an imaginative reconstruction of world history without Europe.
36   A good example of this is provided by Erasmus, who went to Italy in order to learn Greek, and while there was able to study the account of Epicureanism in the *Lives* of Diogenes Laertius, not just in its Latin translation but also in the original Greek, Bietenholz 2009, pp. 115–17.
37   Greenblatt 2011.
38   As demonstrated by the corrections made to DRN manuscripts in the Carolingian age, Butterfield 2013.
39   Passannante 2011, pp. 36–58.

preceded the rediscovery of DRN, namely that from the fourteenth-century onwards a sustained cultural engagement with Greco-Roman antiquity can be seen in Italy.

The refinement of philological methods entailed by this engagement resulted in detailed studies of the language and the meaning of texts, in effect restoring the damaged works to a higher level of sophistication. As noted, this process was greatly aided by the engagement with the Greek language that involved close contacts with Byzantine scholars, especially after the fall of Constantinople in 1453. For example, the rediscovery of the DRN was paralleled by the translation in 1433 of Diogenes Laertius's *Lives of Eminent Philosophers* from Greek into Latin;[40] this, as noted in the previous chapter, contains the main body of texts on and by Epicurus himself. In the hands of scholars such as Lorenzo Valla and Desiderius Erasmus, as well as Thomas More, the writings of Epicurus became important as a way to reconcile Christianity with the Epicurean ethics of pleasure,[41] continuing a theme that we saw was already present in Byzantine times.

As such, we are dealing here with a series of encounters with a number of texts, rather than a single, dramatic one between a man and a book, important though it was. Tracing this series, it is possible to see three main phases, though these should not be conflated with stages, as none was prefigured in its particulars by the one that preceded it:

1. Fleeting encounters with ancient atomism as related in texts by others. Most notable in this regard are the fourteenth-century Italian poets and writers Boccaccio, Dante, and Petrarch.

2. The philological encounter, from the fifteenth century onward, with primary sources on ancient Epicureanism in the form of the DRN and the passages from and on Epicurus from the work of Diogenes Laertius. This encounter started in Italy, but can be seen in lesser form in other areas of Europe such as France, England, and the Low Countries as well.

3. After the philological encounter set up what may be termed the 'tendential laws' of the reception of ancient atomism, the widespread distribution of print editions from the middle of the sixteenth century onwards can be seen as this encounter 'taking hold'.

Before the 'taking hold' of the encounter with Lucretius and the widespread dissemination through print editions of the DRN, it was a rather localised process with a focus on Italy as a whole and Florence in particular. During the

---

40   Palmer 2014, p. 14.
41   Bietenholz 2009, pp. 118–39.

initial phase of reception, the few dozen extant manuscripts of the DRN were comprehensible mostly to a limited set of people skilled at philological methods. Their annotations suggest that the main focus of these readers was on questions of philology and poetry, with due attention to morality, rather than topics such as the early history of humankind.[42] The impact of the radical ideas of Lucretius was therefore initially limited to a handful of scholars and thinkers, but in certain contexts they could reach broader audiences. Such was the case in late fifteenth- and early sixteenth-century Florence. Apart from Machiavelli himself, major figures in this include the Florentine chancellors Bartolomeo Scala and Marcello Adriani, as well as the painter Piero di Cosimo and a host of other scholarly and artistic figures.[43]

Apart from its extraordinary wealth from industry and commerce, Florence stood out both for its learning and for the presence of religious heterodoxy. Of particular note is the undercurrent of Catharism, associated with the Ghibelline faction, which was even conflated with Epicureanism.[44] Slowly but surely, however, conservative attitudes reasserted their power. A first inkling of this can be seen in the mocking of atomism by Savonarola in a sermon given during his brief regime of 1494–98.[45] More important was a Florentine synod of 1516, banning the use of Lucretius in schools and creating a culture of self-censorship.[46] The DRN was not placed on the Inquisition's *Index*, however, owing to the limited, educated audience that had access to it and to a focus of the organisation on combating the Reformation instead.[47] It was only with the appearance of an Italian translation in 1717 that an immediate ban was effected, likely to prevent the ideas from reaching a broader, less elitist audiences.[48] All this has to be taken into account when considering receptions, as later writers especially were labouring under increased risks of persecution.[49]

Turning now to the substance of reception, the focus will lie on the most important 'constants': that is, the invariants of Epicurean philosophy that were actualised in specific ways in the Renaissance. The most notable of these, present in one form or another in most of the figures mentioned earlier, concerns the relation between either a primeval phase without the common good

---

42   Palmer 2014, table 2.4, p. 74.
43   Even if influences may sometimes be more enigmatic, as in the case of Leonardo da Vinci, Beretta 2009.
44   Brown 2010, pp. 10–11; Najemy 2006, pp. 33–4.
45   Brown 2010, p. 49.
46   Brown 2010, p. 14; Palmer 2014, pp. 36–7.
47   Palmer 2014, pp. 37, 238.
48   Palmer 2014, p. 226.
49   See for example the fate of the Academy of Investigators in Naples, Fisch 1953, pp. 552–4.

or the first form of social life, and the contemporary era. Often this juxtaposition of past and present took the form of a qualification of progressive development, using the past to shed light on the present. Hence the first question to address concerns the overall conceptions of historical trajectories. In Chapter 2, we saw that Lucretius conceived of human history as a weave of temporalities, rather than as a linear sequence of stages. In his *historia peri phuseos* account, humankind has to be understood as part of a broader series of encounters, starting with the first-beginnings of the *kosmos* and life. A lack of engagement with the physics of ancient atomism and its cosmological implications, meant that such a broader perspective was never explicitly outlined during the Renaissance.

That is not to say that ancient atomism was unknown in that sense, for the basic principle of things emerging from the fortuitous encounters of atoms was known even before the rediscovery of the DRN.[50] Yet the thinking through of that principle, and its elaboration into a philosophical perspective with which to grasp the world, can hardly be seen in Renaissance Italy. The only exception, of sorts, was Machiavelli. Marginal comments in his hand have been found in his own copy of the DRN in the Vatican library, which can possibly be dated to 1497.[51] His comments show that Machiavelli was concerned precisely with the characteristics of atomic physics in Lucretius, especially their movement and the *clinamen*. Of particular interest is the following marginal comment on lines 256–60 of the second book of the DRN: 'from motion there is variety, and from it we have a free mind'.[52] It should be stressed here that the notion of a 'free mind' is not to be conflated with that of a free will, following closely the intentions of Lucretius in this passage.[53]

Marginal comments like these inevitably give rise to debates as to whether Machiavelli adhered to Epicureanism or not, as we shall see below. Here this debate will be rephrased in somewhat different terms, namely as the question in what sense the philosophical theses of Machiavelli can be said to correspond to the focus on atomic movement and the *clinamen*. In this sense the concep-

50   Boccaccio, in his exposition of Dante from 1373, attributes to Democritus (without mentioning Epicurus) a complex sequence of generation and dissolution, with plants, animals, and 'other things' being created by chance through the combination of seeds, Boccaccio 2009, p. 222.

51   See for an insightful account of this copy as being in Machiavelli's hand, Panichi 2018.

52   Brown 2010, p. 74; Palmer 2014, p. 82.

53   As noted by Brown 2010, p. 74, the notion of a will imposing movement is not present here, rather what is important is the capacity of the mind to be able to act without restraint (determination), something that is in line with the discussion of Epicurean agency as *sponte sua* in the previous chapter.

tion of the aleatory current as based on theses is of use. Morfino has recognised in the writings of Machiavelli five theses, elaborating upon the earlier work of Althusser in this regard.[54] These five theses can be summarised in the following way:

1. The thesis of invariance, which holds that the conditions in antiquity and today are similar enough, being constituted by invariant factors, to enable comparisons between them.[55]

2. The thesis of universal variability, according to which the variation in human affairs derives from fortune, which is unforeseeable to human beings. According to Morfino, this thesis and the first were combined by Machiavelli in order to reject linear causality and the notion of essence entailed by it.[56] Instead causality is plural and all things are 'mixed', as in the opposing classes of the Roman republic, the opposition and struggle between which can be seen as the essence of that state rather than a contradiction existing within it.[57]

3. The thesis of the primacy of the encounter over form, which can be seen in the origins of states as being constituted by meetings of *fortuna* and *virtu* (in conjunctures).

4. The thesis of the primacy of interweaving times over linear time, based on the different times inherent in the cycles of political regimes.[58]

5. The thesis of the disarticulation of truth and memory, which deals with the long-term memory of early times, and the loss of it through human and natural causes.

The key question now is whether, and if so in what sense, these theses can be connected to the marginal comments in the DRN in Machiavelli's hand.[59] We

---

54 Morfino 2015.

55 At the same time, small clues exist in the work of Machiavelli that put into doubt the idea of a timeless order. This can be seen in a reference to a highly destructive hurricane in the Adriatic, where it seemed that: 'the earth, waters, heavens, and entire universe, mingling together, were being resolved into their ancient chaos', Machiavelli 1989, p. 1330.

56 Morfino 2015, pp. 151–8.

57 Morfino 2015, pp. 155–7. Machiavelli's critique of linear causality can be seen in many examples in the *Discourses*, where he notes that similar actions of leaders lead to very different outcomes, based on the particular circumstances in which the action took place, e.g. Machiavelli 1989, pp. 452–3, 477–84.

58 To which can be added the noted longevity of regional customs, as in France and Tuscany, from antiquity to today, Machiavelli 1989, pp. 521–2, these long-term continuities persist irrespective of any cycle of political regimes.

59 The lack of direct references to Lucretius in his major works can hardly come as a surprise, given that they predominantly post-date the 1516 synod banning Lucretius from

may point here first of all to the conception of causality as being not linear but part of a plurality of determining factors, variation being inherent in human affairs. This connects to the first part of the marginal comment on the DRN cited earlier, namely that from motion comes variety. Furthermore, the notion of historical change as coming about through an encounter of *fortuna* and *virtu*, is in harmony with the second part of the comment, which states that from motion and variety we have gained a 'free mind'. In the work of Machiavelli, that free mind seeks not to impose itself on the world by free will, but rather seeks to understand the particular conjuncture in which it finds itself and act accordingly. As such, it is possible to see the marginal comments on the DRN and the theses derived from Machiavelli's work as part of the same aleatory perspective, without immediately demanding that he should be seen as an Epicurean thinker in his own right.

To draw out the implications of this perspective, further insights can be gained by considering the questions of the emergence of states and their long-term trajectories. To start with the latter question, it is well-known that in the *Discourses* Machiavelli uses the cycle of political regimes from the *Histories* of Polybius, the so-called *anacyclosis*. As we saw in the section on the 'two rains' in Chapter 2, this cycle has to be understood as part of the teleological conception of the universe and history of the party of Plato, Aristotle, and the Stoics. Yet, as noted by Althusser and Morfino, Machiavelli in effect takes over the framework of the *anacyclosis* and changes the conception of historical causality and temporality to one more attuned to the role of the aleatory in history.[60] In particular the notion of variable durations and the interaction between different states are important in this, showing how the ideal trajectory of regime changes, from monarchy to oligarchy to democracy, is modified by them. Crucial for understanding the different take on the *anacyclosis* by Machiavelli is also the role of *fortuna* as a driving force in history.

How can we understand *fortuna* in Machiavelli? Certainly it is different from the 'wheel of fortune' notions that prevailed in the medieval era, and which persisted long thereafter. Inklings of a more aleatory perspective can be seen to some degree in Boccaccio.[61] From the fifteenth century there is

---

schools (and through self-censorship largely from public discourse), hardly something that someone in such a precarious position as Machiavelli could easily ignore.

60   The connection between Polybius and the teleological focus of the Academic and Peripatetic philosophical approaches was discussed in Chapter 2.

61   One commentator on Boccaccio's work sees fortune therein as mostly referring to the 'causal interplay of the natural forces of the contingent universe', Hastings 1975, p. 92, yet also with cases of direct divine intervention. There is also little question of human action

a passage from Scala in which a connection is made between fortune and the chance encounters of atoms.[62] There is no 'smoking gun' that allows for the direct connection between the Epicurean *clinamen* and Machiavelli's *fortuna*. Yet there is a passage from the satirical poem the *Golden ass*, where he states on *fortuna* that: 'such a course she who governs us permits and requires, so that nothing beneath the sun ever will or can be firm'.[63] Here *fortuna* follows an aleatory plot, even if it cannot be directly connected to atomistic physics. Its numerous occurrences in the *Prince* and the *Discourses* show the importance of the concept. Furthermore, chance and fortune play key roles in important passages, such as in the beginnings of specific states in the *Discourses*,[64] and the exposition of the actions of different leaders in the *Prince*.[65]

Of course, the most famous use of *fortuna* in Machiavelli comes from chapter twenty-five of the *Prince*, where Machiavelli stresses the potential for human action relative to the variations it creates.[66] Notably he compares fortune to a wild and destructive river, which cannot really be tamed but against the destructive effects of which can be taken precautions. The river metaphor in fact recurs in another text of Machiavelli, the brief *Tercets on Fortune* from an unknown date. Here the river metaphor comes at the end of a summary of the different hegemonic powers, all meeting their fate sooner or later, a canvas of history that is painted by *fortuna*:

> Not a thing in the world is eternal; Fortune wills it so and makes herself
>   splendid by it, so that her power may be more clearly seen.
> Therefore a man should take her for his star and, as far as he can, should
>   every hour adjust himself to her variation.
> All that realm of hers, within and without, is adorned with narrative
>   paintings of those triumphs from which she gets most honour.
> In the first space, painted in vigorous colours, we see that long ago
>   under Egypt's king the world stood subjugated and conquered,

---

here, as the fortune of individuals a providential path along the medieval template of the wheel of fortune, Marchesi 2014, pp. 247–8.

62 Scala, in a work from 1496, brings up, without endorsing it, the Lucretian notion that fortune produces all things, through the fortuitous combination of atoms, Scala 2008, p. 237.

63 Machiavelli 1989, p. 763, the context is a discussion on the transience of good and evil in political and civic life, a theme closely connected to Epicurean connotations of justice.

64 Machiavelli 1989, pp. 196, 197, 200.

65 Machiavelli 1989, pp. 27–34.

66 Machiavelli 1989, pp. 89–92.

and that for long years he held it subject in continuing peace, and that
then the beauties of nature were expressed in writing.

Next we see the Assyrians climbing up to the lofty sceptre, when Fortune did not permit the king of Egypt to wield authority longer.

Thereafter we see her happy to turn to the Medes; from the Medes to the
Persians; and the hair of the Greeks she crowned with the diadem she
took away from the Persians.

Here we see Thebes and Memphis subdued, Babylon, Troy, and Carthage
too, Jerusalem, Athens, Sparta, and Rome.

Here is represented how splendid they were, noble, rich, and powerful,
and how at the end Fortune made them their enemies' booty.

Here we see the noble and god like deeds of the Roman empire; then
how all the world went to pieces at her fall.

As a rapid torrent, swollen to the utmost, destroys whatever its current
anywhere reaches,

and adds to one place and lowers another, shifts its banks, shifts its bed
and its bottom, and makes the earth tremble where it passes,

so Fortune in her furious onrush many times, now here now there, shifts
and reshifts the world's affairs.[67]

What we have here, then, is a view of long-term history and its cycles that is
subject to *fortuna*, a notion that, as we saw, derives from Machiavelli's aleatory perspective. This perspective also shows broad congruence with his marginal comments on the DRN of Lucretius. As noted earlier, this can be seen
as an adaptation of Polybius, replacing his teleological framework with the
aleatory one identified in the theses of Morfino discussed above. The cycle of
states doesn't run along the teleological 'wheel of fortune' but rather follows the
aleatory conception of *fortuna*. Of course, in providing such a view of history,
Machiavelli departs from the Lucretian outline as well. However, this is quite
understandable, as Lucretius gives precious little insights into states and their
trajectories in the DRN beyond brief and generic remarks. In order to look more
closely at the connection between Machiavelli and Lucretius in this regard, it is
necessary to turn to the question of the first emergence of states and political
life.

Here it is first of all important to determine where and when Machiavelli
would locate this process, taking into account the fifth thesis identified by
Morfino: that of the disarticulation of truth and memory. In book II, chapter

---

67   Machiavelli 1989, p. 748.

five of the *Discourses*, Machiavelli discusses the different ways in which historical memory can be lost.[68] This loss can come about through human causes, primarily from the suppression of one power by another, as for Christianity relative to paganism or Rome relative to the ancient civilisation of Tuscany (the Etruscans).[69] In effect, one party here institutes a *damnatio memoriae* on the other, obliterating it almost entirely from the historical record. As such, that record itself has to be seen not just as reflecting objective reality, which to some degree it does given the first thesis of invariance, but also the struggle between powers. Apart from human causes, the loss of historical memory can also come from natural ones, or as Machiavelli puts it: 'from the heavens'.[70] Examples are pestilences, famines, and floods, which have reduced human life in different regions to very basic levels of existence.

While the passage on destruction by natural causes recalls the discussion of historical memory in Plato's *Timaeus*, as Morfino points out Machiavelli is viewing the matter from a perspective that is diametrically opposed.[71] Unlike in Plato, the return to a bare existence does not involve a return to original wisdom as in the *Timaeus*. This difference, together with the distortion of the historical record by human strife, makes historical memory inherently a fragment of reality. That is, the fragment reflects a specific set of conditions brought about by fortune, and can in no way be said to reflect timeless truths. Therefore, accessing historical memory is somewhat like descending into a bottomless pit, as beyond a certain point knowledge becomes too speculative to be credible. Hence, little can be found in Machiavelli that posits a clear outline of the relation between human beings and nature, aside from a marginal comment in his copy of the DRN.[72] The juxtaposition of animals and humans in the *Golden Ass* is insufficient to posit a 'hard primitivism' along Lucretian lines.[73]

---

68 Machiavelli 1989, pp. 339–41.

69 Machiavelli 1989, p. 341, the Etruscans were then just beginning to be recognised properly, Shipley 2013. It is possible to recognise an autochthonous account, with elements of 'hard primitivism', of the emergence of Tuscan social life in Boccaccio's *Ninfale fiesolano* and *Comedia delle ninfe fiorentine*, focused on the town of Fiesole, a place closely associated with the Etruscans, Gittes 2008, pp. 111–12, 118–19.

70 Machiavelli 1989, pp. 340–1.

71 Morfino 2015, pp. 170–1.

72 The marginal comment in question refers to the Earth as a mother, generating not just animals and humans, but also the gods, who enjoy a blissful state of *ataraxia*, Brown 2010, p. 75.

73 As argued in Brown 2010, pp. 83–4. The notion of humans adapting natural phenomena is not present here, however, and in the *Discourses* he discounts the long prehistory of Diodorus Siculus, Machiavelli 1989, p. 340.

Yet examples of Lucretian primitivism are not hard to find in the early Florentine Renaissance. A basic template was already set up by Boccaccio before the rediscovery of the DRN, emphasising two interrelated aspects. First of all, he posited an initial golden age, an ideal kingdom ruled by Saturn similar to that in Virgil's *Aeneid*, existing in a complex and critical relation to his own age.[74] Secondly, in various passages Boccaccio discusses how humans have modelled their works on nature, imitating and emulating it in science and art, as a pupil following the instructions of a teacher.[75] These two aspects are also related to each other by a common factor: the emergence of property and wealth-seeking. For example, Boccaccio argues that usury is diametrically opposed to the arts based on nature, arguing that the usurer 'causes money to bear fruit, which is something that money, by its very nature, can in no way do'.[76] The division between 'mine' and 'yours' also leads to avarice and desires beyond natural needs,[77] the loss of the commons leading to enclosures and conflicts that instigated the turn from the golden age of Saturn to the iron age of war.[78]

Boccaccio's views are broadly similar to Epicurean conceptions of early sociality, the development of technology through the imitation of nature, and the negative role of the emergence of property, even if no direct connection with Lucretius can be inferred. The same themes can also be seen in later Florentine authors, who were directly influenced by the DRN and who by consequence use a more realistic notion of early humans than the golden age template. A good example of this can be seen in the work of Bartolomeo Scala, a chancellor of Florence. In a dialogue with Machiavelli's father Bernardo, Scala explores the beginnings of law, arguing that nature teaches humans an immutable law, the Golden Rule that Christ also taught.[79] In the same dialogue he also

---

74 Golden ages are described in various works of Boccaccio, some of them closer to the 'hard primitivism' of Lucretius, likely mediated through Vitruvius, Gittes 2008, pp. 45–7. The complex temporal relation of this golden age and the present can be grasped from the exposition of Dante, where Boccaccio discusses the four ages of gold, silver, bronze, and iron, describing the effects of former ages as persevering today, Boccaccio 2009, pp. 478–9.

75 Not just in the famous passage on the Vitruvian account of the development of fire, Panofsky 1972, p. 38, but also in Boccaccio's exposition of Dante, where the observation of the heavens and order in nature gave rise to science and the arts, the liberal as well as the mechanical ones, Boccaccio 2009, p. 551.

76 Boccaccio 2009, p. 470.

77 Boccaccio 2003, p. 33; Boccaccio 2009, pp. 362, 367.

78 The mutually supportive destructive properties of iron metallurgy and warfare are juxtaposed in Boccaccio's exposition of Dante, Boccaccio 2009, p. 551.

79 Scala 2008, pp. 174–7.

points to animal ingenuity in creating signs to interact with each other, even if they were not capable of reason or speech.[80] In an apologue called 'the republic', Scala favourably compares the elaborate organisation of cranes in flight with the fragility and inconstancy of human social organisation.[81]

This contrast between simple animal virtue the problematics of human social life foreshadows Machiavelli's *Golden Ass*, but in Scala it is also connected to qualifications of human progress that imply the existence of an original condition without a common good.[82] An example of this state can be found in an early text describing humans as living scattered in the woods.[83] It is also especially prominent in his unfinished poem *On Trees*, which describes early humans as cave dwellers mythically born from tree trunks or from the earth itself, gradually developing culture over time.[84] In the earlier text, Scala furthermore explicitly cites Lucretius on the connection between riches, a lust for purple robes as the source of envy and cause of human self-harm.[85] As such, in Scala the same Lucretian themes occur as in Boccaccio, but now structured by the realistic hard primitivism of the DRN rather than the poetic descriptions of an idyllic Saturnian kingdom.

The Epicurean conception of a process of humans adapting their arts from nature can also be seen in Marcello Adriani, another chancellor of Florence and scholar. Adriani argued that humans not only learned their crafts from animal examples, but also derived political arrangements from them.[86] Directly quoting Lucretius, Adriani counterposed the chaos of the post-Medicean republic in 1495 to the first period of humankind, when there existed no common good. In Adriani, however, it is not riches and property that prompt chaos, but rather the abuse of religion for political purposes, a pertinent topic in an era partially defined by the intervention of the Dominican friar Savonarola in Florentine politics.[87] Indeed, the efforts by Savonarola and church authorities

---

80   Scala 2008, pp. 218–19.

81   Marsh 2004, pp. 94–5.

82   Particularly notable in this regard is the apologue *Sovereignty*, where a savage battle between animals and humans for dominance eventually results in the latter prevailing, Marsh 2004, pp. 164–5. This apologue and others have been connected to a set of stucco friezes in Scala's villa, with a suggested common themes that qualifies the benefits of human progress and civilisation, Brown 2010, pp. 36–8.

83   Scala 2008, pp. 72–5.

84   Brown 2010, p. 40.

85   Scala 2008, pp. 114–17, 126–7.

86   Republics being copied from the ants and monarchies from the bees, Brown 2010, pp. 57–8.

87   Brown 2010, pp. 59–62.

against Lucretius and atomism in general discussed earlier, point to an under-standing of their potential for undermining the existing ecclesiastical order.[88]

One way to understand the broader appeal of the DRN to the Florentine pub-lic at large, is through the adaptation of Lucretian ideas in the arts. Painting is especially suitable in this regard, as it allows for insights not just into the artistic concerns of the painter but also in the structuring role of patronage. The interplay between buyer's demands and artistic impulses signals a dynamic reworking of ancient ideas and myths, rather than passive reflection. As much is evident in the artist most closely associated with the reception of Lucretius in Florence, partially owing to a pioneering analysis by Panofsky, namely the painter Piero de Cosimo.[89] The main impetus for Panofsky's argument were two paintings by Cosimo, which according to him showed the finding of Vul-can on Lemnos, after his fall from Olympus, and his subsequent bringing of civilisation to this Greek island.[90] For him, the main source for these paintings was Boccaccio, mediating Vitruvius and more indirectly Lucretius. From them an account of the beginnings of technology, language, and social life can be gleaned that is broadly congruent with the 'hard primitivism' of Lucretius.[91]

Fire was the key to this process of development, both for its initial begin-nings and as a metaphor for technology and enlightenment in general.[92] Vulcan can be seen as a personification of the historical role of fire, especially in the second painting that shows him directing metal-workers and the construction of a house.[93] Fire also plays an important role in two paintings showing forest fires, to be discussed below, signalling an era before its use by humankind. As such, Panofsky argued that it was possible to see two stages of development in the work of Cosimo, an era *ante vulcanum* and one *sub vulcanum*.[94] That is an era prior to the domestication of fire and another marked off by it. According to him, based on the testimony of Vasari, these paintings would have been com-missioned for the house of Francesco del Pugliese, a wool merchant involved with the anti-Medici faction of Florentine politics.[95] There is no question here,

---

88   Later exacerbated by the religious strife of the Reformation and Contra-Reformation, Palmer 2014, pp. 140–1.

89   See Brown 2010, pp. 103–7, for an overview of artistic figures inspired by Lucretius and atomism in general, see Beretta 2009 for a study on his influence on Leonardo da Vinci.

90   Panofsky 1972, pp. 34–43.

91   Panofsky 1972, pp. 41–2.

92   Panofsky 1972, pp. 38–9.

93   Geronimus 2006, fig. 110, p. 147.

94   Panofsky 1972, pp. 55–6.

95   Panofsky 1972, pp. 57–8, the family had been on the rise for some time, Najemy 2006, p. 327.

however, of a fledgling association of a bourgeoisie and a narrative of progress, for Cosimo shared with Lucretius an ambivalence about civilisation.[96]

Panofsky's reconstruction of the Lucretian overtones in Cosimo's work has met with scepticism and revisions, not always convincing but enough to put the notion of an overarching programme in his work in serious doubt.[97] Yet that Lucretius exerted considerable influence over Cosimo has never been questioned, especially with regard to the two hunting scenes, called *The Hunt* and *The Return from the Hunt*.[98] A number of significant elements can be noted in these two paintings:

1. A clear contrast can be observed between the state of war, between animals as well as between humans and animals, in *The Hunt* and a state of peace in *The Return from the Hunt*. The latter painting is especially notable for the amorous relation between males and females, as well as mutual care extended to animals. The contrast recalls the contrast between Venus and Mars in Lucretius, painted by Cosimo as well as by Botticelli.

2. The hunting group includes not just (sturdy) human beings, but also satyrs and a centaur, reflecting a broader interest by Cosimo in such beings.[99]

3. Even if some technology is present in the form of clubs and boats, fire appears not to have been domesticated yet. Hence the forest fire provides a clear contrast with the two paintings showing the exploits of Vulcan in bringing technology and civilisation to Lemnos.

4. Apart from the relation between males and females, some form of social organisation seems to be indicated by the presence of emblematic masks on the mast of one of the ships in *The Return from the Hunt*.[100]

Notably, viewed from a Lucretian perspective these elements can be assigned to different eras, or rather they can be understood as showing the co-existence

---

96   Panofsky 1972, pp. 65–7.

97   See especially the criticism in Geronimus 2006, p. 125. However, his radical reinterpretation of the Vulcan paintings, Geronimus 2006, pp. 145–61, ignores the connection with the Vitruvian account of early humans and architecture noted in Panofsky 1972, pp. 41–9. See also Chapter 6 for the significance of this connection to Vitruvius.

98   Geronimus 2006, p. 127.

99   Hedreen 2019.

100 Such masks are known from an account of the early history of the Egyptians in book I, chapter 90, of the *Library of History* of Diodorus Siculus, where the earliest human groupings were united by an animal standard, see the discussion in Cole 1990, pp. 64–6. In fact, as noted by Geronimus, the description in Diodorus of early humans coming to each other's aid in a mortal fight with wild animals is an alternative, or supplementary, source for the hunting scenes of Cosimo, Geronimus 2006, p. 129.

of different temporalities. At the very least the state of war without a common good and the state of peace based on sexual coupling and mutual care signals this, while the hybrids and forest fire might, respectively, signal back to the process of anthropogony and forward to the domestication of fire and the beginnings of civilisation. These two elements are also present in another painting of Cosimo called *The Forest Fire*, where another forest fire and human-animal hybrids coexist with settled human life and domesticated flocks.[101] Perhaps such a scene is inconsistent in a narrative sense, but the medium of painting may rather be thought to lend itself well to show the contrasts and interrelation between elements of different areas. In fact, the juxtaposition of different times in Cosimo may well have made his paintings more attractive to patrons like Del Pugliese, by representing the earliest times in such a way that it appears relevant to the contemporary era:

> One can imagine that Lucretius' (and Piero's) textual and visual commentaries on the destabilizing, cyclical forces of nature would have struck a powerful chord with generations of Florentines that found their city in a state of violent flux – and were forced to respond to the dramatic provocations of their time. When examined in the context of Francesco del Pugliese's republican sympathies, Lucretius' text and its unvarnished view of human nature also takes on a possible political significance, providing an alternative to a Medici-styled return to a mythical Golden Age, as conceived by Lorenzo il Magnifico and expressed in his adopted motto *Les temps revient* (Time returns). De rerum natura presented a sobering vision of nature in which humans endure its slings and arrows not by faith or providence alone but by its instincts for survival.[102]

In this sense the sharp contrast between the Lucretian 'hard primitivism' and the tumultuous politics of the Italian Renaissance as it could be recognised in Boccaccio, Scala, and Adriani, had a much broader appeal among Florentine citizens. In this sense, Machiavelli's contrast between animals and humans can be placed in a definitive Lucretian context, even if it lacks even indirect references to the process of anthropogony and the dynamic relation between humans and nature. There is enough in Scala and Adriani that points to the a naturalistic perspective on politics that Machiavelli could share. Indeed, in book I, chapter two of the *Discourses*, Machiavelli notes in a thoroughly

---

101   Geronimus 2006, fig. 100, p. 135.
102   Geronimus 2015, pp. 58–9.

Lucretian vein that 'varieties of government sprang up by chance among men because in the beginning of the world, since the inhabitants were few, they lived for a while scattered in the fashion of beasts'.[103]

Althusser noted the Epicurean connotations in this passage, and it can be seen as the linchpin of the aleatory perspective on the *anacyclosis* of Polybius, which lacks any reference to chance.[104] Brief and enigmatic as it is, this Machiavellian view of the beginnings of political life is of great significance, recurring at crucial moments later on in the 'cycle'. One of the best examples comes from Machiavelli's *History of Florence* of 1525, where a red thread of civil strife runs through the narrative, reaching an apex in the so-called Ciompi revolt of 1378. Named after the wool-workers (the Ciompi), it is one of the first examples of a working class revolution (and accompanying counter-revolution) in Europe.[105] Machiavelli's treatment of this event is notable for including a speech by a nameless leader of the most radical faction of the revolt.[106]

In this speech, the anonymous speaker makes two closely related arguments. First of all, that the riches given by nature and God are more easily stolen than used for labour, and this has led to strife and a division between the stronger and the weaker. Lacking here is any broader consideration of the exploitation of labour and nascent commercial relations. Secondly, he exhorts his comrades not to be cowed by the genealogical claims of antiquity by the nobles, for all are by nature alike. This recalls the partisan character of historical memory discussed earlier. It is only differences in wealth that have generated inequality, and consequentially workers can overthrow this arbitrary order through violence. In fact, at this point in the revolt the speaker argues they should do so, so as to be able to prevent retribution and further violence against themselves.[107]

If there is something unnatural about inequality, then the implication would be that it has some kind of beginning, or, more precisely, a negation of the division between rich and poor and the social structures associated with it.

---

103   Machiavelli 1989, p. 197. The importance of this phrase is rightly emphasised in Brown 2010, pp. 84–5.

104   Instead the picture there is similar to that of book III of Plato's *Laws*, namely a post-apocalyptic humankind that is organised in herds led by individuals on the merit of their natural advantages, Paton 2010, pp. 302–5.

105   A complex sequence of events that included revolution, the crushing of its most radical faction, as well as the eventual counterrevolution and the establishment of an oligarchy. See Najemy 2006, pp. 156–87 for an overview, and Trexler 1998 for more details on the Ciompi workers and their actions.

106   See Winter 2012 for an in-depth analysis of this passage.

107   Winter 2012, pp. 317–19.

Apart from this speech, there is also a notable passage in the *Golden Ass* that sheds some light on this. Here, Machiavelli brings up as a character a boar who provides an extensive critique of humankind. After noting how animals are naturally adapted for survival, but humans are born naked, the boar states: 'nature gave you hands and speech, and with them she gave you also ambition and avarice, with which her bounty is cancelled'.[108] This passage complicates the notion of a negation of inequality at some undefined point in the past, for present in that negation is at the same time another negation: the avarice given by nature to human beings.

As noted above, the juxtaposition of animals and humans can hardly count as a description of early humans, but there is the statement of Machiavelli noted above that the first humans lived scattered like beasts. They would have done so perhaps not in an ideal state of affairs, but certainly in one in which the division between wealth and poverty did not exist. In what follows, states emerge and the cycle of political regimes begins. It is here that the speeches of anonymous rebels and boars gain more serious weight, and where the aleatory perspective of Machiavelli shines through. In book I, chapter five of the *Discourses*, the impact of the division between 'have-nots' and 'haves' on politics is analysed.[109] Machiavelli here comes down against the 'haves', for their avarice, their insecurity and their consequent seeking of more possessions not just creates disturbances in itself, but at the same time invites retribution from the 'have-nots'.

As noted above for the thesis of universal variability, such oppositions are precisely the basis for mixed regimes, and can be the cause for their success or downfall. The histories of both Rome and Florence discussed in the works of Machiavelli provide ample examples of such events, and of the role of fortune in their outcomes. As such, the avarice that the boar of the *Golden Ass* saw as negating the bounty given to humankind by nature and God, recurs as a historical force. Yet the other negating force, that of natural equality, also recurs throughout, in the form of the resistance and revolts of the 'have-nots'. Both started not in some original society forming the template for all that came after, but in the interplay of these two opposing forces developing from a chaotic condition in which humans lived scattered as animals. There is nothing in Machiavelli that suggests any kind of return to an original society; rather these forces have to be understood within the plural temporality of mixed regimes and the impact of *fortuna*.

---

108   Machiavelli 1989, p. 772.
109   Machiavelli 1989, pp. 204–6.

Instead, as discussed in Chapter 1, in an Althusserian sense Machiavelli was a thinker of the conjuncture, of the fact to be accomplished rather than of the accomplished fact. As also noted in Chapter 1, unlike in Rousseau's age there existed neither the nation state nor a social contract theory. The political workers at the Florentine chancellery, as well as their fellow citizens, faced rather a chaotic and unsettled political landscape of city-states and outside invaders. In that context, it is less surprising to see Lucretian ideas being channelled in grasping the disjunction between a situation without the common good and political life in the state. Machiavelli went furthest in his era in thinking this question historically: positing it as an enduring question, while preventing its grounding in a hypothetical state of nature by emphasising the partiality of historical memory. What resulted from this was the comparative method for which Althusser extolled him, the ability to think from within the conjuncture, in his case the non-encounter of the Italian nation-state.[110]

3   Navigation, the European Encounter with the Americas, and the Plurality of Worlds

Overall, then, Machiavelli's historical and comparative treatment of political life is an aleatory one that takes much inspiration from Epicurean atomism, but hardly follows the exact same plot. Old ideas are rather adapted to new times, resulting in the five theses outlined above. And indeed the times were changing rather radically, most importantly as a result of the European encounter with the Americas that took place during Machiavelli's lifetime. Except for an oblique reference, he never seems to have bothered much with the implications of this discovery, which was perhaps too fresh or too far removed from Italian politics to make much of an impact on him.[111] Yet others had clearly grasped that the European voyages of discovery brought an entirely new dynamic. This development had important consequences for philosophy as well, especially for the conception of the early history of humankind. The first to truly grasp this was Boccaccio, who as we saw adapted ancient ideas on early social life and the process of learning from nature.

To this he added, however, an element that is hardly present in the ancient Greco-Roman texts, including the DRN,[112] namely a consideration of the role of

---

110   See Lahtinen 2009, pp. 297–302 for some qualifications on this.
111   Machiavelli 1989, p. 190.
112   At the end of the section 'from metallurgy to the arts' in the previous chapter, the qualifi-

navigation in history. Bocaccio starts by recounting the first naval endeavours in his introduction to the genealogy of Neptune:

> What is it to see, with divine light showing the way, boats, conceived by human genius and fabricated by artifice, now furrowing the waves with oarage, now with a stretched sail driven by the force of the winds, on which every great cargo is carried? What is it to think of the daring of those who first entrusted themselves to unknown waves and untried breezes?[113]

He then goes on to list the benefits of navigation in not just gathering together different materials and products from the different regions of the world, but in bringing peoples and cultures in closer contact with each another, voyaging as far as the Red Sea and Greenland:

> While they exchange their goods with each other, it happens that they marvel at not only their customs, laws, and traits, but nay, while one looks at another as if he is from another world and thinks that he is not circled by one and the same ocean, he mixes practices, shares trust through the exchange of merchandise, and joins in friendships. While they teach their own languages they also become acquainted with foreign ones. And so it happens that those whom geographical distance had made strangers to one another are joined by navigation and made harmonious.[114]

That this process of trading and intermixing was not some afterthought of cultural development for Boccaccio can be grasped from the entry on Nicostrata in his catalogue of famous women. There he notes that while ancient Italy is to be admired for its development, it could never be understood without the importation of Greek philosophy as well as law and techniques and religion from the Middle East.[115] Hence navigation was intrinsic to development in each region, which as a consequence can hardly be understood in isolation and as following a singular trajectory. This notion leads to a different understanding of the

---

cations of progress in Lucretius was cited, including how the vain human quest to satisfy unnatural needs led to the dangers of the deep sea.

113   Boccaccio 2017, p. 483.
114   Boccaccio 2017, p. 485.
115   Boccaccio 2003, p. 109.

first two theses of Machiavelli outlined below. For the thesis of invariance is now applied not just to antiquity and today, but also geographically to world regions far removed from each other, something Boccaccio explicitly endorsed in a letter to Pino de Rossi.[116] At the same time, the thesis of variability is also evident in the diversity of goods, customs, and languages in the different parts of the world.

Another novelty was that Boccaccio's description of a primeval kingdom of Saturn, the golden age of equality discussed earlier, now found support not just in Virgil's poetry but in the societies that were being discovered by European navigators. Notably for Renaissance discourse, the Canary islands were first explored and then subjugated by Europeans in the fourteenth and fifteenth centuries.[117] Basing himself on a navigator's account, Boccaccio wrote a text on the Canaries, with special attention to its native inhabitants, which shows important parallels with his accounts of the golden age.[118] Of particular interest is his description of the Canarians being distinguished in clothing based on marriage and social position, yet also showing a propensity to share their belongings and lacking knowledge of silver and gold.[119] If Boccaccio viewed this account through a golden age perspective, then at least it is one that is open to modification based on accounts of the explorations of these islands in the Atlantic.

The Canaries also make an appearance in the dialogue on laws of Scala mentioned earlier, where they are described as 'previously unknown peoples who live completely without law, like beasts obeying nature'.[120] Yet, they too are taught the immutable Golden Rule by nature itself, and elsewhere in the dialogue, Scala uses the example of animal communication to argue for the existence of some form of law among peoples lacking writing.[121] Here we should recall from the previous section the important role of juxtaposing animals and humans, so as to comment on the relation between past and present and thereby qualify human progress. Hence here, too, a notional connection is made between a generic early state of humankind, with all the philosophical

---

116   Here Boccaccio holds the laws of nature to be universal throughout the globe, while the different peoples scattered over the globe all have much to recommend them, cited in Gittes 2008, p. 61.

117   Abulafia 2002 provides an insightful overview of the European encounter with the Canary islands.

118   Coleman 2014.

119   Cited in Hulme 1994, p. 181.

120   Scala 2008, p. 175.

121   Scala 2008, pp. 218–21.

baggage tied to it, and an actual society in the Atlantic ocean. Furthermore, these early templates can also be traced in the encounter with the Americas after 1492.[122]

Crucial for our purposes is an explicit connection between American Indian cultures and Epicureanism asserted by the Florentine navigator Amerigo Vespucci. In his letter *Mundus novus*, published in 1503, Vespucci describes the way of life of an indigenous tribe he encountered along the coast of what is now known as Brazil:

> They have no cloth either of wool, linen or cotton, since they need it not; neither do they have goods of their own, but all things are held in common. They live together without king, without government, and each is his own master. They marry as many wives as they please; and sons cohabit with mother, brother with sister, male cousin with female, and any man with the first woman he meets. They dissolve their marriages as often as they please, and observe no sort of law with respect to them. Beyond the fact that they have no church, no religion and are not idolators, what more can I say? They live according to nature, and may be called Epicureans rather than Stoics. There are no merchants among their number, nor is their barter. The nations wage war upon one another without art or order.[123]

The trope of these native Brazilian tribes, the Tupi, as following an Epicurean way of life recurs in three more letters attributed to Vespucci.[124] There are some variations in the descriptions, but the common denominator in all is a life that is lived according to nature, negating sovereignty, property, trade, and an official priesthood. In letter VI, for example, more details are provided on communal dwellings in which the Tupi lived, as well as their conception of wealth radically different from the European one.[125] The distinction between the newly discovered peoples and the old continent is emphasised, but neither has an unambiguous moral advantage over the other.[126] No 'noble savage' myth can be readily discerned in Vespucci, who, despite the intrusion of classical templates, adheres to what seems like a perspective of moral realism. In that

---

122 Abulafia 2002, pp. 276–7.
123 Vespucci 1916, p. 6.
124 Vespucci 1992, pp. 42–3, 48–51, 64–5.
125 Vespucci 1992, pp. 64–5.
126 Fernández-Armesto 2007, pp. 158–66.

sense, his descriptions can be likened to the paintings of Piero di Cosimo discussed earlier. Both deploy *fantasia* to show ways of life that are radically different from the contemporary one close to home, but nevertheless share a moralism closely bound up with material realities.

This combination of *fantasia* and realism, of templates from the classics and ethnography, packs a philosophical punch that explains the efficacy of Vespucci's work, despite the controversies with regard to his authorship and overall reliability in scholarly terms. In Chapter 6, we shall explore the important role of such conceptions of the Americas for the formation of European archaeology. More immediately and directly, the influence of Vespucci can be noted in a work published not long after his letters, Thomas More's *Utopia* of 1516. Here the narrator of the Utopian way of life, Hythlodaeus, is introduced as a participant in Vespucci's last three voyages, which as More remarks 'are now universally read of'.[127] Both in More's fictional state and in Vespucci's descriptions of Brazil, things are held in common, but the similarities go deeper. Another 'Epicurean' influence on More was his friend Erasmus, who, like Valla before him, as we saw earlier, emphasised the compatibility of Christ's teachings and the Epicurean ethics of pleasure.

Of course, this did not mean that any of them was fundamentally a follower of Epicurus, for his denial of the immortality of the soul formed an insurmountable obstacle in that regard.[128] Rather, what Valla, Erasmus, and More share with Epicureanism is what may be termed the naturalness of virtuous pleasure.[129] In a remarkable passage in *Utopia*, More draws an explicit contrast between the Stoics, who attributed happiness solely to virtue, while their opponents the Utopians live virtuously according to nature.[130] The dialogue between Christianity and Epicureanism is evident here, as the natural virtue derives from God's creation of nature in the first place, and the command not to injure but help each other is described as one deriving from nature.[131] Continuing this argument further, More makes clear that it forms the basis

---

127 More 1965, pp. 50–1.

128 Though, perhaps seeking to forestall certain charges, More describes the first king of Utopia as having legislated against the notion that 'souls perish likewise with the body or that the world is the mere sport of chance and not governed by any divine providence', More 1965, p. 221. See on this question also Greenblatt 2010.

129 Pleasure is defined in strongly Epicurean terms in More's *Utopia*, as humans are guided to seek it by nature, both in body and mind and at rest or in motion, More 1965, pp. 166–7.

130 More 1965, pp. 162–3.

131 The connections between communism, the ethics of pleasure, and Christianity are treated in Surtz 1957. Notable here, too, is the stance of More against Aristotelianism and its critique of communism, Surtz 1957, pp. 176–9.

for the political economy of Utopia, allowing it to supply to its citizens what he terms the 'material of pleasure':

> Nature calls all men to help one another to a merrier life. (This she certainly does with good reason, for no one is raised so far above the common lot of mankind as to have his sole person the object of nature's care, seeing that she equally favours all whom she endows with the same form.) Consequently nature surely bids you take constant care not to further your own advantages as to cause disadvantages to your fellows.

> Therefore they hold that not only ought contracts between private persons be observed but also public laws for the distribution of vital commodities, that is to say, the matter of pleasure, provided they have been justly promulgated by a good king or ratified by the common consent of a people neither oppressed by tyranny nor deceived by fraud. As long as such laws are not broken, it is prudence to look after your own interests, and to look after those of the public in addition is a mark of devotion. But to deprive others of pleasure to secure your own, this is surely an injustice. On the contrary, to take away something from yourself and to give it to others is a duty of humanity and kindness which never takes away as much advantage as it brings back.[132]

If this passage reflects Epicurean views of pleasure, if in a radically different context, so does the following one dealing with false pleasures. There exist, More argues, pleasures that are neither beneficial nor guided by nature, but rather things that 'mortals imagine by futile consensus to be sweet'.[133] Examples are meaningless distinctions of nobility, hunting, gambling, and the like, which, despite not deriving from nature but from convention, have struck deep roots into society.[134] As in Epicureanism, these false pleasures have been greatly stimulated by money, for as More notes, in a society where money is the standard for everything, luxury and unnecessary crafts proliferate to the detriment of the satisfaction of true, natural pleasures. In effect, it is private property that leads to general poverty, understood from a natural perspective, whereas communism would result in an abundance of the 'material of pleasure'.[135] The

---

132   More 1965, p. 165.
133   More 1965, p. 167.
134   More 1965, pp. 166–73.
135   Thus reversing the Aristotelian argument against communism leading to poverty. A key obstacle for the Utopians to overcome the obstacle to communism was pride, which

ill effects of private property can be seen very well in book one of Utopia, in the great passage where the greed for wool is described as having turned the previously prosperous English countryside into a wilderness.

The comparative aspect implicit in Vespucci comes to the fore here, contrasting the indigenous Americans living according to nature with the hierarchical, monarchical states of Europe where private property dominated.[136] Furthermore, Vespucci's description of their natural social order as Epicurean allowed More to connect his fictional construct, emerging as it were in the interstices between the two worlds, to a theory of pleasure broadly congruent with Epicureanism. Lacking here, however, is an engagement with atomism as a comprehensive doctrine, or the formulation of concrete theses, as we saw with Machiavelli.

It is in another Renaissance author, Michel de Montaigne, that a full engagement between the aleatory current of philosophy and the newly-discovered Americas can be traced most convincingly. Montaigne knew ancient atomism well, as is evident from the flyleaves and marginal comments in his copy of Lambin's edition of the DRN.[137] He used the DRN and other Epicurean sources, as well as their adversaries, to good effect in his *Essais*.

The main concern here is not whether Montaigne was an Epicurean in the strict, sectarian sense, for that he was not. Like the other thinkers discussed in this chapter, he engaged with Epicureanism from his own perspective, addressing his own concerns. Indeed, as the marginal comments in his copy of the DRN show, he ridicules the *clinamen*, yet elsewhere defends Lucretius from distortions by Lambin and Lactantius.[138] As noted by one recent commentator, Montaigne was little interested in the physics of ancient atomism, his primary interest being the relation of human beings, notably himself, to the broader natural order, which he saw in strongly anti-teleological terms.[139] In that sense his ideas are closely related to the aleatory current in philosophy, especially with regard to the thesis of the plurality of worlds, as we shall see shortly.

---

sought not natural advantage but the artificial advantages instituted from the greed of money, More 1965, pp. 240–5.

136 Though note that colonisation in More's *Utopia* is described as bringing common benefits, More 1965, pp. 134–7, and elsewhere wild tribes are described in striking negative terms as a recruiting ground for mercenaries, More 1965, pp. 206–9. Some have interpreted this as an early version of the *terra nullius* doctrine, Hogan 2018, pp. 53–4.

137 Screech 1998.

138 Screech 1998, pp. 114–16, 259.

139 See Hoffman 2005 for an analysis of the anti-teleological positions of Montaigne in relation to Lucretius.

First of all, however, it is important to understand the initial encounter of Montaigne with the Americas, as reflected in his famous essay *On the cannibals*, published in 1580. A number of sources figure in this, the most notable of which is his own encounter with indigenous Brazilians, which he says took place in Rouen in 1562.[140] A recent biography has pointed out that it is highly unlikely that Rouen was the place where this occurred, and that Montaigne's meeting with the Indians took place rather in Bordeaux in 1565.[141] Apart from other motivations he may have had for this, Rouen was significant as the location for one of the main spectacles involving the Americas during the Renaissance. It was during the entry of Henry II in Rouen in 1550 that an entire Tupinamba village was recreated. It was peopled by three hundred people, of whom fifty actually were indigenous Brazilians, depicting their daily life as well as a mock battle with their Tobajaro enemies.[142] There is no evidence that Montaigne was present at this event, but it must have been well-known, and its presentation of Tupinamba life was documented in a woodcut.[143]

Whatever were Montaigne's reasons for locating his encounter in Rouen rather than Bordeaux, he certainly had no intention of glorifying the existing order through some display of exoticism. Rather, he sought to use his audience with them to channel a devastating critique of French and European society, focusing on political and economic inequality:

> In the first place they said (probably referring to the Swiss Guard) that they found it very odd that all those fully grown bearded men, strong and bearing arms in the King's entourage, should consent to obey a boy rather than choosing one of themselves as a Commander; secondly – since they have an idiom in their language which calls all men 'halves' of one another – that they had noticed that there were among us men fully bloated with all sorts of comforts while their halves were begging at their doors, emaciated with poverty and hunger: they found it odd that those destitute halves should put up with such injustice and did not take the others by the throat or set fire to their houses.[144]

Montaigne goes on to describe a conversation with one of their military leaders, a king only in European eyes, discussing his privileges as only slight and based

140   Montaigne 1991, p. 240.
141   Desan 2017, pp. 167–75.
142   Wintroub 2006, pp. 16–17.
143   Wintroub 2006, fig. 1, p. 2.
144   Montaigne 1991, pp. 240–1.

on merit.[145] The contrast drawn between native Brazilians and Europeans is further qualified by a description of the former's way of life. Echoing, though not citing, Vespucci, Montaigne describes indigenous Brazilians as living in large, communal dwellings of up to three hundred persons, their social life being characterised by polygamy, honour-based warfare and cannibalism, a belief in the immortality of the soul, and the absence of private property.[146] Notably, these customs negate psychological problems present in Europe, for polygamy negates the jealousy of European wives, while the lack of private property results in a lack of avarice, envy, cheating, etc. Overall, Montaigne draws a strong contrast between artifice and nature, with the Americas being uncorrupted and the result of nature as she proceeds in her ordinary course.[147] It is precisely this aspect of the opposition between the Old and New Worlds that connects *On the Cannibals* to the main issues of Montaigne's work, most notable in his longest and arguably most important essay, the *An Apology for Raymond Sebond.*

The comment in *On the Cannibals* that human artifice fails to create even something as simple as a spider's web,[148] hints at a theme that is worked out more comprehensively in the essay on Sebond. A major part of that text is dedicated to refuting any notion of human superiority over animals, including with regard to language and religion.[149] Montaigne points out, citing Democritus, that humans have learned most of their arts from the animals, who, too, are capable of learning and teaching what they have learned.[150] In a notable passage, he addresses the DRN critically, going against the notion that nature has ill-supplied humankind, owing to human babies being born naked, providing a contrary example, also from Lucretius, of the Earth giving its fruits freely.[151] In this passage the example given is of 'those people recently discovered', who gain their livelihood without any need for artifice, drawing a clear parallel with *On the Cannibals*. In contrast to humans learning from nature, however, animals have precious little to learn from human artifice, least of all from the enslavement of animals and humans alike, and the warfare it has brought in its wake.[152]

---

145   Montaigne 1991, p. 241.
146   Montaigne 1991, pp. 233–9.
147   Montaigne 1991, p. 233. An argument can be made here that the language is suggestive of the Lucretian account of the spontaneous generation of human beings from the earth, Hoffmann 2002, pp. 211–12. See also a comment added to Lucretius: 'Animate beings are made from insentient basic elements', Screech 1998, p. 113.
148   Montaigne 1991, p. 232.
149   Montaigne 1991, pp. 506–8, 522.
150   Montaigne 1991, p. 519.
151   Montaigne 1991, pp. 510–11.
152   Montaigne 1991, pp. 515–16, 527–30.

More insights into the significance of the contrast between nature and artifice in Montaigne comes from another of his essays. There, he expresses doubts on the practices drawn from the human mind rather than from nature, 'in favour of which we have abandoned nature and her rules and **on to which we do not know how to impose the limits of moderation**'.[153] It is precisely on this point, the connection between convention or artifice and a lack of moderation, that Montaigne converges with Epicurean ethics. In fact, in the essay on Raymond Sebond, he expounds the same distinction between desires as Epicurus did, based on the same distinction between nature and convention:

> Desires are either natural and necessary, like eating and drinking; natural and not necessary, such as mating with a female; or else neither natural nor necessary, like virtually all human ones, which are entirely superfluous and artificial … False opinions and ignorance of the good have poured so many strange desires into us that they have chased away almost all the natural ones, no more nor less than if a multitude of strangers in a city drove out all the citizens who were born there, snuffed out their ancient power and authority, seized the town and entirely usurped it.[154]

One of the things overturned by these false opinions was natural equality, being replaced instead by distinctions based on convention. That from the Epicurean perspective such distinctions were seen to bring little good, Montaigne knew well, for on one of the flyleaves of his copy if the DRN he wrote 'riches, rank, kingdoms delight neither the body nor the soul'.[155] An application of this principle of unnatural distinctions can be seen in the essay *On the inequality there is between us*. There the Epicurean conception of pleasure is deployed against precisely such social distinctions, with an emphasis on the dubious value of being a ruler.[156] It also recurs in the essay on Raymond Sebond, where it is stated that 'the souls of emperors and cobblers are cast in the same mould'.[157] In the same essay, the tendency of human reason to go astray is illustrated by pagan sacrifices that Montaigne condemns as impious, citing here Lucretius on the sacrifice of Iphigenia.[158] All these examples point to a shared conception of the

---

153   Montaigne 1991, p. 866, emphasis added.
154   Montaigne 1991, p. 526.
155   Screech 1998, p. 103. Montaigne had also noted the Lucretian notion of an initial basis for the division of property using natural criteria such as strength and beauty in his essay *On Presumption*, Montaigne 1991, pp. 727–8.
156   Montaigne 1991, p. 290.
157   Montaigne 1991, p. 531.
158   Montaigne 1991, p. 583.

distinction between nature and artifice, as derived from a theory of pleasure. Hence, as in More's *Utopia*, Montaigne's perspective on the Americas broadly follows the Vespuccian template.

However, Montaigne goes far beyond More and Vespucci to think through his conception of the Americas, not just on the basis of a theory of pleasure but of a theory of history as such. As with Machiavelli, it is possible to recognise in his work a set of theses that conceptualise history in aleatory terms, resulting from a similar engagement with the DRN. In fact, more or less the same theses as those of Machiavelli can also be recognised in Montaigne, but there they are structured by another thesis: that of the plurality of worlds. As discussed in the previous chapter, this thesis of Epicurus stretched from the infinite number of *kosmoi* in the universe at large to the plural histories of the different regions of the Earth. Montaigne added comments on the cosmological aspect of this thesis in his annotated copy of the DRN, after highlighting that the sum of atoms is infinite, noting that 'therefore there are other worlds, suns, just as [there are] different men and beasts'.[159] The thesis also figures prominently in the essay on Raymond Sebond, where three key passages can be noted:

1. As part of his argument against human vanity, Montaigne argues against the notion that the world has been brought about for the sake of humankind.[160] He cites passages from various ancient philosophers, including Lucretius, to show the power of the universe compared to the smallness of humanity, demonstrating the philosophical vanity of seeing the Moon as merely another Earth, that is, in our own, human terms.[161]

2. Another argument is that humans only know a small part of the universe, hence can only devise 'laws of nature' that cover this part, not to be extrapolated to the whole.[162] As part of this he brings up the doctrine of infinite worlds as expounded by Democritus and Epicurus. The latter held these worlds both to be similar and dissimilar, pointing here to 'New Lands' discovered by the previous generation, which have neither wheat nor wine, nor the same animals, as the Old World, just as in the distant past grapes and grains were not cultivated.

3. Within an argument on the limits of knowledge, the Epicurean notion of a plurality of worlds is brought up, arguing that it would have been

---

159 Screech 1998, p. 117.
160 Montaigne 1991, pp. 502–5.
161 Ending with his famous anti-teleological observation: 'When I play with my cat, how do I know that she is not passing time with me rather than I with her', Montaigne 1991, p. 505.
162 Montaigne 1991, pp. 585–90.

strengthened if he had known about the New World.[163] Montaigne here points in some detail to similarities in customs between the Old and New Worlds, but also notes that differences exist.

The deployment of the thesis of the plurality of worlds highlights the differences and similarities between the New and Old Worlds, capturing thereby the Machiavellian theses of variance and invariance discussed in the previous section. A good example of the application of these ideas can be seen in Montaigne's critique of natural law. Instead of a singular, underlying one, laws are said to be infinite in number, varying between different cultures.[164] Hence laws can hardly be said to derive from some fundament in nature, but rather vary according to historically grown customs. Moving to the third of Machiavelli's theses, that of the primacy of the encounter over the form, it is evident in another passage from the essay on Raymond Sebond. There, Montaigne juxtaposes *Ecclesiastes* and Lucretius to decry vain human notions of being superior to animals, citing the former: 'Everything under the sky', said the Wise Man, 'runs according to like laws and fortune'.[165] The relevant passages of Lucretius are from DRN V.874 and V.921, on how things move according to their manner and qualities, following here the 'fixed pact of nature' (the *foedera naturae*).[166]

These quotations are used to argue against teleological reasoning, especially as resulting from the human imagination, with Montaigne arguing that humans should forego their arrogance and leave the giving of directions to nature.[167] But what kind of director is nature? The answer, it seems, can be found at the end of the essay on Raymond Sebond, where DRN V.828 is quoted to the effect that everything is constantly modified by nature.[168] Montaigne had noted this passage already in one of the flyleaves of his copy of the DRN,[169] which at any rate abound with references to the generation and perishing of different natural and human phenomena.[170] The notion that the world is in a state of constant flux can also be found in the essay *On Repenting*. There Montaigne argued that all is in a state of constant flux, with 'Everything in it – the

---

163 Montaigne 1991, pp. 644–9.
164 Or as he points out, there are laws enough for 'all those worlds of Epicurus', Montaigne 1991, p. 1208.
165 Montaigne 1991, pp. 513–14. We need to remember here a similar convergence that was highlighted between Spinoza and Epicureanism, also using *Ecclesiastes*, see Montag 2012b and chapter one of this book.
166 Smith 1993, pp. 446–7, 450–1.
167 Montaigne 1991, p. 514.
168 Montaigne 1991, p. 681.
169 Screech 1998, p. 171.
170 Screech 1998, pp. 129–33, 163–4.

land, the mountains of the Caucasus, the pyramids of Egypt – all waver[ing] with a common motion and their own'.[171] As such, the 'fixed compact of nature' cannot be seen as a pre-determined form imposing itself through history, but seems rather a state of flux, the implication being that the different compounds in it constantly perish and regenerate.

The presence in *On Repenting* of two motions, one common to all things on Earth and one particular to individual phenomena, brings up the fourth thesis of Machiavelli, that of the primacy of interweaving times over a single, linear time. Clearly, Montaigne was cognisant of the implications of a world in constant flux for the conception of time, as is evident from the flyleaves of his copy of the DRN.[172] The clearest expression of this perspective can be seen in the second essay dealing with the Americas, the *On Coaches*. Written after *On the Cannibals*, Montaigne here is concerned not so much with the contrast between nature and artifice but rather with the historical trajectories of the different hemispheres. If we remember from Chapter 2 that Lucretius saw the earth as both young and old, after citing precisely these two passages,[173] Montaigne uses them to contrast between the ages of the New and the Old Worlds:

> It is no less big and full and solid than our own; its limbs are as well developed: yet it is so new, such a child, that we are still teaching it its ABC; a mere fifty years ago it knew nothing of writing, weights and measures, clothing, any sort of corn or vine. It was still naked at the breast, living only by what its nursing Mother provided. If we are right to conclude that our end is nigh, and that poet is right that his world is young, than that other world will only be emerging into light when ours is leaving it.[174]

One complication, however, is that Montaigne is not discussing here the tribal societies of Brazil, but rather the urban civilisations of Mexico and Peru. In fact, he extols their urban layout, the sophistication of their crafts, the complex and extensive Inca road system, as well as the astrological and astronomical theories of the Aztecs.[175] Are these not, then, artifices? From a stadialist viewpoint a shift from nature to artifice would certainly be implied, and a lack of references to indigenous American agriculture seems to imply this. Yet there are clues in

---

171   Montaigne 1991, p. 907.
172   Screech 1998, p. 94.
173   They are also commented upon in the flyleaves of his copy of the DRN, Screech 1998, pp. 165–6, 171.
174   Montaigne 1991, p. 1029.
175   Montaigne 1991, pp. 1035–6.

Montaigne's essay for a different perspective. Most notably he contrasts the use of gold in American and European civilisations, where in the former the material was not dispersed in the form of coinage but rather gathered in one place for display.[176] The benefits of 'keeping gold idle' in this way become clearer when Montaigne decries the crimes of the conquistadores, who have wreaked havoc upon indigenous Americans for mere monetary gain, and the perversions that come with it. Here we can recall the critique of European inequality related to Montaigne by the native Brazilians in Rouen from the essay *On the Cannibals*, where there lack of property was described as implying an absence of avarice, envy, etc.

It appears, then, that the central distinction drawn by Montaigne was not between 'natural' and 'civilised', but rather between the artificiality of a property regime based on greed and cultures lacking this. The urban civilisations of Mexico and Peru were cases lacking such property regimes, which, although rather implicitly, suggests a plurality of possible paths of social development. Montaigne seems to suggest as much in another way, by positing the counterfactual of an encounter between the American and Greek and Roman cultures.[177] Without the evils induced by greedily seeking wealth, he argues that this meeting would have been mutually beneficial, entailing a renewal, even a 'restauration of the fabric of the world'. Hence the temporalities of the New and Old World would form a harmonious interwoven tapestry, rather than the clash apparent in Montaigne's time. The theses of the primacy of the encounter and of the interweaving of plural temporalities are couched here within another thesis, that of the plurality of worlds.

The same is true for the fifth and final Machiavellian thesis, that of the disarticulation of truth and memory. Immediately before discussing the distinct temporalities of the Old and New Worlds in the essay *On Coaches*, Montaigne brings up the question of historical memory. He notes Solon's visit to Egypt, where he encountered temple archives stretching back for an immense period of time, citing Cicero on the innumerable forms within the infinite extent of space and time.[178] For Montaigne, what we know of history is but a small fragment compared to what has been lost from our collective memory, which results in shaky foundations for scientific laws:

> A hundred times more is lost for us than what comes to our knowledge, not only of individual events (which sometimes are turned by Fortune

---

176   Montaigne 1991, p. 1035.
177   Montaigne 1991, p. 1031.
178   Montaigne 1991, pp. 1027–8.

into weighty exempla) but of the circumstances of great polities and nations. When our artillery and printing were invented we clamoured about miracles: yet at the other end of the world in China men had been enjoying them over a thousand years earlier. If what we saw of the world were as great as the amount we now cannot see, it is to be believed that we could perceive an endless [C] multiplication and [B] succession of forms. Where Nature is concerned, nothing is unique or rare: but where our knowledge is concerned much certainly is, which constitutes a most pitiful foundation for our scientific laws, offering us a very false idea of everything.[179]

The argument recalls the juxtaposition of *Ecclesiastes* and Lucretius in the essay on Raymond Sebond, where knowledge was bounded within specific conditions of existence. Similarly, in the same essay, in the second passage on the plurality of worlds listed above, Montaigne also brings up the question of historical memory in the context of scientific laws, arguing that small fragments of knowledge cannot stand in for an infinite whole.[180] In the essay *On Coaches*, he once again engages with Lucretius to confront this seeming obstacle of the infinite in history. Montaigne mistranslates DRN v. 327–8, changing the argument of Lucretius that the world is young because no heroic deeds before the Theban and Trojan wars have been immortalised.[181] In Montaigne the argument is that such wars have actually taken place, and that poets sung of them, but that they have vanished into historical oblivion. Furthermore, his step by step movement, as in the traces or *vestigia* of Lucretius – and in contradiction to the DRN – doesn't progress from ignorance to knowledge, but rather wanders about aimlessly.[182]

As in Machiavelli, we can see in Montaigne the catastrophic loss of historical memory, which implies that facing history means facing an abyss rather than standing on solid ground. Montaigne adds a twist to this, however, in framing the disarticulation of truth and memory by reference to the Epicurean mode of explaining through multiple causes when dealing with phenomena for which knowledge is less secure.[183] No 'master cause' can be found in such situations; instead we have to sort through a pile of them so as to find

---

179   Montaigne 1991, p. 1028.
180   Montaigne 1991, pp. 645–6.
181   Montaigne 1991, p. 1027.
182   See also the discussion of Lucretian *vestigia* in Montaigne in Passannante 2011, pp. 114–18.
183   Citing Lucretius on this at the beginning of *On Coaches*, Montaigne 1991, p. 1017.

the one that might be true, at least for the small fragment of knowledge that we possess. Explanation through plural causes is closely related to the thesis of the plurality of worlds in Epicureanism, and Montaigne seems to follow its use in that regard. In a sense, the thesis of the disarticulation of truth and memory in Montaigne follows from the encounter with antiquity and the New World in the Renaissance, together with the realisation that much has been lost or remains to be discovered.[184] The ancient Epicureans never faced the question of past civilisations or newly discovered lands to quite the same degree.

4   From the Plurality of Worlds to Stadialism

The pluralist, Montaignesque perspective on the Americas never gained much of a following beyond radical thinkers like Van den Enden.[185] Even in his own era, the main philosophical template for thinking through the consequences of the encounter with Americas was Aristotelianism. Here we may recall Althusser's notion that idealist philosophy serves as the 'theoretical laboratory' of the ruling class, both to allow it to adapt to new challenges and to prevent resistance to its rule.[186] It was Aristotle's concept of 'natural slavery' that initially framed the (largely Iberian) debate on whether the conquest of the Americas was justified and to what extent its inhabitants could be subjected to European authority.[187] This doctrine also formed the basis for later impositions of racial hierarchies. Even the arguments of what may be called 'left Aristotelians', like those of the famous bishop Las Casas, were defined by this concept. It was rather Montaigne's 'naturalist' perspective that stood completely apart from this debate, not sharing its key tenets.

Despite the mass violence of the conquistadores and the subsequent exploitation and ruthless suppression of indigenous culture, the Spanish sources

---

184   Here Montaigne also points to the astronomical discoveries of Copernicus such as the heliocentric theory, situating it within a broader pattern of discoveries that leave old theories obsolete, citing here DRN V.1276 on the vicissitudes of the human valuation of things according to the shifting sands of time, Montaigne 1991, p. 642.

185   Franciscus van den Enden was involved, together with Cornelis Plockhoy, in an endeavour to establish a new colony in the Dutch territories in North America, established on principles of radical equality, Mertens 2003a, 2003b.

186   Althusser 2017a, pp. 126–7.

187   As epitomised in the early Iberian debates on the humanness and rights of the Indians, most famously between Bartolomé de Las Casas and Juan Ginés de Sepúvelda in 1550, Hanke 1974.

never denied that Aztec and Inca civilisations were states with urban capitals. Furthermore, they did show interest in the philological and ethnographic work to understand Amerindian worldviews, if often with the purpose of obliterating them in practice.[188] From a 'left' position, as in the Inca-Spanish author Garcilaso de la Vega, aspects of indigenous belief could be used to argue that like certain pagan philosophical beliefs they foreshadowed Christianity, as in the *Praeparatio Evangelica* of Eusebius.[189] As much as the author might recognise the value of Inca civilisation and statehood, in the end the goal would be to conform to a European pattern of development. In this way even those sympathetic to the plight of the indigenous Americans, and able to recognise the value of their achievements, remained within the clutches of Eurocentric conceptions of history.

In order to understand these conceptions more systematically, it is instructive to turn to a recent analysis that has emphasised how a stadialist view of history took shape in the European encounter with the Americas,[190] outlining three key important elements of this generic paradigm:

1. A methodological internalism, that is a view of European development as self-contained and self-propelled, its trajectory predominantly shaped by internal factors. The arguments on the role of navigation in cultural development advanced by Boccaccio and others, as discussed above, are completely sidelined in this perspective.

2. European historical priority, as in a distinction between European modernity and Eastern tradition. As we shall see at the beginning of Chapter 6, this view had consequences for the understanding of the deep history of Europe as well, equating its prehistorical social life with that of contemporary Amerindian cultures in the Americas.

3. The unfolding of history according to a linear developmentalism, involving universal stages of social and cultural development proceeding through homogenous time. This notion involves a complete negation of Montaigne's pluralism.

---

188   For example, Diego de Landa is credited with recording important features of the Maya way of writing, yet his chief goal as a bishop in Yucatan was to carry out an inquisition to destroy remaining aspects of Mayan religion and torture or kill its adherents, Tedlock 1993, pp. 142–5. It is more aptly described as gathering intelligence on an enemy than as the enlightened understanding of a culture with different values and beliefs.

189   Especially evident in his account of an Inca prophecy concerning the arrival of the Spanish conquistadores, Garcilaso de la Vega 1966, pp. 576–8.

190   See Anievas and Nisancioglu 2015, pp. 4–5, 128–9 for the first three elements of Eurocentrism.

4. To these three can be added the notion of linear geographical space, concomitant with the imposition of a colonial and territorial system of state sovereignty, thereby excluding any form of Indian self-determination.[191]

It is important, however, to recognise differences between authors and national traditions, which offered very different accounts of development within the broad and generic terms of stadialism. With the shift from feudalism to nascent forms of capitalism, and from the Renaissance to the Enlightenment, more secular forms of Eurocentric finalism would be added that tended to be concentrated in northern European countries and their colonies. It should be stressed that these coexisted with continuing work in the Iberian world, including in the 'left' forms of Christianity that afforded some degree of protection for the Indians.[192] These new strands of Eurocentrism are particularly significant as they stifled attempts such as that of Montaigne, which sought to recognise a plurality of worlds, with important consequences for Marxism as we shall see in the next chapters. Enlightenment discourse strayed from Montaigne, taking its guidance from another thesis, expressed most succinctly by Locke, that 'in the beginning all the world was America'.[193]

Though captured in a single phrase, the thesis in its full complexity encompassed all aspects of history and social and cultural development. Three of them will be emphasised here, namely the role of property, the bio-technological development of the Americas, and the subjugation of Amerindian worldviews to a generic view of mental development. It is important to start with property, for it forms the linchpin, the ideological and political basis for the relevance of the overall thesis for the metropolitan and colonial ruling classes. Its importance can already be glimpsed from the fact that Locke posits his thesis in the chapter on property in the *Second treatise*. In that chapter he makes two important points.[194] The first of these is an acknowledgment that everything on the earth is given to humankind by God in common in the first instance. The second is that through labour and the division of things into private property the common good is advanced.

Specifically, Locke contrasts the low productivity of Amerindian subsistence techniques (hunting) to European wealth, using his labour theory of value to

---

191 Anievas and Nisancioglu 2015, pp. 137–9.
192 See for example the strong parallelism drawn by the Jesuit scholar Peramás between the communism of the missions of his order among the Guarani of Paraguay and that of Plato's Republic, Arbo 2018.
193 Locke 1993, p. 285.
194 Locke 1993, pp. 273–86.

argue that it is just that a new property regime is imposed. In effect this is a *terra nullius* doctrine, building upon earlier legal and philosophical arguments for the right to occupy lands inhabited by other peoples. We may then understand Locke's argument as part of a broader discourse justifying the imposition of new, Europe-derived economic, social, and political practices on the Americas. This connection is made explicit in Locke's proposed constitution for Carolina, published in 1670, long before the *Second Treatise*.[195] This is not the place to discuss this example, nor the great variety of regimes of exploitation in the Dutch, English, French, Portuguese, and Spanish Americas, merely to note how the discourse of exploitation fitted hand in glove with Eurocentric views of Amerindian cultures.[196]

The Lockean connection between subsistence and property regimes brings us to the second element to be discussed, that of the bio-technological development of the Americas. It was a source of great amazement to Europeans, as we shall see, how civilisations could exist without the large-scale use of metals and domesticated animals. Even in Montaigne, as we saw, the issue was muddled, noting on the one hand the existence of large urban centres and extensive road infrastructure, and on the other subsistence on the basis of what the earth provides spontaneously. Later, during the Enlightenment, this question became more vexed, as there was a shift toward the classification of societies based on subsistence and economy, the famous four-stage model of hunting, pastoralism, agriculture, and commerce.[197] Influential in this regard was Montesquieu, who in his 1748 *The Spirit of the Laws* provided a complex, multi-layered argument that connects the laws or manners of different forms of social life to the physical environment in its broadest sense.

Aspects of the environment considered by him included climate, soils, topography, but most notable for our purposes especially the relation between social organisation and modes of subsistence. Here Montesquieu distinguished between economies based on commerce, on agriculture, on herding, and on hunting.[198] He specifically connects hunting to the isolated, dispersed existence of clans in a condition he terms 'savagism', while 'barbarism' denotes herders who are able to unite into smaller nations.[199] Both conditions are contrasted to civilisation, characterised by money and agriculture, with clear struc-

---

195 Locke 1993, pp. 210–32.
196 Anievas and Nisancioglu 2015, pp. 134–41.
197 See chapters three and four of Meek 1976 for the development of the four-stage theory of stadialism.
198 Meek 1976, pp. 31–5.
199 Montesquieu 1777, p. 365.

tural differences with regard to laws and inequality.[200] It should be emphasised that Montesquieu's aims are comparative rather than evolutionist, and that his work includes detailed analyses of specific cases like the Tatars and Franks.[201] But his bio-technological ideas could easily be fit into a stadialist framework. At its most extreme this would place Amerindian societies at the lowest regions of human development, as in the work of Cornelius de Pauw.

If in Montesquieu we can see a notion that American soils were of exceptional fertility, even if the climate had an adverse effect on the indigenous peoples,[202] in De Pauw the picture is one of stark negativity. That his aims were far from impartial can be seen in his distortion of the role of Las Casas in the emergence of the trafficking of African slaves to the Americas,[203] as well as in the generally insulting polemics of his work.[204] A major impetus for De Pauw were the arguments of Buffon on the adverse climatic conditions of the Americas, both for animal life and for the activities of its indigenous peoples.[205] De Pauw used Buffon's ideas to systematically demolish the Spanish sources on the scale of the Inca and Aztec civilisations, inadvertently forcing Buffon to retract his views.[206] Buffon's protestations went largely unheeded, however, and De Pauw's work had considerable impact especially on northern European views on indigenous American cultures.[207] The delineation in De Pauw of different subsistence regimes and the evolutionist principle of parallel development, made his work especially attractive for stadialist views on history.[208]

Ultimately more influential than De Pauw, however, would be the later, more tempered take on the Americas by Robertson in his 1777 magnum opus *History of America*. A scholar with an established record in European history, Robertson had access to more source materials than many of his contemporaries, subjecting them to a sustained Enlightenment critique. Unlike the agglomeration of polemics in De Pauw, he also used a consistent and sophisticated theoretical framework to make sense of the evidence. Robertson developed the thesis that 'in the beginning all the world was America' to build a stadialist

---

200   Montesquieu 1777, pp. 367–9.
201   See especially the long discussion of law among the Franks in this regard, Montesquieu 1777, pp. 372–86.
202   Montesquieu 1777, p. 364.
203   Keen 1998, p. 17.
204   Keen 1971, pp. 261–3.
205   Roger 1997, pp. 179–80.
206   See Roger 1997, pp. 417–21, for Buffon's later more nuanced views on the Americas in his *Epochs of Nature*.
207   Especially in the work of Raynal, itself also of great influence, Keen 1971, pp. 263–6.
208   Meek 1976, pp. 145–50.

framework distinguished by two important axioms, both of which were highly influential on the work of Morgan, discussed in the next chapter. The first of these axioms is that, given that stadial sequences in different regions unfold in a strongly parallel fashion, the lower level of development of Amerindian societies supplied the key to understanding the early phases of Greco-Roman history.[209] Thus, the Americas provide not just analogies for the prehistory of Europe, but also for those proto-historical phases obscured by later periods.

The second axiom of Robertson's stadialism is that history unfolded on two distinct if closely related planes. One of these was the familiar bio-technological line of development from savagery to barbarism to civilisation. The other entailed the development of the mind through a more gradual, sloping trajectory rather than stages.[210] To start with the former, not innovating in a theoretical sense, Robertson attempted to draw up a balance sheet of the level of development of the Inca and Aztec civilisations, noting that in some aspects they were notably advanced, while severely lacking in others.[211] Hampered by a lack of metals such as iron to fabricate tools and of domesticated animals, he provided a qualified argument that both cases belonged in the upper regions of barbarism, or possibly in a transitional phase toward civilisation.[212] This view was considerably more nuanced than that of De Pauw and Smith. However, the focus on mind in Robertson's stadialism proved more significant for the third consequence of Locke's thesis, namely that of the subjugation of Amerindian worldviews to a general outline of mental development.

De Pauw had led the way in this regard, casting doubts on and denigrating the extant indigenous American written sources, especially the *quipus* used to document Inca history by Garcilaso.[213] However, his scattershot approach lacked a solid philosophical basis, which can be found in the work of Robertson. It has been argued that the Lockean notion of the mind as a blank slate, filled gradually through a combination of sense-perception and reflection, played an important role in bringing about a new understanding of Amerindian worldviews.[214] Earlier it had been possible to see them as fully developed, if different, as Montaigne recognised for the Aztec calendar and cosmology. Now the view came to be that the Americans seemed to give insights not just into the origin

209   Keen 1971, p. 276.
210   Robertson 1840b, pp. 268, 275, see also Robertson 1840a, p. 273 for writing specifically.
211   One notable feature that Robertson admired in the Aztecs was their purported use of private property alongside lands held in common, Robertson 1840a, pp. 260–1.
212   Robertson 1840a, pp. 253–5.
213   See for the evaluation and interpretation of the indigenous American documents from Mexico and Peru in De Pauw and Robertson, Cañizares-Esguerra 2001, pp. 118–21.
214   Cañizares-Esguerra 2001, p. 111.

of social life, but of the mind as well. This new paradigm was clearly present in Robertson's work, as can be inferred from the following passage:

> In order to complete the history of the human mind, and attain to a perfect knowledge of its nature and operations, we must contemplate man in all those various situations wherein he has been placed. We must follow him in his progress through the different stages of society, as he gradually advances from the infant state of civil life towards its maturity and decline. We must observe, at each period, how the faculties of his understanding unfold; we must attend to the efforts of his active powers, watch the various movements of desire and affection, as they rise in his breast, and mark whither they tend, and with what ardour they are exerted.[215]

He goes on to note that while the earliest stages of European history are obscured, it is precisely in the Americas that we can find evidence for the early phases of human mental development:

> But the discovery of the New World enlarged the sphere of contemplation, and presented nations to our view, in stages of their progress, much less advanced than those wherein they have been observed in our continent. In America, man appears under the rudest form in which we can conceive him to subsist. We behold communities just beginning to unite, and may examine the sentiments and actions of human beings in the infancy of social life, while they feel but imperfectly the force of its ties, and have scarcely relinquished their native liberty. That state of primeval simplicity, which was known in our continent only by the fanciful description of poets, really existed in the other.[216]

This view of an unfolding of the mind alongside the bio-technological stages of development can be seen in other parts of Robertson's work as well, as for the development of modern ideas in relation to commerce and for religious ideas. But most important here is his take on the Americas, where he seems to follow the De Pauw, Buffon, and Montesquieu in attributing a feebleness and lack of memory to Amerindians in general.[217] However, as has been noted, Robertson

---

215   Robertson 1840b, p. 268.
216   Robertson 1840b, p. 269.
217   Robertson 1840b, p. 291. In Robertson's work this is closely connected to his view that tradition alone was unlikely to preserve historical memory, in the absence of mnemonic devices, especially writing, Robertson 1840a, p. 257.

ranked indigenous American cultures according to his scale of development, and this impacted his view of mental development as well. As with his interpretation of the bio-technological development of the Inca and Aztec civilisations, however, his views on the sophistication of their cultural achievement wavered between admiration and dismissal. Revealing in this regard is Robertson's understanding of surviving Aztec painted manuscripts and the Peruvian quipu's, a mnemonic device made of knots.

Unlike De Pauw, he actually makes some effort to document and interpret the Mexican documents in particular, especially in a later edition after a critical review by Clavigero.[218] Most notable is the passage where Robertson discusses the painted manuscripts as evidence for the evolution of writing, which in his quest to reconstruct a history of human mental development occupies an important place. The overall sequence in the development of writing runs for him from picture writing to plain hieroglyphs, then to allegorical symbols, on to arbitrary characters, and finally culminates in alphabetic writing.[219] All writing from the Americas is picture writing, but the Aztecs are distinct from the rest in that their paintings have composition and design. This allows for features such as a history of the Aztec monarchy, a tribute roll, and a code of military, domestic, political institutions. In a note he gives a more detailed description of different Mexican painted manuscripts, using them to argue that a tentative step to simple hieroglyphic can be seen, as well as signs of convention and numbers.[220] All of this shows for Robertson some advance toward civilisation.

However, it should be clear that while he valued to some degree these painted manuscripts as evidence for the development of the mind, Robertson never uses them in any way as evidence for his history of Mexico.[221] Anyone who does use the indigenous documents in this way, such as Boturini, whose work he was familiar with, is decried as 'credulous'.[222] Given his view of the American Indians as 'improvident', it is not hard to find a passage in which his views on the lower stages of bio-technological and mental development of Aztec civilisation come to the fore. Noting the size of the Aztec army at the siege of Tenochtitlan, estimated by Spanish sources to have involved between 150,000 and 200,000 troops, he comments that this is highly unlikely, and explains that:

218   Robertson 1984oa, note e, pp. 257–8.
219   Robertson 1840a, pp. 275–6.
220   Robertson 1840a, pp. 437–41.
221   Cañizares-Esguerra 2001, pp. 123–4.
222   Robertson 1840a, p. 439.

the quantity of provisions necessary for the subsistence of such vast mul-
titudes assembled in one place, during three months, is so great, that
it requires so much foresight and arrangement to collect these, and lay
them up in magazines, so as to be certain of a regular supply, that one can
hardly believe that this could be accomplished in a country where agriculture was so imperfect as in the Mexican empire, where there were no
tame animals, and **by a people naturally so improvident, and so incap-
able of executing a complicated plan,** as the most improved Americans.[223]

Despite the various nuances imposed by the evidence, in Robertson we can
see the culmination of the Lockean thesis that the indigenous cultures of the
Americas are to be located at the bottom of stadialist scales of development.
The criteria for this were both material and mental, reflected in the inability for largescale organisation, something that can also be connected with the
absence of a property regime and division of labour. All these elements reflect
a movement to discount accounts by certain Iberian sources on the sophistication and high level of development of the pre-Columbian Americas. As such it
also influenced someone like Adam Smith, finding a place in his broader ideas
on economic development in the history of humankind. He is of great significance in this regard not just because of his relation to Marxist thought, but also
because, unlike the authors just discussed, he sought to occupy a position in
the struggle of idealism and materialism in philosophy.

Before turning to that, it is necessary to look at Smith's own take on the
Americas, as it can be seen in the *Wealth of Nations*. Certainly, he recognised the
continent's significance, seeing its discovery by Europeans, together with the
rounding of the Cape of Good Hope, as 'the two greatest and most important
events recorded in the history of mankind'.[224] The spirit in which this is presented is one of mutual benefit through commercial exchange, recalling Boccaccio's praise of navigation for bringing together distant regions and peoples.
However, the seeming concern with the well-being of the indigenous inhabitants of the Americas does not translate into valuing them in their own right.
Discounting most of the continent on the basis that it is occupied by 'savage
nations', he goes on to discount the 'wonderful tales' concerning the civilisations of Mexico and Peru:

---

223   Robertson 1840a, p. 424, emphasis added.
224   Smith 2003, p. 795.

Even the Peruvians, the more civilized nation of the two, though they made use of gold and silver as ornaments, had no coined money of any kind. Their whole commerce was carried on by barter, and there was accordingly scarce any division of labour among them. Those who cultivated the ground were obliged to build their own houses, to make their own household furniture, their own clothes, shoes, and instruments of agriculture. The few artificers among them are said to have been all maintained by the sovereign, the nobles, and the priests, and were probably their servants or slaves. All the ancient arts of Mexico and Peru have never furnished one single manufacture to Europe.[225]

While this passage seems merely to indicate a discounting of indigenous American development similar to De Pauw and Robertson, it is also part of a broader philosophical position. One that connects the Lockean thesis that 'in the beginning all the world was America'. As recently highlighted by Montag, Smith was clearly cognisant of the two opposing tendencies in philosophy, noting the struggle of the 'Socratic school' of Plato and Aristotle with the school of Leucippus, Democritus, and Protagoras (later revived by Epicurus).[226] Owing to his Stoicism-inspired conception of the universe and of society as machines and systems, in which the different parts of the whole interact harmoniously, Smith clearly identified with the idealist tendency in philosophy.[227] Furthermore, this 'harmonious machine' perspective did not just serve to counter anti-teleological, materialist ideas in general, but also can be discerned as a powerful force in his ideas on human nature and history.

In his *Theory of Moral Sentiments*, Smith posits an intrinsic contrast between two views of riches and ambition.[228] One notes that humans tend to imagine the pleasures afforded by riches as part of the harmonious movement of the system or machine of society, which makes their attainment come to be seen as a virtuous and worthwhile endeavour. The other perspective, however, termed

---

225 Smith 2003, p. 276.
226 Montag 2012a, pp. 268–9; Smith 1980, pp. 52–3.
227 Whereas in the *History of Astronomy*, machines or systems are more rational models to describe the movements of the heavenly bodies, Smith 1980, p. 66, in *The Theory of Moral Sentiments*, the notion of the universe as a machine is explicitly connected to Stoicism in the person of the Roman emperor Marcus Aurelius, Smith 1976, pp. 236–7. The actions of the 'Great Conductor' of the universe has in its wisdom 'from all eternity, contrived and conducted the immense machine of the universe, so as at all times to produce the greatest possible quantity of happiness', Smith 1976, p. 236. See later in the same book the conception of society as a similar 'immense machine', Smith 1976, p. 316.
228 Smith 1976, pp. 183–6.

by Smith a 'splenetic philosophy', recognises the emptiness and triviality of these riches and of ambition, a view that he argued is not so much incorrect but rather misses the complete picture:

> If we consider the real satisfaction which all these are capable of affording, by itself and separated from the beauty of that arrangement which is fitted to promote it, it will always appear in the highest degree contemptible and trifling. But we rarely view it in this abstract and philosophical light. We naturally confound it in our imagination with the order, the regular and harmonious movement of the system, the machine or oeconomy by means of which it is produced. The pleasures of wealth and greatness, when considered in this complex view, strike the imagination as something grand and beautiful and noble, of which the attainment is well worth all the toil and anxiety which we are so apt to bestow on it.[229]

Plausibly, this distinction can be related to the distinction between Stoic and Epicurean conceptions of virtue. In Smith's view the latter is intrinsically limited in only recognising pleasure and pain in bodily terms as the basis for ethics, the mind deriving its happiness from them.[230] Following this, he contrasts the philosophical ideas of Epicurus to those of Plato, Aristotle, and the Stoic philosopher Zeno in two ways.[231] First of all, for them virtue did not just consist of bodily pleasure and pain, but a great variety of things, such as knowledge, friendship, country, all worthwhile for their own sake and not reducible to the pleasures of the body. Secondly, the Epicurean conception points only to the passive reception of the body, instead of the natural propensity for the active pursuit of virtue. In the Stoic conception of self-preservation, this active pursuit is based on the capability of the mind to make decisions independently from the immediate sensations of the body.[232] Yet this autonomy is not absolute, for the mind needs to conform to its part within the universe ruled by providence.

In the above quote, then, the Epicurean view of bodily pain and pleasure as the basis for ethics is present in the denial of true satisfaction as flowing from monetary riches. Yet it conveys the Stoic position in its emphasis on the need to conform to the providential order, even if this is based on the imagina-

---

229   Smith 1976, p. 183.
230   Smith 1976, pp. 294–5.
231   Smith 1976, pp. 299–300. See also Montag 2012a, for the contrast between Epicurean and Stoic ethics in Smith.
232   Smith 1976, pp. 272–93.

tion rather than on philosophical reflection. Hence it is unsurprising that Smith here stresses the benevolence of the systemic view, which he argues is the motor behind the development of humankind. Forms of social life with cities and states, industry and technology, the arts and the sciences, these all derive from human ambition as propelled by the first view of riches as something virtuous and worthwhile to attain. Echoing Rousseau, and at the same time implicitly contradicting him, Smith argues that it is this force that has taken humankind out of the 'rude forests of nature' to the cultivation of the soil and the navigation of the seas.[233]

Furthermore, through the invisible hand the selfish drive for riches is transformed into benefits for all, in line with the greatest possible happiness created through the providential order. The wise course of action, then, seems to be to follow this order and to appreciate its harmonious beauty. This can also be seen in the political sphere. There, it is not sympathy with others and a desire to increase their happiness that is effective, but rather a 'spirit of system' that seeks to improve the machine of the state.[234] Here we can see, then, a good demonstration of Althusser's view that the theoretical cause of the 'hidden anthropology' of political economy was older than the bourgeois philosophy, and that it trumps any political cause.[235] For it is the Stoic-derived view of the 'immense machine' of the universe and society, the harmony of this providential order, that shapes Smith's ideas on political life, and the overarching conception of humankind from which they derived.

The 'subject of needs' of classical political economy can therefore only be understood as part of the Origin and End of this teleological order. Its account of development takes the form of 'conjectural history', proceeding from some hypothetical point of origin and moving up through distinct stages.[236] This can be seen in much of Smith's work, for example on the history of astronomy and on the development of language.[237] Most notable, however, is its role in out-

---

233 Smith 1976, p. 183.

234 This 'spirit of system' is contrasted with the 'man of system', who in his self-conceit seeks to overthrow the state and impose a new plan of it, which for Smith inevitably leads to great disorder and disharmony, Smith 1976, pp. 231–4.

235 See his remarks on the emergence of the notion of the subject in European philosophy, Althusser 2017b, pp. 174–5.

236 The term comes from the account of Smith's intellectual trajectory by Dugald Stewart, pointing to Montesquieu as the first one to use such an approach, which then recurs in various thinkers of the Scottish Enlightenment. Stewart notes that Smith 'seldom misses an opportunity of indulging his curiosity, in tracing from the principles of human nature, or from the circumstances of society the origin of the opinions and the institutions which he describes', in Smith 1980, p. 295.

237 For a qualification of the 'conjectural method' as a universal one, see Meek 1976, pp. 234–

lining the four stages of development are Smith's lectures on jurisprudence. In an account of these lectures, Smith introduces his four ages of hunting, pastoralism, agriculture, and commerce, through the Robinsonade of a dozen people coming to an uninhabited island and gradually changing their mode of subsistence to support more people.[238] Detailed explanations are also given as to how these modes of subsistence first bring about property and government, and subsequently change their form.

Here we can see how Althusser's observations on the 'false eternity' of classical political economy gains a quasi-historical form in stadialism, which can be seen as the providential unfolding of the 'immense machine' of society. This unfolding takes place on a hypothetical plane of homogeneous time, imagined by Smith in the form of an uninhabited island, and cannot accommodate even regional divergences from the ideal course. In spite of his extensive knowledge of travellers' reports, and all the diversity they contain, the main focus of Smith was to grasp all this material and contain it within a homogeneous temporal-geographical model of development:

> Adjacent nations in Europe may exist in the same advanced temporal stage or may be separated in time by uneven processes of development. Nations far in physical distance from Europe might lay quite near to Europe temporally (e.g. China), though most of the rest of the world was seen as far-flung both spatially and temporally. However, the paradigmatic case, as seen above, opposes the social space of a developed, civilized Europe to savage or barbarous spaces in Africa, Asia, or the Americas. Smith's primary project in *The Wealth of Nations* is none other than to explain the differences in wealth associated with this temporal distance between savage and civilized nations (and, secondarily, those falling in between). What he does not allow, at least not explicitly (see the next section), is for an overlap of temporal boundaries. In this way, Smith effects a compartmentalization of time into distinct national units, a Westphalian-isation of developmental time.[239]

For, even if the four-stage theory wasn't repeated in the *Wealth of Nations*, the fourth stage of commercial society was nevertheless connected to conjectural

---

40, who argues for a lesser theoretical and more factual focus of the four-stages theory. A broader analysis of conjectural history in Scottish philosophy can be found in Emerson 1984.

238   Smith 1978, pp. 14–17.

239   Blaney and Inayatullah 2006, pp. 157–8.

history through its positing of the origin of economic activity in the division of labour.[240] According to Smith this is based on the natural human inclination to barter and exchange, which is not found in animals to any degree. While there may be downsides to the division of labour, ultimately commercial society as a system provides the poor of commercial society with objectively better conditions than the rich of preceding societies.[241] In sum, the brief discussion of the work of Adam Smith here shows that his philosophical stance in favour of (Stoic-derived) idealism reverberated throughout his conception of social life and its origin. It stretched from Smith's notion of the universe and society as a providential machine, and by extension to his conception of virtue and progress, to include the four-stage developmental model and his account of the origin of the division of labour.

As such, we can see in Smith an explicit anti-aleatory position coupled with the Eurocentric versions of stadialism that placed the Americas at the bottom of the scale. His work can be seen as a providing a philosophical fundament for the Lockean thesis that 'in the beginning all the world was America'.[242] As such, it provided an implicit counterpoint to the thesis of the plurality of worlds as applied to human history, as seen in a fledgling form in Montaigne. The critique of Rousseau also implies a critique of positive valuations of early equality, also notable in Montaigne but also in Vespucci, and in a more dangerous political form in Thomas More. All these writings aimed to counter any resistance to the imposition of a stadialist, Westphalian model on the world both in a historical and in a geographical sense. The success and long-lasting influence of these efforts will become apparent in Chapters 4 and 5, even if Smith's work is perhaps more reflective than constitutive of the broader trend in this direction.

From an aleatory perspective, however, the European encounter with the Americas and its capitalist mode of production should be seen in Machiavellian and Montaignesque terms as a fragment of history that certainly cannot stand for the whole. It was merely one potentiality among many, all of which could, given different circumstances, have become actualities. The thought of these two thinkers furthermore provides the means for thinking history differently. If history is not grounded in an Origin and prefigured in an End, it needs to be understood comparatively. In this sense, the pre-Columbian Americas provide a key opportunity to explore the thesis of the plurality of worlds, given

---

240   Smith 2003, pp. 22–6.
241   Smith 2003, p. 21.
242   Blaney and Inayatullah 2006, p. 154.

the independent development of this continent from that of Afro-Eurasia. Furthermore, the intimations of a strong pattern of American equality in Vespucci, More (and Garcilaso), and Montaigne provide a Lucretian *vestigium* or trace that bears further research, something that will be explored using modern archaeological sources in Chapter 6.

Universal History from a Materialist Perspective

In this chapter the work of Morgan and the adaptation thereof by Engels will be treated, in order to delineate the background of Marxist versions of stadialism from the perspective of the aleatory current in philosophy. Morgan is of particular interest, given that unpublished materials show that Lucretius had considerable impact on his view of the early history of humankind. An important part of the chapter will be devoted to exploring these Epicurean influences in Morgan's work. In particular, the Lucretian outline of early history will be used as a guide to grasp Morgan's own framework in a comparative way, elucidating the similarities and differences. It should be immediately recognised, however, that his use of Lucretius was unlike the historical pluralism of Machiavelli and Montaigne, but rather conformed to Locke's thesis that 'in the beginning all the world was America'. Morgan's stadialism cannot be properly grasped without considering the broader ramifications of this thesis, as they impacted his views on the limited development of the pre-Columbian civilisations of the Americas.

Morgan's ideas entered the Marxist tradition through Engels, in his famous pamphlet on the origins of the state, property, and the family, the influence of which was felt powerfully far into the twentieth century. This work, moreover, has to be understood alongside other late writings of Engels, primarily the *Anti-Dühring* and the *Dialectics of Nature*. Here a stadialist perspective on history is placed within a materialist philosophical system, one that conforms to the notion of materialism as an 'inverted idealism' discussed in Chapter 1. As such, this body of writings of the late Engels allows for a comprehensive engagement via the writings on the aleatory current in philosophy, as outlined in Chapter 1. Of particular relevance in this regard are the theses of trans-individuality, of the primacy of the encounter over the form, and of plural temporality. In this manner it is possible to trace the intellectual background of both Marxist stadialism and the 'teleological' conception of the mode of production, as the result of a universalist conception of materialist philosophy.

1   Morgan's Intellectual Perspective

Morgan's intellectual background has proved puzzling and his positions sometimes seem to be mutually contradictory. These contradictions mainly revolve around the familiar oppositions of materialism to idealism and to theism as well, which has resulted in a fairly large set of perspectives on Morgan, but without an overall intellectual coherence.[1] Arguably this confusion stems partly from the fact that studies on Morgan were dominated largely by a Cold War perspective, in which this quintessentially American scholar became a prop for ideological debates between the USA and the USSR.[2] Lewis Henry Morgan, however, has to be understood within the context of his own time. Morgan was a proud (grand)son of the American Revolution in the broadest sense of the term.[3] His grandfather Thomas Morgan had been a sergeant in the Continental Army, while his father was a well-off farmer and state senator in New York.[4]

Born in 1818, Morgan was educated at Union College and thereafter became a lawyer by profession, settling in Rochester, a town founded shortly after the revolution on land taken from the Iroquois. Morgan joined in the capitalist expansion of Rochester, acquiring considerable wealth and, like his father, becoming a (republican) state senator for New York.[5] Though by all means a man of the liberal establishment, there were also strong elements in Morgan that pointed to what may be termed a 'counter-cultural', if not subversive, perspective. Examples of this are Morgan's esteem for the Iroquois, his ambivalent, though not atheistic, stance toward the church, and his doubts about the benefits of the 'property career' of humankind, though balanced by more

---

1   Early biographies of Morgan include those of Stern 1931 and Resek 1960, containing mainly outlines of his ideas with no sustained engagement with broader intellectual currents. These are now supplemented by Moses 2001, which relates Morgan to the America of his day, but does not address deeper philosophical currents in his work, though the author has recently published an article on Morgan and Epicureanism, Moses 2018. More limited treatments of selected aspects of Morgan that deal with his intellectual background include Feeley-Harnik 2001; Service 1981; Trautmann 1987, 1992.

2   One way to understand this situation is through the biography of the Marxist anthropologist Leslie White, Peace 2004. White would have been eminently qualified to write a book on Morgan, who he viewed as a forerunner to his own evolutionist approach, and was planning to do so, but never managed in the political circumstances of the United States at this time. He made important contributions to scholarship on Morgan, however, by editing his Indian and European travel journals, as well as providing an insightful introduction to the edition of *Ancient Society* used here, Morgan 1964.

3   Morgan's patriotism radiates through his work, as well as his and his wife's journal of their travels to Europe. That of his wife gives a description of a fourth of July party en route where Morgan roused his fellow passengers with a speech extolling the United States as the representative of the highest ideals of liberty and equality, Moses 2001, pp. 351–3.

4   Resek 1960, pp. 2–5.

5   See Moses 2001, pp. 227–66 and Resek 1960, pp. 105–24, for an overview of Morgan's career as a businessman, politician, and aspiring statesman, only really being successful in the first.

reactionary views.[6] One recent biography has sought to frame Morgan's contra-dictions in terms of civilisation versus the wild, considering his participation in, and ambivalent attitude to, the momentous expansion of the USA and its capitalist economic system during Morgan's lifetime.[7]

This idea is of considerable use, but a complementary perspective has to be added, namely that of Morgan's relation to the radical intellectual herit-age of the American Revolution. This heritage consisted of direct influences of Epicureanism and ancient philosophy, as well as of various Enlightenment authors, the most important of whom for Morgan were Locke and Mont-esquieu. Morgan's copy of John Locke's *An Essay upon Human Understanding* was a heirloom from his father Jedediah, while another copy owned by him shows text marks and annotations, indicating a close familiarity with the work of the philosopher.[8] Morgan never cites Locke's notion that 'in the beginning all the world was America' or explicitly discusses his ideas in this regard. Yet it is precisely this thesis, as well as its elaboration in the work of Robertson, dis-cussed in the previous chapter, that had a lingering yet decisive impact on his conception of stadialism in history.

However, Morgan's education at Union College was not just focused on books, it also instilled in him a focus on experimentalism as a central method of science, stimulated by the powerful role of the college's president Eliphalet Nott.[9] It was his knack for scientific experimentalism that led Morgan to de-velop his broad grasp of Epicurean and Enlightenment ideas in new directions, as well as stimulating his search for evidence from the field.[10] The key for under-

---

6   The two coexist in a lecture Morgan gave on the state of affairs of the United States in 1852, discussed more fully below, published as Morgan 1852. What has been interpreted as his Lockean theory of labour and property led Morgan to conservative positions on the personal responsibility of US labourers for their lot, Moses 2001, pp. 215–17.

7   Convincingly framed using Mark Twain's *The Adventures of Tom Sawyer*, see Moses 2001, pp. 1–3. Morgan's library inventory did not list this book, but did include another by Twain, *The Gilded Age*, first published in 1873, Trautmann and Kabelac 1994, p. 137. Its tales of greed and corruption dovetailed with Morgan's critical position on property in the 1870s.

8   Trautmann and Kabelac 1994, p. 197.

9   Resek 1960, pp. 6–11. The atmosphere at this school generally was conservative with regards to questions of property, and Nott's common sense philosophy pointed to a decidedly non-aleatory view of the laws of nature, stimulating his students 'to go out in the world with open eyes, see how it functioned, and accept its iron laws', Resek 1960, p. 9.

10   Morgan carried out extensive fieldwork, not just among the Iroquois but among the Crow and other tribes in Kansas and Nebraska; see his journals collected in White 1962, as well as his study of animal behaviour that formed the basis of his book on the beaver, Morgan 1868. He was greatly interested in material culture and archaeology as well, as is evident

standing these influences relative to his scientific work can be traced in his unpublished manuscripts, which show an intellectual side of Morgan that he was hesitant to express in his published writings.[11] This section will focus on these influences in particular, demonstrating in the next one how these ideas impacted his conception of stadialism. In this way it becomes possible to see Morgan's outline of humankind in relation to nature and history as animated by philosophical ideas that have hitherto not been sufficiently recognised.

When considering Morgan's ontological perspective, it should be noted first of all that Morgan did not write anything of significance about matter in itself.[12] Nevertheless, he must have had a good grasp of Greco-Roman atomism through Lucretius,[13] as well as from his translation of the first book of Cicero's *De Natura Deorum*, which discusses atomic physics and the *clinamen*.[14] The only place where Morgan directly addressed atomism was in his unpublished text on animal psychology, which was originally read in 1857 as a paper to a Rochester intellectual club to which he belonged. This text is notable in that it shows a side of Morgan rarely seen in his published work, a side that engages with broader intellectual currents and takes up more radical positions. Notably, this particular text was later adapted to become the final chapter of Morgan's book on beavers, making it possible to compare his more private views with those he sought fit to publish.

---

from his reports on Iroquois artefacts collected in Tooker 1994. Late in life he was also proposing plans for the investigation of indigenous American architecture not just in the United States but also in Yucatan and central America to the archaeological Institute of America, Morgan 1965, p. v; Resek 1960, p. 148; Stern 1931, pp. 122–5.

11   The two main unpublished texts to be discussed here are a manuscript on animal psychology, Morgan 1857, which was later extensively modified and published in Morgan's book on the beaver, and a text detailing the outline of early humans and the development of civilisation in the Roman poets Horace and Lucretius, Morgan 1872. See Trautmann 1987, p. 173 for the date of this text. The latter manuscript was initially intended as a chapter of *Ancient Society*, but never saw the light of day except in isolated references to both poets in the book, without the coherence of the unpublished text. Page number references in both are to manuscript pages, not to Morgan's own, which are inconsistent.

12   The only example is a very early, unpublished, text on geology from 1841, where Morgan explores the boundary between inanimate and animate matter, also referencing *Genesis*, arguing against the literal reading of it and discussing various geological theories, see Feeley-Harnik 1999, pp. 226–8.

13   Even if there are no references to atomism in the unpublished text on Roman genesis of human development, where Lucretius is nevertheless extensively discussed, Morgan 1872.

14   Trautmann and Kabelac 1994, p. 331. The most relevant passages on Epicurean atomism in book one of this work deal extensively with the swerve, Rackham 1951, pp. 66–9.

In the unpublished text Morgan criticises the views of those authors who posit that animal behaviour is primarily driven by instinct, or as he terms it 'the result either of physical machinery or supernatural power'.[15] Singled out as adherents of this view are Reid and Hamilton of the Scottish common sense school, which is sometimes seen as a key influence on Morgan,[16] as well as Paley's work on natural theology. These represent the notion of instinct as the result of supernatural power.[17] Also mentioned is Descartes, who saw animals as mere physical machines.[18] Counterposed to this is what Morgan terms the 'thinking principle', which is a generic principle that is intrinsic to life and that forms the fundament for his conception of mind.[19] Based on this, Morgan argues, using various forms of evidence, that animals possess minds that are not qualitatively different from those of humans. Notably, it is this argument that is present in the published beaver book, while the two opposing principles and their intellectual pedigrees are present in the unpublished article alone.

According to Morgan the 'thinking principle' is not attached to any particular living body, however, and is unperturbed by the process of the generation and death of specific living forms.[20] Instead it is inseparable from life in general. As such it exists parallel to the material aspect of life, which Morgan conceives along the lines established by Cuvier:

> 'Life is a vortex', according to Cuvier ... 'more or less rapid, more or less complicated, the direction of which is invariable, and which carries along molecules of similar kinds, but into which individual molecules are continuously entering, and from which they are continuously departing; so that the form ... of a living body is more essential to it than its matter. As long as this motion subsists, the body in which this motion takes place is living. When it finally ceases, it dies'. **So in strict analogy is the life of the mind a vortex, into which images and ideas are continuously entering, and from which they are constantly vanishing.**[21]

---

15 Morgan 1857, p. 16.
16 Swetlitz argues that Morgan was influenced by the common sense school throughout his scholarly life, though noting some deviations in the text on animal psychology, Swetlitz 1988, pp. 59–61, see for a similar view Trautmann 1987, pp. 22–3, who counts Locke among the members of this school (in contradiction to Morgan, see below).
17 Most clearly expressed in Morgan's citation of Hamilton's argument that 'an instinct is an agent which performs blindly and ignorantly a work of intelligence and knowledge', linking it closely with Paley's ideas, Morgan 1857, p. 35.
18 Morgan 1857, p. 34.
19 Morgan 1857, pp. 1–2.
20 Morgan 1857, p. 8.
21 Morgan 1857, p. 8, emphasis added.

The notion of parallel orders in a Spinozist sense suggests itself here, even if there is no indication of any kind that Morgan was familiar with his work. Instead it has to be grasped as part of a broader movement within intellectual history, in which Locke may have played an important mediating role.[22] Another clue to his ontological perspective can be found in his general conception of the relation of mind and matter. In a short but revealing passage from the unpublished text on animal psychology, Morgan connects his views on mind and matter to his religious views, furthermore arguing that there exists a scale of both matter and mind:

> The mind of the Deity sees alike the movement of the atom upon the atom, and the movements and mutual relations of the universe of matter. Man, who stands at the head of the animal series, is about as far removed from the zero of matter, the ultimate atom, as he is from the totality of matter, or the Universe; and the subject of knowledge as well as the means of enjoyment below the ken of his rougher intellect and coarser senses which may be open to the more delicate perceptions, and exquisite senses of the tiny insect, **may for ought [sic] we know, or have reason to disbelieve, be as great and wonderful, as the subjects of knowledge, and means of enjoyment which fall within man[']s sphere.** As time is purely a relative term, it has doubtless an expansion as we descend the scale, which furnishes in itself an increased means of knowledge.[23]

Pregnant with meaning, this passage contains a number of intriguing points that can help to grasp Morgan's ontological perspective. Here the discussion will focus on two points in particular, namely the relation of mind and matter and the notion of a scale of mind. To start with matter and mind, the quotation makes clear that Morgan saw the atom as the basis of the 'universe of matter', which consists of the movements and relations of atoms. As far as matter is

---

22   There is a reference to Locke in the unpublished manuscript on animal psychology, where he describes his philosophy as incompatible with the notion of instinct, and opposed to that of Descartes on the question of innate ideas, Morgan 1857, p. 33. It is the only reference to Locke that I have been able to locate in his work. See also Trautmann 1992 for an exposition of Locke's ideas in relation to those of Morgan. The importance of Locke's philosophy in the nascent United States, as well as its possible connections to Spinozism and Epicureanism, have been explored in Stewart 2014. One reference is surely too little to read into Morgan a wholesale subscription to the views as reconstructed by Stewart, but sympathy may be expected based on the 'family resemblances' of ideas.

23   Morgan 1857 pp. 11–12, emphasis added.

concerned this seems as close to Epicureanism as it gets, but what then of the 'mind of the deity' that observes the sum of atomic movements? A solution may be found in a remark of one early biographer of Morgan that put him down as a deist, that is, as positing a creator God that abstained from direct intervention in the universe that had been created.[24] Broadly this definition fits Morgan well enough, as can also be inferred from his earlier treatment of Iroquois religion in his book on them from 1851.

In that book Morgan praises Iroquois religious beliefs, highlighting what he saw as its monotheism and contrasting it in a positive sense to Greco-Roman polytheism.[25] A clear example of a deist attitude can be noted in his argument that the Iroquois had been able to grasp God, or at least the divine conceived in a singular sense, by observing nature rather than through revelation.[26] Another important aspect of this text is that it discusses Greco-Roman philosophical conceptions of God, which in contrast to popular polytheism showed inclinations to monotheism. Of particular interest is the attention Morgan draws to the contrast between the Stoic and Epicurean schools as recorded in Cicero's *De natura deorum*. He highlights the distinction between the Epicurean emphasis on the non-intervention of the gods in either nature or human affairs and the Stoic notion of intervening deities, further expanding the discussion to consider ontology and cosmogony:

> The creation of the world was also a subject which divided the ancient schools. In a belief in the eternity of matter, they, in general, concurred. Plato and the Stoics, however, taught that the visible universe was fashioned and constructed by the direct agency of God. This opinion, **not of the creation of matter**, but of the formation of the world, encountered the ridicule of the Epicureans. This is one of those questions with which human wisdom is unable to cope.[27]

Once again we get here intimations of what we saw in Chapter 1 is a Spinozist and Epicurean perspective on the universe as an endless sequence of encounters that give rise to an infinite plurality of singular things. The valuation of diversity in the conception of the scale of matter and mind quoted above provides another clue to this. So does a remark in the same unpublished text

---

24   Resek 1960, pp. 50–2.
25   Morgan 1962, pp. 150–1.
26   Morgan 1962, pp. 154–6. Also important was their belief in the immortality of the soul, Morgan 1962, p. 168.
27   Morgan 1962, pp. 153–4, emphasis added.

on animal psychology to the effect that the laws of nature originated with the creation of matter.[28] Yet in a stratagem characteristic of deism, Morgan hedges his bets by pronouncing a resolution of the dispute between the Stoics and the Epicureans to be beyond human mental capabilities. Similarly, the valuation of pluralism in the scale of mind in the unpublished text on animal psychology cannot be found in the later published account of the beaver. In that book, the praise of insect senses as an alternative in the overarching scale of mind is instead replaced by a hierarchical view, one that places humans at the summit of the animal kingdom.[29]

Turning to the scale of mind in more detail, there are two statements in the unpublished text on animal psychology that are relevant with regard to the concept of evolution. The first of these considers that in the totality of animal species some have been lost as time has progressed, and, also, that there may exist species more intelligent than humankind.[30] The last part may well refer, although this is not stated, to extra-terrestrial beings.[31] The other passage suggests that, based on the great differences in the intellectual powers of animals and humans, one or more intermediate forms may have existed that are now either extinct or degraded beyond recognition.[32] Morgan immediately disavows this speculation, however, again seeking refuge in the claim that this is something essentially unknowable. If this is not an explicit evolutionary perspective of one form changing into another, it at least suggests that for Morgan these forms were not exactly cast in stone.

Soon after Morgan wrote this, Darwin published his *Origins of Species* (1859), completely redefining the intellectual landscape on the topic. Morgan was initially slow in addressing Darwin's ideas in his own work, and they are not mentioned in his 1868 work on beavers. Yet at least by the early 1870s, and quite possibly by the late 1860s, he had accepted the Darwinian view of evolution.[33] As expressed in a 1872 letter to Lorimer Fison, Morgan explained that he had initially clung to the theory of the fixity of species formulated by Agassiz, but

---

28   Morgan 1857, p. 13.

29   Morgan 1868, pp. 280–2.

30   Morgan 1857 p. 13.

31   There is a close parallel here to a passage from Locke's *Essay on Human Understanding*, where he points to the ideas of other intelligences elsewhere in the universe, precisely in relation to humans, who he argues may be among the lowest of intellectual beings, Locke 1975, pp. 554–55.

32   Morgan 1857 p. 26.

33   The revolution of the enormous expansion of geological time millions of years into the past by Lyell, also played a crucial role in this, see Trautmann 1987, pp. 212–13.

that his work on kinship (published in 1871) had convinced him otherwise.[34] Indeed, in the same year he had paid a cordial and fruitful visit to Darwin, discussing with him his work on kinship and animal psychology.[35] Morgan also saw the usefulness of Darwin's notion of the struggle for existence for his outline of human history as a sequence of modes of subsistence, as a 1873 letter to Joseph Henry shows.[36]

The best evidence, however, of his engagement with Darwinism, comes from the unpublished text on Roman ideas of human development (c. 1872–3). Here Morgan discusses the ideas of Horace and Lucretius on the origin of life in general, and that of human beings in particular. Yet he does not merely summarise these ideas, he also explicitly, and in a way that is highly revealing, connects the ideas of Lucretius on this topic to those of Darwin:

> There is one, however, in which the Darwinian conception of the 'struggle for existence' if not the 'survival of the fittest' of Spencer, seems to have impressed the mind of Lucretius. 'Many kinds of animal life too', he remarks, 'must then have perished, not having been able to continue their species by propagation. For whatever creatures you see breathing the vital air, assuredly their craft or courage, or at least, activity, has preserved and defended their race from the commencement of its existence'. He thus noticed the fact, but without perceiving, perhaps, its significance.[37]

The significance of this quotation is that it carries Morgan's acceptance of Darwin's ideas into the realm of the broader questions of zoogony and anthropogony. While the language at the start of the manuscript remains noncommittal on the question of human origins, presenting Darwin's theory as one among others,[38] the philosophical outlook of the text is coherent and along the lines of Darwin and Lucretius. As the text was intended to be the first chapter of *Ancient Society*, we can assume that the ideas contained therein to be the guiding framework of that book. This notion may seem controversial, as Morgan decided against including the text, but many elements from it recur in the published version. A good example is the opening quotation of the book from Horace's *Satires*, describing in a nutshell the processes of zoogony, anthropo-

---

34 Moses 2001, p. 388.
35 As noted in his travel diary, White 1937, pp. 338–9.
36 Moses 2001, p. 395.
37 Morgan 1872, p. 18.
38 Morgan 1872, p. 1.

gony and cultural development.[39] This passage was extensively analysed in the unpublished text, but in the book is not discussed at all.[40]

In addition to the Horace quotation, there are also two from Lucretius in the chapter on subsistence technologies.[41] He is also cited for the development of language and was of crucial importance for the outline of the different phases of history (both topics will be discussed below). Natural selection is discussed as part of the evolution of the family, though without direct references to Darwin's work.[42] Because of the presence of these elements, the basic outlook of the unpublished chapter is more or less retained, even if implicitly and without elaboration. An important clue as to why the line of Darwin and Lucretius was not made explicit by Morgan in his book can be found in its dedication to the reverend John McIlvaine. Morgan counted him as a long-time friend, sharing with him a passion for scholarly pursuits, but he also has to be counted among the disciplinarian factors of his life.[43] Adamant in his opposition to Darwin, McIlvaine saw in his friend a key supporter of his struggle, as epitomised in the argument of *Ancient Society*.[44]

This seems highly ironic, given the discussion above, but it should not be forgotten that Morgan only expressed his ideas clearly in his unpublished writings and letters. Compare the beaver book to the unpublished manuscript on animal psychology, and both the intellectual background and the more controversial statements can be seen to have been left out of the published version.[45] The same is true for *Ancient society* and the unpublished text on Roman ideas of human development. From the isolated citations of Horace and Lucretius, as well as the use of natural selection, no coherent picture emerges, unless one has the key from the unpublished chapter. Amazingly, Morgan himself seems to point to this, considering the following quotation from Horace on the title page: 'nescit vox missa reverti'.[46] The point of the broader context of this phrase

---

39   Morgan 1964, p. 4.

40   Morgan 1872, pp. 8–9.

41   Morgan 1964, pp. 25, 30.

42   Morgan 1964, pp. 50, 320, 360. The only direct reference to Darwin in the book concerns his questioning of an original state of promiscuity in *The Descent of Man*, Morgan 1964, p. 357.

43   Resek 1960, pp. 50–1.

44   Resek 1960, pp. 94–6, 136–7.

45   Apart from the lack of discussion of the broader intellectual context, the most important difference of the chapter in the published book relative to the unpublished text concerns the scale of mind and the explicit reference to a hierarchy in which humans are superior to animals, as mentioned earlier. Even so, this view is balanced by an exhortation against the slaughtering and eating of animals, Morgan 1868, pp. 282–84.

46   Morgan 1964, p. 1.

lies not just in not being able to take back words spoken, but in the ability to burn unpublished writings if one saw fit.

2 The Scale of Mind and Stadialism in Morgan

The partially hidden intellectual background of Morgan's ideas has to be taken into account when considering his evolutionary history of humankind. Of crucial importance in this is his notion of the scale of mind, which serves both to locate humans in the order of nature and to measure, in a sense, the progress of social development. The interface between these two aspects is our first point of interest here. As discussed in the previous section, Morgan saw the mind as a vortex, on analogy with the metabolism of the body. Ideas and images enter and leave the mind in a continuous process. Even if not directly derived from the notion of *phusiopoiei* of the ancient atomists, it shares with them not just this metabolism but also their notion of 'learning from nature'. This similarity can be seen very well in Morgan's notion of 'natural suggestions', which was defined most succinctly in his 1871 book *Systems of Consanguinity*:

> Natural suggestions are those which arise spontaneously in the mind with the exercise of ordinary intelligence. As suggestions from nature they might spring from internal sources or from the subject; from external sources or from the object; or from both united.

> In the formation of a plan of consanguinity reflection upon the nature of descents, where society recognized the marriage relation, would reveal the method of nature in evolving generations of mankind from common ancestors, through a series of marriages, and thus develop the suggestions of nature from the subject. On the other hand, the uses of a system, when formed, would reach outward upon the condition and wants of society and induce reflection upon the objects to be gained. Whatever deliverances may thus be supposed to come from the voice of nature they are necessarily uniform in all time and to all men, the conditions of society being similar.[47]

Note here how the lessons from nature once systematised in a system, that is as convention, exert a similar impact as nature itself. The notion of learning from

---

47   Morgan 1871, p. 472.

nature recurs throughout Morgan's work, including, as we saw in the previous section, for the conception of the supernatural in his 1851 book on the Iroquois. There the process of inferring a singular Deity from nature was described alongside a short exposition of the Epicurean conception of religion, but the two aspects did not meet. In the unpublished chapter of *Ancient Society* on Roman ideas of human development, Morgan did make the connection between learning from nature and the Lucretian outline of prehistory. Examples of this are the emergence of fire and cooking, as well as of metallurgy.[48] Most notable also is Morgan's emphasis on the step by step character of the sequence of such inventions in Lucretius. These passages show the concurrence between Epicureanism and Morgan's conception of the process of learning from nature, as the linchpin between the natural order and human social development.

This concurrence does not prove, however, that Lucretius was the constitutive influence on Morgan with regard to natural suggestions. By contrast, with regard to the initial emergence and further development of language this influence is unquestionable, given that it was explicitly acknowledged by Morgan in *Ancient Society*. In an all too brief but highly significant footnote, he discusses the development of language by citing Lucretius on the initial form of language being gestural in character.[49] Present still among American indigenous peoples, Morgan describes this as 'a language of natural symbols, and therefore possess[ing] the elements of a universal language'.[50] He also follows Lucretius in noting the development over time of conventional sign systems, superseding in importance the initial natural symbols. Here we see in published form the influence of the longer unpublished account of the Lucretian theory of language.[51]

These comments on the development of language are not further explored in *Ancient Society*, however, especially in relation to the different phases of savagism, barbarism, and civilisation. Some insights can be gained instead from a preparatory table for the book, published in the 1930s by Vinnikov. There gesture language, immediately followed by monosyllabic speech, constitutes the first innovation of humankind, preceding both fire and stone implements.[52] Further steps in the development of language take place in the various later

---

48   Morgan 1872, pp. 14, 19.
49   Morgan 1964, n. 21, p. 38.
50   Morgan 1964, n. 21, p. 38. Note here the difference, however, not so much with Lucretius but with Epicurus in his *Letter to Herodotus* (75–6), where language is stimulated by natural factors that differ between different regions and hence even the first language cannot be understood as a universal one, Inwood and Gerson 1994, p. 16.
51   Morgan 1872, pp. 13–14.
52   Vinnikov 1935, p. 15.

phases of savagism and barbarism, with the refinement of scripts culminating in the alphabet, one of the defining features of civilisation.[53] Yet the first step was in fact of defining importance for all what followed, as can be grasped by Morgan's discussion of the contributions of Lucretius in the unpublished chapter of *Ancient Society*:

> Thirdly: that man came into existence without language, and that the development of articulate speech was a work of time and of experience. The length of the period of time to be assigned to its formation is unquestionably underestimated. Articulate speech is the distinguishing attribute of man. It made him man, and raised him, when formed, immeasurably above the level of the inferior animals. It was the work of ages. As language grew in the infantile human brain the line of separation rapidly widened; and when it was sufficiently perfected to express his thoughts and preserve his increasing knowledge, his great career upon the Earth was inaugurated.[54]

As such, Morgan adapts the Epicurean perspective on the emergence of language as outlined by Lucretius, fitting it within his own stadialist framework. However, the centrality and primary role of language in this scheme, as enabling cumulative development, is readily apparent only in the unpublished materials. Unlike for the process of learning from nature, where the connection with Epicurean ideas is limited to a convergence, for the process of the social application of these lessons Lucretius was a decisive, constitutive influence. Even so, Morgan did not treat all aspects of the Epicurean account of language. Left out of even the unpublished writings is the notion of 'empty words' that derive from convention rather than nature, and which as we saw in Chapter 2 formed the basis of a nexus of religious error and injustice. Closely related to this is the absence of any references to Epicurean ethics, especially with regard to the distinction between the different kinds of pleasures, although Morgan's writings on property reflect a concern with normative ethics.[55]

If natural suggestions and the inability to sustain the lessons learned from them through language were broadly congruent and in important ways stimulated by Epicureanism, what about its impact on the outline of the different

---

53   Vinnikov 1935, pp. 15–17.
54   Morgan 1872, p. 16.
55   See for the interconnections, though not identity, between Morgan's ideas, contemporary Christianity, and Greco-Roman authors like Horace, Lucretius, and Virgil, Moses 2018.

stages of social development? Certainly Morgan was well aware of the Lucretian outline of the sequence of forms of social life, which were summarised
by him in the unpublished chapter of *Ancient Society*. No explicit connection
was made here by Morgan between the sequence of Lucretius and his own outline of savagism, barbarism, and civilisation, though they are often juxtaposed
in the manuscript.[56] It is not unjustified and rather illuminating, therefore, to
try to grasp Morgan's stages from a Lucretian perspective, as the summary in
table 4.1 below aims to show. In particular, as we shall show, it resolves one of
the great contradictions of Morgan's scheme, namely the question of the origin
of the state.

To start with the lower status of savagery, it parallels Rousseau's pure state
of nature discussed in Chapter 1 in a number of ways. First of all, Morgan notes
that there do not exist contemporary parallels to this kind of state, which he can
only reconstruct by the Lucretian stratagem of negating all the extant features
of social life. All that remained was a limited subsistence of fruits and nuts in
a circumscribed geographical area, a gregarious social life that was characterised by promiscuous intercourse.[57] Secondly, and more importantly, this 'zero'
of social life is described in terms of the potentiality of mind. For when all features of development subsequent to the lower status of savagery are negated,
what remains is a kind of mental void:

> In a condition so absolutely primitive, man is seen to be not only a child in
> the scale of humanity, but possessed of a brain into which not a thought
> or conception expressed by these institutions, inventions and discover-
> ies had penetrated; – in a word, he stands at the bottom of the scale, but
> potentially all he has since become.[58]

As we saw, this potentiality derived from the capacity for language, which itself
can be seen in terms of biological evolution. Apart from the contentious issue
of racism, to be discussed below, there is no role for biology in Morgan's outline
of social development. Instead he posits a scheme according to which progress
takes place on two parallel lines, with mutual influence but neither reducible
to the terms of the other.[59] On the one hand there is the line of inventions and

---

56 See for example for the earliest phases of Lucretius and savagery, Morgan 1872, pp. 15–16.
57 Morgan 1964, p. 16; Vinnikov 1935, p. 15.
58 Morgan 1964, p. 38, emphasis added.
59 Morgan emphasised the importance of subsistence as a prerequisite for the human migra-
     tions and gathering in nations, identifying the great advances in progress with new sub-
     sistence regimes, Morgan 1964, p. 24. Yet the series of inventions and discoveries follows its

TABLE 4.1   Juxtaposing the early history of humankind in Epicureanism and in Morgan

Epicureanism	Equivalents in Morgan
Solitary human lifeways	Lower status of savagery, limited to a circumscribed habitat, initial development language. No contemporary parallels of this phase are extant in today's world (reconstructed through description by negation).
First form of social life	Middle and Upper statuses of savagery, further development of language, introduction of technology (fire, flint implements, fishing technology), global migrations, germination of religious ideas, property, organisation of social life on kinship basis of *societas*.
Regional differences of development emerge	Lower and Middle status of barbarism, with distinctions now emerging between the Old and New World in terms of plant and animal domesticates, as well as in the domain of technology (principally metallurgy).
Emergence of kingship	Middle and Upper status of barbarism, development of town life, of a priesthood, the concomitant emergence of both hereditary aristocracies and property regimes. Further development of technology and writing.
Shift to law-bound republics	Civilisation, which is based on the criteria of alphabetic writing and on a radical shift from a plan of government based on *societas* (ordered through kinship) to a plan based on *civitas* (ordered through a state defined by territoriality)
Future society based on Epicurean ethics	Reconstitution of the gentile democracy of *societas* on a higher plane, based on a common and normative democratic principle (negating private property).

discoveries, consisting of language and technologies in the broadest sense of the word, including writing systems and modes of subsistence. The process of learning from nature and accumulating knowledge is the basis for this. On the other hand there is also the line of the growth of institutions, which also derive from nature but are rather captured in principles that 'germinate'.[60]

---

own logic that is different from that of the institutions, which derive from 'a few primary germs of thoughts' that follow from constant human needs, Morgan 1964, pp. 5–6.

60   Morgan had described these principles for government, the family, religious ideas, and property, all having their origins in various phases of savagery, Morgan 1964, pp. 12–13.

It was during the middle and upper statuses of savagery that progress can be noted on both lines.[61] For technology this process starts with the discovery of fire, closely followed by the first flint and bone implements. The discovery of fishing as a mode of subsistence for Morgan allowed for the spread of humans across the different continents, leaving behind the original, circumscribed habitat that provided fruits and nuts. Further inventions notably include the first boats, weaponry, clothes, and huts. Language also continued to develop, still of syllabical form though with some elements of grammar. With regard to the other line, that of the development of institutions, it was during the middle and upper statuses of savagery that the first forms of social life developed. Although there was social interaction in Morgan's lower status of savagery, in the sense that people live together in hordes rather than wandering the forest solitarily, as in Lucretius and Rousseau, this can hardly be described as an organised form of social life.

For Morgan, early social life was based on kin relations, echoing the importance of this in Lucretius but not following his theory of a shift from solitary existence to a husband and wife couple as the basis for social life. Rather than being based on a Lucretian template, Morgan's ideas on kinship derived from his empirical studies that were published in his *Systems of Consanguinity*, only using ancient writers as sources rather than as providing guidelines. In his view the group is present from the beginning, and social organisation proceeds from establishing rules that first limit promiscuous intercourse, a process that ultimately culminated in the monogamous family. It was the first of these rules, that of the division of human groupings into classes on the basis of sex, that not only was the first step away from promiscuity, but also contained in germinal form the so-called gens. Directly derived from the Latin *gens*, a group of Roman families sharing a common ancestor, this form of social organisation came to occupy an important role in Morgan's overall scheme.

For the gens did not just structure the rules of marriage, eventually completely prohibiting intermarriage within it, but also formed the basis for more extensive social forms. Chiefs, tribes, tribal councils, and so on, are all examples of what Morgan referred to as *societas*, a plan of government based on kin relations. Its fundamental distinction to that other form of government, based on political relations and territoriality will be discussed below, when considering the contentious issue of 'the' state in Morgan's work and various interpretations of it. Physically, this form of social life took place in villages, enabled by

---

61 Morgan 1964, pp. 16–17; Vinnikov 1935, pp. 15–16. The exposition of these phases below follows from these references.

the further progress of inventions and discoveries. Other aspects of social life started to appear in germinal form as well. Notably these are religious ideas such as fetishism and the worship of elements, though these are not analysed in any depth in *Ancient society*.[62] Also notable is the appearance of the idea of property.

As we will see below, property played a crucial role in Morgan's account of the development first of forms of social life of larger scale, and especially in the shift to a political plan of government. Yet in the ages of savagery especially, but continuing into barbarism, any social role of property was far outweighed by the dominance of what Morgan term 'communism in living'. This notion is most succinctly defined in his last book on American Indian houses, as reflections of social organisation, where he strongly connects the *societas* based on kin relations to a communism of goods:

> Communism in living had its origin in the necessities of the family, which, prior to the Later Period of barbarism, was too weak an organization to face alone the struggle of life. In savagery and the Older and the Middle Period of barbarism the family was in the syndyasmian or pairing form, into which it had passed from a previous lower form. Wherever the gentile organization prevailed, several families, related by kin, united as a rule in a common household and made a common stock of the provisions acquired by fishing and hunting, and by the cultivation of maize and plants. They erected joint tenement houses large enough to accommodate several families, so that, instead of a single family in the exclusive occupation of a single the [sic] house, large households as a rule existed in all parts of America in the aboriginal period. The community of provisions was limited to the household; but a final equalization of the means of subsistence was in some measure affected by the law of hospitality.[63]

We have described here the broad outlines of the first forms of social life in Morgan, which share a broad resonance with Lucretius, showing similarities for some specific aspects but clear differences for others. In the main, on more speculative matters such as the precise sequence of technological inventions

---

62   The most extensive is a small paragraph, Morgan 1964, p. 13. The table published by Vinnikov allows more insights into the trajectory of religious ideas from fetishism to the worship of the elements, then to personal gods, and even to forms of monotheism, with institutionalisation and complex mythology, as well as Hebrew monotheism, in the statuses of middle and upper barbarism, Vinnikov 1935, pp. 15–18.

63   Morgan 1965, p. 63.

he follows the Lucretian plot more closely than in others, especially in the reconstruction of the role in kinship in early forms of social life. There his own early 'ethnographic' studies of the Iroquois, questionnaires sent out to correspondents in various world regions for his *Systems of Consanguinity* book,[64] as well as similar work by others, led to more elaborate and quite different conclusions. Generally, these differences can be ascribed to two distinct forms of reasoning. One is the more Lucretian theme of description by negation, present especially in the unpublished chapter on Roman ideas of human development but also in *Ancient Society* itself.[65]

The other method of inference is to reason by analogy, mostly through the use of contemporary ethnographic cases like the Iroquois but also using social formations known through historical sources. Notably, all analogies for the middle and upper statuses of savagery are to contemporary cases that are predominantly from the Americas, as well as in Oceania.[66] Morgan would use evidence such as this, supplemented by historical sources and pioneering archaeological research, to outline the differences of the New and Old worlds in a more comprehensive fashion. The description by negation in the Lucretian sense, reduced social phenomena to generic traits, affording little scope for investigating the regional differences highlighted by Epicurus. The use of analogies allowed for more specific and detailed comparisons, even if, as we shall see, it risked reducing specific cases to general templates, thus obfuscating alternative historical pathways.

In that sense, the analogies drawn from American and Oceanic cases for the statuses of middle and upper savagery are applicable to the Old World as well, even if in places like Europe such social forms have long gone. However, for the succeeding phases of lower and middle barbarism, Morgan draws out the differences between the western and eastern hemispheres, rather than merely using the former to illustrate the earliest past of the latter. These differences are held to be exclusive to the strand of inventions and discoveries, not for that of institutions.[67] The lack of domesticated animals in the New World is one of its main distinguishing features, excepting the Llama and Turkey, as is its use of irrigation in maize agriculture and certain kinds of architecture. In

---

64   For a kinship studies perspective on the development of Morgan's ideas, see Trautmann 1987.
65   Morgan 1872, pp. 1–3, compare with Morgan 1964 pp. 32–8.
66   There is very little discussion of the entire continents of Africa and Asia in Morgan, the meagre discussion of which he places together in a single chapter of *Ancient Society* on the forms of the family extant there, noting but not expanding upon 'the early development of Chinese and Indian civilization', Morgan 1964, p. 307.
67   Morgan 1964, p. 17.

the Old World animal domestication rather precedes the cultivation of cereals. Another important difference is the predominance of metallurgy in Eurasia, and the converse lack thereof in the Americas.

Morgan would point to these different continental conditions as part of the explanation for what he saw as differential speeds of development along his stadial outline of history. Another mode of explanation used by him to account for such differences was through race. Morgan's ideas in this regard are hard to fathom, as they are often mentioned in passing and are contradictory when considered together. Moreover, a clear personal bias can be discerned. As much is evident from the travel diaries of Morgan's travels in Europe in 1870 and 1871, where difficulties in his dealings with Italians led him to despair of them in petty racial terms.[68] In the *Systems of Consanguinity* published in 1871, a somewhat more systematic account can be found where nations are defined by what Morgan calls the 'channels of blood'.[69] Through these channels, actual systems of descent are transmitted through the generations,[70] as well as specific cultural phenomena such as sleeping naked that, incredibly, persist even when moving to colder latitudes.[71]

These intimations of a systematic theory of racial differences in the *Systems of Consanguinity* were betrayed by Morgan himself, however, in *Ancient Society*. By instinct and religious doctrine Morgan was a follower of monogenesis, going strongly against the notion of splits within humankind along racial lines.[72] Furthermore, while systems of reckoning genealogical descent as well as idiosyncratic cultural traits were for him transmitted through blood lines, the same is not true for the institutions such as forms of the family, religion, property, and government.[73] There was a singular line of development, so racial differences

---

68   It seems, mainly, from the fact that in the Darwinian competition of street bargaining, Morgan was not carrying the day, coupled with his misgivings about Catholicism, leading him to indefensible comments on the country and its population, though these were limited to his travel diary, White 1937, pp. 314–16.

69   Morgan 1871, pp. vi, 9.

70   A comparison was made by Morgan in this regard between the tracing of the histories of language by philologists and the tracing of descent systems through the 'channels of the blood', Morgan 1871, pp. 505–6. See also the account by Trautmann on the relation of Morgan to the philological methods of his day, Trautmann 1987, pp. 58–83.

71   According to Morgan such customs persist even with greatly changed climatic conditions, for they are strong, being transmitted through the blood, Morgan 1871, pp. 274–5.

72   Morgan's emphasis on the unity of Creation led him to discount the idea of separate origins of races, which was the key doctrine of the racialist science of his day, Trautmann 1987, pp. 27–30.

73   Biology in his scheme only had a minor role compared to the mind and ideas, which were the main determinants for the development of institutions, Swetlitz 1988, p. 72. With

could only speed up or slow down the rate of development. It is questionable what role racial characteristics played as a causal factor in his scheme of development, give that transmission through blood lines was only for traits marginal to it. The one example of an attempt at causal explanation along racial lines is where Morgan speculates that the domestication of animals in Eurasia led to increased brain sizes.[74]

This impact of animal domestication in the Old World for Morgan explains the racial superiority of the Aryan and Semitic families relative to their New World counterparts, these 'representing the central stream of human progress'.[75] Yet the hypothetical connection between animal domestication and brain size does not derive from experimental science, but rather from the accomplished fact, in the sense that Morgan rated the Aryan and Semitic races as further advanced along his yardstick of progress. Furthermore, he himself would diverge radically from his own hypothesis, when positing in his book on American aboriginal houses of 1881 that the 'Iroquois were a vigorous and intelligent people, with a brain approaching in volume the Aryan average'.[76] Quite how this was accomplished without animal domestication was left unsaid, but it is clear that the notion of brain size here is in the eye of the beholder, namely Morgan, rather than constituting a scientific concept properly.

The contradictions in Morgan's statements on race may well be attributed to these deriving more from personal bias than from intellectual reflection. As such, his ideas on race are extrinsic to the stadialist scheme itself, even if they can be latched onto it.[77] This can be observed in the reception of Morgan's ideas. For the Marxist use of his work has been free of racialist biases, though as we shall see below Engels was highly interested in the impact of animal domestication. On the other hand, others like Otis Mason used Morgan's scale of development in a very different way, embedding it within a framework of racial and

---

regard to the 'germs of thought' that formed the basis for institutions, Morgan had noted both transmission 'with the streams of the blood, as well as a logical development', Morgan 1964, p. 12. Yet the blood lines here only serve to transmit these germinal forms, it is the logical sequence of ideas that is universal and recurs independently in different world regions.

74   Through the greater availability of meat as well as dairy products, Morgan 1964, p. 29.

75   Morgan 1964, p. 468.

76   Morgan 1881, p. 40. See also his valuation of the Iroquois relative to the Greeks with regard to their government and religion in his early book on them, Morgan 1851, pp. 139–40, 150–1.

77   Swetlitz reviewed Morgan's ideas on the role of biology in history and pointed out that there was a strong organicist metaphor present in them, yet the underlying causal framework was not based on these metaphors, Swetlitz 1988, p. 73.

geographically determinist notions.[78] Hence, even if race is extrinsic to the sta-dialist framework with regards to its causality, the emphasis on progress as a way to rank social formations, make the scheme susceptible to racialist bias. Morgan's own contradictory and subjective views on race bear testimony to this susceptibility to distortions, whether in positing the superiority of Aryan and Semitic cases or counterbalancing this by extolling the Iroquois.

Returning from this excursus on race to the main topic of the exposition of Morgan's stadialism from a Lucretian perspective, we now turn to the first king-doms in the stages of middle and upper barbarism. As for race, the continental differences in animal domestication and metallurgy served only to speed up or slow down the transition to new stages. According to Morgan no social form-ation in the Americas moved beyond the status of middle barbarism, and he vehemently attacked those who saw in the Mexican and Peruvian cases ana-logies to European kingdoms.[79] Here he seemed to follow the plot established by Robertson and even De Pauw, as discussed in the previous chapter, accord-ing to whom the peoples of the Americas were unable to make the transition to civilisation and the state. As we shall see in Chapter 6, archaeology had first laboured against and then overthrown these notions. Yet it will serve us not to dismiss Morgan's ideas out of hand, for they paint a more complex pic-ture than the generic notion of a coeval birth of the state and class society allows.

If we recall from Chapter 2 the Lucretian account of state formation, then it is clear that it moved through two distinct phases. The first was one in which kings established cities, as well as property regimes, while after their downfall a new form of the state based on laws was established. Quite clearly these two phases are quite different regimes. If we, then, use this perspective to evalu-ate the ideas of Morgan on the state, even if he mentions them only in passing in his unpublished chapter,[80] they become much clearer. For much of the dis-cussion of the later phases of barbarism in Morgan fits the Lucretian outline of the first kingdoms. To be precise in this matter, however, necessitates distin-guishing between the middle phase characterised by the Mexican and Peruvian cases, and the phase of upper barbarism that Morgan mainly illustrates through references to Homer. Both share important commonalities of a kind of social

---

78 Kennedy 2018, especially table 5.1, pp. 170–4.

79 Morgan 1964, pp. 165–6, Morgan expressed himself more strongly in an earlier article, where he ridiculed the Spanish authors, as well as contemporaries like Bancroft, for being carried away by their own preconceptions, resulting in works that have no value save pos-sibly a literary one, 'as Robinson Crusoe', Morgan 1876, p. 268.

80 Morgan 1872, pp. 18–19.

formation that is still a *societas*, its plan of government based on the intricate web of kin relations, yet with emerging elements that signal a departure from existing affair,[81] which can be summed up accordingly:

1. An aristocratic element appears that is focused upon the previously existing office of the chief. This element is closely related to the increased role of property, but still within the overall context of communism in living.

2. Concomitant with the development of the aristocratic element and the expansion of property, the shift to polytheism in religion is paralleled by a more hierarchical organisation of the priesthood, as well as new practices like human sacrifice.

3. What are called military democracies developed from middle barbarism, based on a council of chiefs and a supreme commander, supplemented in the status of upper barbarism by what in Homer was known as the *agora*: the assembly of the people.

Morgan is at pains here to disassociate the middle and upper barbaric chiefs from the medieval and early modern European notions of kingship habitually applied to them. This holds true as much for the *basileus* of Homer, a point wholeheartedly supported by Engels and Marx,[82] as for Moctezuma, the leader of what Morgan termed the Aztec confederacy. The presence of a leadership figure with all the trappings and pomp is hardly the decisive factor, for it depends on the social circumstances whether a leader is a mere chief or an absolutist ruler. By social circumstances, Morgan would mean the plan of government, that of the kinship-based *societas* of Homeric Greece and Mexico in Aztec times. As we shall see below, this plan is radically distinct from that of medieval and early modern Europe, with its territorial states, legal systems, and so on, which he termed *civitas*.

From this perspective, it is less surprising to see Morgan strongly attacking those Iberian and other writers, who couched the indigenous American social formations in the terminology of late feudal Europe. His main point was that the pre-Columbian Americas should be understood according to a plan of government based on *societas*, rather than on *civitas*, and did not constitute a denial of their achievements in the style of De Pauw. Morgan's correspondence with the Swiss scholar Adolph Bandelier, whom he was able to persuade of his views, makes this point particularly clear.[83] Although Morgan expressed

---

81   Morgan 1964, p. 452, see also Vinnikov 1935, pp. 17–18.

82   Engels 1990a, p. 210; Marx 1974, p. 206.

83   Bandelier, who was closely familiar with a broad range of sources on ancient Mexico, was initially sceptical of Morgan's views, arguing for the existence there of territorial states and also of feudalism, see White 1940a, pp. 117–19, 144–7. However, he came round to Mor-

some reservations on population numbers,[84] he did appreciate the complexity of the inventions and institutions evident in the Mexican and Peruvian cases, alongside his esteemed Iroquois. As much can be inferred from his summary of the most advanced phase of middle barbarism in the Americas. After listing numerous inventions, including bronze metallurgy, large scale architecture, conceptual schemas like the Mexican calendars, he goes on to describe institutional development as well:

> A priesthood organized in a hierarchy, and distinguished by a costume, personal gods with idols to represent them, and human sacrifices, appear for the first time in this ethnical period. Two large Indian pueblos, Mexico and Cusco, now appear, containing over twenty thousand inhabitants, a number unknown in the previous period. The aristocratic element in society began to manifest itself in feeble forms among the chiefs, civil and military, through increased numbers under the same government, and the growing complexity of affairs.[85]

Yet, as noted, these social formations were of the *societas* plan of government rather than that of *civitas*, something attributed to the insufficient development of property in them.[86] An obstacle for the further development of property in the Americas was the lack of iron metallurgy. For Morgan iron has to be seen as the 'invention of inventions', being 'without a parallel' and responsible to the largest degree for the ability to transition from barbarism to civilisation.[87] The reason he emphasised this was because, according to him, iron was necessary for field agriculture to develop, allowing humankind to break out from the demographic limitations of horticulture.[88] Morgan cited Lucretius on this, on

---

gan's view of the inappropriateness of the Old World terms in the Spanish sources, White 1940a, pp. 163, 167. Later, during the course of his fieldwork in Mexico, he interpreted the pyramid at Cholula, the largest of its kind in the Americas, as the result of a communal effort, White 1940b, pp. 231–2. See also Pardo 2017 on the relation between Bandelier and Morgan.

84   Morgan 1964, pp. 171–2.
85   Morgan 1964, p. 452.
86   Morgan 1964, p. 187.
87   Morgan 1964, pp. 43, 457.
88   He argued that without field agriculture, dense populations and a common government for groups larger than half a million persons were highly unlikely, except in certain exceptional conditions where irrigation allowed for it, Morgan 1964, p. 30. One such exception Morgan likely had in mind was the Aztec capital Tenochtitlan in the Valley of Mexico.

the forest retreating uphill in the face of expanding cultivation,[89] a common *topos* also seen in Smith and Rousseau in the previous chapter.

He also highlighted the Lucretian sequence of metallurgical development in the unpublished chapter on Roman ideas on the earliest history.[90] The citations and summary of the initial discovery and further steps in metal-working bear witness to the role of chance in this trajectory. Perhaps this had influenced Morgan, for in his conclusions on the overall trajectory from savagery to civilisation, he notes first of all how the Semitic and especially the Aryan streams represent the central strand of progress, yet then makes a half-turn by recognising the aleatory character of this process:

> After reaching the Middle Status of barbarism, civilization hung in the balance while barbarians were feeling their way, by experiments with the native metals, toward the process of smelting iron ore. Until iron and its uses were known, civilization was impossible. If mankind had failed to the present hour to cross this barrier, it would have afforded no just cause for surprise. When we recognize the duration of man's existence upon the earth, the wide vicissitudes through which he has passed in savagery and in barbarism, and the progress he was compelled to make, civilization might as naturally have been delayed for several thousand years in the future, as to have occurred when it did in the good providence of God. We are forced to the conclusion that it was the result, as to the time of its achievement, of a series of fortuitous circumstances.[91]

Notable here is how Morgan's recognition of 'fortuitous circumstances' in the discovery of iron-working, is couched in strongly stadialist terms. It can either speed up or delay the process, just as we saw for the different bio-geographical conditions of the different hemispheres. There is no Lucretian weave of temporalities in evidence here,[92] nor of the Montaignesque valuation of the plural-

---

89   DRN V.1370–1378, Smith 1992, pp. 484–5, cited in Morgan 1964, n. 8, p. 30.

90   Morgan 1872, pp. 19–20. Yet in *Ancient Society* he rejected the Three Age system, of Stone, Bronze, and Iron ages as put forward by nineteenth-century archaeologists, inspired in part by Lucretius, see Morgan 1964, p. 15.

91   Morgan 1964, p. 468.

92   Quite a few temporal 'inconveniences' crop up here and there in Morgan with the potential to disrupt the neat linear temporality of his scheme. Examples are the ancient Britons using iron yet assigned to the status of middle barbarism in *Ancient Society*, Morgan 1964, p. 17, and his observation upon visiting the Assyrian exhibition in the British museum during his European tour that they must have had antecedents that had attained the

ity of historical pathways.[93] The iron logic of the scale of mind evident in Morgan's overall scheme holds captive his appreciation of contingency in history, as well as of his recognition of distinctions between the Eastern and Western hemispheres. Hence what distinguishes the New World are those features that have kept its development limited to the status of middle barbarism, rather than constituting a form of civilisation distinct from those of the Old World. In that sense Morgan was more a pupil if not of De Pauw, than certainly of Robertson and Smith, following, with a twist, the Lockean thesis that in the beginning all the world was America.

Turning now to the transition to civilisation proper, iron-working was its prerequisite but not the decisive factor in bringing it about. Rather it set in motion a complex chain of events, which revolved around the quantitative increase of property enabled by both the iron tools themselves and by the agricultural surpluses of field agriculture they yielded. Significantly, in his unpublished account of Lucretius, Morgan highlighted the initial allotment of flocks and fields based on appearance and strength as fostering in the mind the idea of individual property.[94] Here we can see how close the ideas of Lucretius were identified with Morgan's own notions so as to practically merge. As noted earlier for the phases of middle and upper savagery, property was present then in a latent, germinal form, yet its role was negligible as these social formations were structured on the principles of communism-in-living. Only during middle barbarism did it begin to become more important, connected to the appearance of an aristocratic element in social life.

In order to go into more detail as to how property could become more important in this phase, it is important to recall that Morgan's notion of communism-in-living was closely tied to the necessities of family life. Descent in the female line ensured, moreover, that property was inherited within the gens, an idea that Morgan seems to have taken from Bachofen, with whom he was in

---

status of civilisation already in the third millennium BC, White 1937, p. 252. The latter is especially notable given his use of the Greek case as exemplary for the transition from barbarism to civilisation, yet occurring thousands of years later than in the Middle East.

93 As noted by Morgan, despite the differences between the continents, 'the conditions of society in the corresponding status must have been, in the main, substantially similar', Morgan 1964, p. 22. The focus on similar institutions would seem to follow largely from his use of the universal scale of mind as a yardstick for progress.

94 The passage is very brief but it is the connection with Morgan's understanding of mind that is of the most significance here: 'The allotment of lands, with a division of the domestic animals, and also the gradual formation in the mind of the idea of individual property', Morgan 1872, p. 22.

contact.[95] As the inventions and discoveries multiplied, however, the quantity and quality of potential property grew, in particular in Eurasia for domesticated animals such as cattle. In order for this property to be accumulated, it was necessary to limit inheritance to a smaller group of descendants, passing from a system where goods are inherited within the gens to one where they are passed on to direct descendants.[96] This necessitated a shift from reckoning descent in the female to the male line, something Morgan argued could also be seen in New World cases like the Maya.[97]

At this point the old communism-in-living was still coexisting with the new tendency toward more private forms of property. In the period of upper barbarism, however, the latter induced such tension in the *societas* form based on kinship, that a fundamental change in the plan of government took place. The exemplary case of upper barbarism in *Ancient Society* is the social formation immortalised in the Homeric epics. In Homer's time the introduction of ironworking and the change of reckoning descent in the male line powerfully combine to greatly increase the role of property in social life, evident for Morgan in the poet's mention of fences.[98] He further took from a fragment of Dicaearchus the outline of early Greek social formations as revolving around the gens, phratry, and tribe, that is, the *societas* plan of government based on kinship.[99]

Morgan then traced in some detail the change from *societas* to the new plan of a territorial state, the *civitas*, based on the political relation of citizenship rather than on kin relations. In particular, he focuses on Athens from the heroic era, personified by Theseus, to the political reforms of Solon and Kleisthenes. A number of steps can be recognised in this account, summarised here as follows:

1. The situation in the heroic age created new pressures in social life, in the demands of living together in large walled cities, constant warfare, and the growth of property and thereby also the aristocratic element, necessitating new modes of organisation.[100]

---

95   Morgan 1964, pp. 297–8, see for Bachofen's response to Morgan the letter cited in Stern 1931, pp. 145–52.

96   Morgan 1964, pp. 293–8.

97   Morgan 1964, p. 455.

98   Morgan 1964, p. 459. Marx in his notes on Morgan, questioned that the presence of such fences implied the existence of private property as such, Marx 1974, pp. 134–5.

99   Morgan 1964, pp. 204–5. These Greek terms were of course turned by Morgan into comparative categories, see Varto 2018 for his use of contemporary sources on Greco-Roman antiquity.

100   Morgan 1964, pp. 215, 222.

2.   As a response to these pressures tyrants rose to power, but Morgan argued these were unable to last due to their incompatibility with the pre-existing gentile democratic spirit.[101]

3.   The first great reform, that of Solon, was based on property, but not on territoriality, which was insufficient as a solution, for migrations had resulted in large masses of people being outside the gentile system.[102]

4.   Kleisthenes instituted the second great reform, of a plan of government based both on property and a territorial division of its subjects as citizens rather than kinfolk.[103]

Later scholars have criticised Morgan's use of the Athenian case, typifying it as a second generation state that was distinct from and hence could offer few insights into the development of the first states.[104] Viewed from a Lucretian perspective, however, Morgan's ideas can be seen in a rather different light. While his account does not literally follow that of Lucretius, there is the same dual process in both, with first the emergence of leadership figures and only later a political system bound by law. For Morgan this marked the watershed between ancient and modern life,[105] though of course subsequent to the Greco-Roman civilisations there were added many more inventions, discoveries, and institutions.[106] The great distinction of this 'modern' period, alongside the new plan of government, was that its dynamic was radically changed. Whereas before property was subordinate to the communism-in-living of *societas*, it now became the 'master passion', changing even the form of the family, as for property:

> Governments and laws are instituted with primary reference to its creation, protection and enjoyment. It introduced human slavery as an instrument in its production; and, after the experience of several thousand years, it caused the abolition of slavery upon the discovery that a freeman was a better property-making machine. The cruelty inherent in the heart of man, which civilization and Christianity have softened without

---

101   Morgan 1964, pp. 216–18.
102   Morgan 1964, pp. 228–29.
103   Morgan 1964, pp. 232–4.
104   See for references below for Engels.
105   Morgan 1964, p. 14.
106   Morgan argues through description by negation how modern civilisation rests not just on its ancient counterparts, but also on the preceding ages of barbarism and savagery, see the similar type of argumentation along these lines in Morgan 1964, pp. 32–3 and Morgan 1872, pp. 1, 8.

eradicating, still betrays the savage origin of mankind, and in no way more pointedly than in the practice of human slavery, through all the centuries of recorded history. With the establishment of the inheritance of property in the children of its owner, came the first possibility of a strict mono-gamian family.[107]

This passage brings up two interrelated questions. Firstly, Morgan's phrasing suggests a certain ambivalence about the role of property, leading to a qualific-ation of progress. The second question follows from this and concerns the pos-sibility of a future civilisation organised on principles not subservient to private property. As we saw in Chapter 2, in ancient Epicureanism the conception of a future without slavery and wealth followed from a naturalist ethics of pleasure, which formed a normative framework for evaluating historical changes as well. Morgan did not write about ethics as such, and, as we saw, the crucial Epicurean nexus of 'empty words', religious fear, and greed were absent from his account of Lucretius. Perhaps the tendency to remain circumspect with regard to con-troversial questions, as for Darwinism, extended to his ethics as well. However, even if he did not make his underlying ethical ideas explicit, even in his unpub-lished writings, we can at least grasp their results in his normative evaluations of history and progress.[108]

In Morgan's early writings, three important clues exist that allow us to grasp his valuations. As befitted a grandson of the American, Morgan took an early interest in ancient Athenian democracy. In a published article from 1853 on the topic, he argued that democracy was a timeless principle of history, rather than one of its accidents, and that nations could either ascend to it or sink back into barbarism.[109] Investigating the reasons for the decline and disappearance of Athenian democracy, Morgan argued that the case held lessons for the United States of his day.[110] Another clue comes from his earlier publication on the Iroquois from 1851, where he had briefly discussed the trajectory from heroic

---

107 Morgan 1964, p. 426.
108 See in this regard also Moses 2018, who gives an overview of Morgan's attitudes throughout his scholarly career toward property, civilisation, and progress, especially in relation to Horace and Lucretius, among others.
109 Morgan 1853, p. 341.
110 Morgan 1853, pp. 342–3. Among the deficiencies of Athenian democracy were its reliance on slavery and the degradation of labour, the limitations of the institutions of direct demo-cracy, especially with regard to the territorial expansion of the Athenian state, and what Morgan saw as a lack of a solid moral basis. For unlike Christianity, for Morgan the poly-theism of ancient Greece was unable to furnish a strong sense of morality, Morgan 1853, p. 366.

age to democracy in ancient Greece, juxtaposing it with contemporary trends toward liberty and democracy in Britain.[111] In that book he had also extolled the Iroquois for their liberty, which he, citing the ancient authors Horace and Virgil in support, attributed to the absence of the 'power of gain' from their confederacy.[112] Living in a 'hunter state', the Iroquois were blessed with a natural nobility of character and have no need for the coercive mechanism of the state to live well.

Morgan, though, was a progressive, who may have extolled the Iroquois and ancient Athenians to a degree but was squarely focused on the future of his United States. His views on his country can be readily grasped from one of his lesser known publications, the article 'Diffusion against centralization' from 1852. In this text Morgan emphasises the conflict between labour and capital, the latter always seeking to dominate and exploit the former.[113] The solution to this struggle for Morgan is to diffuse capital, for if scattered into the hands of the many it becomes subservient to labour. This diffusion of property is opposed to its centralisation, which Morgan associates with feudalism and aristocracy in general, arguing that 'the law of primogeniture was the first aggression upon labor'.[114] According to Morgan, industry and commerce have had a great liberating effect, placing great strain upon feudalism and thus in part allowing for the radical break of the American Revolution.[115] In its wake, previous accumulations of property in New York state were annulled, and the land was distributed into the hands of a multitude of smallholders.

Here we should not forget that Morgan himself was a Yankee capitalist, though at this point still at the start of his career. Coupled with his revolutionary patriotism, it is little surprising that the diffusion of not just property but also of access to education and of social dignity were emphasised in an overall vision of the United States as 'paradise regained'.[116] The key to the success of his country, Morgan argues, lies in commerce. Not only does it hold the vast territories of the country together, by bonds more enduring than patriotism, but it also allows the United States to dominate world trade from its central hub loc-

---

111   Morgan 1962, pp. 135–6.
112   Morgan 1962, p. 139. Such ideas can be seen even earlier in Morgan, in 1843, in a lecture he wrote for his fellow members of a club, in which he extolled the simple and enjoyable life of the indigenous Americans, based on the account of the social formations encountered by Columbus, Moses 2018, pp. 36–7.
113   Morgan 1852, pp. 22–5.
114   Morgan 1852, p. 24.
115   Morgan 1852, pp. 26–30.
116   Morgan 1852, p. 53.

ated in New York.[117] The result is what can be seen as a benign empire, breaking down barriers of freedom without any blood being spilt. All of this appears to be far removed, however, from Epicurean *ataraxia*, or indeed any other philosophical system acting as a guide to ethics. It is instead the perspective of the American Revolution, as elaborated by a man of commerce with deeply held democratic ideals.

Later in his life, however, Morgan became disillusioned by commerce, owing to the changed circumstances in the United States. Instead of a further diffusion of property, late nineteenth-century American capitalism tended toward centralisation, which carried with it the danger of aristocratic tendencies re-emerging.[118] If Morgan's views on the United States were expressed mostly in passing references in his correspondence, more information on his general views can be gleaned from the journal he kept on his European travels in 1870 and 1871. In numerous passages in this journal, he not only reiterated his distaste of feudalism,[119] but more importantly now connected it to the new powers of plutocracy. For example, in his discussion of the English aristocracy, Morgan notes that while its traditions are still in place, the real power behind the scenes had shifted to the plutocrats.[120] This group had gained the reins of the state, and now used this institution as an instrument for creating and safeguarding their property.

As a result, the plutocrats now stood opposed to the people, something that Morgan as a democrat would be unable to accept, despite his stated admiration for London as a global capital of trade, and, as such, the pinnacle of the evolutionary process.[121] He describes his own visit to a demonstration of 'workingmen' in Hyde park, expressing his sympathy and admiration, before going on to observe:

> The merchants, capitalists, and middling men keep clear of these meetings because their sympathies are on the other side. Such meetings as this

---

117 Morgan 1852, pp. 44–6.

118 The immediate contexts for this was the bankruptcy of Morgan's own company and the Great Strikes of 1877, in the context of first the ascendancy and then hegemony of monopoly capitalism, Moses 2001, pp. 415–24.

119 White 1937, pp. 235, 237–39.

120 White 1937, pp. 263–64.

121 The man of commerce that Morgan had been earlier in his career was quite animated by the 'great spirit' of the city of London, proclaiming it to be 'the ideal city of the Age of Commerce, which has been reached through the previous ages of Stone, of Bronze, of Iron, of Agriculture, and of the Mechanical arts', White 1937, p. 379.

show the weakness of the republican element in English society. When the time comes, if it ever does, the working men will have to rise upon the merchants and traders as well as the aristocrats and push them out of the way in one body.[122]

Notable, too, are Morgan's thoughts on the Paris Commune, written down in the same journal while visiting the city just after the Communards' demise. He argued that they had been unjustly condemned, especially by the English press, who, he observed, were less enlightened than savages.[123] Describing the situation in the city in some detail, Morgan noted the many places in the city where the phrase 'liberty, equality, fraternity' had been painted or carved on buildings, especially those he described as 'nests of aristocracy'.[124] His emphasis of and sympathy for this revolutionary cry is especially noteworthy, as it recurs in the famous passage of *Ancient Society* in which he formulated his desire for a future form of social life without property. Noting how aristocracy and property had developed hand in glove during the transition from barbarism to civilisation, from *societas* to *civitas*, Morgan argued against their burden on social life and expressed the need for radical change:

> Since the advent of civilization, the outgrowth of property has been so immense, its forms so diversified, its uses so expanding and its management so intelligent in the interests of its owners, that it has become, on part of the people, an unmanageable power. The human mind stands bewildered in the presence of its own creation. The time will come, nevertheless, when human intelligence will rise to the mastery over property, and define the relations of the state to the property it protects, as well as the obligations and the limits of the rights of its owners. The interests of society are paramount to individual interests, and the two must be brought into just and harmonious relations.

> A mere property career is not the final destiny of mankind, if progress is to be the law of the future as it has been of the past. The time which has passed away since civilization began is but a fragment of the past duration of man's existence; and but a fragment of the ages yet to come. The dissolution of society bids fair to become the termination of a career of

---

122   White 1937, p. 376.
123   White 1937, pp. 343–4.
124   White 1937, p. 347.

which property is the end and aim; because such a career contains the elements of self-destruction. Democracy in government, brotherhood in society, equality in rights and privileges, and universal education, fore-shadow the next higher plane of society to which experience, intelligence and knowledge are steadily tending. It will be a revival, in a higher form, of the **liberty, equality and fraternity** of the ancient gentes.[125]

Published six years after his visit to Paris, the recurrence of the revolutionary slogan 'liberty, equality, fraternity' in *Ancient Society* clearly links the opinions in his travel journal to his views on evolution and future progress. The connection between past and future forms of communism is also evident in a passage from his 1881 book on indigenous American architecture. He cites John Lloyd Stephens, an explorer of Maya ruins, on how socialist reformers like Fourier and Owen might take lessons from the communal arrangements of the contemporary Maya.[126] Morgan furthermore connects this observation to the architectural forms found at the nearby Maya ruins of Uxmal, which for him reflect a communist form of social life. For we can read in his work that, rather than reflecting coercion by despotic powers, for Morgan these buildings rather express a communal spirit of equality, or as he puts it: 'liberty, equality, fraternity are emphatically the three great principles of the gens, and this architecture responds to these sentiments'.[127]

In Morgan's words, the ruins of Uxmal seem to echo the slogans he had seen years earlier on the walls of post-Commune Paris, valuing in both the practice of a communist form of social life. In that sense, he certainly used a normative framework, one that was not directly derivative of his views of evolution and history, but rather allowed him to make sense of it on political terms. Even if the underlying ethics of these political views remained implicit in Morgan's writings, and any connection to Epicureanism tenuous, Morgan's linking of past and future freedom is broadly in line with the outline of Lucretius and others of the school. For the Epicurean view, as outlined in Chapter 2, was that the changes introduced after the first form of social life had led people astray, and that philosophical therapy would set things right, not as a return to the past per se, but retaining the benefits of technology and civilisation. Likewise Morgan

---

125   Morgan 1964, p. 467, emphasis added.
126   Morgan 1965, pp. 298–9, already cited in his earlier article on ancient Mexico, Morgan 1876, p. 286. Morgan's friend McIlvaine had earlier preached against the Fourierist phalanxes springing up in New York state, including several that were located close to Rochester, Trautmann 1987, pp. 65–7.
127   Morgan 1965, p. 310.

saw a return to the principles of the past, as inscribed on Parisian walls, rather than a literal turnabout to the initial condition of social life.[128]

In general, Lucretius seems to have been an inspiration for Morgan and to have supplied him with important concepts, especially with regard to evolution and the development of language. At the same time, he was a scientist guided by his own investigations in the field and those of his contemporaries, resulting in findings often at odds with ancient philosophy. The exposition here of Morgan's stages of history from a Lucretian perspective has aimed to show that it can enlighten our understanding of his conceptual framework. This is true as much for the direct influence of Lucretian ideas, especially for early humans, and more indirect resonances, as for the two plans of government of *societas* and *civitas*. Moving from these specific issues to the broader picture, an interesting question is to what degree Morgan can be said to conform to the theses of the aleatory current, as they were outlined in chapter one, which will be summed up accordingly:

1. One aspect of the thesis of trans-individuality can be found in Morgan's understanding of the parallelism of attributes, if there is certainly no reason at all to assume a direct Spinozist connection. It extends to his conception of body and mind in living beings, and even, in a weaker form, to the parallel tracks of inventions and discoveries on the one hand, and institutions on the other, in the progressive sequence of stages. At the same time, Morgan's conception was different in that the qualities of mind, at least in his published writings, are placed on a scale hierarchically ordered from simple to complex.[129]

2. Another aspect of the trans-individuality thesis in Morgan can be seen in the interaction of humans and nature. Rather than starting from an essentialist conception of (the human) species, he emphasised the role of natural suggestions and defined the initial human state in lower savagery as one of potentiality (as a blank slate).

---

128 One other connection, if fleeting, connection between the communism of the gentile *societas* and a later recurrence post-civilisation can be noted in Morgan, when he connects the ordering of kin relations in the ideal communistic state of Plato's *Timaeus* to the consanguine family (the Hawaiian custom), pointing out that Plato may have been familiar with ancient kin relations through extant traditions, Morgan 1964, p. 357. Marx's interest in this passage can be seen from his notebook, Marx 1974, p. 108.

129 In a weak sense, mind is said to gain a greater role in subsistence as the complexity and scale of the production process increases, but not in an idealist sense, given that the material aspects are the conditions, if not the determinants of the development of institutions, Morgan 1964, pp. 24–5.

3.   With regard to the thesis of the primacy of the encounter over the form, this can be traced in the transition from the *societas* to the *civitas* plan of government. For not only was the latter not prefigured in the former, it was also conceived as arising from the chance interplay of factors. Chief among these was the great increase in the means of subsistence, and hence of property, that resulted from the introduction of iron metallurgy, which Morgan argued was itself the outcome of fortuitous circumstances that could well not have been present.

4.   The thesis of plural temporality is not evident in Morgan. For even if the distinct timescales of the eras of savagery, barbarism, and civilisation are noted, there is never any discussion of an interweaving of temporalities. His more detailed outlines of inventions, discoveries, and institutions are provided as sequences, without a more complex view of their distinct temporal character. Each phase has to follow the next, in a relay sequence that can only increase or decrease in speed. This naturally follows from the scale of mind.

As discussed in Chapters 2 and 3, the thesis of plural temporality was closely related to what was termed there the thesis of the plurality of worlds, recognising the regional diversity of historical trajectories. Just as Morgan's strict stadial sequence ignored the possibility of overlapping and intertwined temporalities, so he subsumed regional differences under the overall scheme that is premised on the hierarchical scale of mind. The hemispheric distinctions between the New and Old Worlds were recognised by him, but only insofar as they led to faster or slower movement along the universal pathway of development. There was no inclination on Morgan's part to posit that the indigenous American social formations could be seen as civilisations in their own right, in a different form from that of their Old World counterparts. In that sense he was far removed from the aleatory perspective of Montaigne, and closer to De Pauw, Robertson, and Smith, who followed the Lockean thesis that 'in the beginning all the world was America'. As we shall see in the sections below and in the next chapter, the reduction of temporal and geographical pluralism to a uniform sequence of development formed a considerable obstacle to aleatory conceptions of the early history of humankind in the Marxist tradition.

3   Engels on the Dialectical Unfolding of History

Engels adapted Morgan's stadialist scheme, with some modifications as we shall see, in his *Origin of the Family, Private Property and the State* of 1884, published a year after Marx's death.[130] Yet we would be amiss in seeing this work as merely derivative of that of Morgan, for it has to be grasped within the context of contemporary writings by Engels on dialectics, nature, and history. Most important in this regard are the *Anti-Dühring* of 1878, a manuscript on early German history from 1882, and the *Dialectics of Nature*, which remained unfinished at the time of his death in 1895. No analysis of the Marxist adaptation of Morgan's ideas can ignore the wider body of the late writings of Engels, which were of course completely independent of Morgan's unpublished intellectual background. The late Engels played an important role in twentieth century Marxist debates on dialectics, whether as support for the further development of a dialectics of nature or to formulate arguments against the validity of such a form of dialectics.

Both the texts themselves and the debate they generated are of considerable importance for current debates on aleatory materialism as well. For while the specifics of Epicurean doctrine do not appear central to Engels,[131] Spinoza was close to his heart, as not just his writings but also the testimonies of contemporary revolutionaries reveal. As Georgi Plekhanov recalled: '"So do you think", I asked, "old Spinoza was right when he said that *thought* and *extent* are nothing but two attributes of one and the same substance?" "Of course", Engels replied, "old Spinoza was quite right."'.[132] In the *Anti-Dühring* and *Dialectics of Nature*, Engels does not discuss the parallelism of the two attributes of Spinozist substance, yet he does mention Spinoza a number of times at crucial junctures. He notes that Spinoza (together with Descartes) as 'brilliant exponents' of dialectics in modern philosophy,[133] stressing in particular his notion of *omnis determinatio est negatio*.[134]

In the introduction of the *Dialectics of Nature*, where Engels sketched the historical trajectory of science, he praised Spinoza, together with the French

---

130   See Krader's introduction in Marx 1974, table VII, p. 79, for the utilisation by Engels of Marx's notes on Morgan, which will be discussed in their own right in the next chapter, showing some divergences between the two men.

131   The only exceptions are some excerpts of testimonia from Aristotle and Diogenes Laërtius on the ontology of the ancient atomists in a section of notes on the history of science, Engels 1987a, pp. 470–1, which as noted by the editors are in Marx's handwriting, Engels 1987a, n. 208, p. 672.

132   Cited in Kline 1952, n. 1, p. 15.

133   Engels 1987b, pp. 21, 593.

134   Engels 1987b, p. 131. In chapter four of his book on the relation of Spinozism to Hegel's philosophy, Macherey points out how the emphasis on this phrase derives more from Hegel than from Spinoza himself, who used it in a letter to merely to clarify a point made by his correspondent, Macherey 2011, pp. 127–29; Spinoza 2016, p. 407.

materialists, for 'explaining the world from the world itself'.[135] This reference
to Spinozist *causa sui* recurs later in the book, where it is related to the Hegelian notion of reciprocal action (German: *Wechselwirkung*):

> *Reciprocal action* is the first thing that we encounter when we consider
> matter in motion from the standpoint of modern natural science.* We
> see a series of forms of motion, mechanical motion, heat, light, electri-
> city, magnetism, chemical compound and decomposition, transition of
> states of aggregation, organic life, all of which, if *at present* we *still* make
> an exception of organic life, pass into one another, are in one place cause
> and in another effect, the sum-total of the motion in all its changing forms
> remaining the same. Mechanical motion becomes transformed into heat,
> electricity, magnetism, light, etc., and vice versa. Thus natural science
> confirms what Hegel has said (where?), that reciprocal action is the true
> *causa finalis* of things.
>
> *(Spinoza: substance is *causa sui* strikingly expresses the reciprocal ac-
> tion.) [Marginal note.][136]

Here we see, then, that Spinozist notions are consistently related to the dialectical perspective of nature as an interconnected whole in the late Engels.
However, from the contemporary viewpoint of aleatory materialism this adaptation of Spinoza is problematic. The most significant and sustained analysis of
the late work of Engels from an aleatory perspective is by Morfino. He stresses
that a degree of teleonomy can be detected in his version of dialectical materialism, of a purposefulness to developmental processes, and asks how this is
possible given the apparently significant influence of Spinoza.[137] At the core
of his argument is precisely the juxtaposition of Spinoza's *causa sui* and the
reciprocal action or *Wechselwirkung* of Hegel apparent in the passage from
the *Dialectics of Nature* cited above. Superficially alike, in the sense that both
thinkers emphasise the interconnectedness of things from a universal perspective, Hegel's notion is radically different from the Spinozist whole as a
series of transformations of singular things without beginning or end, as outlined in Chapter 1.

---

135   Engels 1987a, p. 323.
136   Engels 1987a, pp. 511–12, emphasis in the original.
137   Morfino 2014b, pp. 18–22. Recall here also from chapter one the Soviet debate between the
      'mechanists' and Deborin and his followers on Spinoza, in which the recently published
      Dialectics of nature played a significant role.

Instead, Morfino argues that the Hegelian *Wechselwirkung* is marked by what he terms a 'principle of interiority', which turns substance into a subject, one that captures temporality in the diachronic unfolding of its synchronic foundations.[138] In the work of Hegel this was the *Bildungsroman* of Spirit, which in Engels is inverted, resting now on materialist rather than idealist foundations. In place of Spirit, we now have the evolution of worlds, from inorganic matter to life and its highest expression in thinking beings, who are able to leap from the realm of necessity to that of freedom and the mastery of nature.[139] Somehow this sequence of development seems to be inherent in nature. In a passage of the *Dialectics of Nature*, Engels discusses a grand cycle in what seems to be a Spinozist (and Epicurean vein), as a constant process of the emergence and dissolution of a variety of forms. Yet within this process there lurks an inner 'iron necessity' that in fact shepherds the processes of development into a certain direction.

This can be readily grasped from his discussion of the dissolution of the solar system, positing the question whether its remains will become the basis for new processes of development. And though we cannot predict this in exact terms, the very fact of the existence of solar systems seems to imply that this should come about, given enough time:

> We know just as little as Father Secchi knows whether the *caput mortuum* of our solar system will once again be converted into the raw material of new solar systems. But here either we must have recourse to a creator, or we are forced to the conclusion that the incandescent raw material for the solar systems of our universe was produced in a natural way by transformations of motion which are *by nature inherent* in moving matter, and the conditions for which, therefore, must also be reproduced by matter, even if only after millions and millions of years and more or less by chance, but with the necessity that is also inherent in chance.[140]

---

138 Morfino 2014b, pp. 37–9.

139 See especially the outline of development from cosmogony to humankind in Engels 1987a, pp. 327–33, which recalls the *historia peri phuseos* accounts discussed in Chapter 2, with Engels explicitly referring to his Greek predecessors at the beginning. For the leap to freedom, see the comments of Morfino 2014b, pp. 40–3.

140 Engels 1987a, p. 333, emphasis in the original. Here we can recall Althusser's comment in his correspondence with Fernanda Navarro on how in Engels matter 'stands in for ultimate reason', movement being one of its attributes, a parallel to the idealist principle of reason formulated by Leibniz, Althusser 2006, p. 217.

This passage illustrates exactly the teleonomic perspective of Engels, which, attributes a purposefulness to development, if of course one without any kind of divine intervention. The pinnacle of that process are thinking beings, even if like all other things they are eventually destined to perish.[141] No matter, for the process will simply start anew and will, given time, result in another species of thinking beings on another world 'with the same iron necessity'.[142] In effect, we have here in Engels an unfolding of a developmental process from simple to complex, dependent to some degree on chance interplay, but in the end governed by a necessity inherent in the process. As such his work demonstrates how the principle of interiority of reciprocal action or *Wechselwirkung* achieves a similar *Bildungsroman* narrative, if with a different subject than Hegel's. As Morfino has argued, however, this perspective needs to be distinguished from Spinoza,[143] in the following ways:

1. Spinoza distinguished between cause as *causa sui* and *effectus sui*. The former is immanent and infinite, belonging to substance, while the latter is transitive and finite, belonging to specific modes. Each cause is necessary as grasped through the *causa sui* of substance, yet at the same time contingent as understood through its specific mode (as *effectus sui*).

2. Substance exists only 'as the necessity of modal contingency, or as the infinity of necessary relations which maintain between them the contingent existences'.[144] There is no prefigured ontology here in the sense of a hierarchical ordering of categories, according to which thinking beings are ranked above simple organisms, who in turn outrank lifeless things, and so on. Instead in Spinoza there are infinite variations, of the kinds that were discussed in Chapter 1 with regard to singular things.

3. Substance is not a totality in the sense that it has existence as a subject, lacking any kind of interiority. Its eternity lies not in the unfolding of a succession of modes, but rather captures the conditions for the infinite variety of contingent modes. Its attributes of thought and extension are beyond duration, and cannot be understood as pertaining upon a ranked ordering in an evolutionary sense.

4. Hence the Spinozist totality differs from that of Engels in being a space of encounters and clashes between an infinite variety of singular things

---

141 In this regard the remarkable text *Cosmology of Spirit* by Ilyenkov mentioned in Chapter 1 should be recalled, developing these ideas of Engels much further and positing the role of thinking beings as a cosmological force in the Engelsian cosmic cycle, Ilyenkov 2017.

142 Engels 1987a, p. 335.

143 Morfino 2014b, pp. 29–31, 44.

144 Morfino 2014b, p. 30.

and their powers. There is no generic conception of a negation of the negation here that would add form to each particular thing.[145] Furthermore, Spinozism lacks any inherent 'iron necessity' like the one that rules the Engelsian cycle from cosmogony to civilisation.

The implications of these differences between the Spinozist *causa sui* and the Hegelian reciprocal action or *Wechselwirkung* will become further apparent when considering the work of Engels from the perspective of the theses of the aleatory current. As outlined in chapter one, these were the theses of trans-individuality, of the primacy of the encounter over form, and of plural temporality. Starting with the thesis of trans-individuality, it can first of all be noted that for strict parallelism of the attributes of thought and extension the ideas of Engels on this are quite different. As we saw, rather than existing side by side they were expressed in terms of an unfolding from simple matter to complex, sentient beings, in which, as he puts it, 'nature attains consciousness of itself'.[146] This observation has important implications for the conception of the relation of humankind and nature in Engels. From an aleatory perspective this relation should be grasped as a dynamic metabolism rather than a set of essentialist characteristics, as a potentiality that can be actualised in history in one way or another rather than in a prefigured way.

Surveying the, often unfinished, sections of the *Dialectics of Nature*, it is possible to grasp the connection between these aspects of the thesis of trans-individuality in Engels. In his account of the grand cycle of the generation and dissolution of worlds, he had traced the various steps toward the development of thinking beings as dialectical leaps. Each of these leaps stands in a certain proportion to the others,[147] reflecting the overall unfolding process. The dialectical leap of interest here is that of the emergence of humankind, anthropogony, for which the notes and remarks on evolution are of interest too. Engels viewed evolution through the lens not just of Darwin but also through the work of Ernst Haeckel. He was broadly supportive of the work of both scientists, while at the same time offering qualifications and criticisms as well.[148] Engels extols espe-

---

145 It is precisely here that the Hegelian influenced misinterpretation of Spinoza rears its head, for in Engels the negation of the negation becomes something that is present in all phenomena (and consequently reflected in our knowledge of them), even if the particulars of each thing differ: 'the kind of negation is here determined, firstly, by the general and, secondly, by the particular nature of the process', Engels 1987b, p. 131. In Spinoza this general form is absent.

146 Engels 1987a, p. 330.

147 Engels 1987a, pp. 548–9.

148 Haeckel is used mostly for his work showing the morphological sequences of life forms, in a mutual determination of form and function, resulting in a stadialist conception of

cially Darwin, as his theory for him provides the practical evidence for 'Hegel's account of the inner connection between necessity and chance'.[149]

That is, Darwin showed how the rigid distinction between chance and necessity that lay behind the rigid qualification of species into fixed categories was in fact a metaphysical mirage, an arbitrary human construction.[150] Furthermore, Engels appears to recognise in more aleatory terms how each leap at the same time has the result of 'fixing *one-sided* evolution, and excluding the possibility of evolution in many other directions'.[151] Yet in the end the unfolding sequence of evolutionary steps follows an inner logic quite distinct from the theses of the aleatory current. This can be readily grasped when we consider the leap to thinking beings. Engels points out how the nervous system in the vertebrates has brought about the possibility of the emergence of self-consciousness, a Hegelian concept that he sees in strongly Hegelian terms as inhering in the evolutionary process:

> When Hegel makes the transition from life to cognition by means of propagation (reproduction), there is to be found in this the germ of the theory of evolution, that, organic life once given, it must evolve by the development of the generations to a genus of thinking beings.
>
> What Hegel calls reciprocal action is the *organic* body, which, therefore, also forms the transition to consciousness, i.e., from necessity to freedom, to the idea (see *Logik*, II, conclusion).[152]

Even so, Engels does not sharply distinguish between the so-called higher animals and humankind itself in terms of basic forms of cognition, such as induction, deduction, abstraction, synthesis, experimentation, save for dialectics, which only occurs at a higher state of development of social life.[153] Humans are rather distinct in their ability to produce, and by the complex

---

the phases of biological development, but the philosophical bases of his work are more questionable, Engels 1987a, pp. 489–90, 579–82. The critique of Darwin centres mostly on the juxtaposition of natural selection and the survival of the fittest, pointing out that Malthusian population pressure is often not necessarily involved in evolutionary changes and that the struggle for existence is not applicable to social life, given the distinction of human beings as producing animals, Engels 1987a, pp. 582–5.

149   Engels 1987a, p. 582.
150   Engels 1987a, p. 501.
151   Engels 1987a, p. 583, emphasis in the original.
152   Engels 1987a, p. 585, emphasis in the original.
153   Engels 1987a, p. 503.

social forms that come with this, both of which exist only in a rudimentary ways in the animal kingdom.[154] The fact that they produce entails not just a more developed form of social life, but also, with time, a mastery of nature and knowledge of natural laws.[155] All of this implies that the laws governing human history are distinct from those of animal evolution, which makes the transition from the latter to the former, that is, anthropogony, all the more important. From the perspective of the aleatory current, the distinction between animal and human history can be captured by the notion of tendential laws specific to both, without any directional impulse.

To settle the question, the account of anthropogony in Engels is of great importance, and at first sight seems inconclusive in this regard. In the magisterial if incomplete fragment on the transition from ape to human in the *Dialectics of Nature*, Engels follows Darwin in locating it on a continent that has now been lost to the oceans.[156] Furthermore, it depends on what seems to be a chance event, the shift to an erect posture and the consequent differentiation of hands and feet, even if present in a latent form in ape species as well. This alteration in turn set off a cascade of further changes, not just bodily and in the newfound ability to handle tools with greater dexterity (allowing for labour properly), but also in new forms of sociality and language:

> On the other hand, the development of labour **necessarily** helped to bring the members of society closer together by increasing cases of mutual support and joint activity, and by making clear the advantage of this joint activity to each individual. In short, men in the making arrived at the point where *they had something to say* to each other. **Necessity** created the organ; the undeveloped larynx of the ape was slowly but surely transformed by modulation to produce constantly more developed modulation, and the organs of the mouth gradually learned to pronounce one articulate sound after another.[157]

These elements of biology, social life, technology, now mutually reinforced each other (by necessity), leading to the further development of the brain, to the use of fire, to the domestication of animals, as well as other inventions and new forms of social life.[158] Hence while it would be possible to view the initial

---

154   Engels 1987a, pp. 584–6.
155   Engels 1987a, pp. 330–1.
156   Engels 1987a, p. 452.
157   Engels 1987a, pp. 454–5, emphasis in bold added.
158   Engels 1987a, pp. 457–8.

shift to an erect posture and the consequent elaboration of the hand in aleatory terms, the process that follows hardly can be seen along the lines of a tendential law. For the different elements of technology, biology, and language do not just interact, they mutually reinforce each other in a way more suggestive of a singular, teleonomic process. A process that seems to have an interior logic of its own, as when phenomena such as language develop from the necessity inherent in it. The human mastery over nature, and the knowledge of natural laws that results from it, is the driving force of this process, and at the same time sets it apart from the animal kingdom (conceived as the leap to freedom).

Hence human history has a certain autonomy, even 'agency', relative to nature, even if, as Engels emphasises, human control over nature can be fleeting and short-sighted actions often result in unintended, disastrous results.[159] In broader terms, as the human relation to nature is one of mastery rather than of adaptation, Engels completely lacks the notion of learning from nature so central to the accounts of early humans in Lucretius and Morgan. Nor does he follow the Epicureans in their focus on conventionalism as the basis for a fear of death, and consequently greed and religious fear. Instead, he sees a shift to idealism and valuing of mind over 'hand' as the result of class society:

> Law and politics arose, and with them that fantastic reflection of human things in the human mind – religion. In the face of all these images, which appeared in the first place to be products of the mind and seemed to dominate human societies, the more modest productions of the working hand retreated into the background, the more so since the mind that planned the labour was able, at a very early stage in the development of society (for example, already in the primitive family), to have the labour that had been planned carried out by other hands than its own. All merit for the swift advance of civilisation was ascribed to the mind, to the development and activity of the brain.[160]

It is precisely this development of the process of the reversal of the primacy of the hand over the mind that for Engels has led to the dominance of idealism. Here we can observe that the conception of the human relation to nature, as well as the relation of convention to nature, follows a different track in Engels compared to Lucretius and Morgan. It is not so much that Engels posits a metaphysical original state, of the emergence of beings with fixed, essential

---

159   Engels 1987a, pp. 460–2.
160   Engels 1987a, pp. 458–9.

characteristics. Yet his focus on the logic of the overall process that sets him apart from the thesis of trans-individuality of the aleatory current. It is the teleonomy inherent in development of humankind that is emphasised, rather than the potentiality of early humans evident in the thinkers of the aleatory current and in Morgan as well. For all its subtlety, his account would never have been able to grasp the great variation of hominids now being discovered by archaeologists around the world, which fit the aleatory conception of evolution and history far better.[161]

Turning now from the thesis of trans-individuality to that of the primacy of the encounter over the form, the adaptation of Morgan's work by Engels comes to the fore. As noted, in his book Engels took over Morgan's entire stadialist framework. Some important aspects were modified or added to, for example the role of male jealousy in ape and early human sociality,[162] the relation between animal domestication and property,[163] and the formation of national states in post-Roman Europe,[164] among others. Beyond these modifications a more fundamental question lurks in the background as well. For Morgan's stadialism is mostly a factual division of history according to his own, mostly empirical, criteria, his causal explanations lacking by and large any shade of teleonomy. For Engels, of course, the principle of reciprocal action of *Wechselwirkung* was important for grasping any kind of series, including of social forms. As Morfino has shown it was applied by him explicitly when discussing the interaction between different elements of the mode of production, a topic that will be further discussed below.

In his adaptation of Morgan, Engels never uses reciprocal action explicitly in the text, yet its role is evident in the crucial sections. In fact the notion of reciprocal action can illuminate a passage from the work where Engels comments on Morgan's observation that systems of consanguinity often change more slowly relative to other aspects of social life, such as the forms of the family:

And, adds Marx, 'the same applies to political juridical, religious and philosophical systems generally'. While the family continues to live, the system of consanguinity becomes ossified, and while this latter continues to exist in the customary form, the family outgrows it. However, just as

---

161 See in this regard Gamble 2013, where a complex and multi-layered overview of the 'deep history' of humankind is provided, tracing the different hominid species, and the changing geographical and climatological conditions.

162 Engels 1990a, pp. 144–7.

163 Engels 1990a, pp. 162–6.

164 Engels 1990a, pp. 253–6.

Cuvier could with certainty conclude, from the pouch bones of an animal skeleton found near Paris, that this belonged to a marsupial and that now extinct marsupials had once lived there, so we, with the same certainty, can conclude, from a historically transmitted system of consanguinity, that an extinct form of the family corresponding to it did once exist.[165]

Note here that separated from their original form, these systems of consanguinity become merely customary and 'ossified', losing their historical efficacy relative to the new form of the family. Yet their presence demands some earlier form of the family that corresponded to it at an earlier stage of development, based on the causal connection between systems of consanguinity and forms of the family. It should be emphasised that despite the analogy with animal fossils, we do not have here in Engels a kind of organicist perspective. Rather a mutual determination of elements results from reciprocal action or *Wechselwirkung*.[166] Further exemplifications of this can be found in the treatment of Morgan's major historical shifts, first of the emergence of fissures within the gentile system, and then the transition to the state and class society. To both these questions Engels added his own insights, especially focusing on the role of property in bringing about these changes.

One important shift emphasised by Engels was that from group marriage to the so-called pairing form of matrimony, which, if not truly monogamous, severely limited the earlier promiscuity.[167] Each of these corresponded to a particular phase of development, respectively Morgan's statuses of upper savagery and lower barbarism, and they signal a shift from Darwinian natural selection to social factors in determining the forms of the family.[168] One of these social factors, the primary one in fact, is property. Engels outlines how

---

165   Engels 1990a, p. 141. The comment is on a passage from Morgan where he notes that systems of consanguinity are more conservative (passive), and change form only when the form of the family that originally corresponded to them has changed radically as well, see Morgan 1964, pp. 367–8.

166   The commentary by Krader has stressed the organicism in Morgan and connected it to Engels in order to contrast both to Marx, who was more reserved about Cuvier and did not subscribe to any kind of organicism, Krader 1975, n. 19, p. 364. To be fair to Engels, his notion of coherence does not depend on organicism as such, which even for Morgan was not more than an analogy, but rather follows from his conception of dialectics as the science of interconnections, which hold true as much for any living being as for the different forms of social life. See Chapter 5 for Marx's views.

167   The pairing family is the first development after the dissolution of group marriage, with the bond between the two spouses being based on the enduring consent of both, and residing in larger social groups, Morgan 1964, p. 326.

168   Engels 1990a, p. 162.

in the Old World domestication allowed for the mobilisation of surplus from labour through animals, textiles, metals, and agriculture.[169] One result was that, as Engels saw it, this property accumulated in the hands of males, who were unable to pass it on to their children because of the inheritance rules along the female line in the gentile system.[170] Instead of being passed on the children, property was inherited within the gens kin group. As more property accumulated in male hands, so did the pressure increase to change inheritance rules. Eventually this led to a shift from mother to father right, enabling inheritance by one's children, which Engels described famously as 'the world-historical defeat of the female sex'.[171]

The growth of the productive forces and consequently also of property, and the shift from mother to father right that enabled its accumulation over the generations, were mutually reinforcing.[172] Like Morgan, Engels argued that this shift created fissures in the gentile plan of government, which would eventually lead to its overthrow and replacement by the state. Another similarity with Morgan is that Engels, too, saw the Athenian state of the Classical era as an exemplary case, owing to its autonomous development free from outside influences.[173] Engels described the situation in Greece in the status of upper barbarism along similar lines as Morgan in *Ancient Society*, as a military democracy, with field agriculture and towns, inheritance in the male line and a growth of property.[174] He adds to this an emphasis on class and commodity exchange

---

169 Engels 1990a, pp. 162–3. Apart from a chapter on the Iroquois, Engels completely ignored the chapters on the Aztecs from *Ancient Society*, nor is there any recognition of the developments in Mexico and Peru from other sources.

170 Of course there are quite a few cultural assumptions underlying this picture. For why should women not accumulate the new forms of property and pass it on to their daughters?

171 Engels 1990a, p. 165.

172 Before knowing of Morgan's work, Engels had already tried to account for the change from the ancient commune to the state in the *Anti-Dühring*. There he argued that where the commune had remained, it had turned into an obstacle of progress in the form of 'the cruellest form of the state, Oriental despotism, from India to Russia', Engels 1987b, p. 168. It was only through the coming of the slave-owning mode of production that a way out of this 'trap' was found.

173 Engels 1990a, p. 222. It was precisely on this point that twentieth-century Marxism would diverge most radically from nineteenth-century ideas, which side-lined ancient Greece from discussions of the initial formation of the state and class systems, viewing it as a second-generation and derivative case (from its Mycenaean Bronze Age antecedents), Lee 1985. See also Chapter 6 for the comparative concept of the urban revolution developed by Gordon Childe and others, which excludes the Greek and Roman cases to focus on their prehistoric predecessors.

174 Engels 1990a, p. 212.

that, while also present in Morgan, plays an important role in his understanding of the shift from the gentile system to the state,[175] which can be summarised in the following way:

1. Already during the status of upper barbarism, land could be private property, a basic form of exchange of cereals, olives, and wine existed, and prisoners of war were enslaved.

2. The exchange of goods and other factors led to the intermingling of populations, creating frictions within the gentile system. This led to a central administration and a legal code, which divided the people into classes based on occupation. These classes were the *geomoroi* (tillers of the land), *demiurgi* (artisans) and *eupatrides* (nobles), the last exercising control over the central administration and legal system.

3. After this, money emerged as a social power, transforming the products exchanged into commodities proper. Usury also appeared, the land of the *geomoroi* being mortgaged, forcing them in certain cases to sell their children or themselves into slavery.

By now the gentile system had been completely overthrown, and state institutions, military and civil, had emerged on a territorial basis. Within this new framework political battles were being waged by what now were no longer kinfolk but rather fellow citizens, revolving mainly around property. In Greece, the most important initial question concerned the protection of citizens from usury.[176] The laws instituted against this led to further political equality between them in democratic institutions, while at the same time the use of foreign slaves greatly expanded. Extrapolating from this to the subsequent trajectory of states, Engels argued that their main function was the maintenance of private property, and that even revolutions merely supplanted one form for another:

> Solon – the manner in which his reform of 594 B.C. was carried out does not concern us here – started the series of so-called political revolutions by an encroachment on property. All revolutions to date have been revolutions for the protection of one kind of property against another kind of property. They cannot protect one kind without violating the other. In the Great French Revolution feudal property was sacrificed in order to save bourgeois property; in Solon's revolution, creditors' property had to suffer for the benefit of debtors' property. The debts were simply annulled. We

---

175   Engels 1990a, pp. 213–15.
176   Engels 1990a, pp. 219–22.

are not acquainted with the exact details, but Solon boasts in his poems that he removed the mortgage posts from the encumbered lands and enabled all who had been sold or fled abroad because of debt to return home.[177]

As noted, the Athenian case was exemplary for Engels, providing a well-documented direct transition from the gentile system to a political constitution. In other chapters other cases are treated as well. That of ancient Rome provides a close parallel to that of Greece, while state formation in post-Roman Germanic Europe was a subject that Engels had studied independent from Morgan.[178] The latter case was quite distinct, in that the gentile system of the Germans had either been incorporated into Roman state structures, whereas the unconquered tribes later fused with the remnants of the Roman system when they crossed the *limes* border and conquered Roman territories.[179] In the latter instance, the military democracies of upper barbarism status encountered the established, if decayed, Roman civilisation, resulting in a new system: feudalism. In that sense, it can be seen as a variant of the revolutions discussed above, a reorganisation of power and property not from internal strife but rather through conquest from the outside.

In more directly Marxist terms, we can see in this European trajectory the initial emergence of a slave-owning mode of production, as embodied in the Greco-Roman states. The Roman one later gave way to the feudal mode of production, with the fusion of the remnants of its civilisation with the conquering Germanic tribes. The question is whether this sequence should be understood in an aleatory way, or whether it unfolds in the same teleonomic way as biological evolution and anthropogony. Here it is important to remember Morfino's observation that Engels repeatedly used the notion of reciprocal action or *Wechselwirkung* in his correspondence when discussing the concept of the mode of production.[180] A common theme in these letters is the recognition of the historical efficacy of many different kinds of social phenomena, as mutually determining each other, and often in aleatory ways. Yet among these, the economic factor in the end always asserts itself as a necessity, through the good offices of *Wechselwirkung*.

This understanding of the relations between chance and necessity, as well as between matter and thought, can be seen very well in a letter to Bloch of

---

177   Engels 1990a, p. 218.
178   See his *Manuscript on early German history*, Engels 1990b.
179   Engels 1990a, pp. 247–55.
180   Morfino 2014b, n. 76, pp. 41–2.

September 1890. This letter is significant not only for its discussion of *Wechselwirkung* between the political and ideological aspects of the class struggle and the 'economic trend', which in the end (inevitably) always asserts itself as the most important factor among the different determinants.[181] Another aspect discussed here is that of the relation between individual agency and structural forces of the base and superstructure. Here Engels discusses how, in the final analysis, the economic factor asserts itself through *Wechselwirkung*, individual actions combining in 'an infinite series of parallelograms of forces' that result in a specific historical event.[182] In this regard, Engels points to Marx's historical writings as an example of this interplay between agency and structure, most notably the *18th Brumaire*.

Although the term *Wechselwirkung* is not used explicitly in his adaptation of Morgan's work, its role is evident in a passage where he discusses the shift from direct production to commodity exchange. Even if in the chaos and uncertainty of marketplace exchange this new form seems to be beyond human control and lack rationality, as a historical force it has a strong logic of its own:

> But chance is only one pole of an interrelation, the other pole of which is called necessity. In nature, where chance, too, seems to reign, we have long since demonstrated in each particular field the inherent necessity and regularity that asserts itself in this chance. What is true of nature holds good also for society. The more a social activity, a series of social processes, becomes too powerful for conscious human control, grows beyond human reach, the more it seems to have been left to pure chance, the more do its peculiar and innate laws assert themselves in this chance, as if by natural necessity.[183]

The implications of the above exposition of the ideas of Engels for his relation to the thesis of the primacy of the encounter over the form should be clear. Engels never posits a sequence of forms in a metaphysical sense, but at the same time chance is clearly subjected to the necessity of the overall process, unfolding according to a teleonomic conception of dialectical laws. This interpretation of Engels has immediate consequences for the thesis of plural tem-

---

181   Engels 2001, pp. 34–5.

182   Engels 2001, pp. 35–6. The notion of a parallelogram of forces can be seen in the *Anti-Dühring* and the *Dialectics of Nature* as well, including for the dialectical conception of force as such, in a discussion of Newton's conception of gravity, and in a discussion of Dühring's conception of freedom, Engels 1987a, pp. 105; Engels 1987b, pp. 551–2, 559.

183   Engels 1990a, p. 273.

porality, as well as for the accompanying thesis of the plurality of worlds. His outline of Morgan's stages of development resembles the Hegelian 'essential section' of Althusser, the unfolding of a subject through discrete temporal units where all parts are expressions of the whole. The dialectical leaps of Engels closely parallel this notion, for theoretical reasons that, as we saw, Morfino had clarified with reference to the concept of reciprocal action or *Wechselwirkung*.

Plural temporality, then, is either absent or superfluous in Engels.[184] Instead, there exists a close correspondence between different phenomena and the stage of development to which they are assigned.[185] A good example of this is the state, which for Engels corresponds and is the necessary result of a certain level of economic development, but just as surely will become an obsolete, dusty museum piece after the transition to communism.[186] The way in which Engels furthermore views the pathway to communism is further proof that, as with the denial of plural temporality, there is little scope for alternative forms of civilisation, and hence the plurality of worlds. On the contrary, as he puts it in the *Anti-Dühring*, the entire trajectory from the dissolution of the ancient commune to modern socialism is marked by one thing necessarily leading to another:

> *Slavery* had been invented. It soon became the dominant form of production among all peoples who were developing beyond the old community, but in the end was also one of the chief causes of their decay. It was slavery that first made possible the division of labour between agriculture and industry on a larger scale, and thereby also Hellenism, the flowering of the ancient world. Without slavery, no Greek state, no Greek art and science; without slavery, no Roman Empire. But without the basis laid by Hellenism and the Roman Empire, also no modern Europe. We should never forget that our whole economic, political and intellectual development presupposes a state of things in which slavery was as necessary as it was universally recognised. In this sense we are entitled to say: Without the slavery of antiquity no modern socialism.[187]

---

184   Superfluous in the sense of the passage from the adaptation of Morgan cited above, where Engels notes how ossified systems of consanguinity no longer correspond to an actual form of the family. Thus these systems of consanguinity have not just lost their historical efficacy, but in being 'ossified' are placed outside historical temporality as well.

185   In a letter to Bernstein, this applies even to political action, commenting on the futility of the action in the face of the overall trend of development by noting 'as though we or any party in the world could prevent a country from passing through its historically necessary stages of development', Engels 1992a, p. 333.

186   Engels 1990a, p. 272.

187   Engels 1987b, p. 168, emphasis in the original. Engels here seems to follow an 'each accord-

Continuing his argument, Engels discounts any indignation that may be felt with regard to ancient slavery, pointing out that such sentiments prove nothing more than that this institution no longer corresponds with the conditions prevailing today. Indeed, in a remarkable *Wechselwirkung* of the emotive and objective, contemporary indignation simply reflects contemporary conditions, thereby losing its validity relative to the broader progressive vision of Engels himself. This passage from the *Anti-Dühring* can be related to Morfino's argument on how the conception of violence in Engels mirrored the Hegelian view of force as epiphenomenal to the series of dialectical transformations.[188] Instead, he notes how from an aleatory perspective the multiplicity of different forms of violence comes to the foreground, all involving physical and mental pain, as they can be traced in the history of primitive accumulation.[189] From this viewpoint, indeed, the suffering of the slaves of classical antiquity can also be grasped on its own terms, rather than as mere markers on the path towards the dialectical leap to freedom and mastery over nature.

4   Comparing Morgan and Engels

What once may have seemed a rather straightforward adaptation, if with significant modifications, of Morgan's stadialism by Engels, becomes considerably more complex when viewed from the perspective of the aleatory current in philosophy. To begin with, both men had distinct intellectual backgrounds, which shaped their work in decisive ways. Morgan's scientific outlook was balanced by his fondness of the classics, with Lucretius and Horace being especially important for inspiring his views on early humankind. Engels shared with Morgan an interest in science, yet he was shaped neither by scientific experimentalism or fieldwork, nor by the classical past, but rather by a revolutionary philosophical stance that was both Hegelian and materialist. Although he made allusions to Spinozist influences, the analysis of the previous section aimed to show that these were tinged by Hegelianism, and in their use far from the Spinoza of Althusser and Macherey as discussed in Chapter 1. It demonstrates the need to take care when using the term materialism, given the danger of it becoming an 'inverted idealism'.

---

ing to their stage of development' form of reasoning, arguing that the slaves were better off than in the previous era, where instead they were killed 'or even roasted', Engels 1987b, pp. 168–9.

188   Morfino 2014b, pp. 123–6.

189   As part of a broader set of processes involving violence, see Chapter 5 for an aleatory take on Marx's account of primitive accumulation in volume I of *Capital*.

TABLE 4.2 Outline of Morgan and Engels from the perspective of the aleatory current in philosophy

Morgan	Engels
Thesis of trans-individuality	
The body and mind exist as co-occurring dynamic vortices relative to the environment (metabolism). Mind as a principle is posited separate from the body.	Physical changes in the process of anthropogony, starting with the hand, led to a cascade of changes due to the *Wechselwirkung* between elements. These included the emergence of human consciousness and language.
Mind is arranged on a universal scale from simple to complex (despite earlier appreciations of diversity).	In the outline from simple matter to human consciousness, the emergence of the latter is held to be a necessary result from the inherent unfolding from simple to more complex forms (teleonomy in development).
Language is a distinguishing factor between humans and animals, it makes possible cumulative development.	The development of human social life is subject to its own specific laws, distinct from those of the animal kingdom. Qualified view of human mastery over nature.
Biological inheritance of specific characteristics in races. Contradictory statements on relation brain size and development: a) notional impact diet meat and milk on Eurasian brain size, b) Iroquois brain size estimated as similarly sized despite lacking this diet (hunting state).	Engels adopts Morgan's views on the relation between the meat and milk diet in Eurasia and brain size.
Development along the parallel tracks of inventions and discoveries on the one hand, institutions on the other. More *ad hoc* view of their interconnections.	The superstructural aspects have to be traced back to their material base.
Thesis of the primacy of the encounter over the form	
Universal stages of development that group together a specific set of inventions, discoveries, and institutions, without a necessary coherence to them.	Engels modifies Morgan's stages by positing a close correspondence between elements, in line with his views on the base and superstructure in the mode of production.

TABLE 4.2   Outline of Morgan and Engels from the perspective of the aleatory current (*cont.*)

Morgan	Engels
There is no prefiguration of the *civitas* plan of government in the preceding *societas* form. Classes and class struggle over property are the result of this radical shift.	Elements later forms prefigured in earlier ones. Examples are classes before the state and the equalisation of the rate of profit in merchant exchange.
Complex chains of causality, with a role of the aleatory in either slowing down or speeding up development. Points here specifically to the role and timing of iron metallurgy relative to the transition to the stage of civilisation.	Despite having historical efficacy of their own, the superstructural aspects are determined in the last instance by the economic base.
	Individual agency is captured within parallelograms of forces. Through *Wechselwirkung* the different factors of the base and superstructure assert themselves within these interacting forces.
Thesis of plural temporality Different stages have different durations, but there is no interweaving of temporalities between them.	Specific correspondence between political forms such as the state and stages, becoming 'museum pieces' with further (economic) development.
Recognition of different characteristics of distinct world regions (Old and New Worlds), but only sees impact on the speed of development.	
Recurrence of the liberty, equality, and fraternity of ancient *societas* in a future form of communism.	Impact of teleonomic unfolding of history: ancient slavery seen as a necessity for future communism, conceived of as a dialectical leap from the realm of necessity to freedom.

Comparing the two authors, it is apparent that Morgan is closer to the aleatory current than Engels. With regard to the thesis of trans-individuality, we can see in Morgan the parallelism of matter and mind, without the teleonomy of Engels, where cosmogony eventually, yet necessarily, will result in thinking beings. Furthermore, the ancient atomists' notion of *phusiopoiei*, which describes how humans learn from nature and thereby make themselves, was paralleled in Morgan, and a more direct influence can be proven for the emergence of language. In Engels, by contrast, such a process of learning from nature is not evident, the emphasis rather being placed on mastering nature through production and thereby grasping its laws. The situation is similar with regard to the thesis of the primacy of the encounter over the form. Morgan's stadialism is empirical, in that later stages are not prefigured in what comes before, and the tempo of development can vary according to contingencies. While not based on a theory of the encounter, it is far removed from the Engelsian unfolding of stages as ultimately based on the necessities of economic development.

Even if Morgan is closer to the aleatory current, this does not mean that he actually belongs to it. His conception of a universal scale of mind presumes in turn a uniform path of development from simple to complex, even if, unlike in Engels, there is no necessity inherent in traversing the path. Hence there is very little scope for pluralism in Morgan's outline of history, as it moves through stages that are the same in content the world over, excepting some idiosyncrasies that speed up or slow down movement. This view shines through most clearly in Morgan's evaluation of the indigenous civilisations of the Americas, which he denies this status and reinterprets as advanced forms of a gentile rather than a political plan of government. Thus, Morgan was closer to De Pauw, Robertson, and Adam Smith in emphasising the historical priority of Europe relative to America, even if his perspective was informed more by sympathy and science than by prejudice.

Like Smith, too, Morgan saw the seeking of riches as a powerful driving force of development, of turning the forests into the cultivated fields necessary to sustain civilisation. However, Morgan did not extol selfish actions as bringing public benefits, as Smith did. Rather, owing to his democratic impulses, he viewed property as something to be superseded. The universality of Morgan's stages would have appealed to Engels, given his emphasis on the unfolding of history based on the *logos* of economic necessity and the consequent obscuration of pluralism. In the work of Engels the empirical findings of Morgan are tied to his broader view of the dialectical laws of nature. As such, the adaptation of the stadialist scheme of savagery, barbarism, and civilisation by Engels conforms to what Althusser recognised for the teleological conception of the mode of production, where the constituent elements do not encounter each other but rather are predestined to cohere:

> On this hypothesis, each element has, not an independent history, but a history that pursues an end – that of adapting to the other histories, history constituting a whole which endlessly *reproduces* its own [*propre*] elements, so made as to [*propre à*] mesh. This explains why Marx and Engels conceive of the proletariat as a 'product of big industry', 'a product of capitalist exploitation', *confusing the production of the proletariat with its capitalist reproduction on an extended scale*, as if the capitalist mode of production pre-existed one of its essential elements, an expropriated labour-force. Here *the specific histories no longer float in history*, like so many atoms in the void, at the mercy of an 'encounter' that might not take place. Everything is accomplished in advance; *the structure precedes its elements and reproduces them in order to reproduce the structure.*[190]

While Althusser argued that Engels was the true progenitor of the teleological (or better: teleonomic) conception of the mode of production, he also saw it as coexisting with the opposing aleatory conception in distinct chapters of *Capital*.[191] However, the publication history of the works of Marx and Engels was such that initially the weight of the available writings heavily favoured the teleological conception. For the availability of Marx's works in the decades after his death was limited to volume I of *Capital*, the *Communist Manifesto*, the historical writings on the political struggles in France, as well as the second and third volumes of *Capital* that were heavily edited by Engels.[192] Supplementing them were the writings of Engels himself, although the *Dialectics of Nature* was not published until 1925 in the Soviet Union.[193] After the October Revolution, the Marx-Engels Institute there published many important works now crucial to understanding Marx properly, including the *German Ideology*, the so-called *Economic-Philosophical Manuscripts of 1844*, and the *Grundrisse*, including its extensive section on pre-capitalist social formations.[194]

While most of these works were published in the 1930s, it took longer for them to reach broader, global audiences, and still longer for the work of the reinterpretation of Marx to reach a new level of maturity, in the face of increas-

---

190   Althusser 2006, p. 200, emphasis in the original.
191   Althusser 2006, p. 197.
192   Hobsbawm 2011, p. 179.
193   Hobsbawm 2011, p. 187.
194   Hobsbawm 2011, pp. 185–6.

ingly adverse conditions for Marxism itself.[195] Even so, this shift should not be understood as a linear narrative of revision. As noted in Chapter 1, there were sophisticated debates on Spinoza in the 1920s and 1930s in the USSR, and in the next chapter we shall discuss similarly significant debates on history in the thaw period inaugurated by Khrushchev. Yet for most of the twentieth century the Engelsian model held sway, and with it Morgan's stadialist scheme.[196] In order to delineate the differences between the dominant teleological perspective and the newly emerging aleatory opposition, the best way to start is with Marx's own take on Morgan.

---

195   The crisis of Marxism in the 1980s was clearly foreshadowed in the works of Althusser from the 1970s discussed in Chapter 1. Paradoxically, this decade saw both the high-point of Marxist influence, but a hollow form of Marxism devoid of engagement with the sciences and reformist on the economic front, Hobsbawm 2011, pp. 373–4.

196   It held sway not in the sense that it was always, or even in most cases, literally adhered to, but in the sense that it set the terms for improvements, detractions, and the search for alternatives. As we shall see in Chapter 6, twentieth-century Marxist archaeology was the living proof of this, showing both the scholarly successes enabled by the legacy of Engels, as well as the clear limitations of his framework.

Marx and the Thesis of the Plurality of Worlds

Separate from the adaptation of Morgan's work by Engels, Marx's excerpts from and comments on *Ancient Society*, as well as on other works on similar topics, suggests a multilinear approach rather than the unilinealism of Morgan and Engels. This becomes clearer when these excerpts and comments are related to the broader body of writings of the late Marx, as well as to the volumes of *Capital* and the preparatory writings. In this way, an annotated version of Marx's take on Morgan can be created. This analysis can in turn serve as a way to not just understand Marx in his own terms, but also in contrast to Morgan and Engels. Indeed, by considering *Capital* and the preparatory writings it can be shown that Marx diverged more strongly from Engels and Morgan, most particularly for the theses of plural temporality and the pluralism of worlds. The contrast is particulary notable for Marx's take on the indigenous civilisations of the Americas, Peru in particular, which was closer to the pluralism of Montaigne than to the Eurocentrism of Locke and Smith.

Furthermore, the different takes on this issue can be directly related to Marx's view of metabolism and the relation between humans and nature, raising the question of theoretical distinctions between his views and those of Morgan and Engels. In order to grasp the background of these differences, it is useful to consider the methodological ideas of the late and mature Marx and, furthermore, to relate them to his initial philosophical studies. Of particular interest in this regard are the doctoral dissertation and notebooks on ancient atomism, which, if read from the perspective of the later Marx, can provide illuminating insights on the efficacy of his early engagement with Epicureanism. The resulting picture of both Marx's historical analyses and the trajectory of his theoretical ideas can in turn be related to the theses of the aleatory current as discussed in Chapter 1, also used to grasp Morgan and Engels in the previous chapter. In this way that can also serve as comparative terms between the ideas of the three thinkers on the early history of humankind.

1   Marx's Notebooks on Ancient Society and Their Significance

Marx's notes on Morgan were written in 1880–1 and first published in English in the early 1970s.[1] They have to be understood as part of a broader interest in

---

1   Krader's 1974 edition has besides the notes on Morgan also those on Maine and Phear, as well

pre-capitalist social formations and world history in the last phase of his life, as revealed by extensive notebooks on ethnographic, historical, and archaeological works.[2] For many of these books, Marx merely noted down what he held to be their most significant passages, but in some cases he also emphasised certain parts and provided comments of his own.[3] Most notable in this regard are the notebooks on Kovalevsky, on Morgan, Phear, and Maine, as well as those on Roman history, not yet published.[4] The meaning of Marx's emphases and comments deepens when we consider them in relation to his own writings, published and unpublished, in effect creating an annotated version of them. That these notebooks reflect a turn toward the world beyond Europe seems clear, given the sustained effort reflected in the extensive note-taking. Yet it would be too much to conceive this turn as a radical break, from a supposed Eurocentrism or otherwise. For Marx had already started taking an interest in similar works much earlier, as is evident from his London notebooks of 1850–3.[5]

In the main, Marx's excerpts from Morgan follow the outline of *Ancient Society*, which would reflect his broader interest in the historical relations between production, property, gender, and forms of social life. One significant feature is that Marx highlights Morgan's references to Lucretius on the earliest forms of human subsistence and the later expansion of cultivation into the forests,[6]

---

as extensive commentary by Krader himself, while the notes on Kovalevsky are collected in Harstick 1977. There are references to these notebooks earlier, e.g. Lucas 1964a and 1964b, and they were published as early as the 1920s in the Soviet Union, Krader 1974, p. 1. As such, these notes have played a role in discussions on early humankind there, Howe 1980, pp. 112–13, 161–62, which will be discussed further in the next chapter.

2　Anderson 2010 locates them in the broader context of Marx's writings on history outside Europe and on its margins.

3　These notes are useful in themselves to follow Marx's interests, to follow his lines of thought, Hobsbawm 2011, p. 189, but their use becomes much greater when they resonate with writings by Marx himself. One of the best examples of this are Marx's notebooks on atomist philosophy, which deepen considerably the understanding of his doctoral thesis on the differences between its Democritean and Epicurean variations, see below in this chapter.

4　These are scheduled to finally be all published together in the new MEGA series under the entry IV/29, see for a summary of their contents Anderson 2002.

5　See the summary of their contents in Pradella 2014, pp. 175–83, especially interesting are the notes on Prescott's histories of the conquest of Mexico and Peru, which will be discussed in more detail below. These growing recognition of the importance of these notebooks has given rise to stimulating new debates that question Eurocentrism in the earlier phases of Marx's writing, see for an overview of different positions Pradella 2011.

6　Marx in Krader 1974, pp. 99, 101, later in the notebook Marx criticises Morgan for not seeing fire as the main invention ('Hauptinvention!'), Marx in Krader 1974, p. 127. However, as we saw above, fire was in fact more important in Morgan's text on Lucretius and his tables outlining the sequences of institutions and discoveries, both unknown to Marx.

while he overlooks the extensive note on the initial development of language. However, in his critique of the work of Adolph Wagner, written around the same time as the notes on Morgan, the emergence of language crops up in the margins. Criticising Wagner's view of a generic theoretical relation of 'man' to the environment, Marx points out that it is not a question of theory but of practice: located within the social process of production.[7] He emphasises that the starting point of this relation lies in active behaviour to satisfy basic, animal needs, leading in turn to knowledge and concepts as results, rather than as original, theoretical axioms:

> By the repetition of this process the capacity of these things to "satisfy their needs" becomes imprinted on their brains; men, like animals, also learn 'theoretically' to distinguish the outer things which serve to satisfy their needs from all other. At a certain stage of evolution after their needs, and the activities by which they are satisfied, have, in the meanwhile, increased and further developed, they will linguistically christen entire classes of these things which they distinguished by experience from the rest of the outside world. This is bound to occur, as in the production process – i.e. the process of appropriating these things – they are continually engaged in active contact amongst themselves and with these things, and will soon also have to struggle against others for these things. But this linguistic label purely and simply expresses as a concept what repeated activity has turned into an experience, namely that certain outer things serve to satisfy the needs of human beings already living in certain social context //this being an essential prerequisite on account of the language//.[8]

The passage recalls the Epicurean *prolepseis*, the preconceptions in the mind and in language that are formed through repeated sensory encounters, and which we saw in Chapter 2 were crucial for understanding the human-nature relation in the atomism of Epicurus. Of course, this formulation occurs as part of a critique of Wagner's conception of political economy, rather than as an extensive account of early humankind or the relationship between humans and nature. Another glimpse is afforded by Marx's qualification of Morgan's notion of humans gaining a mastery over nature, adding to this phrase both

---

7 Marx 1989a, p. 538, having noted before the historical variation of production processes, pointing out how Wagner's view of the generalisation of capitalism is invalidated by the social production process of pre-capitalist communities such as the South Slavs, Marx 1989a, p. 535.
8 Marx 1989a, p. 539.

exclamation and question marks.[9] Together, these clues point to a rather different view of the human position in the animal kingdom and relative to inorganic nature than those of Morgan and Engels. To grasp this better, it is necessary to consider Marx's notion of metabolism, as put forward in volume I of *Capital*, which in a sense is derivative of the generic process described in the quotation from the notes on Wagner.[10]

At first sight Marx's conception of metabolism seems to follow the ancient atomist's notion of *phusiopoiei* closely, if in a distinctly modern way. Labour here acts as a natural force that mediates between humans and the material world around them, human beings with their organs of labour not just changing their environment but in the process themselves as well.[11] Furthermore, Marx adds to this the well-known distinction between animals making things and human constructions, given the presence of a purposeful plan in human labour:

> A spider conducts operations which resemble those of the weaver, and a bee would put many an architect to shame by the construction of its honeycomb shells. But what distinguishes the worst architect from the best of the bees is that the architect builds the cell in his mind before he constructs it in wax. At the end of every labour process, a result emerges which had already been conceived by the worker at the beginning, **hence already existed ideally.**[12]

Metabolism is a central concept in Marx's thinking and further complexities on it will be explored below. These include the role of geographical differences, the notion of commodity exchange and the division of labour as distinct forms of social metabolism, his conception of technology in general and machinery in specific, and the idea of communism in itself. Although similar to Morgan in the notion of a metabolism and to Engels in the distinction between humans and animals, Marx's views were considerably more complex in terms of the mutual determination of many factors that have to be considered. Furthermore, it should be recognised that traces of these ideas can be found in the early

---

9   Marx in Krader 1974, p. 94.

10   Although suggestive of a process of anthropogony, there are no extant writings on this matter in Marx, even if he did make voluminous excerpts, but with little additions of his own, from contemporary books on prehistory by Dawkins and Geikie, Anderson 2002, table 1, p. 91. See below for intimations on anthropogony in the work of the early Marx.

11   Marx 1976a, p. 283.

12   Marx 1976a, p. 284, emphasis added.

Marx as well. It is in fact possible to trace a complex trajectory that stretches back from the metabolism of *Capital* to the 'species-being' and the engagement with ancient atomism of the earliest Marx. At the end of this chapter, this trajectory will be addressed in detail, including its relation to materialist dialectics.

Whereas the human-nature relation is present in the notebooks only in a shadowy fashion, Marx's appreciation of historical pluralism shines through clearly and various divergences from Morgan and Engels can be noted. To start, the comment by Marx that the relations between systems of consanguinity and forms of the family also extend to political, religious, judicial, and philosophical systems, lacks the reference to Cuvier of Engels.[13] As such, Marx's conception lacks the teleonomic necessity that we saw connected distinct elements of social life, with the final determinant being production, just as it lacks what Krader has described as an analytical organicism in Morgan.[14] As with the human-nature relation, this aspect of the relation of different elements of social life reflects a broader set of ideas on Marx's part, and, as will be shown below, they are in fact closely connected with each other. However, for this aspect the differences with Morgan and Engels manifest themselves concretely, in various aspects of *Ancient Society* commented upon by Marx.

Marx made critical remarks on Morgan's outline of the development of the Greek (Athenian) state from the preceding 'heroic era', as well as providing further remarks on later political developments that are not present in Morgan. First of all, Marx made qualifications to Morgan's use of Homer, pointing out that the enclosed lands and fences mentioned in the *Iliad* by no means prove the existence of private property.[15] Marx shares with Morgan the critique of conceiving of the Homeric heroes, the *basileis*, along the lines of the absolute monarchies of early modern Europe. But unlike Morgan, and unlike Engels as well, he does not share their use of the notion of 'military democracy' as a well-defined stage of development, rather viewing it as a mere transitory, dynamic feature within the communal form. The emphasis on transition can also be seen as Marx highlighting the emergence of (conflicts of) interests within the social life of the communes, as the example of Theseus and the population of Attica shows.[16] The development of such interests is closely connected with the emergence of individuality.

---

13   Marx in Krader 1974, p. 112.
14   Krader 1974, pp. 48–9.
15   Marx in Krader 1974, pp. 134–5.
16   Marx in Krader 1974, p. 210, Krader emphasises the contrast between Marx's more complex view of individuality here and the more generic view of 'unadorned greed' as a driving

The notion of individuality has a special meaning in Marx, which is some-what distinct from ordinary usage in the sense that it does not primarily denote the purely subjective characteristics of distinct human beings. Rather, it is closely tied to objective factors such as interests, which are tied to member-ship of socio-economic classes.[17] In the notes on *Ancient Society*, however, Marx also explores another aspect of individuality, that which is not tied to class but rather to a specific form of the family in Morgan's evolutionary outline. With the emergence of the patriarchal family as a vehicle for holding property in land and livestock, in the upper state of barbarism, family members were reoriented into relations of servility and dependency to the pater familias, to which Marx adds: 'paternal power over the group; with a higher individuality of persons'.[18] Clearly, and here Marx follows Morgan closely, the 'moving power' of this devel-opment was the growth of property and the desire for the inheritance thereof by direct offspring.[19]

However, Marx in his comments paints a more complex picture of the pat-riarchal family than either Morgan or Engels. In Marx we can see not just the impact of property, but also of slavery. For in a comment on Morgan, he notes that the family had earlier been 'sheltered' in the communism-in-living of households composed of several related families, which broke up with the coming of slavery as a social institution (from which later sprang the domestic servants of the monogamian family).[20] Individuality, now constituted as rela-tions of dependency on paternal power, broke up the common personal bonds

---

    force in Engels, Krader 1973, pp. 253–6, fulfilling the function, as noted above, to combine the multiplicity of the parallelograms of individual wills into a coherent movement.

17   See especially also the account of the development of individuality in the section on pre-capitalist social formations in the *Grundrisse*, where this historical process is contrasted to the initial condition of the *Gattungswesen* living as a member of a herd without indi-viduality, Marx 1973, pp. 472, 496.

18   Marx in Krader 1974, p. 119. Krader has emphasised that Morgan saw the Aryan and Semitic patriarchal families as more exceptional in the overall development of forms of the fam-ily, as part of his overall anti-teleological perspective, Krader 1973, p. 251. Certainly, Krader is right that Engels simplified Morgan's scheme of the development of the family. On the other hand, even if the patriarchal family was exceptional in Morgan, what is important is that even if distinctive, it is so on the road to the monogamous form, which is intrinsic-ally connected to the stage of civilisation, and here there is little talk of exceptions, see for the distinction Morgan 1964, pp. 326, 426–7. More interestingly, Brown provides a read-ing of Marx's comments that highlights the historical pluralities of forms of the family, Brown 2012, pp. 157–8. He had already shown an interest in this question as the London notebooks show, Pradella 2014, pp. 113–14.

19   Marx in Krader 1974, p. 121.

20   Marx in Krader 1974, p. 120.

of the gens.[21] The newly emerged familial relations developed further from the patriarchal to the monogamian or 'modern' family, which already carries within it the major antagonisms of civil society and the state:

> *Fourier* charakterisirt Epoche der *Civilisation dch Monogamy u. Grund Privateigenthum*. D. moderne Familie enthält im Keim nicht nur *servitus* (Sklaverei) sondern auch *Leibeigenscft*, da sie von vorn herein Beziegh auf *Dienste für* Ackerbau. Sie enthält in *Miniatur* alle d. Antagonismen in sich, die sich später breit entwickeln in d. Gesellscft u. ihrem Staat.[22]

The wording 'in miniature' should not be taken here in the sense of a *pars totalis* argument, in the sense of implying an overarching principle reflected equally within the family as in slavery and serfdom, as well as the social formations connected to them. Rather it reflects the complex mutual determinations between these elements, without any pre-determined necessity. This reading can be recognised especially well in another context, where Marx comments on the notion that the way of life of pastoral peoples was forced on them by the specific characteristics of the animals they possessed: 'Dies vielleicht nicht Fall bei d. Celts'.[23] Further comments of Marx point to such complex mutual determinations. He cites Morgan's divergence with Maine in arguing against the notion that the patriarchal family formed the basis for the earliest forms of social life, instead it was the result of an evolutionary sequence of institutions, just as for technology.[24] In his notes on Maine, Marx repeats this criticism of the 'blockheaded Englishman',[25] adding to it that it prevents him from recognising

---

21 This process of separation is primarily stimulated by exchange, which dissolves all previous bonds, and the manic seeking of wealth it engenders now confronts each individual in
a purely subjective form, given their separation from the objective conditions (means of
production and subsistence), as their community (*Gemeinwesen*), Marx 1973, pp. 223, 496.
Or as Marx puts it in volume I of *Capital*, when discussing the power of money and the way
it leads to the seeming independence of the relations of production: 'Men are henceforth
related to each other in their social process of production in a purely atomistic way', Marx
1976a, p. 187.

22 Marx in Kader 1974, p. 120, emphasis in the original.

23 Marx in Krader 1974, p. 132. A more significant comment than it may appear as first
sight, as this qualification of economic necessity as enforcing a singular way of life is
precisely what breaks the 'bond of fate' and connects the thesis of the primacy of the
encounter over the form to the thesis of plural temporality (and that of the plurality of
worlds).

24 Marx in Krader 1974, pp. 126–7.

25 Marx in Krader 1974, p. 292.

how the rights of inheritance of women in India are not recent innovations but derive from the preceding *societas*.[26]

The idea that in some ways the greater valuation of women before the emergence of the patriarchal family survived is also emphasised by Marx, pointing to a multi-layered historical picture.[27] Furthermore, it is not a question so much of the mere survival of old elements, as an analysis of Marx's still unpublished notebooks on Roman history from 1879 shows.[28] The overall focus of these notebooks lies on the class conflicts between plebeians and patricians, as well as between these two groups on the one hand and slaves on the other, struggles that themselves are the result of the shift from a form of social life structured by the clan to one dominated by the state.[29] The last aspect was treated especially in the excerpts and comments on Lange, who like Maine made the mistake of positing separate families with property as predating the clan. As noted by Brown, Marx here was especially interested in the complex interactions between forms of the family, law (especially property rights), and class conflict, ultimately leading to the weakening of the patriarchal family:

> Marx's notes on Lange illustrate his interest in understanding the relationship of contradiction and conflict to historical change. Marx paid particular attention to how the conflict among patricians, plebeians and other groups contributed to the weakening of the patriarchical Roman family as the main unit of society, and the concomitant rise in the power of the state. This generally had positive effects on women's position in society, at least among the upper classes, since the men in the family and especially the paterfamilias lost some of their authority over all their relatives, including women. Women were therefore freed, at least to some extent, from some of the worst effects of patriarchical domination.[30]

Concerning this rise of the state, Marx did not provide significant comments on the topic in the notebooks on *Ancient Society*, mostly providing corrections

---

26 Marx in Krader 1974, pp. 308–9.
27 Marx's comment on the position of female goddesses on Olympus as indicating the survival of previously dominant ideas that exalted rather than denigrated femininity, points in this direction, Marx in Krader 1974, p. 121. Brown in her commentary emphasises the discordance between the barbaric treatment of women while Greek civilisation was at its height and the nostalgia for an earlier age of equality, Brown 2012, pp. 160–1.
28 These will be published in the second MEGA series in IV/29. Extensive use is made of these notebooks specifically for gender relation in Brown 2012, pp. 199–207.
29 See Anderson 2010, pp. ix–xi for a short summary of their contents.
30 Brown 2012, p. 207.

to the specific details of Morgan's analysis, as well as adding some material. The most significant addition is a brief discussion of the Athenian state after the reforms of Kleisthenes, which was not treated by Morgan.[31] Here Marx added that after the Persian Wars, the offices of the state were opened to all citizens, regardless of the size of their landholdings, through the law of Aristides. Trade and industry significantly increased in this period, and Marx pointed out that the reform of Aristides benefitted mainly a new class that did not reckon their wealth primarily in land, as its effect was the '*einseitige Bevorzugung d. ländlichen Grundbesitzer aufzuheben u. Gewerbtreibenden u. Kapitalisten ohne Landbesitz Zutritt zu d. Aemtern zo gewähren*'.[32] As we shall see, these comments are significant with regard to Marx's broader ideas on Greco-Roman antiquity, but this topic is not pursued further in these notes.

One significant comment on the state occurs in the notes on Maine, where Marx presents an argument against the notion of sovereignty having its origins in the imposition of minority rule by force.[33] Instead, the state for Marx has to be seen as the 'excrescence of society',[34] that is having its foundations not in an Aristotelian *zoon politikon* but in past and contemporary social forms.[35] It emerges at a certain level of development, with individuation from the communal social bonds through the emergence of class interests. These comments have an important resonance with Marx's earlier writings on the Paris Commune, the significance of which will be discussed for the transition to communism below. For now, the main point of this comment is its complication of the notion of the state as an evolutionist stage. While it begins at a 'certain level' of development, the state is also only a mere 'excrescence' of civil society, itself defined by a complex web of social relations based on the class interests of distinct groups.

---

31   Marx in Krader 1974, pp. 216–17.

32   Marx in Krader 1974, p. 217, emphasis in the original.

33   Marx traces Maine's views back through Austin and Bentham, recognising Hobbes as their true progenitor, based on his theory of force and the dependence of sovereignty on it, inevitably bringing about notions of a state of nature, here represented as a male lording over his wife and children, Marx 1974, pp. 328–9, 333. See on this critique of Maine and his intellectual background also Anderson 2016, pp. 207–8.

34   Marx in Krader 1974, p. 329.

35   Marx comments on Morgan's account of the shift from *societas* to *civitas*, by connecting the latter political condition with the Aristotelian definition of the *zoon politikon* as a city-dwelling political animal, Marx in Krader 1974, p. 196. Both in the *Grundrisse* and in volume I of *Capital*, Marx also brings up Aristotle's notion, in the former to criticise the notion that it can be taken as an original condition, Marx 1973, p. 496, and in the latter to point out that it characterises merely Greco-Roman history, just as other definitions characterise other eras, Marx 1976a, n. 7, p. 444.

Both in his comments on the patriarchal family in the notebooks on Morgan, and on the state for Maine, Marx deploys the notion of individuation to capture the complex dynamics of social change. As such, he adds a new dimension to Morgan's account, away from a strongly stadialist conception of phenomena like military democracy and the state. It also distinguishes him from the strong coherence between different elements implied by the invocation of Cuvier by Engels.[36] Marx adds to the interplay of technologies, subsistence regimes, property, systems of consanguinity and forms of the family, as well as the *societas* and *civitas* plans of government, the notion of historical agency. This agency, however, should not be conceived of in a purely subjective sense but taking into account especially the objective factor of interest, first with the patriarchal families, and then with social classes and the state. Hence the dynamics within and between these interests and social groups play their causal roles among the others, implying a complex, multi-layered causality. In other words, the basis for the thesis of the primacy of the encounter over the form.

This understanding of historical causation also brings up the question of a plurality of historical outcomes, even if this does not mean to invite a voluntarist perspective on history, as agency, objectively conceived, has its own determinants.[37] That Marx valued pluralism in this regard can be inferred from his 1878 letter to the editorial board of the Russian journal *Otechestvennye Zapiski*. In this letter he responded to certain Russian revolutionaries, who had used his account of primitive accumulation in *Capital* to argue that Russia would necessarily have to follow the same historical path.[38] Marx rejects this view, quoting from the French edition of *Capital* to show that he had limited the applicability of his account to western Europe,[39] rather than constituting 'a historico-philosophical theory of the general course fatally imposed on all peoples'.[40] Instead alternatives are possible, for example for the role of the peasant commune in a future Russian revolution, as argued for by Chernychevsky, a notion addressed in more detail by Marx in the draft letters to Zasulich.[41]

---

36   A point emphasised in Krader 1974, n. 19, pp. 364–5.

37   Including superstructural ones, as Marx made clear in the introduction to the *Eighteenth Brumaire* on revolutionary politics and cultural and political traditions, Marx 1979, pp. 103–5.

38   Marx 1983a, pp. 134–5.

39   See for the passage in question – presented in a list of other passages of the French edition not found in the German 1890 edition that was edited by Engels – Marx 1991a, p. 778.

40   Marx 1983a, p. 136. The importance of the French edition is emphasised in Anderson 1983 and Pradella 2011.

41   The context of this late correspondence is provided in Wada 1983. See also Marx's earlier journalistic writings on the autocratic and anti-revolutionary Tsarist state in relation to

Everything, in the sense of the historical outcome, depends on the circumstances, on the specific context, or – and this is a word not used by Marx though it is in line with his train of thought – on the conjuncture. Marx emphasises the importance of context by counterposing the process of primitive accumulation in Britain and western Europe to the case of ancient Rome. Marx notes that in the Rome of the later Republican period a free peasantry, expropriated from its means of production and subsistence, faced the owners of 'big money capitals', yet the outcome here was completely different from the later European process of primitive accumulation:

> What happened? The Roman proletarians became, not wage-labourers, but an idle mob more abject than those who used to be called 'poor whites' in the southern United States; and what opened up alongside them was not a capitalist but a slave mode of production. Thus events of striking similarity, taking place in different historical contexts, led to totally different results. By studying each of these developments separately, and then comparing them, one may easily discover the key to this phenomenon. But success will never come with the master-key of a general historico-philosophical theory, whose supreme virtue consists in being supra-historical.[42]

Indeed, context and pluralism are important not just for social formations in which class struggle is present, but also earlier for *societas*. For while in the Greek case the shift from social bonds of the gens to the individuation of the patriarchal family and class interests was a result, alternative outcomes can be seen in other cases. For example, in a comment on the Kutchin tribes in Canada, Marx pointed out how the petrification of the gens into a caste system is a distinct possibility.[43] As noted by Krader, this should be seen as a 'synchronic' outcome rather than as a succession between stages, based on the complex interplay of the natural factors of kin relations, as well as a host of social factors.[44] However, the situation is still more complicated than this,

---

the emancipation of the serfs, in which the peasant commune makes a brief appearance, Anderson 2016, pp. 55–6.

42 Marx 1983a, p. 136. Precisely the same question also interested Rosa Luxemburg, as her writings on the late Roman republic testify, Luxemburg 2013, pp. 315–25. An insightful and remarkable take on precisely this period and its Marxist significance can be found in Brecht's unfinished *The business affairs of Mr. Julius Caesar*, Brecht 2016.

43 Marx in Krader 1974, p. 183.

44 Krader 1973, p. 247.

when we consider not just Marx's notes on *Ancient society*, but also his long-standing concern with communal forms, already evident both in volume I of *Capital* and its preparatory writings that will be discussed below.

However, it was with his discovery of Maurer's work on the German *Mark* commune in 1868 that Marx started to pay more attention to the historical details of the historical development of the different communal forms. In a letter to Engels, Marx brings up not just the *Mark* and its inferred derivation from a preceding 'Indian type', but also the Celtic world and the contemporary Russian commune.[45] Marx later deepened his knowledge on the subject through the work of his friend Maxim Kovalevsky, making excerpts on the long-term trajectories of communal property in the Americas and India.[46] These notes are interesting in themselves, but Marx's comments on them are fairly limited. One of the most significant concerns Kovalevsky's argument on the emergence of a form of common property based on cooperative labour, as in the Russian *artel*, alongside the existing kin-based forms, as known from various Indian historical law codes.[47] Marx here points to an inconsistency in Kovalevsky, for cooperative labour was present long before the existence of either communal or private property, due to the demands of early hunting in particular.[48]

With regard to the long-term history of communal forms, Marx drew upon analogies with geology, something he had done earlier for the gradual development of manufacturing from handicrafts as well.[49] In a letter to Engels discussing the *Mark* commune, Marx argues that human history is much like palaeontology, in the sense that the best minds often fail to see what lies directly in front of them, criticising here Cuvier.[50] In this way even obvious traces are missed, whether recent ones or ancient sources like Tacitus. In the draft letters to Zasulich, Marx applies a geological metaphor in a more direct way to sketch an outline of the different forms of communal property through time, even in the face of the aforementioned obfuscation of the topic, again emphasising pluralism:

---

45 Marx 1987a, pp. 547–9.

46 The notes on India were published in English in Krader 1975, the complete notes in Harstick 1977, which includes the notes, though few comments of Marx himself, on Kovalevsky's account on development in the Americas from the initial hunting condition to agriculture and the state in Mexico, as well as the imposition of colonial regimes.

47 The subcontinent is notable in allowing for tracing legal conceptions of landholding through a series of law codes, starting with the Manu code, Marx in Harstick 1977, p. 48.

48 Marx in Harstick 1977, p. 49.

49 Marx 1991b, p. 442.

50 Marx 1987b, pp. 557–8.

The history of the decline of the primitive communities has still to be written (it would be wrong to put them all on the same plane; in historical as in geological formations, there is a whole series of primary, secondary, tertiary and other types). So far only rough sketches have been made. Still the research is sufficiently advanced to warrant the assertion that: (1) the primitive communities had incomparably greater vitality than the Semitic, Greek, Roman and a fortiori the modern capitalist societies; and (2) the causes of their decline lie in economic factors which prevented them from going beyond a certain degree of development, and in historical contexts quite unlike that of the present-day Russian commune.[51]

The historical context of the Russian rural commune of the later nineteenth century is different from the German, Celtic, and other cases that had already met their demise. In the draft letters to Zasulich, as well as in the letter actually sent, Marx criticises again the universal application of his account of primitive accumulation in *Capital*, noting that it involved a shift from one form of private property to another.[52] This situation did not apply to Russia, for the starting-point of any rural transition there was based on communal rather than private property, and Marx argues that it could either develop into a new form of communal property or into private property, depending on the historical circumstances.[53] The Russian agricultural commune, Marx notes, may appear obsolete, but one should not be too afraid of a word like 'archaic', pointing here to Morgan's notion of the revival of the equality of the ancient gens on a higher level.[54] That a transition of one form of communal property to another appears as a possibility in Russia is due to its historical context.

Most important in this possible revolutionary future for Russia is the opportunity to take advantage of the productive forces developed in western Europe, without having to follow through the same centuries-long path of development.[55] In this regard Marx's late writings on revolution in western Europe are significant as well, in particular his take on the Paris Commune from 1871 and the *Critique of the Gotha Programme* from 1875. To start with the former,

---

51   Marx 1983b, p. 107.
52   Marx 1983b, pp. 100, 105, 117, 124.
53   Marx 1983b.
54   Marx 1983b, p. 106. See also the reference to the Russian peasant commune, as well as on the South Slavs, in Marx's notes on Morgan's *Ancient Society*, Marx in Krader 1974, pp. 115–16. This point is also emphasised by Tomba in his recent book on insurgent universality, Tomba 2019, p. 228.
55   Marx 1983b, p. 106.

the Commune prompted a renewed engagement of Marx with revolutionary praxis. The significance he attached to the Commune can be grasped from a letter he wrote to Kugelmann, in which Marx describes it as 'a new point of departure of world-historical importance'.[56] The question to be asked here, then, is whether this phrase should be understood in stadialist terms, as part of a universal and necessary sequence, or from an aleatory perspective, as an encounter that may or may not take hold.

The first thing to consider on this topic is Marx's view of the state. Earlier in this section, the description of the state as the 'excrescence of society' in the notes on Maine was discussed, as a counter to ideas on sovereignty. In the first draft of the *Civil war in France*, which deals with the Commune, he uses the same phrase, describing the French state under Louis Napoleon as 'a parasitical [excrescence upon] civil society'.[57] The context here, and in the other drafts and in the final work as well, is the trajectory of the French state from the medieval period onwards, focusing on its use to further class interests, increasingly so for the struggle between capital and labour.[58] In a letter to Kugelmann, Marx connects this view of the state to his earlier work *The Eighteenth Brumaire of Louis Napoleon* of 1851.[59] There he had argued that the next French revolution would have to break rather than take over the machinery of the state, a feat that was precisely what the Paris Commune had now achieved.

Indeed, as described in the *Civil War in France*, the Communards had succeeded in subjecting the state to civil society,[60] thereby instituting a world-historical change of direction from the old form of the state. One important aspect of this change, as we saw in the *Eighteenth Brumaire*, was the question of historical agency. Notably, in one of his letters to Kugelmann on the Commune, Marx treats the role of accidents in vast historical changes such as these. Noting that without accidents history would lack the complexity we can discern in it, Marx argues that chance factors have a causal efficacy but at the same time compensate each other, and hence 'fall naturally in the general course of development'.[61] They cannot alter a development, only the pace at which it takes place. This seems suggestive of the Engelsian parallelogram of forces, but here we have to recall that Marx viewed agency not just in terms of subjective action but also objectively, in terms of interests. There is in his writings

---

56   Marx 1989c, p. 137.
57   Marx 1986a, p. 484, see also Marx 1986b, p. 332.
58   Marx 1986b, pp. 328–30; Marx 1986a, pp. 485–6.
59   Marx 1989d, p. 131.
60   Marx 1986b, pp. 331–4.
61   Marx 1989c, p. 137.

no notion of *Wechselwirkung* that structures individual agency along a teleonomic axis, rather the causal importance of a certain historical direction, which
is itself determined by many factors and far from pre-ordained.

We can see this in more practical terms in Marx's account of the uphill
struggle faced by the Communards in developing their new social formation in
opposition to the old state, facing what he describes as 'slaveholder insurrec-
tions' from the ruling class.[62] In this struggle, the working class follows not an
ideal plan, but rather strives to release those progressive (economic) elements
from their capitalist cradle.[63] Yet these elements in themselves do not prefig-
ure the future in the sense that the part represents the whole, for everything
depends on the new overall order sought by the Communards, representing a
completely new social dynamic in itself:

> They know that this work of regeneration will be again and again relen-
> ted and impeded by the resistances of vested interests and class egot-
> isms. They know that the present 'spontaneous action of the natural laws
> of capital and landed property' – can only be superseded by 'the spon-
> taneous action of the laws of the social economy of free and associated
> labour', by a long process of development of new conditions, as was the
> 'spontaneous action of the economic laws of slavery' and the 'spontan-
> eous action of the economical laws of serfdom'.[64]

Note here the protracted length of the struggle required for the new 'spontaneous actions of the laws' to be established, or in aleatory terms 'to take hold'. As
such the world-historical 'point of departure' started by the Communards can
be understood not as a universal stage, but as a specific, historical step relative
to its (capitalist) context. Further support for this interpretation can be found
in the *Critique of the Gotha Programme*. There Marx famously described the two
phases of communism, the first still involving the right to draw on the means of
consumption according to the quantity and quality of the labour-power expended by the workers.[65] Clearly this is still an imperfect step, the reason for which
is not intrinsic but the result of the fact that the context from which communism has to emancipate itself is capitalism, which stains it with birthmarks.[66]

62   Marx 1986a, pp. 490–1.
63   Marx 1986b, p. 335.
64   Marx 1986a, p. 491.
65   Marx 1989b, pp. 85–7.
66   The important distinction here is that communism did not develop from its own found-
     ations, but from those of capital and 'is thus in every respect, economically, morally and

As a new point of departure, then, the first phase of communism is contingent upon previous points of departure that took hold as 'spontaneous action of the laws'. Just as we saw for the future potential of Russia, or ancient Rome for that matter. Hence context is of prime importance, both temporally and geographically.

For just as important as the recognition of pluralism in the notion of alternative future pathways for Russia, is Marx's emphasis in his notes on Morgan on the intersections between the trajectories of different regions.[67] A good example can be found in his own added comments on the Britons before Roman rule, where he highlights the temporal disjunction, according to Morgan's stages, between iron metallurgy and domestic institutions based on the punaluan family.[68] According to Morgan, and Marx put emphasis on this passage, the ancient Britons were able to achieve a higher technological level, relative to their institutions, by virtue of their nearness to more advanced tribes on the continent. In Morgan's work, however, little can be found to conceptualise the long-distance relations that gave rise to such 'adulterated' trajectories.[69] Therefore, one of Marx's lesser noted insertions in his excerpts from *Ancient Society* is in fact of crucial importance, for it connects his take on Morgan's scheme to the analysis of commodity exchange in his overall work.[70] It is necessary to move beyond the notes on Morgan, and to consider *Capital*, as well as its preparatory writings in more detail, for they reveal the presence of the thesis of the plurality of worlds therein.

---

intellectually, still stamped with the birth-marks of the old society from whose womb it emerges', Marx 1989b, p. 85. A similar use of the term 'birth-marks' can be seen in the third draft of the letter to Zasulich, for the transition between the archaic and agricultural communes, Marx 1983b, p. 119.

67   Marx in Krader 1974, p. 98.

68   Marx in Krader 1974, pp. 97, 109, 115, 118. In his adaptation of Morgan, Engels only discusses the form of the family of the Britons, not their precocious use of iron metallurgy, Engels 1990, p. 150.

69   The reference in *Ancient Society* is to Morgan 1964, p. 117, Marx's excerpt and emphasis in Marx in Krader 1974, p. 97.

70   The observation of one recent Marx biographer that at this point 'Marx abandoned *Capital*', Stedman Jones 2008, p. 201, is misleading. For while his study of the Russian commune deepened the analysis of his mature work, it hardly repudiated it, as the next section will demonstrate. The notion that Marx had abandoned his argument of the importance of the development of the productive forces in capitalism is also belied by his comments in the drafts of the letter to Zasulich that the Russian commune benefitted from the productive forces developed in western Europe, and only by virtue of their existence could follow a different path, Marx 1983b, p. 106.

2   Traces of the Thesis of the Plurality of Worlds in the Mature Marx

Marx's intervention occurs in his excerpts from *Ancient Society* on the topic of
property in heroic-era Greece, which Morgan, drawing especially on Homer,
had defined as being in the stage of Upper Barbarism. As we saw earlier, Marx
evaluated Morgan's analysis in this section with a critical eye, adding a comment of his own to the Homeric references on exchange.[71] Specifically, he noted
the presence in Homer of two forms of equivalency.[72] The first of these was
the 'II Equivalentform', where all commodities (slaves, metals, wine, livestock)
are interchangeable with each other. Then there is the 'III Aequivalentform',
where the value of all commodities is expressed in terms of just one of them,
in this case wine. This use of Homer to demonstrate earlier forms of commodity exchange can be seen both in the *Grundrisse* and in volume I of *Capital*.[73]
Most notably, the latter reference is precisely to the 'II Equivalentform', which
is there called the 'total or expanded form of value', while the use of a single
commodity as a common denominator for the value of all other commodities
corresponds to the 'general form of value'.[74]

    These two forms of equivalency are not tied to specific stages of develop-
ment in Marx, even if a certain sophistication of the productive forces has to
be assumed for the more complex forms.[75] Furthermore, commodity exchange
as such does not develop internally within social formations, but rather at
the boundaries between them, thus requiring common terms to facilitate this
exchange.[76] These common terms were established through the forms of equivalency, which develop from the initial 'simple exchange', to the two forms Marx
discussed in relation to Homer, and, finally, to the money form, where value

---

71   The Homeric passage in question is from book VII of the Iliad, describing how apart from a
      large donation of wine from ships sent from Lemnos, the members of Agamemnon's army
      also bought wine from these ships themselves using a variety of commodities:
          From the rest Achaean soldiers bought their rations,
          some with bronze and some with gleaming iron,
          some with hides, some with whole live cattle,
          some with slaves, and they made a handsome feast.
                  Iliad VII, lines 545–9, FAGLES 1990, p. 230.
72   Marx in Krader 1974, p. 135.
73   Marx 1973, p. 173; Marx 1976a, n. 24, p. 154.
74   See for an outline of these forms of equivalency Marx 1976a, pp. 154–5.
75   For as Marx notes, without it there is no possibility to produce any surplus that can be
      appropriated either through direct exploitation or through commodity exchange, Marx
      1976a, pp. 646–7.
76   Marx 1976a, p. 182.

is expressed abstractly.[77] Exchange carried out through these forms of equivalency results in a new kind of social metabolism, supplementing – but not supplanting – that between humans and nature.[78] It is important to emphasise, however, that this metabolism was not a 'natural' one but rather based on convention, in a way providing a parallel with the Epicurean notion of a shift from natural language and concepts to conventional ones discussed in chapter two.

This conventionality is aligned, furthermore, with a conception of the emergence of exchange value in a way that strongly suggests not just an encounter, but also the need for it to 'take hold':

> Their quantitative exchange-relation is at first **determined purely by chance**. They become exchangeable through the mutual desire of their owners to alienate them. In the meantime, the need for others' objects of utility gradually establishes itself. The **constant repetition** of exchange makes it a normal social process. In the course of time, therefore, at least some parts of the products must be produced intentionally for the purpose of exchange. From that moment the distinction between the usefulness of things for direct consumption and their usefulness in exchange **becomes firmly established**. Their use-value becomes distinguished from their exchange-value. On the other hand, the quantitative proportion in which the things are exchangeable becomes dependent on their production itself. **Custom fixes their values** at definite magnitudes.[79]

Apart from the aleatory character of this process, two other factors are of importance. Firstly, it is important to consider the potential variability of systems of exchange-value, as well as the causal efficacy of this variability. That is, if convention allows for a multiplicity of ways to fix values, these should not be understood just from the perspective of their generic function, but also from that of their specific properties. In volume I of *Capital* and in the preparatory studies, especially in the *Grundrisse*, the focus lies mostly on the role of metals in exchange. In the former work, while noting that while gold and silver are not naturally money, their natural characteristics of durability and divisibility are argued to make them highly suitable for use in exchange,[80] especially in the general form of value and the money-form. Hence the physicality of money as

---

77   Marx 1976a, pp. 162–3.
78   Marx 1976a, p. 198.
79   Marx 1976a, p. 182, emphasis added.
80   Marx 1976a, pp. 183–4.

gold and silver should not be ignored and Marx in the *Grundrisse* spends much effort on outlining their mineralogical characteristics, as well as their initial discovery in prehistoric times.[81]

That is not to say that no other metals were used, for example the copper money of Rome,[82] as well as (not mentioned by Marx) its iron counterpart in Sparta.[83] Apart from these more exceptional uses of different metals for money, Marx also aimed to trace the shifts in value between gold and silver, showing not just changes through time but also remarkable stability.[84] Of course this analysis only pertained to western Eurasia, and was based on a limited of wide-ranging number of cases.[85] It would be invalid to derive a general, historico-philosophical theory from this analysis, especially considering that the initial quantitative determination of exchange value was based on chance rather than on necessity. Indeed, in the *Grundrisse* and other preparatory studies of *Capital*, we can see numerous passages where Marx pointed to New World alternatives to this Old World pattern. These counterpoints seem to highlight both the historical particularity of the use of gold and silver in western Eurasia, as well as the intrinsic relativity of value based on conventionality.

Marx here drew upon his earlier excerpts from Prescott's histories of the European conquests of Mexico and Peru, which are contained in his 1851 London notebooks.[86] Whereas in his account of western Eurasia he had emphasised the natural suitability of gold and silver for the money form, in the American counterpoint he rather stressed how these materials were used for ornamental purposes only.[87] This voids the notion of monetary value as an intrinsic

---

81 In particular pointing to the more easy availability of gold relative to the other metals, something mirrored by their early use for ornamental purposes, and even for tools, Marx 1973, pp. 176–80.

82 Marx 1973, pp. 182, 834.

83 Michell 1947.

84 The fluctuations were the result of a complex interplay between mining technology on the one hand and the hegemony and conquests of imperial states on the other. An example of the Carthaginian use of the Iberian peninsula, which had implications for the value ratio between silver and gold as great as the European conquest of the Americas, Marx 1973, p. 185. Yet on the same page Marx notes that the ratio between gold and silver after the latter epochal historical event was similar to that of the later Roman empire.

85 Most of the cases come from western Eurasia, with East and South Asia only mentioned briefly and with less detail or discussion of sources, excepting the Manu law code from India, Marx 1973, pp. 184–5.

86 Published in MEGA IV/9, Marx 1991c.

87 Marx 1987c, p. 171, elsewhere pointing to the colour of precious metals and their aesthetic appreciation across cultural boundaries, Marx 1987d, p. 386. In the *Grundrisse* he also cites

property of gold and silver, given the more advanced division of labour present in Mexico and Peru.[88] For Mexico specifically, Marx noted the use of a plurality of monies for barter, citing from the Renaissance account of Peter Martyr how the use of cacao beans as currency prevented hoarding and the avarice resulting from it.[89] The Peruvian case was even more significant in that it lacked money and commodity exchange altogether, although a system of weights was present.[90] Yet at the same time the division of labour here had reached 'an exceptionally high degree of development'.[91]

At first sight the presence of an advanced division of labour and the absence of commodity exchange seem paradoxical. But here the other factor present in the quotation on its emergence has to be taken into account, namely that with the establishment of commodity exchange use value becomes separated from exchange value. As Marx points out in volume I of *Capital*, it is possible to grasp the development of the social division of labour parallel or independently from the emergence of commodity exchange, and hence conceive of use value independent from exchange value.[92] Furthermore, the 'reciprocal isolation and foreignness' engendered by commodity exchange does not exist either for ancient communities or for the Inca state.[93] The importance of the Peruvian case will be discussed further below for the division of labour. Here it is important to emphasise that the western Eurasian trajectory of commodity exchange is a historically particular one, proceeding from a starting-point that was shaped powerfully by aleatory factors.

Of course, the result of this trajectory was the capitalist mode of production. As Marx points out in the *Grundrisse*, here the metabolism of commodity exchange comes to fulfil the role of the community (*Gemeinwesen*) in its own right, replacing the previously existing forms of social intercourse.[94] Previously, however, this social metabolism existed between distinct social forma-

---

from Prescott the Peruvian conception of gold as 'the tears wept by the sun', Marx 1973, p. 833, see Marx 1991b, p. 426 for the religious context of this phrase.

88   Marx 1987d, pp. 299–300, see also the mention of this in the introduction to the *Grundrisse*, Marx 1973, p. 102, the implications of which will be explored below and in the next chapter.

89   Marx 1987c, p. 211.

90   Marx 1987c, p. 215. In the excerpts from Prescott Marx mentions a silver balance scale, Marx 1991c, p. 432. There he also mentions periodic fairs where produce was exchanged through barter, Marx 1991c, p. 429. This in contrast to the more developed markets in Aztec Mexico, Marx 1991c, p. 414.

91   Marx 1987d, p. 299.

92   Marx 1976a, p. 131.

93   Marx 1976a, p. 186.

94   Marx 1973, pp. 222–5, 496. This development is emphasised by Tomba in his account of the pre-capitalist modes of production in the *Grundrisse*, Tomba 2013, pp. 67–73.

tions, and hence commodity exchange cannot be conceived of according to the unfolding of stages, defined as they were in Morgan and Engels on the basis of the internal characteristics of social formations. The difference in perspective is clear when Marx points to nomadic peoples as being among the first to develop the money form of equivalency, owing to their high degree of mobility and greater portion of movable, and hence exchangeable, goods.[95] Such peoples hardly figure in Morgan, given his focus on sedentary groups, something that would have lingering effects on later Soviet studies on the pastoral nomadism so dominant in Eurasia.[96]

Furthermore, commodity exchange is not just something that exists alongside social formations, it also exists in a complex relation with the internal dynamics of these formations, including their productive process.[97] Before capitalism, commodity exchange and the money form played more marginal roles, as powerfully captured by Marx through an analogy with the Epicurean gods existing in the spaces between worlds (*kosmoi*):

> In the ancient, Asiatic, Classical-antique, and other such modes of production, the transformation of the product into a commodity, and therefore men's existence as producers of commodities, plays a subordinate role, which however increases in importance as these communities approach nearer and nearer to the stage of their dissolution. Trading nations, properly so called, exist only in the interstices of the ancient world, like the gods of Epicurus in the *intermundia*, or the Jews in the pores of Polish society. Those ancient social organisms of production are much more simple and transparent than those of bourgeois society.[98]

The analogy occurs widely in Marx's writings, and, significantly, in the third volume of *Capital*, he adds to it that usury exists in the pores of social formations as well.[99] Merchant and usury capital were termed by Marx to be 'antediluvian' forms, which played important historical roles, but, as the quotation above makes clear, in the interstices of modes of production rather than as their determinant factor. Marx discussed them in the *Grundrisse*, in *Capital* volume I,

---

95   Marx 1976a, p. 183.
96   The work of Khazanov was important in conceptualising nomadism within a comparative framework based on anthropology and archaeology, see especially the overview of Khazanov 1994 and also Khazanov 1973 for a study of slavery among the ancient Scythians.
97   Marx 1976a, pp. 471–2.
98   Marx 1976a, p. 172.
99   Marx 1981, p. 733.

but especially in volume III. There, the same analysis of commodity exchange emerging at the boundaries of communities as in volume I is presented, but here with the added distinction between exchange based on the value of commodities and that based on their production prices.[100] The latter occurs in a situation in which capital is the primary driving force of the productive process, which entails a division of labour based on wages. This in turn was the result of the separation of the workers from the means of production, something that was present to varying degrees in pre-capitalist modes of production but never completely achieved therein.

Trade and usury had important roles to play in dissolving these pre-capitalist forms, which were discussed in the famous section of the *Grundrisse* on this topic, defining there the Asiatic, ancient, Slavonic, and Germanic forms.[101] Whether these antediluvian forms of capital were able to do so depended both on the specific character of property in these forms, as well as on the specific historical conditions. For example, the Asiatic formations were more resistant to dissolution through commodity exchange, both from their internal dynamics and in their resistance to the imposition of trade from the outside.[102] As already noted above, for the draft letters to Zasulich, it was different for the ancient mode of production, where in the case of Rome there existed, on the one hand, accumulated capitals, and, on the other, workers dispossessed of their means of production. In volume III of *Capital*, Marx had provided more details on how the Roman peasantry, in particular, were separated from the land, with usury playing an important role.[103] But this role was a merely destructive one, rather than one that was constitutive to the emergence of a new, progressive form.

The opposition between the two antediluvian forms of merchant and usury capital on the one hand, and the established forms of landed property on the other, prevented the transformation of these pre-capitalist social formations into a capitalist one. Even with accumulated capitals and the separation of the workers from the means of production, these elements existed only *dunamei* (potentially),[104] in the sense of an encounter. Their actual coming together in a new mode of production depending in the historical circumstances. It was only in England, later to be followed by the rest of western Europe, that the separation of the peasant masses from their primary means of production, their land,

---

100   Marx 1981, p. 278.
101   Marx 1973, pp. 473–85.
102   Marx 1973, p. 486.
103   Marx 1981, p. 734.
104   Marx 1973, p. 267, see also pp. 91, 134 where Aristotle is explicitly discussed.

was accomplished in a way that led to the emergence of the capitalist mode of production. In the famous eighth part of volume I of *Capital*, Marx traced the process of primitive accumulation that shaped this transformation, first from private landownership by smallholders to a class of capitalist farmers, and then further to the emergence of the industrial capitalists.[105]

As noted above, Marx later explicitly discounted to his Russian correspondents that this sequence was one of universal validity, rather than specifically tailored to the case of western Europe. Yet the complexities of the specific historical context within which primitive accumulation took place, are in fact quite evident in *Capital* itself. This can be readily grasped when we consider a passage in which Marx discusses the larger context of the process by which the feudal fetters on transforming the two antediluvian forms of capital into industrial capitals took place, putting special emphasis on the global, colonial context of this western European process:

> The discovery of gold and silver in America, the extirpation, enslavement and entombment in mines of the indigenous population of that continent, the beginnings of the conquest and plunder of India, and the conversion of Africa into a preserve for the commercial hunting of black-skins, are all things which characterize the dawn of the era of capitalist production. These idyllic proceedings are the chief movements of primitive accumulation. Hard on their heels follows the commercial war of the European nations, which has the globe as its battlefield. It begins with the revolt of the Netherlands from Spain, assumes gigantic dimensions in England's Anti-Jacobin War, and is still going on in the shape of the Opium Wars against China, etc.

> The different moments of primitive accumulation can be assigned in particular to Spain, Portugal, Holland, France and England, in more or less chronological order. These different moments are systematically combined together at the end of the seventeenth century in England; the combination embraces the colonies, the national debt, the modern tax system, and the system of protection.[106]

Notably, Marx here starts the sequence of primitive accumulation with Spain, owing to its initial conquests in the Americas and the supply of precious mater-

---

105   See Read 2002, 2013 for the connection of the part on primitive accumulation and the
       Marxist reformulations of both Althusser and the *Lire Capital* group and Negri.
106   Marx 1976a, p. 915.

ials to Europe that was one of its results. Earlier, in the *Grundrisse*, he had noted the great, cascading effect of the abundance of gold and silver, which eventually drew 'distant continents into the metabolism of circulation, i.e. exchange'.[107] Again, as with the prospects for revolution in Russia, historical context is everything, for the great accumulation of money capitals in Spain did not play a progressive role in that country, as was the case also in Rome and Byzantium.[108] In Marx's articles on revolutionary Spain from 1854, he analysed the country's development since the *Reconquista*, pointing to imbalances between various regional powers and the central authority in Madrid, which prevented the absolute monarchy from playing a similar progressive role as it had in other European countries.[109] Instead, the Spanish state resembles more an Asiatic form of the state:

> Thus the absolute monarchy in Spain, bearing but a superficial resemblance to the absolute monarchies of Europe in general, is rather to be ranged in a class with Asiatic forms of government. Spain, like Turkey, remained an agglomeration of mismanaged republics with a nominal sovereign at their head. Despotism changed character in the different provinces with the arbitrary interpretation of the general laws by viceroys and governors; but despotic as was the government it did not prevent the provinces from subsisting with different laws and customs, different coins, military banners of different colors, and with their respective systems of taxation. The oriental despotism attacks municipal self-government only when opposed to its direct interests, but is very glad to allow those institutions to continue so long as they take off its shoulders the duty of doing something and spare it the trouble of regular administration.[110]

Yet, when 'decapitated' by Napoleon of its moribund state, the Spanish people gave the French emperor his first decisive land defeat, one at the hand of the popular masses.[111] All of which goes to show the complexities involved in the

---

107   Marx 1973, p. 227.
108   Marx 1973, p. 506.
109   Marx 1980, pp. 393–6.
110   Marx 1980, p. 396.
111   Indeed, although unquestionably there are many passages from Marx's work that point to views of Asian social forms as stagnating, this did not preclude him from noting the revolutionary potential lurking within them, even in his early journalistic writings on the topic, Anderson 2016, pp. 28–37.

actual historical dynamics of the interaction between the pre-capitalist modes
of production and the antediluvian forms of capital, as they intersected with
the dynamics of states and colonial expansion.[112] The question becomes even
more complex when we consider another element, one not present in Marx's
excerpts from Morgan's *Ancient Society*, but one nevertheless crucial in the
emergence of industrial capital: the impact of the workshop and machinery on
the productive process itself. As noted above, even when commodity exchange
started at the boundaries between communities, this form of exchange also had
the potential to impact the productive process of these communities themselves. Yet, for a long time it did not do so, as production was under strict
regulation within caste or guild contexts.[113]

However, the relation between commodity exchange and manufacturing in
western Europe, as the result of a longer process, should not be conflated with
the development of the division of labour in a generic sense. For as noted
earlier with regard to the role of aleatory factors in the emergence of commodity exchange, the development of use-values through the division of labour can
be grasped parallel or independent from exchange value. In effect, like commodity exchange, the division of labour can be seen as a social metabolism
supplementing that between humans and nature, but one that is more closely
connected to it by virtue of being effected in the productive process. In this
regard it is necessary to recall from the previous section that the metabolism
between humans and nature is generic, the basis for all social formations, but
at the same time it is not an ideal relation but rather an earthly one. This relation can be seen in the section of volume I of *Capital* where Marx notes that
alongside the human bodily organs of labour, the earth itself also supplied not
just natural fruits but also humankind's 'original tool house'.[114]

Through appropriating naturally occurring stone, bone, wood, and shell
objects, as well as animals that are domesticated, these are added to the human
bodily organs as instruments of production.[115] Marx further points out how the
archaeological remains of such instruments of labour provide the real key to

---

112   In particular the dynamic relation between the absolutist monarchical states of early
       modern western Europe, as well as later states, and the development of capitalism points
       to the multiple pathways, Krätke 2018, pp. 32–3.
113   Marx 1981, pp. 452–4.
114   Marx 1976a, p. 285.
115   In a reversal of the Lucretian notion that technology and family life diminished the great,
       hard bodies of the earliest humans, for Marx instead their size increases, in a metaphoric
       sense, through the appropriation of new organs of labour, hence 'adding stature to himself
       in spite of the Bible', Marx 1976a, p. 285.

understanding 'extinct economic formations'.[116] He deploys here an important set of bodily metaphors, conceptually extending the human metabolism with the natural environment to include social and technological aspects:

> Among the instruments of labour, those of a mechanical kind, which, taken as a whole, we may call the muscles and bones of production, offer much more decisive evidence of the character of a given social epoch of production than those which, like pipes, tubs, baskets, jars etc., serve only to hold the materials for labour, and may be given the general denotation of the vascular system of production. The latter first begins to play an important part in the chemical industries.

> In a wider sense we may include among the instruments of labour, in addition to things through which the impact of labour on its object is mediated, and which therefore, in one way or another, serve as conductors of activity, all the objective conditions necessary for carrying on the labour process. These do not enter directly into the process, but without them it is either impossible for it to take place, or possible only to a certain extent. Once again, the earth itself is a universal instrument of this kind, for it provides the worker with the ground beneath his feet and a 'field of employment' for his own particular process. Instruments of this kind, which have been mediated through past labour, include workshops, canals, roads, etc.[117]

Given that the earth is so important in supplying humankind with its tools, we may expect that geographical differences are quite important as well. Marx treats this question in another part of volume I of *Capital*, where the productivity of labour is closely connected to the natural environment. Most notable in this regard is a distinction between natural supplies of the means of subsistence, in the sense of bountiful natural fruits, and of the instruments of production, in the sense of being useful for production, like navigable rivers, wood, metals, and so on.[118] Over time, the advantage shifted from the former to the latter kind, especially in temperate regions with a greater variation of natural products, although Marx hastens to add development was only a potentiality

---

116   Marx 1976a, p. 286, here he also points here to the division of prehistoric times on the principle of the materials used to make the most important tools and weapons, the Stone, Bronze, and Iron Ages, which as discussed in Chapter 3 are in fact derived from Lucretius.

117   Marx 1976a, pp. 286–7.

118   Marx 1976a, p. 648.

rather than a necessary unfolding.[119] At this spatial scale the concern is not direct production, but rather with the reproduction of entire social formations, which prompts the question of the social division more urgently.

In his discussion of geographical differences, Marx had also mentioned the importance of water works, forming the hidden basis for both the industries of Arab Sicily and Spain and the pyramids of ancient Egypt.[120] Such systems for water regulation and irrigation were also one of the rare forms of large-scale cooperative labour in pre-capitalist settings, along with the construction of religious and funerary monuments.[121] Such cooperation entailed a division of labour quite separate from commodity exchange. In order to grasp this distinctiveness more clearly, it is instructive to return to the Peruvian case discussed earlier, where an advanced division of labour was said to exist without commodity exchange. Although only scattered references to the Inca state in Peru and neighbouring countries can be found in the volumes of *Capital* and the preparatory studies, these can be grasped in the context of Marx's excerpts from Prescott mentioned earlier. Marx's take on the Inca state is in fact more significant than has been recognised hitherto, not least given its frequent misrepresentation in the Soviet and Western literature alike.[122]

The exception to this misunderstanding was Krader, who correctly avoided subsuming Marx's conception of this South American polity under a universalist conception of the Asiatic mode of production. For even if ancient India and Peru shared certain characteristics, especially in communal landownership, there was no distinction in the latter between the natural community and the state; rather the state itself embodied the natural community.[123] However,

---

119   Marx 1976a, p. 650.

120   Marx 1976a, pp. 648–49.

121   Marx 1976a, pp. 451–52.

122   This confusion can be recognised in an editorial note in the Soviet *Marx Engels Collected Works*, where the Inca empire is described as 'a slave-owning state with considerable remnants of the primitive-communal system', in Marx 1997, n. 20, p. 530. Outside the Soviet bloc, researchers sought mainly to apply the reinvigorated concept of the Asiatic mode of production to the Inca case, Godelier 1974; Dieterich 1982. Neither approaches take into account the, admittedly scattered, remarks by Marx on the Inca to the fullest extent possible, which, as will become evident below, would show divergences from both the notion of a slave-owning state and that of the Asiatic mode of production.

123   Krader 1975, p. 310. Luxemburg also emphasised the importance of Inca communism, especially in a comparative sense. She argued that the Inca state can be understood as the (violent) subjugation and exploitation by one *mark* community over a multitude of others, Luxemburg 2013, pp. 199–201. Furthermore, it supplies a new perspective on early Greek history, in particular the social arrangements of the Dorians in Crete and Laconia, where exploitation also took the form of one commune subjecting the others to its rule,

it was also distinguished from the natural community as usually understood in the work of Marx by virtue of being planned rather than spontaneous, designed by a state apparatus that deployed unfree labour.[124] In this way Inca labour was communal despite producing a surplus, the system 'in its content and in its effect' being defined by social labour.[125] For Krader these distinguishing features were important enough to posit the 'natural community as the state' as an alternative historical pathway in his reconstruction of the overall historical perspective of Marx in *Capital*.[126]

As noted in the example given earlier of the absence of money and commodity exchange in the Inca case, Marx used this to contrast it with the start of the trajectory that resulted in capitalism in western Eurasia. An example of such usage can be found in volume II of *Capital*, where Marx describes the Inca state as a 'completely isolated natural community'.[127] The contrast here is between its extensive road networks, stretching from Chile to Ecuador, and the notion of classical political economy that circulation costs are universal rather than historically specific to commodity exchange and capitalism. Within this vast realm, through their 'more artificially developed communism',[128] the Inca achieved a scale of cooperative labour that allowed them to overcome the absence of more advanced tools and machinery to some extent.[129] It is instructive in this regard to turn to Marx's excerpts from Prescott's history of the conquest of Peru, in order to grasp the full picture of Inca communism that he had gained through his study of this work.

Marx's references to the Inca adhered closely to his excerpts from Prescott, even if there were few comments of his own in the notebook. The excerpts are mostly from the first book of Prescott's work, which deal with the general characteristics of the Inca realm, ranging from the natural environment to their social, economic, political, and religious arrangements. The copious material on the Spanish conquest and the political events thereafter do not seem to have interested Marx enough to note down. A red thread running through the Inca

---

Luxemburg 2013, pp. 203–5. This comparative argument of Luxemburg was unfortunately not followed up by later Marxist thinkers. A book published by Heinrich Cunow on the Inca state is limited to description and does not contain any significant Marxist theory, Cunow 1937.

124   Krader 1975, pp. 135–6.
125   Krader 1975, p. 140.
126   Krader 1975, table 1, p. 136.
127   Marx 1997, p. 121.
128   Marx 1981, p. 1017.
129   Marx 1973, p. 833. He cites here Prescott 1961, p. 800, likely from his London notebooks, Marx 1991c, p. 428.

order of things is the relation between the central authority located in Cuzco, the residence of the Inca ruler himself, and the different regions of the realm. This relation can be seen for the distinction between the Incas as the core elite group, and the lower nobility of Curacas, regional elites largely left in place after the Inca conquest of their lands.[130] Even so, the central authority sought to interweave the Curacas through the imposition of the Quecha language and new gods that occupied the highest place in the pantheon.[131]

At the same time, a similar intertwining of central control and local organisation can be seen for the relations of production. The territory of the Inca state was subdivided into provinces, districts, and so on, to a very detailed level of administration and regimentation, with laws and regulations strictly enforced.[132] Administrative control extended to the division of the land in each district, and a detailed system for monitoring population, as well as the land and other resources available, were used to set targets for requisitioning. As a general rule a third of the land was set aside for the Inca (the state), another third for the Sun (the priesthood), and a third for the people, with each commoner receiving a temporary and equal share. The Inca land and that supporting persons unable to carry out labour was tilled in common, the allotted lands by households but with mutual support between them.[133] Beyond agriculture, the state was even more directly involved in the productive process, as for the large flocks of llamas and alpacas, mining, and craftwork.[134]

Part of the produce was brought to Cuzco, but much was retained in district storehouses, which aside from serving the needs of the state and the priesthood were also used in times of scarcity and to support the poor.[135] These stores also allowed for the supply of large armies, as well as to support dedicated labour forces for building and maintaining road networks, fortresses, and major centres, including Cuzco.[136] Much labour was also expended on creating irrigation works and terraces, notably in the highlands, to sustain agriculture, with farming having been developed to a high level.[137] As such, the Inca combination

---

130   Marx 1991c, pp. 418–19.

131   Marx 1991c, p. 425.

132   Marx 1991c, p. 420. Idleness was punished as a crime in the Inca realm, Marx 1991c, pp. 421–2.

133   Marx 1991c, p. 421.

134   Marx 1991c, p. 421. Important in this was also the rotation of workers to ensure they did not suffer over prolonged periods from the labour conditions in certain tasks, notably mining, Marx 1991c, p. 423.

135   Marx 1991c, p. 423.

136   Marx 1991c, pp. 423–5.

137   Marx 1991c, p. 428. The more collective arrangements were even reflected in the tools, for

of a strict and detailed execution of central authority and the common ownership and tillage at the local level had yielded spectacular results, especially
given the absence of iron technology. At the same time, however, this state was
ruled by a class unchecked in their authority, even if one of the mildest forms
of despotism, supported by a macabre form of theocracy.[138] Prescott emphasises the pomp used by the Incas to display their rulership, and this is the only
place where Marx adds a comment to the excerpts, terming such displays as
laughable.[139]

The common population of the Inca state were completely subjected to the
state, in the sense that they were unable to increase their property by any means
or ascend the social scale, nor gain the knowledge available to the nobility.[140] In
a sense, even time itself was appropriated from them, given that taxes were in
labour and idleness punishable by law, and in this way free agency was denied
completely to them.[141] Even so, while noting all these aspects so contrary to the
worldview of the American Republic of which Prescott was part, he nevertheless offered measured praise for their system, in a way that is more appreciative
of historical pluralism:

> We must not forget, that, under their rule, the meanest of the people
> enjoyed a far greater degree of personal comfort, at least, a greater exemp-
> tion from physical suffering, than was possessed by similar classes in other
> nations on the American continent, – greater, probably, than was pos-
> sessed by these classes in most of the countries of feudal Europe. Under
> their sceptre, the higher orders of the state had made advances in many
> of the arts that belong to a cultivated community. The foundations of
> a regular government were laid, which, in an age of rapine, secured to
> its subjects the inestimable blessings of tranquillity and safety. By the
> well-sustained policy of the Incas, the rude tribes of the forest were gradu-
> ally drawn from their fastness, and gathered within the folds of civiliza-

---

rather than ploughs being drawn by draught animals common in Eurasia, in the Inca realm
the land was worked with a large stake that was drawn by six to eight men, Marx 1991c,
pp. 428–29.

138 Described in detail in Prescott 1961, pp. 744–9.

139 Marx 1991c, p. 418. Luxemburg in her account of the significance of the Inca cases emphasises the distinction of its form of communism, based on the circumscribed boundaries of
kin and economic relations, and the universal view of communism as universal freedom
and equality as a product of the modern bourgeoisie, Luxemburg 2013, p. 202.

140 Marx 1991c, p. 423.

141 Noted down as 'the power of free agency vernichtet in Peru', Marx 1991c, p. 432.

tion; and of these materials was constructed a flourishing and populous empire, such as was to be found in no other quarter of the American continent.[142]

Here, unlike in Adam Smith, the shift from the rudeness of forest life to civilisation is not travelled on the path of commerce alone, but can take the form of communism as well. Furthermore, a path not shaped by a drive for riches, but rather to satisfy a need for safety from violence and want. Even so, given its nearly complete denial of individuality, it could hardly be taken as exemplary for the western European communism of the nineteenth century, though it would later occupy a significant place in debates by modern Peruvian communists.[143] The main role of the Inca case in Marx is not to give a generic outline of a communist system, but rather to serve as a historical counterpoint to concepts held to be universalist by the classical political economists. Examples already noted above were the development of a complex division of labour without commodity exchange, as well as the provision of a counterpoint to the universality of circulation costs.

Another aspect can be added to this, however. For as Marx argues in volume III of *Capital*, the Inca case voids the naturalisation of capitalist relations of distribution, according to which the value added by labour is distributed among those selling their labour power, capitalists, and landowners.[144] However, as Marx points out here, the only generic feature of social labour, which includes the more developed communism of the Inca, is that after subtracting the part directly consumed a surplus remains. There are no preconditions as to how this surplus is distributed to satisfy socially defined needs, nor 'who functions as the representative of these social needs'.[145] This argument is part of a broader thrust of Marx to demonstrate the historically specific, transient nature of capitalism, a question to which we will return to in more detail in the next section. Here it is important to emphasise that this more general observation connects the Inca case to the broader question of alternatives to universalist conceptions of development.

For in the Inca case an advanced division of labour without commodity exchange gave rise to distribution relations of a radically different kind than those of western Eurasia. As a real alternative it bolsters the case for potential alternatives, especially the future communist pathways that form points

---

142   Prescott 1961, p. 820.
143   Keen 1998, pp. 166–7.
144   Marx 1981, p. 1018.
145   Marx 1981, p. 1018.

of departure from contemporary capitalism. In the previous section, the transition of the Russian rural commune, as well as the first phase of communism in
the *Critique of the Gotha Programme*, involved an advanced division of labour
separating itself from commodity exchange. The historical possibility of such
an independent development of the division of labour was already demonstrated in the Americas, before the ruin of the indigenous states brought about
by the Iberian conquests. The key difference between these potential future
cases and that of the Inca is that in the former the tools and machinery absent
in the latter were available, allowing for a different kind of communism to be
developed.

Moreover, the analysis of the Inca state by Prescott and the use thereof by
Marx in his conception of the state as a natural community, voids the universality of the account of the development of the state in Engels (and by extension
in Morgan).[146] As we saw in the previous chapter, Engels put great emphasis on
the close correspondence between the different elements of social life, which
through a necessary *Wechselwirkung* led to a teleonomic unfolding of stages of
development. For the state specifically this entailed the development of economic classes based on the development of private ownership of land and
commodity exchange. The tensions this induced in social life, especially with
the emergence of money and consequently usury and a higher level of commodity exchange, in turn led to the development of the state. This state then
had as its main function the maintenance of private property, which occasion-
ally changed hands in revolutionary episodes. None of this can be seen in the
Inca state, which neither developed as a result of commodity exchange nor had
as its main function the defence of private property, given the nonexistence
thereof.

Hence it invalidates the notion of a teleonomic unfolding of stages altogether, unless one resorts to the kind of denigrations of indigenous American
civilisations of the kind discussed in Chapter 3 in De Pauw, Robertson, and
Smith. Neither Morgan nor Engels treated the Inca case in any detail, but the
dire consequences for their scheme of doing so should be clear. Incidentally,
the notion that in the Inca state the power of free agency was completely subsumed under the state also shows the distinctions between Marx and Engels

---

146   In a sense the limits of the Engelsian model were also recognised by Luxemburg, who
      emphasised that slavery could emerge already through the subjugation of one commune
      by the other, rather than as the result of the emergence of private property, Luxemburg
      2013, p. 301. However, she did not emphasise the division of labour that can be seen in the
      Inca arrangement, arguing instead that the division of labour 'can only properly develop
      if private property and exchange are already in place', Luxemburg 2013, p. 250.

with regard to the conception of agency. In Engels individual agency was conceived through a parallelogram of forces, the direction of which was in turn shaped by the *Wechselwirkung* of base and superstructure elements. As such it was always present in a generic sense, certainly from the moment that social factors supplanted biological ones in causal primacy. As noted earlier, a distinction could clearly be seen in Marx's conception of individuality through the notion of interests, as part of specific historical trends, as compared to the view of Engels of 'unadorned greed' as a causal factor of agency structured by *Wechselwirkung*.[147]

If individual agency was denied in the Inca state, this is rather inexplicable from the Engelsian conception of the inherent presence of agency as part of a teleonomic process of unfolding. It is as if this civilisation was not just swimming against the tide of history, but also denying an inherent human property of individual agency. Marx's distinction between subjective and objective aspects of agency makes things much clearer. Based on the economic organisation of the Inca realm, there were no distinctive objective interests to distinguish individuals. Certainly, there were distinctions between commoners and the nobility. Yet this hierarchy was captured within the natural community as a state, just as in pre-state natural communities there were social distinctions based on age, gender, and so on. Below the differences with modern views of communism will be noted, especially with regard to the subjective aspect of agency. In this sense, the importance of historical direction and context is crucial for understanding the specific framework of agency, interest, and individuality, distinguishing Marx's approach clearly from the teleonomic views of Engels.

Having outlined the possibility of an advanced division of labour developing without commodity exchange in the New World, it is time to return to the relation between the two in the development of capitalism in the Old World. The key question here is how the development of manufacturing, followed by the large-scale application of machinery should be grasped in its historical context. Just as much as the other forms of social production, the capitalist mode of production was dependent upon the ability of producers to generate surplus through the application of their labour power. In that sense, capitalism is rooted in a long process of the development of the productive forces:

---

147   See on this topic the analysis in Lekas 1988, pp. 228–30, who brings out the nuances of the
        different approaches of Marx and Engels with regard to, respectively, more complex and
        unitary perspectives on the interplay between the communal form, commodity exchange,
        and the formation of the Greco-Roman states.

At the dawn of civilization, the productive powers acquired by labour are small, but so too are the needs which develop with and upon the means of their satisfaction. Furthermore, at that early period, the portion of society that lives on the labour of others is infinitely small compared with the mass of direct producers. As the social productivity of labour advances, this small portion of society increases both absolutely and relatively. Besides, the capital-relation arises out of an economic soil that is the product of a long process of development. The existing productivity of labour, from which it proceeds as its basis, is a gift, not of nature, but of a history embracing thousands of centuries.[148]

Yet the soil in which capitalism developed was rather distinct from that of Inca communism, in that in Eurasia the development of the division of labour was parallel, and mutually interacting with, the development of commodity exchange. In an important passage from volume I of *Capital*, Marx traced the different starting points of the division of labour and how they were influenced by commodity exchange,[149] which can be summed up accordingly:

1. One starting point for the division of labour can be found in the physical differences of age and gender in familial and tribal forms, that is the commune.

2. A second point of departure was the restriction of individual labourers to certain vocations, notably in caste or guild contexts. This would later form the basis for manufacturing.

3. The impact of commodity exchange on these two forms of the division of labour took distinct forms. In the case of the physiological division of labour in the commune, labourers would be separated from the whole, the communal bond being replaced by the social metabolism of commodity exchange. For caste and guild the effect was the opposite, for, through the same metabolism, these formerly independent branches of production could now be related to each other in a collective process of production.

4. The result of this combination of a developed division of labour and commodity exchange is the division between urban and rural, for which Marx observes that 'the whole economic history of society is summed up in the movement of this antithesis'.[150]

---

148 Marx 1976a, p. 647.
149 Marx 1976a, pp. 471–2.
150 Marx 1976a, p. 472.

Even so, there were many factors that prevented the encounter between the division of labour and commodity exchange taking hold in a definitive way. Examples of this are the insulation of the rural communes from commodity exchange in the Asiatic mode of production, the primacy of the production of use values in antiquity, as well as the guilds of medieval and post-medieval western Europe.[151] The antediluvian forms of merchant and usury capital, present in varying degrees, existed, as we saw earlier, only in the interstices, unable to direct the productive process. This situation changed decisively and radically with the development of the manufacturing workshop in western Europe, as one of the results of primitive accumulation.[152] Manufacturing initially drew upon the craft skills developed under the guild system that had developed under feudalism, but was characterised by fundamentally different relations of production as based on wage labour. It was the structuring of cooperative labour through wages, not the development of the productive forces as such, that was decisive in bringing about this change.[153]

Whereas in pre-capitalist modes of production cooperative labour had been forced and was either of a limited scope or limited by the relative simplicity of the tools available, in capitalism it became a general principle. That is, even if coeval with the first incarnation of the manufacturing workshop, it remained basic to all successive iterations of industrial capitalism.[154] With the workshop a number of things change relative to guild handicrafts. First of all, unlike the guilds where there was a limit to the number of apprentices and no separation of labour and the means of production, the fledgling capitalist could hire more workers using wage labour.[155] Secondly, the way in which these workers cooperated was also different. With the expanding number of labourers in the workshop, it was no longer the worker but the productive process that was central, as 'a productive mechanism whose organs are human beings'.[156] In this way a 'collective worker' emerged, who became a working part, an *automaton*, lacking control over a productive process increasingly shaped by science.[157]

---

151   Marx 1973, pp. 497–503; 1976a, pp. 477–9.
152   Marx 1976a, p. 480.
153   Marx 1976a, p. 452.
154   Marx 1976a, pp. 453–4.
155   At the same time there ensued a diversification of tools, in this way enabling workers to carry out more specific tasks as part of an overarching productive process, thereby creating 'at the same time one of the material conditions for the existence of machinery, which consists of a combination of simple instruments', Marx 1976a, p. 461.
156   Marx 1976a, p. 457.
157   Marx 1976a, pp. 482–3.

It was this mechanism that was the revolutionary core of industrial capital, even if it initially was limited in its scope, given the available handicraft techno-logy.[158] With the development of motive power, notably the steam engine, this changed, as this device could drive the exemplary form of the *automaton*, the machine. The principle of the machine had been available already in antiquity, in the form of the water mill,[159] and the application of steam as a moving force can be observed in the *aeolipile* described by Vitruvius.[160] Yet it was with the modern steam engine and principles of production of the manufacturing workshop that machinery was applied comprehensively, leading to an enorm-ous expansion of the productive forces. Furthermore, different machines were combined with each other in a way that marks a change relative to manufac-turing. For the isolation of working parts (including workers) and their cooper-ation in the workshop now becomes the factory, acting as an *automaton* on a Cyclopean scale and driven by 'a self-acting prime mover'.[161]

With the deployment of machines on a vast scale, Marx observed that the roles of merchant capital and industrial capital were reversed, and that the lat-ter now controlled the former.[162] Yet it is not a question of a shift from one stage to the next, for the coming of machinery has to be grasped within the broader development of the capitalist mode of production. In volume I of *Capital*, Marx used an analogy with geological formations to point to the temporal complex-ity of the relation between manufacturing and machinery,[163] just as he did for the sequence of communal types in the draft letters to Zasulich discussed earlier. A more elaborate version of this argument can be found in the eco-nomic manuscripts of 1861–3, where the same metaphor is used, pointing also to the technological and scientific aspects of the development of machinery, adding further:

> But the *general law* which is valid throughout, is that the material pos-sibility of the later form is created in the earlier form; both the techno-logical conditions and the economic structure of the workshop which corresponds to them. Machine labour is directly called into existence as a

---

158 Marx 1976a, pp. 490–91.
159 Marx 1976a, p. 468; Marx 1991b, pp. 394–5.
160 Rowland 1999, p. 163.
161 Marx 1976a, p. 502. The clock was also of crucial importance in this, as it enables for the uniform measurement of time, including the labour-time captured in the commodity, Marx 1991b, p. 403.
162 Marx 1981, p. 448.
163 Marx 1976a, p. 492.

revolutionising element by the excess of needs over the possibility of sat-
isfying them with the old means of production. But this excess of demand
is itself given by the discoveries made still on the handicraft basis, by
the colonial system founded under the domination of manufacture, and
by the world market relatively firmly established by the colonial system.
Once the revolution in the productive forces has been achieved – which is
displayed in technological terms – a revolution also starts in the relations
of production.[164]

A complex set of mutual determinations exists here, adding manufacturing and
machinery to the broader question of primitive accumulation, which itself has
to be grasped within the opposition between landed property and the antediluvian forms of merchant and usury capital. These are determinations that
play out dramatically in historical terms, as in the example of the trajectory
of Spain, which started the sequence of primitive accumulation by plundering
the resources of the New World, destroying Inca communism and the other
indigenous civilisations in the process. The country then languished for centuries, before performing a dramatic revolutionary turnabout as the result of a
foreign invasion. Needless to say, this perspective is far removed from a stadialist outline of fixed phases of development. Rather, it can be seen as a cascade
of distinct but related trends that interweave in what can be recognised now
as stratigraphic layers. None of these trends were preordained, and nor was the
mutual interaction between them structured by the Engelsian notion of *Wechselwirkung*.

However, there are also a number of passages in Marx that refer to the historical role of capitalism. Here he argued that, unlike the preceding modes of
production, it has developed the productive forces and relations of production
in such a way that communism becomes possible. Examples of such praise for
capitalism can be found especially in the *Grundrisse*.[165] To focus in particular
on the extensive account of the development of machinery in volume I of *Capital*, Marx here points out how the technical aspects of machinery have resulted
in relations of production that favour associated labour in a way that the manufacturing workshop did not:

> Large-scale industry, on the other hand, possesses in the machine sys-
> tem an entirely objective organization of production, which confronts the

164   Marx 1991b, p. 442, emphasis in the original. See also Marx 1986c, pp. 335–6.
165   Marx 1973, pp. 163, 409–10, 540–2, 589–90, 712.

worker as a pre-existing material condition of production. In simple co-operation, and even in the more specialized form based on the division of labour, the extrusion of the isolated worker by the associated worker still appears to be more or less accidental. Machinery, with a few exceptions to be mentioned later, operates only by means of associated labour, or labour in common. Hence the co-operative character of the labour process is in this case a technical necessity dictated by the very nature of the instrument of labour.[166]

Yet this production by associated labour had as its starting point the manufacturing workshop based on wage labour, which entailed an inherent drive to maximise surplus labour. In the *Grundrisse*, Marx had focused mainly on the role of manufacturing and machinery in reducing the socially necessary labour time, which had the progressive effect of increasing productivity.[167] Because of the separation of labour from the ownership of the means of production, this increase in productivity is rather played out in terms of the dispossession of labour. Marx notes, however, that this opposition between productive forces and workers is not inherent for production, but rather constitutes 'a merely **historical** necessity, a necessity for the development of the forces of production solely from a specific historic point of departure'.[168] He continues in the same vein, pointing out that it is quite possible to envision a different historical foundation of production where, unlike with wage labour, the machines and other means of production are owned by associations of workers.[169]

In volume 1 of *Capital* this analysis is deepened, as Marx provides a more complex argument, notably positing science as a free resource for capitalism to exploit.[170] More importantly, the sheer force of the exploitative power of capital is emphasised, seeking to reduce not just the socially necessary labour time but also to increase absolute surplus value by increasing the length of the working day.[171] The horrific results for the workers are exposed through a rigorous use of official English sources, but at the same time Marx makes clear that this drive to maximise exploitation is the result of specific historical conditions. For in the middle of his discussion of the appalling conditions of English factory workers, he contrasts modern capitalism to references to machines in Aristotle and

---

166   Marx 1976a, p. 508.
167   Marx 1973, pp. 708–9.
168   Marx 1973, pp. 831–2, emphasis in the original.
169   Marx 1973, pp. 832–3.
170   Marx 1976a, pp. 508–9.
171   Marx 1976a, pp. 517–42.

other ancient Greek writers. In these authors the emphasis is on the possibility of such hypothetical machines doing away with the conditions of slavery, and even bringing about the return of the Golden Age.[172] These passages are in line with the ancient Greek emphasis on the production of use values and the disparaging of seeking money for its own sake.[173]

Unlike the case of Inca communism, the contrast drawn here is not with a real alternative in the use of machinery but rather with an alternative ideal conception of their use. Nevertheless, this contrast was in the end based on a real contrast in the respective modes of production. Just as in Marx's late writings on the transition to communism discussed in the previous section, historical context and the point of departure of historical trends are the primary factors. These factors established tendential laws, which can be changed in the transition to communism. The notion discussed there of capitalism stamping the initial phase of communism with birthmarks, can also serve to help grasp the passages on the transition to communism in the mature writings, especially those in volume III of *Capital*. There Marx points out how certain elements that have emerged within capitalism serve either to abolish key features of it as a mode of production or to form, potentially, a constitutive part of a future communist mode of production.[174]

The latter kind concerns the element of cooperative factories, which have abolished the opposition of capital to labour by making the labourers themselves the capitalists, building upon the previously established factory and credit systems.[175] Hence, much as in the writings from the 1870s, the building of communism here proceeds from a capitalist point of departure. Indeed, the reference to the Communards setting free elements developed under capitalism within a new kind of tendential law, that of the associated producers, is closely related to the analysis in volume III of *Capital*. Indeed, the late writings in general are aligned with the volumes of *Capital* and the preparatory studies in a broader sense, sharing more than the view of the historical determination of the transition to communism. For example the discussion of the missed encounter between the dispossessed proletariat and the owners of money in

---

172   Marx 1976a, p. 532.

173   Especially evident in the Aristotelian distinction between economics, conceived as the satisfaction of natural and limited needs, and chrematistics, the unbounded seeking of wealth for its own end, Marx 1976a, n. 6, pp. 253–4. Also relevant in this regard is the passage where Marx discusses Plato's conception of the division of labour in his *Republic* from the perspective of use-value, Marx 1976a, pp. 487–9.

174   Marx 1981, pp. 566–73. See also Hudis 2013, pp. 176–9.

175   Marx 1981, pp. 571, 991.

the later Roman Republic in the letter to *Otechestvennye Zapiski*, is in line with the discussion of this case in the mature works.

Even more importantly, the analogy of geological stratigraphy used to capture the complex mutual determinations in the trajectory from manufacturing to machinery, could also be seen for the succession of communal forms in drafts of the letter to Zasulich. Hence the shared perspective involved not just the notion of encounters, taking hold in tendential laws, but also a multi-layered view of temporality. The trajectory of early modern Spain is a good example of how this plays out in specific historical cases. Both the theses of the primacy of the encounter over the form and that of plural temporality are in evidence here, the latter following from the former. For it is the complex interplay between different elements in encounters and the tendential laws that they engender that create the uneven layers of temporality. Important in this regard are also the causal efficacy of historical agency and elements of the superstructure.

In table 5.1 below the various aspects of the theses of the aleatory current in Marx's work are outlined, as well as his differences with Morgan and Engels. With regard to the thesis of plural temporality, the distinctiveness of Marx relative to Morgan and Engels is clear, for they both lack any notion of 'stratigraphy', positing instead a universal pathway of history. In Morgan this was the result of the uniform scale of mind as applied to social development. The universalism of Engels rather derived from the teleonomic effect of *Wechselwirkung* in his *Dialectics of Nature*, leading to an unfolding of stages according to a necessary sequence. As noted in the previous chapter, this universalist perspective also led to the denial of the thesis of the plurality of worlds in Engels. However, this thesis is certainly present in the work of Marx, and furthermore intertwined with his mature work, surfacing in distinct ways as the entries in the table show.

TABLE 5.1   Contrasting Marx to Morgan and Engels

Marx	Similarities and differences with Morgan and Engels
Thesis of trans-individuality	
The interaction between humans and nature is through the metabolism of labour, whereby humans do not just change their natural environment but also themselves.	Similar use of metabolism in Morgan, if mind is posited as a separate entity. In Engels the interaction with nature is conceived of solely through the process of anthropogony.

TABLE 5.1 Contrasting Marx to Morgan and Engels (*cont.*)

Marx	Similarities and differences with Morgan and Engels
Human labour is distinguished from animal activity by virtue of it being planned in advance, in that what is made existed already in an ideal sense before being produced.	Conception of the human distinction from animals in terms of language in Morgan and in terms of consciousness in Engels.
The metabolism of humans and nature is supplemented by two forms of social metabolism: the division of labour and commodity exchange.	Commodity exchange and the division of labour absent in Morgan. In Engels can see a change from natural to social laws, rather than coexistence. Mastery over nature in both.
The earth was the original toolhouse of human beings, adding instruments of production to the natural organs.	Not present in either Morgan or Engels.

Thesis of the primacy of the encounter over the form

Marx	Similarities and differences with Morgan and Engels
The development of new social forms is conceived of in terms of an encounter. Furthermore, it is an encounter that can fail to take hold, as with the owners of capitals and the proletariat of the later Roman Republic.	Absent in Morgan. In Engels, by contrast, a teleonomic unfolding of stages can be observed, with elements closely corresponding to each other through *Wechselwirkung*.
Chance factors play an important role in the initial encounter, as with the equivalent forms established in the development of commodity exchange. Through repetition these forms take hold as tendential laws.	Recognition of the role of aleatory factors in Morgan with regard to invention of iron, but only slows down or speeds up development on a universal pathway.
Future changes in social forms depend on previous forms, as well as their broader social environment, forming their point of departure. The specific, historical circumstances should not be conflated with any overarching historico-philosophical theory.	Not present in either Morgan or Engels, contrary to their notion of a universalist path of development.

TABLE 5.1   Contrasting Marx to Morgan and Engels (*cont.*)

Marx	Similarities and differences with Morgan and Engels
Agency is conceived of in both subjective and objective terms, the latter mainly conceived through interest. Notion of individualism is variable according to the presence or absence of interests favouring its development. Individual action has causal efficacy relative to historical trends.	No conception of individual agency in Morgan. Generic presence of individual agency or action in Engels, with the interaction of the parallelograms of forces being structured through *Wechselwirkung*.
State as an excrescence of society, determined by complex causality yet as a political form it has causal efficacy, as have other superstructural elements.	Complication of the state as strongly coherent stage of development in Morgan and Engels, as well as of the dominance of the base to the superstructure in Engels.

Thesis of plural temporality and the plurality of worlds

Conception of a sequence of forms on the analogy of geological stratigraphy, with a complex set of mutual determinations between a variety of elements.	Not present in either Morgan or Engels, contrary to their notion of a universalist path of development.
Geographical differences in the natural bounties or instruments of production supplied by distinct regions. These differences potentially, but not necessarily, structure the development of these regions along different lines.	Different characteristics of the New and Old Worlds only impact speed of development in Morgan. More use of the Old World particularities relative to the development of property in Engels, but no comparison with the Americas.
Commodity exchange as social metabolism emerges at the boundaries of communities. Furthermore, the antediluvian forms of usury and merchant capital exist in 'interstices between worlds', that is, relative to modes of production.	Absent in Morgan. No complication of the universalist stages of development in Engels. Merchant communities viewed instead as parts prefiguring the capitalist whole.

TABLE 5.1   Contrasting Marx to Morgan and Engels (*cont.*)

Marx	Similarities and differences with Morgan and Engels
Division of labour as a social metabolism can develop independently of commodity exchange, including within a state framework, as with Inca communism.	Marx's argument is not of relevance to Morgan given absence of these concepts in his work. Voids the Engelsian universalist conception of the state as the result of commodity exchange.

The notion of 'worlds' is in fact implied by the emergence of commodity exchange at the boundaries between communities, forming a new social metabolism that interweaves distinct social formations to different extents (based on their degree of resistance). Eventually, the antediluvian forms of merchant and usury capital give way to the capitalist mode of production, wherein commodity exchange itself becomes the new community, a *Gemeinwesen* based on wage labour. Even within the world market, however, there remains unevenness, in the sense that the different regional trajectories, each with their distinct characteristics and temporalities, are connected in a complex set of mutual determinations. The case of Russia and the intersection of capitalist elements there with the communal property of the peasantry, itself the result of a layered stratigraphy of forms, is a case in point of such uneven, yet interwoven, coexistences on a global scale. In this sense, commodity exchange as a social metabolism is inherently a connecting, interweaving force, not an organicist whole. It cannot be conflated with an evolutionary stage of development, nor viewed as an element that in its more simpler form prefigures the future capitalist mode of production, as in Engels.

Marx's divergence from the notion of a singular and universal path of development is further underlined by his use of Inca communism as a counterpoint to classical political economy. Here an advanced division of labour developed without commodity exchange, directed by a state that was in effect still a natural community. Unlike the conception of state formation in Engels, its basis was not a class struggle engendered by commodity exchange, demonstrating that it constituted a truly distinct historical pathway. As in the case of commodity exchange, the division of labour can be seen as a social metabolism that supplements the metabolism between humans and nature. This natural metabolism was not a mere generic abstraction in Marx, but earthly in the sense that he pointed to the natural environment as supplying the first instruments of production. Furthermore, geographical differences in this regard also provided different potentialities for development, which may or may not be realised according to the historical context.

Here the regional differences in environment lead to a diversity of outcomes, whereas in the outline of the distinctions between the Old and New World in Morgan these could only speed up or slow down the progression through universal stages. Marx's valuation of pluralism in this sense, in contrast to the universalism of Morgan and Engels, was based on two things. First of all, there is his emphasis on the importance of historical context, as captured in the primacy of specific points of departure in a complex stratigraphy of mutually determined elements. As such, the notion of plural temporality here follows from the primacy of the encounter over the form, as could be seen in the account of the emergence of commodity exchange. It also follows from the causal efficacy of agency and of superstructural elements. Another source of pluralism is based on the differences of the environments of different regions, as well as the social variation in systems of commodity exchange and their relation, or lack thereof, with the division of labour.

The potentiality and historical particularity of natural and social distinctions between world regions conforms to the thesis of the primacy of the encounter over the form. In turn these distinctions are evidence to support the thesis of trans-individuality, both in the role of agency and in the natural and social metabolisms. Both theses furthermore support the theses of plural temporality and the plurality of worlds. Marx's appreciation of pluralism therefore can hardly be taken to be accidental to his perspective, for it is present in the central concepts of his late and mature writings. It is enlightening to relate the analysis of Marx presented here not just to the work of Morgan and Engels, but also to his earlier self, in particular to his engagement with Epicureanism. Doing so will allow not just for a better understanding of the presence of the aleatory current in Marx, but will also serve to better elucidate his views on the higher form of communism as the realm of freedom in historical rather than universalist terms.

3   Marx's Method in relation to His Encounter with Epicureanism

The picture of Marx we have gained from this extensive annotation of his excerpts and notes on Morgan differs greatly from both Morgan and Engels, especially with regard to the theses on pluralism, but in ways that are distinct. An added complication is that there are certain passages in the work of Marx himself, as we shall see below, that seem to be at odds with pluralism. In order to understand these complexities better, it is necessary to relate the picture we have gained to Marx's theoretical ideas in a broader sense. An important aspect of this concerns the thesis of trans-individuality, in particular the relation of matter and thought. We saw earlier that in his notes on Wagner, Marx, rather in passing, described a form of embodied knowledge that seemed close to the Epicurean notion of *prolepseis*. This observation prompts the question of the relation of the late Marx to the earliest Marx, the one who wrote a thesis on Epicurean and Democritean atomism.

In order to do so it is important to avoid locating in the early Marx an 'origin' for the late Marx, in the sense that the end was already prefigured in the beginning. Rather, it is useful to retrace the movement of ideas from the later to the earlier writings, so as to grasp the dynamics of his intellectual development and the later efficacy of some of his earliest ideas.[176] In following Marx's steps back to his beginnings, it is also important to consider his own statements on the relative worth of ancient philosophy. In a 1857 letter to Lasalle, Marx notes his fondness for Heraclitus, but above all for Aristotle, while at the same time stating that his emphasis on Epicureanism in the doctoral thesis was for political rather than philosophical reasons.[177] His attitude to Epicureanism can also be seen in his doctoral thesis itself and in the notebooks. While on the one hand praising Epicurus as 'the greatest representative of Greek Enlightenment',[178] Marx was far from uncritical with regard to the specific doctrines of Epicurus and his followers.

Marx's exposition of the ideas of the Democritean and Epicurean 'schools' is couched in the terms of the Hegelian dialectic, and at the same time engages with the account of these ancient atomists presented in Hegel's own history of philosophy.[179] In so doing he breaks important new ground, most notably with regard to the interpretation of the *clinamen*, which later won him high praise by some of the major scholars of ancient Epicureanism.[180] In the end, however,

---

176   In much the same way as capitalism supplies the key for understanding the preceding modes of production, in a comparative sense and to be taken with a grain of salt; see below for a discussion of this aspect of Marx's method.

177   Marx 1983c, p. 226, the word 'political' here is inferred, given the damaged state of the original.

178   Marx 1975a, p. 73.

179   There are a number of works that engage with the Hegelian character of Marx's dissertation, notable recent studies include Finelli 2016; Levine 2012; McIvor 2008; Schafer 1999. As noted in the introduction to this book, the aim here is solely to grasp Marx from the perspective of the aleatory current rather than to add to existing debates on his relation to Hegel. At the same time, we wish to approach his work by addressing the later efficacy of his early ideas.

180   One of the main interpreters of Epicureanism reviewed Marx's dissertation when it was recovered and afforded it high praise, especially for the perspective on the *clinamen*

Marx concludes in his notebooks presenting his exposition of the 'immanent dialectics' of Epicurean philosophy that its doctrines are found wanting due to its inconsistencies.[181] Yet he values this ancient philosophical perspective nevertheless for its lack of the prejudices of contemporary philosophy, giving it qualified praise:

> If, according to Hegel (see *Gesamtausgabe*, Vol. 14, p. 492), the Epicurean philosophy of nature deserves no great praise when judged by the criterion of objective gain, from the other point of view, according to which historical phenomena do not stand in need of such praise, the frank, truly philosophical consistency with which the whole range of the inconsistencies of his principle in itself is expounded, is admirable. The Greeks will for ever remain our teachers by virtue of this magnificent objective naiveté, which makes everything shine, as it were, naked, in the pure light of its nature, however dim that light may be.[182]

This passage should give considerable pause to efforts to see in Marx's doctoral thesis and the notebooks associated with it, some kind of foundational 'atomist dialectics' that then acts as a 'hidden hand' in Marx's later work.[183] Instead Marx's stance towards the ancient authors seems to be that of a connoisseur rather than that of a follower of one doctrine or the other, something that seems borne out by his use of the ancient authors to illustrate and deepen certain points. This holds true not just for Epicurus and Lucretius, but especially for Aristotle as well.[184] These authors are, furthermore, not central presences in Marx's major theoretical reflections. For Epicureanism in particular, Marx stated 'political reason' may have played a role in this as well, as will be argued below. Hence it can hardly be argued on this basis that Marx was some kind of 'hidden Epicurean', as one might plausibly argue for Morgan based on his unpublished texts, nor that there is an 'Aristotelian ontology' behind his views on communism.[185]

---

offered in it, Bailey 1928. Current scholars of Greco-Roman philosophy still find enough of interest to return to his work, e.g. Asmis 2020.

181   Marx 1975b, pp. 413, 500.
182   Marx 1975b, p. 500.
183   A recent attempt to do so, Nail 2020, leaves me unconvinced.
184   Most notably in the account of the value-form in volume I of *Capital*, Marx 1976a, pp. 151–2.
185   Pike 1999, a position also associated with the work of Alasdair MacIntyre, Knight and Blackledge 2011.

Instead we can note traces of these thinkers in his work, and of others like Hegel and Spinoza too, and consider how these relate to Marx's broader theoretical concerns. Hence the major theoretical texts have to be taken into account as well. Here our concern is solely with the Epicurean traces, the latest of which we could see in the notes on Wagner and the excerpts on Morgan discussed in the previous section. Moving back in time from these texts from the 1880s, our next signpost on this matter is the postface to the second edition of volume I of *Capital*, containing his most extensive discussion of dialectics. Marx starts this discussion by citing from a review of volume I of *Capital* by the Russian economist I.F. Kaufman. He had argued that in his book Marx had combined a realistic mode of inquiry with a dialectical mode of exposition, in this way recognising that there are no universal laws of history, but only particular laws that apply to specific historical eras.[186]

Marx appreciated these comments by Kaufman. Yet he also noted that his description of the architecture of *Capital* was nothing but the result of applying the dialectical method to the specific phenomenon of the capitalist mode of production, adding to this that

> Of course the method of presentation must differ in form from that of inquiry. The latter has to appropriate the material in detail, to analyse its different forms of development and to track down their inner connection. Only after this work has been done can the real movement be appropriately presented. If this is done successfully, if the life of the subject-matter is now reflected back in the ideas, then it may appear as if we have before us an *a priori* construction.
>
> My dialectical method is, in its foundations, not only different from the Hegelian, but exactly opposite to it. For Hegel, the process of thinking, which he even transforms into an independent subject, under the name of 'the Idea', is the creator of the real world, and the real world is only the external appearance of the idea. With me the reverse is true: the ideal is nothing but the material world reflected in the mind of man, and translated into forms of thought.[187]

Here we have the parallelism discussed in Chapter 1 for strategies of reading, in the distinction between the mode of inquiry as the reflection of the world

---

186   Cited in Marx 1976a, pp. 100–2.
187   Marx 1976a, p. 102.

and the mode of presentation in the realm of ideas. It is important to note here that this view is more or less identical to the view of the initial formation of linguistic concepts in the notes on Wagner. Also significant is that when Marx draws the famous contrast between the mystic and reactionary form of the dialectic and its rational and revolutionary counterpart, he emphasises in the latter its recognition of transience, in that its understanding of the existing world implies 'a simultaneous recognition of its negation, its inevitable destruction'.[188] As such, the dialectical method as used by Marx is inherently critical, as it engages both with what exists and with the negation of that existence. To sum up, Marx's dialectics is realist rather than idealist, historical rather than universal, and critical rather than empirical.

From this description, the expectation would be that Marx's method would be inherently favourable to the theses of plural temporality and the plurality of worlds, as evident in the annotated account of his notes on Morgan given above as well. However, this notion would seem to clash with certain writings of Marx himself, principally the preface to his 1859 book *A Contribution to the Critique of Political Economy*. Therein he unequivocally makes three points on method that suggest a more unilinear rather than a pluralist view of history,[189] which can be summed up accordingly:

1.   The totality of the relations of production form the economic basis of a social formation, on which rests a superstructure of laws and political life, as well as 'definite forms of social consciousness' that correspond to this base.

2.   Social revolution follows from the conflict between the forces and relations of production, occurring when the former have developed up to a point where the latter become fetters on their further development. The revolutionary struggle on the political and ideological planes are derivative of this economic contradiction, and the further development of the material conditions completely determines whether or not an 'era of social revolution' begins.

3.   The Asiatic, ancient, feudal, and capitalist modes of production are described as 'epochs marking progress in the economic development of society', of which capitalism is the last of the 'antagonistic' ones, closing out the 'prehistory' of humankind.

With regard to the second position on revolution, here the context in which the preface was written has to be taken into account. As pointed out by Prinz,

---

188   Marx 1976a, p.103.
189   Marx 1987d, pp. 263–4.

the desire to publish the book in Prussia entailed a need to prevent the censor for banning it, leading Marx to couch his notion of revolution in a way that seems to emphasise a gradualism that could hardly upset the status quo.[190] Of course, the notion of capitalism fostering an enormous growth while at the same time putting fetters on their further development through co-operative labour was, as we saw earlier, a fairly common theme in Marx's mature writings. What is contentious, however, is the mechanical view of revolution presented, as well as the seeming formulation of a 'historico-philosophical theory' for the transition between modes of production in general, rather than specifically for the contradictions of the capitalist mode. Naturally, this view of revolution had its ramifications on how the relation between base and superstructure was conceived of, as well as the conception of modes of production in a progressive series, without implying this to be a singular and unilinear sequence.[191]

Further complications abound. As noted by Althusser, in the text of the book itself more aleatory formulations can be discerned.[192] On the other hand, in the 1867 preface to the first edition of volume I of *Capital*, a more unitary conception like that in the 1859 preface is evident. There Marx argues that industrial development in England foreshadowed developments in other European countries like Germany, this being a question of the tendential laws 'working themselves out with iron necessity'.[193] Such an application of the dialectic was in fact realist, historical, and critical, and its results were certainly seized upon by Engels, but it does seem to contradict notions of plurality in history. However, this may have more to do with the brevity and didactic value of the prefaces, and in the 1859 case also censorship. In the more expansive 1857 introduction to the *Grundrisse*, Marx provided an outline of his method more amenable to the theses of pluralism.

---

190   Prinz 1968, pp. 449–50.

191   In his review of *A Contribution to the Critique of Political Economy*, Engels emphasises precisely those aspects of Marx's exposition that lend themselves to a unilinear perspective, arguing against taking a more historical approach owing to the vagaries and contingencies of history, Engels 1980, pp. 475–77. He comes close in this review to conflating the logical and historical orders, the former based on a sequence from simple to complex forms, something lacking in Marx, and in this way reducing the latter to a more illustrative, demonstrative function.

192   In the interview with Fernanda Navarro, Althusser 2006, p. 263. In an important passage in the book, Marx makes clear that economic laws depend on their historical (pre)conditions, in this case also pointing to the advanced division of labour among the Inca that developed without commodity exchange, Marx 1987d, pp. 299–300.

193   Marx 1976a, p. 91.

Marx starts his introduction by criticising the state of nature theories of the political economists, as well as Rousseau, who project back into the earliest times an ideal that mimics the essence of the current state of affairs.[194] Important in this is especially his discounting of individualism in the early history of humankind, noting instead the dependency of persons on familial and communal ties. Individuality for Marx is the result rather than the origin of social intercourse, a theme that recurs widely in other sections of the *Grundrisse*.[195] What is important, then, are the different forms of social life, and Marx's narrower methodological concern in this introduction is with the economic categories that are the basic analytical means for interpreting these forms. Or more precisely: for the mode of exposition of the analysis in dialectical terms. He delves into great detail with regard to specific questions on this topic, some of which are of great theoretical significance, as for example the question of the relation or identity of production and consumption.[196]

Our concern here, however, is more with the general thrust of Marx's argument on the economic categories as ideational forms in themselves, rather than with the interpretation of specific ones such as production or consumption. To begin with, we need to consider the general perspective in the 1857 introduction, which Althusser highlighted as important to his own exposition of Marx's thought. This perspective can be said to revolve around two opposite poles: production in general and the specific perspective allowed for by the capitalist mode of production. With regard to the former, which is production irrespective of the particular mode of production, it is crucial to remember that this can be no more than a rational abstraction, not a universal law that stands outside history as in political economy.[197] Instead Marx provides a basic definition of production as 'appropriation of nature on the part of an individual within and through a specific form of society',[198] an abstraction that should never be conflated with a particular (original) mode of production.

---

194   The specific objection to Rousseau and the Robinsonades of classical political economy alike is that they start with independent individuals, Marx 1973, p. 83, a conception that as we shall see below was rejected by Marx from the outset and also coloured his relation to Lucretius and Epicurean political doctrines.

195   Indeed, as Tomba has convincingly argued the conception of the social individual is what connects the section on the pre-capitalist forms with the so-called fragment on machines, Tomba 2013, pp. 79–83.

196   Most notably the quotation of Spinoza's phrase *determinatio est negatio* in this context, Marx 1973, p. 90, discussed in chapter one. See also on this phrase chapter two of Lezra 2018.

197   Marx 1973, pp. 85–7.

198   Marx 1973, p. 87.

Furthermore, and this is the crucial point, he contrasts the realist and idealist uses of economic categories, so as to show that simple economic categories do not exist in their own right. The context is Marx's outline of distilling from a chaotic whole categories as simple as possible, thus gaining a sophisticated view of the whole as 'unity of diverse', but risking idealist misconception:

> In this way Hegel fell into the illusion of conceiving the real as the product of thought concentrating itself, probing its own depths, and unfolding itself out of itself, by itself, whereas the method of rising from the abstract to the concrete is only the way in which thought appropriates the concrete, reproduces it as the concrete in the mind. But this is by no means the process by which the concrete itself comes into being. For example, the simplest economic category, say e.g. exchange value, presupposes population, moreover a population producing in specific relations; as well as a certain kind of family, or commune, or state, etc. It can never exist other than as an abstract, one-sided relation within an already given, concrete, living whole.[199]

Not being able to proceed from an idealist original position, instead the economic categories are to be considered in their (historical) relations, in the way they 'hang together', and from the perspective of the most recent, most progressive form. Here we can find the famous analogy between the anatomy of humans and apes. More precisely, the categories and their interrelations in capitalism allow 'for insights into the structure and the relations of production of all the vanished formations **out of whose ruins and elements it built itself up**, whose partly still unconquered remnants are carried along within it, whose mere nuances have developed explicit significance within it, etc.'[200] Marx emphasises that the understanding of the pre-capitalist modes of production from this perspective requires a self-criticism of the capitalist mode itself, a recognition of its historicity.[201] Specifically, he points out that the truth that its categories express for the earlier forms 'is to be taken only with a grain of salt'.[202] Instead, what is needed is a comparative approach, which looks not just to similarities between past and present forms, but also to their differences.

---

199   Marx 1973, p. 103.
200   Marx 1973, p. 105, emphasis added.
201   Also emphasised in the first volume of *Capital*, Marx 1976a, pp. 174–5.
202   Marx 1973, p. 106.

We can see this at work in Marx's argument on money in capitalist and pre-capitalist forms.[203] On the one hand, he noted that here an idealist path from simple to complex can be noted, as money had existed in a simpler form before capitalism. On the other hand, it is possible to note both an advanced division of labour in Peru, existing here without any kind of money, and money playing only a marginal role at the boundaries of Slav communities. Further, he adds the familiar themes of the marginal trading nations in Greco-Roman antiquity, as well as the limited scope of monetisation in the Roman empire, existing fully only in its army.[204] These differences, revealed by comparison, show the senselessness of any idealist scheme moving from simple to complex. Most interestingly, one of the cases used by Marx to complicate the economic category of money was that of Peru. This case is important for two reasons, which enhance the substantive and theoretical case for pluralism.

First of all, its form of communism had a complex division of labour yet lacked commodity exchange, a combination that fascinated Marx. Secondly, if we ignore its plundering by colonial powers, strictly speaking the Peruvian case, by virtue of its isolation from Eurasia, was not an ancestral form of the capitalism that emerged in western Europe. To argue it to be ancestral would imply invoking an idealist, universalist conception of an 'Asiatic' mode of production, while ignoring its particularities in which Marx delighted. This point rather emphasises the argument on pluralism, challenging even the use of the economic categories of capitalism to grasp the global diversity of social formations. Marx seems to recognise this when in shorter remarks at the end of the 1857 introduction he makes cryptic remarks on the appearance of necessity and legitimising chance, before noting that 'World history has not always existed; history as world history a result'.[205]

A similar use of the Peruvian case is made in volume III of *Capital*, where Marx argues against viewing distribution relations (an economic category) as natural rather than as products of history, a view according to which pre-capitalist modes of production can only be seen as underdeveloped capitalist forms.[206] Instead, the simpler Indian communities and the 'more ingeniously developed communism of the Peruvians' show that distribution relations can be very different from those assumed by political economists. From this, Marx goes on to observe the historically transient character of capitalism, which, by extension, holds for its distribution relations as well:

---

203   Marx 1973, pp. 102–3.
204   Marx 1973, p. 103.
205   Marx 1973, p. 109.
206   Marx 1981, pp. 1017–18.

The scientific analysis of the capitalist mode of production proves the contrary, i.e. that this is a mode of production of a particular kind, and **a specific historical determinacy**; that like any other particular mode of production it assumes a given level of social productive forces and of their forms of development as its historical precondition, a condition that is itself **the historical result and product of a previous process** and from which the new mode of production proceeds as its given foundation; that the relations of production corresponding to this specific and **historically determined** mode of production – relations into which men enter in their social life-process, in the production of their social life – have **a specific, historical and transitory character**; and that finally the relations of distribution are essentially identical with these relations of production, the reverse side of the same coin, so that **the two things share the same historically transitory character.**[207]

This passage gives Marx an almost Montaignesque flavour, especially considering the Peruvian counterpoint to the Old World that we have emphasised here, which was also present in the 1857 introduction. As in the 1859 preface, here the realist and historical dialectic is contrasted to its ideal and universal form. Unlike in that text, and in those similar to it, in the passage from the third volume of *Capital* and in the 1857 introduction the critical aspect of the dialectic receives great emphasis, following from the inherent transience of things. It is this aspect of Marx's dialectics that favours the theses of pluralism, its absence in the 1859 preface rendering it susceptible to didactic uses that legitimise the existing order of things, as we saw in Chapter 1 for Stalin. Both aspects of the dialectic are in fact connected to the ideas that the early Marx grappled with. Yet as we made clear above, he drew inspiration rather than a doctrine from his work on ancient atomism, leaving for interpreters only faint traces with which to fathom its influence.

The strongest and most straightforward claim for recognising such traces can in fact be made for the critical, transient aspect of the dialectic. Here the connection between the late and early Marx appears strong, despite the 'break' of the theses on Feuerbach. This critical aspect of the dialectic was based on the recognition of the inevitable destruction of the existing state of affairs. Hence also the transience of the economic categories, which do not have existence as simple forms but are only knowable from the way in which they 'hang together' in forms like capitalism, which will in turn, as all states of affairs, pass away.

---

207   Marx 1981, p. 1018, emphasis added.

Most significantly, there exists a direct and strong link here with the Epicurean view of the natural world, one that ties with one of the tenets of the fourfold cure (*tetrapharmakos*) not to fear death, which also seems to have appealed to Marx.[208] Again, it is instructive to move back in time from the later to the earlier texts, in this case starting with Marx's critique of Proudhon in the *Poverty of Philosophy*, where the relation between the inherent transience of the economic categories and Epicureanism is made explicit.

An important element in the critique of Proudhon is the broader argument against Hegelianism. In the first observation on Proudhon, Marx shows that when the Hegelian dialectic is applied to the economic categories, they are placed in an ideal, logical sequence rather than understood historically.[209] In the second observation, he rather points out that these economic categories are based not on the reflections of Proudhon, who has turned the correct order of investigation upside down.[210] One should start with the material, with the productive forces and the social relations that apply them, giving a short sketch of his materialist outlook:

> In acquiring new productive forces men change their mode of production; and in changing their mode of production, in changing the way of earning their living, they change all their social relations. The hand-mill gives you society with the feudal lord; the steam-mill, society with the industrial capitalist.

> The same men who establish their social relations in conformity with their material productivity, produce also principles, ideas and categories, in conformity with their social relations.

> Thus these ideas, these categories, are as little eternal as the relations they express. They are *historical and transitory products*. There is a continual movement of growth in productive forces, of destruction in social relations, of formation in ideas; the only immutable thing is the abstraction of movement – *mors immortalis*.[211]

---

208 As evident from a letter of Engels shortly after Marx's death, Engels 1992b, p. 462.
209 Marx 1976b, pp. 162–5. See especially here the remarks on *logos*, which infests everything by virtue of its abstraction into logical categories, Marx observing 'if the whole real world can be drowned thus in a world of abstractions, in the world of logical categories – who needs to be astonished at it?', Marx 1976b, p. 163.
210 Marx 1976b, pp. 165–66, emphasis in the original.
211 Marx 1976b, p. 166.

The formulation is important as an early sketch of historical materialism, but for our purposes is all the more significant through the presence of the *mors immortalis* phrase. This phrase refers to a line in Lucretius, in line 869 of book III of the DRN: 'mortalem vitam mors cum inmortalis ademit', translated as 'when death the immortal has taken away his immortal life'.[212] The immediate context of this phrase was an argument by Lucretius against the fear of death. For Marx, however, it had to be understood in broader terms. We can see this in a passing remark in the *German Ideology*, where he argues that *mors immortalis* was the principle of the Epicurean atomist view of nature.[213] The phrase occurs in the doctoral thesis itself as well, in the context of the relation between atoms as principles and atoms as elements in the world of appearance.[214] It is also present in a more elaborate form in comments in Marx's notebooks on Epicurean philosophy:

1. Although the Lucretian phrase is not mentioned here, the same principle is present in the contrast between Epicurus and Plutarch on immortality and the fear of death, the former contrasting the transience of animate beings with the immortality of the atoms.[215] This has to be understood more broadly as part of the political aspect of the critique of Epicurean theology by Plutarch, more on which below.

2. In another notebook, Marx discussed in more detail the Lucretian account of atomism given in book II of the DRN, extending his excerpts to the account of human beings in book III. For the former book he focuses especially on the *clinamen*, how it relates the atoms as mere ideal principles and as the constituent elements of transient things.[216] He then excerpts a passage from book III on the mortality of the mind, as well as on the futility of the fear of death. Here again the mors immortalis line is cited, and Marx observes: '*It can be said that in the Epicurean philosophy it is death that is immortal.* The atom, the void, accident, arbitrariness and composition are in themselves death'.[217]

Here, then, we can see a recognition of a series without beginning or end, just as discussed for the convergences of Epicureanism and Spinozism in chapter one.

212   Smith 1993a, pp. 254–55.
213   Marx and Engels 1975, p. 139.
214   Marx 1975a, p. 62.
215   Marx 1975b, pp. 454–5.
216   Marx 1975b, pp. 472–5. One notable passage of the commentary stresses the martial character of Lucretian poetics, the atoms existing in a Hobbesian war of 'all against all', Marx observing that 'here the world takes shape to the ringing war games of the atoms', Marx 1975b, p. 475.
217   Marx 1975b, p. 478, emphasis in the original.

Marx certainly did not view Spinoza in these terms, but his use of the Lucretian *mors immortalis* specifically in the context of economic categories unambiguously connect his dissertation writings to his critique of political economy. In the very same passage, as quoted above, the critique of the Hegelian inversion of ideal and realist views of the world, as evident in Proudhon's writings, also highlights the realist and historical aspect of the dialectic. The question can then be posed whether for this aspect, too, traces be detected between the late and the earlier Marx. However, the answer here is considerably more complex than for the critical, transient aspect of the dialectic. In simple terms, however, a connection can be established between Marx's view of concept formation in his notes on Wagner quoted earlier and the Epicurean notion of *prolepseis* discussed in the doctoral dissertation.

We can see this in the short but highly significant chapter on time in the dissertation, which has been somewhat overlooked in favour of the focus on 'atomist dialectics'. Marx here notes how in Epicurus time is accidental to things, existing only for the transient world of appearance and not for atoms and void as ontological principles, and furthermore is connected to human sensuousness. That is, the human sense of the world is 'embodied time', and its physical form are the *eidola*:

> The *eidola* are the forms of natural bodies which, as surfaces, as it were detach themselves like skins and transfer these bodies into appearance. These forms of the things stream constantly forth from them and penetrate into the senses and in precisely this way allow the objects to appear. Thus in hearing nature hears itself, in smelling it smells itself, in seeing it sees itself. Human sensuousness is therefore the medium in which natural processes are reflected as in a focus and ignited into the light of appearance.[218]

In a sense, this is connected with *mors immortalis* as well, as the *eidola* reflect the transient states of affairs that generate them, which are perceived through the human senses as having a temporal character. Notably, in one of the notebooks Marx also refers to how the historical account of Epicurus of the formation of knowledge, embodied in the *prolepseis*, is important both for the exposition of his system and for distinguishing it from Scepticism.[219] The notion of

---

218 Marx 1975a, p. 65. Marx continues on the same page to note that in this way the senses are the only objective criterion for the world of appearance, as opposed to abstract reason for that of essence (atoms and void as principles).

219 Marx 1975b, pp. 427–8.

nature reflecting on itself through the human senses can be seen in a modi-fied form in the 1844 manuscripts, where nature is described as the 'inorganic body' of humans, observing that 'man's physical and spiritual life is linked to nature means simply that nature is linked to itself'.[220] This text in fact shows the complexities of Epicureanism in the early Marx, for central to its concep-tion of the relation between humans and nature are not the *eidola*, but rather the mediating force of industry.[221]

Indeed, despite the similarities between the *Notes on Wagner* and the doc-toral dissertation with regard to both the *eidola* and the primacy of sense-perception, the latter writings do not contain any references to the production and labour in the former text. As we saw earlier, the basis of the realist and historical aspect of the dialectic is to start with the productive forces. From the analysis of the atomist's views on the relation of humans and nature in Chapter 2, especially in the notion of *phusiopoiei*, it seems strange that Marx completely ignores this aspect of their philosophy. Instead, two other elements are emphasised in particular. The first and best known of these concerns the critique of the political use of religion to instil fear in the population, so as to be able to consolidate the existing regime and state of affairs. Marx emphasises this point in the contrast he draws between Plutarch, who defended this point of view, and Epicurus, who criticised it, notably also drawing in the modern arguments of Holbach and Spinoza on this question as well.[222]

One comment of Marx on this question is particularly astute. In a notebook he points out that the Epicurean critique of the political usefulness of religious fear is motivated not by concerns of pleasure or science, but rather to assert the freedom of the mind from external determination.[223] This has to be understood as part of the main thrust of the dissertation on the nature of the Epicurean doctrine. Marx argued that the *clinamen* is not a particular physical explana-tion of atomic movement but rather a general philosophical principle, hence the gods in their independence 'swerve away from the world' and cannot be the cause of fear.[224] It is important to keep this argument in mind, for it connects

---

220   Marx 1975c, p. 276.

221   Marx 1975c, pp. 302–3.

222   Marx 1975a, pp. 74, 102; Marx 1975b, pp. 452–3. The reference to the work of Spinoza occurs in a later commentary contrasting Plutarch to Lucretius, but is significant for this topic, too, citing from part V, P42 of the *Ethics*, where Spinoza states against a transactional view of religion that 'blessedness is not the reward of virtue, but is virtue itself', Marx 1975b, p. 469.

223   Marx 1975b, pp. 447–8.

224   Marx 1975a, pp. 50–1; Marx 1975b, pp. 408–9.

to the second element of human social relations. In the dissertation, Marx discusses this question using the notion of repulsion, which refers to the atoms combining into compound forms as a consequence of the *clinamen*.[225] And even though he does not treat the human productive relation to nature, Marx does pay attention to consciousness:

> And in truth: the immediately existing individuality is only realised conceptually, inasmuch as it relates to something else which actually is itself – even when the other thing confronts it in the form of immediate existence. Thus man ceases to be a product of nature only when the other being to which he relates himself is not a different existence but is itself an individual human being, even if it is not yet the mind [*Geist*]. But for man as man to become his own real object, he must have crushed within himself his relative being, the power of desire and of mere nature. *Repulsion is the first form of self-consciousness*, it corresponds therefore to that self-consciousness which conceives itself as immediate-being, as abstractly individual.[226]

An important connection with the critique of the use of religion can be made here. Firstly, the only part of book V of the DRN excerpted by Marx in his notebooks on Epicurean philosophy concerns Lucretius' account of religion as it arose from the sensory perception of the earliest humans.[227] This provides a historical connection to the commentary of Marx on the deployment of the fear of the gods in 'religious feudalism', being a state in which 'man is determined as an animal'.[228] That is, as in the quote above, as a 'product of nature'. An echo of this can be seen in the journalistic article on the law of the theft of wood from 1842, in a remarkable passage on feudalism. Marx there attacks the customary privileges of the idle classes, which are contrary to law and derive from animality:

---

225 Marx 1975a, p. 51.
226 Marx 1975a, p. 52, emphasis in the original. The importance of this passage is underlined by Heinrich, who stresses the relation between this view of social relations and its metaphoric uses in Epicurean philosophy in general, Heinrich 2019, pp. 307–9. From an Epicurean perspective, the passage is also significant in departing from Lucretius' view that the earliest humans were isolated wanderers, in fact completely determined by a wandering, animal existence. Marx's location of humanity in itself as defined by the outset by sociality marks a decisive break with this Lucretian view of early humankind, and by extension also with the similar views of Rousseau.
227 Marx 1975b, p. 490.
228 Marx 1975a, p. 74.

Their origin dates to the period in which human history was part of *natural history*, and in which, according to Egyptian legend, all gods concealed themselves in the shape of animals. Mankind appeared to fall into definite species of animals which were connected not by equality, but by inequality, an inequality fixed by laws. The world condition of unfreedom required laws expressing this unfreedom, for whereas human law is the mode of existence of freedom, this animal law is the mode of existence of unfreedom. *Feudalism* in the broadest sense is the *spiritual animal kingdom*, the world of divided mankind, in contrast to the human world that creates its own distinctions and whose inequality is nothing but a refracted form of equality.[229]

Marx here points to a 'naive' form of feudalism in the caste system, and the religious worship of animals therein. He also drew an analogy between the predatory struggle between species and the exploitation of fellow human beings, as well as later connecting the worship of animals with fetishism.[230] This emphasis on the distinction between humanity and animality, provides, perhaps, a connecting link between the Epicurean self-consciousness of the dissertation and Marx's inspiration by the humanist materialism of Feuerbach.[231] If that is accepted, there are perhaps a host of themes in the early Marx that might suitably be understood in Epicurean terms. The most notable of these is the notion of species-being in the 1844 manuscripts, where human production is said to be able to adapt the standards of the other species, which seems to mimic the notion of learning from nature, of *phusiopoiei*, of the atomists.[232] This is in fact a crucial point, as the notion of species-being is the main basis of the critique of the Hegelian dialectic in the same text.[233]

Another example from the 1844 manuscripts is the reference to spontaneous generation, which is also present in the *German Ideology*, and its context within a broader argument against creation.[234] These, of course, are familiar

---

229 Marx 1975d, p. 230, emphasis in the original.
230 Marx 1975d, pp. 230–1, 262–3.
231 In the sense that Marx describes in *The holy family*, Marx 1975f., p. 125.
232 Marx 1975c, pp. 276–7.
233 Marx 1975c, pp. 332–3.
234 In the passage in the 1844 manuscripts, Marx locates anthropogony within a broader argument against creation, Marx 1975c, pp. 304–6. He argues that the notion of creation is not just the wrong answer in itself, but that the questions that inform it are misguided. For rather than positing a state of non-existence before the creation of nature in an idealist fashion, nature is to be grasped in terms of the theoretical and practical sensuousness that is an inherent part of praxis. In that sense, the understanding of nature is bound up with

themes from Epicurean philosophy and its reception contexts in early modern European philosophy.[235] Yet as suggestive and even plausible as these connections might be, there is no direct evidence for them in the form of explicit statements of Marx to this effect. Instead, Marx in the dissertation and the notebooks focuses on another aspect of Epicurean philosophy, namely its conception of the emergence of social life and especially of the state. We can see this in the dissertation, where he moves from the basic repulsion of the self-consciousness of human beings to the covenant as a political form of repulsion, and friendship as a social one.[236] The source cited for the former is the *Principal Doctrines* of Epicurus, which contrasts the human ability to achieve something like the common good to the inability of animals to do so, an inability that can also be seen in certain human tribes.[237]

In the notebooks, too, only the *Principal Doctrines* are excerpted, whereas the views of Lucretius, as well as those of Democritus, on the emergence of social and political life are left out completely.[238] Marx introduces the passages on justice and law in Epicurus by pointing out that they 'represent Epicurus' views on spiritual nature, the state', based on the contract and having utility as its end.[239] No further comments are added to these excerpts, but the last citation is notable, in that Epicurus here argued for assurance from the 'external circumstances' in gaining only the possible, avoiding what is alien to oneself.[240] This relates to what we have seen earlier for religion, namely the freedom of the mind from external determinations such as the fear of the gods. With these references we come to the crux of the matter concerning the Epicurean influence on Marx. For as we saw above it was for a political reason that Marx was drawn to this philosophy, and, as argued here, it was for the same reason that Epicureanism was only an explicit, inspirational presence in his later work.

---

humankind's own development. In the *German Ideology*, however, Marx asserts the independent existence of nature from human history and praxis by referring precisely to the process of anthropogony, Marx and Engels 1975, p. 40.

235 See for the specific context of Marx's passages on this topic Foster 2000, pp. 118–20.

236 Marx 1975a, p. 53.

237 Marx 1975a, n. 32, p. 91. Most notable is Marx's emphasis in these excerpts on the notion of Epicurus that justice does not exist by itself, but in the mutual relations between people.

238 Any notes of Marx on this topic are certainly not lost, for there are excerpts from books IV through VI of the DRN in the notebooks, with those from book V being limited to the preconceptions or *prolepseis* of the gods induced by the impression of the particles they emitted, the *eidola*, on the earliest humans, Marx 1975b, pp. 489–90.

239 Marx 1975b, p. 409.

240 Marx 1975b, p. 410.

This political reason can be found in a section written by Marx in the *Holy Family*, entitled 'Critical battle against French materialism'. There he gives a complex outline of the history of early modern materialism, tracing the succession of British and French materialist thinkers, who developed their ideas in opposition to metaphysical systems, including that of Spinoza. Leaving no doubt as to what the source of materialism was, Marx pointed out that 'French and English materialism was always closely related to Democritus and Epicurus'.[241] And, furthermore, this current had a clear political role, namely in that its anti-metaphysical, materialist perspective, based on the evidence of the senses, led directly to socialism and communism.[242] We can see this influence first of all for the primacy of human sensuousness for understanding the world, which we saw was central to Marx's exposition of Epicureanism in his dissertation and remains so here:

> There is no need for any great penetration to see from the teaching of materialism on the original goodness and equal intellectual endowment of men, the omnipotence of experience, habit and education, and the influence of environment on man, the great significance of industry, the justification of enjoyment, etc., how necessarily materialism is connected with communism and socialism. If man draws all his knowledge, sensation, etc., from the world of the senses and the experience gained in it, then what has to be done is to arrange the empirical world in such a way that man experiences and becomes accustomed to what is truly human in it and that he becomes aware of himself as man.[243]

Marx then continues with a passage that has important resonances with the Epicurean conception of justice, as summarised in the excerpts he made from the *Principal Doctrines* in one of the notebooks used for his dissertation. He summarises the connection between the aforementioned materialism and its implications for political life as follows:

> If correctly understood interest is the principle of all morality, man's private interest must be made to coincide with the interest of humanity.

---

241   Marx 1975e, p. 126.
242   Marx 1975e, p. 125.
243   Marx 1975e, p. 130. In the terms of the dissertation, this becoming aware of oneself as human was phrased, as we saw in terms of gaining self-consciousness and thus move beyond relative, natural existence.

If man is unfree in the materialistic sense, i.e., is free not through the negative power to avoid this or that, but through the positive power to assert his true individuality, crime must not be punished in the individual, but the anti-social sources of crime must be destroyed, and each man must be given social scope for the vital manifestation of his being. If man is shaped by environment, his environment must be made human. If man is social by nature, he will develop his true nature only in society, and the power of his nature must be measured not by the power of the separate individual but by the power of society.[244]

These key tenets of eighteenth-century materialism are then further demonstrated in selected quotations from the works of Bentham, Helvetius, and most notably Holbach.[245] Furthermore Marx shows the connections between these ideas and various currents of nineteenth-century English and French socialism and communism, for example that of Fourier and Owen, among many others.[246] Here we can then grasp the political significance of ancient Epicureanism, for through its influence on English and French materialism, it was, if indirectly, the mainspring of modern socialism and communism in a theoretical sense. If we leave aside the more complex aspects of the relation to Hegelianism and Feuerbach's humanism, this clearly shows, conforming to Marx's own words, the efficacy of these ancient ideas in the early Marx. Unfortunately, despite this, they can hardly be taken to be original to Marx as a whole, in the sense of providing a clear foundation for all of his work. For the very same political reason that led Marx to Epicurus, somewhat later also served to draw him away from 'political Epicureanism' as conceived by (early) modern European philosophy.

The argument and controversies on the 'epistemological break' signalled by the theses on Feuerbach and the *German Ideology* of 1845 are well-known and need hardly be elaborated here. On the Epicurean front, at least, the evidence for a break is unambiguous. Leaving aside the overall thrust of the argument against Feuerbach, Marx also repudiates Epicurus in two of the theses. Indirectly, we can see this in the first thesis, where 'all previous materialism' is seen as being limited by mere contemplation, rather than taking an active stance,

---

244   Marx 1975e, pp. 130–1.
245   Marx 1975e, pp. 132–4. The reference to Holbach is especially notable given that his *System of Nature* is excerpted in the appendix of Marx's doctoral thesis on the critique of Plutarch on the Epicurean conception of the gods, Marx 1975a, p. 102. The importance of Holbach for the early Marx is set out comprehensively in Lecompte 1983.
246   Marx 1975e, p. 131.

or as Marx put it in the eleventh and last thesis, seeking to merely understand the world rather than to change it.[247] Epicurus is certainly implicated as part of the totality of preceding materialisms. Even if he shares much with the outlook of some the theses, and should not be conflated with the main target of Feuerbach, Epicurus can hardly be argued as harbouring the revolutionary practice called for by Marx.[248] Yet a more direct distinction can be seen in thesis nine and ten, which pertains directly upon the political importance of Epicurus.

In thesis nine Marx argues that the preceding forms of contemplative materialism, which cannot grasp that practical activity is the basis for sensuousness, are limited to 'the contemplation of single individuals in "civil society"'.[249] Such contemplation is, of course, precisely what we saw for Marx's interpretation of the Epicurean state as based on a contract that has utility as an end. The same interpretation is in fact also repeated in the *German Ideology*, where Marx points out that the notion of the social contract, of the state as derived from mutual agreement, derives from Epicurus.[250] In the tenth thesis on Feuerbach, Marx adds to the preceding one the following contrast between two opposing standpoints, that of the 'old materialism' being located in civil society, and that of its new successor that of 'associated humanity'.[251] Again, the contrast is also present in the *German Ideology*, which can be seen very well in the following passage:

> Up till now association (by no means an arbitrary one, such as is expounded for example in the *Contrat social*, but a necessary one) was simply an agreement about those conditions, within which the individuals were free to enjoy the freaks of fortune (compare, e.g., the formation of the North American state and the South American republics). This right to the undisturbed enjoyment, within certain conditions, of fortuity and chance has up till now been called personal freedom. – These conditions

---

247   Marx 1975 f., pp. 6, 8.
248   If we recall from Chapter 2 the Epicurean emphasis on the philosophical therapeutic of the *tetrapharmakos* as the basis for gaining the life of the gods, proceeding from inner reform in the company of friends toward the emergence of a new form of social life, then we can grasp how different this is from Marx's emphasis on revolutionary practice and class struggle in bringing about such changes, as captured in the third thesis on Feuerbach, Marx 1975 f., p. 4.
249   Marx 1975 f., p. 8.
250   Marx and Engels 1975, p. 141.
251   Marx 1975 f., p. 8.

of existence are, of course, only the productive forces and forms of inter-course at any particular time.[252]

Here the contrast between Marx's new perspective and a contemplative materialism that advocates a social contract that allows for the freedom of the individual for 'undisturbed enjoyment', is now drawn out explicitly. For it is an intrinsically different perspective from that of a social formation based on the associated use of the productive forces (communism). Given that Marx in al his pre-1845 writings that directly refer to Epicureanism only refers to the social contract of Epicurus, and not to the broader canvas painted by Lucretius, suggests that this for him was the most important, defining aspect. Marx broke not just with his kind of social contractual thinking, but also with the previously existing communisms of people like Owen.[253] The very same communisms he had argued in the *Holy Family* to have been crucially influenced by eighteenth-century materialism, itself a historical successor to ancient atomism, all now relegated as 'contemplative materialisms'. Hence the same political reasons that once drove Marx to Epicureanism now led him, not perhaps to disassociate himself from the ancient thinker, but to treat him more as an inspiration than as a foundational influence.

This can be seen quite well in Marx's notion of metabolism (*Stoffwechsel*), a concept discussed in the previous section, where its importance for the relation between humans and nature and the thesis of the plurality of worlds was emphasised. The influences of contemporary science on Marx has been traced in great detail.[254] What is rather striking, however, is the missed encounter with Epicureanism and Lucretius in particular. If we take the basic outline of metabolism from volume I of *Capital*, there, in their interaction with nature, human beings do not just act on external objects, but at the same time change their own nature as well.[255] At this level the similarity with the *phusiopoiei* of the ancient atomists is striking, and the possible connection through the 1844 manuscripts has to be born in mind. Marx also used the Lucretian account of the earliest history in book V of DRN for illustrative purposes, in the discussion of the shifts in the use of different metals for money in the *Grundrisse*.[256]

Yet the atomists are absent from Marx's account of metabolism, whether in the passages of volume I of *Capital* or in any of his other texts that deal with the

---

252   Marx and Engels 1975, pp. 80–1.
253   Marx and Engels 1976, pp. 514–17.
254   In chapter five of Foster 2000 and in Kohei 2017.
255   Marx 1976a, p. 283.
256   Marx 1973, p. 182.

concept. Lucretius is present, however, in another passage, which is concerned with the role of constant capital relative to the creation of value, to which Marx adds a remarkable footnote

> What Lucretius says is self-evident: '*nil posse creari de nihilo*', out of nothing, nothing can be created. 'Creation of value' is the transposition of labour-power into power. Labour-power itself is, above all else, the material of nature transposed into a human organism.[257]

Labour-power, being central to the metabolism of humans and nature, is here connected not with the notion of *phusiopoiei*, but with another, central aspect of Epicurean philosophy. For as we saw in the account of the convergences between Epicureanism and Spinozism in Chapter 1, the notion that nothing can come from (nor disappear into) nothing was central to Epicurean ontology. In opposition to idealist notions of Origin, it posits an eternal 'sum of things' with a constant coming and passing away of compound forms, in other words the principle of *mors immortalis* inherent in nature. The citation of Lucretius hence has to be seen as a show of force of inspiration, for it shows the efficacy of the encounter of the early Marx with Lucretius, in the new framework of *Capital*. In this sense, it is also noteworthy that in another passage of volume I, the very same ideas are present but with different authorities cited. This concerns the citation from Verri, which is used to the effect that when humans produce, they 'can only proceed as nature does herself, i.e. he can only change the form of the materials', given the impossibility of acts of creation.[258]

The inspirational force of Epicureanism, then, is not to be discounted, and Marx seems to have been powerfully shaped in his thinking by the qualification 'magnificent naivety' that we have already seen that he used to describe ancient philosophy. In the dissertation he would go so far as to claim that the great Hellenistic schools of philosophy, of Epicureanism, Scepticism, and Stoicism, might well deserve 'full spiritual citizenship' in the modern world.[259] The great endeavour of historical materialism had brought Marx far beyond the limited writings of Lucretius on the emergence of fire, metallurgy, the first cities, and property within the narrow confines of the Mediterranean and adjacent areas. Now, the question is of the world market, and with it world history, and of Cyc-

---

257 Marx 1976a, n. 2, p. 323. The importance of this passage is highlighted in Foster 2000, p. 168; Morfino 2012a.
258 Marx 1976a, pp. 133–4, note the gendered language, also present in the subsequent citation from Petty on the earth as the 'mother' of material world.
259 Marx 1975a, p. 35.

lopean machines that develop human powers far beyond what was possible in antiquity. In this sense it is instructive to compare the Greek naivety in philosophy with that of their art, based as it was not just on Greek mythology, but also their broader imagination of nature and social relations:

> It is well known that Greek mythology is not only the arsenal of Greek art but also its foundation. Is the view of nature and of social relations on which the Greek imagination and hence Greek [mythology] is based possible with self-acting mule spindles and railways and locomotives and electrical telegraphs? What chance has Vulcan against Roberts & Co., Jupiter against the lightning-rod and Hermes against the Crédit Mobilier? All mythology overcomes and dominates and shapes the forces of nature in the imagination and by the imagination; it therefore vanishes with the advent of real mastery over them. What becomes of Fama alongside Printing House Square? Greek art presupposes Greek mythology, i.e. nature and the social forms already reworked in an unconsciously artistic way by the popular imagination.[260]

In this passage from the 1857 introduction, Marx shies away from historical relativism, however, for there is an 'eternal charm' to the naivety of Greek art,[261] a notion that rather closely parallels his views on the pull of the naivety of Greek philosophy. Both still have the power to draw moderns, to inspire them and even set models to attain. Given the extensive drawing upon and rationalisation of mythology by Lucretius, they are also by no means completely separable.[262] If these sources served as great inspirations for Marx personally, as well as in his most important ideas, then the analysis here serves to deepen our knowledge of his work. While it would be quite possible to grasp Marx from his major theoretical statements in themselves, his sources of inspiration show rather more clearly the processes of thinking behind it. Knowing these processes can prevent Marx's theoretical statements from hardening into lapidary doctrines, and furthermore allows them to be understood in a more flexible way within the framework of the theses of the aleatory current.

---

260 Marx 1973, p. 110.

261 Marx 1973, p. 111. Marx had planned to write more on Greek art and philosophy, see Rose 1984 for context.

262 In this sense we can perhaps understand Marx's remark that 'little use can be made of Lucretius', Marx 1975b, p. 466. Lezra has argued, however, for the powerful force of the work of Lucretius in Marx, as an interlocutor of Epicurean ideas in his work, see the first chapter of Lezra 2018, especially pp. 50–4 on *vestigia*.

4   Marx, the Aleatory Current, and the Realm of Freedom

It is now possible to relate the analysis of Marx's early engagement with Epicureanism to the earlier evaluation of his mature and late works, using the theses of the aleatory current. The connecting element here is the conception of the dialectic as critical and transient on the one hand, and realist and historical on the other. Starting with the former aspect, it can be readily observed that if the only thing that is immutable is the mutability of everything (*mors immortalis*), there can be no question of a universalist conception of historical development. For if the economic categories are inherently transient, there can be no historico-philosophical theories, as in the adaptation of Marx's primitive accumulation to Russia by some of his followers there. If a similar trajectory can be observed in different cases, it is a result of probabilities, given the existence of tendential laws, not of a necessary sequence reflecting logical categories.

In a similar vein, the transient character of *mors immortalis* invalidates Morgan's concept of a hierarchical scale of mind from simple to complex. For there can be no unchanging, simple category of mind in Marx to serve as a foundation for this. Hence while Marx shares with Morgan the notion of a metabolism between humans and nature, one that also has an ideal aspect, there is no prefigured path of development in Marx. The notion of a unilinear pathway cannot even be grasped in terms of a tendential law in itself, as will be shown in the discussion on communism below. Finally, an important difference with Engels can be found in the critical, transient aspect of the dialectic, which voids any notion of universal laws governing it. As an immutable principle, *mors immortalis* is purely negative, denying the universal applicability of any principle. Therefore, it is incompatible with and opposed to the notion of *Wechselwirkung*, in the sense of necessity structuring the interaction between elements, which shapes a teleonomic unfolding of development from simple matter to consciousness.

With regard to the realist, historical aspect of Marx's dialectic, however, the difference with Engels is more subtle. For the emphasis on different historical laws valid for different eras could support different views on historical development in Marx, from the unilinear outline of the 1859 preface to the comparative, pluralist method of the 1857 introduction. In the former text Marx is more closely aligned with Engels, as is clear also from the use made of that text by Engels. Yet even if a sequence of different economic epochs is posited, the succession between them structured by a contradiction between the forces and relations of production, what is still lacking here in Marx is a teleonomic conception of development in itself. Although the different epochs are seen as a progressive series, there is no causal connection between them in the sense that there is posited a single historical pathway that traverses all of them. That is, there is no posited set of general dialectical laws and no view of a hierarchical progression from simple matter to complex forms of consciousness. The linearity of the process is not an inherent necessity, but rather results from what is arguably an abbreviated presentation of a succession of distinct historical laws from a realist perspective.

Indeed, unlike in Engels, there is no question here of proceeding from generic dialectical principles to the more detailed and specific knowledge of a specific phenomenon. Instead the realist mode of inquiry in Marx is separate from the dialectical exposition. As such, the realism is not so much based on a specific conception of matter, but rather on the primacy of the human interaction with nature that includes sense-perception. This realism is in contradistinction to idealist impositions of logically constructed schemes on the world, as in Hegelianism. While not exactly identical to the metabolism of humans and nature in the productive process, this realism nevertheless shared the same practical conception of knowledge. As argued earlier, in spite of the break with 'all preceding materialisms' in the *Theses on Feuerbach*, it is still possible to see traces of the early Marx's engagement with Epicureanism in his later realist conception of the dialectic. Particularly relevant in this regard is his discussion of the Epicurean *eidola* as the perception of nature by itself in human consciousness, in other words the human sense of things as constituting 'embodied time'.

From this perspective it can be said that Marx's realist mode of inquiry proceeds not from an ontology of matter but from the sensory perception of the natural world, not from universal laws of dialectics but from the recognition of the inherent transience of all things. It is a practical grasp of things, and in that sense variable by definition, for nature is always changing and not necessarily according to what was previously assumed by humans to be lawful. Hence it is not surprising that Marx, unlike Engels, was appreciative of historical pluralism, as can be seen in the Montaignesque passages in the 1857 introduction. This valuation of historical differences was a strong current that runs throughout his work, despite the important discontinuities and breaks, and the role of some traces of the early engagement with Epicureanism in this should certainly not be discounted. Indeed, one aspect in which the early Marx should be related to his later iterations concerns one that has yet to be considered: that of the higher phase of communism, that of the realm of freedom.

In the previous sections, the discussion has remained limited to the first phase of the transition to communism, with emphasis being given to the specific, capitalist point of departure and its impact on this phase. However, another form of communism can be found in Marx, one defined by freedom rather than by necessity. A crucial question in this regard is how this form should be understood in an aleatory and historical sense, rather than as aspirational, as in Morgan, or as the result of a teleonomic unfolding of historical stages, as in Engels. The crux of the problem is that the realm of freedom appears to be an ideal notion, given its seeming independence from a specific historical context. Yet from an aleatory perspective such an ideal concept of communism would be impossible, for there is nothing immutable to support it but only the principle of *mors immortalis* that would signal its inevitable demise or transformation. In order to resolve this question, therefore, it is necessary to show that the realm of freedom is a historical concept, in the sense that it follows from practice (human beings) rather than from theory (humankind as an abstraction).

The best way to grasp the realm of freedom historically is by relating it to its (potential) historical point of departure, the first phase of communism that still exists in the realm of necessity. There are two important passages where Marx relates these two realms to each other, one in the *Critique of the Gotha Programme* and the other in volume III of *Capital*. In the latter work, moreover, this passage occurs within a broader discussion of surplus value, where Marx pointed out how capital had developed both the productivity of labour and elements contradictory to its own persistence. This is the familiar historical point of departure for the first phase of communism, but Marx here also relates it to what comes after it:

> The real wealth of society and the possibility of a constant expansion of its reproduction process does not depend on the length of surplus labour but rather on its productivity and on the more or less plentiful conditions of production in which it is performed. The realm of freedom really begins only where labour determined by necessity and external expediency ends; it lies by its very nature beyond the sphere of material production proper. Just as the savage must wrestle with nature to satisfy his needs, to maintain and reproduce his life, so must civilized man, and he must do so in all forms of society, and under all possible modes of production. This realm of natural necessity expands with his development, because his needs do so too; but the productive forces to satisfy these expand at the same time.[263]

---

263   Marx 1981, pp. 958–9.

A number of important points are raised by this passage. Notably Marx discounts the notion that material production by itself can lead to freedom, for just as it increases, so do human needs. In this sense, the 'civilised' is not better off than the 'savage', even if the necessities they face are very different. The juxtaposition of the two in this passage can be connected to another one in volume I of *Capital*. There, in his discussion of the earthly basis of differences between regions, Marx brings up the subsistence on the natural fruit of the sago tree on certain islands in the East Indies.[264] The ease of gathering and consuming these fruits allows for only a small expenditure of labour to meet the extant needs of the islanders, serving as a counterpoint to a supposed natural drive to supply a surplus value beyond them.[265] Economic life on these islands lacks the compulsion to 'pump out' surplus value, instead being naturally blessed by nature in a way allowing for much leisure, even if with the limited tools available there is little potential to use this time for productive uses.

The islanders of the East Indies, then, are limited by what nature can provide, even if they are not compelled to labour for the benefit of the others. By contrast for their 'civilised' counterparts in western Europe the situation is the exact reverse. For they possess a greater power relative to nature based on machinery, yet are at the same time enslaved to a system of needs that compels them to work a great many more hours.[266] As such, the contrast between 'savage' and 'civilised' goes to the core of the distinction between the realms of necessity and of freedom: that of external determination, whether by natural or social forces. This point is reinforced by the continuation of the passage on the two forms of communism in volume III of *Capital*:

> Freedom, in this sphere, can consist only in this, that socialized man, the associated producers, govern the human metabolism with nature in a rational way, bringing it under their collective control instead of being dominated by it as a blind power; accomplishing it with the least expenditure of energy and in conditions most worthy and appropriate for their human nature. But this always remains a realm of necessity. The true realm of freedom, the development of human powers as an end in itself,

---

264 Marx 1976a, pp. 650–1.

265 Marx's analysis finds an (unacknowledged) echo in the notion of the 'original affluent society', Sahlins 1968. This concept has recently been restudied, with findings in line with Marx's insight, Bhui et al. 2019.

266 See in this regard also the second volume of Capital, where it is emphasised that the goal of the capitalist is not to enjoy the fruits of labour, but rather to increase surplus value, Marx 1997, p. 125.

begins beyond it, though it can only flourish with this realm of necessity as its basis. The reduction of the working day is the basic prerequisite.[267]

In this sense the reduction of the working day within the context of a productive process based on machinery, implies a move beyond both 'savage' and 'civilised' as defined by Marx. For unlike as for the 'savage' there is a (relative) freedom from being determined by natural necessity, and unlike the 'civilised' there is no compulsion to maximise surplus value. Labour in this state can be said to have been freed from both its natural and conventional constraints, which resonates with the description of the second, higher phase of communism in the *Critique of the Gotha Programme*.[268] Notably, there the division of labour itself was questioned as a foreign imposition on natural human inclinations, echoing an earlier famous passage on communism from the *German Ideology*.[269] This view of communism, then, negates the two social metabolisms of commodity exchange and the division of labour. They are replaced by the common direction of the associated producers, in effect a new social metabolism, one that governs the metabolism with nature in a rational way, using nature in ways beneficial to humans but without implying a mastery over it.[270]

As a potential historical form, this social metabolism stands relative to two historical points of departure. First of all there are the social metabolisms of commodity exchange and the division of labour, with which it marks a break. Given that these two were themselves developed in various ways in different world regions, the transition to communism as the realm of freedom should be understood as a potentiality in relation to them. That is, there is no specific path of progress, no necessity of a past form for future developments, as in the notion of slavery being a necessity for modern socialism in Engels. For if that is a necessity at all, it is so purely by virtue of the specific, historical point of departure among a number of potential alternatives. The second break is with the determination of nature by necessity, equally present in all previously existing forms of social life. Like the 'sago eaters' of the East Indies, future communists will face no more than the socially necessary labour time, without any compulsion to work longer so as to produce surplus value. Unlike the inhabitants of these blessed islands, however, they will have the means to develop their copious leisure time productively, owing to the greatly developed productive forces.

---

267   Marx 1981, p. 959.
268   Marx 1989b, p. 85.
269   Marx and Engels 1975, pp. 80–1.
270   Marx 1981, p. 911.

As such, communism as the realm of freedom can be understood in a historical sense, as a potential form relative to existing ones, negating previous forms. The possibility of such a negation is highlighted precisely by the examples discussed for the thesis of the plurality of worlds, which showed that the historically particular trajectory of commodity exchange and the division of labour in western Europe. As the existence of other 'worlds' can be demonstrated, so can the transience of the current, capitalist world. Yet even if it is a historical concept, the source of this form of communism is not purely historical. For part of the impetus behind it is the conception of revolutionary praxis in the theses on Feuerbach, and the break these marked with all previously existing strands of communism and materialism, as discussed in the previous section. In the sense that this praxis is defined as 'the coincidence of the changing of circumstances and of human activity or self-change',[271] it points to an active, practical stance rather than to a contemplative life within a democratic republic.

Yet at the same time there are continuities with those previously existing systems of thought as well. Taking into account the discussion of English and French materialism in relation to various communism in the *Holy Family*, it should be noted that it has some resemblance to Marx's realm of freedom in three ways. Firstly, there is the freedom from external determination. Secondly, the rearrangement of the empirical world in accordance with inferred human needs based on sensory experience. Thirdly, and finally, the primacy of collective power as the most beneficial for both the group and the individual. Given that Marx observes the close relation between ancient atomism and English and French materialism, it is little wonder that all three aspects could be related to ideas current in Epicureanism, as the previous section showed. Certainly, the revolutionary praxis and use of the concept of metabolism are inspired rather than directly derived from Epicurus and Lucretius, but the common inspiration is strong. It is based on the notion that the good life can be realised by a combination of practical and theoretical means, not in the form of a utopia but in a potential form of social life that negates the ills of the present. In that sense Marx's view of communism as the realm of freedom shares much with the Epicurean future inscribed on the walls of ancient Oenoanda.[272]

271   Marx 1975 f., p. 4.
272   As discussed in Chapter 2. The first fragments of this inscription were discovered in 1884, after Marx's death.

'The Relics of Bygone Instruments', Marxist Archaeology and the Thesis of the Plurality of Worlds

The previous chapters aimed to demonstrate two things. First of all to show how the theses of the aleatory current can shed light on the conceptions of history in thinkers usually grouped together in the materialist category. This can be seen as a 'current' (in the sense intended by Heraclitus) stretching from its emergence in the ancient atomists to the nineteenth-century writings of Marx and Engels. Secondly, the aim was to show how the historical perspectives of these thinkers reflects back on the understanding of the aleatory current itself, pointing to the potential to deepen the theses already proposed and to formulate new ones. As such, it has been a mutually supportive endeavour, combining philosophy and the history of ideas in a comparative investigation of thinkers in different ages and regions. A major impetus in this was to grasp the influence specifically of the Epicurean ideas on early human history, in relation to natural history in a broader sense, which so far had received less attention in debates on the aleatory current in philosophy.

Chapter 2 dealt with these ideas in depth, focusing especially on the Lucretian outline of early human history as an extension from anthropogony, zoogony, and cosmogony. The theses of the aleatory current were used to grasp this account, in which two major aspects stood out in particular. The first of these concerned the notion of two camps in ancient philosophy, which are usually seen as those of the idealists and the materialists. Yet perhaps the more important distinguishing features were, respectively, a theoretical and teleological perspective as counterposed to a realist and aleatory one. This translated into two views of human history, on the one hand the 'idealist' camp of Aristotle, Plato, and the Stoics, and on the other the 'materialists', of which the ancient atomists were the exemplary case. The other great contribution of the aleatory current was to recognise the plural temporality inherent in the Lucretian account of early history, as distinct from approaches seeing it as a stadialist outline based on a succession of social forms. In return, the Epicurean source material allowed for the formulation of a new aleatory thesis: that of the plurality of worlds.

In the Epicurean sources the thesis of the plurality of worlds follows from two things. First of all, from a realist conception of knowledge as based on the senses, it follows that it is impossible to gain definitive certainty with regard to the heavenly phenomena. Hence a plurality of different possible causes for the same phenomenon cannot be ruled out. Secondly, in the conception of the emergence of worlds, the chance encounter of atoms shapes these newly formed *kosmoi*. The same also holds true for the subsequent beginnings of animate beings, social forms, technology, and so on. It is not surprising, there-fore, that in the same passage in the *Letter to Herodotus* on the plurality of worlds, Epicurus also emphasises the different trajectories of social develop-ment in distinct world regions (partly from chance, partly from natural causes). However, this aspect of the thesis was developed into an entirely new direction as a result of the late Renaissance encounter with the Americas.

In Machiavelli it was already possible to note a new conception of the past, based both on his notion of the encounter and the comparative approach it engendered in his work, and on the recognition of the fallibility of historical memory. As he emphasised, most knowledge of the past has been lost, owing to human and natural causes, leaving moderns with only a fragment of knowledge on ancient events. A fragment, moreover, that cannot stand for the whole, as historical knowledge is inherently uncertain and unwieldy for anyone seeking order in it. Instead, one has to live, in a Machiavellian sense, by one's wits, using a comparative approach to delineate whatever patterns one can. The implicit valuation, or rather recognition, of pluralism, enhanced by Machiavelli's under-standing of historical causation, later became more explicit in Montaigne. For in his work a similar conception of historical memory is juxtaposed with the different social forms encountered by Europeans in the Americas, a discussion framed by references to the plurality of worlds in Epicureanism.

In Montaigne, then, there is not a single template for the development of civilisation, the New World having taken a different course than the Old. In the same way, there might be different human worlds, too, in the deep past that is now lost. Hence one cannot use the fragment of knowledge rooted in one's own culture as the criterion for judging history as a whole. Montaigne decried the violence inflicted by the Europeans, motivated by greed, on the indigen-ous Americans and their cultures. He also imagined a counterfactual encounter between the American and ancient Greco-Roman civilisations, based not on genocide and plunder but rather a peaceful and mutually beneficial meeting of different worlds and temporalities. In the tendential laws that established European colonialism, it was impossible for such a meeting of minds to take place. Instead a consistent denial of the historical achievements of the Amer-ican civilisations can be observed, paralleling the wholesale subjection and exploitation of its surviving peoples. One of the philosophical justifications of this denial can be found in Locke's thesis that 'in the beginning all the world was

America', which effectively relegated the continent's civilisations to a position on the lowest rung of a stadialist ladder of development.

Of course, Locke has to be understood within a broader Eurocentric current, which involved not just positing the historical primacy of Europe but also the internal, linear character of social development in geographical spaces bounded by state sovereignty. This perspective is directly opposed to any Montaignesque valuation of pluralism in history. Most notably, in the hands of men like De Pauw and Robertson the Lockean thesis was broadened into a comprehensive critique of the descriptions of indigenous American civilisations in the Spanish sources. Their civilisational status was found by them to be doubtful and mistaken in the terms defined by Europeans, with inferiority even posited for the mental development of indigenous Americans. This perspective was wholly adopted by Adam Smith, as part of his overall philosophical views. A perspective that saw progress as being structured as a 'harmonious machine', in which the seeking of riches fulfilled a paramount systemic role. We are far removed here from Machiavelli and Montaigne, and it is this perspective that proved more influential, and retains influence even today.[1]

For Marxism, the greatest impact of Locke's American thesis and its later elaborations was through the influence of Morgan's work. Morgan was greatly influenced by the Lucretian outline of early human history, and recognised the role of the aleatory even in his stadialist outline of development. Yet his notion of a universal scale of mind structuring development led him to discount the causal efficacy of the continental differences he recognised for the New and Old Worlds, except for its influence upon the pace of development. Furthermore, based in part on his fieldwork with the Iroquois and other North American Indian tribes, Morgan joined in with the criticism of the Spanish sources, denying the Aztec and Maya the status of civilisation and statehood. This denial of the thesis of the plurality of worlds was adapted without question in the reworking of *Ancient Society* by Engels, if from a rather different theoretical perspective than Morgan's.

---

1   Especially in the notion that the indigenous Americas lagged a quantifiable amount of time relative to development in the Old World, usually measured in a few millennia, see for examples Diamond 1997, pp. 360–70; Morris 2015, fig. 5.5, p. 153. Many of Diamond's assumptions are highly questionable, most notably his notion of Eurasia possessing 'more effective food production', Diamond 1997, p. 370, which will be shown below was rather the reverse. Furthermore, his notion of a great distinction between continental axes oriented according to longitude or latitude, the latter being less conducive to cultural contact, is belied by the transmission of metallurgy from the coastal areas of South America to Mesoamerica, Dewan and Hosler 2008. An amusing counterfactual argument to Diamond's ideas can be found in the first part of a recent novel by Laurent Binet, see Binet 2020.

Engels was not influenced by Lucretius nor familiar with the Iroquois, like Morgan, but rather had developed a dialectical and materialist scheme to account for evolution on a cosmic scale, rivalling rather than imitating the ancient atomists. The resulting picture was that of a teleonomic outline of a progressive unfolding of stages from simple matter to complex consciousness. In the development of social forms this led to an even lesser appreciation of pluralism than in Morgan, due to a conception of the necessary relations between elements captured in the notion of *Wechselwirkung*. Hence Engels did not just adapt Morgan's view of the New World, but also posited the necessity of ancient slavery for modern socialism to exist in strongly teleonomic terms. Using the theses of the aleatory current, it was possible to more clearly distinguish the views of Engels from those of Marx, specifically with regard to their respective valuation of pluralism.

Through a close reading of Marx's excerpts and comments on Morgan's *Ancient Society*, as well as their resonances in his mature and late work, these distinctions become apparent. Furthermore, this argument was extended to show how in the interstices of the volumes of *Capital* and the preparatory studies, a version of the thesis of the plurality of worlds can be recognised. Most notably, Marx used another set of excerpts from a work on the indigenous civilisations of the Americas, Prescott's work on the Spanish conquests of the Aztec and Inca realms, to bolster his case against the classical political economists. His main thrust here was to counter their assumptions, showing their historical relativity, rather than providing his own analysis of these civilisations. Most notably, the Inca case showed that the development of the division of labour need not be coeval with the emergence of commodity exchange. This case hence throws into doubt the universality of the role of commodity exchange in the formation of the state, as argued for by Engels.

The use of the Inca case needs to be grasped together with other aspects favouring pluralism in Marx's mature work, such as the earthly basis of the metabolism of humans and nature in relation to geographically differences. The different regional trajectories these engendered were not subsumed under a universalist outline of history in Marx, unlike as in Morgan and Engels, who argued instead for a comparative method to evaluate their distinctive characteristics. This comparative perspective followed from his view of dialectics as both historical and critical, as seen in both volume I of *Capital* and the 1857 introduction to the *Grundrisse*. Furthermore, aspects of this dialectical method can be related to the engagement of the early Marx with the ideas of the ancient atomists, despite the break instituted by the *Theses on Feuerbach*. This observation allows for recognising in Marx not so much a hidden doctrine of Epicureanism, but rather a powerful source of inspiration that shaped his work not in the application of preconceived ideas but rather in valuing the aleatory and pluralism.

In this epilogue the two views of Marxism that result from the distinctions of Marx and Engels will be traced within the application of these ideas in a particular historical science, that of archaeology. First of all, the emergence of archaeology will be related to the late Renaissance encounter with both ancient Epicureanism and the contemporary Americas, as discussed in Chapter 3. For this encounter had a formative influence on the first major archaeological theory, the Three Age system that divided prehistory into a Stone, Bronze, and Iron Age. This theory, however, would be shaped in powerful ways by the institutional context in which it not just emerged but 'took hold', most notably in the dominating influence of European nationalism and its colonialist and imperialist offshoots. As such, it provided the context for another encounter, that between archaeology and Marxism, which despite passages in Marx's mature writings pointing to a pluralist conception was shaped mostly by the work of Morgan and Engels.

This influence can be traced especially well in Soviet archaeology, both for the initial emergence of humankind and the first forms of social life, and for the subsequent unfolding of the sequence of the five modes of production in the *pyatichlenka*. Most importantly, the conceptions of materialism discussed in Chapter 1 for the early Soviet philosophical debates between the 'mechanists' and Deborin and his followers, can be traced here as well. This connects the archaeological and historical studies to the broader critiques of their philosophical premises through the theses of the aleatory current. Indeed, the trajectory of historical debates in the USSR shows a move away from both the *pyatichlenka* and the framework of ideas that sustained it. Efforts to preserve it merely served to show its intellectual fallacy, despite strenuous official efforts to preserve it from critique. In that sense, these debates also had a clear political role. For the debates that pitted unilineal views of history against more pluralist conceptions of it also had clear implications for the understanding of the (world) historical role of the October Revolution and the Soviet model of development.

If the *pyatichlenka* was obsolete both scientifically and politically, and with it the ideas of Morgan and Engels, the further scientific development of archaeology has rather vindicated the Marxist thesis of the plurality of worlds. This is true especially of the comparative study of the emergence and further development of class systems and of their broader geographical and social contexts. Through extensive fieldwork, the scale and advanced character of the indigenous civilisations of the Americas, and many other cases in Africa and Asia as well, have been recognised, allowing for them to be compared on a global scale without prejudice. Furthermore, it is increasingly recognised that such civilisations cannot be grasped in isolation from the interaction with their peers in larger geographical areas, such as the Mediterranean and Mesoamerica. This shift dovetails with Marx's emphasis on 'worlds' rather than the stadialist sequences of Morgan and Engels. As such, the scientific analysis of the differences between such 'worlds' can now be used to evaluate the plausibility of the thesis of the plurality of worlds.

1   The Aleatory Emergence of Modern Archaeology

In Chapter 3, Locke's thesis that 'in the beginning all the world was America' was treated, and its negative impact on the thesis of the plurality of worlds was noted. Yet in another way, the connection between the pre-Columbian Americas and early European prehistory proved to be an important catalyst to the development of the science of archaeology. For it was through the demonstration of a resemblance between artefacts as used in contemporary Amerindian societies and those found in European archaeological contexts, that the antiquity of the latter was demonstrated. Conceptually, this connection was made early on during the European encounter with the Americas. The clearest initial example comes from the description of the earliest architecture in chapter 1 of Book II of *De Architectura* by Vitruvius. In a passage that strongly emphasises that technology and architecture derive from the imitation of nature, the first buildings are described in terms that are of considerable significance for our discussion:

> **First they erected forked uprights**, and weaving twigs in between they covered the whole with mud. Others, letting clods of mud go dry, began to construct walls of them, joining them together with wood, and to avoid rains and heat they covered them over with reeds and leafy branches. Later, when these coverings proved unable to endure through the storms of winter, they made eaves with molded clay, and set in rainspouts on inclined roofs.[2]

Notable in this account, too, is the description of a variety of such constructions in far-flung, 'barbarian' regions, as well as remnants of them in Athens and Rome. It is precisely the use of such unworked tree trunks in the earliest

---

2   Rowland 1999, p. 34, emphasis added.

architecture that is illustrated in the Renaissance manuscripts of Vitruvius, as well as in a Vulcan-themed painting of Piero di Cosimo.[3] They can also be seen in the 1521 edition of *De Architectura* by Cesare Cesariano, where a connection is made between the early humans of Vitruvius and recently discovered cave dwellers in India.[4] A connection with the Americas is evident in unsquared tree trunks in the house depicted in the oldest extant European image of indigenous Americans, a German woodcut dated to 1505, as well as in a later work by the painter Jan Mostaert.[5] The connection between the Vitruvian account of the earliest times and indigenous Brazilians is also evident in the 1555 staging of their way of life for the entry of Henry II in Rouen,[6] already referred to in Chapter 3.

Thus, art history suggests not only a connection between the earliest history of humankind and the contemporary Americas, but also the influence of specific Greco-Roman texts such as that of Vitruvius. One element depicted in a woodcut from Cesariano's 1521 edition is the use of stone tools, which notably were not present in the text of Vitruvius.[7] The significance of this becomes clearer when we consider that Greco-Roman accounts of the first ages regularly describe a lack of metals, cultivation, writing, and so on, but rarely describe the extant technology.[8] In fact, the use of stone tools is only explicitly described in Lucretius. It can be found in his account of the beginning of metallurgy, precisely after the section on the shifts in the esteem within which different metals were held, which is then extended to account for the emergence of iron metallurgy:

> The ancient weapons were hands, nails, and teeth, and stones and branches also broken from forest trees, and fire as soon as they were known. Later was discovered the power of iron and of bronze. The use of bronze was known before iron, because it is more easily worked and there is greater store. With bronze men tilled the soil of the earth, with bronze they stirred up the waves of war, and sowed devastating wounds, and seized cattle and lands; for when some were armed, all that was naked

---

3　Panofsky 1972, p. 44.
4　Kim 2014, p. 50.
5　See for the German woodcut Schuller 1930; for an interpretation of Mostaert's painting Snyder 1976.
6　Kim 2014, fig. 2.10, p. 52.
7　Schnapp 1996, p. 73.
8　For the interest seems to have been more focused on the earliest state of affairs negating the technological prowess current in the Greco-Roman world, Lovejoy and Boas 1935, p. 14.

and unarmed readily gave way to them. Then by small degrees the sword of iron gained ground, and the fashion of the bronze sickle became a thing of contempt; then with iron they began to break the soil of the earth, and the struggles of war now become doubtful were made equal.[9]

One problem with the Lucretian account of the development of technology, for its interpreters in Renaissance Europe and afterwards as well, was that it directly contradicted Scripture. For in *Genesis*, only a few generations after Adam and Eve, Tubal-cain is described as an 'instructor of every artificer in brass and iron'.[10] Notwithstanding the great longevity of Biblical figures like Methuselah, this account hardly leaves any space for a metal-less 'stone age'. Mounting scientific evidence would eventually overturn this and establish the Three Age system of stone, bronze, and iron ages, following the Lucretian template. It should be noted, however, that the adoption of this scheme was a drawn out struggle, and that as late as the middle of the nineteenth century doubts were still expressed about the validity of the concept of a stone age.[11] The first step toward breaking down the prevalence of such doubts in earlier centuries involved dissociating stone tools, then known as thunderstones or *ceraunia*, from mythological lore and establishing them as objects of science.[12] As with the growing recognition of fossils as the remains of past life forms, this entailed establishing analogies between fossil objects and present day natural and social processes.[13]

Given that close parallels were established between the indigenous Americas and Greco-Roman accounts of early history, including Epicurean ones as we saw, the analogy between the use of stone tools in prehistoric Europe and contemporary America naturally suggested itself. This analogy was in fact made by a number of Seventeenth and Eighteenth century authors.[14] The most important work in this regard was that of Michele Mercati, a man with broad historical interests, as his investigations of the different forms of symbolic writing in Egypt and Mexico show.[15] As a superintendent of the botanical gardens of the Vatican, Mercati had access to a collection of *ceraunia* and added more specimens to it. Based on this body of evidence he was able to make distinctions

---

9   DRN V.1283–1296, Smith 1992, pp. 477, 479.
10 Chagall 2008, p. 25.
11 Trigger 2006, p. 96.
12 Schnapp 1996, p. 151.
13 Trigger 2006, pp. 92–3.
14 Goodrum 2002b, 2008.
15 Cañizares-Esguerra 2001, p. 96.

between the stones and to posit different functional uses for them as tools in his *Metallotheca Vaticana*.[16] Furthermore, his grasp of the material allowed him to posit the analogy with the contemporary use of stone tools in the Americas with a greater degree of scientific credibility, noting how they were used there to fashion ships and houses.[17]

Apart from his scientific precision, another aspect of Mercati's work is that he closely connected technological development to warfare and moral degeneration. This connection was of course present in Lucretius as well, in his account of the emergence of metallurgy. Hence it is instructive to quote here the passage from Mercati in which he discusses Lucretius:

> 'Ceraunite' has the same shape as these, hence the opinion according to which the ancients, before the working of iron, cut sicilices from flint and that 'ceraunite' comes from this. It seems that among mortals, hate, from small beginnings grew to immense proportions, and the Africans made war on the Egyptians with clubs, which are called phalanges. Before this, the Phoenicians (according to Pomponius Mela and Pliny) were the originators of war. Nor is what Lucretius describes true, that 'ancient weapons were hands, nails and teeth'.
>
> Since these are of little use to man as weapons, he used his intellect, and his hands provided him with weapons which were very suitable for killing so that someone who could not kill in a simple, savage way, could kill more nobly. First, his intellect showed hint stones and sticks as weapons that he should master to attack and overcome an enemy from afar. Whereas originally fighting was restricted to individuals' disagreements, eventually whose peoples and nations took to war. Then ever more terrible weapons of war were occasioned by envy, greed and ambition, in their unquenchable thirst for human blood.[18]

The finding fault with Lucretius here is entirely disingenuous, as a comparison with the text of DRN cited above shows. It can only reflect an attempt on Mercati's part to distance himself from the dangers involved with any association with Lucretius, given the policies of the Inquisition discussed in chapter three. He also sought to forestall any charge of him criticising the Biblical account of

---

16   Goodrum 2008, pp. 493–7.
17   Schnapp 1996, p. 347.
18   Cited in Schnapp 1996, pp. 347–8.

Tubal-Cain as a metallurgist, arguing that metallurgy was lost after the Deluge and only rediscovered in some regions afterwards.[19] Despite these precautions the *Metallotheca Vaticana* was published only posthumously in 1719, though it may have circulated earlier in manuscript form.[20] In the course of the eighteenth century the analogy between the stone tools of prehistoric Europe and contemporary America became more strongly established, and the Lucretian notion of a stone age was seriously considered in scholarly circles.[21] The key problem, however, was that apart from positing such an age, there was as yet little to say about it.

Apart from glimpses afforded by excavations like that of the Cocherel tomb, there was no way to delineate the stone age in chronological terms, let alone to interpret the forms of social life that characterised it. The true breakthrough that established the Three Age system as a scientific concept, rather than a mere hypothesis, came from early nineteenth-century Denmark, based on the work of Christian Thomsen, the first curator of its National Museum of Antiquity. He devised a method for ordering the collection under his care, helped by the evidence of their find contexts.[22] Through such 'closed finds' (artefacts belonging to the same find context), he could determine those that regularly occurred together and those that did not. Important distinguishing features in this regard were the materials and method of fabrication of artefacts, as well as styles in decoration if present. The result was a series of distinct groups of co-occurring artefacts, arranged in a historical order that started with simple stone tools and ended with iron metallurgy.

This scheme was initially supported by limited stratigraphic evidence, yet subsequent excavations would both demonstrate its validity and further refine it. One of these refinements involved the recognition of regional differences between artefact groups, based mainly on stylistic distinctions, which would become connected to nationalism.[23] Other kinds of research connected the tools typical for the phases of the sequence to ethnographic parallels of stone use, and scientific analysis of bone and plant remains allowed for the reconstruction of past environments and means of subsistence.[24] In this way, science made it possible to reconstruct the (economic) ways of life in the different ages. As such, Scandinavian archaeologists advanced over a broad front, even if

---

19   Schnapp 1996, p. 348.
20   Schnapp 1996, p. 267.
21   Trigger 2006, pp. 104–5.
22   Trigger 2006, pp. 123–7.
23   Trigger 2006, pp. 110–14.
24   Trigger 2006, pp. 129–31.

fundamental questions such as determining the true antiquity of humankind would be resolved elsewhere. It has been rightly argued, therefore, that here a new template for archaeology was established, the Three Age system 'taking hold' as it were, in which three strands can be recognised:

> Thus, in early Scandinavian prehistoric archaeology we discover the origins of the evolutionary, culture-historical, and functional-processual approaches that have characterized prehistoric archaeology ever since. In the early nineteenth century, Scandinavian archaeologists evolved a prehistoric archaeology that exhibited in an embryonic form all the main features of modern prehistoric archaeology. Although the database and the analytical resources of prehistoric archaeology have expanded enormously in the interval, the founders of prehistoric archaeology would experience little difficulty in discussing their goals and aspirations with modern archaeologists. Romantic and evolutionary interests had combined to produce a complex and multifaceted interest in prehistoric times.[25]

These three aspects of course sprang from different sources. The evolutionary understanding of the Three Ages derived from Enlightenment ideas, and so did the scientific analysis that allowed for functional-processional reconstructions. More complex is the culture-historical strand. For this derived not just from the recognition of regional differences between archaeological finds, or from the Romantic and/or nationalist inclinations of scholars, but also from the institutional contexts in which archaeological work was carried out. Thomsen had laboured, after all, in a museum, and furthermore not just any museum but the *National* Museum of Antiquity. As such, there was a tendency for cultural sequences to become associated with nation states, even if their characteristics were completely meaningless for understanding prehistoric times. In effect this can be seen as a Westphalianisation of the past, analogous to the geographical imposition of state sovereignty on the New World discussed in Chapter 3. The difference is that here the unit was not so much a spatial one, but more of a temporal one defined by a variety of ideas of nationality.[26]

From such national, institutional contexts it is only a short step to the ideologies used by modern states to legitimise their existence, as had been the case in

---

25   Trigger 2006, p. 137.

26   As different and opposed to an universalism understood as the stadialist process through which 'universal civilisation' is attained, instead being contrary to the existing order, Tomba 2019, p. 21. Cases discussed by him include the French revolution, the Paris Commune, the early phase of the October revolution, as well as the Zapatistas.

a rather different form in pre-capitalist social formations.[27] Of course, distinct kinds of states exist, and archaeologists have noted the distinctions between nationalist, colonialist, and imperialist regimes with regard to the past.[28] More complex patterns have since been recognised, notably of the archaeological practices of the French revolutionary era.[29] Of the three, the nationalist variant was in a sense the foundational one, structuring the others as well. For it was the basis not just for national sequences of archaeological phases, but also for the notion of the superiority of certain nations relative to others. A notion that would be applied in colonialist settings and also formed the ideological basis for the competition between imperialist powers. Because of this, cases that seem far removed from each other in effect share more than commonly assumed, due to the underlying Eurocentric and nationalist framework.

Consider, for example, the discovery and subsequent display in the 1790s of a statue of the Aztec goddess Coatlique. As pointed out by Diaz-Andrue, even if Mexico was nominally still a Spanish colony at the time, its European elites would invoke the statue for patriotic reasons, while the poor indigenous population started to worship Coatlique again before being denied this by the state.[30] Here the official, institutional view of the indigenous past, shared by a wider intelligentsia, was completely divorced from the beliefs and practices of indigenous communities. In this way a European understanding of nations was deployed in a firmly established colonial state, suppressing the actual progenitors and descendants of the ancestral national cultures of Mexico. Of course, this followed the European practice of the primacy of one ethnic group over others, its sovereignty in effect, which of course was also present in Europe itself. Most notable in this regard was the work of the German archaeologist Kossinna, who connected specific archaeological cultures to ethnic groups, their presence being connected to the legitimacy of contemporary claims on territories.[31]

Not out of line with his own beliefs,[32] Kossinna's nationalist perspective was later used in Nazi Germany to provide historical legitimacy for its policies of

---

27   Such efforts can be recognised as early as Bronze Age Egypt and Mesopotamia, Trigger 2006, pp. 43–5. In China, notably, the theories concerning the early history of humankind noted at the beginning of chapter three, also were accompanied by work that related certain kinds of (archaeological) material to these eras, Schnapp 1996, pp. 318–21.
28   Trigger 1984.
29   Díaz-Andrue 2008, pp. 60–78; Wengrow 2010, pp. 163–73.
30   Díaz-Andrue 2008, pp. 56–7.
31   Trigger 2006, pp. 238–9.
32   Trigger 2006, p. 240.

genocidal conquest and occupation.[33] Yet, while distinguished by its extreme violence, Kossinna and the Nazis were a development upon patterns that were widely shared in the culture-historical strand of archaeology, as well as in the Eurocentric conception of evolutionism. Incidentally, this is a problem that reverberates in present day archaeological discourse, despite the extremely watered down ideological context of archaeology in some world regions such as western Europe.[34] Given its institutional embedding and dependence on state support, it is of little surprise that such ideological conceptions enjoy a dominant position, both in education and in the dissemination of knowledge to the public. Yet within archaeology, owing to its intrinsic materiality and scientific ethos of most of its practitioners, the scientific strand cannot be easily subdued by ideological factors. New discoveries always have a potential to undermine ideology, whether by themselves or in combination with philosophical ideas, always present in the shadows, as with Lucretius and the Enlightenment for the Three Age system.

As a development from Enlightenment ideas, Marx's work presented a potential philosophical partner for archaeology, one that could enable it to draw away from the ideological strangleholds of nationalism, colonialism, and imperialism. An encounter between the two would be beneficial for Marxism itself as well, supplying it with new scientific evidence to evaluate existing theses and to formulate new ones. Of course, as we saw in the discussion of Marx's notion of metabolism in the previous chapter, he himself had highlighted the importance of knowledge of 'bygone instruments of production'.[35] Furthermore, he developed this point at some length for the 'earthly basis' of this metabolism, pointing in particular to the first tools and domestication. However, this perspective was for a long time overshadowed by the stadialism of Morgan and Engels. For, as noted earlier, their texts were better known and widely circulated, while those works of Marx containing a more favourable view of historical pluralism only become known well into the twentieth century.

No justice can be done here to Marxist archaeology as it has developed from 1917 to today, given that from the outset a multiplicity of approaches can be discerned. As a global phenomenon, with different streams in all world regions, it is still perhaps not fully understood, especially given that it exis-

---

33   Arnold 1990.
34   See Volker 2017 for the contemporary problematics of genetics in relation to (resurgent) nationalist ideas.
35   Marx 1976, p. 286.

ted in opposition to hegemonic discourses of the 'West' (i.e. NATO). Instead the focus here will lie more narrowly on the fate of the *pyatichlenka* in relation to Soviet archaeology and more recent scientific and comparative work in archaeology. It was this scheme that best embodied the universalist stadialist outlines of Morgan and Engels, even if it should not be taken as exactly identical with their works. As a product of Stalinism it structured early Soviet archaeology and the communist states influenced by it.[36] The main interest in the *pyatichlenka*, however, is that it shows the encounter between stadialism and the scientific process. Over decades of refinement, critique, and reformulation, Soviet scholars comprehensively demonstrated the notion of universal stages of development to be an inadequate way of conceptualising history.

In so doing, they were in dialogue with other Marxist approaches, most notably the work of Gordon Childe, and those influenced by him, on the notion of the urban revolution. This perspective was highly influential among a broad spectrum of scholars in western Europe, and Latin and North America.[37] The detailed study of specific case studies of the urban revolution, as well as global comparative studies of its occurrence in distinct, independent world regions, allows for new Marxist perspectives on the development of class systems. Most notably, these are more in line with Marx's inclinations toward pluralism and the thesis of the plurality of worlds, as recent studies emphasising contrasts in the development of Old and New World civilisations show. As such, the demise of the *pyatichlenka* shows the potential for another way of grasping history. The interest here is not merely with the history of ideas, but follows from the connection of stadialism and the *cul de sac* in which the great revolutions of the twentieth century found themselves. In that way, the encounter of the science of archaeology and the philosophical thesis of the plurality of worlds can lead to a new historical perspective that breaks with the 'bonds of fate' shackling revolutionary politics.

2 The Fate of the Pyatichlenka in Twentieth-Century Science

Soviet archaeology had started many years before the publication of the *Short Course*. To be precise, on 18 April 1919, when Lenin signed a decree to establish the Russian Academy of the History of Material Culture (RAIMK, later changing to the better known State Academy of the History of Material Culture or

---

36   See the contributions in Lozny 2016 for archaeology in a number of Soviet bloc countries.
37   See the papers in Manzanilla 1987 and Harris 1994.

GAIMK).[38] This is not the place to expand upon the history of Soviet archaeology in general, given that the focus here lies on the fate of the *pyatichlenka*. However, a number of key aspects have to be taken into account to understand what follows:

1. The new Soviet state enabled an enormous expansion of scientific research. For archaeology this involved not just an increase in the number and scale of expeditions, but also the use of new scientific techniques to study the artefacts recovered.[39] In this aspect Soviet archaeology was ahead of its imperialist adversaries, even if in more traditional areas of archaeological inquiry the level of research sometimes left something to be desired.[40]

2. Within the vastness of the Soviet Union, the archaeological record was characterised by very distinct phenomena. The record of the Palaeolithic era was rich and especially suitable for the new field methods and methods for analysing artefacts, as will be discussed below for the study of sites such as Kostenki. When it came to the emergence and further development of class systems, Soviet archaeologists were initially faced with cases that seemed more peripheral to the great civilisations of Indian subcontinent, Middle East, and eastern Mediterranean.[41] Examples are the Caucasus and Central Asia during the Bronze Age, and the Crimea for the Classical era. Then there was the vast Eurasian interior, which initially existed in a kind of conceptual void, being unable to be captured by 'national' sequences of the kind seen in western Europe. It was only from the medieval era onwards that something like Russian archaeology can be seen as a plausible research subject.[42] Hence the conceptual unity,

---

38   Trigger 2006, p. 326.

39   For example in reconstructing tool use, Semenov 1964.

40   Chapter six of Klejn 2012 discusses in some depth the tensions between the historical focus of Soviet Marxism and the traditional culture-historical methods of archaeology. See especially his take on the regionalist focus of Soviet research, compared to the broader geographical scale of western European research, Klejn 2012, pp. 130–1, which owed something to the stadialist focus of both the *Short Course* and of the tracing of national origins.

41   Russian and later Soviet conceptions of antiquity were broader than the western European and North American focus on Greece and Rome, including most of the Middle East as well as the Caucasus, Central Asia, and the Indus, in effect the area of early urban civilisations outside of China. Khatchadourian 2008 explores the Soviet use of the concept of *Antichnost* for the Caucasus.

42   Based on an 'archaeology of the Slavs', mixing a nationalist perspective with the feudalism of the stadialism of the *Short Course*, creating an interpretive framework modelled on European templates and quite at odds with preceding developments in the Soviet space,

or even relatedness of aspects, of the country's past was far from clear in archaeological terms.

3.   In disciplinary terms, archaeology was seen as part of history in a Marxist sense, rather than as part of natural history as under the Tsarist regime, or as part of anthropology as in the USA.[43] The implication of this conception is that apart from their special physical and technical characteristics, archaeological remains were seen primarily as historical sources.

4.   With regard to Marxist theory, Soviet archaeologists from the late 1920s onwards had access to a much greater selection of previously unpublished works of Marx and Engels that dealt with pre-capitalist modes of production. These included the anthropogony section of Engels, to be grasped together with the *Dialectics of Nature*. For Marx there were the notebooks on Morgan, Maine, and others, as well as the *German Ideology*, the drafts and letter to Vera Zasulich, and somewhat later also the *Grundrisse*. Many of these texts would not be widely known in western Europe and North America for decades.

5.   As in philosophy the notion of *partiinost*, party-mindedness, was a central factor in scholarly discourse, and in the same way as in philosophy increased in scope and intensity as the 1930s progressed and the Purges started. Similar lists of victims can be assembled, subject to the same kinds of shifts in doctrine to suit the needs of the state. Of particular note was an earlier extreme emphasis on stadialism that even denied the autonomy of the history of languages, a doctrine known as Marrism.[44] This trend was eventually denounced in favour of a greater emphasis on nationalities and the tracing of ethnic groups in the archaeological record, in particular with regard to the long term history of the Slavs.[45] In both cases these approaches fell in and out of favour according to the regime's desires, with often disastrous consequences for those who had formerly found favour.

As might be inferred from the above enumeration of factors, the application of *partiinost* to suit political needs was in fact faced with a myriad set of difficulties. For science is not easy to count upon to serve ideological needs, nor

---

as the synthetic work of Mongait 1959 shows. This perspective had to be guarded against facts at odds with it, such as the influence of the Varangians on early medieval Russia, Klejn 2012, pp. 115–20.

43   Even so, its role within history would be debated throughout the Soviet period, Klejn 2012, pp. 89–98.

44   See chapter 11 of Klejn 2012 for an overview of Marr's career.

45   Klejn 2012, p. 53. See on this topic also Schnirelmann 1995.

were the writings of Marx and Engels necessarily in accordance with the ideas of their ostensible followers, and not just in the case of the *Short Course*. A second, more subtle and indirect, danger concerns threats to the coherence of official doctrine, due to its inability to account for the broader historical picture in a convincing way. This second threat is in fact the most dangerous, for unlike the first one is unable to be remedied by quick ideological fixes, and risks overturning the entire foundations of the ruling ideology. Arguably this is what happened to the *pyatichlenka*, which needed constant patching up to face various challenges both in terms of new evidence and in terms of new ideas. As a result the scheme became stuck in its own ideological snares, which rendered it incoherent in the face of the historical record as a whole.

In a way, the challenges to the *pyatichlenka* can be traced to the early efforts of Soviet archaeology to interpret the material remains of the past according to the ideas of Marx, Engels, and Morgan. Although later disciplined by the intensification of *partiinost* in the 1930s, the early ideas and the evidence gained through new scientific work would always remain as a subterranean current to threaten the status quo. At the beginning of Soviet archaeology in the 1920s, however, there was no dogma facing its practitioners, but rather the challenge to develop a new Marxist archaeology. This was no mean feat given the limits of the field methods at the time, as well as a lack of any precedent on how to connect the ideas of Marx and Engels to such sources. Furthermore, in the early 1920s many of their works on early humankind and pre-capitalist modes of production remained to be published. In addition, the ideas of the Second International still carried considerable weight, with the particular influence of its version of Darwinism and a general unilinear perspective.[46]

For example, an early influence was the view of the earliest human communities of Cunow and Kautsky, which differ in important aspects from Marx and Engels.[47] First of all, it was not much of a social form at all, but rather a loosely aggregated collection of monogamous families struggling with each other for resources. Contrary to Engels, these authors believed that males dominated the social interaction of early humankind, and the notion of communism, if it existed at all, only consisted of the forced and unequal sharing of the hunter's spoils. This biological perspective in Kautsky also extended to the Asiatic mode of production, emphasising its unity with 'primitive' forms in the primacy of biological rather than economic factors. A rather Eurocentric

---

46   Blackledge 2006, pp. 56–9.
47   Howe 1980, n. 5, pp. 162–3.

conception, given the opposition of both forms to the progressive 'Western' ancient, feudal, and capitalist modes of production.[48] Clearly, this was hardly promising material for Soviet archaeologists to work with, and the publication of the works of Marx and Engels, as well as the attention given to Morgan, was a much needed corrective to these restrictive Second International theories.

Pioneering scientific research also played a crucial role in reshaping views. For example, Soviet archaeologists were the first to carry out horizontal excavations on a larger scale for Palaeolithic and Neolithic sites.[49] The evidence gained in this way allowed them to make sense of the social relations in these settlements, rather than merely trace the stratigraphic succession of different eras. One example, among a number of others, was that of the Palaeolithic site of Kostenki in the south of the Russian SFSR. Here a long standing research project started by Efimenko in 1923 resulted in the recognition of the outline of Upper Palaeolithic dwellings, which were interpreted as reflecting a larger community that carried out its affairs in common.[50] Such findings played an important role in applying Morgan's ideas about the role of kinship in early human social forms, as well as the adaptation thereof by Engels and his own theory of anthropogony. A number of different schemes for the early development of humankind were developed, paying close attention not just to kinship and social relations, but also especially to the emergence of productive activity.

Of these schemes that of Ravdonikas stands out for its completeness, spanning the sequence from anthropogony to the earliest states, as well for his philosophical position and the issue of *partiinost*. With regard to the latter factors, Ravdonikas placed himself in the camp of Deborin, arguing against the application of 'mechanist' ideas in archaeology.[51] These 'mechanist' ideas were introduced into archaeology mainly through the influence of Bukharin, who was the main figure in the RANION group of social science institutes, which served as an incubator for a new generation of graduates while also drawing upon existing specialists.[52] One of the main ideas expounded by Bukharin was the centrality of Marx's notion of metabolism of humans and nature, which he conceived of as an external equilibrium of society and nature captured in the productive forces.[53] From the productive forces, he reasoned his way upwards

---

48   Howe 1980, n. 5, p. 163.
49   Trigger 2006, pp. 334–5.
50   Mongait 1959, p. 78.
51   Howe 1980, n. 39, pp. 167–8.
52   Joravsky 1961, pp. 68–9.
53   Bukharin 1965, pp. 111–18.

a chain of phenomena, starting with the relations of production, and moving on to political arrangements, as well as the arts, philosophy, and religion.[54]

The relations between these different social phenomena were for him the internal equilibrium of society, which coexisted with the external equilibrium with nature rather than superseding it.[55] As such, this perspective provided a rich set of ideas for a new generation of archaeologists to work with, under the guidance of the preeminent pre-revolutionary archaeological specialist Gorodtsov.[56] The graduates now formulated the so-called 'ascending method', which reasoned from the archaeological remains of the instruments of production to social relations and superstructural phenomena.[57] This method came under heavy attack from Ravdonikas and similarly minded archaeologists, through the same kind of *Partiinost* line of critique forced them to abandon the 'ascending method'.[58] Ravdonikas rather argued for the internal, dialectical unfolding of anthropogony and developed social forms.[59] In this sense, his work can be seen as a precursor to the separation of natural history and the sequence of social forms in the *Short Course*, the former becoming irrelevant for the latter.

Instead, it can be argued that natural factors became internalised in the process of human development in the scheme of Ravdonikas, inspired by the references to natural selection in kinship relations in Morgan and Engels. As discussed in Chapter 4, Engels in particular had emphasised a shift from natural factors to social factors as the dominant determinants, which he saw as taking place at the transition from upper savagery to early barbarism. Property was the most important of these social factors, with the particulars of domestication in Eurasia allowing for its accumulation in greater quantities. Ravdonikas developed these ideas in a rather more radical way, overlooking some of the qualifications by Engels on the specifics of Morgan's scheme.[60] Soviet archaeologists had from the beginning emphasised this aspect of kin relations in their study of early humans, but recognising these in the archaeological record was far from easy. Often the result was to present an analysis of early production relations in the garb of kinship terms.[61]

---

54   Bukharin 1965, pp. 120–3, 150–1.
55   Bukharin 1965, pp. 240–1.
56   Klejn 2012, p. 318.
57   Klejn 2012, pp. 239–40.
58   Klejn 2012, p. 243.
59   Howe 1980, pp. 128–9.
60   As noted by Soviet scholars in the 1930s, Howe 1980, pp. 152–3.
61   Howe 1980, pp. 148–9.

Ravdonikas rather argued for the identity of kin and production relations in the first mode of production, which in Stalin's outline of the *pyatichlenka* would be termed the 'primitive communal' one. The reasoning was that during the Upper Palaeolithic period the first form of the matrilineal descent group (Morgan's *gens*) can be recognised, with a division of labour based on age and sex and as such completely identical to the form of the family that structured age and sex relations.[62] As a result, this perspective assumed the historical priority of kin relations, production relations being derivative from them, which would become a major point of contention in Soviet debates in the decades that followed. The primitive communal form established in the Upper Palaeolithic was for Ravdonikas characterised by a central contradiction, that between the division of labour and the development of the productive forces on the one hand, and on the other hand the necessity of collective relations of production at this stage.[63]

It is of some interest how this contradiction came about according to Ravdonikas, who provided a sketch of biological, technological, and social development over hundreds of thousands of years. Notable in particular are his views on the transition between the Lower and Middle Palaeolithic.[64] In the former era, there was a reliance on gathering and the hunting of small animals, without the use of fire or any division of labour. The evidence of the Middle Palaeolithic, of cave dwellings, more advanced tools, and fire, points to a rudimentary division of labour, first based on age but later also on sex. The emergence and further development of this division of labour was accompanied by changes in kin relations, Ravdonikas here following Morgan's outline of family forms. Other notable aspects in his account concern the emergence of language from the gestural 'kinetic speech' and the initial development of religious ideas in what he termed totemism.[65] These aspects are more peripheral to the central concern with technology, the division of labour, and kinship.

The Palaeolithic stages of Ravdonikas develop from the dialectical interplay of these factors, according to an internalist logic that resembles the *Wechsel-*

---

62   Howe 1980, p. 136.
63   Howe 1980, pp. 129–30.
64   Howe 1980, pp. 138–40.
65   Both of these concepts had been elaborated by others. The 'totemic society' was used by Tolstov to account for the ideological aspects of early human social groupings, most notably the sexual taboos that allowed for social cohesion, Howe 1980, pp. 227–35. The role of such taboos was further explored by Yuri Semenov, as will be discussed below. The notion of 'kinetic speech' was connected to the ideas of Marr, and connected earlier ideas about the role of gestures in the development of language to the mimetic aspects of making tools, Howe 1980, pp. 245–50.

wirkung of Engels. This conforms to his critique of the 'mechanist' perspective
noted above, the interaction with external nature having become secondary to
the dialectical interplay between production, kinship, speech, and cognition.
As pointed out by Howe, even exogamy developed from the internal trajectory
of isolated groups in Ravdonikas, rather than from the (external) interaction of
distinct groups.[66] With the transition to the Upper Palaeolithic, all the different factors are combined in a new social form, that of the 'primitive commune',
cohering together in a radically distinct way compared to what came before:

> And so the society of the Upper Paleolithic consisted of exogamous
> groupings subdivided by age and sex possessing a developed natural divi-
> sion of labor and various forms of group marriage, the nature of which
> awaits future research, as does the historical dynamic of the age. It is upon
> the complexification of socio-economic relations at this moment in his-
> tory that verbal speech develops. The social ideology of this stage in the
> history of society is characterized by the flourishing of totemic thinking,
> manifest especially in Paleolithic art.[67]

As the result of a process spanning an almost immeasurable time, the 'primitive communal' form of Ravdonikas occupies a paradoxical position in history.
As noted earlier, the matrilineal descent group defining this form was characterised by a contradiction between the development of the productive forces
and the collective relations of production. Further development of the former
would result in households becoming the main productive units and increasingly standing in opposition to communal ties, eventually leading to the patriarchal family and the social division of labour.[68] These in turn would form the
prerequisites for class systems and the state. In this way the first form of social
life occupied a liminal position. For rather than becoming a building block for
what followed, its operating principles were negated by the social division of
labour, thereby also negating the principles of human development traced by
Ravdonikas in the various phases of the Palaeolithic era. In effect it formed a
watershed between two distinct processes of development, sharing the formal
model of the dialectical unfolding of stages but not the respective contents.

The outline of social development of Ravdonikas seems far removed from
Marx's stratigraphic analogy for the historical trajectories of communal forms

---

66   Howe 1980, pp. 149–50.
67   Howe 1980, p. 151.
68   Howe 1980, pp. 154–6.

in different historical contexts. Such a perspective is theoretically impossible for him, for his 'primitive commune' is based on principles that lose their force when development based on the social division of labour takes over. The latter's principles are inherently contradictory to the communal form, and at any rate themselves progress along an internal trajectory defined by a necessity that precludes alternatives. In effect, it can be said that in rejecting the emphasis on the metabolism of humans and nature of the 'mechanists', Ravdonikas also precluded a more complex account that would posit the 'primitive commune' as the development of a social metabolism of labour. Doing so would have allowed for a nuanced view of the break engendered by the transition to the Upper Palaeolithic, being able to trace continuities and discontinuities between the processes of anthropogony and subsequent social development.

From the perspective of the aleatory current, the scheme of Ravdonikas provides a fascinating play on Rousseau.[69] As in his *Second discourse*, there is in the Soviet author what may be seen as a pure state of nature, negating the notion of a stable foundation or juridical definition of humankind. Nor can his 'civil society' be said to be developed upon solid ground, for the 'primitive communal' form is structured along lines negated by its successors. In this sense, as in Rousseau, there is no Origin or End. Yet unlike Rousseau, development is inherent in Ravdonikas, rather than being driven by the accidents of external nature. It is through the internal unfolding of stages, structured by the laws of dialectical materialism, that the teleological pair of Origin and End return through the backdoor, even if in the teleonomic form of Engelsian dialectics. In effect, the account of the development of early humans and the first forms of social life in Ravdonikas grounds the *pyatichlenka* in nature, but at the same time separates its own logic of development from natural history.

Even as this outline of prehistory served ideology, it was not in itself purely ideological. By all accounts, by no means all friendly, Ravdonikas was both a gifted theoretician and fieldworker alike.[70] He and his colleagues from the era can be seen as modern day Lucretians, seeking to infer from the faint traces of the Palaeolithic a picture of the biological and social development of early humankind. Nothing like this existed in western European and North American archaeology for a long time.[71] Audacious and overly speculative as these

---

69   As noted in Chapter 1, Rousseau was one of the thinkers part of the aleatory current. See Althusser 2019, p. 75 for a schematic overview of his take on the vicissitudes of early humankind.

70   Klejn 2012, pp. 225–9.

71   At least not on a large scale until the so-called New Archaeology of the 1960s, see for an extensive account of this movement by a Marxist archaeologist, Trigger 2006, pp. 392–444.

early Soviet studies no doubt were, they could also serve as the basis for further research, which had the potential to weed out the ideological notions from the scientific ones. As noted, however, Soviet archaeology failed to achieve such a critical, scientific discourse because of 'its failure to operationalise its theory by connecting it more systematically to its data'.[72] Of course, this had little to do with the researchers themselves, but everything with the pervasive pressure to adhere to an increasingly ferocious application of *partiinost* in the course of the Stalin years from the early 1930s onwards.

In the interplay of science and ideology the risk was not just that some inconvenient fact or theory might emerge, but also, probably more seriously, that previously accepted and celebrated schemes would become incompatible with *partiinost*. As noted in Chapter 1, changes in the party line created serious problems for scientists in this regard, leading to a potential lethal mixture of scientific and ideological critique. Schemes as that of Ravdonikas were especially fraught with risk in this regard, given that precisely in their more creative application of Marxist ideas the notion of 'plural Marxisms' was contained, with potential conflicts with the party line.[73] Far better, in this sense, fared works that provided only obligatory quotations from Marx and Engels, safely insulated from the scientific content of said works. Little surprise then that Ravdonikas, himself not shy from using the language of *partiinost* in scholarly disputes, in the end faced a dose of his own medicine, even if he remained unharmed and was able to escape his predicament through early retirement.[74]

The role of *partiinost* can also be seen in another major debate from the late 1920s and early 1930s that pertained upon the later development of the *pyatich-lenka*, namely that on the Asiatic mode of production. Unlike the debates on early humans, this debate was prompted specifically by a political question: the failed Chinese revolution of 1925–7 and the position of the Comintern in relation to it. Briefly, Comintern policy drove the CPC to ally itself with the Kuomintang, with disastrous results in the April 1927 massacre of its cadres and supporters in Shanghai. Among other things, this policy was driven by the notion that the presence of strong feudal remnants necessitated a bourgeois-democratic revolution, a transition to socialism being premature.[75] Shortly after the Shanghai massacre, Stalin put forward a set of 'theses for propagand-

---

72   Trigger 2006, p. 344.
73   Howe 1980, pp. 158–9.
74   Klejn 2012, pp. 231–2.
75   In close connection with the critique of Trotsky, Dunn 1982, pp. 31–5. Trotsky's position on the question of the Chinese revolution as democratic or socialist can be found in Trotsky 1966, pp. 29–33.

ists' on the Chinese revolution, in which he continued to argue the need for an alliance with the 'left' Kuomintang government in Wuhan, a strategy that would soon show itself to be futile indeed.[76]

In his commentary on Stalin's theses, Trotsky focused on the inconsistencies, omissions, and faulty reasoning evident in them, notably also for the section on the 'errors of the opposition'.[77] According to Trotsky, the main errors of Stalin are his notion of the bourgeoisie as an ally against strong feudal remnants, as well as his emphasis on the adherence to necessary steps in the revolutionary process. The theses follow from what Trotsky terms a *chvotists* logic, according to which no deviations or skipping of steps or stages is possible, and which leads to a certain passivity.[78] Here we can see the difference between the Trotskyist international revolutionary perspective, with its recognition of a process of combined and uneven development, and the internalist stadialism of 'socialism in one country'. Although the proponents of the Asiatic mode of production argued from a different position than that of Trotsky, they nevertheless fell foul of the *partiinost* induced by this struggle over revolutionary strategy and the victory of 'socialism in one country'.

These factors can be observed in the debates on the Asiatic mode of production in 1930 and 1931. Ludvig Mad'iar, a Comintern official in China in 1926 and 1927, was one of its chief proponents. In one of his contributions, he meticulously traced the development of the concept in Marx and Engels, as well as in relation to Hegel, and considers the implications of it as a model for contemporary China.[79] In his argument the remnants of the Asiatic mode of production were predominant, though in some areas alongside feudal elements, and exploitation was often through usury.[80] Given the connection of the bourgeoisie with imperialism and the usurious exploitation of the countryside, the implication is that the revolutionary dynamic of China is quite distinct from the earlier analysis of the Comintern. For if China lacked the contradiction between feudal forces and the bourgeoisie on which the notion of a bourgeois-democratic revolution is based, then the necessity of that form of revolution is called into question.

In that sense, the proponents of the Asiatic mode of production (the *Aziatiki*) were aligned in broad terms with Trotsky in their evaluation of the Chinese revolution, even if from a political perspective that was not necessarily

---

76   Stalin 1954, pp. 226–8.
77   Trotsky 1966, pp. 44–6.
78   Trotsky 1966, pp. 23, 68.
79   See his contribution to the 1931 debate on the Asiatic mode of production, Mad'iar 1981.
80   Mad'iar 1981, pp. 92–4.

identical. The main sin of the *Aziatiki* was not to advocate the Asiatic mode as a historical category, but rather to deny the presence of strong feudal remnants in China.[81] The arguments against the *Aziatiki* were in fact varied, but the primacy of political arguments against their position is clear. Yet these were accompanied by theoretical arguments as well. For example, the extensive treatment of the Asiatic mode of production in Marx and Engels by Mad'iar, was now argue to be a selective set of quotations without an understanding of the underlying logic behind them.[82] This logic, and this was the main argument, was that of a unilineal and internal dialectic of development. As such, the *Aziatiki* neglected the 'historical necessity and inevitability' of transitions from one mode to another, problematising crucial role of the class struggle, as well as their controversial 'mechanist' emphasis on the role of merchant capital.[83]

Once again, we can see here the counterposing of 'mechanist' ideas of the interplay of internal and external factors, and the emphasis on an internal and unilinear stadialism. From the latter followed a strong emphasis on the unitary character of human history. This emphasis was contrasted with 'mechanist' ideas as well, or as Kovalev put it: 'in place of a unified process, we obtain a multiplicity of historical processes – i.e. a mechanistic conception'.[84] No such perspective was accepted by the critics of the Asiatic mode of production, for they argued that, save for some particularities, China 'in a very unique fashion' went through the same sequence of stages as observed for Europe.[85] In this sense, the unilinealism of the *pyatichlenka* can be traced to debates that occurred years before the *Short Course*, which can be seen as a canonisation of this view of dialectics and historical development. As with the trajectory of early humankind, it was structured by an Origin (the 'primitive' communal form) and an End (the future communist mode).

Of course, where the 'primitive' communal form was the Origin of the historical sequence of modes of production, it was at the same time the End of the processes of anthropogony and sociogenesis that had its Origin in the primeval horde. The teleonomic processes of unfolding stages in these two distinct pairings of Origin and End in turn fitted in the overall movement of matter in the universe, which in the Engelsian view would necessarily evolve to higher forms of consciousness. Given the echoes of this view in Soviet thinkers such

---

81 Dunn 1982, p. 36.
82 In other words 'to distinguish between the letter and essence of Marxism', pointing to Stalin's polemics with Trotsky and the opposition in this regard, Godes 1981, p. 103.
83 Godes 1981, p. 101.
84 Cited in Dunn 1982, pp. 21–2.
85 Godes 1981, p. 103.

as Deborin and Ilyenkov, it is certainly relevant as part of the theoretical background of the dialectics of historical development. Of course, as a strand of thought it should not be conflated with Stalin's formulation of the *pyatichlenka*, for that was shaped by a powerful thrust of *partiinost* rather than primarily by philosophical ideas. The dialectical and historical materialism of the *Short Course* can instead be seen as a stunted, political version of this perspective, which as noted in Chapter 1 should not be conflated with the philosophical outlook of Soviet scientists and philosophers following the Engelsian path.

Yet at the same time there was a shared perspective of a teleonomic conception of dialectics, with a focus on internal development according to a series of unfolding stages, whether it concerned the process of anthropogony or that of socialist revolution. At the same time, the practical consequences of the theoretical repudiation of the 'mechanists' discussed in Chapter 1 becomes apparent as well. For teleonomic internalism cannot conceive the role of external relations to the degree that the 'mechanists' could. This can be seen for the process of anthropogony, where the metabolism of humans and nature became subsumed under the identity of kin and productive relations. It can also be seen in the denial of a significant role for merchant capital in the internal development of a country like China. Indeed, it was explicitly recognised that such 'mechanist' views would result in the valuation of the multiplicity, or plurality, of historical processes and forms. Apart from reasons of a *partiinost* character, this emphasis on unilinearity and unicity was the main reason for the disinheritance of the Asiatic mode of production from the Marxist tradition.

Even when after the Twentieth Party congress of 1956 the *pyatichlenka* was retained, powerful scientific sources were set loose that became a mortal threat not just to the scheme itself, but also to its historico-philosophical premises. The spectre of a multiplicity beyond the 'set of five', so carefully contained previously, now cropped up again, and not only with regard to historical studies in themselves but also to the political consequences that derived from them. A new generation of historians, part of the broader movement of the *Shestidesyatniki* (people of the 1960s), developed the so-called New Direction in Soviet historical studies. The most important innovation of this new tendency, being so central that it was sometimes conflated with it, was the concept of 'multi-structuredness'.[86] The meaning of this term can be grasped from its Russian

---

86   As applied to a number of central historical questions in Soviet scholarship, ranging from the characteristics of the absolute Tsarist state, the emergence of capitalism, the nature of the October revolution, as well as the future socialist pathways of the newly independent former European colonies, all discussed in chapter three of Markwick 2001.

original *mnogoukladnost*, meaning a multiplicity of, in this particular case, socio-economic formations, one of which may be held to be the dominant one structuring the others.[87]

The source of this concept of multistructuredness can be found in Lenin's polemics against the communist critics of state capitalism. Shortly after the October revolution, Lenin described the economic conditions of the country as not yet socialist but transitional toward it, a form containing 'elements, particles, fragments of *both* capitalism and socialism'.[88] He went on to enumerate five main economic structures, ranging from patriarchal forms (peasant, nomadic, or a combination thereof), petty commodity production (including agricultural), private and state capitalism, as well as socialism.[89] The historians of the New Direction took this brief outline by Lenin of the specific situation of post-revolutionary Russia, and developed it into a complex and multifaceted theory, in which a number of important aspects can be discerned:

1. The interpretation of the Tsarist state diverged in important ways from the viewpoint that it was a superstructural expression of the economic base, emphasising instead that absolutism in Russia did not have its roots in capitalism.[90] Instead there was a non-correspondence, in the sense that a strong state developed relative to a weak economic base: 'the state got ahead of itself'.[91] Later this would have repercussions for the development of capitalism, in which the Tsarist regime played an active, stimulating role rather than passively reflecting economic developments.[92] In that sense the military and feudal aspects of the state existed parallel to its capitalist and imperialist aspects, being of a multistructured character.

2. The historical specificity of the Tsarist state relative to Western European absolutism, was also paralleled by a conception of Russian capitalism as belonging to a 'second echelon' of the development of capitalism.[93] This later form of capitalism was distinguished from earlier developments by virtue of a greater role of the state, and retained strong feudal remnants.

---

87   But not dominant in the sense that the capitalist *uklad* as the leading one should be confused with the capitalist economy viewed as a whole, Markwick 2001, p. 98.

88   Lenin 1974, p. 335, emphasis in the original.

89   Lenin 1974, pp. 335–6.

90   Markwick 2001, pp. 106–7.

91   In this view, the absolutist Tsarist state enjoyed a relative independence and would gradually evolve out of itself a bourgeois state of sorts, Markwick 2001, pp. 107–8.

92   Markwick 2001, pp. 81, 83–4.

93   Markwick 2001, pp. 91–3.

Consequently, capitalism had not, as in western Europe, taken root in the rural areas, and, furthermore, great regional variations existed within the Tsarist empire.[94]

3. Given that, according to the perspective of multistructuredness, pre-revolutionary Russia was neither fully capitalist nor fully feudal, the conception of the October revolution could not follow the template of a transition from capitalism to socialism through class struggle. Instead the bourgeois and democratic revolution was held to be insufficient, because of the presence of monopoly capitalism, necessitating a socialist revolution.[95] However, as feudal and other remnants were present as well, this revolution had to accomplish some of the tasks of the skipped bourgeois and democratic one as well.[96]

4. The distinction between the earlier forms of capitalism of western Europe and the later form of Russia had contemporary relevance, in that the latter was held to be more representative for the 'developing world'.[97] For, like Tsarist Russia, many of these countries were also characterised by multi-structuredness, with strong pre-capitalist remnants and a large role for the state in developing capitalism. By extension, the view of the October revolution as multistructured also had consequences for grasping the future trajectory of the 'developing world', in particular in the possibility of (a) non-capitalist path(s).[98]

5. Although rarely articulated, the concept of multistructuredness could also be applied to the Soviet Union itself. In this view a plurality of future paths would be possible without a pre-determined victory for socialism, the October revolution either going 'backwards toward some form of primitive capitalism or forwards to genuine communism'.[99]

The concept of multistructuredness in this way was developed to a degree that transcended the brief analysis by Lenin of a very specific situation, that

---

94 Markwick 2001, pp. 94–5.

95 Markwick 2001, pp. 101–2.

96 Significant in this regard is Danilov's account of the two stages of the October revolution, with socialism developing from the preceding bourgeois-democratic stage, the transition taking place in the Summer of 1918 when the alliance of the proletariat with the peasantry as a whole shifted to class conflict within the peasantry, Markwick 2001, pp. 87–8.

97 Markwick 2001, p. 92.

98 Hough 1986, pp. 54–60.

99 These options are inferred by Markwick 'after the fact' so to speak, yet seem strongly implied by an aside on the multistructured character of the Soviet Union by Mikhail Gefter, which followed from his main analysis on how Tsarist era serfdom had 'digested' the capitalist structure for its own purposes, Markwick 2001, p. 99.

of the early years of Soviet power. Neither can it be said to be derivative of Trotsky's notion of combined and uneven development.[100] Rather, it was an original formulation that emerged from within the Khrushchev Thaw, parallel-ing contemporary engagements with Marxist theory such as the *Lire Capital* group in Paris.[101] As we shall see below, the Brezhnevite reaction and ensuing stagnation prevented the encounter of multistructuredness and revolutionary practice. However, the New Direction did throw open the Pandora box of his-torical multiplicity, which, among other things, also led to the rekindling of the debate on the Asiatic mode of production. Or rather, it brought a slumbering debate back to the forefront, for in science the disavowal of the Asiatic mode had already created significant problems. After an initial idea that the cases formerly grouped under the Asiatic rubric could be understood as feudal, they were instead argued to be part of the slaveholding mode.[102]

The problem here was that, as Soviet scholars such as Kovalev and Struve had noted in the 1930s, the large scale slavery of classical antiquity was typical to these cases and not to the other cases that were now supposed to be slavehold-ing formations as well.[103] Hence it was necessary to broaden the conception of the slaveholding formation, so as to be able to accommodate more cases. Publication of Marx's *Grundrisse* in 1941 added further complexities, given the extensive discussions of both the Asiatic and Classical modes of production therein. The ground shifted accordingly. In a 1947 editorial in a Soviet historical journal, it was held argued that to focus mainly on the antagonism of slaves and slaveowners was too narrow an approach.[104] Instead, more attention should be given to a broader set of aspects, including the role of the free peasantry, the division of town and country, as well as that between industry and trade within cities. In a 1952 editorial, things were carried further as a division was now made between two distinct stages of the slaveholding formation, with the first phase of 'patriarchal slaveholding' characterised by 'an Oriental form of property'.[105]

These changes were spurred in part by the pioneering Marxist approaches to the earliest cities and states in the Middle East, the first ones being the Sumerian city-states of southern Iraq and the Pharaonic state in Egypt. A

---

100   See for the differences and the centrality instead of Lenin, Markwick 2001, pp. 103–5.
101   Markwick 2001, p. 109.
102   Especially in the work of Struve on the most ancient states of the Middle East, Dunn 1982, pp. 42–51.
103   Dunn 1982, pp. 63–5.
104   Cited in Dunn 1982, pp. 65–6.
105   Cited in Dunn 1982, p. 67.

new generation of specialists on these cases would carry the argument much further. This can be seen in a discussion paper from 1963 by Igor D'iakonov, which generated considerable scholarly excitement and drew many responses. D'iakonov retained the notion of the slaveholding epoch, but in a rather paradoxically way argued that it was not be defined by slavery.[106] Central to his view of this formation was the role of the commune. He argued that the commune in the early Middle East, and by extension in the Mediterranean as well, should not be seen as a mere survival from the 'primitive communal' formation, but rather followed 'the laws of the economics of slaveholding society itself'.[107] Even so, the commune of the slaveholding epoch emerged from the 'primitive' in D'iakonov's account by a fairly conventional rendering of the contradiction between the equalising distribution of the matrilineal structuring of kin relations and the social division of labour.[108]

What rather distinguished his sketch of this transition was his emphasis on the emergence of a new form of the commune, compatible with but not identical to forms of the family, which he termed the 'neighbourhood commune'.[109] Drawing further away from kinship, he emphasised its character as a civil organisation, defining for the free peasantry a set of duties, obligations, and rights, drawing attention to the work of Jacobsen on forms of democracy in early Mesopotamia.[110] In the early phases of Sumerian civilisation, these rights had included the common ownership of the land and its periodic redistribution, but this aspect weakened in the later phases of Mesopotamian history. He also recognised different forms of state formation and of slavery for the later phases as well, noting for the Mediterranean especially the greater roles of commodity exchange.[111] Yet here, too, the free peasantry and the commune as a civil organisation remained basic building blocks, regardless of the disappearance of holding land in common.

In the ensuing discussion on D'iakonov's paper, two main themes came to the fore, which each in its own way could be related to debates then gaining traction in Soviet scholarship. The first theme concerned the class character of the free peasantry organised in neighbourhood communes, now part of a slaveholding mode of production expanded greatly beyond Marx's original formu-

---

106   D'iakonov 1963, p. 32.
107   D'iakonov 1963, p. 35.
108   D'iakonov 1963, p. 36.
109   D'iakonov 1963, pp. 36–8.
110   D'iakonov 1963, p. 35.
111   D'iakonov 1963, p. 33. See also D'iakonov 1976 for a more in-depth account of the different phases of communal forms in relation to different kinds of exploitation.

lation. D'iakonov had emphasised the diachronic aspect in this, distinguishing between an early and later phase of slaveholding, with the commune as a civil institution a common denominator between them. It would be just as possible, however, to recognise in these two phases instead two distinct modes of production, adhering respectively to Marx's Asiatic and Classical-antique modes. Indeed, it was at this time that the debate on the Asiatic mode of production was revived in Soviet scholarship.[112] This debate was spurred on not just by scientific concerns, but also by the process of decolonisation and the possibility of different, socialist pathways of development for the nations that had just gained independence from the European colonisers.[113]

The comeback of the Asiatic mode of production raised again the spectre of multiplicity, something recognised from the outset.[114] Whereas in the *pyatichlenka* the unicity of the historical process as unfolding on a single line of development was emphasised, now multiple pathways of development structured on different principles were proposed. D'iakonov's paper and the ensuing discussion also had another, more indirect, impact, namely that the commune as a civil institution was conceptually separated from kinship groupings such as the clan. This discussion pertained to the early phases of history, rather than the 'primitive' communal mode, but soon doubts would be voiced on the notion on the identity of kin and production relations for this form as well. Indeed, many of the theories on the emergence of humankind and the first forms of human life in the Palaeolithic were now thrown into doubt, as the result of new evidence from archaeology and ethnography.

Engagement with foreign ethnographic studies on the indigenous peoples of Australia, New Guinea, and other areas, put into grave doubt the universality of the matrilineal clan as the basis for the 'primitive' communal mode.[115] This observation led to reformulations, most notably the daring hypothesis that a 'pairing family' was already present in the initial 'primitive' horde stage. New archaeological studies of Palaeolithic settlements, furthermore, demolished previous interpretations of settlement structures as evidence for the presence of matrilineal clans.[116] Such revisions followed from a more rigorous applica-

---

112   An overview can be found in Dunn 1982, pp. 77–120. Also significant in this shift is the critique of Stalinist views on the role of the natural environment in history and its implications for the recognition of a pluralist rather than unilinear view of the different modes of production, Sawer 1977, pp. 128–36.

113   Danilova 1966, p. 4.

114   Struve 1965, p. 45.

115   Howe 1980, pp. 287–88, 295–301.

116   Howe 1980, pp. 306–7, 317–20.

tion of archaeological methods and limiting interpretations to what the evidence allowed, making superfluous notions such as Morgan's group marriage. The disproving of both scientific and ideological concepts had important consequences for Marxist theory as well. For as one participant in the debate noted, the focus on reconstructions of kinship and social form had led to a neglect of conceptualising the role of technology, even as technological studies of Palaeolithic stone tools, as well as later ones, again came to the fore.[117]

The impact of these studies was profound. Whereas the revival of the Asiatic mode of production had brought back the question of multiplicity, Palaeolithic revisionism confronted the *pyatichlenka* with an existential crisis. For if the adaptation of the schemes of early human development based on kinship of Morgan and Engels were comprehensively disproved, the 'primitive' communal mode would lose its liminal, mediating status. This created an enormous problem, as this mode formed a boundary between two distinct processes of dialectical unfolding. On the one hand, the 'primitive' communal form was the End of the processes of anthropogony and sociogenesis, while it also formed the Origin of the sequence of socio-economic formations on the other hand. The End in this sense was the basis for social life in the matrilineal clan, the outcome of a process based on the specialisation of labour along kin lines (based on age and sex). The Origin on the other hand can be found in the contradiction put forward by Ravdonikas and others, between the equalising tendencies within the matrilineal clan and the further development of the social division of labour.

Hence, without the matrilineal clan as the lynchpin, and at the same time the liminal boundary, between 'nature' and 'history', the *pyatichlenka* faced, to put it in Rousseauist terms, the abyss of the pure state of nature. That is, the scheme faced a complete unmasking and dissolution in both a logical sense and in terms of the evidence stretching its inconsistencies to a breaking point. The consequences of this breakdown involved not just the *pyatichlenka* itself, but most importantly also the political concept of 'socialism in one country' and the denial of historical pluralism. For the 'primitive' communal mode was precisely conceived in such a liminal way as to preclude the notion of multiple pathways toward the state and class systems, which also precluded multilinear conceptions of a transition to communist social forms.[118] Of course, alternative theories had been evident in early Soviet debates on Marxist theory, notably in the ideas of the 'mechanists', which, as we saw earlier, extended from philo-

---

117   Howe 1980, p. 296.
118   Plotkin and Howe 1985, p. 276.

sophy to archaeological methods, with ramifications for grasping both early humankind and historical multiplicity in the form of the Asiatic mode of production.

That such conceptions were still possible in Soviet scholarship is shown by a remarkable and highly significant article from the late 1960s by Lyudmila Danilova. This work combines the findings from the aforementioned debates threatening the *pyatichlenka* with the early debates of the 1920s and 1930s, drawing upon an important 'mechanist' source by Bogdanov and Stepanov from that era.[119] The critical debates on the slaveholding mode of production are noted and its geographical limitedness to European history emphasised, calling into question the universality of the sequence of socio-economic forms and raising the spectre of multiplicity:

> The concept developed in the 1930s does, of course, allow for the skipping of certain stages of development, and even of entire social orders, but it allows for this either as a deviation from the main line of world history or as an exception owing to special conditions (primarily the accelerating influence of more advanced systems). But, in the first place, deviations and exceptions proved more numerous than cases which fit the rule; and second, and most important, the regularities operative here proved to be so tied to a specific set of circumstances as not to be explicable merely by the influence of the historical environment. Science was faced with the problem of a multiplicity of forms of societal evolution.[120]

Most importantly, she starts her diagnosis of the ailments of the Soviet Marxist historiography of the time with the conundrums of the 'primitive' communal mode. Going beyond the boundaries between biology and history, as well as qualifying the focus on the role of kinship in early human social life, she argued instead for the need to grasp the economic factor in more precise terms. Referring back to Marx and recent studies by the Soviet economist Kolganov, she traces distinct methods for appropriating material goods, from obtaining the natural fruits of the earth to producing those goods that nature does not supply.[121] Each of these methods of appropriation constitutes a different config-

---

119   The work in question is the book *A Course in Political Economy* by Bogdanov and Stepanov, which she cited extensively throughout the article, which was one of the main points of the critique of Danilova and her colleagues in the official journal *Kommunist*, Danilov 1969, p. 94. See on this critique also Markwick 2001, pp. 177–9.

120   Danilova 1971, p. 273.

121   Danilova 1971, pp. 282–3. Apparently this was part of a broader thrust among political eco-

uration of the metabolism of humans and nature, in a way that also connects it with social phenomena such as property regimes. Hence it provides a way of analysing both a group of early humans subsisting upon natural fruits, as well as the modern industrial nations, thus moving beyond the strict dichotomy between the dialectics of sociogenesis and of economic formations.

Danilova proposed a thorough revision of the periodisation of history, replacing the one based on the distinct modes defined by forms of property of the *pyatichlenka* with one based on different forms of appropriation. She points for example to the work by Bogdanov and Stepanov as an early example of the wholesale revision of the relation between humans and nature through agriculture and animal domestication, now known as the Neolithic revolution.[122] She argues that this shift 'became the basis for the subsequent formation of world civilization',[123] based on the form of appropriation through the agricultural exploitation of land. The modes of production of this phase have, however, been misunderstood by the extrapolation of capitalist relations of production to the interpretation of their characteristic features. This is incorrect for two reasons. First of all, the mode of appropriation is based on the land rather than on a productive process based on machinery.[124] Secondly, in the pre-capitalist modes of production there was no separation between labour and its conditions, given the lack of control of commodity-exchange over production.[125]

As a result, the appropriation of surplus in these modes was not through economic means, but rather through 'extra-economic', primarily political, means.[126] In the end there was a powerful economic factor behind this development, namely the expanding division of labour (itself the result from the earlier Neolithic revolution).[127] Such a conception of pre-capitalist modes of production made it possible to think the Asiatic formation in its complexity. Danilova conceptualised this mode of production as a combination of the state and inequality on the one hand, and collective forms of organisation of the

---

nomists to rethink early Soviet debates, considering also the work of Bogdanov, Markwick 2001, n. 119, p. 284.

122 Danilova 1971, nos. 48–9, pp. 320–1.

123 Danilova 1971, p. 295.

124 Danilova 1971, pp. 296–7.

125 Danilova 1971, p. 297.

126 A crucial point, Danilova 1971, pp. 293, 301. She also points out how this distinction became blurred by Stalin's conception of feudalism, Danilova 1971, n. 41, p. 320. It was this point that formed the main critique of her work, and most significantly this was also connected to her recognition of the role of extra-economic relations of power that existed in the contemporary Soviet Union and other socialist countries, Markwick 2001, p. 178.

127 Danilova 1971, pp. 302–4.

free peasantry on the other.[128] As such, it could now be understood in relation to the previous 'primitive' communal mode in other terms than a strict dichotomy between two distinct dialectical processes. Rather it can be seen as a specific development upon a previous form, based on the processes of the Neolithic revolution and the elaboration of the division of labour. Both are grasped through the common factor of the Marxist understanding of the metabolism of humans with nature and with each other, as actualised in the forms of appropriation of the productive process.

Danilova's article was originally published as the introduction to a volume on the 'problems of pre-capitalist formations', as part of a prospective series of collective works to comprehensively rethink Marxist historiography. Future titles included a work on slavery in world history, one on Lenin and the conception of class struggles, as well as a volume on social revolutions in world history and a book by Danilova herself on feudalism, all discontinued, with the second volume on pre-capitalist modes of production ready but simply left unpublished.[129] Brezhnevite reaction had now 'taken hold', in the person of Sergey Trapeznikov, who reasserted *partiinost* and mounted a defence of stadialism along these lines against those who in high acrobatic form were designated as 'apologists of capitalism'.[130] It would take more theoretical sophistication, however, to fend off the spectre of multiplicity and the redemption of 'mechanist' conceptions by Danilova. As noted earlier, this task was accomplished by Yuri Semenov, who in effect 'held the line' for the *pyatichlenka* in spirit if not in all details.

The most remarkable aspect of Semenov's work is perhaps his account of anthropogony and the emergence of society, which one commentator has described as a 'Marxist book of Genesis'.[131] His conception of the main outline and outcome of the process during the course of the Palaeolithic is roughly similar to that of Ravdonikas, but Semenov uses scientific concepts of Darwin and Pavlov to explain it more deeply. Central to this is his adoption of Pavlov's unconditioned (instinctual) and conditioned (learned) reflexes, which are used to delineate a series of stages in cognition from pure unconditioned reactions to the capacity for complex, conditioned behaviour.[132] Semenov uses these ideas to explain how humankind acquired the capacity for productive labour, as well as for morality and agency in social life. This process involved a

---

128   Danilova 1971, p. 287.
129   Markwick 2001, p. 193.
130   Markwick 2001, pp. 238–9.
131   Gellner 1988, p. 18.
132   Howe 1980, pp. 357–9.

complex interaction between the human brain and bodily morphology, technological development, Darwinian (sexual) selection, as well as what he
termed 'biosocial selection'.[133] In a sense, it can be said that through this mutually reinforcing process, and the Pavlovian notion of reflexes in particular, the
human metabolism with the natural environment became 'internalised' in the
resultant human constitution.

This internalised 'human nature' is expressed externally in social forms. The
exogamous kin group as such is the starting point of human history, being the
outcome of a process that started with primate alliances and moved through
the herd and notably the 'totemic horde' of the Neanderthals.[134] A strong
emphasis on this internalisation of the human relation with nature in essential characteristics leads, as in Ravdonikas, to a preference for unilinear views of
history. Much like Morgan's scale of mind, there will be a tendency to emphasise the causal connection between development as based on its essential characteristics, relegating 'external' factors of the physical and social environment
as secondary ones. Even if Semenov's use of Pavlov's ideas strongly diverged
from Morgan, his scheme did provide a robust, if at many turns hypothetical
and speculative, defence of the historical priority of the matrilineal clan.[135] He
recognised the same contradiction posited by Ravdonikas between the collective ownership of property and the development of the productive forces, which
tended to be located in smaller domestic units and entailed a potential for accumulation in them.[136]

The result is a rather similar conception of the shift from kin to class to the
one we saw in Morgan and Engels in Chapter 4. It involved the mutual interaction between the developing productive forces, allowing for a more regular
surplus, property now being located mainly in households, the use of slave
labour, and the development of distinctions within the commune.[137] A 'military democracy' of the Aztec and Homeric kind develops, and kin relations
become decisively separated from the relations of production and assume a
superstructural character. Interestingly, however, Semenov, unlike Ravdonikas,

---

133   Humans could internalise Pavlovian habits in the form of 'dynamic stereotypes' that can
      also be seen in other species with significant social interaction, Howe 1980, pp. 365–6. Such
      stereotypes formed the starting point for a complex interaction between generic charac-
      teristics of the species and specific adaptations of specific social groups, especially forms
      of social interaction and tool use, leading to a form of group selection, Howe 1980, p. 382.
134   Howe 1980, pp. 420–6.
135   Even trying to reconcile it with a peculiar form of pairing marriage, in which the spouses
      did not cohabit but rather reside in their respective kin groups, Howe 1980, pp. 434–35.
136   Howe 1980, pp. 439–40.
137   Howe 1980, pp. 444–9.

accepts the Asiatic mode of production, which in his outline of the sequence of social formations is the first class-based one.[138] There is a certain dissonance here between the view of slavery and distinctions in property as undermining the communal order, following the ideas of Morgan and Engels, and the Asiatic mode, where the commune remains the mainstay of social life and slavery plays an insignificant role.[139] Semenov here seems to prefer not to think through D'iakonov's findings on the role of the commune in the most ancient states of the Middle East, lest the consequences for the views of Morgan and Engels become apparent.

However, the Asiatic mode of production is held to be the first of the sequence of socio-economic formations, which continues with the slaveholding, feudal, capitalist, and socialist forms, in what he terms 'a natural-historical process'.[140] Unlike the process of anthropogony, where speculative theories are used to buttress an existing scheme, Semenov makes more modifications to the *pyatichlenka*. Partly, this follows from his desire to counter Danilova's emphasis on multiplicity and plurality in history, arguing instead for a strongly unitary conception of world history.[141] Apart from reinstating the Asiatic mode of production, he also introduces the notion of 'social organism'. This term refers to specific societies, which show a greater degree of variation than the socio-economic formations, even if they are bound by 'inner objective necessity' to the laws of the specific socio-economic formation to which they belong.[142] In this way the concept of the social organism allows for some multiplicity of a secondary order, while the unity of socio-economic history is retained.

More importantly, however, he addresses the notion of alternative pathways, and especially the idea that the slaveholding mode represents a particular path not universally followed, by introducing a new concept: the 'global-historical centre'. This concept denotes the presence in a region of a number of social organisms characterised by the most advanced socio-economic formation, as seen from a global perspective. The first example of such a centre is the most ancient Middle East, the first region globally where the Asiatic mode of production emerged.[143] After that, the centre shifted to the Mediterranean with the

---

138   Semenov 1980, p. 42.
139   For his account of the dissolution of the kingroup commune and the transition to class society follows the standard Morgan-Engels scheme, and as such can hardly afford an Asiatic mode of production.
140   Semenov 1980, p. 29.
141   Semenov 1980, pp. 53–4.
142   Semenov 1980, pp. 33–4.
143   Semenov 1980, pp. 42–3.

slaveholding mode, before moving to western Europe with the onset of feudalism. The transition from feudalism to capitalism takes place in Europe, but the system has a truly global reach, which eventually leads to the emergence of a new global-historical centre at the margins, that of socialism.[144] The key point is that although social organisms may vary considerably as historical phenomena, not following the sequence of the *pyatichlenka*, on a global scale this sequence is followed and history assumes a unitary character.

The Hegelian connotations of this scheme of shifting global-historical centres are acknowledged by Semenov, and he quotes specifically the argument of Engels in the *Anti-Dühring* that the slavery of the ancient world was necessary for modern socialism to emerge.[145] After the collapse of the USSR, he modified his theory accordingly, arguing that the Soviet system can be understood as a variant of the Asiatic mode with modern industry, by necessity giving way after it had exhausted its historic mission.[146] This disavowal of the socialist character of the Soviet Union, while at the same time using his version of historical materialism to grasp its demise, shows that Semenov followed a similar trajectory to the one discussed in Chapter 1. That is, the same conception of historical necessity that posited the inevitability of 'developed socialism' as a historical stage was reversed, explaining its demise as equally necessary and inevitable. As such, the analysis of this reversal in Chapter 1 is now deepened, and its theoretical roots can be grasped more comprehensively.

Semenov's account of anthropogony, sociogenesis, and the sequence of socio-economic formations certainly cannot be closely tied to the *Short Course* alone. Rather it has to be grasped as part of the dominant current in Soviet historiography, one that is also apparent in the discussions on the Asiatic mode of production and early humans of the late 1920s and 1930s. The influence of the ideas of Morgan and Engels discussed in Chapter 4 in this current is clear. With regard to Morgan, there was a tendency to cling to certain concepts even in the face of studies showing them to be outmoded already in the 1930s, but more decisively so in the 1960s. The concept of the matrilineal *gens* as the outcome of a long evolutionary process, forming the basis for *societas*, was maintained in the face of clear evidence to the contrary, leading to the speculative acrobatics of Semenov on dislocal marriage. Furthermore, the shift to a patrilineal reckoning of descent as part of a broader shift to class rather than kinship, was

---

144   Semenov 1980, pp. 45–8. Explicitly connecting this movement from East to West to the Absolute Spirit of Hegel, its idealism being substantiated by the sequence of socio-economic formations, Semenov 1980, p. 48.

145   Semenov 1980, p. 47.

146   Luehrmann 2005, p. 867.

also maintained largely according to the ideas of Morgan and Engels. However, their ideas on the breakup of the commune and the consequent formation of the state were incompatible with the concept of the Asiatic mode of production, seen as the first class formation.

Less attention was paid to Morgan's ideas on the scale of mind and metabolism with nature, nor to his more aleatory conception of the transition from his stage of 'upper barbarism' to 'civilization'. What seems to have mattered primarily in this Soviet take on Morgan were concepts that Engels used in his adaptation of *Ancient Society*, most notably the aforementioned forms of kinship and the trajectory toward classes and the state. Yet with regard to Engels the question concerns not just this or that concept, but also their place within his conception of dialectics, as evident in late works like the *Anti-Dühring* and *Dialectics of Nature*. In Chapter 4 these ideas were discussed in relation to his adaptation of Morgan, as well as his own take on the emergence of humankind. These concepts of the late work of Engels were certainly influential upon this current in Soviet historiography. This influence can be seen in the ideas discussed above for the history of early humankind, as well as in the debates on the Asiatic mode and the spectre of a multiplicity of socio-economic formations.

Two aspects of this Engelsian influence stand out in particular. The first concerns the separation in Engels between the dialectical process of anthropogony and the emergence of consciousness, which he grasped as part of a grand cosmic cycle, and the wholly different laws of social development. As a result these processes in this current of Soviet thinking were kept strictly apart, the 'primitive' communal form constituting a liminal boundary between them. In effect, in the course of the first process the human relation with nature became internal to the developing human constitution, and as such formed the basis for the unilinear sequence of socio-economic formations that followed in the second process. The notion of a dialectical unfolding of a process according to a series of stages was intrinsic to Engelsian dialectics, based on the *Wechselwirkung* between different elements and the teleonomy inherent in every development from simple to more complex forms. This explains the strong emphasis on internal development, rather than the interplay with external factors.

The influence of Engels on the dominant currents of Soviet thought was noted in Chapter 1, in the discussion of the early reception of Spinoza's ideas in the USSR. The interpretations of Deborin and his followers, and especially their resonance in the later official line of the 1930s, favoured the view of dialectics espoused by Engels, including his conception of *Wechselwirkung* and emphasis on internal development. This can be observed in philosophy, history, as well as in the historiography of philosophy itself, being defined by the unfolding struggle of materialism and idealism in relation to socio-economic development. As an extension of this, it also shaped how the transition from capitalism to socialism, and onwards to communism, was conceived. In this sense, the failings of the Engelsian perspective are evident both in its inadequate conception of history and in its inability to support a transition to communism. Instead, it can be seen as the theoretical *cul de sac* accompanying the very real one facing the socialist revolutions of the twentieth century.

However, it was also possible to recognise alternative concepts and strategies in the 'mechanists' of the philosophical debates of the 1920s and the New Direction in Soviet historiography of the 1960s and 1970s. As we saw in Chapter 1, the 'mechanists' did not grasp dialectics as an internal, teleonomic unfolding from simple to complex through a sequence of stages, but rather emphasised mechanical causality within an infinite series of finite modes. The contrast between the two approaches can be clearly discerned in approaches to history as well. Engelsian dialectics posits that each form of motion has to be grasped in its own terms, with other forms of motion that formed constituent parts being relegated to a secondary role. In this sense, it is less surprising that between the distinct processes of anthropogony and sociogenesis on the one hand, and the sequence of socio-economic formations on the other, a strong qualitative break was posited. The human relation with nature that became 'internalised' in the former process, had a secondary role in the latter one.

By contrast, the 'mechanists' started with the most simple mechanisms to grasp the specificity of the whole through the way its parts fit together. For a living organism this would imply starting with the chemistry of life, including the metabolic process, moving up to biological phenomena such as genetics. For human history, as we saw above, Danilova did not start with chemistry as such but rather with the metabolism of humans and nature. In her analysis she distinguished between forms of appropriating material goods, as specific expressions of the human relation with nature. In this way she was able to grasp early prehistory and later history from a common analytical perspective. Furthermore, in this way it was also possible to provide a more satisfactory account of later changes in the human relation to nature during the Neolithic revolution and the emergence of machine-based production. In this way, Danilova could also account for the multiplicity of history, in the sense that the specificity of modes of production could be thought through. Examples are the Asiatic mode of production, as well as the distinguishing features of the capitalist one relative to its predecessors.

As noted above, Brezhnevite reaction and censorship prevented the New Direction of Danilova and her colleagues in realising their ambitious plans to rethink Marxist historiography, and to provide a new, critical method to aid in the transition to communism. As such, they were never able to provide a comprehensive theoretical perspective as part of a broad, comparative research programme. Rather we have now only elements of such a theory. Certainly, gaps can be noted. Most notable is the small role that commodity exchange plays in Danilova's account, even if it is mentioned. There was little attention to the interconnections between the multiplicity of social formations. In this sense the critique of Semenov and his use of the notion of the global-historical centre is significant, even if his theory of it remains oblique. The notion of multistructuredness of the New Direction would be useful in this regard, but was only applied by them to multiplicity within social formations. As such, there were few theoretical means to grasp not just social formations themselves but also the specific connections between them, and the causal efficacy of these connections on internal development.

In order to develop the theoretical means to grasp the interplay among social formations, it is necessary to return to Marx. The historical perspective sketched by Danilova has important points in common with the interpretation of Marx's ideas provided in the previous chapter, especially with regard to the role of the metabolism with nature and the valuation of historical pluralism. Marx as read along the lines of the aleatory current provided more, however, in the form of a theory of encounter and the primacy of specific historical points of departure. It was also argued there that not only is it possible to recognise plural temporality in Marx's stratigraphic metaphor of historical development, but also that the Epicurean thesis of the plurality of worlds has important resonances in his work. In the next section the contemporary relevance of these ideas are explored, again with reference to the historical and archaeological records. The aim is to show how Marx's ideas, as well as those of Danilova and the New Direction, relate to the findings of contemporary science.

3   Marx, the Thesis of the Plurality of Worlds and Twenty-First Century Science

Recalling the argument made in the previous chapter, a Marxist version of the thesis of the plurality of worlds is based on three aspects of Marx's work. First of all there is the metabolism of humans and nature, and the earthly and historical character of this relation that is evident in distinctions between different world regions. Secondly, there was the encounter and specific point of departure of commodity exchange in western Eurasia, forming the basis for a long-term trajectory that resulted in the capitalist mode of production. However, the evidence from the Americas was counterposed to this Old World trajectory, pointing to its historical and particular character rather than its universality. Thirdly, the case of the Inca state showed that it was possible for an advanced division to emerge without commodity exchange, in contradistinction to the ancient Mediterranean states posited as universal cases by Morgan and Engels. This plurality of social formations derives both from the earthly basis for the metabolic interaction with nature, and from distinctions in the way the social metabolisms of commodity exchange and the division of labour were consti- tuted historically.

Earlier in this chapter, we saw that the European encounter with the Amer- icas was instrumental in the development of archaeology as a science, demon- strating the validity of the Three Age system initially formulated by Lucretius. Intrinsic to this was the analogy made between the contemporary use of stone tools in the Americas, and ancient artefacts found in Europe. By contrast, what twenty-first century science shows is not an analogy between the Old and New Worlds, but rather the great differences between them. Distinctions that seem to support the thesis of the plurality of worlds. In order to understand this, however, it is necessary to start with the Old World first. Following from Marx's arguments on different metals, in relation to the origin of metallurgy, in the development of commodity exchange and the money-form, this would be a natural way to grasp the interaction among the different social formations of western Eurasia. Furthermore, Marx's ideas were known already from then already published volumes of *Capital*, even if the later published *Grundrisse* added more details and evidence.

Yet neither the initial development of commodity exchange, nor the inter- action between distinct social formations, can be recognised as important research topics in Soviet archaeology. Rather, the emphasis was on tracing first of all the *pyatichlenka*, and from the late Stalin era onwards do so from the per- spective of the various nationalities that made up the USSR.[147] Archaeology in the various republics returned to a form closer to the European nation- alist frameworks discussed earlier in this chapter, with little critical Marxist archaeology being accomplished.[148] Of course, this should take into account the specific form that the nationalities question assumed in its Soviet context, just as the perspective of the centre cannot be simply denoted as imperial- istic.[149] Rather, it should be understood as a variation on the triad of nationalist,

---

147   Each stage was argued to have corresponding ethnic unit, see Gellner 1988, table 6.1, p. 132
       for a reconstruction.
148   Khatchadourian 2008 gives an overview for the Caucasian republics.
149   It is important in this sense to note a sense of internationalism, perhaps even more pro-

colonialist, and imperialist archaeologies, much like the archaeology of the French revolutionary regime earlier. The main point in this is that the archaeological centres in Leningrad, Moscow, as well as in the capitals of republics and provinces, followed an ideological template that could hardly think the history of the Soviet space as such.

Take as an example a synthesis of Soviet archaeology by Alexander Mongait, a more liberal scholar, from the later 1950s.[150] This book describes in various chapters the occurrence of slaveholding and feudal modes in various parts of the Soviet Union, creating a rather disjointed spatial picture of the *pyatich-lenka* in space and time. As noted above, connections to the broader world are noted, most especially for the Crimea and southern Ukraine, the Caucasus, and Central Asia relative to the broader world of antiquity. Viewing these areas as margins of a world beyond, the interior of the Soviet space became a kind of conceptual void, given its lack of the internal development according to the sequence of socio-economic stages. Confronted with geography, the notion of a universal trajectory from simple to complex turns into an incomprehensible, motley map of regions out of joint with each other. As such something like the Hegelian Spirit was needed to save it from the confrontation with (scientific) reality, as could be seen for Semenov's 'global-historical centre'.

The problem was recognised by Marxist archaeologists outside the Soviet Union, however, most notable by the Australian scholar Vere Gordon Childe. His work is especially significant as it took place largely contemporary to the formative phases of Soviet archaeology, independent of it but also interacting with it.[151] Indeed, his work was a formative influence on both Marxist archaeology outside the countries ruled by Communist Parties, and from the 1960s onwards on certain Soviet scholars as well.[152] Apart from his fieldwork in Scot-

---

nounced among scientists, as several short profiles of Soviet archaeologists indicate, Kohl 2008, pp. 122–5, 241–3. It is hard in this sense to see any kind of 'Russian imperialism' in this sense.

150   Later he became involved in debates on the definition of archaeological cultures, arguing against the identification of these with ethnic groups, see Markwick 2001, pp. 137–8 for this debate.

151   A good overview of Childe's archaeological ideas can be found in Trigger 1980. A recent biography, Irving 2020, traces Childe's political background in pacifist, socialist, and trade union circles, pointing also to his own philosophical development relative to Hegel, Marx, and contemporary philosophy. Notably, too, together with Jack Lindsay, Childe had formulated some of the key tenets of what later became the New Left, Irving 2020, pp. 320–3.

152   Childe played a crucial role in what would become known as 'Latin American Social Archaeology', an important strand of Marxist archaeology that emerged in Latin America in the 1970s, Trigger 2006, p. 496. Soviet archaeologist Vadim Masson also drew extensively

land, Childe's contribution to archaeology was twofold. First of all, he was a master of archaeological synthesis, piecing together the varied sequences as reconstructed by culture-historical archaeology into grand narratives, starting with *The Dawn of European Civilisation* of 1925. This book presented an account of what he saw as an indigenous European civilisation, in close interaction with the civilisations of the Middle East, a work that he would keep refining up through the 1950s. Its intellectual sources were not Marxist, however, even if he added Marxist elements to it in later versions.[153]

The other major contribution did derive from Marxism, and has to be understood in the context of the engagement with Marxism by a number of British scientists such as John Bernal and Joseph Needham from the 1930s onwards.[154] Childe developed an outline of human history according to a sequence of revolutions, rather than stages of development.[155] This sequence started with the 'human revolution', which enabled the accumulation of technological and cultural traits, moving to the 'Neolithic revolution' that initiated a food-producing economy through agriculture, both radically altering the relation of humans and nature. Then came the 'urban revolution', the coeval emergence of cities, socio-economic classes, the state, and civilisation. These revolutions are more flexible concepts, with Childe noting important distinctions between the urban revolution in Mesopotamia and Egypt, both in terms of the process through which they emerged and in their characteristics.[156] He also emphasised the complex temporality of development, including the phenomenon of the long-term stagnation of social development.[157]

Initially, Childe identified these revolutions with the transition between different archaeological ages, as evident in the naming of the Neolithic one, but

---

on Childe in his work on the Neolithic and urban revolution in Central Asia, as part of his broader thrust for a Marxist and comparative archaeology, e.g. Masson 1972, 1988.

153   Meheux 2017.

154   Very much stimulated by the presentations of the Soviet delegation at the *Science at the Cross Roads* conference of 1931, which included Bukharin and Vavilov, among others, Werskey 1971. Childe was an active collaborator in these efforts and friends with some of its key participants, Peace 1992, pp. 143–5; Trigger 1980, pp. 136–43.

155   Greene 1999 gives an overview of these revolutions, which were first comprehensively outlined together in 1936 in his work *Man makes himself*, Childe 1965.

156   In particular with regard to the different ways of extracting surplus, Childe 1954, pp. 47–50.

157   Childe clearly related such stagnation to the parasitical exploitation of farmers and craftworkers by newly emerged political and priestly elites as they became entrenched, Childe 1965, pp. 229–30. He certainly recognised how class systems in this regard could lead to periods of stagnation that lasted for many centuries, even millennia, as could also be seen for pre-state social forms in prehistoric Scotland, Childe 1946, p. 96.

notably for the metal ages as well.[158] He even posited an additional 'iron revolution', given the great impact of the adoption of iron metallurgy on Eurasian history (and indeed African history, but this was not explored by him).[159] These studies proved highly fruitful in grasping the specific development of western Eurasia, but at the same time clashed with the universalist tendencies of the Marxist stadialism of the day. In close contact with Soviet archaeologists from the 1930s onwards, Childe attempted to critically engage with the schemes of Morgan and Engels.[160] This engagement certainly did not lead to his adoption of reconstructions of a shift from matrilineal to patrilineal clans, deeming Soviet arguments on this topic speculative relative to the available archaeological evidence.[161] However, it did lead him to qualify the connection between the metal ages of the Old World and stages of economic development.

He now recognised that the correspondence between archaeological ages and his revolutions was not as close as he previously assumed, based on two observations. First of all, the identification of the urban revolution with the Bronze Age faltered on the evidence from the New World, where the Inca and Maya urban civilisations had both developed from a Neolithic technological base.[162] For the Old World, he observed that the Bronze and Iron Ages showed in fact a great deal of variation in the characteristics of the different regional trajectories of development.[163] Indeed, in tracing a number of them in parallel, Childe showed rather that they could not be grasped independently but only through mutually induced changes. Such changes were brought about not just by trade itself, but also by the transfer of ideas accompanying it, conceived together by Childe as 'intercourse'.[164] Important cases of this are the spread of

---

158   Childe 1965, pp. 34–5.
159   Childe 1944, p. 23, see also the many passages from *What Happened in History*, where he traced the revolutionary social changes after the large-scale introduction of iron metallurgy, Childe 1942, pp. 182–83, 204–9.
160   This was something of a reversal, for earlier Childe had provided a scathing critique of the adaptation of Morgan's work by Engels, Irving 2020, pp. 286–7. Yet in his *Social Evolution* of 1951, he paid considerably more attention to the ideas of Morgan, as well as the use made of them by Soviet archaeologists.
161   Childe 1951, pp. 28–9.
162   Childe 1951, pp. 26–7, 162. See also his remarks on the inclusion of ancient Maya civilisation among the cases of the urban revolution, Childe 1950, p. 9.
163   His comparative cases were temperate Europe, the Mediterranean, the Nile valley, and Mesopotamia, investigating the parallels between them to ascertain the existence of 'general stages', Childe 1951, p. 161.
164   Most notable external exchange, which in Mesopotamia had developed to such an extent that dedicated merchant communities existed, Childe 1951, pp. 152–3. Long-distance ex-

lapis lazuli artefacts many thousands of kilometres from their mining areas in Afghanistan and Pakistan, as well as the spread of technologies like iron metal-lurgy. Important in this is that the acceptance, or lack thereof, of such features follows internal needs.[165]

Childe posited an analogy here with the modern spread of railway techno-logy from Britain to a set of very different countries, with highly distinct cultural norms.[166] In the same way, the prehistoric trajectories of Western Eurasia can-not be grasped as existing completely independent of each other, but rather have to be understood in a complex pattern of mutual interaction:

> In any case the evidence cited leaves no doubt that intercourse went on between the diverse geographical regions where relatively full cul-ture sequences are available throughout the whole period when barbar-ism reigned in each. That intercourse helps to explain the convergences observed in very diverse natural environments. It also shows why we have failed to define in all regions similar stages, intermediate between barbar-ism and civilization. For on the one hand the processes of change have been too rapid to allow of the total integration of the societies affected by diffusion into stable new configurations. On the other hand, the sev-eral series considered are not in fact so completely independent of one another as to constitute distinct "instances" from which inductions can legitimately be drawn.[167]

The notion of diffusionism had always been central to culture-historical ar-chaeology, most notably to its grand narratives like those posited by Childe in his aforementioned work *The Dawn of European Civilisation*. Now, however, he proposed to grasp it from a Marxist perspective, drawing a contrast between biological and cultural evolution, the latter based on the capabilities for pro-ductive labour and cultural accumulation made possible by the human revolu-tion. Whereas in biological evolution the 'mechanism of organic evolution' brings differentiation through mutations and sexual selection, in cultural evol-

---

change is also one of the key traits of the urban revolution, Childe 1950, pp. 15–16, which therefore cannot be seen as a purely endogenous phenomenon. Of course, the possibil-ity to carry out such external trade on a significant scale depended on the possibility of extracting surplus.

165   As well as being 'socially approved' by the social norms of a specific culture, Childe 1951, pp. 172–3.
166   Childe 1951, pp. 167–8.
167   Childe 1951, pp. 173–4.

ution new 'mutations' such as technological inventions can be shared with others through acculturation.[168] In this way, there exists not just differentiation but also convergence between different social formations, which can explain phenomena such as the distinctiveness of the indigenous European civilisation that Childe recognised. Indeed, convergence for him exerted such a strong pull on history that he conceived of history in a strongly unitary way, based on a central stream of development that incorporated the others.[169]

In the work of Childe, then, we can find a mechanism for the mutual interaction of distinct regions that could form the basis for 'worlds', even if he subsumed plurality under a universal conception of progress. Quite apart from this frankly Eurocentric perspective, the limits of his culture-historical framework became obvious in relation to the archaeology of the USSR as well. Even if many of the criticisms he made of Soviet archaeological practices were true, his inability to provide a coherent account of its archaeology cannot be put down to these inadequacies.[170] For subsequent research has shown that rather than the reconstructions of archaeological cultures being inadequate in empirical terms, it is precisely the culture-historical framework that is insufficient for understanding the material record. From the 1960s onwards some Soviet archaeologists would break with the narrow mould of the notion of cultures as the alpha and omega of research, and turn away from a regional focus to consider wider horizons.

Interestingly, the impetus for this change in direction came not from theory but from the practical study of artefacts, in particular of metal finds. Under the direction of Yevgeny Chernykh, a new laboratory set up in the 1960s in Moscow for archaeo-metallurgical studies became one of the most important centres for the study of the development of metalworking.[171] Its geographical focus was not limited to the Soviet Union, but through collaborative fieldwork also included countries in eastern Europe and the Middle East (notably Iraq).[172] The main initial research output of the work of the laboratory was the 1992

---

168   Emphasising here the different mechanisms of cultural evolution, Childe 1951, pp. 175–9.
169   This unity is the red thread that runs through *What Happened in History*, Childe 1942.
170   It should be emphasised that not only have these areas seen more intensive archaeological fieldwork, starting in many cases already in the nineteenth century, they are also smaller than their northern counterparts. It simply will take more time to understand the northern regions in the same detail, and this will require different methods and theories appropriate to the available sources.
171   Chernykh 1992, pp. 16–17.
172   See Avilova 2009 for the evidence from Iraq. Specialists from these areas initially did not engage with the notion of metallurgical provinces, but see now Wilkinson 2014.

book *Ancient Metallurgy in the USSR*, authored by Chernykh.[173] Even if subsequent laboratory studies and fieldwork at sites such as Kargaly have added much that is new, the book remains important for having posited the main concepts and findings of this research effort. In it, Chernykh defines its focus as the delineation of what he terms the Early Metal Age (EMA), temporally wedged in between the Neolithic and the Early Iron Age.

Given the scientific evidence then available to him, the area covered by the book is limited to the Soviet Union and parts of eastern Europe. Yet he emphasises the implications of the findings from these areas for understanding the broader Eurasian context of the EMA. The main concept for understanding the EMA is what Chernykh terms a 'metallurgical province', which refers to long-term continuities in forms of metalworking that extended over very large geographical areas. It had long been obvious that the uneven distribution of copper ores, as well as of the major materials for making bronze alloys such as arsenic and more importantly tin, implied the existence of mining and production foci.[174] What the Moscow laboratory studies further revealed, however, was uniformity in the morphology of artefacts and in their manufacturing techniques, persisting over centuries and in areas stretching for thousands of kilometres. Chernykh captured this uniformity in the notion of the aforementioned metallurgical province, which itself consisted of a number of different zones with metallurgical and metalworking foci.[175]

The (understated) revolutionary impact of the metallurgical province is not just that it presents a new way of grasping the history of a particular era, that of the EMA, but also that it shows the limited, secondary status of traditional archaeological cultures. Given that metallurgical provinces were of such geographical and temporal scopes that they encompassed many distinct archaeological cultures, they have to be understood as the more fundamental unit of analysis. For whereas each metallurgical province was 'independent', the individual cultures within it were to some extent entangled within the larger unit of which they were a part.[176] Implied by this is the incompleteness of the

---

173 No Russian language edition of this book exists, owing to the crisis befalling the Soviet scientific community during *Perestroika* and after, Chernykh 2017, p. 586.

174 To relate metal finds to the specific mining context from which they derived is possible in principle but fraught with difficulties in practice, limiting but not preventing attempts to trace the sequence of steps between the mining of ores and the deposition of metal objects in archaeological contexts, Chernykh 1992, pp. 18–22; Wilkinson 2014, pp. 153–68.

175 The metallurgical provinces themselves consist of different foci, both metallurgical and metalworking ones, the latter only involving the working of raw material rather than mining and copper smelting, Chernykh 1992, pp. 8–10.

176 Chernykh 1992, p. 7.

'internalist' perspective of both culture-history, with its focus on the histories of cultural or ethnic groups, and the evolutionary view of the unfolding of developmental stages in a specific region. For in reality in each culturally or geographically defined region, the internal dynamic was always determined in part by something external to this, as reflected in the metallurgical provinces.

Unlike the general assumption of gradual development in single cultures and geographical regions, the history of the metallurgical provinces was characterised by a distinct dynamic of stagnation and sudden, rapid change. That is, the formation (and dissolution) of such a formation took place quickly and marked a radical break with the preceding arrangement. It is possible to recognise a certain periodicity in this, often marked by waves of destructions and migrations, but the causality behind this process is still insufficiently understood.[177] After a new metallurgical province was established, there was a tendency towards conservatism, even stagnation.[178] These processes of the emergence and collapse of various metallurgical provinces did greatly impact the different social formations that existed within their fold, their fate being to a large extent bound up with it:

> The emergence of such metallurgical systems and their subsequent disintegration nearly always signifies a major turning point in the historical development of the peoples of the EMA period, as does the end of the EMA itself. It should be particularly emphasized that the formation and collapse of provinces marked more than just metallurgical changes. These never occurred in isolation but invariably coincided with and were closely linked with other very important historical events. These included the formation of new archaeological cultures and historico-cultural communities, the emergence of new ethnic groups, the transformations of various systems of production, changes in the orientation of the links between various extensive population groups, and changes in ideological conceptions. It is also apparent that the formation and collapse of provinces most often took place more or less simultaneously over a vast area (such as that stretching from the Pacific to the Atlantic ocean, in the case of the end of the EMA itself).[179]

---

177 Chernykh 1992, p. 307.

178 This stagnation is connected to the operation of 'normative factors', which insulate from the circumstances facing a culture, as well as the larger framework of the metallurgical province, eventually leading to contradictions and a possible breakdown of order, Chernykh 1992, pp. 298–9. See also chapter 39 of Chernykh 2017.

179 Chernykh 1992, pp. 12, 15.

Chernykh explains this decisive influence of metallurgical trends as being based on the social impact of metalworking and metal tools and other artefacts. According to him metallurgy allowed for an increase in labour productivity, as well as leading to the first professionally defined artisans, thereby generating more social wealth as a basis for social stratification and the state.[180] Another aspect he emphasises is the use of metal to fashion weaponry, notably that used by the mounted warriors in the northern steppe areas of the EMA area.[181] However, metalworking was not the only important economic activity during the EMA era, and social stratification and the state can emerge in its absence as well.[182] Just as important, and possibly more so, are the domesticated animal and plant species that allow for the production of surpluses of foodstuffs, including those to feed dedicated groups of metalworkers. Chernykh certainly recognises this factor and in later work places great emphasis on the different geoecological zones of Eurasia, and the interaction they engendered between hunter-gatherers, pastoral nomads, settled agriculturalists, as well as hybrid forms.[183]

At the same time, he resists changing the periodisation based on metallurgi-cally-defined phases to include other aspects, such as distinct episodes of domestication and other aspects.[184] Instead, he proposes to grasp the Neolithic revolution and succeeding phases of domestication as part of a 'complex pro-ductive economy', which combines the different factors of agriculture, metal-lurgy, and other kinds of economic activity.[185] As such, this conception of the economy constitutes a form specific to the EMA, while the Neolithic revolu-tion was global in character. The EMA, then, is not a universal model but rather captures a particular part of Eurasian history. Chernykh thinks through this specificity of the EMA comprehensively, shifting away from a general sequence of metallurgical phases in the Three Age fashion to a more contextualised view

---

180 Chernykh 1992, pp. 4–5.
181 There are important archaeological indications for this in the so-called Seima-Turbino phenomenon of mounted nomads that practiced metallurgy, emerging in the Altai moun-tain range at the end of the third millennium BC and rapidly spreading across a vast spatial extent in Eurasia, Chernykh 1992, pp. 215–33, Chernykh 2017, chapter 15.
182 As per the aforementioned New World cases. Conversely, it is now recognised that (low-density) urban sites in the EMA could develop without the state as well, as the Tripolye culture of the Carpatho-Balkan Metallurgical Province shows, Gaydarska 2016; Kohl 2007, pp. 39–46; Wengrow 2015.
183 Chapter 2 of Chernykh 2017 outlines the different geological and ecological zones of Eurasia, as well as major geographical divisions like the Dzungarian Gate.
184 Chernykh 1992, p. 11.
185 Chernykh 2017, pp. 27–9.

in which the metallurgical provinces define distinct phases. In that sense the metal ages become embodied in a particular succession of spatio-temporal forms, rather than being valid for all regions,[186] and can be summed up accordingly:

1.   A Protometal period that dates from the Ninth through the Sixth millennia BC, focused on Mesopotamia and parts of Anatolia and Iran. This age is roughly coterminous with the initial development of agriculture in the Fertile Crescent.

2.   The Copper Age dating to circa 5500–3500 BC. Apart from the expansion of metallurgy from the Middle East northwards through the Caucasus, an eastern European focus can now also be noted. This focus was the first metallurgical province, the so-called Carpatho-Balkan Metallurgical Province or CBMP.

3.   With the transition to the Bronze Age, the CBMP collapses but new metallurgical provinces can be recognised for the Early Bronze Age (circa 3500–2500 BC). Two can be noted: the Circumpontic Metallurgical Province (or CMP), as well as an Irano-Afghan Metallurgical Province or IAMP. The CMP encompassed the entire area that during the Copper Age showed evidence for metalworking, while the IAMP is a new one.

4.   During the Middle Bronze Age (2500–1750 BC) the CMP and IAMP continue.

5.   A radical change can be seen during the shorter Late Bronze Age (1750–1250 BC), with both a proliferation of metallurgy to the north, west, and east, and the emergence of a large number of metallurgical provinces to fill the void left by the collapse of the CMP and IAMP.

As noted, the transition between each phase also resulted in a comprehensive reordering of social formations. Furthermore, in most cases it also led to an expansion of the total area covered by the sum of metallurgical provinces, expanding into new zones such as temperate Europe, the northern parts of Eurasia, and China. In this way, Chernykh's account provides a good way to grasp the broad outlines of a particularly crucial part of human history. However, the causal mechanisms driving not just the formation and dissolution of metallurgical provinces but also their internal dynamics, remain somewhat oblique. Trade must have been extensive, given the scale of production evident from the archaeological record. For example, from the mine at Ai Bunar in Bulgaria, which was mainly exploited in the CBMP era, it is estimated that as much

---

186   See the overview in Chernykh 2011, fig. 5, p. 67, and also Wilkinson 2014, figs. 5.19–22, pp. 178–9.

as 20,000 tonnes of copper ore have been mined.[187] Furthermore, copper from this mine and other ones in the Carpatho-Balkan region has been traced far afield, in artefacts found in Tripolye settlements in the Ukraine.[188]

Later, in the CMP era, similar flows of metals can be detected, most notably a persistent transfer of copper from southern agricultural productive centres to northern steppe pastoralists.[189] Little is known about the way in which these metals were exchanged, however, and factors other than trade such as military force may have played a role too.[190] Even when more detailed evidence is available for specific sites, it is frustratingly difficult to ascertain the mechanisms through which metals were transferred from one region to another. The fieldwork of Chernykh and his colleagues at the site of Kargaly in the Urals demonstrates this difficulty. Exploited mainly during the Second millennium BC, as much as 100,000 tonnes of copper may have been produced at Kargaly from millions of tonnes of ore, and artefacts made from this copper have been found across a large geographical area.[191] Just as remarkable as the output of copper production were the enormous amount of animal bones that have been found at the settlement site of Gorny next to Kargaly, which consist mainly of cattle bones.[192]

On the basis of this juxtaposition of both mining and the deposition of animal bones at such a large scale, Chernykh hypothesised that metal and animals were exchanged for each other in what he termed a 'primitive market economy'.[193] Yet the evidence also allows for a potential alternative, in the form of a seasonal exploitation of the Kargaly mines by pastoral nomads.[194] At present there is no conclusive evidence to warrant decisive support for either hypothesis. In this sense, Marx's idea that forms of money developed early among the nomads of the Eurasian steppes remains profound, but still depends

---

187   Kohl 2007, p. 33.
188   Chernykh 1992, pp. 41, 46–7. It now appears that these metals came not exactly from Ai Bunar itself, but rather from other mines in Romania that were closer to the Black sea coast, but the outline of a long-distance exchange network that included metals remains the same, Kohl 2007, pp. 33–4, 38–9.
189   Chernykh 1992, pp. 158–62.
190   A later parallel to this can be seen in the tribute of gold paid by the Huns by the later Roman empire, Bayless 1976.
191   Chernykh 2011, pp. 66–7.
192   Furthermore, natural scientific analysis of the bone remains indicates that cattle was imported, rather than being part of a 'mixed regime' of different forms of economic activities that included stockbreeding alongside metallurgical activities, Antipina and Morales 2006.
193   Chernykh 2011, p.67.
194   Kohl 2007, pp. 176–8.

on further exploration and material studies. The only way to know more about exchange in the Early Metal Age, is to turn to the southern belt of literate state formations, which stretched from the Aegean in the West to the Indus valley in the East. Here there exists both textual and material evidence for the exchange of metals and other goods, and it is also more easy to grasp the broader social, economic, political, and ideological contexts in which it took place.

Texts dating to the EMA from various Middle Eastern states allow for insights into the mechanisms of long-distance exchange. At a general level a considerable level of variation can be observed in this regard. A more 'commercial' or 'market' kind of exchange can be discerned in texts from the Old-Assyrian period, while the Amarna letters show that an entirely different dynamic of gift-exchange existed between the great powers of the region.[195] It is important to keep in mind that these forms of exchange involved not just metals but many other materials as well, both naturally occurring ones such as lapis lazuli and other precious stones, as well as ones artificially made such as glass and textiles.[196] Other than through texts, such trade can also be followed through material proxies, which are of considerable importance for grasping the particular circumstances within which commodity exchange took hold in western Eurasia. These proxies can be noted in two forms: first of all standardised forms of the materials to be exchanged, and, secondly, the means through which trade equivalencies were reckoned, mainly in the form of weighing systems.

As for standardised forms of materials for exchange the main evidence comes from shipwrecks, which is not surprising given that such forms are unlikely to occur in settlement, workshop, and other contexts.[197] Standardised 'ox-hide' shaped ingots of copper and tin, as well as of glass, were found in the Uluburun shipwreck off the coast of Anatolia, which has been dated to the late fourteenth-century BC.[198] It has been suggested that these standardised forms for copper formed a standard of value for both the Mediterranean and Black Sea areas, but many specific details such as the relation of state-sponsored trade relative to unregulated commercial activity remain oblique.[199]

195　Wilkinson 2014, p. 193.

196　The interactions between which is one of the main themes in Wilkinson 2014.

197　Given the scarcity of materials such as metal and glass, workshop contexts show much evidence for recycling, Brysbaert 2011. As such, it is of little surprise that ingots are only very rarely found in normal deposition contexts.

198　Mee 2008, p. 364.

199　One shipwreck at Cape Gelidonya from the later Thirteenth century BC, shows evidence not just of trade in ingots, but of scrap metal as well, which would have been more congenial to trade in metal at a smaller scale by merchants or even the smiths themselves, Sherratt 2000, pp. 87–8.

Certainly, the widespread use and fairly standardised forms of weighing systems, even at smaller sites, points to an important role for commerce that cannot have been completely controlled by state bureaucracies.[200] In that sense, Marx's notion of the coexistence of merchant capital with landed forms of property is still useful, especially compared to twentieth-century approaches that sought either to deny or to hypostatise exchange in the earliest forms of social life.[201]

Weighing systems were of crucial importance, as they allowed for the measurement of specific amounts of materials, which could then be exchanged for specific quantities of other materials. In that sense they work well in relation to the ingots, as these represent not just standard forms but in effect standard weights as well. In this way these weighing systems enabled the second and third forms of equivalency outlined by Marx in *Capital*, the ones that he also recognised in Homer and added to his excerpts and notes on Morgan. Archaeologists have also noted their centrality in the development of economic life in western Eurasia, as the basis for a 'commodity nexus' that started with weighing systems and later developed into coinage and other forms of universal money.[202] For our purposes, it is notable that the weighing systems are closely related to the trade in metals and can be found precisely in the area stretching between the Aegean and the Indus Valley.

As noted earlier, this area is precisely the southern belt of state or state-dependent social formations of the Early Metal Age. We can now understand this area as an elaboration of Chernykh's notion of the 'complex productive economy', which for him involved mainly metals and domesticates. It is necessary to add to this the economic mechanisms that as of yet cannot be easily recognised in the northern part of the EMA. These mechanisms involved not just the trade in metals and other goods that is evident from the texts, the artefacts themselves, and the means of exchange of weights and later, after the EMA, coinage. It also involved the mechanisms through which the surplus goods needed to carry out this trade were mobilised, that is the means through which 'surplus value was pumped out of the direct producers'. In the Bronze Age of the Middle East and selected regions of the Mediterranean such as the Aegean, the largescale mobilisation of agricultural produce, as well as the pro-

---

200 Indeed, in the Late Bronze Age site of Akrotiri, the finds of weights in several houses points to economic interaction at a larger scale, Michailidou 2010, pp. 77–9, away from direct control by state bureaucracies.

201 In the debate between the neo-classical 'formalists' and 'substantivists' such as Karl Polanyi, see for a sophisticated Soviet interpretation of this debate Semenov 1974.

202 Renfrew 2012, pp. 253–5.

duction of textiles, took place mainly within 'administrative' contexts. Mainly, these would be palaces, but they could also involve temples and even larger households.[203]

The key means through which economic life in such institutional contexts was structured was through writing on clay tablets and other media for administrative purposes, as well as the use of seals and sealings.[204] It is no longer thought that the palatial economies completely dominated economic life, but they could mobilise resources and labour in ways that were unparalleled in these social formations. For example, in the Mycenaean state of Pylos in mainland Greece, the palatial administration shows evidence for a great range of economic activities both in the archaeological and textual records. These activities included the management of large herds of oxen for agricultural work and sheep for wool, the redistribution of metals, as well as supporting large groups of textile workers, among other things.[205] It also provided testimony for the mobilisation of resources for different religious festivals, as well as for various military tasks.[206] The scale with which the palatial state was able to do this can be seen in the landscape as well, such as in the large harbour that was created in this region of Greece, parallels for which exist in other regions.[207]

Another thing highlighted by the Pylos texts is the role of certain prestigious artefacts, which have to be understood in terms of both the value inherent in them and the power of the expression of those values in visual display.[208] The role of the palace as such was both to act as a centre of redistribution of such treasured objects, as well as to put them on display within its walls.[209] Indeed these values were expressed in a more expansive way on its walls as well, in the

---

203   Earlier models from the 1960s emphasised a greater degree of state control, whereas contemporary ones recognise a greater diversity of economic actors, a shift that can be recognised well for the Aegean, e.g. Nakassis 2013.

204   Notably, the use of seals and sealings is attested long before the emergence of the state, as evidence from Neolithic Syria shows, Duistermaat 2010. It is to be connected more closely with distinctive forms of property that developed before the emergence of the state, deriving from the particulars of Eurasian agriculture and animal husbandry.

205   See for an overview Killen 2008.

206   Palaima 2015.

207   Zangger et al. 1997, pp. 613–23.

208   In this way the palatial centres could be seen as foci for the creation and display of value and prestige, Dakouri-Hild 2012, pp. 477–9; Killen 2008, pp. 177–81.

209   As well as beyond the territories of the Mycenaean states themselves, as the large numbers of impressive *krater* vessels in Late Bronze Age Cyprus shows, where they have been found mostly in burials, Steel 2013, pp. 209–16.

form of wall-paintings that expressed key themes not just of political power but of the worldview within which that power was conceived.[210] Much later, Homer would describe a palace in terms that are especially indicative of the way in which prestigious metals and precious stones such as lapis lazuli were conceived, as the following passage from the Odyssey shows:

> A radiance strong as the moon or rising sun came flooding
> through the high-roofed halls of generous King Alcinous.
> Walls plated in bronze, crowned with a circling frieze
> glazed as blue as lapis, ran to left and right
> from outer gates to the deepest court recess,
> and solid golden doors enclosed the palace.
> Up from the bronze threshold silver doorposts rose
> with silver lintel above, and golden handles too.
> And dogs of gold and silver were stationed either side,
> forged by the god of fire with all his cunning craft
> to keep watch on generous King Alcinous' palace,
> his immortal guard-dogs, ageless, all their days.
> Inside to left and right, in a long unbroken row
> from farthest outer gate to the inmost chamber,
> thrones stood back against the wall, each draped
> with a finely spun brocade, women's handsome work.[211]

The influence of esteem and aesthetic values of metals and related materials should be clear. This pattern was powerfully present not just in the palaces of the mighty, but also in the elite burials that can often be seen to precede them. In the case of Pylos this is evident from the recent spectacular discovery of the Griffin Warrior tomb that preceded the emergence of the palace.[212] Yet many other notable examples exist, such as the Royal Cemetery at Ur.[213] It is precisely this funerary display of metallic and other forms of wealth that can also be seen in the northern zone of the EMA, in the so-called *kurgan* burial mounds.[214] This aspect of prestige, and the aesthetic values that underpinned it, should be recognised as a key factor in the development of class systems in this period. Even so, it was far from inevitable that this template was imposed

---

210 A connection that I have explored elsewhere in some depth, Bajema 2017a, pp. 144–59.
211 Fagles 1996, p. 182.
212 Davis and Stocker 2016.
213 Woolley 1934.
214 See for some examples from the Maikop culture of the Caucasus Kohl 2007, pp. 72–86.

on the era as a historico-philosophical theory applicable to all cases. For the civilisations of Crete and the Indus Valley show the emergence of largescale urban economies without first the funerary and then the monumental rulership seen in the other examples, but rather point to a more collective form of governance.[215] Similarly, the *kurgan* model is hardly applicable to the Kargaly case, which instead shows the 're-emergence of equality'.[216]

From the above account of the Early Metal Age, as defined by Chernykh, two main conclusions can be drawn. First of all, much more research is needed for the northern belt, which lacks the copious data record of its southern counterpart, amply helped by the particular forms of evidence afforded by shipwrecks and textual archives preserved by accidental conditions. Secondly, and this is the main point, the particular outline of the EMA allows both for the ability to think this phase of 'middle Eurasian' history in its specificity and in comparison with the trajectories of other regions. Through the metallurgical provinces it becomes not just possible to conceive of the specific characteristics of the historical trajectories of the (former) Soviet space. It also enables conceiving the southern belt in a broader perspective, one that is less focused on the narrow confines of each individual civilisation within it. In this sense it builds upon the earlier work of Childe on the 'sociological' and historical interpretation of the metal ages, but in a way that traces and explains his notion of the 'intercourse' between cultures more concretely and showing the central role of exchange in it.

Another distinction is that Chernykh emphasises the historical particularity of the different phases of the Early Metal Age, as being effectively embodied in the different metallurgical provinces. He emphasises that they are not universal models of development, for in Africa the EMA had been skipped with a direct transition to the Iron Age and in the Americas metallurgy was still precocious at the time of the European conquest.[217] In a short collaborative article with Philip Kohl, Chernykh compared the Eurasian EMA with later Mesoamerican history, noting the common occurrence of long-distance exchange in highly valuable goods and their use by elites.[218] At the same time, they also emphasised a number of differences between these world regions:

1. They argue that while Eurasian development takes place over a vast area, in Mesoamerica it was limited to a more tightly bound and well-

215   Driessen 2001; Possehl 2000.
216   Kohl 2007, pp. 178–9.
217   Chernykh 1992, p. 1.
218   Kohl and Chernykh 2003, pp. 307–8.

defined area, though not taking into account here the contacts between Mesoamerica and the western coastal areas of South America.[219]

2. The size of cities in Mesoamerica tends to be larger than their Eurasian counterparts, in part owing to the higher productivity of maize agriculture compared to the wheat and barley of western Eurasia.[220] Furthermore, the farming regimes were quite distinct as well, based more on intensification in Mesoamerica, and more on the use of animal labour in Eurasia. As we shall see below, this had important implications for patterns of inequality.

3. The widespread use of pastoralism on the Eurasian steppes, with specific economies and polities acting as important military and political forces, has no parallels in Mesoamerica, owing to the absence of suitable animal domesticates there.[221]

4. They argue that, partially owing to geographical circumstances, new inventions spread more slowly in Mesoamerica compared to the speed with which they did so in Eurasia.[222]

5. Not only did metallurgy develop later in Mesoamerica it also developed along different lines than the Eurasian EMA, to such an extent that the Three Age periodisation hardly fits it.[223] While as in the Old World, Mesoamerican metalworking was focused initially mostly on ornamental objects, the shift to large-scale production of metal weaponry and agricultural tools characteristic of the Eurasian Bronze Age was not present here.

This kind of comparative perspective, based on the characteristics of larger macro-regions rather than those of single cultures or regions, has so far been insufficiently pursued. Of course, this is the result not just of the conceptual limitations imposed by nationalist, imperialist, colonialist, as well as Soviet stadialism. Limits are also imposed by the scarcity of the evidence and the difficulties of mastering it that make even the comparison of singular cases a daunting task. In fact, it would take a scientific enterprise on the scale of Needham's *Science and Civilisation in China*, organised perhaps along the lines of the collective works of Moscow's ill-fated 'sector of methodology'. So far such work has been carried out mostly by individual researchers or in the form of

---

219 Kohl and Chernykh 2003, p. 308.
220 Kohl and Chernykh 2003, pp. 308–9.
221 Kohl and Chernykh 2003, p. 309.
222 Notably given the absence of domesticated animals to transport goods in Mesoamerica, Kohl and Chernykh, p. 310.
223 Kohl and Chernykh 2003, p. 311.

edited volumes with varying degrees of synthetic interpretation.[224] The result is that while much significant work has been conducted, there has been no breakthrough either in the results of comparative work, nor in the use of a method for comparison that is widely accepted without controversy.

However, comparison based on singular cases has allowed for recognising the sophistication of the early civilisations of the New World, and enables them to be understood in their global context.[225] Even so, the limitations of using only single cultural and regional cases, and only a limited part of their histories at that, imposes clear constraints on what can be said.[226] Such constraints are not always appreciated in studies in which strong claims about universal validity are made.[227] Yet the pitfalls of using single cases and ignoring their broader macro-regional contexts should be apparent from an aleatory perspective, in case fragments are used to stand in for the whole. In chapter five Marx's use of the Inca case to demonstrate the particularity of capitalism was highlighted, as well as how that case invalidated the strong causal connection made by Engels between commodity exchange and the emergence of the state. However, the broader picture of the Andean regions shows that some form of market exchange had been present, and that in fact the Inca state had suppressed these markets during its expansion.[228] In that sense the Inca case cannot stand for the Andean whole.

Hence, just as we saw for Eurasia, there always cases that are 'exceptional', a term that itself has to be taken with a grain of salt as it derives from extrapolation backwards in time of the 'accomplished facts' of succeeding periods.

---

224   Usually such volumes are collections of papers on different cases, with little attention to the actual comparison of the different cases, but see Lillios 2011 for an example where more in-depth comparison of cases is applied consistently, using the evidence of a great number of specialists.

225   Important studies in this regard are Adams 1966 and Trigger 2003, both of whom developed the ideas of Gordon Childe on the urban revolution much further, see in this regard also Masson 1988. My earlier comparative work has to be located in this tradition as well.

226   Certainly, the character of the evidence as well as the temporal depth of the historical and archaeological records can vary considerably, as can be seen for the seven cases compared by Trigger. Some of these were encountered by European colonialists, which heavily influenced interpretation, while others are known primarily through archaeology and textual records that were deciphered later, Trigger 2003, pp. 54–8.

227   A recent attempt to establish a database to be used for comparative purposes is a case in point, using a sophisticated method and peer review, Turchin 2018, but at the same time using mere lists of social and cultural traits. Such abstract measures of complexity in effect arguably embody the empty, homogenous time recognised by Benjamin.

228   Hirth and Pillsbury 2013.

Ideally, comparative studies should take multiple temporal and geographical scales into account, to show how macro-regional characteristics are distinct between different world regions, and how this is reflected in a variety of cases in each. To carry out such a study is clearly far beyond the scope of this chapter, but at least Marx's insights on the distinctive character of the pre-Columbian civilisations can be related to the current findings of comparative studies. In doing so, it is important to recall that Marx noted not just the Inca case, but also the distinctive uses of money in markets in Mesoamerica. What is most important in this is the general thrust of his argument, the notion of alternative pathways of development, rather than the specific reconstructions of cases based on the state of knowledge current in the nineteenth century.

Perhaps the most significant finding has been the result of archaeologists seeking new methods to measure inequality, based not on texts but on the surviving material record. Such studies had been pioneered in Soviet archaeology, and subsequently by other archaeologists as well, but these had focused on distinctions in burials.[229] In themselves such results cannot be held to unambiguously reflect social distinctions, as religious and other factors come into play as well, which make any kind of quantification along a Gini scale more problematic. However, more recent studies seek to focus on other sources of evidence as well, most notably distinctions in the sizes of houses that are less obviously influenced by worldviews and may be held to reflect social distinctions more clearly.[230] In this way a broad sample of Gini scores has been generated, given the wide availability of settlement evidence from various archaeological sites around the world. These different data points could then be plotted on a timescale in a figure, showing the trajectory of inequality as time progressed, with a distinction being made between Old World and New World (mostly Mesoamerican) cases.[231]

Comparing the two hemispheres based on time elapsed since the first plant domestication (in other words, since the Neolithic revolution), a number of observations can be made based on this figure. The first is that in the first 2,500 years there were no significant differences between the trajectories of inequality in the New and the Old Worlds. According to the aforementioned figure the

---

229 A method still popular in Russian archaeology, Kradin 2011, and in itself not without merit. For example, the relations between social classes in the early Athenian *polis* can be traced in this way, Morris 1987. Yet at the same time burials are not merely, or even primarily, about display and prestige, but as much about emotions and religious life.

230 See Fochesato et al. 2019 on the methodological issues for estimating Gini coefficients based on archaeology.

231 Kohler et al. 2017, fig. 3, p. 621.

Gini coefficient increased from an initial figure of under 0.2 to between 0.3 and 0.4, with those in the New World being slightly higher. Yet after this first phase of 2,500 years, the trajectories diverge. In the Old World the curve of inequality surpasses that of the New World in a more significant way, even if the dramatic increase in equality generally does not occur until 3,000 to 4,000 years after the first emergence of domesticates. Gini coefficients of up to 0.6 to 0.7 are then visible. Yet this did not occur in the New World, where if anything there seems to be a decrease in the Gini coefficient, with even a case as late as the Aztec capital Tenochtitlan having a coefficient below 0.4.[232] Significantly, however, there are New World case that do show higher coefficients, most notably the Maya kingdom of Tikal and the site of Cahokia from the southwestern United States that are close to 0.6.

Kohler and colleagues offer a number of arguments to explain the difference between the trajectories of the two hemispheres, focusing mainly on their distinct agricultural regimes. Their argument, elaborated in specific studies, is that a particular form of agricultural extensification in western Eurasia based on the use of draft animals for agricultural work, especially ploughing, enabled higher levels of inequality.[233] In a nutshell, a shift from more intensive horticulture to extensification allowed both for increased surpluses in the hands of the owners of draft animals. At the same time the greater use of land resulted in its scarcity and the consequent marginalisation of a group of landless producers. Here, then, we have an essentially Engelsian argument, if reached from the perspective of scientific studies rather than Marxist theory. Furthermore, this pattern had been recognised earlier by other scholars as well, especially drawing upon the differences in farming regimes across the world and their implications for socio-economic development.[234]

According to Kohler and colleagues, the agricultural strategies of extensification allowed for increases in inequality, later supplemented by two additional factors.[235] The introduction of bronze metallurgy and mounted warriors some 3,000 years after the first domesticates allowed for increases in polity size. Together with the greater role of long-distance trade in Eurasia, this stimu-

---

232   The evidence is summarised in more accessible form in Kohler et al. 2018, table 11.1, pp. 293–5.

233   Kohler et al. 2017, pp. 620–1. See on this also Bogaard et al. 2019.

234   Most notably in the comparative work of Scarborough 2003, based on the earlier insights in the particular qualities of rice-based farming regimes in Bray 1986. See also Masson 1988, pp. 127–32, for a Soviet Marxist understanding of the role of agriculture in distinctions between early civilisations.

235   Kohler et al. 2017, p. 621.

lated a further possible increase in inequality, based on new forms of political economy. In essence, these suggested ways of explaining the different trajectories of the Old and New Worlds, capturing some of the points of Kohl and Chernykh outlined earlier but in a more succinct form. However, a number of qualifications have to be made concerning their arguments. For it is not so much that the Old World curve shows an upward curve at 2,500 years after the first domesticates but rather that the New World one showed a clear depression after this. A depression that in turn can be qualified by the outliers of Cahokia and Tikal. The pattern to be explained, then, is rather the depression of Gini coefficients in the Americas, while isolated cases show higher ones to be possible.

In order to understand this better, it is instructive to look at the findings of Kohler and colleagues in more detail, especially with regard to their later inferences with regard to the correlation between Gini coefficients and demographic scale. If anything, the differences between the Old and New Worlds are brought out more dramatically when plotting Gini coefficients relative to regional and site populations, showing an average of 0.2 in both cases.[236] Notably, too, the inequality difference between the hemispheres actually increases for larger sites, which is an extremely important result in itself. For study upon study had emphasised a strongly unitary pattern in the increase of social scale and the development of inequality and class systems, in something of a prehistoric version of the so-called Iron Law of Oligarchy.[237] The evidence from Mesoamerica seems to suggest, rather, that this has to be rethought. Indeed, as mentioned by Kohler and colleagues, theories based on the evidence provided by this world region have highlighted the presence of more collective forms of the state, in contrast to more autocratic ones such as the Classic period Maya.[238]

However, again there has to be a qualification to the qualification. For while Kohler and colleagues note the high Gini coefficient of 0.62 of Tikal, another Classic period Maya capital of Caracol shows a much lower score at 0.34.[239] Hence this cannot be ascribed to a generic conception of the Classic Maya as autocratic. Instead, more attention should be paid to the second point of

---

236   Kohler et al. 2018, fig. 11.3, p. 300.
237   As following the classic and controversial argument of Robert Michels, based mostly on the experience of the German SPD, that the development of oligarchy is all but inevitable even in the most democratic of organisations, a notion that still engenders considerable debate within sociology, Leach 2015.
238   Kohler et al. 2018, pp. 302–5.
239   Kohler et al. 2018, table 11.1, p. 293.

Kohl and Chernykh's argument, concerning the differences in settlement trajectories and agricultural intensification. For while Kohler and colleagues had noted the potential for increased inequality based on agricultural extensification, they had not investigated the impact of intensification on Mesoamerican strategies of obtaining farming surpluses and their implications for the development on inequality. Another study by Blanton is highly significant in this regard, comparing the evidence of settlement patterns and their long-term changes in the Mediterranean and central Mesoamerica.[240] The latter area is especially significant, as it contained some of the most equal urban states of Mesoamerica, most notably the early site of Teotihuacan but also the Aztecs and other Postclassic states.[241]

A major benefit of Blanton's study is that he considered at the outset the different agronomic regimes in Mesoamerica and the Mediterranean, by focusing especially on the main grain staple foods of, respectively, maize and wheat. As noted earlier, to gain wheat surpluses extensification and the application of draft animals and metal tools is required, which do not result in higher yields but rather in a decrease of the labour input relative to the amount of produce. In the case of maize, on the contrary, surpluses are gained by increasing yields through applying labour in irrigation works and other measures. These are two fundamentally different strategies in a political economic sense, the Mediterranean one conforming to what Scarborough has called a 'techno-tasking' strategy, and the Mesoamerican one as 'labour-tasking'.[242] Another important finding of Blanton was calculating the degree to which Mesoamerican maize was more productive than Mediterranean wheat. Whereas in the Mediterranean one farming household could support from 0.25 to 1.01 non-farming households, in Mesoamerica this figure was initially 0.61 before increasing to 1.72.[243]

Hence maize as the main staple of Mesoamerican farming is distinguished from the Mediterranean by two crucial factors. Namely that the acquisition of greater surplus depends on labour rather than 'capital' such as draft animals

---

240 Based on the evidence of settlement patterns in both macro-regions, gained from so-called 'surface surveys' of archaeological remains from different persons on the surface, Blanton 2004, pp. 207–8.

241 Teotihuacan in particular has a very low estimated Gini coefficient at 0.12, but scores from the same area dated to the Late Postclassic period (the apogee of the Aztecs) remain low, Smith et al. 2014, table 1, p. 318. Work is underway to recalculate the Teotihuacan score based on newly available evidence, Smith et al. 2019, p. 415.

242 Scarborough 2003, pp. 13–16.

243 Based on Blanton 2004, tables 15.3–15.5, pp. 212–13.

and metal tools, and secondly, that the surpluses gained through this labour are more substantial. So whereas in Mesoamerica it was not possible to increase inequality through extensification in agriculture, the maize surpluses nevertheless allowed for the building and maintenance of great urban centres such as Tenochtitlan, Teotihuacan, and Tikal, among a great many others.[244] In this regard another finding of Blanton's study is of significance, namely that the relation between centres and their hinterlands were quite distinct in the two world regions. Whereas in Mesoamerica there were fewer but larger centres that were surrounded by dozens of villages, in the Mediterranean more centres can be seen, but these are smaller in size and surrounded by only a handful of villages.[245] What this points to is a more 'commercialised' landscape in Mesoamerica, with centres acting as market areas for a large and densely populated hinterland.

By contrast in the Mediterranean, populations seem more tightly bound towards the centres, which is also reflected in the administrative control over the economy in the case of the Mycenaean state of Pylos, also discussed above.[246] Blanton in fact argues that the dynamics of state formation were quite distinct.[247] Whereas in Mesoamerica states and urban centres developed quickly through agricultural intensification, subsequently drawing in peripheral regions, in the Mediterranean state expansion was 'thalassocratic'. That is, it depended on the projection of naval power from a centre, thus capturing other regions but without intensification in the core region. Of course, this view has to be qualified somewhat, given the importance of other crops in the Mediterranean such as olive trees and vines.[248] All the same, these hardly represent a divergence from the 'techno-tasking' focus, but rather have to be understood as part of the developing 'complex productive economy'. One that was distinct in crucial ways from that of Mesoamerica, which also had a complex arboriculture.[249]

In this way, to use Marxist terms, we can see how the distinct character of the (agricultural) forces of production in Mesoamerica influences the rela-

---

244 The high productivity of maize was noted in particular in Braudel 1981, pp. 158–63.

245 Blanton 2004, pp. 220–4.

246 As noted by Blanton, the scale of early Mesoamerican state was quite similar to that of Pylos, yet what is lacking there is any significant evidence of administrative mechanisms, Blanton 2004, pp. 225–6.

247 Blanton 2004, pp. 226–8.

248 The importance of which was emphasised by Renfrew in his classic account of the emergence of civilisation in the Aegean, Renfrew 1972, pp. 480–3, and recently emphasised as well in Margaritis 2013.

249 Especially in the lowland Maya area, Houston and Inomata 2009, pp. 237–9.

tions of production, in the form of markets. More can be said about these
relations of production, for the distinctiveness of Mesoamerica in their distinct form of monies had not just been noted by Marx. In a number of articles,
Kowalewski has emphasised those features of Mesoamerican economies that
distinguish them from those of western Eurasia. The main thing for him is that
in Mesoamerica households are the main productive units and that economic
interaction between them takes place on marketplaces.[250] To establish equivalencies between goods in these places, a variety of quasi-moneys such as cacao
beans were used that in the main could not be hoarded, excepting textiles. In
effect this constitutes something of a mixture of Marx's second and third forms
of equivalency. For not only can the exchange value of any commodity be measured by any other commodity, some commodities can also establish value in a
more general sense, even if they cannot do so exclusively given the presence of
competitors.

What is important to Kowalewski is not just the absence of exclusivity, but
also something closely related to this: the absence of a means of exchange
established and sanctioned by the state.[251] For in Eurasia coined money derived
from the state, and previous to coinage weight quantities of metals such as
silver had been exclusively used to establish the value of various commodities, most notably of staple grains.[252] This observation dovetails with the pattern recognised by Blanton, that of a central role for marketplace exchange in
Mesoamerica in contradistinction to a clearer focus on economic control of
centres over their hinterlands in the Mediterranean. Yet this dominance of marketplace commerce should not be taken to mean that anything was for sale, for
unlike in the Mediterranean there was no trade in persons and land and large-
scale slavery was never present in Mesoamerica.[253] Neither was it the case that
households could participate in marketplace exchange in a kind of abstract
and rational way, for these were embedded in Mesoamerican cultural institutions.[254]

---

250   Kowalewski 2012, pp. 220–2.
251   This observation arose from his own fieldwork on the development of cities, states, and
      markets in the Mexican state of Oaxaca, the nascent states drawing upon rather than con-
      trolling economic life, Kowalewski 2016, pp. 25–8. His conclusion dovetails with Blanton's
      aforementioned contrast between the closely administered Mycenaean state centred at
      the palace of Pylos and Oaxaca.
252   Kowalewski 2012, p. 222. See also Wilkinson 2014, pp. 193–4, 198–9, for a similar perspective
      on Eurasia.
253   Kowalewski 2020, pp. 32–3.
254   Most notably, Mesoamerican marketplaces themselves were cultural institutions of this
      kind, to which Bakhtin's notion of the carnivalesque has been applied, Hutson 2000.

In my own comparative work on the Mediterranean and Mesoamerica, the main attention was on the initial phases of the urban revolution in the lowland Maya and Mycenaean cases.[255] Among other things, a key finding was that even if the scale of urban centres and states was rather similar in both cases, the specific characteristics of class relations were notably different.[256] In the Aegean, it is possible to see a pattern based on a 'modular household'. This household could potentially be incorporated in hierarchical relations such as patron-client ones, as well as incorporating dependents within itself, such as servants and slaves. In that sense this household was truly a microcosm of the state, replicating its hierarchy at a lower scale. The lowland Maya case, on the contrary, showed an enduring role for extended households as reflected in the ritual articulation of lineage ancestors. The location within which this took place was the community, in effect the multiplicity of the smaller places surrounding the centres in Blanton's reconstruction.

When considering the situation prior to the emergence of the first states in the lowland Maya, the evidence points to a situation in which many important aspects of later Maya civilisation were already present at the community level.[257] Importantly, this included irrigation works, showing that this kind of agricultural intensification was not limited to the 'Oriental despotism' of Cold War lore.[258] Also significant is the evidence for the elaboration of communal religion in the laying out of central plazas, some of which also show indications for rites revolving around ancestors. Maize played an important role in this, both in an iconographic sense, especially in relation to cosmography, and through its metaphoric associations with jadeite and similarly coloured materials. In this sense, the valuation of jadeite and other precious materials provides a parallel to the Eurasian aesthetical valuing of metals and related materials, something that can be seen well in the iconography of succeeding periods of Maya history.[259] The main point here, however, is that this ideology has its roots in communities that existed before the emergence of the first states. Furthermore, in later periods these communities retained their access to jadeite and other precious materials.

In that sense, the trajectory of state formation in the Maya area shows a rather different dynamic compared to that of Mycenaean Greece.[260] For

255   Based on my PhD research, published as Bajema 2017a.
256   Bajema 2017a, pp. 256–60.
257   As at the small Maya site of Chan, Wyatt 2012, but elsewhere as well, Marcus 2003, pp. 80–1.
258   Erickson 2006.
259   As traced in Taube 2000. See also Houston 2014 for an interpretation of the Maya view of the material world.
260   Bajema 2017a, pp. 260–2.

whereas in the Aegean a series of transformations can be recognised that play out wholesale, correlated across all scales of social life from the local context to long-distance trade, Maya history shows a somewhat different pattern. Rather than a process of more uniform change, despite important correlations like the Classic Maya collapse, a dynamic interplay has been recognised for the relation between communities on the one hand and states on the other. Notably, this is also associated with two distinct form of the economy, the 'social' one that existed at the communal level and a 'political' one of the various city-states. Just as the royal courts drew upon the ideology of the communities in the elaboration of their monumental and iconographic legitimation of sovereignty, so the political economy drew upon communal patterns of labour mobilisation. In fact, it may well be that it was precisely the initial mobilisation of labour that provided one of the key factors behind the emergence of states.[261]

This dynamic of Maya history should not be seen as one of a cyclical trajectory of states relative to an unchanging communal form. For detailed case studies show individual communities to develop new features of their own outside the orbit of states, as well adapting to the harsh regime imposed by the European conquest of Mexico.[262] It is also necessary to take into account the importance of marketplace exchange noted by Blanton and Kowalewski, which existed in a complex relation to both communities and states. A number of key characteristics can be recognised for markets in the Maya area and for Mesoamerica more broadly:

1. Marketplace exchange is carried out through commodity or quasi-monies, unable to be hoarded and neither issued nor regulated by states, even if the political elites would sometimes draw upon these monies for their own purposes.[263]

2. Access to rare goods by commoners was enabled through marketplaces, both at small sites such as the lowland Maya site of Chan and in 'poorer' neighbourhoods of Teotihuacan.[264]

3. The scale of markets expanded over time, as the lowland Maya area shows.[265] Furthermore, the expanded trade of the Postclassic period Maya was connected to what has been interpreted as a wider Mesoamerican world-system.[266]

261   Estrada-Belli 2012, pp. 219–22.
262   Eric Wolf's classic account remains important in this regard, Wolf 1959, but more detailed accounts are available now on specific regions, e.g. Restall 1997 for the Maya area.
263   Kowalewski 2012, pp. 203–6.
264   Meierhoff et al. 2012, fig. 14.1, p. 278; Carballo et al. 2019, p. 109.
265   Braswell 2010, fig. 6.4, p. 139.
266   Berdan et al. 2003.

4. Economic growth can be clearly recognised, not just in terms of the development of technology and in a broader sense the productive forces,[267] but also in the great increases in the supply of products evident in marketplaces and the contexts of the political economy.[268]

It should be clear from this that we are far here from stereotypes of stagnant 'Asiatic' communities. Rather, the development of economic life through marketplaces and long-distance exchange led to a complex dynamic relative to communal and state forms of organisation. It could be argued that marketplace exchange to some degree allowed for the prospering of the (relative) equality inherent in communities, allowing access to goods irrespective of political control. In fact, the interaction between this triad enables the formulation of an explanation of the paradoxical findings of a high Gini coefficient at Tikal, relative to contemporary and later Maya states. For as noted, Classic Maya marketplaces are thought to be administered ones, potentially allowing state elites to control not just the social economy through different kinds of tribute but also the marketplace. Such a situation may well have been the case at Tikal. Yet given the counterpoint of contemporary Caracol, this situation seems not to have been a given even for the Classic period.

As noted, during the succeeding Postclassic period there is an expansion of marketplace exchange. This expansion can also be seen at the site of Mayapan with its relatively low Gini score, which is broadly congruent with the interpretation of the Maya polities of this era being more collective than autocratic.[269] This pattern seems to signal that the high Gini coefficient of Tikal is more of an exception, resulting from an unparalleled ability to control the economic output of both the markets and communities within its realm. Certainly, there was no steady increase of inequality within either the lowland Maya area or Mesoamerica as a whole. Rather, there were structural factors inhibiting a steady increase of inequality in the Eurasian fashion. Firstly, there are the specific characteristics of the forces of production, with a primacy of labour relative to capital, given the lesser importance of domesticated animals and tools, as well as the high productivity of the main staple of maize. Even smaller communities in this way could generate agricultural and other kinds of surpluses.

Given the relative autonomy of these communities from the state, as well as a greater emphasis on marketplace exchange, there were limits to the ability for elites to entrench their property. Certainly, the absence of evidence of

267 Stark et al. 2016.
268 Blanton et al. 2005.
269 Blanton et al. 1996, p. 12.

direct elite control over most of the means of production is striking, as is the lack of institutionalisation of the means of exchange. For unlike the weighing systems and coinage of western Eurasia, the quasi-monies in the form of cacao beans and textiles were less amenable to state control, even if states certainly drew upon them within the 'political' economy. Indeed, as Kowalewski points out, quasi-monies may favour more egalitarian economic regimes:

> Mesoamerica had wealth, growth, specialization, urbanization, markets, but was not monetized and did not allow for much accumulation by economic means (as opposed to force). Mesoamerican currencies were relatively less liquid and fungible than the minted silver of the ancient Mediterranean. It is possible, although this proposition is not well established, that goods monies could be fundamentally more egalitarian in themselves, perhaps because goods retain some of their use value, or because with multiple types of goods as currencies none is a monopoly money, or because goods money exchanges are more intricate, distributed, and embedded and thus less subject to control by the state or other large actors. Unfortunately we do not have much ethnographic or historical description of how such systems worked.[270]

Indeed, the Mesoamerican case is profound for its distinctive economic structure and egalitarian institutions, which are not easily understood from the perspective of the western Eurasian patterns that have come to dominate the globe after 1492. Marx had an inkling of this in his recognition of the distinctive characteristics of Mesoamerican monies, which are now amply recognised by scholars. Obviously more studies are needed, not least to incorporate the particularities of the Inca state, and its predecessors as well, given its ability to combine a heavily administered economy with egalitarian social arrangements. The Inca case is also important with regard to the development of metallurgy, given that it has to be located in a long history of metal use that dates back to the second millennium BC. Kohl and Chernykh's observation for the different pattern of the development of metallurgy in Mesoamerica can to a considerable extent be attributed to its lateness, as well as deriving from contact with regions along the central and south American coastline.

Yet in the broader Andean area, metallurgy developed alongside the first states, yet as in Mesoamerica the trajectory of the usage of metals was different here, too, even if in a technical sense a roughly similar trajectory as in the

---

270   Kowalewski 2020, pp. 28–9.

Old World can be discerned.[271] Hence what will be particularly interesting to investigate when Gini scores and other measures of inequality from different sites in the Andean area become available, is how these relate to the different development of metalworking in this area. Most notably, it will be possible to draw interesting contrasts between the Inca state's suppression of marketplace exchange and the flourishing thereof in Mesoamerica. In this sense, Marx's scattered references on the Aztec and Inca cases in the preparatory studies of *Capital* may turn out to be remarkably prescient, in his recognition of not just one generic alternative to western Eurasian development but rather a plurality of forms. This plurality should of course include many other world regions not discussed here, such as Africa, eastern Eurasia, other parts of the Americas, as well as Australia and Oceania.

Some of these regions existed in close contact with developments in western Eurasia, notably China and Africa, whereas the Americas and Australia were isolated from the Old World until conquered and colonised by European states. During this process of subjugation, the indigenous American civilisations were confronted with key material factors that were in fact inherited from the Early Metal Age. Most directly, the large-scale production of metal weapons and armour in this period gave the Spanish conquistadores a clear military advantage, given that Andean and Mesoamerican metalworking did not pursue the production of such artefacts. More indirectly, the closeness of humans and domesticated animals in Eurasia resulted in a greater resistance against pathogens. At contact with Europeans these diseases were unleashed on largely defenceless indigenous American populations, leading to mass mortality.[272] These two factors decisively weakened the resistance toward European colonisation, opening the door to wholesale social transformation.

Surviving indigenous peoples were now enchained in a new regime, one structured by new economic relations. Like the weapons of the conquistadores, these economic relations ultimately derived from the Early Metal Age, when the commodity nexus typical of western Eurasia came into being. Here we have a clear example of Marx's argument noted in the previous chapter, of the metabolism of commodity exchange replacing the previously existing forms of social life, becoming the new *Gemeinwesen*. Within this new community, the particularities of indigenous American histories and forms of social life were made subservient for a supposedly universal trajectory modelled on the Eurasian case. The Americas, we are told by contemporary authors, are simply

271 Especially in the use of arsenic and tin to produce bronze alloys, Lechtman 2014, pp. 381–3.
272 Rodolfo et al. 2004.

latecomers to the party and consequently left with the crumbs.[273] Yet, to think
with Montaigne, what is particularly admirable about a form of civilisation that
prevailed because of its means to kill and economically enslave fellow human
beings? It might be said that it was rather the pre-Columbian civilisations were
more admirable in certain aspects, if not in all, including their relatively limited
inequality.[274] There is no reason not to think that these patterns would not have
led to further development along these particular lines, if not for their demise.

4   Breaking the Bonds of Fate

In the previous section, Marx's intimations of a version of the thesis of the plurality of worlds were related to current findings from archaeology. These findings
show rather well how his writings on the development of commodity exchange
in Eurasia, as well as American alternatives thereof, remain relevant for contemporary scientific thought. They also show how the 'earthly basis' of the
metabolism of humans and nature varied, and what the consequences of this
variation are. Further lines of investigation could be developed in this regard,
tracing the development of humankind through the various 'worlds' of Palaeolithic migrations.[275] The importance of metabolism and pluralism is also what
connects this perspective to the 'mechanist' one of Danilova discussed earlier,
as well as to the New Direction in Soviet historical studies more generally. The
aborted comparative work of the New Direction might well have led to a recognition of some of the patterns discussed in the previous section, given Soviet
interest in New World archaeology.[276]

      This perspective never took hold in Soviet historical studies. Yet the criti-
cism of the *pyatichlenka* by New Direction historians, as well as the responses
and modifications by scholars like Semenov, in effect demonstrate its demise.

---

273   Especially in the ideas of Diamond and Morris discussed at the beginning of this chapter.
274   This observation is not to ascribe any kind of absolute moral perfection to Mesoamer-
      ican cultures, given the presence therein of practices such as human sacrifice, Tiesler and
      Cucina 2006.
275   Gamble makes an important argument in this regard in his book, thinking the different
      human expansions across the world, from deep history to recent migrations such as the
      Polynesian expansion into Oceania, Gamble 2013. In it, he recognises different 'terras' that
      reflect different geographical expansions of humankind. A perspective like this is espe-
      cially worthwhile as it can rethink the human experience as such from a natural, even
      Montaignesque perspective that decisively transcends any nationalist attempt seeking to
      locate a national Origin in some notional roots.
276   Bashilov and Gulyaev 1990.

Both the set of five modes of production arranged in a unilinear way as well as the account of anthropogony and sociogenesis underlying it, were shown to be incompatible with either Marx's ideas or contemporary scientific evidence. Twentieth-century archaeology in particular has shown the notion of two spiralling dialectical processes meeting in the primitive-communal mode of production to be false. The philosophical bases for this view could be recognised in the debates between the 'mechanists' and Deborin and his followers in the 1920s and early 1930s. As noted in Chapter 1, Deborin derived from Engels the importance of *Wechselwirkung* in dialectics, which is reflected in his interpretation of Spinoza. Essentially, science has now shown the practical and logical limits inherent in the Engelsian historico-philosophical perspective.

Of course Engels cannot be held to account for what was made of his work under Stalin's regime. Nor should the results of his 'science of dialectical interconnections' be discounted out of hand, for in contexts where its teleonomic aspects were not emphasised it could produce fruitful results. Yet at the end of the day, as in teleology of which it forms a variant, the highest form of knowledge that can be achieved using a teleonomic perspective remains within Spinoza's imaginary realm. So while the Engelsian-Soviet paradigm could achieve insights into aspects of anthropogony or the formation of Greco-Roman states, its view of the whole was fatally tied to chaining these fragments to an imaginary teleonomic order. New forms of evidence showing aspects of the work of Engels to be correct for this or that aspect cannot essentially change this conclusion. The theories of Engels and in Soviet adaptations of his ideas may to an extent have reflected the state of knowledge and ideological context of specific eras, but were not able to explain and adapt to new evidence and social contexts without losing their logical coherence.

By contrast, Marx's ideas seem more adaptable. This can be partially ascribed to Marx being a more far-sighted and careful thinker, with an eye for details such as Mesoamerican forms of currencies, which certainly would not be highlighted in nineteenth-century political economy. More important than his critical faculties, however, was Marx's understanding of dialectics as critical, as well as the historical and realist aspects that are also present in the Engelsian version. As argued in the previous chapter, it is this critical aspect of Marx's dialectics that prevents his ideas becoming lapidary, and hence prone to the inevitable erosion that affects all solid things. Rather, inspired by the Epicurean phrase of *mors immortalis*, Marx recognised that the categories of political economy are inherently transient, and that a scientific understanding of history therefore has to be comparative. For history is founded not upon some kind of essential nature, but only on the abyss of more history, that of the infinite sequence of the transformation of things found in Epicureanism and Spinoza.

In this way, the thesis of the plurality of world breaks with the 'bonds of fate' inherent in stadialism. The implications of this shift in perspective are manifold. First of all, the recognition of a different pattern of development in Mesoamerica and its distinctive correlation between social scale and measures of inequality, has a number of consequences for Marxism. The role of communities in this alternative pathway strengthens and deepens Marx's view of the history of communal forms in stratigraphic terms. Their enduring historical role should be emphasised in this regard, not as being inevitably tied to the dissolution of the 'primitive-communal' mode of production. Another important historical role can now be seen for the commodity monies noted by Marx, which in Mesoamerican marketplaces were enabling both the persistence of the equality within communities and long-term economic development. Both factors powerfully undercut the Engelsian account of the development of the state, with its inevitable and wholesale transformation of social life based on the fatal imposition of property as the central determinant of social life.

Of course, this perspective had a practical aspect as well, in the conception of the transition toward communism along stadialist lines. Among other things, this led to the conception of 'developed socialism' as a transitional stage. In effect this 'stage' became a cul de sac that entrenched a regime that was unable to make any kind of progressive transition, partially as a result from increasing inequality within it, instead changing into a particularly parasitical form of capitalism. The active suppression by the ideological guardians of this state of alternative conceptions of historical understanding, based both on the study of Marx's writing and new forms of evidence, was one of the factors that doomed 'developed socialism'. For rather than conceiving revolutionary strategy according to the complex causality of history, as the New Direction in Soviet historical studies sought to do through its concept of multistructuredness, stadialism was enshrined as a sacrosanct dogma. Indeed, the replacement of this dogma by another one, that of a vicious form of capitalism, marks a continuation of a stadialist, unitary ideology, now serving new masters.

Instead, there is more variation of states than was previously assumed by Marxists, if not by Marx given his use of the particular characteristics of the Inca state to show the transience of capitalist categories. Here there exists a need to think through the notion of more collective states, which entail mechanisms that prevent the imposition of socio-economic equality by elites. The aforementioned different pattern of Gini scores relative to social scale in Mesoamerica, is spectacularly expressed in some of its most famous states. Pride of place in this regard goes to Classic period Teotihuacan, but the same pattern persists in the succeeding Postclassic era. Based on these Mesoamerican cases, attempts have been made to study collectivist state arrangements comparatively, yielding promising results that nevertheless lack a sufficient understanding of class systems.[277] Certainly, there were examples of more collective states in Eurasia as well, including the cases of Minoan Crete and the Indus valley from the Early Metal Age mentioned earlier. The presence of such cases in fact invites a more radically Montaignesque reflection on the history of the western Eurasian 'world'.

As noted in Chapter 4, Engels viewed modern socialism as the outcome of a long trajectory that culminated in modern Europe, itself based on the Roman empire, and on ancient Greece. Given that the ancient world, in his view, was only possible based on slavery, his argument goes that modern socialism was in fact only made possible by ancient slavery. This view from the perspective of the aleatory current is dubious in itself, given that it reasons from the accomplished fact, conceiving the encounter that 'took hold' in a teleonomic way. Rather, if we view this trajectory from a New World perspective, it may be argued that it was just one of a plurality of outcomes. That is, things might have turned out rather differently. For even given the specifics of the 'complex productive economy' that emerged during the Early Metal Age, it was possible for more collective polities to emerge and prosper. Indeed, during the heyday of Greco-Roman slaveholding and associated forms of unfreedom, such as the helots under Spartan rule, there emerged new democratic forms of rule that were accompanied by greater economic equality within the body of (male) citizens.[278]

As argued by Geoffrey de Ste. Croix, the shift from the Classical period to the empires of the Hellenistic era at the same time witnessed a prolonged struggle between oligarchic and democratic forms of rule.[279] The Roman republican regime in particular promoted oligarchic factions as part of their agenda of conquest, which of course was accompanied by the mass enslavement of foreign peoples. As noted in the previous chapter, Marx took particular note of the situation in late republican Rome. According to him it was the influx of slaves on a massive scale that decisively changed the Roman republic itself, its proletariat being turned into an 'idle mob'. This process can be understood as a failed encounter between the 'moneybags' and the proletarians stripped of the

---

277 The main argument for collective states is contained in Blanton and Fargher 2008, a work that sometimes makes a caricature of Marxism. Elsewhere, I have sought to address their work by relating the presence of class systems to more collective socio-political arrangements, Bajema 2017b.

278 Morris 1997.

279 See especially the last sections of chapter six of his *The Class Struggle in the Ancient Greek World*, Ste. Croix 1981.

ownership of the means of production. Yet the inevitability of this outcome may well be challenged. Rome in the first-century BC was in fact severely challenged by foreign and civil wars, as well as various slave uprisings in Sicily and, most famously, on the Italian mainland with the Spartacus revolt. Its victory and later establishment of a more durable imperial state were far from certain.

Tongue in cheek, we could well imagine a counterfactual to the Engelsian argument, according to which there would have been no modern socialism without the sacking of Rome by the slave army of Spartacus.[280] For while this momentous event did not establish any kind of utopia nor abolish slavery wholesale, it severely weakened Rome. In this way the oligarchic factions both within and outside of Rome lost their previous advantage, leading to a Mediterranean dominated by different powers and with a greater variation of political regimes. Such alternatives were in fact pointedly recognised by the Classical authors themselves.[281] The point of such counterfactuals was not so much to sketch a story of how things might be, but rather to weigh the likelihood of this or that outcome and thereby understand the causal pattern better.[282] A similar weighing of factors should be undertaken for the formation and dissolution of social formations and modes of production. In this sense, the focus in Engels on slavery and the Roman transformation of Europe is decidedly one-sided, overlooking the causes for the result.

For there is a need to grasp in more detail the interaction between a plurality of elements. These include the relations between Roman mass slavery, the state's oligarchic focus, the petrification of its proletariat into a mob on the one hand, and the alternative economic and political regimes that can be recognised in the contemporary Mediterranean. Another question concerns the relation of these different regimes to the development of the productive forces, most notably the incipient machinery evident both in practical technology and theoretical discourse. In the teleological conception of the mode of production there can be only one way in which these different elements 'hang together', as evident in the strict correspondence between elements in

---

280   Unlike in the Mediterranean, and Europe more broadly, in China peasant revolts did effect major change, either by weakening the established dynasty or by completely overthrowing it. See Harrison 1965 for the impact of the greater scope and historical efficacy of the Chinese peasant revolts on CPC ideology.

281   See for examples from the *Histories* of Sallust, Gerrish 2018.

282   Note in this regard also the discussion of Machiavelli in Chapter 3, in particular Morfino's attribution to him of the thesis of universal variability, as well as the constant drawing of analogies between different political events in relation to the specific circumstances in which they took place. It is precisely the causal force of these circumstances that become more clearly apparent through comparative counterfactuals.

Engels noted in Chapter 4. By contrast, seen from the aleatory perspective different combinations may be possible, as could be seen in the discussion of the emergence of machine-based production in the work of Marx discussed in Chapter 5. There it was noted that, as with the history of communal forms, the development of machinery can be grasped according to a stratigraphic outline emphasising a plurality of interacting aspects.

Indeed, in this way the conditions in the English factories of the nineteenth century have to be understood as conforming to a specific set of social and economic conditions. Being a particular and contingent outcome of history, it is certainly possible for machinery to be deployed in a very different way in a future communist form of social life. Of course, Marx also contrasted the specific modern use of machinery with the imagined counterfactual uses thereof in ancient authors. Again, the point here is not to sketch any specific alternative outcome of antiquity, wherein it resulted in communism and flying cars rather than the misery of feudalism. It is rather to point out, with the ancient authors and Machiavelli, that similar historical circumstances can have different outcomes. To their arguments should be added the Marxist observation that this holds not just for the actions of military and political leaders, but also for the more significant interplay of the forces and relations of production, as well as of the superstructural aspects of politics and ideology.

Hence just as there existed in the Americas alternatives to the western Eurasian trajectory that resulted in capitalism, so there were lurking within this 'world' alternatives capable of producing vastly different outcomes. All of this makes a mockery of universal histories that reason from the result of capitalism, or for that matter 'developed socialism', connecting this End to a hypothetical Origin in some faraway historical or prehistorical land. Such universalism is, in Spinozist terms, nothing more than a mode of the imagination. The theses of the aleatory current in philosophy decisively break these 'bonds of fate', which have shackled not just the understanding of history but also practical attempts to change it through the building of communism. As argued in the conclusion of Chapter 5, communism as the realm of freedom has to be understood historically, in relation to external determination by both natural and social forces. Indeed, insofar as these conditions are present in different degrees in all social formations, communism itself is also 'universal'.

Yet this 'universalism' in this sense can only be understood as such in a Benjaminian way, from the perspective of the oppressed. For it is they who face the compulsion and violence of the social forces oppressing them, which are often combined with natural ones like hunger, disease, and inadequate protection from catastrophic events such as storms and flooding. As Benjamin recognised, there is nothing universal in the barbarous and cruel historical justifications of

these forms of oppression. The need to create an alternative historical understanding of the different forms of resistance to this oppression has recently
been emphasised by Massimiliano Tomba with his conception of 'insurgent
universality'.[283] From this perspective he sketches a plurality of forms of resistance and collective forms of organisation that exist parallel to capitalism:

> Overcoming temporal provincialism means that it is not the European
> Middle Ages that show us the 'feudal' nature of the *obshchina*; on the con-
> trary, it is the latter that shows us the Middle Ages as a field of possibilities
> for alternative possibilities that streak across the European continent.
> With this spirit, the Communards retrieved medieval juridical material
> to activate alternative institutions for that nation-state. Similarly, the *ayl-*
> *lus*, the indigenous forms of self-government in South America, instead of
> being an obstacle to capitalist modernization, constitute an opportunity
> to experiment with different forms of life and politics that connect to the
> Russian *mir* and the soviets, as well as the Paris Commune. These forms
> are not relics but, rather, are social structures that have existed elsewhere
> since before modernity – not in remote geographical spaces or in some
> oceanic atoll, but in temporalities that flow alongside the dominant one
> of capitalist modernity.[284]

Although formulated separately from the aleatory current, the notion of 'insurgent universality' in fact has much in common with this strand of Marxism, and
can be enriched through its theses. For it is through the theses of the aleatory
current that both the oppressed themselves and their insurgent forms of resistance can be thought of not as accidental sideshows of a sequence of unfolding
stages. Rather these have to be understood as the lifeblood of the Benjaminian
form of a true universal history, one that not merely treats oppression and the
violence that comes with it as a triviality and even as an inevitable necessity of
a stadialist march to communism. At the same time, the comparative understanding of different social formations and modes of productions in distinct
world regions points to something else too, namely the complex interaction
between different elements. In this sense, there is considerable truth in the
realist and historical approach of the 1859 preface, to start with the product-

---

283   As different and opposed to universalism understood as the stadialist process through
      which 'universal civilisation' is attained, instead being contrary to the existing order,
      Tomba 2019, p. 21. Cases discussed by him include the French revolution, the Paris Com-
      mune, the early phase of the October revolution, as well as the Zapatistas.
284   Tomba 2019, p. 228.

ive forces and to work upward from them to the relations of production and the different aspects of the superstructure.

What matters, however, is not to see this approach in terms of *Wechselwirkung* and unilinearity, but rather from an aleatory and pluralist point of view. According to the latter perspective, comparative history can show not just the transience of the capitalist mode of production, it can also demonstrate two further aspects. First of all, the transience of capitalism is further underlined by its contingent roots, based on encounters that 'took hold' but just as well could not have done so. Secondly, the more collective and equal states of the indigenous Americas, paralleled by certain Eurasian cases, invalidates an abstract sequence of modes of production. In this way the 1857 introduction nuances the unilinear reading of the 1959 preface, while leaving intact the interaction between the main elements mentioned therein. To study this interaction is important not just for understanding these specific historical cases, but also for contemporary revolutionary strategy. For the question of the state occupies a rather central place in this, not just in terms of resistance to capitalism and imperialism but also in the dangers of Soviet style bureaucratic stagnation.

In effect, what is needed is an aleatory understanding of the state, one that disentangles it from the stadialist notion that the state corresponds in a fatally deterministic way to a specific level of social development. Closely related to this is the notion that the state is a mere tool of class oppression, as a superstructural reflection of the economic base. A more nuanced view is required, one that is able to recognise not just class oppression, which is certainly very real, but also collectivist aspects that are overlooked in the Engelsian conception of sovereignty. For the evidence from Mesoamerica shows that the correlation between inequality and scale of western Eurasia cannot be automatically applied to the New World, and, moreover, that more collective state forms can be recognised there. This observation is of crucial importance for strategic thinking about the transition away from the current state of affairs to a communist form of social life, which in its initial phases will have to depend, quite simply, on what came before it, as Marx recognised.

Hence given that the historical point of departure is a world based on state power and sovereignty, existing parallel and in combination with the capitalist mode of production, any transitional form will have to incorporate elements of the old. In this way the comparative study of collective state forms serves a dual purpose. Firstly, it can help to understand the flaws in the Soviet state form, which would parallel the criticisms of its philosophical and historical underpinnings offered in this chapter and the previous ones. Especially relevant in this regard are historical examples of mechanisms for enforcing equality, as well as for the proper and accountable management of public goods, both of which were wanting in the Soviet state.[285] Secondly, it can help to support both thinking through the institutions required for building communism and to grasp the relation between collective states and a variety of other institutions such as communities. This latter aspect is crucial in connecting the oppressed to the institutional means that can enable the revolutionary encounter not just to occur, but to 'take hold' in a lasting way as well.

Furthermore, that ability to 'take hold' has to take into account the international context as well, lest the mistakes of 'socialism in one country' are blindly repeated. Here it is important to carry the notion of 'combined and uneven development' further, to think not just in terms of the skipping of stages, which tacitly still assumes some form of stadialism. Rather, the 'insurgent universality' of the oppressed can be held to exist as a potentiality in the interstices of the capitalist world system, just as Marx observed for the merchants of the ancient world.[286] It is precisely the thesis of the plurality of worlds that allows for thinking through this in the most radical way possible. It completely subverts the conventions of the Westphalian system, and its visions of sovereignty and history, with a perspective rooted in nature, the same perspective that, as we saw in the conclusion of the previous chapter, shaped Marx's conception of communism as the realm of freedom. As such it breaks the 'bonds of fate' of stadialism and inevitability to which Marxist theory has been shackled like a postmodern Prometheus.

---

285   As the state itself acknowledged: see the account of the work of the 'anti-waste' commission, Lewin 2005, pp. 351–6.
286   Fernanda Navarro has emphasised the importance of interstices for the aleatory current in relation to organisation and the question of the transition to communism, Navarro 2015, pp. 53–5.

Bibliography

Abulafia, David 2002, 'Neolithic meets medieval: first encounters in the Canary islands', in *Medieval frontiers: concepts and practices*, edited by David Abulafia and Nora Berend, Aldershot: Ashgate.

Acuna-Soto, Rodolfo, David Stahle, Matthew Therrell, Richard Griffin, Malcolm Cleaveland 2004, 'When half the population died: the epidemic of hemorrhagic fevers of 1576 in Mexico', *FEMS Microbiology Letters*, 240: 1–5.

Adams, Robert 1966, *The evolution of urban society. Early Mesopotamia and Prehispanic Mexico*, Chicago, IL: Aldine Publishing.

Akselrod, Lyubov 1952, 'Spinoza and materialism', in *Spinoza in Soviet philosophy. A series of essays*, edited by George Kline, London: Routledge and Paul.

Alexeev, Michael and Clifford Gaddy 1993, 'Income distribution in the U.S.S.R. in the 1980s', *Review of Income and Wealth*, 39, 1: 23–6.

Allen, Robert 2003, *Farm to factory. A reinterpretation of the Soviet industrial revolution*, Princeton, NJ: Princeton University Press.

Althusser, Louis 1976, *Essays in self-criticism*, London: New Left Books.

Althusser, Louis 1977, *For Marx*, London: New Left Books.

Althusser, Louis 1990, *Philosophy and the spontaneous philosophy of the scientists*, London: Verso.

Althusser, Louis 1993, *De toekomst duurt lang, gevolgd door, De Feiten*, Amsterdam: Prometheus.

Althusser, Louis 1999, *Machiavelli and us*, London: Verso.

Althusser, Louis 2003, *The humanist controversy and other writings*, London: Verso.

Althusser, Louis 2006, *Philosophy of the encounter. Later writings, 1978–1987*, London: Verso.

Althusser, Louis 2014, *On the reproduction of capital. Ideology and ideological state apparatuses*, London: Verso.

Althusser, Louis 2015a, 'From *Capital* to Marx's philosophy', in *Reading Capital. The complete edition*, edited by Louis Althusser, Etienne Balibar, Roger Establet, Jacques Ranciere and Pierre Macherey, London: Verso.

Althusser, Louis 2015b, 'The object of *Capital*', in *Reading Capital. The complete edition*, edited by Louis Althusser, Etienne Balibar, Roger Establet, Jacques Ranciere and Pierre Macherey, London: Verso.

Althusser, Louis 2017a, *How to be a Marxist in philosophy*, London: Bloomsbury.

Althusser, Louis 2017b, *Philosophy for non-philosophers*, London: Bloomsbury.

Althusser, Louis 2019, *Lessons on Rousseau*, London: Verso.

Althusser, Louis 2020, *History and imperialism*, Cambridge: Polity.

Anderson, Kevin 1983, 'The 'unknown' Marx's Capital, vol. I: the French edition of 1872–75, 100 years later', *Review of Radical Political economics*, 15, 4: 71–80.

Anderson, Kevin 2002, 'Marx's late writings on non-Western and precapitalist societies and gender', *Rethinking Marxism*, 14, 4: 84–96.

Anderson, Kevin 2010, 'Not just capitalism and class: Marx on non-Western societies, nationalism and ethnicity', *Socialism and Democracy*, 24, 3: 7–22.

Anderson, Kevin 2016, *Marx at the margins. On nationalism, ethnicity, and non-Western societies (expanded edition)*, Chicago, IL: University of Chicago Press.

Andrianov, Boris 2016, *Ancient irrigation systems of the Aral Sea area. The history, origin, and development of irrigated agriculture*, Oxford: Oxbow Books.

Anievas, Anievas and Kerem Nisancioglu 2015, *How the West came to rule. The geopolitical origins of capitalism*, London: Pluto Press.

Antipina, Ekaterina and Arturo Morales 2006, 'Archaeozoological approach to complexity: animal remains from two metallurgical sites from the eastern and western corners of Europe', *Archaeology, Ethnology & Anthropology of Eurasia*, 27, 3: 67–81.

Arbo, Desiree 2018, 'Plato and the Guarani Indians', in *Antiquities and classical traditions in Latin America*, edited by Andrew Laird and Nicola Miller, Chichester: Wiley.

Arnold, Bettina 1990, 'The past as propaganda: totalitarian archaeology in Nazi Germany', *Antiquity*, 64, 244: 464–78.

Asmis, Elizabeth 2020, 'A tribute to a hero: Marx's interpretation of Epicurus in his dissertation', in *Approaches to Lucretius. Traditions and innovations in reading the De rerum natura*, edited by Donncha O'Rourke, Cambridge: Cambridge University Press.

Avilova, Lyudmila 2009, 'Models of metal production in the Near East', *Archaeology, Ethnology & Anthropology of Eurasia*, 37, 3: 50–8.

Badiou, Alain 2012, *Plato's Republic. A dialogue in sixteen chapters, with a prologue and an epilogue*, Cambridge: Polity Press.

Bai, Shouyi 2002, *An outline history of China*, Beijing: Foreign Languages Press.

Bailey, Cyril 1928, 'Karl Marx on Greek atomism', *Classical Quarterly*, 22: 205–6.

Bajema, Marcus 2017a, *Bodies of maize, eaters of grain. Comparing material worlds, metaphor and the agency of art in the Preclassic Maya and Mycenaean early civilisations*, Oxford: Archaeopress.

Bajema, Marcus 2017b, 'Variation on a theme: Mycenaean early civilisation in a comparative perspective', *Journal of Greek Archaeology*, 2: 81–114.

Bakhurst, David 1991, *Consciousness and revolution. From the Bolsheviks to Evald Ilyenkov*, Cambridge: Cambridge University Press.

Balibar, Etienne 1998, *Spinoza and politics*, London: Verso.

Barker, Tim 2017, 'The bleak left: on *Endnotes*', *N+1*, 28.

Barlow, Tani 2019, 'Semifeudalism, semicolonialism', in *Afterlives of Chinese communism. Political concepts from Mao to Xi*, edited by Christian Sorace, Ivan Franceschini and Nicholas Loubere, London: Verso.

Bayless, William 1976, 'The treaty with the Huns of 443', *The American Journal of Philology*, 97, 2: 176–179.

Benjamin, Walter 1994, *The correspondence of Walter Benjamin, 1910–1940*, Chicago, IL: University of Chicago Press.

Benjamin, Walter 1999, *The Arcades project*, Cambridge, MA: The Belknap Press of Harvard University Press.

Benjamin, Walter 2006a, 'Paralipomena to "On the concept of history', in *Selected writings. Volume IV: 1938–1940*, edited by Howard Eiland and Michael Jennings, Cambridge, MA: Harvard University Press.

Benjamin, W. 2006b, 'On the concept of history', in *Selected writings. Volume IV: 1938–1940*, edited by Howard Eiland and Michael Jennings, Cambridge, MA: Harvard University Press.

Berdan, Frances, Marilyn Masson, Janine Gasco and Michael Smith 2003, 'An international economy', in *The Postclassic Mesoamerican world*, edited by Michael Smith and Frances Berdan, Salt Lake City, UT: University of Utah Press.

Beretta, Marco 2009, 'Leonardo and Lucretius', *Rinascimento*, 49: 341–72.

Berryman, Sylvia 2009, *The mechanical hypothesis in ancient Greek natural philosophy*, Cambridge: Cambridge University Press.

Bhui, Rahul, Maciej Chudek and Joseph Henrich 2019, 'Work time and market integration in the original affluent society', *PNAS*, 116, 44: 22100–5.

Bietenholz, Peter 2009, *Encounters with a radical Erasmus. Erasmus' work as a source of radical thought in early modern Europe*, Toronto: University of Toronto Press.

Binet, Laurent 2020, *Beschavingen*, Amsterdam: Meulenhoff.

Blackburn, Robin (ed.) 1991, *After the fall. The failure of communism and the future of socialism*, London: Verso.

Blackledge, Paul 2006, *Reflections on the Marxist theory of history*, Manchester: Manchester University Press.

Blaney, David and Naeem Inayatullah 2006, 'The Savage Smith and the temporal walls of capitalism', in *Classical theory in international relations*, edited by Beate Jahn, Cambridge: Cambridge University Press.

Blanton, Richard 2004, 'Settlement pattern and population change in Mesoamerican and Mediterranean civilizations: a comparative perspective', in *Side-by-side survey. Comparative regional studies in the Mediterranean world*, edited by Susan Alcock and John Cherry, Oxford, Oxbow.

Blanton, Richard, Gary Feinman, Stephen Kowalewski and Peter Peregrine 1996, 'A dual-processual theory for the evolution of Mesoamerican civilization', *Current Anthropology*, 37, 1: 1–14.

Blanton, Richard and Lane Fargher 2008, *Collective action in the formation of premodern states*, New York: Springer.

Blanton, Richard, Lane Fargher and Verenice Heredia Espinoza 2005, 'The Mesoamerican world of goods and its transformations', in *Settlement, subsistence, and social complexity. Essays honoring the legacy of Jeffrey R. Parsons*, edited by Richard Blanton, Los Angeles, CA: Cotsen Institute of Archaeology Press.

Bloch, Ernst 1970, *A philosophy of the future*, New York: Herder and Herder.

Boccaccio, Giovanni 2003, *Giovanni Boccaccio Famous women*, Cambridge, MA: Harvard University Press.

Boccaccio, Giovanni 2009, *Bocaccio's expositions on Dante's Comedy. Translated, with introduction and notes, by Michael Papio*, Toronto: University of Toronto Press.

Boccaccio, Giovanni 2017, *Giovanni Boccaccio Genealogy of the pagan gods: books VI–X*, Cambridge, MA: Harvard University Press.

Bogaard, Amy, Mattia Fochesato and Samuel Bowles 2019, 'The farming-inequality nexus: new insights from ancient Western Eurasia', *Antiquity*, 93, 371: 1129–43.

Brandenberger, David and Mikhail Zelenov 2019, *Stalin's master narrative. A critical edition of the history of the Communist Party of the Soviet Union (Bolsheviks), short course*, New Haven, CN: Yale University Press.

Braswell, Geoffrey 2010, 'The rise and fall of market exchange: a dynamic approach to ancient Maya economy', in *Archaeological approaches to market exchange in ancient societies*, edited by Christopher Garraty and Barbara Stark, Boulder, CO: University Press of Colorado.

Braudel, Fernand 1981, *Civilization and capitalism, 15th–18th century, volume 1. The structures of everyday life: the limits of the possible*, New York: Harper & Row.

Bray, Francesca 1986, *The rice economies. Technology and development in Asian societies*, Oxford: Blackwell.

Brecht, Bertolt 2016, *The business affairs of Mr. Julius Caesar*, London: Bloomsbury.

Brown, Alison 2010, *The return of Lucretius to Renaissance Florence*, Cambridge, MA: Harvard University Press.

Brown, Heather 2012, *Marx on gender and the family. A critical study*, Leiden: Brill.

Brushlinski, Vladimir 1952, 'Spinoza's substance and finite things', in *Spinoza in Soviet philosophy. A series of essays*, edited by George Kline, London: Routledge and Paul.

Brysbaert, Ann 2011, 'Technologies of re-using and recycling in the Aegean and beyond', in *Tracing prehistoric social networks through technology: a diachronic perspective on the Aegean*, edited by Ann Brysbaert, London: Routledge.

Bukharin, Nikolai 1965, *Historical materialism. A system of sociology*, New York: Russell & Russell.

Bury, Robert 1926, *Plato XI: Laws, book 1–6*, London: William Heinemann.

Butterfield, David 2013, *The early textual history of Lucretius' De rerum natura*, Cambridge: Cambridge University Press.

Campbell, Gordon 2003, *Lucretius on creation and evolution. A commentary on "De rerum natura", book five, lines 772–1104*, Oxford: Oxford University Press.

Campbell, Gordon 2006, *Strange creatures. Anthropology in antiquity*, London: Duckworth.

Cañizares-Esguerra, Jorge 2001, *How to write the history of the New World. Histories, epistemologies, and identities in the Eighteenth-Century Atlantic world*, Stanford, CA: Stanford University Press.

Carballo, David, Kenneth Hirth, Daniela Hernández Sariñana, Gina Buckley, Andrés Mejía Ramón and Douglas Kennett 2019, 'New research at Teotihuacan's Tlajinga district, 2012–2015', *Ancient Mesoamerica*, 30: 95–113.

Chagall, Marc 2008 *The Bible: Genesis, Exodus, the Song of Solomon. Illustrations by Marc Chagall*, San Francisco, CA: Chronicle Books.

Chase, Adrian 2017, 'Residential inequality among the ancient Maya: operationalizing household architectural volume at Caracol, Belize', *Research Reports in Belizean Archaeology*, 14: 31–9.

Chernykh, Evgeny 1992, *Ancient metallurgy in the USSR. The early metal age*, Cambridge: Cambridge University Press.

Chernykh, Evgeny 2011, 'The archaeology paradigm through the prism of natural science methods', *Herald of the Russian Academy of Sciences*, 81, 1: 62–74.

Chernykh, Evgeny 2017, *Nomadic cultures in the mega-structure of the Eurasian world*, Brighton: MA, Academic Studies Press.

Childe, Gordon 1942, *What happened in history*, London: Penguin Books.

Childe, Gordon 1944, 'Archaeological ages as technological stages', *The Journal of the Royal Anthropological Institute of Great Britain and Ireland*, 74: 7–24.

Childe, Gordon 1946, *Scotland before the Scots*, London: Methuen.

Childe, Gordon 1950, 'The urban revolution', *Town Planning Review*, 21, 1: 3–17.

Childe, Gordon 1951, *Social evolution*, London: Collins.

Childe, Gordon 1954, 'Early forms of society', in *A history of technology*, edited by Charles Singer, Eric Holmyard, Alfred Hall and Trevor Williams, Oxford: Clarendon Press.

Childe, Gordon 1965, *Man makes himself*, London: Collins.

Clark, Gillian 2000, *Porphyry's On abstinence from killing animals*, Ithaca, NY: Cornell University Press.

Clay, Diskin 2009, 'The Athenian garden', in *The Cambridge companion to Epicureanism*, edited by James Warren, Cambridge: Cambridge University Press.

Cockburn, Alexander 1991, 'Radical as reality', in *After the fall. The failure of communism and the future of socialism*, edited by Robin Blackburn, London: Verso.

Cogniot, Georges 1954, *De la nature des choses. Lucrèce; textes choisis, préf., comment. et notes explicatives par Georges Cogniot*, Paris: Éditions Sociales.

Cohen, Bernard 1964, ''Quantum in Se Est': Newton's concept of inertia in relation to Descartes and Lucretius', *Notes and Records of the Royal Society of London*, 19, 2: 131–55.

Cole, Thomas 1990, *Democritus and the sources of Greek anthropology*, Atlanta, GA: Scholars Press.

Coleman, James 2014, 'Boccaccio's humanistic ethnography', in *Boccaccio: a critical guide to the complete works*, edited by Victoria Kirkham, Michael Sherberg and Janet Levarie Smarr, Chicago, IL: University of Chicago Press.

Cooper, Melinda 2003, 'Marx beyond Marx, Marx before Marx: Negri's Lucretian critique of the Hegelian Marx', in *Reading Negri. Marxism in the age of empire*, edited by Pierre Lamarche, Max Rosenkrantz and David Sherman, Chicago, IL: Open Court Publishing.

Cullhed, Eric 2017, 'Theodore Prodromos in the Garden of Epicurus: the Amarantos', in *Dialogues and Debates from Late Antiquity to Late Byzantium*, edited by Averil Cameron and Niels Gaul, Abingdon: Ashgate.

Cunow, Heinrich 1937, *Geschichte und Kultur des Inkareiches. Ein Beitrag zur Kulturgeschichte Altamerikas*, Amsterdam: Elsevier.

Curd, Patricia 2007, *Anaxagoras of Clazomenae. Fragments and testimonia*, Toronto: University of Toronto Press.

Dakouri-Hild, Anastasia 2012, 'Making *la différence*: the production and consumption of ornaments in Late Bronze Age Boeotia', in *Kosmos. Jewellery, adornment and textiles in the Aegean Bronze Age*, edited by Marie-Louise Nosch and Robert Laffineur, Leuven: Peeters.

Dale, Stephen 2006, 'Ibn Khaldun: the last Greek and the first Annaliste historian', *International Journal of Middle East Studies*, 38, 3: 431–51.

Danilov, A. 1969, 'On the question of methodology in historical science', *Translations from Kommunist*, 5: 80–95.

Danilova, Lyudmila 1966, 'A discussion on an important problem', *Soviet Anthropology and Archaeology*, 4, 4: 3–12.

Danilova, Lyudmila 1971, 'Controversial problems of the theory of precapitalist societies', *Soviet Anthropology and Archaeology*, 9: 269–328.

Davidson, Neil 2018, 'The frontiers of uneven and combined development', *Historical Materialism*, 26, 3: 52–78.

Davis, Jack and Sharon Stocker 2016, 'The lord of the gold rings: the Griffin Warrior of Pylos', *Hesperia*, 85, 4: 627–55.

Dawson, Doyne 1992, *Cities of the gods. Communist utopias in Greek thought*, Oxford: Oxford University Press.

Deborin, Abram 1952, 'Spinoza's world-view', in *Spinoza in Soviet philosophy. A series of essays*, edited by George Kline, London: Routledge and Paul.

Deleuze, Gilles 1990, *The logic of sense*, London: The Athlone Press.

Desan, Philippe 2017, *Montaigne: a life*, Princeton, NJ: Princeton University Press.

Dewan, Leslie and Dorothy Hosler 2008, 'Ancient maritime trade on balsa rafts: an engineering analysis', *Journal of Anthropological Research*, 64, 1: 19–40.

Di Pasquale, Giovanni 2016, 'Vitruvius's image of the universe: architecture and mechanics', in *Vitruvianism. Origins and transformations*, edited by Paolo Sanvito, Berlin: De Gruyter.

D'iakonov, Igor 1963, 'The commune in the ancient East as treated in the works of Soviet researchers', *Soviet Anthropology and Archaeology*, 2, 1: 32–46.

D'iakonov, Igor 1976, 'Slaves, helots, and serfs in early antiquity', *Soviet Anthropology and Archaeology*, 15, 2–3: 50–102.

Diamond, Jared 1997, *Guns, germs and steel. A short history of everybody for the last 13,000 years*, London: Vintage.

Diaz-Andreu, Margarita 2008, *A world history of Nineteenth-century archaeology. Nationalism, colonialism, and the past*, Oxford: Oxford University Press.

Dieterich, Heinz 1982, 'Some theoretical and methodological observations about the Inca empire and the Asiatic mode of production', *Latin American Perspectives*, 9, 4: 111–32.

Driessen, Jan 2002, ' "The king must die": some observations on the use of Minoan court compounds', in *Monuments of Minos. Rethinking the Minoan palaces*, edited by Jan Driessen, Ilse Schoep and Robert Laffineur, Liege: Universite de Liege.

Duistermaat, Kim 2010, 'Administration in Neolithic Societies? The first use of seals in Syria and some considerations on seal owners, seal use and private property', in *Die Bedeutung der minoischen und mykenischen Glyptik. VI. Internationales Siegel-Symposium, Marburg, 9.–12. Oktober 2008. Corpus der minoischen und mykenischen Siegel – Beiheft nr. 8*, edited by Walter Müller, Mainz am Rhein: Verlag Philipp von Zabern.

Dunn, Stephen 1982, *The rise and fall of the Asiatic mode of production*, London: Routledge & Kegan Paul.

Einarson, Benedict and Philip De Lacy 1967, *Plutarch's Moralia XIV*, London: William Heinemann.

Emerson, Roger 1984, 'Conjectural history and Scottish philosophers', *Historical Papers/Communications historiques*, 19: 63–90.

Engels, Friedrich 1980, 'Karl Marx, *A contribution to the critique of political economy*', in *Marx and Engels Collected Works, Vol. 16*, Moscow: Progress Publishers.

Engels, Friedrich 1987a, 'Dialectics of nature', in *Marx and Engels Collected Works, Vol. 25*, Moscow: Progress Publishers.

Engels, Friedrich 1987b, 'Anti-Dühring', in *Marx and Engels Collected Works, Vol. 25*, Moscow: Progress Publishers.

Engels, Friedrich 1990a, 'The origin of the family, private property and the state. In the light of the researches by Lewis H. Morgan', in *Marx and Engels Collected Works, Vol. 26*, Moscow: Progress Publishers.

Engels, Friedrich 1990b, 'Manuscripts on early German history', in *Marx and Engels Collected Works, Vol. 26*, Moscow: Progress Publishers.

Engels, Friedrich 1992a, 'Engels to Eduard Bernstein, 22 September 1882', in *Marx and Engels Collected Works, Vol. 46*, Moscow: Progress Publishers.

Engels, Friedrich 1992b, 'Engels to Friedrich Adolph Sorge, 15 March 1883', in *Marx and Engels Collected Works, Vol. 46*, Moscow: Progress Publishers.

Engels, Friedrich 2001, 'Engels to Joseph Bloch, 21[–22] September 1890', in *Marx and Engels Collected Works, Vol. 49*, Moscow: Progress Publishers.

Erickson, Clark 2006, 'Intensification, political economy, and the farming community: in defense of a bottom-up perspective of the past', in *Agricultural strategies*, edited by Joyce Marcus and Charles Stanish, Los Angeles, CA: The Cotsen Institute of Archaeology at UCLA.

Erler, Michael 2009, 'Epicureanism in the Roman empire', in *The Cambridge companion to Epicureanism*, edited by James Warren, Cambridge: Cambridge University Press.

Essler, Holger 2011, *Glückselig und unsterblich. Epikureische Theologie bei Cicero und Philodem: mit einer Edition von PHerc. 152/157, KOL. 8–10*, Basel: Schwabe Verlag.

Estrada-Belli, Fernando 2012, 'Early civilization in the Maya lowlands: monumentality and placemaking, a view from the Holmul region', in *Early new world monumentality*, edited by Richard Burger and Robert Rosenswig, Gainesville, FL: University Press of Florida.

Evans, Alfred 1986, 'The decline of developed socialism? Some trends in recent Soviet ideology', *Soviet Studies*, 38, 1: 1–23.

Fagles, Robert 1996, *Homer: Odyssey*, London: Penguin.

Fairclough, Henry 1935, *Virgil Eclogues, Georgics, Aeneid I–VI*, London: William Heinemann.

Farnesi Camellone, M. 2017, 'Fraternitas militans: time and politics in Ernst Bloch', in *The government of time. Theories of plural temporality in the Marxist tradition*, edited by Vittorio Morfino and Peter Thomas, Leiden: Brill.

Farrell, Joseph 1994, 'The structure of Lucretius' anthropology', *Materiale e discussioni per l'analisi dei testi classici*, 33: 81–95.

Farrington, Benjamin 1953, '*Vita prior* in Lucretius', *Hermathena*, 81: 59–62.

Feeley-Harnik, Gillian 1999, ''Communities of blood': the natural history of kinship in Nineteenth-Century America', *Comparative Studies in Society and History*, 41: 215–62.

Feeley-Harnik, Gillian 2001, 'The ethnography of creation: Lewis Henry Morgan and the American beaver', in *Relative values. Reconfiguring kinship studies*, edited by Sarah Franklin and Susan McKinnon, Durham, NC: Duke University Press.

Fernández-Armesto, Fernando 2007, *Amerigo. The man who gave his name to America*, New York: Random House.

Filtzer, Don 2014, 'Privilege and inequality in communist society', in *The Oxford handbook of the history of communism*, edited by Stephen Smith, Oxford: Oxford University Press.

Finelli, Roberto 2016, *A failed parricide. Hegel and the young Marx*, Leiden: Brill.

Fisch, Max 1953, 'The Academy of the Investigators', in *Science, medicine and history. Essays on the evolution of scientific thought and medical practice written in honour of Charles Singer*, edited by Edgar Underwood, London: Oxford University Press.

Fochesato, Mattia, Amy Bogaard and Samuel Bowles 2019, 'Comparing ancient inequalities: the challenges of comparability, bias and precision', *Antiquity*, 93, 370: 853–69.

Fortenbaugh, William and Eckart Schutrumpf (eds) 2001, *Dicaearchus of Messana. Text, translation, and discussion*, Piscataway, NJ: Transaction Publishers.

Foster, John 2000, *Marx's ecology. Materialism and nature*, New York: Monthly Review Press.

Fowler, Harold 1921, *Plato VII: Theaetetus, Sophist*, London: William Heinemann.

Fowler, Don 1989, 'Lucretius and politics', in *Philosophia Togata*, edited by Mirian Griffin and Jonathan Barnes, Oxford: Oxford University Press.

Fowler, Don 2002, *Lucretius on atomic motion. A commentary on De rerum natura, book two, lines 1–332*, Oxford: Oxford University Press.

Frazer, James 1921, *Apollodorus The library: volume 1*, London: William Heinemann.

Frischer, Bernard 1982, *The sculpted word: epicureanism and philosophical recruitment in ancient Greece*, Berkeley, CA: University of California Press.

Fuentes-Ramirez, Ricardo 2017, 'The updating of the Cuban model: precursor socialism and cooperativism', *Latin American Perspectives*, 45, 6: 140–55.

Fukuyama, Francis 1992, *The end of history and the last man*, New York: Free Press.

Fukuyama, Francis 2011, *The origins of political order. From prehuman times to the French Revolution*, London: Profile Books.

Furley, David 1989, *Cosmic problems. Essays on Greek and Roman philosophy of nature*, Cambridge: Cambridge University Press.

Gale, Monica 1994, *Myth and poetry in Lucretius*, Cambridge: Cambridge University Press.

Gale, Monica 2009, *De rerum natura V / Lucretius*, Warminster: Aris & Phillips.

Gamble, Clive 2013, *Settling the earth. The archaeology of deep human history*, Cambridge: Cambridge University Press.

Garani, Myrto 2013, 'Lucretius and Ovid on Empedoclean cows and sheep', in *Lucretius: poetry, philosophy, science*, edited by Daryn Lehoux, Andrew Morrison and Alison Sharrock, Oxford: Oxford University Press.

Garcilaso de la Vega 1966, *Royal commentaries of the Incas and general history of Peru*, Austin, TX: University of Texas Press.

Gaydarska, Bisserka 2016, 'The city is dead! Long live the city!', *Norwegian Archaeological Review*, 49, 1: 40–57.

Gellner, Ernest 1988, *State and society in Soviet thought*, Oxford: Basil Blackwell.

Gera, Deborah 2003, *Ancient Greek ideas on speech, language, and civilization*, Oxford: Oxford University Press.

Geronimus, Dennis 2006, *Piero di Cosimo: visions beautiful and strange*, New Haven, CT: Yale University Press.

Geronimus, Dennis 2015, 'No man's lands: Lucretius and the primitive strain in Piero's art and patronage', in *Piero di Cosimo: the poetry of painting in Renaissance Florence*, edited by Dennis Geronimus and Gretchen Hirschauer, Washington, DC: National Gallery of Art.

Gerrish, Jennifer 2018, 'The Blessed Isles and counterfactual history in Sallust' *Histos*, 12: 49–70.

Gittes, Tobias 2008, *Boccaccio's naked muse. Eros, culture, and the mythopoeic imagination*, Toronto: University of Toronto Press.

Godelier, Maurice 1974, 'On the definition of a social formation: the example of the Incas', *Critique of Anthropology*, 1, 1: 63–73.

Godes, Mikhail 1981, 'The reaffirmation of unilinealism', in *The Asiatic mode of production: science and politics*, edited by Anne Bailey and Josep Llobera, London: Routledge.

Goodman, Lenn 2015, 'How Epicurean was Razi?', *Studia Graeco-Arabica*, 5: 247–80.

Goodrum, Matthew 2002a, 'Biblical anthropology and the idea of human prehistory in late antiquity', *History and Anthropology*, 13, 2: 69–78.

Goodrum, Matthew 2002b, 'The meaning of ceraunia: archaeology, natural history and the interpretation of prehistoric stone artefacts in the eighteenth century', *The British Journal for the History of Science*, 35, 3: 255–69.

Goodrum, Matthew 2008, 'Questioning thunderstones and arrowheads: the problem of recognizing and interpreting stone artefacts in the Seventeenth century', *Early Science and Medicine*, 13: 482–508.

Gordon, Pamela 1996, *Epicurus in Lycia. The second-century world of Diogenes of Oenoanda*, Ann Arbor, MI: University of Michigan Press.

Gordon, Pamela 2012, *The invention and gendering of Epicurus*, Ann Arbor, MI: The University of Michigan Press.

Goshgarian, Michael 2013, 'The very essence of the object, the soul of Marxism, and other singular things', in *Encountering Althusser. Politics and materialism in contemporary radical thought*, edited by Katja Diefenbach, Sara Farris, Gal Kirn and Peter Thomas, London: Bloomsbury.

Gourevitch, Victor 2000, 'Rousseau on providence', *The Review of Metaphysics*, 53, 3: 565–611.

Graham, Loren 1971, *Science and philosophy in the Soviet Union*, London: Allen Lane.

Greenblatt, Stephen 2010, 'Utopian pleasure', in *Cultural reformations. Medieval and Renaissance in literary history*, edited by William Simpson and Brian Cummings, Oxford: Oxford University Press.

Greenblatt, Stephen 2011, *The swerve. How the world became modern*, New York: Norton.

Greene, Kevin 1999, 'V. Gordon Childe and the vocabulary of revolutionary change', *Antiquity*, 73, 279: 97–109.

Guthrie, William 1969, *A history of Greek philosophy, volume III: the fifth-century enlightenment, part 1 the Sophists*, Cambridge: Cambridge University Press.

Hanfmann, George 1998, 'Giants', *The Oxford companion to Classical civilization*, edited by Simon Hornblower and Antony Spawforth, Oxford: Oxford University Press.

Hanke, Lewis 1974, *All mankind is one. A study of the disputation between Bartolomé de Las Casas and Juan Ginés de Sepúlvelda in 1550 on the intellectual and religious capacity of the American Indians*, DeKalb, IL: Northern Illinois University Press.

Hardt, Michael and Antonio Negri 2000, *Empire*, Cambridge, MA: Harvard University Press.

Hardt, Michael and Antonio Negri 2019, 'Empire, twenty years on', *New Left Review*, 120: 67–92.

Hardie, Philip 1986, *Virgil's Aeneid. Cosmos and imperium*, Oxford: Clarendon Press.

Harmon, Austin 1915, *Lucian: volume II*, London: William Heinemann.

Harmon, Austin 1921, *Lucian: volume III*, London: William Heinemann.

Harmon, Austin 1925, *Lucian: volume IV*, London: William Heinemann.

Harris, David (ed.) 1994, *The archaeology of V. Gordon Childe. Contemporary perspectives*, London: UCL Press.

Harrison, James 1965, 'Communist interpretations of the Chinese peasant wars', *The China Quarterly*, 24: 92–118.

Harstick, Hans-Peter (ed.) 1977, *Karl Marx über Formen vorkapitalistischer Produktion. Vergleichende Studien zur Geschichte des Grundeigentums 1879–80*, Frankfurt am Main: Campus-Verlag.

Hastings, Robert 1975, *Nature and reason in the 'Decameron'*, Manchester: Manchester University Press.

Hedreen, Guy 2019, 'The question of centaurs: Lucretius, Ovid, and Empedokles in Piero di Cosimo', in *Piero di Cosimo: painter of faith and fable*, edited by Dennis Geronimus and Michael Kwakkelstein, Leiden: Brill.

Hegel, Georg 1955, *Hegel's lectures on the history of philosophy*, London: Routledge & Kegan Paul.

Hegel, Georg 2001, *The philosophy of history*, Kitchener: Batoche Books.

Heinrich, Michael 2013, 'The 'fragment on machines': a Marxian misconception in the *Grundrisse* and its overcoming in *Capital*', in *In Marx's laboratory. Critical interpretations of the Grundrisse*, edited by Riccardo Bellofiore, Guido Starosta and Peter Thomas, Leiden: Brill.

Heinrich, Michael 2019, *Karl Marx and the birth of modern society. The life of Marx and the development of his work, volume 1: 1818–1841*, New York: Monthly Review Press.

Heyd, Volker 2017, 'Kossinna's smile', *Antiquity*, 91, 356: 348–59.

Hine, William. 1995, 'Inertia and scientific law in sixteenth-century commentaries on Lucretius', *Renaissance Quarterly*, 48, 4: 728–41.

Hirth, Kenneth and Joanne Pillsbury 2013, 'Redistribution and markets in Andean South America', *Current Anthropology*, 54, 5: 642–47.

Hobsbawm, Eric 1994, *The age of extremes. A history of the world, 1914–1991*, New York: Pantheon Books.

Hobsbawm, Eric 2011, *How to change the world. Tales of Marx and Marxism*, London: Abacus.

Hoffmann, George 2005, 'The investigation of nature', in *The Cambridge companion to Montaigne*, edited by Ullrich Langer, Cambridge: Cambridge University Press.

Hogan, Sarah 2018, *Other Englands. Utopia, capital, and empire in an age of transition*, Stanford, CA: Stanford University Press.

Holmes, Brooke 2005, 'Daedala lingua: crafted speech in De Rerum Natura', *The American Journal of Philology*, 126, 4: 527–85.

Holmes, Brooke 2013, 'The poetic logic of negative exceptionalism: from a state of nature to social life in Lucretius, book five', in *Lucretius: poetry, philosophy, science*, edited by Daryn Lehoux, Andrew Morrison and Alison Sharrock, Oxford: Oxford University Press.

Houston, Stephen 2014, *The life within. Classic Maya and the matter of permanence*, Yale, CT: Yale University Press.

Houston, Stephen and Takeshi Inomata 2009, *The Classic Maya*, Cambridge: Cambridge University Press.

Howe, Jovan 1980, *The Soviet theories of primitive history: forty years of speculation on the origins and evolution of people and society*, Seattle, WA: University of Washington.

Hough, Jerry 1986, *The struggle for the Third World. Soviet debates and American options*, Washington DC: The Brookings Institute.

Hudis, Peter 2013, *Marx's concept of the alternative to capitalism*, Chicago, IL: Haymarket Books.

Hulme, Peter 1994, 'Tales of distinction: European ethnography and the Caribbean', in *Implicit understandings. Observing, reporting and reflecting on the encounters between Europeans and other peoples in the Early Modern era*, edited by Stuart Schwartz, Cambridge: Cambridge University Press.

Hutson, Scott 2000, 'Carnival and contestation in the Aztec marketplace', *Dialectical Anthropology*, 25: 123–49.

Ilyenkov, Ewald 1977, *Dialectical logic. Essays on its history and theory*, Moscow: Progress Publishers.

Ilyenkov, Ewald 2012, 'Dialectics of the ideal', *Historical Materialism*, 20, 2: 149–93.

Ilyenkov, Ewald 2017, 'Cosmology of the spirit', *Stasis*, 5, 2: 164–90.

Inwood, Brad and Lloyd Gerson (eds) 1994, *The Epicurus reader. Selected writings and testimonia*, Indianapolis, IN: Hackett Publishing Company.

Irving, Terry 2020, *The fatal lure of politics. The life and thought of Vere Gordon Childe*, Clayton: Monash University Publishing.

Israel, Jonathan 2001, *Radical Enlightenment. Philosophy and the making of modernity, 1650–1750*, Oxford: Oxford University Press.

Israel, Jonathan 2019, *The Enlightenment that failed. Ideas, revolution, and democratic defeat, 1748–1830*, Oxford: Oxford University Press.

Johnson, Monte 2013, 'Nature, spontaneity, and voluntary action', in *Lucretius: poetry, philosophy, science*, edited by Daryn Lehoux, Andrew Morrison and Alison Sharrock, Oxford: Oxford University Press.

Jones, Horace 1923, *Strabo The geography: volume II*, London: William Heinemann.

Joravsky, David 1961, *Soviet Marxism and natural science, 1917–1932*, London: Routledge.

Kahn, Charles 1997, 'Greek religion and philosophy in the Sisyphus fragment', *Phronesis*, 42, 3: 247–62.

Kaldellis, Anthony 2012, 'Byzantine philosophy inside and out: orthodoxy and dissidence in counterpoint', in *The many faces of Byzantine philosophy*, edited by Borje Byden and Katerina Ierodiakonou, Bergen: Norwegian Institute at Athens.

Kaldellis, Anthony and Niketas Sinniosoglou, N. 2017, *The Cambridge intellectual history of Byzantium*, Cambridge: Cambridge University Press.

Keen, Benjamin 1971, *The Aztec image in Western thought*, New Brunswick, NJ: Rutgers University Press.

Keen, Benjamin 1998, *Essays in the intellectual history of colonial Latin America*, Boulder, CO: Westview Press.

Kennedy, Rebecca 2018, 'Otis T. Mason and Hippocratic environmental theory at the Smithsonian Institution in the Nineteenth and Early Twentieth Centuries', in *Brill's companion to classics and early anthropology*, edited by Emily Varto, Leiden: Brill.

Keyes, Clinton 1928, *Cicero XVI: On the republic, On the laws*, Cambridge, MA: Harvard University Press.

Khatchadourian, Lori 2008, 'Making nations from the ground up: traditions of classical archaeology in the South Caucasus', *American Journal of Archaeology*, 112, 2: 247–78.

Khazanov, Anatoly 1973, 'On the character of slaveholding among the Scythians', *Soviet Anthropology and Archaeology*, 11, 4: 415–38.

Khazanov, Anatoly 1994, *Nomads and the outside world, second edition*, Madison, WI: University of Wisconsin Press.

Khrushchev, Nikita 1961, *Report of the Central Committee of the CPSU to the 22nd congress of the Communist Party of the Soviet Union*, New York: Crosscurrents Press.

Kradin, Nikolai 2011, 'A panorama of social archaeology in Russia', in *Comparative archaeologies. A sociological view of the science of the past*, edited by Ludomir Lozny, New York, Springer.

Kilburn, K. 1959, *Lucian: volume VI*, London: William Heinemann.

Killen, John 2008, 'Mycenaean economy', in *A companion to Linear B. Mycenaean Greek texts and their world*, edited by Yves Duhoux and Anna Morpurgo Davies, Louvain-la-Neuve: Peeters.

Kim, David 2014, *The traveling artist in Renaissance Italy. Geography, mobility, and style*, New Haven, CT: Yale University Press.

Kitromilidis, Paschalis 2013, *Enlightenment and revolution. The making of modern Greece*, Cambridge, MA: Harvard University Press.

Klejn, Leo 2012, *Soviet archaeology. Trends, schools, and history*, Oxford: Oxford University Press.

Klever, Wim 2005, *Spinoza classicus. Antieke bronnen van een moderne denker*, Budel: DAMON.

Kline, George 1952, 'Introduction', in *Spinoza in Soviet philosophy. A series of essays*, edited by George Kline, London: Routledge and Paul.

Knight, Kelvin and Paul Blackledge (eds) 2011, *Virtue and politics. Alasdair MacIntyre's revolutionary Aristotelianism*, Notre Dame, IN: Notre Dame University Press.

Kohei, Saito 2017, *Karl Marx's ecosocialism. Capital, nature, and the unfinished critique of political economy*, New York: Monthly Review Press.

Kohler, Timothy, Michael Smith, Amy Bogaard, Gary Feinman, Christian Peterson, Alleen Betzenhauser, Matthew Pailes, Elizabeth Stone, Anna Prentiss, Timothy Dennehy, Laura Ellyson, Linda Nicholas, Ronald Faulseit, Amy Styring, Jade Whitlam, Mattia Fochesato, Thomas Foor and Samuel Bowles 2017, 'Greater Post-Neolithic Wealth Disparities in Eurasia than in North America and Mesoamerica', *Science*, 551: 619–622.

Kohler, Timothy, Michael Smith, Amy Bogaard, Christian Peterson, Alleen Betzenhauser, Gary Feinman, Rahul Oka, Matthew Pailes, Anna Marie Prentiss, Elizabeth Stone, Timothy Dennehy and Laura Ellyson 2018, 'Deep inequality: summary and conclusions', in *Ten thousand years of inequality. The archaeology of wealth differences*, edited by Timothy Kohler and Michael Smith, Tucson, AZ: University of Arizona Press.

Kolganov, Andrey 2016, 'Political economy of Russian capitalism's "Jurassic park"', in *Special English-language edition of the journals Questions of Political Economy and The Economic Revival of Russia*, edited by Aleksandr Buzgalin and Natalya Yakovleva, Moscow: URSS.

Konstan, David 2008, *A life worthy of the gods. The materialist psychology of Epicurus*, Las Vegas, NV: Parmenides.

Konstan, David 2011, 'Epicurus on the gods', in *Epicurus and the Epicurean tradition*, edited by Jeffrey Fish and Kirk Sanders, Cambridge: Cambridge University Press.

Kouvelakis, Stathis 2016, 'Syriza's rise and fall', *New Left Review*, 97: 45–70.

Kowalewski, Stephen 2012, 'A theory of the Mesoamerican economy', *Research in Economic Anthropology*, 32: 187–224.

Kowalewski, Stephen 2016, 'It was the economy, stupid', in *Alternative pathways to complexity*, edited by Lane Fargher, and Verenice Heredia Espinoza, Boulder, CO: University of Colorado Press.

Kowalewski, Stephen 2020, 'Economic institutions in ancient Greece and Mesoamerica', *Social Evolution & History*, 19, 1: 21–42.

Krader, Lawrence 1973, 'The works of Marx and Engels in ethnology compared', *International Review of Social History*, 18, 2: 223–75.

Krader, Lawrence 1974, *The ethnological notebooks of Karl Marx*, Assen: Van Gorcum.

Krader, Lawrence 1975, *The Asiatic mode of production. Sources, development and critique in the writings of Karl Marx*, Assen: Van Gorcum.

Krätke, Michael 2018, 'Marx and world history', *International Review of Social History*, 63, 1: 1–35.

Lahtinen, Mikko 2009, *Politics and philosophy. Nicolo Machiavelli and Louis Althusser's aleatory materialism*, Leiden: Brill.

Langermann, Tzvi 2009, 'Islamic atomism and the Galenic tradition', *History of Science*, 47, 3: 277–96.

Leach, Darcy 2015, Oligarchy, iron law of, in *International encyclopedia of the social & behavioral sciences, 2nd edition, Vol. 17*, edited by James Wright, Oxford: Elsevier.

Lechtman, Heather 2014, 'Andean metallurgy in prehistory', in *Archaeometallurgy in global perspective. Methods and syntheses*, edited by Benjamin Roberts and Christopher Thornton, New York: Springer.

Lecompte, Denis 1983, *Marx et le baron d'Holbach*, Paris: Presses Universitaire de France.

Lecourt, Dominique 1977, *Proletarian science? The case of Lysenko*, London: New Left Books.

Lee, Richard 1985, 'Greeks and Victorians: a re-examination of Engels' theory of the Athenian polis', *Culture*, 5, 1: 63–73.

Lekas, Padelis 1988, *Marx on classical antiquity. Problems of methodology*, Brighton: Wheatsheaf.

Lenin, Vladimir 1974, *Collected works, volume 27: February–July 1918*, Moscow: Progress Publishers.

Lenin, Vladimir 1977, *Collected works, volume 14: materialism and empirio-criticism*, Moscow: Progress Publishers.

Lenin, Vladimir 1981, *Collected works, volume 38: philosophical notebooks*, Moscow: Progress Publishers.

Lesher, James 1991, 'Xenophanes on inquiry and discovery: an alternative to the 'hymn of progress' reading of Fr. 18', *Ancient Philosophy*, 11: 229–48.

Leszl, Walter 2007, 'Democritus' works: from their titles to their contents', in *Democritus: science, the arts, and the care of the soul. Proceedings of the International Colloquium on Democritus (Paris, 18–20 September 2003)*, edited by Aldo Brancacci and Pierre-Marie Morel, Leiden: Brill.

Levine, Norman 2012, *Marx's discourse with Hegel*, London: Palgrave Macmillan.

Lewin, Moshe 2005, *The Soviet century*, London: Verso.

Lezra, Jacques 2018, *On the nature of Marx's things. Translation as necrophilology*, New York: Fordham University Press.

Liddell, Henry and Robert Scott 1940, *A Greek-English lexicon*, Oxford: Clarendon.

Lillios, Katina (ed.) 2011, *Comparative archaeologies. The American Southwest (AD 900–1600) and the Iberian peninsula (3000–1500 BC)*, Oxford: Oxbow.

Lloyd, Geoffrey 2012, *Being, humanity and understanding*, Oxford: Oxford University Press.

Lloyd, Geoffrey and Jingyi Zhao (eds) 2018, *Ancient Greece and China compared*, Cambridge: Cambridge University Press.

Locke, John 1975, *An essay concerning human understanding*, Oxford: Oxford University Press.

Locke, John 1993, *Political writings*, London: Penguin.

Long, Anthony and David Sedley 1987, *The Hellenistic philosophers. Volume 1: translations of the principal sources with philosophical commentary*, Cambridge: Cambridge University Press.

Lovejoy, Arthur and George Boas 1935, *Primitivism and related ideas in antiquity*, Baltimore, MD: The John Hopkins University Press.

Löwy, Michael 2005, *Fire alarm. Reading Walter Benjamin's 'On the concept of history'*, London: Verso.

Lozny, Ludomir (ed.) 2016, *Archaeology of the communist era. A political history of archaeology of the 20th century*, Cham: Springer.

Lucas, Erhard 1964a, 'Die Rezeption Lewis H. Morgans durch Marx und Engels', *Saeculum*, 15: 153–76.

Lucas, Erhard 1964b, 'Marx' Studien zur Frühgeschichte und Ethnologie 1880–1882. Nach unveröffentlichten Exzerpten', *Saeculum*, 15: 327–43.

Luehrmann, Sonja 2005, 'Russian colonialism and the Asiatic mode of production: (post-)Soviet ethnography goes to Alaska', *Slavic Review*, 64, 4: 851–71.

Luria, Solomon 2016, 'Democritus. Texts, translation, investigations', available at https://www.academia.edu/25014428/S.Y_Luria_Demokrit_English_translation_by_C.C.W_Taylor, (last accessed 7.6.2017).

Luxemburg, Rosa 2013, *The complete works of Rosa Luxemburg. Volume 1: economic writings 1*, London: Verso.

Macherey, Pierre 1998, *Introduction à l'Ethique de Spinoza. 1: La première partie: la nature des choses*, Paris: Presses Universitaires de France.

Macherey, Pierre 2011, *Hegel or Spinoza*, Minneapolis, MN: University of Minnesota Press.

Machiavelli, Niccolò 1989, *The chief works and others. Volume 1*, Durham: Duke University Press.

Mackey, Jacob 2015, 'New evidence for the Epicurean theory of the origin of language: Philodemus, *On poems* v (PHerc. 403, Fr. 5, Col. 1)', *Cronache Ercolanesi*, 45: 67–84.

Mad'iar, Ludvig 1981, 'The legitimacy of the AMP', in *The Asiatic mode of production: science and politics*, edited by Anne Bailey and Josep Llobera, London: Routledge.

Maffie, James 2013, *Aztec philosophy. Understanding a world in motion*, Boulder, CO: University of Colorado Press.

Maidansky, Andrey 2003, 'The Russian Spinozists', *Studies East European Thought*, 55: 199–216.

Maidansky, Andrey 2017, 'The Ilyenkov triangle: Marxism in search of its philosophical roots', *Stasis*, 5, 2: 136–63.

Mansfeld, J. 2016, 'Doxography of ancient philosophy', in *The Stanford Encyclopedia of Philosophy* (*Winter 2016 Edition*), edited by Edward Zalta, available at: https://plato .stanford.edu/archives/win2016/entries/doxography-ancient/, (last accessed 14.10. 2017).

Manzanilla, Linda (ed.) 1987, *Studies in the neolithic and urban revolutions. The V. Gordon Childe Colloquium, Mexico, 1986*, Oxford: BAR.

Marchesi, Simone 2014, 'Boccaccio on fortune (*De casibus vivorum illustrium*)', in *Boccaccio: a critical guide to the complete works*, edited by Victoria Kirkham, Michael Sherberg and Janet Levarie Smarr, Chicago, IL: University of Chicago Press.

Marcus, Joyce 2003, 'Recent advances in Maya archaeology', *Journal of Archaeological Research*, 11, 2: 71–148.

Margaritis, Evi 2013, 'Distinguishing exploitation, domestication, cultivation and production: the olive in the third millennium Aegean', *Antiquity*, 87, 337: 746–57.

Markwick, Roger 2001, *Rewriting history in Soviet Russia. The politics of revisionist historiography, 1956–1974*, New York: Palgrave Macmillan.

Marsh, David 2004, *Renaissance fables. Aesopic prose by Leon Battista Alberti, Bartolomeo Scala, Leonardo da Vinci, Bernardino Baldi*, Tempe, AZ: Arizona Center for Medieval and Renaissance Studies.

Marx, Karl 1973, *Grundrisse*, London: Penguin.

Marx, Karl 1975a, 'Difference between the Democritean and Epicurean philosophy of nature', in *Marx and Engels collected works, Vol. 1*, Moscow: Progress Publishers.

Marx, Karl 1975b, 'Notebooks on Epicurean philosophy', in *Marx and Engels collected works, Vol. 1*, Moscow: Progress Publishers.

Marx, Karl 1975c, 'Economic and philosophic manuscripts of 1844', in *Marx and Engels Collected Works, Vol. 3*, Moscow: Progress Publishers.

Marx, Karl 1975d, 'Proceedings of the sixth Rhine province assembly. Third article debates on the law on thefts of wood', in *Marx and Engels collected works, Vol. 1*, Moscow: Progress Publishers.

Marx, Karl 1975e, 'The holy family: critical battle against French materialism', in *Marx and Engels Collected Works, Vol. 4*, Moscow: Progress Publishers.

Marx, Karl 1975 f., 'Theses on Feuerbach [original version]', in *Marx and Engels Collected Works, Vol. 5*, Moscow: Progress Publishers.

Marx, Karl 1976a, *Capital: volume 1*, London: Penguin.

Marx, Karl 1976b, 'The poverty of philosophy. Answer to the poverty of philosophy by M. Proudhon', in *Marx and Engels Collected Works, Vol. 6*, Moscow: Progress Publishers.

Marx, Karl 1979, 'The Eighteenth Brumaire of Louis Bonaparte', in *Marx and Engels Collected Works, Vol. 11*, Moscow: Progress Publishers.

Marx, Karl 1980, 'Revolutionary Spain', in *Marx and Engels Collected Works, Vol. 13*, Moscow: Progress Publishers.

Marx, Karl 1981, *Capital: volume III*, London: Penguin.

Marx, Karl 1983a, 'A letter to the editorial board of Otechestvennye Zapiski', in *Late Marx and the Russian road. Marx and the peripheries of capitalism*, edited by Teodor Shanin, New York: Monthly Review Press.

Marx, Karl 1983b, 'Drafts of a reply to Vera Zasulich', in *Late Marx and the Russian road. Marx and the peripheries of capitalism*, edited by Teodor Shanin, New York: Monthly Review Press.

Marx, Karl 1983c, 'Marx to Ferdinand Lasalle, 21 December 1857', in *Marx and Engels Collected Works, Vol. 40*, Moscow: Progress Publishers.

Marx, Karl 1986a, 'Drafts of the *Civil war in France*', in *Marx and Engels Collected Works, Vol. 22*, Moscow: Progress Publishers.

Marx, Karl 1986b, 'The civil war in France', in *Marx and Engels Collected Works, Vol. 22*, Moscow: Progress Publishers.

Marx, Karl 1986c, 'Outline of the critique of political economy (rough draft of 1857–58) [first instalment]', in *Marx and Engels Collected Works, Vol. 28*, Moscow: Progress Publishers.

Marx, Karl 1987a, 'Marx to Engels, 14 March 1868', in *Marx and Engels Collected Works, Vol. 42*, Moscow: Progress Publishers.

Marx, Karl 1987b, 'Marx to Engels, 25 March 1868', in *Marx and Engels Collected Works, Vol. 42*, Moscow: Progress Publishers.

Marx, Karl 1987c, 'Outline of the critique of political economy (rough draft of 1857–58) [second instalment]', in *Marx and Engels Collected Works, Vol. 29*, Moscow: Progress Publishers.

Marx, Karl 1987d, 'A contribution to the critique of political economy, part one', in *Marx and Engels Collected Works, Vol. 29*, Moscow: Progress Publishers.

Marx, Karl 1989a, 'Marginal notes on Wagner's Lehrbuch der politischen Oekonomie', in *Marx and Engels Collected Works, Vol. 24*, Moscow: Progress Publishers.

Marx, Karl 1989b, 'Critique of the Gotha programme', in *Marx and Engels Collected Works, Vol. 24*, Moscow: Progress Publishers.

Marx, K.H. 1989c, 'Marx to Ludwig Kugelmann, 17 April 1871', in *Marx and Engels Collected Works, Vol. 44*, Moscow: Progress Publishers.

Marx, Karl 1989d, 'Marx to Ludwig Kugelmann, 12 April 1871', in *Marx and Engels Collected Works, Vol. 44*, Moscow: Progress Publishers.

Marx, Karl 1991a, *Karl Marx Friedrich Engels Gesamtausgabe* (MEGA). *Zweite Abteilung 'Das Kapital' and Vorarbeiten: Band 10, 2 apparat*, Berlin: Dietz Verlag.

Marx, Karl 1991b, 'Economic manuscript of 1861–63 (continuation)', in *Marx and Engels Collected Works, Vol. 33*, Moscow: Progress Publishers.

Marx, Karl 1991c, *Karl Marx Friedrich Engels Gesamtausgabe* (MEGA). *Vierte Abteilung Exzerpte, Notizen, Marginalien: Band 10, Exzerpte und Nitizen Juli bis September 1851*, Berlin: Dietz Verlag.

Marx, Karl 1997, 'Capital, volume II', in *Marx and Engels Collected Works, Vol. 36*, Moscow: Progress Publishers.

Marx, Karl and Friedrich Engels 1975, 'The German ideology', in *Marx and Engels Collected Works, Vol. 5*, Moscow: Progress Publishers.

Marx, Karl and Friedrich Engels 1976, 'Manifesto of the communist party', in *Marx and Engels Collected Works, Vol. 6*, Moscow: Progress Publishers.

Masson, Vadim 1972, 'The problem of the Neolithic revolution in the light of new archaeological data', *Soviet Anthropology and Archaeology*, 11, 2: 123–54.

Masson, Vadim 1988, *Altyn-depe*, Philadelphia, PA: University Museum.

Mayor, Adrienne 2000, *The first fossil hunters. Paleontology in Greek and Roman times*, Princeton, NJ: Princeton University Press.

Mayor, Adrienne 2018, *Gods and robots. Myths, machines, and ancient dreams of technology*, Princeton, NJ: Princeton University Press.

McGinnis, Jon 2019, 'A continuation of atomism: Shahrastānī on the atom and continuity', *Journal of the History of Philosophy*, 57, 4: 595–619.

McIvor, Martin 2008, 'The young Marx and German idealism: revisiting the doctoral dissertation', *Journal of the History of Philosophy*, 46, 3: 395–419.

Mee, Christopher 2008, 'Mycenaean Greece, the Aegean, and beyond', in *The Cambridge companion to the Aegean Bronze Age*, edited by Cynthia Shelmerdine, Cambridge: Cambridge University Press.

Meek, Ronald 1976, *Social science and the ignoble savage*, Cambridge: Cambridge University Press.

Meheux, Katie 2017, '"Dawn of European Civilization": a celebration of the UCL Institute of Archaeology's 80th Anniversary', *Archaeology International*, 20: 91–105.

Meierhoff, James, Mark Golitko and James Morris 2012, 'Obsidian acquisition, trade, and regional interaction at Chan', in *Chan. An ancient Maya farming community*, edited by Cynthia Robin, Gainesville, FA: University Press of Florida.

Mertens, Frank 2003a, 'Enden, Franciscus van den (1602–74)', in *The dictionary of Seventeenth and Eighteenth-Century Dutch philosophers*, edited by Wiep van Bunge, Bristol: Thoemmes Press.

Mertens, Frank 2003b, 'Plockhoy, Pieter Corneliszoon (c. 1620–c. 1700)', in *The dictionary of Seventeenth and Eighteenth-Century Dutch philosophers*, edited by Wiep van Bunge, Bristol: Thoemmes Press.

Michailidou, Anna 2010, 'Measuring by weight in the Late Bronze Age Aegean: the people behind the measuring tools', in *The archaeology of measurement. Comprehending heaven, earth and time in ancient societies*, edited by Lian Morley and Colin Renfrew, Cambridge: Cambridge University Press.

Michell, Humfrey 1947, 'The iron money of Sparta', *Phoenix*, 1: 42–4.

Miller, Walter 1913, *Cicero XXI: On duties*, Cambridge, MA: Harvard University Press.

Mongait, Alexander 1959, *Archaeology in the U.S.S.R.*, Moscow: Foreign Languages Publishing House.

Montag, Warren 2012a, 'To disorder and discompose the whole machine of the world: Adam Smith, Epicurus and Lucretius', *Rivista di storia della filosofia*, 67, 2: 267–77.

Montag, Warren 2012b, 'Lucretius Hebraizant: Spinoza's reading of Ecclesiastes', *European Journal of Philosophy*, 20, 1: 109–130.

Montag, Warren 2013, *Philosophy's perpetual war. Althusser and his contemporaries*, Durham: Duke University Press.

Montag, Warren 2016, 'From clinamen to conatus: Deleuze, Lucretius, Spinoza', in *Lucretius and modernity. Epicurean encounters across time and disciplines*, edited by Jacques Lezra, Blake, New York: Palgrave Macmillan.

Montaigne, Michel 1991, *The complete essays*, London: Penguin.

Montesquieu, Charles Louis 1777, *Complete works, volume 1. The spirit of the laws*, London: T. Evans.

More, Thomas 1965, *The complete works of St. Thomas More, volume 4*, New Haven, CT: Yale University Press.

Moreau, Pierre-Francois. 2006, *Problèmes du Spinozisme*, Paris: Vrin.

Morel, Pierre-Marie 2007, 'Démocrite et l'objet de la philosophie naturelle. Sur les sens de phusis chez Démocrite', in *Democritus: science, the arts, and the care of the soul. Proceedings of the International Colloquium on Democritus (Paris, 18–20 September 2003)*, edited by Aldo Brancacci and Pierre-Marie Morel Leiden, Brill.

Morel, Pierre-Marie 2008, 'Method and evidence: on Epicurean preconception', *Proceedings of the Boston area colloquium in ancient philosophy*, 22, 1, 25–55.

Morel, Pierre-Marie 2009, 'Epicurean atomism', in *The Cambridge companion to Epicureanism*, edited by James Warren. Cambridge: Cambridge University Press.

Morfino, Vittorio 2012a, 'L'interpretazione marxiana di Lucrezio', *Rivista di storia della filosofia*, 67, 2: 277–93.

Morfino, Vittorio 2012b, 'The misunderstanding of the mode: Spinoza in Hegel's *Science of logic* (1812–16)', in *Between Hegel and Spinoza. A volume of critical essays*, edited by Hasana Sharp and Jason Smith, London: Bloomsbury.

Morfino, Vittorio 2014a, 'The multitudo according to Negri: on the disarticulation of ontology and history', *Rethinking Marxism*, 26, 2: 227–38.

Morfino, Vittorio 2014b, *Plural temporality. Transindividuality and the aleatory between Spinoza and Althusser*, Chicago, IL: Haymarket Books.

Morfino, Vittorio 2015, 'The five theses of Machiavelli's 'philosophy'', in *The radical Machiavelli. Politics, philosophy and language*, edited by Filippo Del Lucchese, Fabio Frosini and Vittorio Morfino, Leiden: Brill.

Morgan, Lewis 1852, *Diffusion against centralization. A lecture delivered before the Rochester Athenæum and Mechanics' Association, on its third anniversary, January 6, 1852*, Rochester, NY: D.M. Dewey.

Morgan, Lewis 1853, 'Athenian democracy', *New York Quarterly*, 2: 341–67.

Morgan, Lewis 1868, *The American beaver and his work*, Philadelphia, PA: J.B. Lippincot & Co.

Morgan, Lewis 1871, *Systems of consanguinity and affinity of the human family*, Washington, DC: City of Washington.

Morgan, Lewis 1876, 'Montezuma's dinner', *North American Review*, 122: 265–308.

Morgan, Lewis 1962, *League of the Iroquois*, New York: Corinth Books.

Morgan, Lewis 1964, *Ancient society*, Cambridge, MA: The Belknap Press of Harvard University Press.

Morgan, Lewis 1965, *Houses and house-life of the American aborigines*, Chicago, IL: University of Chicago Press.

Morris, Ian 1987, *Burial and ancient society. The rise of the Greek city-state*, Cambridge: Cambridge University Press.

Morris, Ian 1997, 'An archaeology of equalities? The Greek city-states', in *The archaeology of city-states*, edited by Thomas Charlton and Deborah Nichols, Washington, DC: Smithsonian Institution Press.

Morris, Ian 2015, *Foragers, farmers, and fossil fuels. How human values evolve*, Princeton, NJ: Princeton University Press.

Moses, Daniel 2001, *Lewis Henry Morgan's "barbaric yawp". The making of a Victorian anthropologist*, Rochester, NY: University of Rochester.

Moses, Daniel 2018, 'Dialogue among cellmates: Lucretius, Horace, and Lewis Henry Morgan', in *Brill's companion to classics and early anthropology*, edited by Emily Varto. Leiden: Brill.

Naddaf, Gerard 2005, *The Greek concept of nature*, Albany, NY: State University of New York Press.

Nail, Thomas 2020, *Marx in motion. A new materialist Marxism*, Oxford: Oxford University Press.

Najemy, John 2006, *A history of Florence, 1200–1575*, Malden, MA: Blackwell.

Nakassis, Dimitri 2013, *Individuals and society in Mycenaean Pylos*, Leiden: Brill.

Naumova, Natalia and Vadim Rogovin 1989, 'The task of justice', in *New directions in Soviet thought: an anthology*, edited by Murray Yanowitch, Armonk, NY: Sharpe.

Navarro, Fernanda 2015 'Celebrating Althusser's legacy', *Crisis and Critique*, 2, 2: 46–61.

Needham, Joseph 1959, *Science and civilisation in China, volume 3: mathematics and the sciences of the heavens and the earth*, Cambridge: Cambridge University Press.

Needham, Joseph 2004, *Science and civilisation in China, volume 7. Part 2: general conclusions and reflections*, Cambridge: Cambridge University Press.

Negri, Antonio 1990, *The savage anomaly. The power of Spinoza's metaphysics and politics*, Minneapolis, MN: University of Minnesota Press.

Negri, Antonio 2003, *Time for revolution*, London: Continuum.

Obbink, Dirk 1984, 'POXY. 215 and Epicurean religious theoria', in *Atti del XVII Congresso Internazionale di Papirologia*, Naples: Centro Internazionale per lo Studio dei Papiri Ercolanesi.

Obbink, Dirk 1996, *Philodemus On piety. Part 1: critical text with commentary*, Oxford: Clarendon Press.

O'Brien, Michael 1985, 'Xenophanes, Aeschylus, and the doctrine of primeval brutishness', *The Classical Quarterly*, 35, 2: 264–77.

Oizerman, Teodor 1988, *The main trends in philosophy. A theoretical analysis of the history of philosophy*, Moscow: Progress Publishers.

Oldfather, Charles 1933, *Diodorus Siculus The library of history: volume I*, London: William Heinemann.

Oldfather, Charles 1939, *Diodorus Siculus The library of history: volume III*, London: William Heinemann.

Palaima, Thomas 2015, 'The Mycenaean mobilization of labor in agriculture and building projects: institutions, individuals, compensation and status in the Linear B tablets', in *Labor in the ancient world*, edited by Piotr Steinkeller and Michael Hudson, Dresden: ISLET-Verlag.

Palmer, Ada 2013, *Reading Lucretius in the Renaissance*, Cambridge, MA: Harvard University Press.

Palmer, Martin 1996, *The book of Chuang Tzu*, London: Penguin.

Panichi, Alessio 2018, 'At the root of an ongoing debate: Machiavelli, Lucretius, and the Rossiano 884', *Culture del Testo e del Documento*, 56, 20: 5–32.

Panofsky, Erwin 1972, *Studies in iconology. Humanistic themes in the art of the Renaissance*, Boulder, CO: Westview Press.

Passannante, Gerard 2011, *The Lucretian renaissance. Philology and the afterlife of tradition*, Chicago, IL: University of Chicago Press.

Paton, William 2010, *Polybius The histories III: book 5–8*, Cambridge, MA: Harvard University Press.

Peace, William 1992, *The enigmatic career of Vere Gordon Childe*, New York, Columbia University.

Peace, William 2004, *Leslie A. White. Evolution and revolution in anthropology*, Lincoln, NE: University of Nebraska Press.

Phelan, Anthony 2013, '"Im Augenblick Der Gefahr": Brecht, Benjamin and Die Geschäfte Des Herrn Julius Caesar', *The Modern Language Review*, 108, 3: 881–97.

Pike, Jonathan 1999, *From Aristotle to Marx. Aristotelianism in Marxist social ontology*, London: Routledge.

Piketty, Thomas 2020, *Capital and ideology*, Cambridge, MA: The Belknap Press of Harvard University Press.

Pines, Shlomo 1997, *Studies in the history of Jewish thought*, Jerusalem, Magnes Press: Hebrew University.

Pines, Yuri and Gideon Shelach 2005, 'Using the past to serve the present: comparative perspectives on Chinese and Western theories of the origins of states', in *Genesis and regeneration. Essays on conceptions of origins*, edited by Shaul Shaked, Jerusalem: The Israel Academy of Science and Humanities.

Plekhanov, Georgi 1981, 'Civilisation and the great historical rivers', in *The Asiatic mode of production: science and politics*, edited by Anne Bailey and Josep Llobera, London: Routledge.

Plotkin, Vladimir and Jovan Howe 1985, 'The unknown tradition: continuity and innovation in Soviet ethnography', *Dialectical Anthropology*, 9, 1: 257–312.

Pollock, Ethan (ed.) 2001, 'Conversations with Stalin on questions of political economy. Cold War International History Project, Working Paper No. 33'., available at: https://www.wilsoncenter.org/sites/default/files/media/documents/publication/ACFB07.pdf, (last accessed 4.4.2020).

Possehl, Gregory 2000, 'Harappan beginnings', in *The breakout. The origins of civilization*, edited by Martha Lamberg-Karlovsky, Cambridge, MA: Peabody Museum of Archaeology and Ethnology, Harvard University.

Pradella, Lucia 2011, 'Kolonialfrage und vorkapitalistische Gesellschaften: Zusätze und Änderungen in der französischen Ausgabe des ersten Bandes des *Kapital*', *Marx-Engels-Jahrbuch 2010*: 82–100.

Pradella, Lucia 2014, *Globalisation and the critique of political economy. New insights from Marx's writings*, London: Routledge.

Prescott, William 1961, *The history of the conquest of Mexico and history of the conquest of Peru*, New York: Random House.

Rackham, Harris 1944, *Aristotle Politics: volume XXI*, London: William Heinemann.

Rackham, Harris 1951, *Cicero XIX: De natura deorum, Academica*, Cambridge, MA: Harvard University Press.

Read, Jason 2002, 'Primitive accumulation: the aleatory foundation of capitalism', *Rethinking Marxism*, 14, 2: 24–50.

Read, Jason 2013, 'To think the new in the absence of its conditions: Althusser and Negri and the philosophy of primitive accumulation', in *Encountering Althusser. Politics and materialism in contemporary radical thought*, edited by Katja Diefenbach, Sara Farris, Gal Kirn and Peter Thomas, London: Bloomsbury.

Renfrew, Colin 1972, *The emergence of civilisation. The Cyclades and the Aegean in the third millennium BC*, London: Methuen.

Renfrew, Colin 2012, 'Systems of value among material things: the nexus of fungibility and measure', in *The construction of value in the ancient world*, edited by John

Papadopoulos and Gary Urton, Los Angeles, CA: Cotsen Institute of Archaeology Press.

Resek, Carl 1960, *Lewis Henry Morgan, American scholar*, Chicago, IL: University of Chicago Press.

Restall, Matthew 1997, *The Maya world. Yucatec culture and society, 1550–1850*, Stanford, CA: Stanford University Press.

Robertson, William 1840a, *The works of William Robertson. Volume 7: The history of America, books 5–8*, London: T. Cadell.

Robertson, William 1840b, *The works of William Robertson. Volume 6: a catalogue of Spanish books and manuscripts and The history of America, books 1–4*, London: T. Cadell.

Robinson, Kim Stanley 2002, *The years of rice and salt*, London: HarperCollins.

Roger, Jacques 1997, *Buffon: a life in natural history*, Itaka, NY: Cornell University Press.

Rogovin, Vadim 1989, 'Social justice and the socialist distribution of vital goods', in *New directions in Soviet thought: an anthology*, edited by Murray Yanowitch, Armonk, NY: Sharpe.

Rose, Margaret 1984, *Marx's lost aesthetic. Karl Marx and the visual arts*, Cambridge: Cambridge University Press.

Rose, Peter 1976, 'Sophocles' Philoctetes and the teachings of the Sophists', *Harvard Studies in Classical Philology*, 80: 49–105.

Roskam, Geert 2007, *Live unnoticed. On the vicissitudes of an Epicurean doctrine*, Leiden: Brill.

Ross, David 1952, *The works of Aristotle. Volume XII: select fragments*, Oxford: Clarendon Press.

Rowland, Ingrid 1999, *Vitruvius Ten books on architecture*, Cambridge: Cambridge University Press.

Sahlins, Marshall 1968, 'The original affluent society', in *Man the hunter*, edited by Richard Lee and Irven DeVore, New York: Aldine Publishing Company.

Ste. Croix, Geoffrey 1981, *The class struggle in the ancient Greek world*, London: Duckworth.

Sandys, John 1937, *The odes of Pindar*, London: William Heinemann.

Sawer, Marian 1977, *Marxism and the question of the Asiatic mode of production*, The Hague: Martinus Nijhoff.

Sawer, Marian 1980, 'Socialism and the legitimation of inequality', *The Australian and New Zealand Journal of Sociology*, 16, 1: 56–62.

Scala, Bartolomeo 2008. *Essays and dialogues*, Cambridge, MA: Harvard University Press.

Scarborough, Vernon 2003, *The flow of power. Ancient water systems and landscapes*, Santa Fe, NM: SAR Press.

Schafer, Paul 1999, *The praxis of philosophy. Nature, reason, and freedom in the young Marx's criticism of Hegelian idealism*, Chicago, IL, DePaul University.

Schiefsky, Mark 2005, *Hippocrates On ancient medicine*, Leiden: Brill.

Schiesaro, Alessandro 2007a, 'Lucretius and Roman politics and history', in *The Cambridge companion to Lucretius*, edited by Stuart Gillespie and Philip Hardie, Cambridge: Cambridge University Press.

Schiesaro, Alessandro 2007b, 'Didaxis, rhetoric, and the law in Lucretius', in *Classical constructions. Papers in memory of Don Fowler, classicist and Epicurean*, edited by Stephen Heyworth, Oxford: Oxford University Press.

Schnirelmann, Victor 1995, 'From internationalism to nationalism: forgotten pages of Soviet archaeology in the 1930s and 1940s', in *Nationalism, politics, and the practice of archaeology*, edited by Philip Kohl and Clare Fawcett, Cambridge: Cambridge University Press.

Schrijvers, Piet 2007, 'Seeing the invisible: a study of Lucretius' use of analogy in De Rerum Natura', in *Oxford readings in Lucretius*, edited by Monica Gale. Oxford: Oxford University Press.

Schuller, Rudolph 1930, 'The oldest known illustration of South American Indians', *Indian Notes*, 7: 484–97.

Screech, Michael 1998, *Montaigne's annotated copy of Lucretius. A transcription and study of the manuscript, notes and pen-marks*, Geneve: Librairie Droz S.A.

Sedley, David 1998, *Lucretius and the transformation of Greek wisdom*, Cambridge: Cambridge University Press.

Sedley, David 2011, 'Epicurus' theological innatism', in *Epicurus and the Epicurean tradition*, edited by Jeffrey Fish and Kirk Sanders, Cambridge: Cambridge University Press.

Semenov, Sergey 1964, *Prehistoric technology. An experimental study of the oldest tools and artefacts from traces of manufacture and wear*, London: Cory, Adams & Mackay.

Semenov, Yuri 1974, 'Theoretical problems of 'economic anthropology'', *Philosophy of the Social Sciences*, 4, 2: 201–31.

Semenov, Yuri 1980, 'The theory of socio-economic formations and world history', in *Soviet and Western anthropology*, edited by Ernest Gellner, London: Duckworth.

Serge, Victor 2014, *Midnight in the century*, New York: New York Review Books.

Service, Elman 1981, 'The mind of Lewis H. Morgan', *Current Anthropology*, 22, 1: 25–43.

Sherratt, Susan 2000, 'Circulation of metals and the end of the Bronze Age in the eastern Mediterranean', in *Metals make the world go round. The supply and circulation of metals in Bronze Age Europe*, edited by Christopher Pare, Oxford: Oxbow.

Shipley, Lucy 2013, 'Guelphs, Ghibellines and Etruscans: archaeological discoveries and civic identity in Late Medieval and Early Renaissance Tuscany', *Bulletin of the History of Archaeology*, 23, 1: 1–9.

Schnapp, Alain 1996, *The discovery of the past. The origins of archaeology*, London: British Museum Press.

Shorey, Paul 1935, *Plato v: Republic, part i*, London: William Heinemann.

Shorey, Paul 1937, *Plato vi: Republic, part ii*, London: William Heinemann.

Smith, Adam 1976, *The theory of moral sentiments*, Oxford: Clarendon Press.

Smith, Adam 1978, *Lectures on jurisprudence*, Oxford: Clarendon Press.

Smith, Adam 1980, *Essays on philosophical subjects*, Oxford: Oxford University Press.

Smith, Adam 2003, *The wealth of nations*, New York: Putnam's sons.

Smith, Michael, Timothy Dennehey, April Kamp-Whittaker, Emily Colon and Rebecca Harkness 2014, 'Quantitative measures of wealth inequality in ancient Central Mexican communities', *Advances in Archaeological Practice*, 2, 4: 311–23.

Smith, Michael, Abhishek Chatterjee, Angela Huster, Sierra Stewart and Marion Forest 2019, 'Apartment compounds, households, and population in the ancient city of Teotihuacan, Mexico', *Ancient Mesoamerica*, 30, 3: 399–418.

Smith, Martin 1992, *Lucretius On the nature of things*, Cambridge, MA: Harvard University Press.

Smith, Martin 1993, *Diogenes of Oinoanda. The Epicurean inscription*, Naples: Bibliopolis.

Smith, Martin 1996, 'An Epicurean priest from Apamea in Syria', *Zeitschrift für Papyrologie und Epigraphiek*, 112: 120–30.

Snyder, James 1976, 'Jan Mostaert's West Indies landscape', in *First images of America. The impact of the New World on the Old*, edited by Fred Chiappelli, Berkely, CA: University of California Press.

Snyder, Jane 1983, 'The warp and the woof of the universe in Lucretius' *De rerum natura*', *Illinois Classical Studies*, 8: 37–43.

Sotiris, Panagiotis 2014, 'Rethinking structure and conjuncture in Althusser', *Historical Materialism*, 22, 3–4: 5–51.

Sotiris, Panagiotis 2020, *A philosophy for communism. Rethinking Althusser*, Leiden: Brill.

Spinoza, Baruch 1985, *The collected works of Spinoza: volume i*, Princeton, NJ: Princeton University Press.

Spinoza, Baruch 2016, *The collected works of Spinoza: volume ii*, Princeton, NJ: Princeton University Press.

Spufford, Francis 2010, *Red plenty*, London: Faber.

Stalin, Iosif 1939, *History of the Communist Party of the Soviet Union (bolshevik)*, Moscow: Progress Publishers.

Stalin, Iosif 1952, *Economic problems of socialism in the u.s.s.r.*, Moscow: Foreign Languages Publishing House.

Stalin, Iosif 1954, *Works. Volume 9: December 1926–July 1927*, Moscow: Progress Publishers.

Stark, Barbara, Matthew Boxt, Janine Gasco, Rebecca Gonzalez Lauck, Jessica Hedgepeth Balkin, Arthur Joyce, Stacie King, Charles Knight, Robert Kruger, Marc Levine,

Richard Lesure, Rebecca Mendelsohn, Marx Navarro-Castillo, Hector Neff, Michael Ohnersorgen, Christopher Pool, Mark Raab, Robert Rosenswig, Marcie Venter, Barbara Vorhies, David Williams and Andrew Workinger 2016, 'Economic Growth in Mesoamerica: Obsidian Consumption in the Coastal Lowlands', *Journal of Anthropological Archaeology*, 41: 263–82.

Stedman Jones, Gareth 2008, 'Radicalism and the extra-European world: the case of Karl Marx', in *Victorian visions of global order. Empire and international relations in nineteenth century political thought*, edited by Duncan Bell, Cambridge: Cambridge University Press.

Steel, Louise 2013, *Materiality and consumption in the Bronze Age Mediterranean*, London: Routledge.

Stern, Bernard 1931, *Lewis Henry Morgan: social evolutionist*, Chicago, IL: University of Chicago Press.

Stewart, Matthew 2014, *Nature's God. The heretical origins of the American republic*, New York: W.W. Norton & Company.

Struve, Vasily 1965, 'The concept of the "Asian mode of production"', *Soviet Anthropology and Archaeology*, 4, 2: 41–6.

Sun, Yan 1995, *The Chinese reassessment of socialism, 1976–1992*, Princeton, NJ: Princeton University Press.

Surtz, Edward 1957, *The praise of pleasure. Philosophy, education and communism in More's Utopia*, Cambridge, MA: Yale University Press.

Swetlitz, Marc 1988, 'The minds of beavers and the minds of humans: natural suggestion, natural selection, and experiment in the work of Lewis Henry Morgan', in *Bones, bodies, behavior. Essays on biological anthropology*, edited by George Stocking, Madison, WI: The University of Wisconsin Press.

Tanner, Jeremy 2009, 'Ancient Greece, early China: Sino-Hellenic studies and comparative approaches to the Classical world', *Journal of Hellenic Studies*, 129: 89–109.

Taub, Liba 2009, 'Cosmology and meteorology', in *The Cambridge companion to Epicureanism*, edited by James Warren, Cambridge: Cambridge University Press.

Taube, Karl 2000, 'Lightning celts and corn fetishes: the Formative Olmec and the development of maize symbolism in Mesoamerica and the American southwest', in *Olmec art and archaeology. Social complexity in the Formative period*, edited by John Clark and Mary Pye, Washington, DC: National Gallery of Art.

Taylor, Christopher 1999, *The atomists: Leucippus and Democritus*, Toronto: University of Toronto Press.

Tedlock, Dennis 1993, 'Torture in the archives: Mayans meet Europeans', *American Anthropologist*, 95, 1: 139–52.

Tiesler, Vera and Andrea Cucina 2006, 'Procedures in human heart extraction and ritual meaning: a taphonomic assessment of anthropogenic marks in Classic Maya skeletons', *Latin American Antiquity*, 17, 4: 493–510.

Tomba, Massimiliano 2013, *Marx's temporalities*, Leiden: Brill.

Tomba, Massimiliano 2019, *Insurgent universality. An alternative legacy of modernity*, Oxford: Oxford University Press.

Tomba, Massimiliano and Riccardo Bellofiore 2014, 'The 'fragment on machines' and the *Grundrisse*: the Workerist reading in question', in *Beyond Marx. Theorising the global labour relations of the Twenty-first century*, edited by Marcel van der Linden and Karl Roth, Leiden: Brill.

Trautmann, Thomas 1987, *Lewis Henry Morgan and the invention of kinship*, Berkeley, CA: University of California Press.

Trautmann, Thomas 1992, 'Whig ethnology from Locke to Morgan', *Journal of the Anthropological Society of Oxford*, 22: 208–18.

Trautmann, Thomas and Karl Kabelac 1994, *The library of Lewis Henry Morgan and Mary Elizabeth Morgan*, Philadelphia, PA: The American Philosophical Society.

Trexler, Richard 1998, *The workers of Renaissance Florence. Power and dependence in Renaissance Florence*, Asheville, NC: Pegasus Press.

Trigger, Bruce 1980, *Gordon Childe. Revolutions in archaeology*, London: Thames and Hudson.

Trigger, Bruce 1984, 'Alternative archaeologies: nationalist, colonialist, imperialist', *Man*, 19, 3: 355–70.

Trigger, Bruce 2003, *Understanding early civilizations: a comparative study*, Cambridge: Cambridge University Press.

Trigger, Bruce 2006, *A history of archaeological though, second edition*, Cambridge: Cambridge University Press.

Trotsky, Leon 1966, *Problems of the Chinese revolution*, New York: Paragon Book Reprint Corp.

Trotsky, Leon 1969, *The permanent revolution, and Results and prospects*, New York: Merit Publishers.

Trotsky, Leon 1974, *The history of the Russian revolution*, Ann Arbor, MI: University of Michigan Press.

Turchin, Peter 2018, 'Translating knowledge about past societies into SESHAT data', *Cliodynamics*, 9, 1: 143–47.

Van der Linden, Marcel 2007, 'The 'law' of uneven and combined development: some underdeveloped thoughts', *Historical Materialism*, 15, 1: 145–65.

Vardoulakis, Dimitris 2019a, 'Neo-epicureanism', *Philosophy Today*, 63, 4: 1013–24.

Vardoulakis, Dimitris 2019b, 'Spinoza's law: the epicurean definition of the law in the Theological Political Treatise', *Radical Philosophy*, 2, 5: 23–33.

Vardoulakis, Dimitris 2020, 'Freedom as overcoming the fear of death: epicureanism in the subtitle of Spinoza's Theological Political Treatise', *Parrhesia*, 32: 33–60.

Varoufakis, Yanis 2017, *Adults in the room. My battle with Europe's deep establishment*, London: Vintage.

Varto, Emily 2018, 'The tinted Lens of Ancient Society: classical history and American experience in the ethnology of Lewis Henry Morgan', in *Brill's companion to classics and early anthropology*, edited by Emily Varto, Leiden: Brill.

Vavilov, Nikolai 1996, *Five continents*, Rome: IGPRI.

Vavilov, Sergey 1948, 'Lucretius' physics', *Philosophy and Phenomenological Research*, 9, 1: 21–40.

Vespucci, Amerigo 1916, *Mundus novus. Letter to Lorenzo Pietro di Medici*, Princeton, NJ: Princeton University Press.

Vespucci, Amerigo 1992, *Letters from a new world. Amerigo Vespucci's discovery of America*, New York: Marsilio.

Vinnikov, Isaak 1935, *Materials from the archives of Lewis H. Morgan*, Moscow: Academy of Sciences USSR.

Wada, Haruki 1983, 'Marx and revolutionary Russia', in *Late Marx and the Russian road. Marx and the peripheries of capitalism*, edited by Teodor Shanin, New York: Monthly Review Press.

Wengrow, David 2010, *What makes civilization? The ancient Near East & the future of the West*, Oxford: Oxford University Press.

Wengrow, David 2015, *Cities before the state in early Eurasia*, Munchen: Max Planck Gesellschaft.

Wersky, Gary 1971, 'Introduction: on the reception of *Science at the cross roads* in England', in *Science at the cross roads*, edited by Nikolai Bukharin, London: Frank Cass & Co. Ltd.

White, Leslie (ed.) 1937, 'Lewis H. Morgan's European journal', *The Rochester Historical Society Publications*, 16: 219–389.

White, Leslie (ed.) 1940a, *The Bandelier-Morgan letters, 1873–1883. Volume I*, Albuquerque, NM: The University of New Mexico Press.

White, Leslie (ed.) 1940b, *The Bandelier-Morgan letters, 1873–1883. Volume II*, Albuquerque, NM: The University of New Mexico Press.

White, Leslie (ed.) 1959, *Lewis Henry Morgan: The Indian journals, 1859–62*, Ann Arbor, MI: University of Michigan Press.

Wicksteed, Philip and Francis Cornford 1957, *Aristotle Physics I–IV: volume IV*, London: William Heinemann.

Wilkinson, Toby 2014, *Tying the threads of Eurasia. Trans-regional routes and material flows in Transcaucasia, eastern Anatolia and western Central Asia, c. 3000–1500 BC*, Leiden: Sidestone Press.

Wilson, Catherine 2008, *Epicureanism at the origins of modernity*, Oxford: Clarendon Press.

Winter, Yves 2015, 'Plebeian politics: Machiavelli and the Ciompi uprising', in *The radical Machiavelli. Politics, philosophy and language*, edited by Filippo Del Lucchese, Fabio Frosini and Vittorio Morfino, Leiden: Brill.

Wintroub, Michael 2006, *A savage mirror. Power, identity, and knowledge in early modern France*, Stanford, CA: Stanford University Press.

Wolf, Eric 1959, *Sons of the shaking earth*, Chicago, IL: University of Chicago Press.

Woolley, Leonard 1934, *Ur excavations: volume II. The Royal Cemetery: a report on the predynastic and Sargonid graves excavated between 1926 and 1931*, London: The Trustees of the Two Museums.

Wyatt, Andrew 2012, 'Agricultural practices at Chan: farming and political economy in an ancient Maya community', in *Chan. An ancient Maya farming community*, edited by Cynthia Robin, Gainesville, FA: University Press of Florida.

Xi, Jinping 2014, *The governance of China*, Beijing: Foreign Languages Press.

Yakhot, Yehoshua 2012, *The suppression of philosophy in the USSR (the 1920s & 1930s)*, Oak Park, MI: Mehring Books.

Yuan, Xingpei and David Knechtges (eds) 2012, *The history of Chinese civilization. Vol. I: Earliest times–221 B.C.E.*, Cambridge: Cambridge University Press.

Zangger, Eberhard, Michael Timpson, Sergey Yazvenko, Falko Kuhnke and Jost Knauss 1997, 'The Pylos Regional Archaeological Survey part II: landscape evolution and site preservation', *Hesperia*, 66, 4: 549–641.

Zizek, Slavoj 2015, 'Sinicisation', *London Review of Books*, 37, 14: 30.

Zweynert, Joachim 2014, '"Developed socialism" and Soviet economic thought in the 1970s and early '80s', *Russian History*, 41: 354–72.

Index